MW01106043

INTRODUCTION
TO
EDUCATION

INTRODUCTION
TO
EDUCATION

Second Edition

TOM E.C. SMITH

University of Alabama at Birmingham

WEST PUBLISHING COMPANY

St. Paul • New York • Los Angeles • San Francisco

COVER IMAGE Superstock
COVER DESIGN Pollock Design Group
INTERIOR DESIGN Diane Beasley
COMPOSITION Carlisle Communications, LTD
COPYEDITING Cindi Gerber
INDEXING E. Virginia Webb

COPYRIGHT © 1987   By WEST PUBLISHING COMPANY
COPYRIGHT © 1990   By WEST PUBLISHING COMPANY
                   50 W. Kellogg Boulevard
                   P.O. Box 64526
                   St. Paul, MN 55164–1003

97   96   95   94   93   92   91   90   8   7   6   5   4   3   2   1   0

LIBRARY OF CONGRESS CATALOGING-IN-PUBLICATION DATA

Smith, Tom E.C.
   [2nd ed]
   Introduction to education / Tom E.C. Smith.
     p. cm.

   Includes bibliographical references.
   ISBN 0-314-66315-0
   1. Teachers—Training of—United States.   2. Education
—Study and teaching—United States.   I. Title.
LB1715.S4847   1990

370'.973–dc20   89–39660
                                                         CIP

PHOTO CREDITS

2 top Dale Lewis; **2 bottom** Dale Lewis; **13** Susan Lapides, ©1983, Design Conceptions; **19** Dale Lewis; **26** Dale Lewis; **30** Dale Lewis; **44 top** Arlene Casto Lewis; **44 bottom** Historical Picture Services, Chicago; **61** Historical Picture Services, Chicago; **63** Historical Picture Services, Chicago; **65** Dale Lewis; **72 top** Dale Lewis; **72 bottom** Dale Lewis; **81** Dale Lewis; **87** Dale Lewis; **94** Dale Lewis; **100 top** Dale Lewis; **100 bottom** James Shaffer; **105** James Shaffer; **118** Dale Lewis; **126** Arlene Casto Lewis; **146 top** David A. Krathwohl, Stock Boston; **146 bottom** Dale Lewis; **158** Dale Lewis; **166** Dale Lewis; **175** Dale Lewis; **188 top** Dale Lewis; **188 bottom** Dale Lewis; **199** Arlene Casto Lewis; **207** Arlene Casto Lewis; **214** Dale Lewis; **220 top** Dale Lewis; **220 bottom** Dale Lewis; **224** Eileen Christelow/Jeroboam, Inc.; **240** Dale Lewis; **242** Dale Lewis; **246** Susan Lapides, ©1985, Design Conceptions; **254 top** Arlene Casto Lewis; **254 bottom** Dale Lewis; **260** Dale Lewis; **272** Elizabeth Crews, Stock Boston; **278** Cary Wolinsky, Stock Boston; **280** Bruce Wellman, Stock Boston; **296 top** Arlene Casto Lewis; **296 bottom** Dale Lewis; **301** Dale Lewis; **315** Dale Lewis; **332** Laimute E. Druskis, Stock Boston; **338 top** Arlene Casto Lewis; **338 bottom** Dale Lewis; **349** Frank Siteman/Jeroboam, Inc.; **352** Dale Lewis; **357** Frank Siteman, Stock Boston; **366 top** Jeff Dunn, Stock Boston; **366 bottom** Dale Lewis; **371** Jean-Claude Lejeune, Stock Boston; **374** Dale Lewis; **387** Frank Siteman/Jeroboam, Inc.; **396 top** Arlene Casto Lewis; **396 bottom** Susan Lapides, ©1986, Design Conceptions; **409** Susan Lapides, ©1986, Design Conceptions; **411** Fredrick D. Bodin, Stock Boston; **426 top** Arlene Casto Lewis; **426 bottom** Dale Lewis; **432** Dale Lewis; **434** Frank Siteman, Stock Boston; **440** Dale Lewis; **442** Donald Dietz, Stock Boston; **458 top** Arlene Casto Lewis; **458 bottom** Dale Lewis; **463** Cary Wolinsky, Stock Boston; **465** Dale Lewis; **480** Dale Lewis.

To
Bonnie,
Jake,
and
Alex

∎

ABOUT THE AUTHOR

Dr. Tom E. C. Smith is currently the Director of the Division of Special Education and Vocational Rehabilitation at the Sparks Center, University of Alabama at Birmingham. He also has an appointment as a Professor of Special Education. Prior to coming to the University of Alabama at Birmingham, Dr. Smith taught in the Department of Teacher Education at the University of Arkansas for ten years, where he was the Program Coordinator of the Special Education Program for four years. Before receiving his Doctor of Education degree from Texas Tech University in 1977, Dr. Smith taught at the elementary and secondary levels in public schools and community special education programs.

Dr. Smith has written four college textbooks and published more than thirty articles in refereed professional journals. He has made numerous presentations at international, national, regional, and state conferences, and is currently the Vice President for the Division on Mental Retardation, Council for Exceptional Children. He has served on several editorial boards for professional journals and has been on various committees for the MidSouth Educational Research Association and Kappa Delta Pi.

Currently, Dr. Smith is a member of the Alabama Comprehensive System of Personnel Development. He also participated in teacher education task forces and committees for the Arkansas Department of Education.

TABLE OF CONTENTS

PREFACE

When the first edition of *Introduction to Education* was published, it was stated that the American system of public education was at a crossroads. Several years later, it still is at the crossroads. Although we are still in an era of reform in public education, the intensity of the reform movement has diminished significantly since the mid-1980s. We have learned a few things about educational reform, the most important being that a massive public educational system cannot be "fixed" with political ideas such as longer school days, longer school terms, more homework, and a simple return to a basic curriculum. While some of the reforms implemented during the past five years have had a positive effect on the quality of public education, others already have been pushed aside as meaningless actions that primarily resulted from actions initiated in political environments without sound data or even a sound theoretical base.

Even with some failures and a lot of frustrations, the reform movement in public education continues. Although it may not be front-page news, it is still receiving a great deal of attention from professional educators. The result should be a continually improving public education system that evolves to meet the ever-changing needs of our highly technological society. Maybe reforming our public schools has finally passed from the hands of politicians and headline grabbers to professional educators who can have a significant impact on the system.

The objective of this revision is to provide students preparing to be teachers with a current, general overview of the field of public education. The text is designed for students who are beginning their coursework in education. The book clarifies many issues related to education and public schools and focuses on the positive aspects of our educational system and of teaching as a profession. Its aim is to provide a basis for advanced coursework in education and to provide beginning education majors with some answers concerning what teaching is all about.

Although this is the first revision of *Introduction to Education*, major changes have been made from the first edition. Significant changes include the addition of two new chapters—Early Childhood Education and Legal Issues in Education. The chapter on vocational education was combined with the secondary education chapter, and the chapter on educational financing was made a part of the chapter discussing who controls American public education. A great deal of new information was added to the chapter on Philosophy of Education. In every chapter, a significant number of new references were added bringing the text up to date in every area covered. Although the original text was published in 1987, a great deal of new information has been added to the literature in every aspect of public education.

As with the first edition, two topics discussed throughout the text include multicultural education and special education. Information related to multicultural education is interpolated in several chapters, while content concerning special education is presented in a separate chapter. These two topics receive extensive coverage because of their importance to our educational system today, and because the National Council for the Accreditation of Teacher Education (NCATE) requires that content related to these areas be included in teacher education curricula.

TEXTBOOK ORGANIZATION

The textbook is organized into fourteen chapters. Chapter one provides an introduction to education in the United States. The focus is on the magnitude of public education, as well as the status of the reform movement that began in the late 1970s and early 1980s. The outcome of several of these reforms are discussed, as well as information related to where public education is moving in the 1990s. Chapters two and three focus on foundations of our educational system with a chapter on the history of our educational system and a chapter describing how philosophy and education are related. Chapter four deals with the complicated issue of who controls our American system of public education. A new section of this chapter focuses on the financing of public schools. This is added to show a relation of finance to other control issues.

Chapter five, Legal Issues, is a new chapter. The focus of this chapter is on the many different legal issues involved in providing public education. Topics such as education and religion, teachers' rights, and the rights of students are included. Chapter six is a new chapter that deals with early childhood education. In the 1990s and beyond, more and more emphasis will be placed on preschool educational programs. This chapter traces the history of early childhood education and describes the components of early childhood educational programs.

Chapters seven and eight deal with elementary schools and secondary schools. The secondary education chapter has been reorganized to include content previously included in a chapter on vocational and career education. Chapter nine contains information about special education and students with disabilities. As a result of federal legislation and extensive litigation, more and more regular classroom teachers at elementary and secondary levels have children with disabilities in their classrooms. Chapter ten focuses on the administration of our schools.

Information related to careers in education and how teachers are educated are included in chapters eleven and twelve. These two chapters were significantly updated to reflect the results of various reforms in teacher education generated from the Holmes and Carnegie reports. Chapter thirteen is about educational technology. Finally, the fourteenth chapter focuses on the future and public education. Trends in public education, as well as global trends, are discussed. Predictions made by several authors during the past fifteen years are discussed, and a new set of predictions for the 1990s is presented. An epilogue is provided to tie together all content presented in the text.

INSTRUCTIONAL AIDS

Highlights, which focus on current newspaper and magazine articles, have once again been included. These contain the most current information available and reflect much of what is happening nationally and in local communities in public education. Each chapter also includes an in-the-field section which is meant to give students participating in field placements some questions to investigate during their in-school time. A report form for in-the-field activities is again included in the appendix. Chapter objectives and advance organizers are also provided in each chapter.

ACKNOWLEDGEMENTS

I would like to gratefully acknowledge my family for their support and encouragement during this revision. Thanks to my daughter Alex, son Jake, and wife Bonnie for always being there to provide me with whatever support was necessary at the time. I would also like to thank all those who provided formal reviews of the first edition. Their many suggestions helped make the revision a much better textbook. These reviewers include:

Mary Ann Chapko	Indiana University-Northwest
Roderick M. Thronson	Carroll College
Johanna Nel	University of Wyoming
Sharon Thomas	Miami-Dade Community College
William D. Hallock	Hartford Community College
Katherine B. McIntosh	College of Charleston
Peter H. Yaun	College of Charleston
Thelma Bobo	State Community College of East St. Louis

Finally, I want to thank the "family" at West Publishing Company. Special thanks go to Mr. Clark Baxter, my editor, and his more than able-bodied assistant, Ms. Nancy Crociere. Also, thanks to Mr. Tom Modl who made sure the production of the text went smoothly. As always, the staff at West Publishing is a truly professional group and a joy to work with.

Tom E. C. Smith

1

INTRODUCTION

OBJECTIVES

After reading this chapter you will be able to

- describe the magnitude of public education in the United States;

- discuss the reform reports that emerged in the early 1980s;

- specify some of the reforms that have been initiated in states in response to the critical reports;

- discuss the results of the latest reform movement;

- define and discuss multicultural education;

- discuss the changing role of the federal government in education;

- describe the role of the conservative movement in public education;

- discuss some of the trends in public education in the United States.

ADVANCE ORGANIZERS

1. How many pupils are served in public education in the United States?
2. What were the major criticisms voiced in the reports on education that were published in the early 1980s?
3. What is the status of reforms initiated during the early 80s?
4. What are the purposes of public education?
5. What role is the conservative movement playing in public education?
6. What has been, and is emerging as, the federal government's role in public education?
7. What is multicultural education?
8. Which teacher organizations have influence in education?

INTRODUCTION

The public educational system in the United States is a model for many countries. What started as an idea in Colonial America—that citizens of this country needed to be educated in order to maintain their free form of government—has evolved into a massive, publicly supported effort to provide basic educational opportunities to all children. While the educational system has gone through periods of praise, criticism, and neglect, it has endured as a strong foundation for the country.

The 1980s likely will be remembered as a decade of educational reform. Public education received more attention during this period than at anytime since the Soviet launching of the satellite Sputnik (Timar and Kirp, 1989). What started as a public bashing of the educational system quickly turned into local, state, and federal efforts to improve the system. Although the fervor surrounding the critical reports issued in the early 1980s has subsided, reforms still are being suggested and tried. The verdict is still out on many of the reforms. While some obviously have been successful, others have been failures.

Beginning in the late 1970s, an increasing degree of criticism was directed at schools about the quality of education provided. Attention was drawn to adults who could not read, write, or verbally communicate at a functional level after twelve years of public education. America's difficulty in maintaining technological leadership in the industrialized world was pointed out; that students in some other countries achieve at a higher level than children in this country caused concern; and that students graduate from high school without adequate vocational or college preparatory skills embarrassed educators.

Schools were also criticized for including too many extracurricular activities in the curriculum, diluting the quality of academic instruction.

In response to these highly publicized problems, reformers came forward with myriad solutions. Suggestions included everything from lengthening school days and school years to competency tests and/or basic skills tests for teachers. Politicians, professional educators, parents, and other interested persons offered advice. An indication of public support for reforms can be found in the results of a survey conducted by Freeman, Cusick, and Houang (1985). The survey, from a nationwide sample of twelve hundred adults, found that more than eighty percent of the sample supported

1. a requirement that students pass high school exams in reading and math;
2. a requirement that junior-high students pass exams in reading and math;
3. at least half of all classes being required courses;
4. a system to reduce unexcused absences from school;
5. a requirement that teachers pass state or national teacher exams;
6. a requirement that teachers spend one month each summer improving their teaching skills.

The Gallup Poll of the Public's Attitude Toward the Public Schools (1988) indicated that 40 percent of the respondents gave the schools either an A or B rating. This compared with only thirty-one percent of the public rating schools with an A or B in 1983 but still reflects dissatisfaction by many.

The American system of public education needs to be supported by a higher degree of public confidence if the system of equal educational opportunities for all children is to become stable. To prevent further erosion of public confidence and to support more positive public attitudes toward education may take many years of serious efforts by educators, parents, and politicians. That attention has been called to problems in the educational system is a positive step to needed reform. Caution must be used however, in implementing change. Much of the educational system today is excellent. There are excellent teachers, curricula, and buildings, and highly motivated students. The positive things about education must be developed to strengthen the system. Great American educators such as Dewey, Mann, Conant, and Goodlad, as well as many parents and professionals, have worked diligently over the years to build a sound system of public education. Much of this system should remain in place.

American education is, however, at a crossroads. Several critical reports issued in the early 1980s indicated that the educational system in this country had reached a point where major changes needed to be made if the United States was to maintain its role of leadership in the world. While isolated concerns about education have been voiced for many years, education's loss of credibility and prestige was widely acknowledged by the public in the early 80s (Weiler 1982).

Although discounted by many professionals, the report that created the most concern was issued by the National Commission on Excellence in Education in 1983. The Commission, formed in 1981 by Secretary of Education Terrell Bell, published *A Nation at Risk* (1983) after a two-year study of the condition of education in the United States. The report began with the conclusive statement that "Our nation is at risk" and listed several indicators of this risk: (1) twenty-three million American adults are functionally illiterate; (2) thirteen percent of all seventeen-year-olds in this country, and as many as forty-eight percent of minority seventeen-year-olds, are functionally illiterate; (3) scores on the Scholastic Aptitude Test (SAT) declined steadily from 1963 to 1980; (4) science achievement scores of seventeen-year-olds declined in testing in 1969, 1973, and 1977; and (5) remedial math courses in colleges increased seventy-two percent between 1975 and 1980. These are but a few of the findings included in the report that indicated that the effectiveness of American education has seriously declined.

The following statements further clarify why the Commission concluded that the nation was "at risk":

- The number of students taking a general curriculum in high schools increased from twelve percent in 1964 to forty-two percent in 1979.
- Only thirty-one percent of high-school graduates completed intermediate algebra.
- Twenty-five percent of the credits earned by general-track high-school students were in areas of health, physical education, remedial math, English, and work outside the school.
- Homework for high-school seniors had decreased while grades had increased and academic achievement decreased.
- Students in other industrialized countries spent up to three times as much time in math and science courses as students in the United States.
- Twenty percent of all four-year public universities had to accept all high-school graduates from state high schools.
- Fifty percent or more of the credits earned for graduation could be electives in thirteen states.
- The amount of time spent in school was less in the United States than in many other industrialized countries.
- The average school provided only twenty-two hours of instruction per week to students.
- Too many teachers came from the bottom of their high-school and college graduating classes.

■ The average salary for teachers with twelve years of experience was only $17 thousand.

The reforms called for in the Commission's report were far reaching. They ranged from lengthening the school day and school year to decreasing the amount of time allotted for nonacademic electives.

Many of the educational practices and perceived practices in our schools were being challenged (Campbell 1983). Several other reports issued in 1982 and 1983 also focused on problems of public education in the United States (see table 1.1).

TABLE 1.1
Selected Recommendations of Six Reports on Education
(and Sponsoring Organization), 1982–1983

	FEDERAL ROLE (OR OTHER SUPPORT ROLE)	SCHOOL PRACTICES	CURRICULUM OBJECTIVES
TIME FOR REFORM (Council for Basic Education 1982)	School people, with parents and community members, should establish educational goals and academic standards. Role of federal government is minimal.	Increase time devoted to learning. Consider the role of the principal and community in reforming schools.	Strengthen academic standards; emphasis on liberal arts and science; raise college entrance requirements.
ACADEMIC PREPARATION FOR COLLEGE (The College Board, 1983)	Develop a national standard for academic achievement in secondary education.	Emphasize improvement of study and independent learning skills.	Improve preparation in English, math, science, computers, foreign languages, the arts. Improve student competencies in reading, writing, speaking, listening, reasoning, math, study skills. Raise college entrance requirements.
MAKING THE GRADE (Twentieth Century Fund, 1983)	Emphasis on the federal government providing special education programs for the poor, minority, immigrant and handicapped student. Similar emphasis on the federal government providing programs to develop scientific literacy among all citizens and advanced math and science training for secondary students.	No comparable provision.	Improve English language and advanced learning in math and science. Initiate alternative programs for students with learning problems, and a voucher program for disadvantaged students.

TABLE 1.1
(Continued)

	FEDERAL ROLE (OR OTHER SUPPORT ROLE)	SCHOOL PRACTICES	CURRICULUM OBJECTIVES
EDUCATING AMERICANS FOR THE 21ST CENTURY (National Science Foundation, 1983)	Federal government should maintain a national mechanism for measuring student performance; it should have input in establishing national goals for education.	Consider longer school day, week, and/or year.	Require one hour daily of math and thirty minutes of science in grades K–6. Devote more time to math and science in the secondary grades, and provide more advanced courses. Raise college entrance requirements.
ACTION FOR EXCELLENCE (Education Commission of the States, 1983)	Create policies which foster partnerships between the private sector and education. Federal government has an essential supporting role in financing education.	Consider longer school day. Emphasize order and discipline and more rigorous grading with periodic testing. Assign more homework. Revitalize the curriculum to encourage independent learning and reduce dropouts.	Establish and improve minimum competencies in reading, writing, speaking, listening, reasoning, economics. Strengthen programs for gifted students. Raise college entrance requirements.
A NATION AT RISK (The National Commission on Excellence in Education, 1983)	Federal government, in cooperation with the states and localities, should help meet the needs of special populations such as the disadvantaged, minority and bilingual students, the handicapped, gifted, and talented. Advocates national standardized tests, and the identification of the national interest in education.	Consider 7-hour school day and 200-day school year. Tighten attendance and discipline. Provide periodic testing and more rigorous grading. Place and group students by performance rather than age. Assign more homework, improve textbooks and other instructional materials.	Strengthen graduation requirements in the five New Basics; English, math, science, social studies, and computer science. Increase foreign languages for college-bound. Provide rigorous courses in vocational education and arts. Raise college entrance requirements.

Reprinted with permission. Ornstein, 1985.

Although most of the attention during the 1980s focused on education's problems, there is good news: states, local districts, and professional groups have taken and are taking actions to improve public schools in this country. Nationally, more than 700 statutes were enacted between 1984 and 1986 that impact on teaching (Timar and Kirp 1989). The Education Commission of the States reported that more than 250 task forces dealing with educational issues were established during the early and mid 1980s (Chance 1988). In one year alone, between June, 1983, and July, 1984, twenty-seven states initiated reforms, fourteen states were refining plans for reform, and five states had already completed reforms (Action in the States 1984). These reforms were responses to recommendations made by the National Commission on Excellence in Education and other task force reports, and ranged from lengthening the school day to implementing merit pay plans for teachers. Specific actions have included improved teacher and administrator salaries (Carter and Rosenbloom 1989), changes in teacher education programs (Tafel and Christensen 1988), and higher standards for high-school graduation (Orlich 1989).

While education in this country will not turn back the "rising tide of mediocrity" cited by the Commission's report, the improvement process has begun. The first step was simply to publicize concerns. The future will determine if the reforms called for in the various reports are implemented and, if implemented, whether the suggested reforms actually improve the quality of education.

Although no proof exists that the changes implemented thus far have had a significant effect, students' test scores have begun to improve. Stedman and Kaestle (1985) reported that student's scores on Iowa Test of Basic Skills improved dramatically between 1977 and 1984 and that test scores on the American College Testing Program (ACT) and the Scholastic Aptitude Test (SAT) had bottomed out. Graham (1984) reported that verbal and math test scores on the SAT increased slightly. While these reports indicated improvements in test scores, more recent reports suggest these improvements have subsided.

Not all professionals view the reports of the early 1980s and the resulting reforms as helpful to education. For example, Albrecht (1984) states that the report of the National Commission on Excellence in Education encouraged overgeneralization of the condition of public education. The Commission's report" . . . would have us believe that a school is a shool is a school." Other criticisms of the Nation at Risk report include the following: (1) the report suggests that the welfare of the college-bound student should be the criterion for judging the success of schools; (2) action should be taken immediately, before thorough thought has been applied; (3) the report legitimizes a way to get rid of children who have difficulty with school; and (4) what is good for one student, such as more math and science, is good for all students (Albrecht 1984).

In addition to these criticisms of the Nation at Risk report, critics have also reacted to other national reports. Omstein (1985) lists the following general criticisms of the reports:

1. Reports are too idealistic and too unrealistic.
2. Narrow nationalistic interests are served at the expense of the public interest.

3. Too much attention is focused on course requirements and standards.

4. Most of the recommendations reflect previous suggestions.

5. Most of the reports ignore knowledge about school change.

6. Elitist solutions are supported, such as advanced courses and programs for gifted and talented children.

7. Most of the recommendations are very expensive.

Although these criticisms have been expressed at various times by various people, the reports of the early 1980s caught the public's attention. State legislators, governors, and others got on the bandwagon to improve education, to restore it to its previous place with what some regard as "quick-fix" solutions (Albrecht 1984). While few educators would suggest that all is right with education in this country, many would have suggested different modifications. Too frequently, the reforms that were tried were "contradictory in nature, poorly implemented, and eventually abandoned" (Orlich 1989, p. 513). One of the major criticisms of many of the recent reforms is that they were implemented with little or no teacher involvement, this despite the fact that many of the problems were student- and teacher-centered. While the reforms frequently made good political headlines, teachers frequently remained without a voice in their conception and implementation (Henley 1988).

Although some of the reforms resulted in positive outcomes, many individuals involved in the movement have been disappointed at the rate of progress. William Bennett, Secretary of the U.S. Department of Education, recently stated that "This year the news is not what it should be: test scores are in a dead stall. In saying that I am disappointed, I think I speak for the American people. The very substantial and ever-increasing dollars spent for education have not yet given us the results our children deserve" (*Education Reports*, February 29, 1988, p. 1).

A summary of Bennett's analysis of the educational reform effort includes the following facts:

- ACT and SAT scores either dropped or remained stable during the past two years.

- Test scores for minority students have increased recently.

- The graduation rate decreased between 1985 and 1986.

- Average teacher salaries have risen thirty-eight percent between 1982 and 1987.

- Average per-pupil expenditure has increased from $2,726 in 1982 to $3,752 in 1986.

- Twelve states require minimum competency testing for grade promotion.

- Twenty-four states have planned or implemented minimum competency testing for graduation.

The success of the educational reforms initiated in the 1980s is viewed differently by various individuals. For example, while Secretary Bennett considers many of the changes as positive, others consider the changes to this point to be of limited value. Terrell Bell, a previous U.S. Secretary of Education, believes that the current reform movement is stagnant due to a lack of attention and that the only way meaningful reform can occur is when the failures of the education system become a national obsession (Bell 1988). Other critics of the movement have concluded that the majority of the reforms were misguided and were implemented by federal and state policymakers unaware that American schools have remained virtually unchanged for decades (Cuban 1988). In the most recent edition of The Gallup Poll of the Public's Attitudes Toward the Public Schools (Gallup and Elam 1988), only twenty-nine percent of the respondents indicated that schools had improved during the past five years. During this five-year period, when many reforms were taking place, thirty-seven percent felt the schools stayed the same while nineteen percent thought the schools had gotten worse.

The issues in education today are particularly difficult, because they are not clearcut. They are matters of value. Since different people value different things, disagreement is inevitable. The need seems to be for compromise/consensus rather than winners and losers and forced agreement. The reform movements have hopefully pointed out these facts and will lead to a better educational system.

EDUCATION IN THE UNITED STATES TODAY

Magnitude of Public Education

Public education in the United States is big business. The number of individuals directly and indirectly affected by education is difficult to estimate. Directly, students and their families and professional educators are involved. Indirectly, many other groups must be considered when describing the magnitude of public education, including employers; citizens who support schools with their tax dollars; and businesses that depend on schools for their existence, such as textbook companies, school supply businesses, and enterprises that provide transportation capabilities to schools. The list is endless.

Number of Students in Public Education. To grasp the extent of public education, an understanding of the number of children involved is needed. In the 1987–88 school year, 40.1 million students were enrolled in public education programs in the United States. Of this number, 24.9 million, or sixty-two percent, were enrolled in elementary schools, while 15.1 million were in secondary schools. Enrollment by states ranged from a high of 4.5 million in California to a low of 102,000 in Alaska (National Center for Education Information 1988). Although enrollments in public schools began declining in 1970, recent evidence suggests that the decline has ended. The 1985 enrollment in elementary schools reflected the first major enrollment increase in fourteen years (Elementary Enrollment Up 1985).

School Districts. To provide public educational programs for the approximate forty million students enrolled in public school programs, states are divided into school districts. During the 1986–1987 school year, there were 15,713 such districts. The number of districts per state ranged from one each in Hawaii and the District of Columbia to 1,092 in Texas. Fifty-five percent of the districts enrolled fewer than 1,000 students; twenty-two percent enrolled between 1,000 and 2,499 students; and only twenty percent had enrollments of more than 2,500 (Digest of Education Statistics 1988).

Private Education. In addition to the forty million students enrolled in public educational programs in 1985, approximately 5.6 million students, or 12 percent of all students, were enrolled in private schools. In some states, fifteen percent or more of students were in private schools, while other states had very few students enrolled in private programs (Snyder 1988).

Purposes of Public Schools

Unlike public schools of the 1800s, which were designed primarily for academic and religious training, today's schools are expected to accomplish many goals. Many believe that too much is expected of American schools.

Even the academic purposes have expanded. The original goal of developing students' skills in the basic academic areas of reading, writing, and arithmetic has expanded to include many areas of knowledge. Besides the academic purpose of schools, society expects schools to provide instruction and experiences in civic, vocational, and personal goals. The expectations of schools now range "from mechanics in the basic skills, understanding of social and natural phenomena, and the highest levels of cognition to getting along with others, relating to humankind, and developing personal interests and capacities" (Goodlad 1983, p. 468).

Not only are schools supposed to provide instruction and experiences in all these areas, but they are supposed to accommodate myriad children in the process. The purposes would be difficult enough if all students were equal in abilities, came from similar environments, and had the same needs. A condition much to the contrary exists in public schools. Students range from the low to the high end of the intellectual continuum; represent many different racial, cultural, linguistic, and socioeconomic groups; and have different attitudes concerning education. The task of being all things to all students has proved to be difficult and has led to much dissatisfaction.

■ *Unlike the schools of the 1800s, today's public schools have many different purposes, including preparation for life after high school.*

Current Trends and Problems in American Education

Educators in this country always seem to be implementing one trend or another. Many critics have suggested that educators are more interested in fads and quick fixes than in thought-out, well-researched solutions based on empirical evidence. Concerning the reactions to the Nation at Risk report, Albrecht (1984) believes that reforms are being implemented too fast to answer some of the points made by the report. Effective change must consider the interaction among numerous variables, each of which may affect combinations of others. Change must occur after a feasible plan for action has been developed. Without such a focus, as well as the necessary resources to implement the plan, change will not succeed (Tyler 1987). The remainder of this chapter will describe other conditions, goals, and problems that need to be addressed if change is to be effective.

Curricular Reform. Back-to-the-basics started as a reform movement in the 1970s. Since then, the merits of emphasizing the three Rs at the

QUESTIONS RAISED ON EFFICACY OF STIFFER MATH, SCIENCE GRADUATION REQUISITES

Lynn Olson

This decade's raised high-school graduation requirements have primarily affected low- and middle-achieving students, who are taking more science and mathematics courses as a result, a new study has found.

But the report by the Center for Policy Research in Education, a federally funded research consortium, questions whether the new courses are as challenging or as rigorous as they could be.

Most of the added classes are for noncollege-bound students, it found, and are concentrated at the remedial, general, or basic level.

Thus, the report argues, they do little to rectify the stratified curriculum that already exists in most high schools.

"The problem is that the extra courses may not fulfill the reform objectives very well," said William H. Clune, Voss-Bascom Professor of Law at the University of Wisconsin Law School and primary author of the report.

"Insofar as the reformers had educational objectives, they intended to produce a more uniform academic curriculum and raise student achievement," Mr. Clune said, "And the problem is that a couple of extra low-level courses doesn't move very far in that direction."

A Popular Reform

The report, by Mr. Clune and two associates—Paula White and Janice Patterson—provides the first in-depth study of how selected schools across the country have carried out mandates to increase academic requirements.

State mandates on the number of required "core" courses have been the most common reform of the 1980's.

Since the beginning of the decade, 45 states have either specified for the first time, or increased, the total number of courses required for high-school graduation.

Of those states, 42 increased course requirements for math or science, or both. At least 18 added language-arts requirements; and about half raised social-studies requirements.

The report focused on changes in graduation requirements in six states—Arizona, California, Florida, Georgia, Minnesota, and Pennsylvania. It also studied a select number of schools and districts in each state, except Minnesota.

In each instance, school administrators, teachers, school-board members, union leaders, and parent representatives were asked for their views on the reforms.

In addition, the study examined actual changes in course offerings in four states—Arizona, California, Florida, and Pennsylvania.

Bypassed High Achievers

In general, the report found, affluent schools and districts and college-bound students were not affected by the reforms, because they already met or exceeded the new curriculum requirements.

Instead, the reforms were felt most by noncollege-bound students: those traditionally considered low- or middle-achievers.

Approximately 27 percent of these students took an extra math course, and 34 percent an extra science course, as a result of the reforms, the study found. Many also took a new or added course in social studies.

Given the relatively low number of math and science courses previously taken by such students, the study noted, the in-

continued

creases represent a "potentially significant increment of educational content."

But it cautioned that most of the new math courses were focused on a relatively low level of skills, such as general math, remedial math, consumer math, algebra, geometry, and math applications.

And although science courses were added in such traditional subjects as physical science, chemistry, physics, and biology, the additions also tended to be at the "basic" level.

The 'Major Casualty'

Respondents complained that the new requirements substantially reduced the number of courses that students took in home economics, industrial arts, physical education, vocational education, business, psychology, and the performing arts.

"Vocational courses were the major casualty of the increased academic course-taking," Mr. Clune said. "We saw evidence that the new requirements made it difficult to complete logical, and even required, sequences of vocational courses."

"*A Nation at Risk,* the so-called bible of the reform movement, spoke of eliminating weak academic courses in favor of higher-quality academic courses and vocational courses," he added. "In some cases, the real impact [of these reforms] may have been the reverse. You got low-quality academic courses replacing higher-quality vocational ones. But we don't have the precise data to support that."

Increased Dropout Rate?

Respondents also worried that the increased standards would push marginal students out of school, although they admitted that they lacked data to support that view.

The report itself cited previous research findings linking higher standards to lower mean dropout rates, and indicating that graduation rates are improving slightly nationwide.

A longitudinal study of students in Dade County, Fla., for example, found a significant decline in the dropout rate during the same period that students' academic course load was rising.

"I actually can't explain the discrepancy between school-level perceptions of dropout problems as a result of these higher standards and the lack of objective data," Mr. Clune said.

"It's possible that we'll see the [dropout] rates go up later on because there's been some sort of lag," he said. "Also, school people may have a bias toward seeing the problems of higher standards and not seeing the benefits, such as increased motivation for students resulting from more interesting material. There is research supporting that type of effect."

'Watered Down' Courses

The study did not gather systematic data on the actual content of the new courses. But it did find scattered evidence of attempts to "water down" the curriculum.

The evidence included shortened class periods, courses with repetitious material, science "labs" held in regular classrooms, and some inadequately qualified teachers.

In some instances, students were also steered toward less-demanding classes. In two Florida districts, for example, high-school counselors reported advising students in danger of failing to take easier courses in order to meet the new standards. The counselors said that in the past they had advised such students to take more-challenging classes in order to stretch themselves.

In two of four Pennsylvania districts studied, students were allowed to substitute vocational courses for their academic requirements. One district was considering substituting courses like "nursing math, baking math, and carpentry math."

"Lacking systematic data, we cannot tell how common such practices were," the study noted. "But there are deeper reasons for doubting that the new courses were the best possible."

First, it said, schools typically offer low- and middle-achieving students "dull, factual, repetitive material," and there was no reason to believe that most schools changed their tactics in adding the new courses.

continued

Second, designing the right kinds of academic courses for such students is extremely difficult, the report argued. But states focused almost no attention on the need to upgrade instruction at the same time that they increased course requirements.

Moreover, state mandates included almost no provisions for technical assistance to either districts or schools.

California offered the one exception in the study. The state specifically created "bridge" courses that would allow students to upgrade their skills and make the transition from the general to the academic track.

Streamlined Core Curriculum'

In general, Mr. Clune concluded, the reforms produced mixed results: Schools added the best courses they could manage for low- and middle-achieving students on short notice. But they fell "far short" of providing real academic rigor.

He suggested that to attain the latter goal, policymakers would have to take a serious look at the content of academic courses, and not just their labels.

"At a certain level of requirements, you begin to get high costs and unclear benefits," he said. "States with very high graduation requirements may be choosing quantity over quality. At some point, students lose all of their electives and the opportunity to take vocational courses. Or they spend a lot of time retaking courses they have failed."

Instead of adding more and more course requirements, Mr. Clune advised, states should pare back the number of credits required for graduation and work to strengthen the content of the courses they do require.

In particular, he advocated the creation of a "streamlined core curriculum" for all students. Within that curriculum, he said, states should create a very specific set of learning objectives that focus on higher-order skills and that are as "demanding as possible" for everyone.

"Ways must be found to identify the most important part of the core curriculum and to make sure students reach at least that level," according to the report. "States, districts, and schools need to design workable paths from remedial and weak courses to more demanding ones."

New Look at Voc. Ed.

Mr. Clune also suggested that the role of vocational education "deserves a second look." It can be a "superior method" of introducing students to both basic and higher-order academic skills, he said, and can also be "an excellent means of motivating some students to stay in school."

The Center for Policy Research in Education is a federally funded research consortium that includes Rutgers University, Michigan State University, Stanford University, and the University of Wisconsin-Madison. The opinions expressed in the report are those of the authors and do not necessarily reflect the views of CPRE's institutional partners.

Copies of the report may be obtained for $5 each prepaid, including postage and handling, from the Center for Policy Research in Education, Eagleton Institute of Politics, Douglass Campus, Rutgers, the State University of New Jersey, New Brunswick, N.J. 08901, Attention: Publications Discounts for bulk orders are available on request.

Reprinted with permission from *Education Week*, vol. VIII, no. 21, p. 5.

---

expense of other curricular areas has been debated. The issue is whether to base the entire curriculum on these basic subjects or include them within other subject areas.

Critics often refer to current educational practices as moving away from teaching the skills necessary to develop competencies in these three basic areas. In reading for example, Bussis (1982) believed that an emphasis on "essential" reading had greatly reduced the time spent on reading. To change this practice, it was recommended that teachers make a wide range of reading materials available to students, read to children daily, encourage writing, set aside a reading time, and work individually with children. Similar changes in writing as well as in other basic curricular areas, are frequently recommended by others.

William Bennett, Secretary of the U.S. Department of Education during the last part of the Reagan administration, believes that the best way to develop a curriculum is to determine what students should know at the end of a particular school period. For example, asking the question "What should children know by the end of the eighth grade?" will enable school leaders to determine what should be included in the curriculum. Bennett recommends that the elementary curriculum include reading, writing, mathematics, science, social studies, cultural literacy, the arts, foreign languages, and health and physical education. Bennett advocates an emphasis in reading, writing, and computing because of the importance on these skills in later school and life (Bennett 1986).

State Initiatives in Response to Reports of the Early 1980s. Many states responded quickly to the Nation at Risk report and other critical reports of the early 1980s. By the middle of 1984, more than 250 task forces had been established to examine the state of education and recommend changes. Many of the task forces responded to a report by the Education Commission of the States, which recommended actions in eight areas:

1. Develop and implement state plans to improve education in public schools.
2. Create broader partners for improving the schools.
3. Acquire the resources necessary for improving the schools.
4. Express a new and higher regard for teachers.
5. Make academic experiences more intense and productive.
6. Provide quality assurance in education.
7. Improve leadership and management in public schools.
8. Provide better services to those underserved and unserved (Action for Excellence 1983)

The actions range from minimal to far reaching, all having the intent of responding to critics of public education in the early 1980s (see table 1.2).

Multicultural Education. Multicultural education developed out of the racial turmoil of the 1960s (Banks 1983). Just what multicultural education is cannot be precisely agreed upon. What can be stated is that multicultural education "is a concept predicated upon a fundamental belief that all people must be accorded respect, regardless of age, race, sex, economic class, religion, physical or mental ability" (Grant 1982,

TABLE 1.2
Examples of Early Actions Taken by States in Response
to Education Reports of the Early 1980s

STATE	ACTIONS
Arkansas	■ Approved most comprehensive education program in state's history in a special legislative session in 1983. ■ Passed sales tax increase to fund reforms ■ Adopted new standards that will —reduce student/teacher ratios —increase number of principals and counselors per district —increase course offerings in high schools —initiate competency testing in grades 3, 6, and 8
Tennessee	■ Passed a comprehensive reform act in 1984 ■ Passed tax increases to fund reforms ■ Established a five-step career ladder for teachers with annual salary incentives ranging from $500 to $7,000
Florida	■ Passed stiffer high-school graduation requirements ■ Established twenty-eight regional coordinating councils to review and recommend programs to assure timely and needed vocational education programs ■ Established new academic performance standards for graduation and participation in interscholastic extracurricular activities
Ohio	■ Increased funding for public education 15.4 percent for FY 1984 and 7.3 percent for FY 1985 ■ Increased gaduation requirements ■ Passed procedurs for ensuring that students achieve minimum academic competencies ■ Lowered student/teacher ratios in grades 1–4
Massachusetts	■ Established the Commonwealth Inservice Institute to fund inservice programs. Examples of funded programs: —Middle management training model focusing on time management, staff development, computer education, and curriculum planning for administrators —Program to assist elementary teachers in coordinating reading programs —Training to assist administrators in programs for gifted and talented students
California	■ Developed the Mathematics, Engineering, Science Achievement (MESA) Program. Program objectives: —Increase minority students' participation in math, science, and engineering training programs —Promote career awareness in minority students

Source: Action in the States, Task Force on Education for Economic Growth. *Education Commission of the States, 1984.*

p. 485). The term is sometimes used as a catchall for anything innovative dealing with the education of minorities (Ivie 1978).

Currently the area of multicultural education is taking on greater significance because of the large numbers of immigrants. Between 1970 and 1979, more than 4.3 million immigrants entered the United States legally. It is estimated that this number will be more than 8 million

■ *Multicultural education attempts to provide all children with equal opportunities, regardless of cultural background.*

between 1980 and 1989 (Kellogg 1988). In the state of California, no one racial or cultural group currently accounts for a majority of the student population. A recent survey of states determined that 24 states plus the District of Columbia had multicultural education programs; $81 million was spent in these programs (Mitchell 1987).

Melting Pot Theory. The multicultural education movement began in the early 1960s as educators responded to the demands of ethnic and racial minority groups who wanted a more balanced presentation in textbooks about minority groups and wanted more minority professionals involved in education (Banks 1983). The movement resulted from the realization that the melting pot theory of American culture had not occurred, and probably would not occur. This idea is called cultural pluralism. "Pluralists reject the traditional 'Americanizing' function of the public school because it has meant assimilation into the white, middle class pattern of American society" (Ivie 1978, p. 442).

Cultural pluralism is much more than simply integrating minority children into the American mainstream (Emihovich 1988). Educators need to acknowledge that assimilation has not taken place. Multicultural education is an attempt to realize this fact.

Our society appears to be growing more rather than less diverse (Kellogg, 1988). The recent immigration of Hispanics, Cubans, Haitians, Vietnamese, and others adds to our cultural diversity. Many parents and children still have strong ties to racial, linguistic, nationalistic, ethnic, or Waspish traditions (Ehlers and Crawford 1983). These strong ties probably will not change in the near future.

Purposes of Multicultural Education. The initial purpose of multicultural education was to promote racial equality and harmony. Correcting errors of omissions, stereotyping, and misinformation, as well as providing information about ethnic minorities, has been replaced by the promotion of ethnic pluralism. The purposes have moved from primarily political to pedagogical (Gay 1983). Multicultural education currently attempts to assimilate reliable information about cultural pluralism into the entire curriculum.

Components of Multicultural Education. Multicultural education is not accomplished in a simplistic, single course taught to high-school students. Rather, multicultural education includes

1. Professional staffing that reflects the pluralistic nature of our society;
2. Curricula that are unbiased and present appropriate information about individuals of different sex, race, ethnic background, socioeconomic class, and ability;
3. Acknowledgement of the knowledge and use of different languages as acceptable;
4. Instructional materials free of bias and representative of various groups. (Grant 1982)

Bilingual education is a component of multicultural education. It focuses not on teaching equal skills in English and another language, but rather attempts to teach English skills to non-English speakers (Foster 1982). Students are taught in their native language until they become proficient enough in English to receive the majority of instruction in English (Ovando 1983). This model, used in the majority of cases, is referred to as the transitional model. An alternative model focuses on maintaining the child's native language by giving it equal attention as English. The goal in this model is to enable the child to continue to develop the native language as well as English (Foster 1982). Forty-nine percent of those responding to the recent Gallup educational poll oppose local schools providing instruction in a student's native language (Gallup and Elam 1988).

Beginning with a federal budget of $7.5 million in the early 1970s, bilingual education had reached federal expenditures of $160 million by 1982 (Foster 1982). The mere size of federal financial involvement in bilingual education indicates the importance of this program. The role of the federal government in bilingual education will affect its future.

The Future of Multicultural Education. Positive results of multicultural education include more minority students graduating from high school, the acknowledgment in textbooks of contributions made by minority individuals, and a more accurate representation of minority groups in textbooks and other instructional materials. U.S. Secretary of Education William Bennett notes another major indicator of the positive results of multicultural education in his analysis of the results of educational reforms in the 1980s. In his report, he indicated that test scores of minority students had increased consistently while those of white students had declined slightly or become static (Educational Reports, February 29, 1988). However, multicultural education is at a crossroads. Although teachers involved in multicultural education play a significant role in successfully implementing its concepts (Ehlers and Crawford 1983), the movement is confronted by two factors that could lead to its demise: economics and ideology. Economics could affect multicultural education because, in a time of budget cutbacks, government-supported multicultural education programs could be cut. Ideologically, the current movement toward conservatism and the promotion of the majority culture could limit multicultural programs (Gay 1983). If multicultural education is to continue to be a positive force in American education, it must have the support of government policymakers, as well as those in business and education (Banks 1983).

Improved Teachers. One of the reforms called for in *A Nation at Risk, Action for Excellence,* and other reports is improved teachers (Tracy, Sheehan, and McArdle 1988). *A Nation at Risk* reported the following about teachers:

- Too many teachers come from the bottom quarter of graduating classes.
- Teacher preparation curricula are heavily weighted with educational methods courses.
- Average teacher salary after twelve years of teaching is only $17 thousand.
- Severe teacher shortages exist in some subject areas, most notably math and science.
- Half of the newly hired math, science, and English teachers are not qualified to teach these courses.

The two most noted national reports calling for reform in teacher education were the Carnegie Task Force on Teaching as a Profession and the Holmes Group. These two reports recommended academic standards for students majoring in education, curricular options for teacher education, and financial support for teacher education programs and teachers' salaries. Many colleges of education have implemented reforms that address these areas. However, some areas, such as eliminating undergraduate teacher education programs and fifth-year teacher education programs, have encountered significant resistance (Tracy, Sheehan, and McArdle 1988).

To improve the quality of teachers, many states initiated reforms including increasing salaries, screening prospective teachers before they enter teacher education, providing merit pay for outstanding teachers, providing more flexibility in teacher certification, requiring teachers to pass competency tests to remain certified, and requiring teachers to pass tests before initial certification. In addition to these suggestions, a congressional task force called for school districts to develop sabbatical programs for teachers, for the federal government to fund leave time for study through a talented teacher fellowship program, and for school administrators to try different ways to improve the work environment for teachers (Congressional Report Waffles on Merit Pay 1983). Several initiatives have been implemented by states to improve the quality of teachers.

Providing merit pay for superior teachers is being investigated by several states. The issue is controversial, but is strongly supported by the public (Gallup and Elam, 1988). Most professionals agree that those teachers who do the best job should receive the most pay; questions concerning how such a system would be developed remain unanswered. Should teachers be rewarded based on their continuing education, the achievement levels of their students, ratings by supervisors, peer evaluations, or other measures?

Even though a merit pay plan that is without criticism may be difficult to develop, several states and local districts have implemented merit pay programs. Some of the states and their plans include the following (Pipho 1983):

California	Recommend rules, regulations, and guidelines for the California Mentor Teacher Program
Florida	Appoint the Florida Quality Instruction Incentives Council to develop and implement a plan for incentives for teachers
New Jersey	Develop the Master Teacher Program
Tennessee	Revamp the Master Teacher Plan
	Appoint an Interim Commission on Master Teacher-Administrator Certification
Virginia	Budget $500 thousand in 1984–86 to field-test several performance-based teacher pay plans

Besides these statewide efforts, many local districts have taken the initiative to implement teacher incentive-merit pay plans. In Round Valley School District, California, teachers assist in the development of their own merit pay program. They can earn merit points for (1) teacher initiative, (2) teacher cooperation, and (3) principals' evaluations (Burke 1982). Various rewards are provided for teachers in the Catalina Foothills School District in Tucson, Arizona, for excellence in the classroom. The most popular reward for teachers in the program has been trips to professional meetings, although cash, instructional materials, and computers can also be earned (Frase, Hetzel, and Grant 1982).

An alternative to merit pay plans is the career ladder concept. Career ladder plans, enacted in more than seventy-five percent of the states, enable teachers to "gain responsibility, status, and pay as they grow in experience and acquire more work skills" (Engelking and Samuelson 1986, p. 137). Leadership development is a key element of career ladders; teachers share in leadership decisions with school administrators. Similar to university professorial ranks, various teacher levels are the basis for the career ladder. As teachers gain in experience and skills, they are promoted up the ladder to positions with more rewards and leadership responsibilities (Engelking and Samuelson 1986).

While many states and districts are experimenting with merit pay plans, a great deal of controversy over the issue still exists. Although teacher unions have traditionally opposed merit pay plans, a recent reversal of this policy was suggested by the President of the National Education Association (NEA), Mary Futrell (Olson 1989). Often, merit pay plans that are developed and implemented are not successful. One example of a failed merit pay plan is in Kalamazoo, Michigan. The plan was started in 1974 to reward administrators and teachers based on evaluations by administrators, peers, pupils, self, and pupil performance. The program ended with a great deal of controversy, having never achieved its goal (Doremus 1982).

The Conservative Movement. The political climate in the United States has been conservative since the mid-1970s. The conservative trend has had an impact on public education. Calls for returning to the basic purposes of public schools have been voiced by conservative educators, parents, and politicians. Some of the recommended changes include (1) a return to emphasizing the basic academic subjects; (2) a deemphasis on extracurricular activities; (3) an emphasis on moral education; (4) inclusion of school prayer; and (5) more control of the educational process by the family.

Most supporters of conservative reform of public schools are not extremists. They are well-intentioned, well-informed citizens who have the welfare of their children in mind. They are firmly convinced that the public schools of today have moved too far away from the appropriate purposes of public education. Some of the questions asked by these reformers include:

- Do parents have the primary rights and responsibilities in the education of their children?
- Do educators in public schools have the right to programmatically enter the "affective domain" of the child without the prior, informed consent of parents?
- What is the primary purpose of education—social and psychological development or academic and vocational achievement? (McGraw 1982, p. 94)

Parents who ask these questions want more of a say in the educational system than they currently feel they have.

Some professional educators also feel that public education has ventured too far from its original purposes. In Ebel's view (1982) much of what schools do today does not emphasize student achievement and, therefore, should be changed. His proposals for strengthening public education are similar to the ideas held by Horace Mann and other traditional educational theorists. To determine whether schools are promoting achievement, Ebel suggests asking: (1) Is there evidence of student learning? (2) Are teachers' instructional goals appropriate? (3) Are teachers' instructional methods effective? and (4) How can the school facilitate teachers' efforts?

The New Right. In 1980, Park wrote that a new coalition was being formed among ultraconservative and right-wing groups in the United States. This coalition, called the New Right, includes traditional conservative groups and certain fundamentalist religious groups. The New Right is a potentially powerful force that deserves the attention of educators. The aim of the coalition is to change the ways children in this country are educated (Brodinsky 1982). People who hold New Right views differ from other conservative educational reformers in the extent to which they would go to alter public education. They agree with other conservative reformers, but would go further in implementing changes in schools.

The New Right has focused on public education as a target for change. Among the aims of the movement are:

- developing and propagating "model" legislation for states;
- promoting prayer in public schools;
- promoting creationism;
- censoring textbooks and school library books;
- ending unionism and union tactics in education;
- promoting the interests of Christian schools;
- cutting taxes and school expenditures;

- nurturing conservative ideas;
- fighting "secular humanism" in public schools;
- channeling corporate gifts and funds into colleges and universities that promote "free enterprise." (Brodinsky 1982, p. 88)

Supporters of the New Right suggest that schools in this country "have been deliberately sabotaged by a core of elitist educators" who "through such exotic titles as values analysis, values clarification, situation ethics, death education, sex education, environmental education, and now the new global education . . . are bent on totally stripping from children those traditional American values that parents and the majority of those who pay teachers' salaries still espouse" (Dixon 1982, p. 97). They believe that books expounding on traditional values have been banned from public schools (Gabler and Gabler 1982).

Censorship in school libraries is a major focus of the New Right; since the mid-1970s, individuals espousing New Right views have attempted to remove books from school libraries that are considered objectionable for a variety of reasons (Pincus 1984). The censorship activities have involved areas other than books. As a result of the attacks of right-wing groups, teachers are often questioned about classroom discussions, content of school plays and assemblies, and the circulation of materials (Kemerer 1984). Individuals identifying with the New Right want more control over what is presented to their children and press for the right to veto any information that they consider objectionable.

An area related to censorship is the desire by conservative groups to have creationism taught in lieu of or in combination with evolutionism. This area alone has caused a great deal of debate between individuals who believe in the scientific approach to creation and those who believe in the creationist view. Those who believe religion should be in the schools and those who strongly advocate strict adherence to separation of church and state are also at odds. Those who favor inclusion of creation science base their request on the fact that students have a right to know all sides to the creation question (Hahn 1982); those opposing creation science in public schools argue that creationism is not science but religion and should therefore be separate from education, which is an arm of the state (Strike 1982).

Home Schooling. Another movement that parallels the conservative movement is home schooling. Parents in many parts of the country are beginning to formally educate their children at home, rather than sending them to public school programs. Although this might be viewed as encouraging truancy and breaking mandatory attendance laws, many states have given parents the legal right to provide home schooling.

Until just a few years ago, educating children at home was viewed as a subversive activity. Parents who educated their children at home

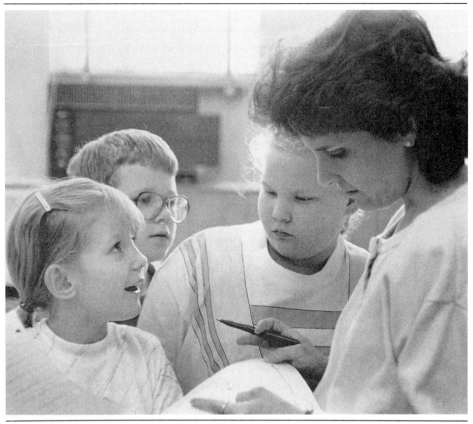

■ *Many states have implemented merit pay plans to reward excellence in teaching.*

would keep them indoors during school hours for fear that neighbors would report them to the local school authorities. As a result of a rapid expansion of home schooling during the past several years, most parents involved with the movement are currently members of a community of home schooling parents (Knowles 1988). Although many home schools develop out of a common political and cultural background, there appears to be great diversity in their structure. For example, the range of methods and materials used vary in home schools just as they vary in public school classrooms (Ray 1988).

While the majority of individuals involved in the home schooling movement are probably religious fundamentalists who believe that schools do a poor job of adequately educating their children, especially in fundamental values (Divoky 1983), they represent a cross-section of our society and approach home schooling in a variety of ways (Knowles 1988). A minority of home schoolers provide educational programs in the home because they feel they can do a better job than the schools have done in educating their children. With the movement picking up supporters, school officials should begin to cooperate with home schoolers and develop a close working partnership (Holt 1983). A large majority of Americans are still opposed to home schooling (Gallup and Elam 1988).

Technology. Our world is experiencing a technological explosion. New technologies are being developed that affect all aspects of our lives, including education (Mecklenburger, 1988). The most obvious technologies are in the area of machines and equipment (Hatch 1984). The use of microcomputers in education appears to have become a major force in education. The National Center for Education Statistics (1983) reported that the number of computers available in public schools tripled between 1980 and 1982. The number of schools with microcomputers increased from 13,986 in 1982 to 30,493 in 1983, an increase of over 200 percent in one year alone (National Center for Education Statistics 1984). During the latter part of the decade, computer usage increased even more dramatically. A recent report noted that the number of elementary and secondary schools using computers increased from sixteen percent in 1982 to ninety-five percent in 1988. The report also indicated that ninety-one percent of schools use videocassette recorders. Currently, twenty-one states and the District of Columbia require schools to provide some level of computer education (Quality Education Data 1988).

The potential of computers to revolutionize education may never be realized if computer purchases and program implementation precede adequate planning. To avoid this occurrence, Boyer (1984) suggests acceptance of three high-priority goals for computer usage by students. First, students need to learn about technology. This includes teaching students about the social impact of technology and computers, not hands-on instruction. The second priority is to teach students how to learn with computers or use computers to gather information. Finally, students should learn from computers. This requires interactive learning between students and computers, or "conversing" between students and computers to improve thinking skills.

While computers are capable of becoming a major force in education, some professionals argue that the overuse of computers and other technologies can have a negative effect. For example, Hatch (1984) believes that the technology in education can "isolate us from the very processes by which we define our humanity." These human processes, defined as those things that differentiate humans from other living organisms, such as loving, knowing, and making decisions, can become devalued as a result of overdependency on technology.

Regardless of concerns, the use of technology in education today is definitely increasing. Microcomputers will likely continue to become a major instructional tool. While there are problems in the widespread use of this technology and concerns from some educators about dehumanizing the educational process, the future promises increased use of microcomputers in most aspects of education.

Fiscal Problems. In the fall, 1979, Chicago School Board members realized that they would not receive any bids on $124.6 million in general obligation notes that were required to keep the school system fiscally solvent. As a result, several things occurred: (1) more than forty thousand teachers and school staff did not know if they would receive paychecks, (2) the school board was unable to meet its payroll three times, (3) a one-week walkout by teachers occurred, (4) a full strike by teachers occurred, (5) 2,465 jobs in the district were lost, (6) the school superintendent resigned, and (7) a rescue plan was formulated by the state legislature, city of Chicago, and teacher unions (Banas 1980).

Since the Chicago fiscal crisis, other school districts have faced similar problems. The San Jose district in California, the eighth largest in the state, filed for bankruptcy when it faced a $14 million deficit after having closed fourteen schools and laying off five hundred teachers during the previous year (A California school district goes broke 1983). Money is the basis for public educational programs; without funds schools will discontinue to be a force in our society. Some reasons that schools today face increasing difficulties include:

- Constituency of the local community—fewer people with children; smaller families; population shifts from urban to rural, from industrialized to the sunbelt.
- Declining economy—the country has been experiencing economic decline, coupled with an astronomical federal deficit. Local communities have also experienced declining tax bases.
- Deemphasis of funding educational programs by the federal government.
- Inflation—increasing costs for transportation, utilities, building maintenance, and personnel.

In a time when state and local governments must assume a greater funding burden for public schools, their ability to do so is declining. A tax revolt, which began in the early 1970s, has had an impact on state and local governments. Between 1977 and 1980, sixteen states reduced sales taxes and twenty-two reduced income taxes. In the 1978 general election, tax reduction or limitation measures were voted on in thirteen states, with ten passing (Archambault and Duncombe 1979). States now provide the biggest share of the public school funding, approximately 50 percent, compared with 6 percent from the federal government. Unfortunately, during the past several years, state tax collections have not kept pace with inflation (National Center for Education Statistics, 1988). (See figure 1.1).

The tax revolt of the late 1970s is a reversal of the situation during the 1960s and early 1970s. From 1959 until 1976, forty-one new taxes and 586 tax increases were passed in the states. This substantially increased the tax money available for public school programs (Adams 1982). Two of the biggest tax reversals occurred in California and Mas-

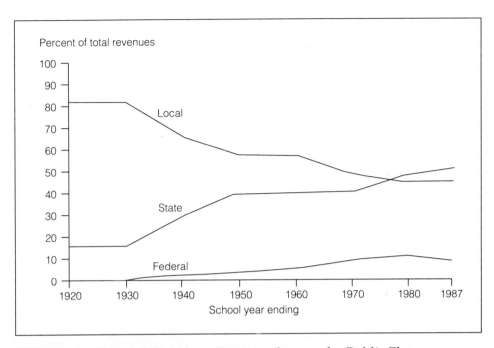

Percent of total revenues

FIGURE 1.1 National Trends in Revenue Sources for Public Elementary and Secondary Education: Selected School Years Ending 1920–1987
SOURCES: National Center for Education Statistics, Digest of Education Statistics, 1988. National Education Association, Estimates of School Statistics, 1986–87.

sachusetts. In 1978, California voters passed Proposition 13. This legislation limited property taxes to one percent of their 1975 assessed valuation (Hoban 1979). In Massachusetts, Proposition 2½ was passed in 1980. This act stipulated that no community could levy property taxes in excess of 2½ percent of its total assessed value. Furthermore communities that already taxed at higher rates had to reduce taxes at a rate of fifteen percent per year until the lower maximum was reached (Bumstead 1981).

The reform movements of the 1980s have reversed the negative funding trends. Many states, responding to demands that education be improved and shocked by the reports indicating that schools were declining rapidly, passed substantial tax increases to fund new and improved programs. In July 1984 the Education Commission of the States reported that

- Fifteen states had passed or were considering increases in state sales or income taxes to support educational reform.
- Revenues increased from $69 billion in 1969 to $89 billion in 1984.
- Since 1982 increased state and local funding has offset part of the federal government's reduction in funding.
- Corporate, business, and foundation support for public education amounts to more than $50 million annually.

■ *Current information suggests that citizens are willing to pay more taxes to support school reform.*

The most recent "Gallup Poll of the Public's Attitudes Toward the Public Schools" (Gallup and Elam 1988, p. 38) reported a statistically significant increase in the number of taxpayers willing to increase property taxes to finance school reform. "Today 64% of respondents say they are willing to pay more taxes for this purpose; 29% are opposed. Comparable figures for 1983 were 58% in favor and 33% opposed."

Changing Enrollments. The enrollment in elementary and secondary public schools declined significantly during the 1970s and early 1980s. Between 1971 and 1981, overall enrollment in public schools dropped thirteen percent, or 5.9 million students. Declines occurred in forty-two states and the District of Columbia. The decline in elementary schools was greater than in secondary schools, suggesting that the overall decline will continue (National Center for Education Statistics 1983). National population projections indicate that there will be twenty-six percent fewer eighteen-year-olds in 1991 than in 1978 (Wharton, Baudin, and Griffith 1981).

INTRODUCTION TO EDUCATION

CENSUS BUREAU FORECASTS U.S. POPULATION DECLINE

The size of the U.S. population will most likely peak at 302 million over the next 50 years and then shrink to about 292 million by the year 2080, the U.S. Bureau of the Census predicted last week.

The projections were the first by the bureau since the pre-World War II era to show either a leveling or a decline in the size of the future American population, an official said.

In 1983, when the bureau for the first time issued a 100-year set of projections, it foresaw population growth continuing to the year 2080—for a total at that point of 311 million Americans.

But the new report's "middle" scenario—its most commonly used calculations, and the mean between its "high" and "low" projections—shows the population growing by 56 million between now and the year 2038—up 25 percent from its current level of 246 million—and then beginning to shrink.

The new, lower projections reflect primarily the bureau's revision of the fertility rate over the next century, from 1.9 births per woman to 1.8.

If the middle scenario—which also takes into account immigration, fertility among subgroups, and mortality—proves accurate, the nation's population will grow at its slowest rate since the Great Depression over the next six years, and at its slowest rate ever between 1995 and 2038.

The School-Age Population

Among the bureau's new projections for school-age populations are these:

■ For the next 50 years, the elementary-school population will remain above its 1987 level of 30.8 million.

By 1995, that population (ages 5 to 13) will have grown by about 3 million, reaching 33.9 million. It will shrink again, by 2 million, between 1995 and 2005, but will not dip below the 1987 level until the year 2038.

Over the subsequent four decades, it will decline to 28.3 million.

(Only in the bureau's "highest" series of projections would the elementary population again reach, around the year 2010, its 1970 record level of 36.7 million. In that series, the numbers would then continue to rise, to 58.2 million in 2080.)

■ The population of children under age 5 will grow slightly by 1990—to 18.4 million from the 1987 level of 18.3 million—and then shrink to 16.8 million by the year 2000. It will hover at between 16 and 17 million until the year 2050, and then drop slowly to 15 million by 2080, according to the mean projections.

■ The high-school population (ages 14 to 17) is expected to decline from 14.5 million in 1987 to 13.2 million in 1990, but will rebound to the 1987 level by 1995. It will remain at or slightly above that level, according to the projections, until at least the year 2010. It will then drop slowly, to 13.1 million in 2080.

(The highest series projects growth in the high-school population after the year 2000, up to 25.6 million in 2080; the lowest series envisions declines from the 1987 level after the year 2005—to 7.2 million in 2080.)

■ In the Census Bureau's middle projections, the college-age population (ages 18 to 24) will never again achieve its 1987 level of 27.3 million.

That age group, which shrank by 3 million between 1980 and 1987, is projected to decline by another 3 million by 1995—to 24.3 million. It will then rebound, according to the bureau, to 25 million in the year 2000 and 27.1 million by 2010. But the group will shrink again, by 4 million, over the next seven decades.

Immigration Impact Uncertain

One of the biggest uncertainties in their latest long-range forecast, Census officials

continued

acknowledged, is assessing future levels of immigration. An upward drift in actual immigration rates could affect school-related projections in particular, as well as over-all population-growh rates, their report suggests, because immigrants tend to be of child-bearing age.

Such unanticipated effects of immigration are already causing serious problems in many districts.

But the Census Bureau's middle population projections are based on a steady net immigration rate after 1997 of 500,000 annually, far below current estimates of illegal immigration alone. The net-immigration figure, the report notes, assumes that various immigration-control efforts now under way will be effective.

If the annual net immigration rate averages 800,000, the bureau estimates, the U.S. population could reach 333 million by the year 2080—14 percent above the total that year under the middle projections.

Proportional Shifts

The bureau also notes that:

- The proportion of the population under age 35—now 55 percent of all Americans—will not be that large again over the next 100 years. It is expected to shrink to 48 percent in the year 2000, and to 41 percent by 2040.

- The proportion that is white will drop from 85 percent to 77 percent in 2040. The white population will grow from 206.1 million in 1987 to 235.2 million in 2030, and then decline to 212.3 million in 2080.

- Black Americans, who now constitute 12 percent of the population, will represent 15 percent by 2040. The population will grow from 29.9 million to 46.2 million over the period.

- Other minority populations—including Asians, Pacific Islanders, and American Indians—will triple in size by the 2040, rising from 8 million to 24 million and from 3 percent of total population to 8 percent.

- By 2000, the U.S. population will include 9 million immigrants who entered the country after 1986; by 2030, it will include 32 million such immigrants and their families, or 12 percent of the total population that year.

- The high, middle, and low population projections all show declining rates of teenage childbearing for all races.

- After rising slowly for the next 20 years, the number of Americans over 65 will jump from 39.4 million in 2010 to 65.6 million in 2030; that group will represent 22 percent of the 2030 population.

Reprinted with permission from *Education Week*, vol. VIII, no. 20, p. 6.

Recent predictions by the U.S. Bureau of the Census (Census Bureau 1989) include the following relative to school enrollments:

- Enrollment in elementary schools for the next fifty years will remain above the 1987 level of 30.8 million.

- The student population for five to thirteen-year-olds will reach 33.9 million in 1995, decline to 31.9 million between 1995 and 2005, and decline to 28.3 million after the year 2038.

- Preschool population will grow to 18.4 million in 1990 and shrink to 16.8 million by the year 2000.

- The number of high school students fourteen–seventeen will decline from the 1987 level of 14.5 million to 13.2 million in 1990 and return to 14.5 million by 1995. A decline will begin in 2010 and level off at 13.1 million in 2080.

Changing enrollments have a major effect on the educational system, specifically (a) affecting state funding, (b) impacting on the number of teachers needed, (c) altering class sizes, (d) causing redistricting of school boundaries, and (e) changing school plant needs (King-Stoops and Slaby 1981). (See figure 1.2)

Instructional programs are also affected by changing enrollments. Subject areas most affected include language arts, social studies, science, fine arts, and foreign language, which results in reduced course offerings and fewer jobs in these subject areas (Gay, Dembowski, and McLennan 1981).

Accurate predictions of enrollments aids in planning and implementing quality educational programs. With changing enrollments, accurate predictions are even more critical. Unfortunately, being able to predict enrollments is not easy (King-Stoops and Slaby 1981). Variables such as the strength of the economy at the local, state, and national levels, also difficult predictions for economists, make predicting enrollments for schools even more difficult. Still, schools must attempt to accurately predict enrollment figures in order to adequately plan fiscal needs, personnel needs, and space needs.

Changing Federal Role. The role played by the federal government in education has been changing and should continue to change. Terrell Bell, the Secretary for the Department of Education during the first Reagan term, stated that "During the first two years of the Reagan administration, responsibility for administering the nation's education system began to be returned to the states and localities" (Bell 1984,

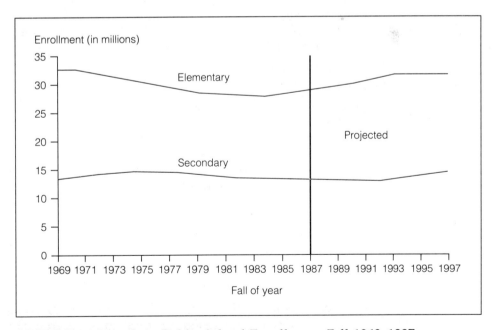

FIGURE 1.2 Trends in Public School Enrollment: Fall 1969–1997

SOURCE: National Center for Education Statistics, Projections of Education Statistics to 1997–98, forthcoming.

p. 531). A primary aim of the Reagan Administration was indeed to return to states and local agencies certain decision-making powers. Concomitant with this shift of responsibility came a shift of funding. The administration's request for federal funding for education in 1983 was $2.1 billion less than the previous year. Nearly 20 percent of the previous federal aid to education was cut (Clark, Astuto, and Rooney 1983). These budget cuts marked the beginning of a federal pullback from public education. President Reagan's final budget proposal for education included a $9.4 million increase for the U.S. Department of Education. This marked only the third Reagan budget that did not propose an overall cut in education spending (Miller 1989). Although the Bush administration may take a different approach to funding for educational programs, the trend of reduced or limited increases is expected to continue.

Besides sharply reducing the federal share of fiscal support to education, the Reagan administration also sought to decentralize federal education policy. A major avenue to effect this was through block grants. During the first Reagan term, twenty-nine categorical programs were consolidated into one block grant (Bell 1984). By consolidating programs the administration succeeded in shifting more authority to states and local agencies to carry out education programs. Although the future federal role in education cannot accurately be predicted at this point, the consensus is that the push to decentralize will continue (Clark, Astuto, and Rooney 1983).

Teacher Unions. Teacher unions have grown in membership and influence. The two major unions are the National Education Association (NEA) and the American Federation of Teachers (AFT). The NEA has long held the distinction of being the larger and more powerful of the two organizations. Currently the memberships of both groups collectively exceed two million members.

Although considered to be a necessary force several years ago, the NEA and AFT are currently losing some power and credibility. Lieberman (1979), who advocated a collective bargaining role for teacher organizations in the early 1960s, now thinks that they have become too powerful and that their representational rights should be reduced. In clarifying this position. Lieberman points out the following:

- Teacher unions may have more than $500 million annually to support their causes.
- Pupil welfare is a secondary or tertiary consideration in teacher bargaining.
- The widespread use of collective bargaining techniques has made it virtually impossible for teaching to be considered a profession.

Many citizens now consider strong unions to be a barrier to educational reforms.

Bush's Revisions Add $441 Million to E.D. Budget

By Julie A. Miller

WASHINGTON—President Bush last week unveiled 1990 budget revisions that would provide an additional $441 million for the Education Department, most of it for a series of new initiatives.

They include a "Merit Schools" program awards for outstanding teachers, a science-scholarship program, an alternative-certification initiative, and a new magnet-schools program.

The Bush plan reportedly would rescind a Reagan Administration proposal to cut the school-lunch program. In addition, it calls for a child-care tax credit, increased funding for the National Science Foundation and the Head Start program, and a youth-service initiative that would cost $1 billion over four years.

In the Feb. 9 address to lawmakers, marking Mr. Bush's first speech before a joint session of the Congress, he called efforts to improve education "The most important competiveness program of all," and reaffirmed his campaign pledge to be the "education President."

"We must reward excellence and cut through bureaucracy," he said. "We must help schools that need help the most. We must give choice to parents, students, teachers and principals, and we must hold all concerned accountable."

"In education," he declared, "we cannot tolerate mediocrity."

The $441 million Mr. Bush proposed adding to President Reagan's last education budget includes $4 million to fully fund education programs for homeless children and adults; an additional $10 million for historically black colleges; and an additional $25 million for the Drug-Free Schools and Communities Act.

Part of a $1-billion plan to "escalate the war on drugs," the increased money for anti-drug-abuse activities would be distributed in the form of "urban emergency grants' to inner-city districts, according to budget documents.

But the Bush Administration otherwise kept intact the $21.9 billion Education Department budget that had been submitted by Mr. Reagan.

That budget proposed eliminating 25 programs and reallocating about $750 million to other programs, mainly those targeted at the disadvantaged. It boosted total spending for fiscal 1990 by only $9.4 million over 1989 levels.

"Growth above inflation in federal programs is not preordained; not all spending initiatives were designed to be immortal," Mr. Bush told the lawmakers, echoing a Reagan theme.

But the new Administration's proposals, coupled with an additional $150 million that department officials said would be needed for the Stafford student-loan entitlement program, would bring the department's total budget to $22.5 billion—a 2.7 percent increase from 1989.

The department's discretionary spending—all programs other than guaranteed loans—would rise from $13.7 billion to almost $19.4 billion. The only time Mr. Reagan proposed a comparable increase for the department was during the Presidential campaign year of 1988.

In addition, Mr. Bush proposed a gradual increase in funding for his new programs from $410 million in 1990 to $651 million in 1993.

The President aims to pay for his initiatives by freezing growth in defense spending and freezing discretionary domestic spending at 1989 levels over all, but he did not specify which domestic programs he would cut to balance the new spending.

In his address, he urged bipartisan cooperation, and called for negotiations on the

continued

budget. Mr. Bush will also need Congressional help with his new education initiatives, as they require the passage of legislation.

Many of the proposals echo themes and promises from Mr. Bush's campaign. For example, he requested $250 million for "Merit Schools" and $8 million for awards to outstanding teachers.

The Merit Schools program, for which Mr. Bush proposed gradually increasing funding to $500 million a year, would reward schools that demonstrate educational improvement, with "emphasis on" schools enrolling many disadvantaged students. The other program would give competitive awards "averaging $5,000" to about 25 teachers in each state.

Mr. Bush also proposed fleshing out the "Youth Entering Service" plan he unveiled during the campaign by spending $25 million a year for four years on a national "YES Foundation" that would aid and promote youth-service programs.

Two other familiar proposals spring from Mr. Bush's advocacy of parental choice, reiterated last week.

I will work for choice for American families, whether in the housing in which they live, the schools to which they send their children, or the child care they select," he said.

One proposal would provide a tax credit for low-income families of up to $1,000 per child. It would also make the existing child-care tax credit refundable to families that pay no taxes. Mr. Bush has touted this proposal as an alternative to Congressional child-care bills.

The other "choice" proposal would provide magnet-schools aid to districts using such programs "for other than desegregation purposes." Mr. Bush requested $100 million for that purpose for 1990.

The Senate included a similar initiative in its omnibus education reauthorization bill last year, but House conferees insisted that it be dropped from the final bill. Opponents contended that the magnet program's proper purpose was desegregation, and that the federal government should not fund efforts that could widen racial imbalance.

Other new initiatives include:

■ **Alternative certification.** Mr. Bush requested $25 million for grants to states and school districts to develop alternative-certification systems for teachers and principals.

■ **Science scholarships.** This program would fund 570 college scholarships of up to $10,000 "to encourage high-school seniors to take more courses in the sciences and mathematics." The members of the Congress would each select one recipient; the President would select 30. Mr. Bush proposed spending $5 million for the awards in 1990, increasing to $20 million by 1993.

■ **Experimental projects.** Mr. Bush asked for $13 million in 1990 to "expand experiments in educational innovation and data collection to help states and localities find out what can work in their schools." According to budget documents, the program could fund efforts ranging from school-management projects to curriculum development.

Mr. Bush's most costly education proposal could prove to be a decision to abandon his predecessor's plan to cut school-lunch subsidies for non-poor children, which would cost some $900 million. Budget Director Richard G. Darman reportedly said the plan would be dropped, but Agriculture Department spokesmen said they could not confirm that.

Education advocates had been gearing up to fight Mr. Reagan's cuts both in budget deliberations and in the upcoming debate on reauthorizing child-nutrition programs.

Mr. Bush also proposed a $250-million increase for Head Start in 1990 and increased spending in later years to raise funding from $1.2 billion in 1989 to $1.6 billion in 1993. Mr. Reagan had proposed level funding for 1990.

The President also raised Mr. Reagan's $2.15-billion proposal for the National Science Foundation to $3.08 billion, but did not specify how much would be earmarked for pre-collegiate programs, which were allotted $190 million by Mr. Reagan.

Reprinted with permission from *Education Week*, vol. VIII, no. 21, p. 1.

AIDS Education. A new area of concern for educators is AIDS (Acquired Immune Deficiency Syndrome) education. This health epidemic is affecting more and more Americans every year. Schools are concerned about AIDS for two reasons. First, children with AIDS, usually born with the condition or acquiring it through blood transfusions, are enrolling in public schools. Second, educating children about AIDS to help control the disease is viewed as a responsibility of the schools.

The most recent Gallup poll concerning attitudes toward public schools revealed overwhelming support for AIDS education. Ninety percent of those responding felt that AIDS education should be a part of the school curriculum (Gallup and Elam 1988). A recent poll of school superintendents' views on AIDS found similar support (Keough and Seaton 1988, p. 359):

- Every respondent said that education about AIDS should be part of the regular school curriculum.
- Every respondent said that schools and outside health agencies should coordinate their efforts in order to better meet the needs of students with AIDS.
- Ninety-eight percent of the respondents said that schools should help students who are seeking information about AIDS testing.
- Ninety-seven percent of the respondents agreed that school districts should have a policy on dealing with teachers and students with AIDS.

In order to help with the AIDS education effort, the federal government is making available AIDS Education Grants. The first of these funds made available $11.6 million to state and local education agencies to help develop and implement AIDS education (Reed 1988).

FUTURE OUTLOOK OF EDUCATION

Although attention has been focused on education in the past, the reform movements that began in the early 1980s have surpassed previous periods of interest. Not only are community members concerned about schools in their neighborhoods, but all segments of American society are concerned about the state of education and ways to improve education. Politicians, parents, professional educators, and other groups of people have all become involved in the reform of public education.

Several trends are already well entrenched and can be expected to continue during the next decade, including

- decreased role of the federal government;
- decreased funding by the federal government;
- increased emphasis on basic curricular areas;

- increased emphasis on competency testing;
- increased emphasis on teacher improvement;
- increased need for local and state funds for education;
- increased use of technology;
- continued influence from conservatives;
- continued opportunities for handicapped and other minority groups;
- continued emphasis on accountability.

We do not know whether the heightened public interest in education will continue. Interest generated by the many national reports may be replaced by more pressing issues. If so, the gains in student performance made by the recent attention to reform may have propelled American education into a position of providing children with an educational opportunity never attained. Whether the public educational system in this country has benefited from the reforms cannot be determined until the reforms have been evaluated.

ORGANIZATION OF THE TEXTBOOK

The remaining thirteen chapters include discussions on the history and philosophy of education; who controls and finances American education; preschool, elementary, and secondary education; special areas of special education and vocational education; educational administration; careers in education and teacher education; educational technology; futurism; and an epilogue that attempts to draw some conclusions concerning public education. Information on multicultural education is included in several chapters to provide an understanding of the concept and how it relates to public education.

Each chapter contains questions related to field observations for students to consider during field placements. Since many introductory education courses include a field component, these questions are included to encourage students to ask questions and make certain observations during their field experiences. The questions provide topics for classroom discussions following exposure to schools and students. They are also intended to raise issues relating to educational theory, policy, and practice.

SUMMARY

This chapter has provided general information about public education in the United States. The first part of the chapter focused on the current state of education, including discussions of the critical reports on public education issued in the 1970s and 1980s.

The next section of the chapter included information on the magnitude of public education in this country. Approximately forty million students are enrolled in public schools each year. Various demographic information on these students was presented. The final section of the chapter focused on current trends in public education, including curriculum reform, improved teachers, multicultural education, the conservative educational movement, the New Right, technology, changing enrollments, and the reduced federal role in public education. Finally, a section on the future outlook for public education was included.

IN THE FIELD

1. Does the school district have a document stating the purposes of the schools? If so, where is it located, and are teachers and students aware of its existence?

2. Have any district or school actions resulted from the critical reports issued in the early 1980s? Examples could include longer school days, longer school year, more required academic subjects.

3. Is there any evidence of multicultural education in the classroom through instruction or materials? What evidence did you observe?

4. Are teachers in the district on any kind of merit pay plan? If so, what are the provisions? If not, is there a plan to develop such a program?

5. Are teachers actively involved in professional organizations such as the NEA and AFT? Does one of these groups or another group represent the teachers in collective bargaining?

6. Are computers available for student use? If so, what kinds of computers and at what levels? Who makes the decision regarding adoption of particular kinds of computers and software?

7. Has the district been experiencing declining or increasing enrollments? What is the future projection concerning district enrollment? What are the reasons for the enrollment trends in the district?

8. What problems, concerns, and/or controversies exist in the school or district?

REFERENCES

A California school district goes broke. *Newsweek*, July 11, 1983, 26.
A Nation at Risk: The Imperative for Educational Reform. The National Commission on Excellence in Education. U.S. Department of Education, 1983.

Action for Excellence. Task Force on Education for Economic Growth. Education Commission of the States, 1983.

Action in the States. Task Force on Education for Economic Growth. Education Commission of the States, July, 1984.

Adams, E. K. 1982. The fiscal condition of the states. *Phi Delta Kappan* 63(9), 598–600.

Albrecht, J. E. 1984. A nation at risk: Another view. *Phi Delta Kappan* 65(10), 684–85.

Archambault, E. D., and H. S. Duncombe. 1979. Incompatible messages of the property tax revolt. *Phi Delta Kappan* 61(1), 26–27.

Banas, C. 1980. The Chicago school finance catastrophe. *Phi Delta Kappan* 61(8), 519–22.

Banks, J. A. 1983. Multiethnic education at the crossroads. *Phi Delta Kappan* 64(8), 559.

Bell, T. H. 1984. American education at a crossroads. *Phi Delta Kappan* 65(8), 531–34.

Bell, T. H. 1988. On the need for national leadership to make American education work. *Phi Delta Kappan* 70(1), 8–10.

Bennett, W. J. 1986. A critical look at curriculum goals. *Principal* 66(2), 11–15.

Bonner, P. 1984. Computers in education: Promise and reality. *Personal Computing* 8(9), 64–77.

Boyer, E. L. 1984. Education's new challenge. *Personal Computing* 8(9), 81–85.

Brodinsky, B. 1982. The new right: The movement and its impact. *Phi Delta Kappan* 64(2), 87–94.

Bumstead, R. A. 1981. One Massachusetts school system adapts to proposition 2½. *Phi Delta Kappan* 62(10), 721–25.

Burke, B. T. 1982. Merit pay for teachers: Round Valley may have the answers. *Phi Delta Kappan* 64(4), 265–66.

Bussis, A. M. 1982. Burn it at the casket: Research, reading instruction, and children's learning of the first R. *Phi Delta Kappan* 64(4), 237–41.

Campbell, R. F. 1983. Time for vigorous leadership in the public schools. In J. Frymier (Ed.), *Bad Times, Good Times.* West Lafayette, IN: Kappa Delta Pi.

Carter, M., and C. Rosenbloom. 1989. Compensation survey for school and university administrators. *American School & University* 61(5), 21–25.

Clark, D. L., T. A. Astuto, and P. M. Rooney. 1983. The changing structure of federal education policy in the 1980s. *Phi Delta Kappan* 65(3), 188–93.

Congressional report waffles on merit pay. 1983. *The American School Board Journal* 170(12), 14.

Cuban, L. 1988. A fundamental puzzle of school reform. *Phi Delta Kappan* 69(5), 341–344.

Divoky, D. 1983. The new pioneers of the home schooling movement. *Phi Delta Kappan* 64(6), 395–98.

Dixon, G. 1982. The deliberate sabotage of public education by liberal elitists. *Phi Delta Kappan* 64(2), 97.

Doremus, R. R. 1982. What ever happened to Kalamazoo's merit pay plan? *Phi Delta Kappan* 63(6), 409–10.

Ebel, R. L. 1982. Three radical proposals for strengthening education. *Phi Delta Kappan* 63(6), 375–78.

Ehlers, H. And D. Crawford. 1983. Multicultural education and national unity. *The Educational Forum* 47(3), 263–77.

Elementary enrollment up, total enrollment down. 1985. *Phi Delta Kappan* 66(10), 736.

Emihovich, C. 1988. Toward cultural pluralism: Redefining integration in American society. *The Urban Review* 20(1), 3-7.

Engelking, J. L., and E. V. Samuelson. 1986. Career ladders: Choices for school districts. *The Clearing House* 60(3), 137-140.

Estimates of School Statistics. 1985-86. National Education Association.

Foster, C. R. 1982. Defusing the issues in bilingualism and bilingual education. *Phi Delta Kappan* 63(5), 342-44.

Frase, L. E., R. W. Hetxel, and R. T. Grant. 1982. Merit pay: A research-based alternative in Tucson. *Phi Delta Kappan* 64(4), 266-69.

Freeman, D. J., P. A. Cusick, and R. T. Houang. 1985. Secondary school reform: What does the public say. *NASSP Bulletin* 69(483), 52-62.

Gabler, M., and N. Gabler, 1982. Mind control through textbooks. *Phi Delta Kappan* 64(2), 96.

Gallup, A. M. 1985. The 17th annual Gallup poll of the public's attitudes toward the public schools. *Phi Delta Kappan* 67(1), 35-47.

Gallup, A. M., and S. M. Elam. 1988. The 20th annual Gallup poll of the public's attitudes toward the public schools. *Phi Delta Kappan* 70(1), 33-46.

Gay, G. 1983. Multiethnic education: Historical developments and future prospects. *Phi Delta Kappan* 64(8), 560-63.

Gay, G., P. L. Dembowski, and R. L. McLennan. 1981. Preserving quality of education during enrollment declines. *Phi Delta Kappan* 62(9), 655-57.

Goodlad, J. I. 1983. A study of schooling: Some findings and hypotheses. *Phi Delta Kappan* 64(7), 465-70.

Graham, A. M. 1984. SAT results: Student achievement is up and the President's education policies are working. *American Education* 20(7).

Grant, C. A. 1982. *Bringing Teaching to Life.* Boston: Allyn and Bacon, Inc.

Hahn, G. E. 1982. Creation-science and education. *Phi Delta Kappan* 63(8) 553-55.

Hatch, J. A. 1984. Technology and the devaluation of human processes. *The Educational Forum* 48(2), 243-52.

Henley, M. 1987. Something is missing from the education reform movement. *Phi Delta Kappan* 69(4), 284-285.

Hoban, G. 1979. The untold golden state story: Aftermath of proposition 13. *Phi Delta Kappan* 61(1), 18-21.

Holt, J. 1983. Schools and home schoolers: A fruitful partnership. *Phi Delta Kappan* 64(6), 391-94.

Ivie, S. D. 1978. Multicultural education: The Mexican experience. *The Educational Forum* 42(4), 441-49.

Kellogg, J. B. 1988. Forces of change. *Phi Delta Kappan* 70(3), 199-204.

Kemerer, F. R. 1984. Censorship, academic freedom, and the right to know. *Kappa Delta Pi Record* 20(3) 73-76.

Keough, K. E., and G. Seaton. 1988. Superintendents' views on AIDS: A national survey. *Phi Delta Kappan* 69(5), 358-361.

King-Stoops, J., and R. M. Slaby. 1981. How many students next year? *Phi Delta Kappan* 62(9), 658-62.

Knowles, J. G. 1988. Introduction: The context of home schooling in the United States. *Education and Urban Society* 21(1), 5-15.

Lieberman, M. 1979. Eggs that I have laid: Teacher bargaining reconsidered. *Phi Delta Kappan* 60(6), 415–19.

McGraw, O. 1982. Where is the public in public education? *Phi Delta Kappan* 64(2), 94–95.

Mazzoni, T. L., and V. D. Mueller. 1980. *Phi Delta Kappan* 61(6), 406–10.

Mecklenburger, J. A. 1988. What the ostrich sees: Technology and the mission of American education. *Phi Delta Kappan* 70(1), 18–19.

Miller, I. 1980. Tax referendum strategies: A perspective for the eighties. *Phi Delta Kappan* 62(1), 22–23.

Miller, J. A. 1989. Budget projects little growth but many funding shifts. *Education Week* 8(17), January 18, 1+.

Mitchell, B. M. 1987. Multicultural education: A second glance at the present American effort. *Educational Research Quarterly* 11(4), 8–12.

National Center for Education Statistics. 1988. *Digest of Education Statistics, 1988 Edition.* Washington D.C.: U.S. Department of Education.

National Center for Education Statistics. 1983. The Condition of Education, 1983 edition. Washington, D.C.: U.S. Department of Education.

National Center for Education Statistics. 1984. The Condition of Education, 1984 edition. Washington, D.C.: U.S. Department of Education.

National Center for Education Statistics. 1988. *The Condition of Education, 1988 edition.* Washington, D.C.: U.S. Department of Education.

Olson, L. 1989. Futrell backing full funding for a merit-pay plan. *Education Week.* 8(2), February 8, 1+.

Orlich, D. C. 1989. Education reforms: Mistakes, misconceptions, miscues. *Phi Delta Kappan* 70(7), 512–517.

Ornstein, A. 1985. The national reports on education: Implications for directions and aims. *Kappa Delta Pi Record* 21(2), 58–64.

Ovando, C. J. 1983. Bilingual/bicultural education: Its legacy and its future. *Phi Delta Kappan* 64(8), 564–68.

Park, J. C. 1980. Preachers, politics, and public education: A review of right-wing pressures against public schooling in America. *Phi Delta Kappan* 61(9), 608–12.

Passow, A. H. 1984. Tackling the reform reports of the 1980s. *Phi Delta Kappan* 65(10), 674–83.

Pincus, F. L. 1984. Book bargaining and the new right: Censorship in the public schools. *The Educational Forum* 49(1), 7–21.

Pipho, C. 1983. Merit pay/master teacher plans attract attention in the states. *Phi Delta Kappan* 65(3), 165–66.

Quality Education Data. 1988. *Microcomputer and VCR Usage in Schools.* Denver, Colorado: Author.

Ray, B. D. 1988. Home schools: A synthesis of research on characteristics and learner outcomes. *Education and Urban Society* 21(1), 16–31.

Reed, S. 1988. I have AIDS please hug me. *Phi Delta Kappan* 69(5), K2–K12.

Say, E., and L. Miller. 1982. Phi Delta Kappan 64(4), 270–71.

Snyder, T. D. 1988. Trends in education: Get ready for crowded classrooms and minority majorities. *Principal* 66(1), 26–30.

Stedman, L. C. and C. F. Kaestle. 1985. The test score decline is over: Now what? *Phi Delta Kappan* 67(3), 204–10.

Strike, K. A. 1982. The status of creation-science: A comment on Siegel and Hahn. *Phi Delta Kappan* 63(8), 555–57.

Tafel, L., and J. Christensen. 1988. Teacher education in the 1990s: Looking ahead while learning from the past. *Action in Teacher Education* 10(3), 1–6.

Timar, T. B., and D. L. Kirp. 1989. Education reform in the 1980s: Lessons from the states. *Phi Delta Kappan* 70(7), 504–511.

Tracy, S.J., R. Sheehan, and R. J. McArdle. 1988. Teacher education reform: The implementors' reactions. *Action in Teacher Education* 10(3), 14–21.

Tyler, R. W. 1987. Educational reforms. *Phi Delta Kappan* 69(4), 277–280.

Weiler, H. N. 1982. Education, public confidence, and the legitimacy of the modern state: Do we have a crisis? *Phi Delta Kappan* 64(1), 9–14.

Wharton, J. H., J. J. Baudin, and O. Griffith, 1981. The importance of accurate enrollment projections for planning. *Phi Delta Kappan* 62(9), 652–55.

Williams, D. A., P. King, D. Shirley, and S. Steptoe. The merits of merit pay. *Newsweek*, June 27, 1983, 61–62.

2

HISTORY OF EDUCATION

OBJECTIVES

After reading this chapter, you will be able to

- trace the historical development of education in Europe;
- describe the educational systems developed in colonial America;
- describe the public school movement;
- trace the development of secondary education;
- discuss the role of litigation and legislation in the development of public education in the United States;
- describe the major criticisms of American education today;
- describe some of the recommendations made by critics for American schools;
- discuss the future of reforms currently being made in American schools.

OUTLINE

ADVANCE ORGANIZERS

1. What was the system of education like in ancient Greece and Rome?
2. How were the Greek and Roman educational systems different and similar?
3. What were the differences in the educational systems established in the Colonies?
4. Why did the high school emerge as the model for secondary education?
5. What ideas existed that supported the Common School Movement?
6. What was the role of John Dewey in American education?
7. What legislation affected education in the twentieth century? How did this legislation impact public education and how did it relate to changes in society?
8. What were the Cardinal Principles issued by the National Education Association?
9. What major criticisms were leveled at American schools during the 1950s? Were they reactions to any events or publications?
10. What recommendations did James Conant make concerning the high school?
11. What is the status of reforms initiated during the 1970s and 1980s?
12. What do you predict will be the next reforms or changes in American education?

INTRODUCTION

Why study the history of education? Many prospective teachers ask this question, expecting the content to be uninteresting and to have little relevance to becoming a teacher. However, teachers need a general understanding of the historical foundations of education for many valid reasons. By understanding some of the historical forces that helped shape our current educational system, teachers may avoid misconceptions and misunderstandings concerning our public schools today (Pulliam 1987).

John Dewey understood this a half century ago when he wrote that "knowledge of the past is the key to understanding the present. History deals with the past, but this past is the history of the present" (1916, p. 251). We understand what we currently are doing by understanding

INTRODUCTION TO EDUCATION

our past; current educational practices are partly explained by historical practices.

Many of the issues facing education today are not new. The relationship between education and government, providing adequate financing for public education, ensuring equal educational opportunity for all members of society, and providing quality education programs are issues that have plagued education in the United States for more than three hundred years. By understanding the past, better solutions are likely to be made for the future. An understanding of the history of education can provide insight into education just as knowledge of the history of man can provide insight into society (Gutek 1970). This chapter presents an overview of the history of education in the United States so the reader will have a basic understanding of the foundations of the current educational system.

EUROPEAN FOUNDATIONS IN EDUCATION

Education in the United States had its beginning in Europe. Therefore, a quick look at the way the European educational system emerged will provide a foundation for the present public educational system in the United States. The exact location and time of the beginning of education programs is impossible to determine. Formal schools existed in China and Sumer as early as 2000 B.C.; however, educational systems that developed in Greece are considered the beginning of the framework for education in the United States (Pulliam 1987).

The Greek Period

Education in Greece became somewhat formalized during the days of the Greek city states of Sparta and Athens. Since the Greek peninsula was politically organized around cities, the educational systems of the time reflected the basic philosophies of the city states. In Sparta which was a militarized city, schools attempted to assist in making citizens totally obedient and subservient to the state. The content of the educational program was basically physical and moral, with little emphasis on academic subjects (Cordasco 1970). The goal of education was to educate children to serve the state.

The Greek city state of Athens was considerably different from Sparta, although it was in existence during the same period—approximately 800 B.C. Differences between the cities were reflected in the educational programs each devised. While the government of Sparta tried to destroy the family, the government of Athens preserved the family. Athens' educational programs focused on reading, writing, and literary elements. Music, which was provided for students, included poetry, drama, history, oratory, and science as well as typical music education (Cordasco 1970). The educational program in Athens was the beginning of a liberal arts curriculum. The emphasis was on educating for "wholeness": body, mind, and spirit.

The Roman Period

Roman education was heavily influenced by Greek education. Roman education can be divided into two distinct periods: that period without Greek influence and that period with Greek influence. From approximately 750 to 250 B.C., Roman education was not influenced by Greek education. Schools during this period offered rudimentary instruction in reading and writing. The home, however, remained the primary moral instruction center. Greek influence began about 350 B.C. and continued until 200 A.D. Schools were of several types, ranging from providing instruction in basic reading and writing to preparing students for public careers. The Latin Grammar School, which was developed during this period, remained the most persistent part of Roman civilization until the Roman Empire was destroyed. Subjects studied in the Latin Grammar School included literature (history, poetry, and scientific writings), math, music, and rudimentary dialects. Gymnastics and dancing, which were found in Greek schools, were not included (Cordasco 1970).

The Medieval Period

The medieval period covers approximately 800 years, from A.D. 476 (the Fall of the Roman Empire) to A.D. 1300. Education went into a severe decline during the first five hundred years of this period (the Dark Ages) and was somewhat revived during the last three hundred years.

During the Dark Ages, the Roman Catholic church became a powerful political force. By stressing gaining admission into heaven, the church deemphasized life on earth, including any knowledge acquired through education. Significant amounts of knowledge that had been generated were lost. During this period, Charlemagne came to power and attempted to infuse some life into education. However, despite his efforts, little progress was made and education continued to decline (Johnson et al. 1982).

The last part of the medieval period has been termed by some as the Age of the Revival of Learning. The reconciliation of religion and philosophy and the renewed interest in previous writings, mainly those of Aristotle, provided the impetus for many positive developments (Johnson, Collins, Dupuis, and Johansen 1982).

Renaissance and Reformation

During the Renaissance and Reformation periods, lasting from approximately 1300 to 1700, education continued to make significant gains. Some of the positions that had a later effect on American education included replacing God with man as the focal point for art and literature, transfering some power from the church to individuals and governments, and a revival of interest in Greek and Roman classical cultures. An interest on the individual encouraged an expansion of the educational system (Pulliam 1987).

Religious activities during this period had a major impact on every aspect of life, including social, political, and economic. Before Martin Luther posted his Ninety-five Theses on the church door in 1517, the Catholic church was the primary educational institution in the world. The main effect of the Reformation on education was the desire to expand literacy to the masses (Ornstein and Levine 1981). This created the need for schools in all cities and towns and the need for their control to be other than that of the Roman Catholic church. The result was that all children were encouraged to learn to read in order to understand the Scriptures. "While the schools were often rudimentary, they offered universal education for all children regardless of wealth and were supported by both church and state." (Pulliam 1987, p. 10)

During this period the scientific movement also gained momentum. Francis Bacon popularized the scientific method, Copernicus and Galileo made astronomical discoveries, and Isaac Newton discovered the basic laws of physics. While science was becoming more accepted, it was still suspect by many people who viewed it as a materialistic movement. Still, it challenged certain beliefs and laid a foundation for the Enlightenment of the eighteenth century (Pulliam 1987).

The Enlightenment

Following the Renaissance and Reformation came a period (eighteenth century) when reason emerged as a factor in schools. Called variously the Enlightenment or the Age of Reason, this period was a revolt against the authoritarianism of the Reformation, and education reflected the political, economic, and religious changes (Cordasco 1970). The Enlightenment emphasized science and humanism. Based on the naturalistic and social theories of Comenius and Locke, this period emphasized the dignity of each individual. A renewed interest in studying the classics emerged in schools. The Enlightenment "created an attitude of distrust for despotic monarchs and all other forms of centralized government" (Pulliam 1987, p. 48) and enabled the American revolution to occur.

EDUCATION IN THE UNITED STATES

Many historians divide American educational history into two major periods: the colonial period (1607–1788) and the national period (1787–present). The national period is further divided into the period from

1787 through the nineteenth century and the twentieth century (Cordasco 1970).

The Colonial Period

During the early days of the United States, the thirteen original colonies took on distinctly different characteristics. For the most part, the colonies were divided into three different groups: the New England colonies, the Middle colonies, and the Southern colonies. Many of the political practices in the colonies, and the educational systems as well, reflected the religious beliefs of the citizens of each section. New Englanders were predominantly Calvinists, following the dictates of John Calvin; the Middle colonies were composed of religious dissenters, including Quakers and Anabaptists; and the Southern colonies were mostly Anglican (Cordasco 1970).

The New England Colonies. The New England colonies included Massachusetts, Connecticut, New Hampshire, Vermont, and Rhode Island. Most New Englanders were neither poor nor wealthy. Generally they had some form of house and a small amount of land to plant. In addition, most had a limited number of livestock, generally a cow, horse, hogs, and poultry. They led simple lives; the work was hard and visiting with neighbors was the primary source of socialization. Social cohesiveness, a common language, and similar heritage all facilitated the interest in education found in the New England colonies (Madsen 1974).

Massachusetts was settled by Puritans who followed the teachings of John Calvin (Gutek 1986). The educational system developed in the New England colonies was heavily influenced by Calvinism. Education was the primary method of indoctrinating children in the Calvinist dictates, the Bible, and the general laws of the colonies. A major motivating factor in the establishment of schools was to prevent Satan from corrupting an illiterate society (Gutek 1970). "The New England schools were designed to create educated Puritans who would perpetuate the religious, social, political, and economic beliefs of the adults" (Gutek 1986, p. 6). Education was to prepare an educated ministry and a literate and productive citizenry (Gutek 1986).

In order to combat the evils of illiteracy, Massachusetts passed the School Act of 1642, which marked the beginning of elementary education. This act was considered important in maintaining the commonwealth of Massachusetts (Commager 1983). It required that parents and guardians be responsible for ensuring that their children receive instruction in reading and that they understand religious principles and commonwealth law. The law did not order school attendance, but simply placed the educational responsibility on parents (Gutek 1970).

Massachusetts went a step further in 1647 when the General Court of Massachusetts passed the Old Deluder Satan Law. This act, which was designed to outwit Satan, required towns of fifty or more families to provide a teacher for reading and writing; towns of one hundred or more families also had to provide children with instruction in Latin (Gutek 1986). Similar laws were enacted in Connecticut in 1650 and New Hampshire in 1680. Rhode Island was the only New England colony that did not pass laws regarding education and allowing for taxes to be collected to support education (Cordasco 1970).

New England schools included town schools, or elementary schools, and secondary schools called Latin Grammar Schools. Town schools were governed by the community's selectmen. Whereas the Latin Grammar School was found in larger towns and had the primary objective of preparing boys for college, town schools were found in the more predominant rural areas. These town schools could be excellent or extremely poor. The quality was totally dependent on the teacher. There were two terms, one in the winter and one in the summer. Recitation was an extremely popular teaching method; students would memorize lessons and recite them before the class and teacher. A typical curriculum in the town school included reading, writing, grammar, and arithmetic (Madsen 1974).

In addition to this basic academic school, other educational arrangements were available for young children, including apprenticeships, which had originated in medieval Europe, and dame schools. Dame schools were for very young children, were taught by women in their homes, and focused on simple skills such as learning the alphabet (Gutek 1986).

Puritan-influenced schools stressed reading (Gutek 1986). The major reading material used for education was the Hornbook, which was a paddle with a sheet containing the alphabet, vowels, syllables, the doctrine of the Trinity, and the Lord's Prayer. In 1690 another famous textbook, the *New England Primer*, became available. This book included twenty-four rhymes to assist in learning the alphabet, vowels, and syllables, as well as lessons for children such as "An Alphabet of Lessons for Youth," "The Dutiful Child's Promises," the Lord's Prayer, the Creed, the Ten Commandments, and "The Duty of Children Toward Their Parents." In later versions, the *New England Primer* contained about one hundred pages and included woodcut illustrations. Its popularity continued until the nineteenth century when several other primers became available. These included the *Boston Primer*, *New York Primer*, and *Albany Primer*. Other textbooks available during the later eighteenth century included the reader, *The American Preception*, and a grammar book, *The Young Lady's Accidence* (1785), both written by Boston schoolmaster Caleb Bingham, and a popular math book written in 1788 by Nicholas Pike, *New and Complete System of Arithmetic* (Madsen 1974).

Memorization was the principal method of learning (Gutek 1970). The most important part of the *New England Primer* was an outline of Puritan theology (Gutek 1986).

Reading, writing, spelling, and arithmetic, or ciphering, were also subjects taught in New England elementary schools. Spelling required students to memorize long lists of difficult words, while arithmetic focused on basic computation, decimals, fractions, weights, and measures (Gutek 1986).

Unlike elementary education, secondary education in the New England colonies was not for the masses. Patterned after secondary schools in Europe, these schools were primarily designed to prepare students for college (Cordasco 1970). Students were mostly from economically well-to-do families.

The Middle Colonies. The Middle colonies were composed of very divergent groups, having no common religion, language, or value structure. (In Pennsylvania alone there were at least twenty different religious denominations.) Germany, Holland, Spain, France, Sweden, and the West Indies are examples of the many homelands of these colonists (Madsen 1974). Consequently, contrary to the homogeneity of educational programs established in the New England colonies, programs developed in the Middle colonies varied considerably. In New York, which was controlled by the Dutch, the Dutch Reformed church operated schools that taught reading, writing, and religion. Some private schools, called academies, were established to prepare children for careers in specific trades or skills. The most famous of these schools was the Philadelphia Academy founded by Benjamin Franklin in 1751 (Ornstein and Levine 1981). Academies expanded very rapidly during the early 1800s and became the dominant secondary educational model during that era (Button and Provenzo 1983).

The Southern Colonies. A major difference between the Southern colonies and those in the middle and New England regions was population distribution. While population centers were common in other parts of colonial America, the South was characterized by large, rural areas. While the South was settled by individuals from Scotland, Ireland, and France, the majority of Southerners were English. Because of the rich farmland and climate, this region quickly became dominated by farms. Large plantations became the dominant social and economic force of the region. These were able to operate because of the slaves. The first slaves arrived in 1619; by 1800 the slave population was approximately 1 million (Madsen 1974). The impact this rural nature had on education was that there were few areas where ample numbers of people lived to facilitate the development of school programs. The result was an emphasis on private and tutorial education. Landowners who could afford private tutors for their children did so, while poor white children and children of black slaves did without education.

The National Period

The success of the American Revolution and the adoption of the Constitution ended the colonial period and marked the beginning of the national period. Many major historical events occurred between 1787 and the beginning of the twentieth century, including the United States gaining independence from England, the Civil War, and the emergence of the United States as a great industrial and political power. During the nation's first fifty years, several important developments occurred that affected education.

Constitutional Developments. In 1788 the United States Constitution was ratified. This document, which still provides the legal basis for our country, included many elements of Enlightenment political theory and British law. It provided for a system of checks and balances among the three branches of government, guaranteed basic individual rights, and established the principle of separation of church and state. The Constitution, however, did not specifically address education.

As a result of the Tenth Amendment reserving to states items not included in the Constitution, education was made a state responsibility (Gutek 1986). Several states made provisions for education in their constitutions. State constitutions of Pennsylvania (1776), North Carolina (1776), Georgia (1777), Massachusetts (1780), New Hampshire (1784), and Delaware (1792) included some provisions for the establishment of schools. In 1779 Thomas Jefferson, who thought education was critically important for a democratic society, introduced the Bill for the More General Diffusion of Knowledge in the Virginia Assembly. The bill would have made free public schools available for all children for three years, would develop secondary schools, and would establish a state university for higher education that would be free from religious influences. Although the bill was rejected in 1779 and later in 1817, it laid the foundation for public education in the United States (Pulliam 1987).

The federal government became involved in education even before the current Constitution was passed (Unks 1985). Under the Articles of Confederation the new government passed the Land Ordinance of 1785, which required each township to reserve lot number 16 for the support of public schools. The Northwest Ordinance of 1787 reinforced the 1785 act by encouraging education as being important to good government and happiness. Article Three of the 1787 ordinance expressed a commitment for education by stating that "Religion, morality, and knowledge being necessary to good government and the happiness of mankind, schools and the means of education shall forever be encouraged" (Gutek 1986, p. 30).

Following the passage of the current Constitution, the federal government made outright financial grants to states to support education beginning with the Ohio Enabling Act of 1802, which returned five percent of the earnings from the sale of public lands to newly admitted states. This was followed by other acts that enabled states to use federal funds to support educational programs. "Federal grants to public education prior to the Civil War reflect the fusion of two basic Jeffersonian principles: the belief that government governs best when it governs least and the almost holy belief in the power of education to create a reasonable citizen for a democracy" (Unks 1985, p. 138).

The Academy Movement. Academies began in the mid-1700s and flourished until the Civil War, when high schools began to emerge. Between the years 1781 and 1825, academies were the most rapidly growing type of school in the United States. There were slightly more than one hundred academies in 1800 and more than one thousand in 1830 (Button and Provenzo 1983). In 1855, it was reported that there were 6,185 academies with 263,000 students (Binder 1974). Benjamin Franklin was instrumental in the development of the first academy in 1751 (Cordasco 1970). The focus of Franklin's academy was on a broad and practical curriculum. It was much more like an English Grammar School than the old Latin Grammar School (Gutek 1970).

Academies varied considerably in organization, control, and support. Some were operated for profit by private groups; some were under the control and support of churches; and still others received some support and were controlled by local government units. Programs offered by academies were diverse, including college-preparatory curriculum for students who would be attending college; English-language curriculum for students who would complete their formal education with the academy; and the normal curriculum, which prepared students to be teachers in common or elementary schools (Gutek 1986).

Although there was widespread support for academies, and many existed, the majority of American youth did not participate. One reason that some youth did not attend academies was the negative impact the absence of a teenager would have on the family's financial status. Without the physical labor of adolescent children, many farms and small shops simply would not survive. Another reason some adolescents did not attend academies was financial. Although the cost amounted to approximately $1.50 per day, this proved prohibitive to many families (Binder 1974).

Courses provided at academies included

- Latin and Greek
- English

- Natural Sciences
- History
- Modern Languages
- Commercial Subjects
- Mathematics
- Music and Art (Gutek 1986)

Academies were the forerunner to the current comprehensive high school in the United States. In fact, a major reason for their decline was the growth of the high school (Binder 1974).

Elementary Education. Because of states passing legislation for education and of localities receiving funds from the federal government either through land grants or direct funding, elementary education began to grow in the United States during the first years following the American War of Independence. The infant school, which served children ages four to eight, was supported financially by the city of Boston in 1818. This practice was duplicated in many other communities and states, thus creating a network of elementary schools. After further development of elementary schools, infant schools became synonymous with the lower level of elementary schools (Cordasco 1970).

Another model developed during the first years of the Republic was called monitorial schools, where teachers would teach their brightest students who in turn would teach their peers. This model of education enabled one headmaster to teach many more students than the teacher alone could have taught. These schools, also known as Lancasterian schools after the founder of the idea, Joseph Lancaster, were started in many states after a Lancasterian school was opened in New York City in 1806 (Cordasco 1970).

Education in the Nineteenth Century

Public education in the United States made significant progress during the nineteenth century. Some of the reasons include the common school movement, state laws and state boards of education, and permanent sources of funding.

The Common School Movement. Public education as it is known today had its beginnings with the common-school movement in Massachusetts, led by Horace Mann. Proponents of mass education for all children defined the common school "as an institution that would provide its students with basic cultural and literary skills. . . . Common did not mean lowly or base-born, but expressed the idea of a cultural community in which ideas, experiences, beliefs, aspirations, and values would eventually become uniquely American" (Gutek 1970, p. 52).

Pre-nineteenth-century forces contributed heavily to the common-school movement. These included district schools in New England, the Massachusetts school laws of 1642 and 1647, and the ideals of the American Revolution. Along with state school laws, these forces helped lay the foundation for public education (Cordasco 1970).

Many arguments were heard both supporting and opposing universal education for all children. Arguments supporting the idea included

- education would benefit political enlightenment;
- individuals from diverse backgrounds could develop common values and loyalties;
- educated individuals would have job skills;
- education could lead to social improvement and economic advancement. (Gutek 1970)

Public education was thus viewed as a vehicle for preparing children from various ethnic and religious backgrounds for citizenship in the United States as well as for participation in the economic system. The movement sought to mold citizens into a force with common values, ideals, loyalties, and purposes.

Many did not support the common-school movement. Reasons for the opposition included the facts that class distinctions would be dismantled, cultural heritages would be lost, and religion would be removed from the schools (Binder 1974). While some supported the common-school movement for the reason of melting various heritages into one, others opposed the movement for the same reason. Some conservative religious leaders were staunchly opposed to the common school idea. "They considered all this to be part of the movement to completely sever ties that had existed between church and commonwealth since Puritan days" (Binder 1974, p. 59).

The one individual who is given most of the credit for the success of the common-school movement is Horace Mann. Mann was an attorney, legislator, and president of the Massachusetts senate. As president of the senate, Mann supported a law in 1837 that created the first Massachusetts State Board of Education. Prior to this bill, he had supported a bill passed in 1834 that established the Common School Fund and a bill passed in 1836 that prohibited factories from employing children who had not spent at least three months of the previous twelve months in school (Field 1976). In 1837 Mann was appointed as the first secretary of education for the state of Massachusetts. Because of his efforts in establishing the common school, Mann is considered the father of American free public schools (Fain, Shostak, and Dean 1979).

When Mann was appointed as the secretary of education for Massachusetts, several problems were paramount in the public education system: incompetent teachers, poor physical facilities, inadequate curricula, and a lack of leadership by the local school committees. Mann viewed many of these problems as resulting from inadequate local control and saw two objectives as critical in the revitalization of public education: bringing back into public schools students in private education and limiting the control of schools by local citizens. That the State Board of Education had been created in Massachusetts indicated a direct challenge to local autonomy (Field 1976). Overall, Mann was very successful in his efforts to reform public education in Massachusetts. Other states were also making significant progress in their efforts in public education.

Several elements were necessary for the success of common schools. These included

1. The common school would be free and open to all.

2. The common school would be of such excellent quality that all parents and guardians would be willing to send their children.

3. The school would be common in the sense that all children would attend and that it would serve as a unifying force in welding communities together, assimilating the great numbers of immigrants pouring into the country. The premise was that if children from all classes of society would attend the same school, they would learn to understand and appreciate each other.

4. The common school would be publicly supported through taxation of the entire community.

5. The common school would be publicly controlled through elected or appointed public officials responsible to the whole community and not to any political, economic, or religious group.

6. The common school would be nonsectarian in character, with morality being taught without reference to the tenets of any particular sect.

7. The common school would provide the basic skills and knowledge essential for students of diverse backgrounds to assume the responsibility of citizenship. (Fain, Shostak, and Dean 1979, p. 34)

Horace Mann and others made the common-school movement of the early 1800s successful. By 1860 approximately half of all elementary-aged children were being served in public school programs, and free school systems were established in most states (Armstrong, Henson, and Savage 1981). Although many children attended school sparingly, the system of public education at public expense had been established and was the framework for the current educational system.

State Legislation. For the common-school movement to be successful, states had to pass legislation that promoted public education and es-

TABLE 2.1
State Legislation Supporting the Common School Movement

STATE	LEGISLATION
New York	Passed legislation in 1784–1787 that established the University of the State of New York, a state school board
New York	Established a state school fund in 1805
New York	Established the office of the superintendent of common schools in 1812
Pennsylvania	Established the right to levy taxes for education in 1834
Massachusetts	Set up a state board and a state education superintendent in 1837

Source: Cordasco, F. *A Brief History of Education*, 1970.

tablished permanent funding sources for public education (see table 2.1).

Development of Secondary Schools. The American high school evolved from the Latin Grammar School and academies. While the common elementary school was established by the late 1800s, high schools were just being developed. The Latin Grammar School, which focused on a curriculum emphasizing Greek and Latin writings, declined in popularity after the American Revolution because of a desire for a more utilitarian secondary school. Private academies appeared to meet the public demand for a more practical curriculum. While offering classical courses for college preparation, academies also included practical courses such as bookkeeping and surveying in their curricula. The broader based curricula of the academies was much more popular than the narrow opportunities of the Latin Grammar School (Gutek 1970).

In the late 1800s, private academies gave way to publicly supported high schools. This was a continuation of the trend started by the common-school movement for elementary education. High schools in the United States formally date from 1821 with the founding of the English Classical School in Boston (renamed the English High School in 1824). Legislation supporting high schools was first enacted in Massachusetts with the Massachusetts Law of 1827, which required that towns with more than five hundred families have high schools (Binder 1974).

Although formally beginning in the early 1800s, high schools developed very slowly. In 1860 only 321 high schools existed in the United States (Cordasco 1970); New York State did not require the maintenance of high schools until 1864. As late as 1890 only 2,526 high schools were operational in the entire country (Commager 1983), and only 3.5 percent of all seventeen-year-olds graduated from high school (James and Tyack 1983).

INTRODUCTION TO EDUCATION

In 1880 enrollment in high schools surpassed the enrollment in academies; from that point, high schools grew significantly. Reasons for the rise of popularity of the high school included

- the change from an agrarian to an urban society where people were required to have certain skills;
- the industrialization that accompanied urbanization;
- the public's growing sensitivity of the needs of children and youth;
- the better financial capabilities to support public schools resulting from industrialization;
- the Kalamazoo court case of 1874 supporting the right of taxation for high schools. (Gutek 1986)

Although high schools made major gains during the latter part of the nineteenth century, they suffered from one major problem—a lack of standardization. High schools offered such a wide range of curricula that they almost repeated the demise of the academy. To rectify the situation, the National Education Association (NEA) established the Committee of Ten, a group of ten professionals, largely college presidents and professors, who were charged with the task of standardizing high schools (Cordasco 1970).

In 1893 the Committee of Ten made its report. Included in the recommendations were that

- children receive eight years of elementary school;
- children receive four years of high school;
- four separate curricula be offered: classical, Latin-scientific, modern language, and English;
- students be exposed to a smaller number of subjects for intense study as opposed to many different subjects for shorter periods. (Gutek 1986)

Besides standardizing high-school curricula, the Committee of Ten was charged with improving the preparation of high-school students for college. In so doing, the committee members attempted to determine what scholarly content should be included in each of the four basic curricula offered in high schools (James and Tyack 1983).

The Committee of Ten was the first reform group for high schools. While many of its recommendations never were implemented, the process of having groups of professionals assess the needs of education was established as a precedent.

Education in the Twentieth Century

The growth of education in the United States during the twentieth century has been phenomenal. A comprehensive public education system has developed that supports all children from approximately five years of age to eighteen years. Unlike the educational programs in many countries, the American public education system attempts to provide twelve years of equal educational opportunity to all students, not only those with certain intellectual characteristics. "Schooling is available to a larger proportion of U.S. youth than is the case in other developed countries, yet the top five percent of U.S. young people attain the same high scores reached in nations where advanced schooling is reserved for an elite" (Tyler 1981, p. 307). Although the educational system in this country certainly has problems, as was amply pointed out in chapter one, it remains a model system for many countries to emulate.

Education from 1900 to World War II. During the early part of the twentieth century, public education began to take on its current form. By 1918 all states had mandatory attendance laws, and by 1930 the school year had increased to an average of 172 days (Cordasco 1970). The concept of elementary education for all children was widely accepted, and American high schools continued to grow rapidly.

John Dewey was the overriding influence over education in the United States during the first half of the twentieth century. Dewey was born in Vermont in 1859 and received his formal training in philosophy. He wrote several books that had a great impact on education, including *The School and Society* in 1898 and his classic text, *Democracy and Education*, written in 1916 (Gutek 1986), which was considered by a group of eighty-four curriculum specialists to be one of the two most important writings in education (Shane 1981).

In 1896, while at the University of Chicago, Dewey established an experimental laboratory school. In this setting he implemented some of his ideas in the classroom: (1) students should learn using the scientific process (Armstrong, Henson, and Savage 1981); (2) teachers should emphasize class discussions, sharing experiences and testing ideas (Lazerson 1987); (3) furniture should be movable to facilitate large and small group work; (4) activities should replace teacher-dominated drills; and (5) students should have available to them a large array of toys, materials, and books (Parker 1981).

Although Dewey's educational programs, which were based on his experimental philosophy, were not exactly like programs espoused by the progressive education movement, they were related. The major difference was that progressive education had a broader base among educators and was less specific than Dewey's ideas. Progressive education, supported by several of Dewey's followers, focused on the scientific method, the individual child, and society. However, some leaders of the progressive movement put more emphasis on the individual than on society, which met with much criticism, especially during the depression years (Gutek 1970).

During the first half of the twentieth century, the National Education Association issued a major report that had a great impact on secondary education. The report, issued by the NEA's Commission on the

■ *John Dewey was the primary influence in American education during the first half of the 20th century.*

Reorganization of Secondary Education, became known as the Cardinal Principles and is considered "one of the most influential documents on secondary education in American history . . ." (Lazerson 1987, p. 79). The goals of the report included

1. Health
2. Command of fundamental processes
3. Worthy home membership
4. Vocational preparation
5. Citizenship
6. Worthy use of leisure time
7. Ethical character

These principles laid the foundation for current comprehensive secondary schools. They suggested that high schools have a greater purpose than simple academic instruction (Armstrong, Henson, and Savage 1981) and thus reflected Dewey's notion of "using secondary education as an instrument for transforming the everyday lives of citizens in an industrial democracy" (James and Tyack 1983, p. 402).

The Cardinal Principles emphasized a major thrust away from the purely academic high school. The report (1) stressed activities, democracy, and efficiency; (2) reflected the hope that schools could eliminate social problems; (3) brought focus on the drop-out rates of high schools; and (4) placed educators at the center of social reform. Overall, the Cardinal Principles won considerable public support and had a significant impact on secondary education (James and Tyack 1983).

Education in the United States during the depression era faced many problems. The depression hit all aspects of the country: the gross national product dropped, personal income declined, unemployment soared, stocks fell, and corporate profits plummeted (Tyack and Hansot 1984). For school-age children, the depression meant unemployment, apathy, unrest, and despair (James and Tyack 1983). Abounding throughout the entire society these problems should have produced a major blow to education. Surprisingly, public education emerged from the depression in relatively good condition. Professionals were united, schools were viewed with a great deal of confidence by the public, and states had dramatically increased their contribution to public education (Tyack and Hansot 1984). Better guidance programs, more extensive social programs, and a more appealing curriculum were advocated by the teaching profession (James and Tyack 1983).

Although some of the tangibles appeared to have emerged from the depression on a positive note, the educational system still faced severe problems. For one thing, there was little equality of opportunity. School districts with strong economic bases continued to prosper, while those with unstable economic foundations were destroyed. The one positive thing to come out of this inequity was the recognition by many mem-

■ *The depression affected all aspects of American society, including education.*

bers of society that the American system maintained certain class differentials, that inequities existed (Tyack and Hansot 1984).

The belief that the public school system in the United States "owed all youths either an education through secondary school or guaranteed public service jobs" (James and Tyack 1983, p. 404) was a new philosophy that emerged as a result of the depression.

Education from 1940 to Present. In the early 1940s, the progressive education movement was widely adopted. Individuals supporting this curricular approach referred to it as life-adjustment education. Emphasis on academic subject matter was limited, while other areas of the curriculum flourished (Armstrong, Henson, and Savage 1983).

Major criticisms of the schools began to emerge in the 1950s. Critics attacked low academic standards, which were considered a major reason for society's problems. Low academic standards were viewed as synonymous with life-adjustment education, child-centered learning, and other titles associated with the progressive movement. Targets for criticisms included watered-down curriculum, incompetent teachers, and a lack of programming for gifted children. The crest of public criticism came as a result of the 1957 launching of Sputnik, a Soviet satellite (James and Tyack 1983).

Reformers called for more science, more math, a stricter adherence to discipline, less individualization, fewer extracurricular activities, and fewer nonacademic subjects. One of the most ardent critics of the time was James Conant, former president of Harvard University. In 1959 Conant published *The American High School Today*, which presented twenty-one recommendations for American high schools. Among these recommendations were

- comprehensive counseling programs to assist students in selecting appropriate electives;
- more individualized instruction;
- ability grouping by subject;
- a core academic curriculum, consisting of English, social studies, and math and science;
- relevant vocational programs;
- special programs for slow readers;
- programs for gifted students;
- more choices in science and foreign languages. (Conant 1959)

Responding to the critics, especially since the Sputnik launch concerned many Americans about national defense issues, the federal government passed the National Defense Education Act (NDEA) in 1958. This act was a major effort by the federal government to get involved in American education. It provided large amounts of money and stimulated curricular changes in science, math, and social studies. In addition, the NDEA supported teacher training, the development of better teaching materials, and an upgrade in the quality of textbooks (Lazerson 1987).

The revolt against progressive education did not last long. In the mid-1960s social issues—such as racial segregation, poverty, equal opportunities for disabled children and women, and eventually the Vietnam War—shifted attention from heavy emphasis on academic educational programs and programs for selected students to programs aimed at wiping out poverty and inequalities. Diversity characterized the opinions held about public education: conservatives demanded more discipline and stricter academic standards, and libertarians and radicals declared that schools were unnatural and called for alternative schools, more electives, and experience-based curricula (James and Tyack 1983).

An important set of events in public education during this period dealt with integration. Prior to the mid-1950s most minority racial children were educated in separate, segregated schools. This dual system

■ *Science and math were emphasized after the launching of Sputnik.*

of education was legally maintained, based on legal precedent in the case of *Plessey v. Ferguson* in 1896. The dual school systems provided minority racial children "putatively inferior training" (Braddock, Crain, and McPartland 1984, p. 260). This changed in 1954 when the United States Supreme Court issued its ruling in the *Brown v. Board of Education, Topeka, Kansas* case. The decision stated that "separate" is inherently unequal and required that schools desegregate with all deliberate speed. What followed was more than twenty-five years of turmoil, litigation, and disruption. By 1980, however, most of the nation's schools had been desegregated. Dual school systems, one for black children and one for white children, were mostly history. The actions from the *Brown v. Board of Education* case had a major impact on public education (Lazerson 1987).

Studies investigating the effects of desegregation have abounded. For the most part, they prove that desegregation had positive outcomes for education and socialization. Braddock, Crain, and McPartland (1984) reviewed ten studies that show desegregation having a significant impact on socialization (see table 2.2).

TABLE 2.2

Summary of Recent Research Evidence on the Effects of Desegregation

STUDY	DATA	INDEPENDENT VARIABLE	DEPENDENT VARIABLE	CONTROL VARIABLES	FINDINGS
Braddock (1980)	Survey in 1972 of black students attending four colleges in Florida (N = 253)	High school racial composition	Racial composition of college	Socioeconomic status, sex, high school grades, college costs and reputation, financial aid, and proximity to college	Black students from majority-white high school are more likely to enroll at majority-white four-year colleges.
Braddock and McPartland (1982)	Black subsample of the National Longitudinal Study (NLS) High School Class of 1972 (N = 3,119)	Elementary/secondary school racial composition	Racial composition of college	Socioeconomic status, sex, high school grades and test scores, region, and proximity to college	Black students from majority-white elementary/secondary schools are more likely to enroll in and persist at majority-white two- and four-year colleges.
Braddock, McPartland, and Trent (1984)	Black and white subsamples of the NLS Class of 1972 merged with survey data from their 1976 and 1979 employers (blacks = 1,518; whites = 1,957)	High school and college racial composition	Racial composition of employing firm	Sex, age, public vs. private employment, educational attainment, region, and community racial composition	Blacks and whites from desegregated elementary/secondary schools are more likely to work in desegregated firms; blacks from predominantly white colleges are also more likely to work in desegregated firms.
Crain and Weisman (1972)	Survey in 1966 of blacks living in North and West (N = 1,651)	Elementary/secondary school racial composition	Interracial contact, neighborhood racial composition, racial composition of occupation	Socioeconomic status, age, sex, region of birth	Blacks from desegregated elementary/secondary schools are more likely to have white social contacts, live in integrated neighborhoods.
Braddock and McPartland (1983)	Two-year follow-up of black subsample of NLS 1980–81 Youth Cohort (N = 1,074)	High school racial composition	Racial composition of co-worker groups and attitudes toward white supervisors and white co-workers	Sex, age, public vs. private employment, job status, and community racial composition	Northern blacks from majority-white high schools are more likely to have white co-workers. In the South, this relationship is also positive but confounded with community racial composition. Desegregated blacks evaluate white co-workers and supervisors more positively than do segregated blacks.

66

TABLE 2.2 – Continued
Summary of Recent Research Evidence on the Effects of Desegregation

STUDY	DATA	INDEPENDENT VARIABLE	DEPENDENT VARIABLE	CONTROL VARIABLES	FINDINGS
Green (1981; 1982)	Ten-year follow-up of 1971 black college freshmen surveyed by American Council on Education (N = 1,400)	High school and college racial composition	Racial composition of co-worker and friendship groups	Sex, high school grades, college major, etc.	Black adults who graduated from majority-white high schools or majority-white colleges and who grew up in majority-white neighborhoods are more likely to have white work associates and friends.
Crain (1984a)	Survey in 1982 of Project Concern participants (N = 660)	Elementary/secondary school racial composition	Interracial contact and neighborhood racial composition	Socioeconomic status, age, and test scores	Blacks who attend desegregated schools are more likely to move into integrated neighborhoods and to have a greater number of white friends.
Crain (1984b)	Survey of employers of NLS respondents (N = 4,080)	Inner-city school vs. suburban school	Employment decisions about applicants	Race, age, sex, education, and how applicant came to firm	Employers give preference to blacks from desegregated (i.e., suburban) schools.
Pearce (1980)	14 communities	Change in school segregation indices	Change in degree of desegregation in housing and in marketing policies in housing	Communities matched by size, region, racial composition	Communities with a communitywide school desegregation plan have more integration in housing and less "racial steering" by the real estate industry.
Pearce, Crain, and Farley (1984)	25 large cities	Change in school segregation indices	Change in housing segregation indices	City size, racial composition, previous level of segregation	Central cities where schools are desegregated have more desegregation in housing.

Reprinted with permission. Braddock, Crain, McPartland (1984) p. 260–261.

During this period litigation became a major variable in public education. Court cases dealing with integration, with programs for the disabled and disadvantaged, and with student rights were heard in state and federal courts, from the district level all the way to the United States Supreme Court. In addition to the *Brown* case, a landmark court case dealing with handicapped children brought significant changes to schools. In the *PARC v. Pennsylvania* case, filed in 1971, a consent decree was reached in which Pennsylvania agreed to provide appropriate educational programs to mentally retarded children in the state. This case was followed by other similar right-to-education cases in which the majority were ruled in favor of handicapped children's rights to access public educational programs (Smith, Price, and Marsh 1986).

Concomitant with litigation, legislation was passed that greatly affected public education. Presidents Kennedy and Johnson, champions of civil rights and the rights of the disabled and disadvantaged, were leaders in enacting legislation that guaranteed these groups equal educational opportunities. During the 1960s and 1970s a great deal of federal legislation was enacted that supported programs for these minority populations. A prime example of this legislation was Public Law 94–142, the Education for All Handicapped Children's Act, which was passed in 1975. This act required all schools to provide a free, appropriate public education for all handicapped children; when possible, this education was to be provided with nonhandicapped children.

As was discussed in the beginning of the text, national reform movements became pervasive in the late 1970s and early 1980s. Reformers of this period reflected many of the same concerns and recommendations heard in the 1950s. Indeed, "The editorials and articles on public education in popular magazines of the 1950s might be reprinted today without any substantial change and be fashionable once again" (James and Tyack 1983, p. 406).

Whether the reforms initiated in the early 1980s have significant, long-term effects on public education remains to be seen. The public's lack of confidence in the public educational system in the United States has been extensively documented. Much of the public will likely be eager to grasp and encourage the implementation of recommended reforms. The fallacy in accepting reforms without adequate research will undoubtedly lead American education into still another swing of the pendulum. One of these days, educators, parents, government officials, and others must look at the history of education and learn from it. Constantly revolving on a never-ending cycle of change will not likely lead us to as sound an educational system as we could achieve with better planning and judgment.

SUMMARY

This chapter presented information concerning the history of education in the United States. The first section of the chapter discussed the

INTRODUCTION TO EDUCATION

importance of studying history and education. Information was then presented that traced education from the Greek city states of Athens and Sparta to the current educational activities in the schools. It was pointed out that education in colonial America was regionalized, with the New England, Middle, and Southern colonies differing significantly in their approach to public education.

Public education, as it is known today, had its beginnings in the common-school movement of the mid-1800s. Its leader, Horace Mann, believed that public education should be available to all children during the elementary school years. From this beginning came mandatory public school attendance laws and the beginning of the public education system in the United States. Major events that affected education during the twentieth century were also presented.

IN THE FIELD

1. When were public schools first started in the school district? Who were some of the local founders of the school system and what were their motivations?

2. Were secondary schools started at the same time as elementary schools?

3. How many elementary, junior high, and high schools are in the district? Has the growth in the number of schools been steady, or was there a period when rapid growth was apparent?

4. How many professional teachers and administrators are employed in the district?

5. How many students graduate each year, and what percentage of these students go on to higher education programs?

REFERENCES

Armstrong, D. G., K. T. Henson, and T. V. Savage. 1983. *Education: An Introduction.* New York: Macmillan.

Binder, F. M. 1974. *The Age of the Common School, 1830–1865.* New York: John Wiley and Sons.

Braddock, J. H., R. L. Crain, and J. M. McPartland. 1984. A long-term view of school desegregation: Some recent studies of graduates as adults. *Phi Delta Kappan* 66(4), 259–64.

Button, H. W. and E. F. Provenzo. 1983. *History of Education and Culture in America.* Englewood Cliffs, NJ: Prentice-Hall.

Commager, H. S. 1983. A historian looks at the American high school. *American Journal of Education* 91(4), 531–48.

Conant, J. B. 1959. *The American High School Today.* New York: McGraw-Hill Book Company.

Cordasco, F. 1970. *A Brief History of Education.* Totowa, NJ: Littlefield, Adams & Co.

Dewey, J. 1916. *Democracy and Education: An Introduction to the Philosophy of Education.* New York: Macmillan.

Fain, S. M., R. Shostak, and J. F. Dean. 1979. *Teaching in America.* Glenview, IL: Scott, Foresman and Company.

Field, A. J. 1976. Educational expansion in mid-nineteenth-century Massachusetts: Human-capital formation or structural reinforcement? *Harvard Educational Review* 46(6), 521–52.

Gutek, G. L. 1970. *An Historical Introduction to American Education.* New York: Thomas Y. Crowell.

Gutek, G. L. 1986. *Education in the United States: An Historical Perspective.* Englewood Cliffs, NJ: Prentice-Hall.

James, T., and D. Tyack. 1983. Learning from past efforts to reform the high school. *Phi Delta Kappan* 64(6), 400–406.

Johnson, J. A., H. W. Collins, V. L. Dupuis, and J. H. Johansen. 1982. *Introduction to the Foundations of American Education.* Boston: Allyn and Bacon.

Lazerson, M. 1987. *American Education in the Twentieth Century.* New York: Teachers College Press.

Madsen, D. L. 1974. *Early National Education, 1776–1830.* New York: John Wiley and Sons.

Ornstein, A. C., and D. U. Levine. 1981. *An Introduction to the Foundations of Education.* Boston: Houghton Mifflin.

Parker, F. 1981. Ideas that shaped American schools. *Phi Delta Kappan* 62(5), 314–19.

Pulliam, J. 1987. *History of Education in America,* 4th ed. Columbus, OH: Merrill.

Shane, H. G. 1981. Significant writings that have influenced the curriculum: 1906–1981. *Phi Delta Kappan* 62(5), 311–14.

Tyack, D., and E. Hansot. 1984. Hard times, then and now: Public schools in the 1930s and 1980s. *Harvard Educational Review* 54(1), 33–66.

Tyler, R. W. 1981. The U.S. vs the world: A comparison of educational performances. *Phi Delta Kappan* 62(5), 307–10.

Unks, G. 1985. The illusion of intrusion: A chronicle of federal aid to public education. *The Educational Forum* 49(2), 133–56.

3

PHILOSOPHY OF EDUCATION

OBJECTIVES

After reading this chapter, you will be able to

- understand the branches of philosophy;

- understand the reasons for studying philosophy;

- define philosophy;

- list the purposes of educational philosophy;

- describe the components of the major schools of philosophy;

- relate the schools of general philosophy to the major schools of educational philosophy;

- describe the relationship between philosophy and teaching;

- discuss your philosophy of education as it relates to a formal philosophy.

OUTLINE

ADVANCE ORGANIZERS

1. What is philosophy?
2. Why should educational philosophy be studied by prospective teachers?
3. What are the purposes of educational philosophy?
4. What are the three branches of philosophy?
5. What are the major schools of philosophy?
6. What are the major schools of educational philosophy?
7. Which schools of general philosophy gave rise to schools of educational philosophy?
8. What is the role of teachers?
9. How does educational philosophy influence teachers' actions?
10. How will you respond to interviewers and colleagues when they ask you "What is your philosophy of education?"

INTRODUCTION

Philosophy of education is a broad and complex subject. This chapter is not intended to provide students with an in-depth study of philosophy, but it does provide an overview of philosophy and the philosophy of education. General philosophical concepts are presented to enable students to understand the role of philosophy in education.

Many students will ask why they must study philosophy and the philosophy of education. Just as the study of the history of education is relevant, so is the study of educational philosophy. First of all, "philosophy and education are not at all antithetical" (Phillips 1983, p. 3). Educational philosophy can help teachers clarify concepts, assess arguments, and expose assumptions (Phillips 1983). It can help teachers and other educators focus on questions that are speculative, prescriptive, and analytical; it can help enlarge thoughts so better personal choices can be made (Kneller 1971), and it helps in self-evaluation of beliefs and self-knowledge (Levison 1974).

"Perhaps, after all is said and done, the major role of philosophy in education is not to devise some system or school of thought, but to help develop the educator's thinking capacity" (Ozmon and Craver, 1976, p. 223). For example, do you believe that some students are just bad? Do you think that there are ultimate truths that should be taught? Do students learn better by being lectured to or by getting involved with learning activities? Should teachers accept the educational system as it is, or should they become radical change agents and attempt to change the system? These are the types of questions that philosophy of education addresses.

Understanding educational philosophy requires some knowledge and understanding of general philosophy, because "many of the educational implications of philosophical views have not been made explicit. One needs to be familiar with philosophical problems to see their relevance to education" (Broudy, Parsons, Snook, and Szoke 1967, p. 7). When philosophy is related to problems in education, an understanding of general philosophy is required in order to see the relationship between these educational issues and philosophy (Broudy et al. 1967).

Although the basis for actions and beliefs, philosophy often is ignored or simply not considered essential in teacher education programs. Viewed in a general sense, philosophy is thought of as boring and meaningless. Opponents of teaching educational philosophy to prospective teachers rally around three basic arguments. Some think that teaching educational philosophy slows up the process of producing teachers. These individuals would encourage the emphasis of practical methods and materials courses or courses that give students something tangible to take with them into the classroom. Others feel that teaching philosophy confuses students. It might raise questions in students' minds whereas other courses give students ready-made answers to persistent educational questions. Others wonder why we should teach philosophy when philosophers themselves cannot agree. This argument fails to recognize that some philosophers do agree, in principle, and also that disagreement often leads to better understanding (Ozmon 1972).

A lack of a general understanding of philosophy precludes individuals from understanding how philosophy actually affects everyday actions (Marler 1975). Plato viewed philosophy as encompassing all knowledge into a "semireligious synthesis" (Park 1974, p. 3).

From a technical point of view, philosophy includes an interrelationship among activities, content, and attitudes. Synthesizing, speculating, prescribing, and analyzing are the activities in philosophy (Marler 1975). Synthesis enables educators to show the relationship of ideas to practice (Ward 1981). Speculative philosophy is a search for orderliness applied to all knowledge; it applies systematic thinking to everything that exists. The activity that attempts to establish standards for assessing values, judging conduct, and appraising art is prescriptive philosophy (Kneller 1971). It structures or restructures norms based on facts that have been synthesized (Marler 1975). Analyzing allows the use of language to analyze such words as *mind, freedom,* and *equality.* The analytic activity is currently the dominating activity of American and British philosophers (Kneller 1971).

Definition of Philosophy

Describing what philosophy is *not* might be more meaningful than describing what philosophy is. First, philosophy is not like science on three counts: It presents no proofs, there are no theorems, and there are no questions that can be answered with yes or no (Waismann 1969). Philosophy is an attempt to understand the world, discover how life should be lived, determine what things people should strive for, and improve social organization. It has been used to analyze almost every problem faced by man (Henderson 1947).

"Philosophy is the human being's attempt to think most speculatively, reflectively, and systematically about the universe and the human relationship to that universe" (Gutek 1988, p. 2). Philosophy can be viewed as a means of answering basic, almost unanswerable questions, such as "What is real?", "What is good?", "What is bad?", and "What is the nature of man?" The different ways in which individuals answer these questions reveal their philosophies and will affect their daily actions. For teachers and school administrators, actions in the schools are affected by these kinds of beliefs.

Purposes of Educational Philosophy

Philosophy of education is the application of formal philosophy to the field of education. When most educators speak of their philosophy of education, they are talking about a loose set of beliefs that indicates their feelings about children and education. In an academic sense, philosophy of education is a particular, specific way of dealing with problems found in education (Taylor 1983). Problems such as what methods of instruction should be used and what should be included in the curriculum are focal points in educational philosophy.

Viable philosophies of education are based on general philosophy. Any philosophy of education should answer three questions: (1) what is education? (2) what should education accomplish? and (3) how should it be accomplished? (Henderson 1947).

The study of philosophy will not dictate teachers' actions in classrooms, rather, it will give teachers

1. explications of philosophical assumptions commonly held in American culture that are of special import to the American school;
2. hypotheses concerning the possible contributions of philosophy to increasing the rationality of educational practices and increasing the opportunities to become involved in testing them;
3. speculative opportunities to analyze the philosophical reasons underlying observed professional practices and to synthesize these reasons with nonphilosophical factors that also contributed to the practices;
4. opportunities to explicate personal assumptions as to the basic problems of man and his world, thus taking one more step in relating beliefs, knowledge of facts, and habitual practices;

5. opportunities to become involved in a most systematic, comprehensive, penetrating, and open-minded inquiry into the present state and future possibilities of American education, which, it is suggested, is one important function of any truly professional educator. (Marler 1975, p. 21–22)

Educational philosophy, therefore, has many purposes, including: (1) planning for the best education; (2) providing directions for the best education in various political, social, and economic contexts; (3) correcting mistakes about educational policy and practices; (4) focusing on educational activities that require resolutions; and (5) inquiring about the entire process of education (Power 1982). Teachers need to be involved in educational philosophy and go beyond simply teaching skills to students based on textbook organizations. An understanding of various educational philosophies will help clarify the role of teachers in classrooms.

BRANCHES OF PHILOSOPHY

Traditionally the subject matter of philosophy has been regarded as the whole of reality. Since it is almost impossible to study and write about philosophy using such a broad viewpoint, philosophers have focused the study of philosophy on three basic questions: "What is real?", "What is true?", and "What is good?" (Taylor 1983). These questions have resulted in three branches of philosophy: metaphysics, epistemology, and axiology.

Metaphysics

Metaphysics is the branch of philosophy that deals with ultimate reality. It is primarily within the speculative activity. With the avalanche of scientific knowledge, metaphysics was considered unnecessary by many who felt that scientifically verifiable truths deleted the need for metaphysical assumptions about reality. Today, however, metaphysics has once again emerged as an important area. Scientists, Albert Einstein being the most noted, have even made metaphysical assumptions based on scientific fact. Currently metaphysics and science are considered as two separate activities, each with relevance for the other (Kneller 1971).

Metaphysics focuses on four concepts and assumptions: (1) basic reality, (2) human nature, (3) free will and determinism, and (4) God and faith. The concept of human nature can be described as inherently evil, inherently good, inherently superior or inferior, or as resulting from experiences or internal choices (Marler 1975). A teacher's view of human nature will undoubtedly affect trust, disciplinary methods, and daily interactions with students. If a teacher holds the view that people are inherently evil, classroom rules will reflect this mistrust. On the other hand, teachers who believe that the human nature is inherently good will rely less on structured classroom rules and more on individual responsibility.

Metaphysics is related to educational curriculum, in that a large part of the subject matter in schools attempts to describe what is real. "For example, subjects such as history, geography, chemistry, and so on, describe certain phases of reality to students" (Gutek 1988, p. 2).

Epistemology

Epistemology deals with knowledge. As an epistemologist, the philosopher would ask questions such as:

- What is there that is common to all the different activities that are involved in knowing?
- What is the difference between knowing and, say, believing?
- What can we know beyond the information provided by the senses?
- What is the relation of the act of knowing to the thing that is known?
- How can we show that knowledge is "true"? (Kneller 1971, p. 18)

Concepts of epistemology include the mind, ideas, experience, objectivity, frame of reference, and knowledge and truth (Marler 1975). Educators' views of knowledge have an immediate effect on the way information is transmitted. If the teacher believes that experience is the key to all knowledge, the teacher attempts to have children participate and to actively experience everything. On the other hand, teachers who believe that knowledge can be acquired without direct experiences will be more inclined to instruct children using a lecture approach or simply by having children read materials. Epistemology, therefore, is directly related to the instructional methods employed by teachers (Gutek 1988).

Axiology

The third branch of philosophy, axiology, is the study of values. The basic questions in axiology include: are values personal or impersonal, changing or constant, and are they hierarchical in nature? Ethics deals with moral values, while aesthetics focuses on the value of beauty (Kneller 1971). Concepts and assumptions of axiology include (1) value: its nature and locus, (2) value judgments: validation, (3) values: classifying and ordering, (4) morality, (5) obligation and conscience, and (6) ends, means, and process (Marler 1975). In education the area of values has received a great deal of attention. Should schools teach values and, if so, which values? Is moral education something schools should provide, or should this domain be left to parents? Teachers' views on these topics will affect their classroom behaviors regardless of a school's policies. If teachers feel that they should have a part in moral education, they may provide instruction on a variety of topics that they would not include in their curriculum if they did not support the idea of moral education. Values clarification is a good example of the relationship between education and axiology.

Today our society is frequently made up of clashing values and mores. Within our pluralistic society exists a great variety of religions, ideas, values, and customs. Schools frequently face the predicament of promoting certain values which can lead to problems with certain groups (Gutek 1988). School prayer is an example. Although school prayer is a legal issue, in actuality it is an axiological issue.

SCHOOLS OF PHILOSOPHY

Although the three branches of philosophy are discussed by philosophers, most nonphilosophers are more familiar with schools of philosophy. Schools are orientations to philosophy and result from a consensus or near-consensus regarding the answers to the basic questions of philosophy. Several of these schools of philosophy have endured for centuries; others are relatively new. Some of these are related to general philosophy, while others have emerged as specific philosophies of education. Schools of philosophy can be divided into basic and educational (see table 3.1). Educational philosophies that have evolved from these basic philosophies include perennialism, essentialism, progressivism, reconstructionism, and behaviorism. A brief description of each of the basic and educational philosophies will provide a basis for understanding each viewpoint.

Basic Philosophies

Idealism: Idealism had its roots in ancient Indo-European culture; Plato is considered the "Father of Idealism." Idealism was assimilated into

TABLE 3.1
Schools of Philosophy

BASIC PHILOSOPHY	EDUCATIONAL PHILOSOPHY
Idealism	Essentialism
Realism	Behaviorism
Pragmatism	Progressivism Reconstructionism
Existentialism	Existentialism

the Christian movement and was dominant throughout the Middle Ages. The philosophical base of colonial education in the New England colonies was idealism; it spread with the advent of the common-school movement. Idealism suffered a severe blow with Darwin's scientific approach to knowledge and did not recover until the 1930 attack on progressivism, when it was more commonly known as essentialism (Marler 1975).

The basis of idealism is that there are certain universal, absolute concepts, such as Truth and Honor. These concepts are considered "higher truths" and are not to be questioned by scientific inquiry. Deductive logic, or going from a universal truth to a specific conclusion, is used to develop knowledge (Marshall 1973). Idealism can be related to metaphysics, epistemology, and axiology of the traditional schools of philosophy (see table 3.2).

Idealism was very popular in the United States during the 1880s. Individuals who represented idealistic philosophy included Ralph Waldo Emerson (1803–1882), Henry David Thoreau (1817–1862), and William Torrey Harris (1835–1909) (Gutek 1988). A description of the most noted idealists follows.

Plato. Plato, a follower of Socrates, is most often associated with idealism. Basically he believed that man should be concerned with the search for truth. While Plato did not believe that man created knowledge, he did think that man discovered knowledge. Plato believed that a dichotomy exists between ideas and matter; he believed that ideas are the only true reality because matter is flawed. As a result, Plato believed that students should be taught to think abstractly and should move away from the study of physical matter. To Plato, the abstract concept of values was permanent (Taylor 1983).

The development of modern idealism resulted from the works of several other philosophers who were considered idealists—René Descartes, George Berkeley, Immanuel Kant, and George Hegel. Descartes (1596–1650), a Frenchman educated by Jesuits, believed that man could doubt the existence of everything except his own existence. His famous principle, "I think, therefore I am," formed the basis for his philosophy. He believed that matter outside of self was perceived by the senses, which frequently were in error. Other than self, the only other thing that Descartes believed was undeniable was the existence of God (Ozmon and Craver 1976).

George Berkeley (1685–1753) believed, that for a thing to exist, a person must be present to know that it exists. He did not believe that a material world existed independent of mind. To the old question, "Does a tree that falls in the forest make a noise?" Berkeley would answer "no." "Berkeley's efforts may be viewed as a kind of 'last ditch' stand against the encroachments of science and scientific realism which held to the materialistic thesis" (Ozmon and Craver 1976, p. 11).

Immanuel Kant (1724–1804) was born in Germany and is considered one of the world's great philosophers. He readily accepted modern science and developed his philosophy on human thought processes (Ozmon and Craver 1976). Kant believed that concrete, physical objects could be explained by science, but also held that man had the freedom to make moralistic choices. He viewed the "development of humanity as the outcome of the complex interaction of man, nature, and society" (Brumbaugh and Lawrence 1963, p. 101).

Realism. Realism also has ancient roots, and Aristotle is considered the "Father of Realism." Because idealism had such a monopoly on thought, through religion, realism remained a rather uninfluential philosophy until the expansion of science during the Enlightenment period in Europe. Realism gained a foothold in the United States during the eighteenth and nineteenth centuries. It was the dominant philosophy underlying education in the Middle colonies; several academies were founded by adherents of realism. In the twentieth century, realism expanded rapidly with the scientific movement. It was influen-

■ *Realists believe that knowledge can be derived from the senses.*

TABLE 3.2
Metaphysics, Epistemology, and Axiology of the
Traditional Schools of Philosophy

■

Idealism
- Metaphysics   ■ Ultimate reality is spiritual, not physical
- Epistemology   ■ True knowledge comes from reason
- Axiology   ■ Values and ethics are absolute
  - ■ Good and beautiful do not change but are constant from society to society

Realism
- Metaphysics   ■ Matter is the ultimate reality
  - ■ Matter exists even when it has not been discovered
- Epistemology   ■ The world is as it is, not as it has been created by man
  - ■ True knowledge is that which corresponds to the way the world is
- Axiology   ■ Fundamental values are permanent

Pragmatism
- Metaphysics   ■ Reality is what we experience
  - ■ Reality results from experience
- Epistemology   ■ Knowledge results from the interaction of man and the environment
- Axiology   ■ Values are relative
  - ■ Worth of values should be tested, not simply accepted

Source: G. Kneller. *Introduction to the Philosophy of Education.* New York: John Wiley & Sons, Inc., 1973.

■

tial in the development of educational testing and educational psychology. In the 1930s realists and idealists both attacked progressive education; following Sputnik in the late 1950s, realism became popular and was a force in the push for more science education (Marler 1975).

Realism holds the position that reality exists without knowledge of its existence. The world is a physical world, governed by various laws which exist even if they have not been discovered. Individuals discover these laws through scientific study. Realism also can be related to the three branches of philosophy (see table 3.2).

Aristotle. Aristotle was one of Plato's students. He believed that ideas can exist without matter, but that the study of matter could help man develop better, more specific ideas. Aristotle was both a philosopher and scientist, believing that the study of one could actually lead to a better understanding of the other. He believed in an orderly universe where things occur in a predictable matter. For example, kittens grow up to be cats and seeds grow into flowers (Ozmon and Craver 1976).

Aristotle advocated using the method of syllogism to determine knowledge. A famous example is the following (Golden, Bergquist, and Coleman 1989):

All men are mortal.
Socrates is a man;
therefore, Socrates is mortal.

This method generally follows deductive reasoning principles whereby truths are derived from generalizations. The process works well as long as the generalization is true. Should the generalization be false, then the entire reasoning process becomes faulty (Ozmon and Craver 1976). The work of Aristotle is very important because of the break from the idealistic position that truths are enduring and that they are arrived at abstractly.

In addition, Aristotle and other realists believed that knowledge also can be derived from the senses. These realists included Francis Bacon, John Locke, Alfred Whitehead, and Bertrand Russell. Francis Bacon (1561–1626) seriously challenged the Aristotelian approach to science. Rather than using a deductive reasoning approach, Bacon suggested that an inductive method be used starting with observable, verifiable truths rather than with nonverifiable generalizations (Ozmon and Craver 1976). Bacon is generally credited with popularizing the scientific method of inquiry (Pulliam 1987).

John Locke (1632–1704) was an English philosopher who contributed to both the Declaration of Independence and the American system of government. His political writings related to man's inalienable rights, were almost universally accepted by Thomas Jefferson and other American revolutionaries and were used as a basis for declaring independence from England. In the area of education, Locke's idea that humans were born with a blank slate, without innate ideas, greatly impacted education. He believed that children's minds at birth were blank, ready to be "written on" by experiences. Consequently, Locke believed that all ideas and knowledge are gained from experiences (Pulliam 1987).

Alfred Whitehead (1861–1947) is considered a contemporary realist. Originally a mathematician, Whitehead became a full-time philospher only after the age of 60. The central theme in Whitehead's philosophy was "process." He believed that process is reality. Like Plato, he believed that ideas were the important things to learn in education; however, Whitehead focused on living ideas, or ideas related to everyday experiences of the learner (Ozmon and Craver 1976).

Bertrand Russell (1872–1970) is the most recent noted philosopher aligned with realism. A maverick realist, Russell was associated with many socially activist causes during the years before his death. For example, he was a staunch opponent of the Vietnam war and an advocate for banning nuclear weapons. Russell's philosophy was based on scientific inquiry. He believed that science should be the basis of philosophy since science provided the only way to acquire knowledge. Russell advocated using science to gain two different kinds of information: hard and soft. Hard data includes facts which can be verified using the scientific method; soft data includes beliefs, thoughts, and other constructs which simply cannot be denied or proved with science (Ozmon and Craver 1976).

St. Thomas Aquinas (1225–1274) combined the philosophy of Aristotle realism with church doctrine to develop religious realism, or scholasticism. Some philosophers label this Neo-Thomism. Scholasticism is the official philosophy of the Roman Catholic church. It is based on the belief that matter and spirit were created by God (Kneller 1971). Thomas Aquinas considered reason the basis of the organization of the universe, but any conflict between conclusions arrived at by reason and faith were the result of inaccurate reasoning (Johnson et al. 1982).

Pragmatism. Pragmatism is primarily an American philosophy. Its beginnings can be traced to an essay published in 1878 by Charles S. Peirce (Leight 1984). The development of pragmatism into a philosophy occurred during the late nineteenth century and early twentieth century. In comparison to idealism and realism, this is a modern philosophy. Although it had some roots in ancient Europe, the primary bases for its development were Darwin, Newton, the progressive movement, and social philosophy in the United States (Marler 1975).

Pragmatism is a philosophy based on scientific analysis. It "ideally aims at intellectually honest solutions based upon an objective and dispassionate scientific analysis of all the evidence before any solution is even considered" (Marshall 1973, p. 47). Pragmatists consider the human mind as a tool to be used to discover knowledge. The basis of pragmatism is the inductive reasoning approach through human experience. The most noted American pragmatists include Charles Peirce, William James, and John Dewey. Peirce believed that the verification of true knowledge could only be made through actual experience. Ideas could only be considered hypotheses until tested through experience. William James believed that truth and experience were one in the same. "James called upon thinkers to concentrate on experience in lieu of essences, abstractions, and universals." (Ozmon and Craver 1976, p. 82)

Considered the foremost pragmatist, John Dewey (1859–1952) always felt that schools and society were to be closely coordinated within education (Leight 1984). For example, he believed that the only way to create a true democracy was through education and the schools. Dewey and other pragmatists believed that children learn best through experiences. Therefore, he believed in organizing learning experiences in which children could participate (Perkinson 1987).

Dewey is one of the few philosophers whose philosophy and educational theory are almost the same. Unfortunately for Dewey, many of his ideas were misconstrued because of his links to progressivism. Foremost, Dewey was an advocate of progressive education. However, when the progressive education movement took on a "hands-off-let-the-bud-unfold" technique, Dewey tried to distance himself from the movement. Allowing children of any age to determine their own educational curriculum and methods of learning was not an acceptable approach for Dewey (Brumbaugh and Lawrence 1963).

Dewey's educational philosophy and, therefore, his educational theory include the following guidelines (Brumbaugh and Lawrence 1963):

- young children are not to be presented with unlimited choice in self development;
- the three Rs are vital to higher levels of learning;
- selection and organization of subject matter is critical in education;
- teachers should have a significant amount of control over what occurs in the classroom; and
- teachers need to understand and be able to implement a systematic method of inquiry for students to follow.

Specifically, Dewey rejected three doctrines of progressive education: "(1) self-development through student choice of materials . . . ; (2) nondirective supervision on the part of the teacher; (3) an educational science with a content of its own" (Brumbaugh and Lawrence 1963, p. 129–130). Pragmatism can also be related to the three branches of philosophy (see table 3.2).

Existentialism. Although existentialism had origins in ancient Europe, modern existentialism developed in Europe following the morass of two world wars. Basic themes of existentialism include the following:

1. The human situation is one of meaninglessness, alienation, anguish, and death.
2. Man has both absolute freedom and absolute responsibility to authenticate himself, make meaning in the world, and avoid meaningless, unauthentic life.
3. In so doing, he must have the courage to be, make decisions in the face of despair, and realize that truths and values are created by his subjective choice.
4. The Other represents a great danger to self-actualization, but a meaningful relationship with him is probably necessary to the achievement of one's own self. (Marler 1975, p. 382)

True existentialists would have students direct much of what occurs in schools, from setting the curriculum to the methods and rate at which the curriculum is presented (Marler 1975). While science would be a part of the curriculum, science would be taught as a tool, not as a decision maker. Man must retain control over science rather than science over man. Like pragmatism, existentialism would have students use psychology and sociology as a base. Students would be encouraged to learn about the diversity of cultures rather than be praised for stereotypical behavior patterns (Marshall 1973). While the effect of existentialism on education likely will remain minimal, it will continue to affect small pockets, such as the Summerhill school, which is based on existentialism philosophy (Marler 1975). Also, existentialism undoubtedly will continue to influence individuals' philosophies to a great extent.

TABLE 3.3
Views of Leading Existentialists

INDIVIDUAL	SUMMARY OF VIEWS
S. Kierkegaard	■ Was a devout Christian who attacked convential Christianity ■ Called for man to accept Christianity on faith, not facts ■ Believed that men need to come to an understanding of their souls, destiny, and the reality of God ■ Believed education should be subjective and religious
Martin Buber	■ Was a Jewish philosopher-theologian ■ Man needs to realize that every individual has his own intense, personal world of meaning ■ Felt that men are treated as objects ■ Believed that students and teachers should have mutual respect and feelings for each other
Martin Heidegger	■ Believed that man comes into the world without his own consent ■ Anxiety is a primary feature of being ■ Focused his studies on "Being" ■ Studied the question "Who am I?"
Jean-Paul Sartre	■ Probably the best known existentialist philosopher ■ Views humans as individuals in an absurd world ■ Thought that the development of meaning for life was an individual process ■ Thought that man was absolutely free

Source: H. Ozmon and S. Craver 1976. *Philosophical Foundations of Education.* Columbus, OH: Merrill.

Existentialism is a truly unique philosophy. It represents a radical departure from other schools of philosophy—existentialism is an irrational position (Taylor 1983). The numerous and different interpretations of existentialism are due, in part, to its emphasis on individuality. "Its seemingly tortured and mixed varities may be due to the very return of the existentialist credo—the lonely, estranged, and alienated individual caught up in a meaningless and absurd world" (Ozmon and Craver 1976, p. 158). Several noted existentialists include Soren Kierkegaard, Martin Buber, Martin Heidegger, and Jean-Paul Sartre. Table 3.3 summarizes the views of these existentialists.

Educational Philosophies

Perennialism. Perennialism is a developed form of realism that had its beginnings with St. Thomas Aquinas. It is based on Aristotle's realism and on the belief that there are certain everlasting values. As a result of this orientation, perennialists based the entire college curriculum on the "Great Books" of the world (Marshall 1973).

The basic principles of perennialism include the following:

■ Human nature is the same everywhere; therefore, education should be the same.

- Man must use rationality to control his instincts.
- Education must teach knowledge of eternal truth.
- Education prepares man for life.
- Students should be taught about the world's permanence.
- Great works of literature, philosophy, and other subjects should be a major component of the curriculum (Kneller 1971)

Perennialists believe that the universal aim of education is truth. Education should help students pursue this truth through subjects such as history, language, literature, science, and the humanities. The curriculum should be logical and should help students develop principles and ethics (Gutek 1988).

Essentialism. Essentialism had its beginnings in the early 1930s. Like perennialism, essentialism holds that subject matter should be the center of education. Essentialism differs from perennialism, however, in denying the existence of everlasting values. Essentialism focuses on (1) learning as hard work, (2) teacher-directed learning, (3) assimilation of knowledge, and (4) mental discipline (Kneller 1971). Back-to-the-

- *Essentialism is the foundation for the back-to-the-basics movement.*

EXPERTS SAY AMERICA NEEDS TO LAUNCH INTENSIVE PROGRAM TO COUNTER ECONOMIC THREAT

Richard Higgins

Thirty-two years ago, the threat to American eminence in science and engineering was palpable: The world's first space satellite, *Sputnik 1*, blipped and beeped across the night sky.

The American response also was highly visible: public alarm followed by the 1958 National Defense Education Act, an intensive effort to upgrade the teaching of math and science. The proof of its success was the fulfillment of President John F. Kennedy's 1961 pledge to put a man on the moon by the end of the decade.

Today, the threat is more diffuse, as the United States slips behind a growing number of countries in math and science literacy at the same time it is losing its advantage in the world marketplace.

A recent international study that ranked the United States last in math and science skills among 12 nations generated national headlines, but other changes have been more subtle.

Earlier this year, for example, the United States was displaced as the No. 1 provider of foreign aid for the first time since 1946. Japan, using the enormous budget surpluses it built upon its technological prowess, has assumed that role.

Such changes may be less obvious than a singular satellite, but a growing number of educators believe that the nation must now embark on a program as intensive as that of the post-*Sputnik* era to avoid losings its position as a world leader.

"The threat now is by far more critical, and the consequences higher, than was the case in the immediate post-*Sputnik* era," said Bassam Shakharishi, chief of science and engineering education for the National Science Foundation.

The nation's population has grown by 50 million since 1957, he said, yet the pool of qualified science and math teachers has declined during the last decade after increasing during the 1960s and early 1970s.

"*Sputnik* was perceived as a national security threat, and the country responded," Shakharishi said. "The threat now is one of slow economic corrosion, and our response can be no less emphatic."

The National Science Foundation education office awards $100 million in federal funds to enhance science and math instruction at the pre-college level. Shakhashiri said more will be needed to increase the number of qualified science, math and engineering teachers and create a more "supportive public environment" for working scientists.

"We live in a much more technologically and scientifically advanced world, one in which the United States can't compete if it doesn't have an educated work force and citizenry that knows the difference between astronomy and astrology, that can comprehend the issues of pollution control or genetic engineering," Shakhashiri said. "Sadly, we don't."

F. James Rutherford, education officer for the American Association for the Advancement of Science, said the United States is still dealing with essentially the same problem it faced after *Sputnik*.

"Our schools have not been able to keep up with the pace of technological change since the beginning of this century," he said. "World affairs and developments in science have moved faster than the schools can handle them. That was the fundamental problem then, and remains so."

The problem with the post-*Sputnik* push on the teaching of science and technology was only that it petered out too soon— sometime in the mid-1970s. From 1968 to 1982, the year it was almost wiped out, the

continued

National Science Foundation's education budget dropped from $135 million to $20 million. Many schools are still using laboratory equipment they got under the National Defense Education Act in the early 1960s, Rutherford said.

"This is a truly long-term problem and can only be addressed by truly long-term solutions," he said. "If you are going to invest in the training of teachers, it has to be persistent and systematic. Once-a-year training sessions for four weeks are not enough. We ought to be using our satellite and computer technology to make materials available in order to do some of that training on a year-round basis."

Several educators said that while an increased federal role is necessary, simply spending more money is not, by itself, the solution.

"The impact of federal money was much greater right after *Sputnik* because we still had good teachers around," said Sheldon Glashow, a Harvard University physicist and Nobel laureate. "We don't have good teachers anymore."

Today, school systems are much more decentralized than they were after *Sputnik*, said Marshall Smith, dean of education at Stanford University.

While decentralization has had its benefits, one negative result, he noted, is that science and math teacher-training programs, curriculums and classroom standards are adequate in some states and extremely lax in others.

Smith and other educators said standards for minimum proficiency in science and math should in general be higher as well as more uniform. In the United States, he noted, high school science and math standards are far below those of Japan, the Soviet Union and many European countries. "Our math and science teachers tend to have low expectations, and that gets communicated to the kids."

A key to addressing science and math illiteracy is understanding where the battle is being lost—in kindergarten through eighth grade, said Smith.

"Few students enter high school equipped to handle high school-level science," he said. "They're already turned off." Another problem, he said, is that the teacher themselves do not understand enough about science or math to teach it well. "They'll teach what they feel comfortable with," he said, "and avoid what they don't understand, or else teach it badly."

Margaret MacVicar, dean for undergraduate education at the Massachusetts Institute of Technology, said that while improving elementary education in math and science is crucial, all of the remedial attention cannot be focused on children.

"The problem is more immediate. What about the educationally disabled people from say, age 20 to 35, who are the products of this school system we've been deploring for 10 or 15 years. Are we just going to write them off? What can we do to empower them to participate knowledgeably in addressing the complex scientific and technological problems we face.

MacVicar said the response needs a political focal point as dramatic as *Sputnik*. "I'd like to see a national emergency declared," she said. A measure that sweeping, she said, may be necessary to "cut across the huge education bureaucracy."

One thing MacVicar said she would like to see would be for each state to devise a "coordinated statewide vision for science and math education from kindergarten all the way up through Grade 26—the advanced graduate-school level."

Reprinted courtesy of the Boston Globe.

basics, or the three Rs as a curricular focus, should be considered the core of the school curriculum in essentialism philosophy (Marshall 1973).

Today's back-to-the-basics movement is a resurgence of the essentialist philosophy. The current conservative education movement also contains elements in common with essentialism (Gutek 1988).

Progressivism. The progressive education movement peaked in this country in the early 1900s; however, its beginnings date back to the eighteenth century Enlightenment period. Adherents to the progressive philosophy believe that human beings are basically good and can improve their environment with intelligence and science. The social reform movement of the early twentieth century also influenced the progressive education movement. While progressives were heavily influenced by John Dewey, not all were ardent followers of Dewey's pragmatism (Gutek 1988). The general thread holding progressives together was the desire to break away from the dehumanizing traditional educational philosophies of the time.

Advocates of progressivism are in favor of individuals learning effective problem-solving techniques. Progressivists do not believe there is a need to search for eternal truths, either through philosophy or science. In application, it is a practical approach to learning and education (Ozmon 1972).

Reconstructionism. The philosophy of reconstructionism was developed in the mid-twentieth century. It called for schools to get involved and support social reform. Although they did not believe that schools should take the lead in developing a new social order, reconstructionists thought that schools should cooperate with social reform movements. Adherents to this philosophy believe that schools should help establish a new social order that brings to realization basic cultural values. The new society should be truly democratic and directed by the people; the role of teachers should be to encourage students to identify with and support such a social revolution (Kneller 1971).

Reconstructionists advocate two major premises: (1) society is always in need of change, and (2) education must be changed and also used as a force in changing society. A major tenet underlying reconstructionism is that individuals should attempt to make life better. Proponents of reconstructionism more likely would be classified as social activists than philosophers (Ozmon and Craver 1976).

Behaviorism. Individuals adhering to the philosophy of behaviorism favor manipulating people through the use of rewards and punishments. Operant conditioning and classical conditioning are the two primary methods used in behaviorism. Well-known individuals who advocate this philosophy include Ivan Pavlov, John Watson, and B. F. Skinner.

Some proponents of behaviorism do not use punishments, but use a combination of positive and negative reinforcers. Positive reinforcers are pleasant things that occur following a behavior that will act as a reward. After being rewarded, or positively reinforced, the individual is more likely to repeat the appropriate behavior than if no reward were given. Negative reinforcers, on the contrary, are negative consequences that are removed when an individual performs in an appropriate manner. This differs from punishment in that punishment is something unpleasant that is provided following an inappropriate behavior, whereas a negative reinforcer is removed when the behavior is appropriate. For example, if a child cries because of a loud noise and the loud noise goes way, the child stops crying. This is a form of negative reinforcement. Punishment would occur if the child cries and is spanked for crying.

Behaviorists believe that behavior is learned and can be extinguished with proper stimulus/response interventions. They are not concerned about eternal truths or causes of certain behavior. On the other hand, behavioral engineers *are* concerned with the causes of behavior.

Behavioral Engineering. Behavioral engineering is a philosophy of education that focuses on controlling the learner's environment. Through manipulating the environment with rewards and punishment, behavior can be changed in the desired direction. "Behavior engineers feel that much of human behavior reflects attitudes and actions already conditioned by the environment, and that these attitudes and actions should be engineered along paths that are more useful and productive" (Ozmon 1972, p. xiv). Skinner has been the leading promoter of behavior engineering.

Practitioners of behavior engineering arrange reinforcers to encourage repeated appropriate behavior. Operant conditioning, sometimes referred to as behavior modification, is the primary methodology that implements this philosophy. Although this strategy is used extensively with disabled learners in special education programs, it has also been shown to be very effective with all students.

PHILOSOPHY AND EDUCATIONAL PRACTICE

The influence of philosophy on educational policies and practices cannot be overemphasized. A teacher's philosophical beliefs generally affect what occurs in classrooms. Administrators' philosophies affect policies and the implementation of policies. Building principals' philosophies affect the manner in which students are disciplined and teachers are entrusted with professional responsibilities. For example, if teachers hold the view that all men are inherently evil, they will likely routinely distrust students. Similarly, if they support the ideas of perennialism, they are likely to include in their daily teaching activities information from the "Great Books" of history.

Just about anyone can read a teacher's guide and present information in a sensible order. Understanding *why* it is presented in a particular way, *if* it should be presented in a particular way, or if it should be presented *at all* requires a different kind of knowledge. Educational philosophy can provide a background for questioning practices, which should lead to better educational programs for students.

Without the desire and ability to question, teachers are often at a loss concerning how to deal with various issues that confront students and schools. Ethnic, religious, and ideological controversies require that teachers make decisions. They must be able to evaluate these kinds of issues and deal with them effectively in the educational process (Ozmon 1972).

Tables 3.4 and 3.5 briefly summarize some general influences philosophy has on teaching and some specific teaching methods related

TABLE 3.4
Examples of the Influences of Philosophy on Educational Practice

PRACTICE	BASE PHILOSOPHY
Students are mistrusted and expected to cheat when they get the chance	Idealism
Curriculum is based on the "Great Books"	Perennialism
Students should choose why they want to learn and how they want to learn it	Existentialism
Teachers should arrange learning through experiences	Pragmatism
The three Rs should be the primary focus of education	Essentialism
Students and teachers should support social changes that will lead to a new social order	Reconstructionism
Well-defined values should be taught to children by teachers	Realism
Students should be taught values and how to live with them	Idealism
Ideas are judged as true only after they have been tested	Pragmatism

Source: G. F. Kneller, 1973. *Introduction to the Philosophy of Education.* New York: John Wiley & Sons, 1973.

TABLE 3.5
Philosophy and Teaching Methods

PHILOSOPHY	BASIC METHOD(S)
Idealism	Lecture Discussion
Realism	Demonstration Recitation
Neo-Thomism	Formal drill Memorization
Experimentalism	Problem solving Project method
Existentialism	Individual study Individual questioning

Source: Morris and Pai. *Philosophy and the American School.* New York: Houghton Mifflin. 1976.

INTRODUCTION TO EDUCATION

to particular philosophies. The next section describes in more detail specific philosophies and their effects on teaching methods and curriculum.

Philosophy and Teaching Methods and Curriculum

Philosophy impacts education through both teaching methods and curriculum. While many teachers use a hodgepodge approach to teaching, most consistently adhere to a certain philosophical approach, even though they may not realize it. Their methods and the curriculum usually can be associated with a specific school of philosophy.

Idealism: Methodology and Curriculum. Idealists are opposed to students learning facts in a regimented manner, believing those students will later become narrow specialists unconcerned about fellow humankind. Rather, they would prefer that students be allowed to learn through contemplation or the dialectic. Although not used in schools today, the approach was widely used through the Middle Ages. Today, idealists rely on allowing students to learn through reading classical writings and art that express great ideas (Ozmon and Craver 1976).

The curriculum of idealists focuses on teaching students to think as opposed to teaching facts. Rather than teaching specific technical skills, idealists would teach broad concepts. During elementary years, this means an emphasis on teaching the habits of understanding, patience, tolerance, and hard work. Although the lecture method would not be used extensively, it still could be used to help students understand truths. Library experiences and art would be more appropriate ways to learn (Ozmon and Craver 1976).

Realism: Methodology and Curriculum. For realists the goal of education is "to aid human beings to attain happiness by cultivating their potentiality for excellence to its fullest" (Gutek 1988, p. 46). Realists focus on intellectual learning over social and recreational activities. The curriculum at the elementary level should contain the basic academic areas of reading, writing, and arithmetic. At the secondary and post-secondary levels, the curriculum focus should shift to content courses that comprise the wisdom of humankind. Courses would include social studies, science, math, and literature (Gutek 1988).

Realists advocate a simple instructional approach. They focus on the teacher, the knowledge to be taught, and the actual instruction. Instructional methods include a wide repertoire of traditional approaches, such as lecture, discussion, and experiential activities. Specific methods used should be chosen based on the individual needs of students (Gutek 1988).

Pragmatism: Methodology and Curriculum. John Dewey's writings form the basis for much of pragmatism. Basically, Dewey and other

■ *Pragmatism utilizes a problem-solving and experiential learning model.*

pragmatists advocate the use of a problem-centered learning approach. Dewey's pragmatism has been called experimentalism, reflecting the emphasis on problem solving and experiential learning (Pulliam 1987).

Some of the permissive progressivists mixed some of Dewey's ideas with those of Jean-Jacques Rousseau and with some social philosophies (Pulliam 1987). Unlike them, Dewey did not encourage anarchy, or students doing just what they desired. Dewey's approach was much more structured, though he did emphasize the student getting actively involved in the learning process. The teacher, rather than impose restrictive structure, would provide guidance and direction to the student (Gutek 1988).

Pragmatism focuses on problem solving, personal experiences, and an interaction between student and environment (Pulliam 1987). Dewey espoused a curriculum organized into three levels. Level one, making and doing, enabled students to do projects using raw materials from their environments. Level two focused on history and geography. At this level, students started learning about their immediate environments and expanded outward to enable them to understand where they fit into the total scheme of society. Finally, Dewey's third level was organized subjects of science. At this level, students used the experiential approach to solve their problems while learning about science (Gutek 1988). The primary education implications of pragmatism can be summed up as dealing with experiences and problem solving.

Existentialism: Methodology and Curriculum. This philosophy is not a uniform, well-coordinated system. Rather, the philosophy of existentialism is unique and individualized, which makes generalizing difficult. Still, some general assumptions made by most existentialists about education include the following (Gutek 1988):

1. Education should help individuals become aware of their own freedom.
2. The standardization of the schools is counter to existentialist philosophy.
3. A goal of schools should be to increase student self-awareness.
4. The existentialist curriculum should include skills and subjects that explain physical reality and social reality and that depict human choices.
5. Humanistic studies, such as history, the arts, literature, and philosophy, should be included to encourage self-examination.
6. Teachers should foster an environment of openness and the expression of subjectivity.
7. Education and schooling should be organized to give to students many choices concerning goals and the curriculum.

Essentialism: Methodology and Curriculum. The revival of essentialism is reflected in the back-to-the-basics movement. Adherents to this educational philosophy believe that there are certain subjects and skills that are "essential" to learn. Essentialists have used the findings of the "Nation at Risk" report to substantiate their claims that our public schools have gotten too far away from their purpose of teaching basic skills. Essentialism emphasizes these points:

1. The elementary curriculum should emphasize basic tool skills that contribute to literacy.
2. The secondary curriculum should include history, mathematics, science, literature, and language.
3. Discipline is necessary in order for systematic learning to occur in school situations.
4. Respect for legitimate authority, both in school and in society, is a value to be cultivated in students.
5. The mastering of a skill or a subject requires effort and diligence on the part of the learner.

6. The teaching of these necessary skills and subjects requires mature and well-educated teachers who know their subjects and who are able to transmit them to students. (Gutek 1988, p. 257)

Basically, essentialists believe in a no-frills approach to education. They believe the curriculum should be made up of basic subjects and that the primary teaching methodology is drill and rote memorization. Progressive curricula and teaching methods are severely attacked by essentialists.

WAR BETWEEN THE CLASSES

Tim Padgett

It is frustrating for educators when the poor and affluent share the same school. The problem isn't the children. It's their parents. One night last week Richard Stephenson, district superintendent for Chicago's new South Loop Elementary School, was trying to calm yet another raging quarrel over parent-council elections. One angry faction was from the integrated, middle-class Dearborn Park neighborhood, the other from a public-housing project nearby, Hilliard Homes. The condo-and-townhouse crowd fears South Loop will become a remedial school for the ghetto; the project parents worry it will turn into an exclusive academy for the well off. "It's chaos," Stephenson says. "These people have vastly different expectations about who this school is for."

The conflict in South Loop is over one issue: who's going to get what little quality remains in public schools like Chicago's. Middle-class parents who have stayed in the city don't want inner-city educations for their children. And poorer parents don't want their kids treated as untouchables by the system.

The problems began even before South Loop opened. The affluent Dearborn Park residents fought to make the school a fine-arts magnet; Hilliard parents demanded a neighborhood elementary school that would serve their needs. The board of education crafted a compromise that has managed to

peeve both sides. Half of the current 440 pupils are from low-income homes, one fourth from Dearborn Park, and the rest bused in for the magnet program. Hilliard parents now plan to sue the board because their kids cannot enter South Loop until the third grade; instead they spend their first two years in a barrackslike school surrounded by junkyards.

As South Loop prepares to take in 100 more students next fall, the parental conflict has intensified. Michael Gipson, a black middle-class parent heading up the Dearborn Park group, believes enrollment of Hilliard children should be curtailed. "If the intent is to improve their environment," he reasons, "how can you do that if they're the dominant force in the classroom?" Gipson's Hilliard counterpart, Sheila Garrett, insists her community's children are not sluggards and troublemakers. "What do they expect our kids to be when they've never seen a test tube let alone a science lab?" she says. "My kids are damn well going to get what those other kids get."

Inside South Loop, principal Joan Fron says her pupils from different worlds study amicably together in a curriculum that forces them "to learn from each other." That's a theme that can seldom be heard above the parental hubbub, and it's one that is drawing new attention from intellectuals. Educa-

continued

---

tional philosopher Mortimer Adler argues that schools like South Loop deserve more help and attention. In his new book, "Reforming Education: The Opening of the American Mind," Adler assails "oligarchs" like Allan Bloom and insists that so-called "inferior" pupils and "their betters" can—and must—benefit from a common classroom setting if urban public education is to survive. But Adler's egalitarian vision doesn't impress skeptics. Gipson says Dear-born Park parents would like to see Adler's ideas flourish, but "so far there hasn't been a teaching method brought forth to make us feel at ease."

Ease isn't what South Loop is about. Last week, proposed by-laws for the school's local improvement council were voted down, sending Stephenson back to square one in his efforts to unite the communities.

Perennialism: Methodology and Curriculum. Perennialists believe that education should help students understand basic truths and values. Advocates of this philosophy originally organized to attack Dewey's pragmatism. Perennialists assert that the key purpose of education is to promote intellectualism, not to teach students to learn through problem solving (Pulliam 1987).

Like essentialism, perennialism recently has regained popularity in some segments of our society. The revival of perennialism is in the form of the "Paideia proposal," developed by Mortimer Adler. This proposal encourages equal educational opportunity for all in both quantity and quality of public education. Proponents of this view oppose any form of tracking, ability grouping, or special programming. Rather, they advocate the same education for all students (Gutek 1988).

The Paideia curriculum would be the same for all students throughout the twelve years of public education. The curriculum would include language, literature, fine arts, math, science, history, geography, and social studies. Basic academic skills would be taught in the early years to enable students to take advantage of later learning opportunities. Teaching methods primarily would be didactic, using well-organized narratives, using coaching in basic skills, and using the Socratic model of probing questions when teaching the great works of art and literature. The "Great Books" would be an important part of materials used (Gutek 1988).

SUMMARY

This chapter presented information concerning the philosophy of education in the United States. Philosophy, it was discussed, is an all-encompassing field. The three branches of philosophy are metaphysics, the study of the nature of reality; epistemology, the study of knowledge; and axiology, philosophy dealing with values.

The many different schools of philosophy include general philosophies—idealism, realism, pragmatism, and existentialism—and educational philosophies that have evolved from these basic philosophies—perennialism, essentialism, progressivism, reconstructionism, behaviorism, and behavioral engineering. The chapter discussed the relationship among the different branches of philosophy and the schools of philosophy, pointing out the different orientations for each school. Finally, the role of philosophy to educational practice was presented. Philosophy affects policies and practices at all levels of education: administration, teaching, and learning. With such direct and important relationships, professional educators should determine their own individual philosophies and determine if there are unwanted effects in the classroom from this philosophical base.

IN THE FIELD

1. Does a written statement of philosophy exist for the school system? If so, where is it located, and do teachers and students have access to it?

2. Did you observe an instance of
   behavior modification?
   inquiry/problem solving?
   values clarification?
   drill and rote memorization activities?
   lecturing?

3. How can you perceive a person's philosophy by classroom actions?

4. Would you say the school and classroom reflect a general liberal or conservative philosophy or something in between? How did you determine this?

REFERENCES

Broudy, H. S., M. J. Parsons, I. A. Snook, and R. D. Szoke, 1967. *Philosophy of Education*. Urbana, IL: University of Illinois Press.

Brumbaugh, R. S., and N. M. Lawrence. 1963. *Six Essays on the Foundations of Western Thought*. Boston: Houghton Mifflin.

Golden, T. L., B. Bergquist, and C. L. Coleman. 1989. *Philosophy of Education*. Englewood Cliffs, NJ: Prentice-Hall.

Gutek, G. L. 1988. *Philosophical and Ideological Perspectives on Education*. Englewood Cliffs, NJ: Prentice-Hall.

Henderson, S. V. P. 1947. *Introduction to Philosophy of Education*. Chicago: The University of Chicago Press.

Johnson, J. A., H. W. Collings, V. L. Dupuis, and J. H. Johansen. 1982. *Introduction to the Foundations of American Education*. Boston: Allyn and Bacon.

Leight, R. L. 1984. Three pragmatic philosophers. *The Educational Forum* 48(2), 191–206.

Levison, A. B. 1974. The uses of philosophy and the problems of educators. In J. Park, ed., *Selected Readings in the Philosophy of Education.* New York: Macmillan.

Marler, C. D. 1975. *Philosophy and Schooling.* Boston: Allyn and Bacon.

Marshall, J. P. 1973. *The Teacher and his Philosophy.* Lincoln, NE: Professional Publications, Inc.

Morris, V. C., and Y. Pai. 1976. *Philosophy and the American School.* New York: Houghton-Mifflin.

Ozmon, H. 1972. *Dialogue in the Philosophy of Education.* Columbus, OH: Merrill.

Ozmon, H., and S. Craver. 1976. *Philosophical Foundations of Education.* Columbus, OH: Merrill.

Park, J. 1974. *Selected Readings in the Philosophy of Education.* New York: Macmillan.

Perkinson, H. J. 1987. *Two Hundred Years of American Educational Thought.* New York: University Press of America.

Phillips, D. C. 1983. Philosophy of Education: In extremis? *Educational Studies* 14(1), 1–30.

Power, E. J. 1982. *Philosophy of Education: Studies in Philosophies, Schooling, and Educational Policies.* Englewood Cliffs, NJ: Prentice-Hall.

Pulliam, J. D. 1987. *History of Education in America*, 4th ed. Columbus, OH: Merrill.

Taylor, A. J. 1983. *An Introduction to the Philosophy of Education.* New York: University Press of America.

Waismann, F. 1969. How I see philosophy. In R. S. Guttchen and B. Bandman, eds., *Philosophical Essays on Curriculum.* Philadelphia: J. B. Lippincott.

Ward, S. A. 1981. The philosopher as synthesizer. *Educational Theory* 31(1), 51–72.

4

WHO CONTROLS EDUCATION IN THE UNITED STATES?

OBJECTIVES
—■—

After reading this chapter, you will be able to

- describe the way the federal government controls public education;
- discuss teacher organizations and other national controlling influences;
- list the methods used by the state government to control education;
- discuss local influences in public and private education;
- discuss state influence in public and private education;
- describe local tax support for public schools;
- discuss the property tax and the issue of equity; and
- discuss the methods in which states support public education.

OUTLINE
—■—

ADVANCE ORGANIZERS

1. What does the United States Constitution say about education? Why is there no mention of education, learning, teaching, or related concepts in the Constitution?
2. How different would our educational system be if there were explicit statements about education in the Constitution?
3. What federal legislative acts have affected education?
4. Which federal court decisions have affected education, and how have they affected education?
5. What role do teachers' organizations play in the control of education?
6. What groups in state government influence education?
7. How do accreditation agencies and textbook publishers influence education?
8. What is the role of local boards of education?
9. Who does control public education in the United States?
10. What are taxes?
11. How did public support for schools develop?
12. How are property taxes used to support public schools?

INTRODUCTION

The control of education in the United States has been debated for decades. Although initial consideration of the question suggests a simple answer that local school boards control the schools, more extensive investigation into the issue indicates that the control of education in this country is a complex arrangement. Various groups and agencies that exert some control include the federal government, state governments, local school boards, and local communities. Other less obvious organizations include accreditation agencies, textbook publishers and authors, teachers' unions, curriculum reform groups, and the press.

Who actually controls education in the United States is very difficult to determine. With so many different groups exerting influence, perhaps no one group controls education, but a number of groups and factors collectively provide the control. This chapter will investigate the various groups that have some influence over what occurs in our schools and will attempt to conclude which forces exert the most significant control over education in the United States.

ROLE OF THE FEDERAL GOVERNMENT

The role of the federal government in public education in this country has been controversial. Many individuals believe that the federal government should have nothing to do with public education, because the Tenth Amendment to the United States Constitution reserves for states matters not specifically given to the federal government. Since education is not a topic in the Constitution, the conclusion is drawn that education is the responsibility of the states, not the federal government. This should have ended the debate (Harder 1983).

Most people seem to believe that the federal government has too much influence over public education. In the 1986 Gallup Poll of the Public's Attitudes Toward the Public Schools, fifty-three percent of the respondents indicated that the federal government should have less influence in educational matters. Only twenty-six percent of those responding wanted more federal involvement with public education (Gallup 1986). When asked if they thought the federal government should have more or less influence on improving the public schools, thirty-seven percent responded "more" and thirty-nine percent responded "less" (Gallup and Clark 1987).

Legislative Branch

Although this argument has been expressed for years, the federal government has been increasing its involvement in education for many years. This increased involvement started early in the history of the country with several pieces of legislation.

The first national legislation related to education was enacted by the Continental Congress. This act, the Land Ordinance Act of 1785, required that every township set aside one section for the establishment of public schools. While not far reaching, this legislation enabled Congress to establish "an early precedent for making its voice heard in education whenever it is desired" (Koerner 1968, p. 4).

The Northwest Ordinance of 1787 further indicated a commitment from the federal government by stating that "Religion, morality, and knowledge being necessary to good government and the happiness of mankind, schools and the means of education shall forever be encouraged" (Strahan and Turner 1987). The next federal legislative action affecting education was the Morrill Land Grant Act of 1862. The passage of this act gave federal land to states to establish land-grant colleges. The federal government ended up giving seventeen million acres of land to states for this purpose. Sixty-eight land-grant colleges exist today (Pulliam 1987). A second Morrill Act, passed in 1890, provided funding to land-grant institutions for instruction in various subject areas.

The Smith-Hughes Act of 1917 was unprecedented, with the primary purpose of providing categorical aid to vocational education programs in public schools. The legislation met the needs of both state and federal governments in that it recognized and supported vocational education (Harder 1983). The legislation differed from previous federal legislation in that it did much more than provide land; it provided money for programs.

Other federal legislative actions related to education were enacted during the depression and World War II years. They were considered temporary and affected education only indirectly. Some of these included (1) the use of funds from the Public Works Administration to construct schools, (2) payment for some teachers from the Federal Emergency Relief Funds, and (3) the Lanham Act of 1941 that reimbursed local schools for serving military dependents (Kaestle and Smith 1982).

By 1950 federal involvement in education continued to be limited to such things as vocational education, school lunches, aid to military dependents, and aid to native Americans. Although various lobby groups, such as the National Education Association, advocated general federal aid to education, Congress resisted (Kaestle and Smith 1982). In 1958 the National Defense Education Act (NDEA) was passed. This represented a major effort on the part of the federal government to become involved in curricular matters. Passed in response to the launching by the Soviet Union of two satellites, Sputnik I and Sputnik II, the legislation funded the strengthening of science education programs and programs in foreign languages (Pulliam 1987).

The 1960s marked the beginning of significant federal involvement. During this period, Congress became involved in education through the passage of numerous acts. These included the Manpower Development Training Act of 1962, the Vocational Education Act of 1963, the Economic Opportunity Act of 1965, the Higher Education Act of 1965, the Elementary and Secondary Education Act (ESEA) of 1965, the Bilingual Education Act of 1968, and the Education for All Handicapped Children Act of 1975, as well as amendments to the ESEA.

The most comprehensive act affecting public education was the Elementary and Secondary Education Act of 1965 and its subsequent amendments. This act provided funds for economically disadvantaged children, demonstration programs, innovative programs, libraries and assistance to improve secondary education programs. With the passage of this legislation, Congress began influencing educational reform with financial incentives. With the passage of ESEA, federal spending on public education doubled and continued to increase throughout the 1970s (McCarthy and Cambron-McCabe 1987). Future amendments to the ESEA focused on non-English-speaking students, on students with disabilities, and on students classified as gifted and talented (McCarthy and Cambron 1981).

The Elementary and Secondary Education Act of 1965 started out small compared with its current provisions. Initially, there were only five titles and twelve programs. Currently there are thirteen titles and more than one hundred different programs. With each program having its own director, staff, and procedures, the bureaucracy grew with the proliferation of programs (Kaestle and Smith 1982).

Civil Rights Legislation. In addition to legislation passed by Congress that attempted to improve programs, other legislative acts were passed that were designed to ensure equal opportunities in education. These included Titles VI and VII of the Civil Rights Act of 1964, Title IX of the Education Amendments of 1972, the Rehabilitation Act of 1973, the Bilingual Education Act of 1968, and the Education for All Handicapped Children Act of 1975. These legislative actions were intended to protect the rights of minority races, of women, and of persons with disabilities (McCarthy and Cambron-McCabe 1987).

Judiciary Branch

Originally the federal court system did not hear cases dealing with educational issues (McCarthy and Cambron-McCabe 1987); however, for the past thirty years, the judiciary branch of the federal government

■ *The judicial branch has become very involved in education during the past thirty years.*

has been heavily involved in education issues. Prior to the landmark *Brown v. Board of Education* civil rights case in 1954, educational issues and legal issues were kept separate. Even the Supreme Court, through its various decisions, indicated that it had no desire to become a "super school board" (Fischer 1979, p. 109). More recently, courts have become involved in most aspects of education, "including students' rights to free expression, compulsory attendance, and mandatory curriculum offerings, school finance reform, employment practices, student discipline, educational malpractice, sex discrimination, collective bargaining, employees' rights to privacy, desegregation, and the rights of handicapped and non-English-speaking students" (McCarthy and Cambron 1981, p. 13).

Through the process of litigation, the courts seek to exercise judicial review, establish legal principles, and settle disputes using principles of law. Courts do not deal with issues until there is a conflict or controversy. Further, the decisions of courts only apply to the geographic area where courts have jurisdiction. Only the rulings of the Supreme Court have national application (McCarthy and Cambron-McCabe 1987).

In two different situations the federal judiciary does become involved with cases—where cases involve citizens from more than one state and when there are questions about federal law (Valente 1987). Federal court cases dealing with educational issues may be based on either of these criteria.

Court Structure. The United States has two court systems: federal and state. The federal court system comprises three levels. The lowest federal court level is the trial court, called district courts. There are approximately ninety-two district courts in the country. This is the entry level for litigation in the federal court system.

There are thirteen circuit courts of appeal. These include a court of appeal in each of eleven districts (see figure 4.1), a District of Columbia court of appeal, and a federal circuit court of appeal which has national jurisdiction on specific claims (McCarthy and Cambron-McCabe 1987).

Federal circuit courts of appeal have between three and fifteen judges, depending on the caseload for that particular district. Decisions rendered in circuit courts are binding only on the geographic area in that district. These decisions are extremely important, however, because they may be used as precedents in similar cases in other districts (McCarthy and Cambron-McCabe 1987).

The highest federal court, and the ruling court of the United States, is the United States Supreme Court. No appeal can be made beyond the Supreme Court. Decisions rendered by the Supreme Court are binding on the entire country and may overturn previous decisions, as well as bring consensus to issues resolved differently by various courts of appeal (Valente 1987).

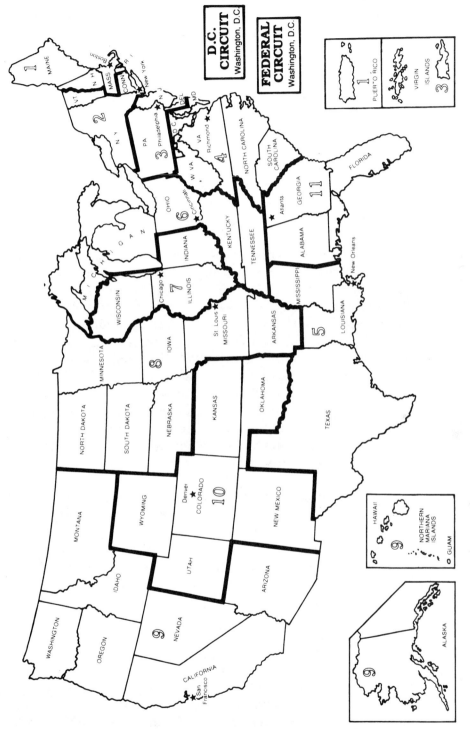

D.C.
CIRCUIT
Washington, D.C.

FEDERAL
CIRCUIT
Washington, D.C.

FIGURE 4.1. U.S. Courts of Appeals.

The United States Supreme Court deals with approximately five thousand cases per year. A written opinion is issued in fewer than five percent of these cases, with the remaining cases being considered by the Court to be inappropriate or of too little significance to require review. A determination not to hear a case does not imply agreement by the Supreme Court with the lower court; it merely signifies that the Court leaves the decision to a lower court's jurisdiction (McCarthy and Cambron-McCabe 1987).

Litigation in Federal Court. Most educational issues are resolved in state courts (Valente 1987). However, the federal court system has become increasingly involved in education cases as a result of federal legislation protecting students' rights and guaranteeing certain groups of children educational opportunities. An analysis of student litigation dealing with civil rights cases filed between 1977 and 1981 cataloged 1,632 cases. Cases involving handicapped children were the most numerous, with cases involving discipline, regulation of sports, and equal protection also represented in large numbers. Approximately forty-five percent of the cases were filed in federal court (Marvell, Galfo, and Rockwell n.d.).

That federal courts have become a factor in public education in the United States should be obvious. Some critics would say that the courts have become too involved. In cases such as *Brown v. Board of Education* (1954), which struck down segregated schools, *PARC v. Pennsylvania* (1973), which required schools to provide appropriate educational opportunities to handicapped children, and the case of *New Jersey v. T.L.O.* in 1985 when the U.S. Supreme Court ruled that the Fourth Amendment does not apply to searches of students by school officials (Pulliam 1987), the federal courts have made a major impact on public education (see table 4.1).

Prior to the federal court's intervention in education, public schools were primarily responsive to the needs and desires of the white and financially middle and upper-middle class. "Court decisions altered the balance of authority" (Kirp and Jensen 1983, p. 207). The decisions gave rights to individuals and groups that had previously been ignored and caused schools to make attempts to provide appropriate services for a broader population of students.

Since the landmark decisions that guaranteed certain rights and access to public education, the legislative and executive branches have assumed a greater role in shaping educational policy. Still, the federal court system is involved in public education. The system still creates rights and "may offer a forum for challenges to proposed federal cutbacks." Federal courts may continue to create rights, respond to challenges of federal cutbacks, and expand their domain (Kirp and Jensen 1983, p. 207).

TABLE 4.1
Significant Federal Court Decisions

◾

CASE	DESCRIPTION
Issue: School Finance/Organization	
Attorney General of Michigan v. Lowrey (1905)	Upheld the right of state legislatures to make and change boundaries of school districts
San Antonio Independent School District v. Rodriquez (1973)	Upheld a state funding model where local property taxes are used to provide a minimum educational program for all students
Issue: Church-State Relationships	
Illinois ex rel. v. Board of Education (1948)	Court ruled as unconstitutional a school program that permitted students to attend religious instruction in school during school hours
Abington School District v. Schempp, Murray v. Curlett (1963)	Ruled as unconstitutional a law that required the reading of ten Bible verses and recitation of the Lord's prayer during school hours, on school grounds, conducted by school personnel
Epperson v. Arkansas (1968)	A law forbidding the teaching of evolution was ruled unconstitutional
Sloan v. Lemon (1973)	The Supreme Court ruled as unconstitutional, a law allowing for partial reimbursement by the state for tuition paid by parents sending their children to private schools
Wallace v. Jaffree (1985)	The U.S. Supreme Court upheld a lower court's ruling that a daily period of silent prayer or meditation violated the Constitution.
Edwards v. Aguillard (1987)	The U.S. Supreme Court upheld a lower court's ruling striking down a Louisiana law that required schools to teach creation science.
Issue: Student Rights	
Tinker v. Des Moines Independent Community School District (1969)	The ruling was that it was unconstitutional to suspend students from wearing arm bands or other symbolic expressions unless such interferes with school
New Jersey v. T.L.O. (1985)	The U.S. Supreme Court ruled that students have protections from search and seizure guaranteed by the Fourth Amendment to the Constitution; however, schools only have to have a "reasonable suspicion" to search, not "probable cause."
Issue: Race, Language, and Sex Discrimination	
Sweatt v. Painter (1950)	U.S. Supreme Court ruled that a black student could not be denied admission to the University of Texas Law School for the sole reason of race

TABLE 4.1 – *Continued*
Significant Federal Court Decisions

Brown v. Board of Education, Topeka, Kansas (1954)	The Court ruled that children could not be denied admission to public schools on the basis of race; ruling declared segregated public schools to be unconstitutional
Green v. County School Board (1968)	Ruling declared that a "freedom of choice" plan in a previously segregated school district offers little likelihood for desegregation; required that an effective plan for desegregation be implemented.
Swann v. Charlotte-Mecklenburg Board of Education (1971)	Upheld busing as a legitimate means for desegregating schools; gave district courts wide discretion in remedying long standing segregated school systems
Pennsylvania Association for Retarded Citizens (PARC) v. Pennsylvania (1971)	Required local schools to provide a free appropriate public education for all school-aged handicapped children
Arline v. School Bd. of Nassau County	A U.S. Circuit Court of Appeals ruled that tuberculosis was a contagious disease that entitled a teacher to protections under Section 504 which set a precedent for persons with AIDS.

Source: Zirkel, 1978; McCarthy and Cambrom-McCabe 1987.

Executive Branch

The executive branch of the federal government has also been involved in public education and has expanded its involvement since the late 1960s. No federal agency dealt with education until 1867, when Congress created the Federal Department of Education. The department was created to

- collect statistics and facts on the condition of education;
- disseminate information concerning organization and management of schools and teaching methods; and
- promote the cause of education.

After an unproductive first year of operation, the department was downgraded to an "office" (Koemer 1968).

During the first one hundred years of operation, the United States Office of Education (USOE) had minimal impact on public education. In fact, it never efficiently accomplished its purpose of collecting and disseminating information. In 1930 the Office moved from the Department of the Interior and was given separate status. In 1939, it moved to the Federal Security Agency. It became a part of the newly formed Department of Health, Education, and Welfare in 1953 (Pulliam 1987). Following the launch of Sputnik by the Soviet Union in 1958, the USOE took on greater significance and grew greatly in size and power. Although Congress continued to identify the general purposes of programs administered by the USOE, detailed guidelines and qualifications were established by the Office (Koemer 1968).

The USOE was hampered by many variables. Silberman (1980) indicated that a major problem in the USOE was the constant competition among three groups: elite reformers, power brokers, and professional educators. Elite reformers included the higher level bureaucrats in the Office of the President, department deputies and their assistants, consultants, and individuals from federal budget offices. Members of Congress and their powerul constituents made up the power broker group, while the professional educator group included civil service managers and their grantees. Constant bickering among these three groups created major problems for the USOE (Silberman 1980).

In 1979, supported by the Carter administration, Congress passed legislation authorizing the Department of Education as the eighth department in the federal government. The passage of the legislation authorizing this department was difficult, with many opponents to the concept. Those in opposition basically focused their arguments on the department's creation as adding to the federal budget and federal bureaucracy. As late as June 1979 the likelihood that the legislation would be passed by the House of Representatives was no better than fifty-fifty (Neill 1979a). The bill authorizing the establishment of the Department of Education did pass, however, and was signed into law in 1979. Provisions in the legislation stated that the department was to be operational within 180 days after the law's passage, and on May 7, 1980, the department was officially opened.

Creating the Department of Education was a major step forward in consolidating federal programs dealing with education. More than 150 agencies and programs that had operated in six different departments—Department of Health, Education, and Welfare; Department of Justice; Department of Defense; Department of Housing and Urban Development; Department of Labor, and Department of Agriculture— were placed in an agency that was without precedent (Neill 1979b). Indeed, this was a major shift in education policy at the federal level.

The five purposes listed for the Department of Education were the following:

1. To ensure equal educational opportunities for all citizens.
2. To strengthen the federal commitment to support state and local efforts to meet educational needs.
3. To encourage increased involvement of the public, parents, and students in federal education programs.
4. To promote improvements in the quality of education through research, evaluation, and information sharing.
5. To improve coordination, management and accountability of federal education programs. (Neill 1980, p. 670)

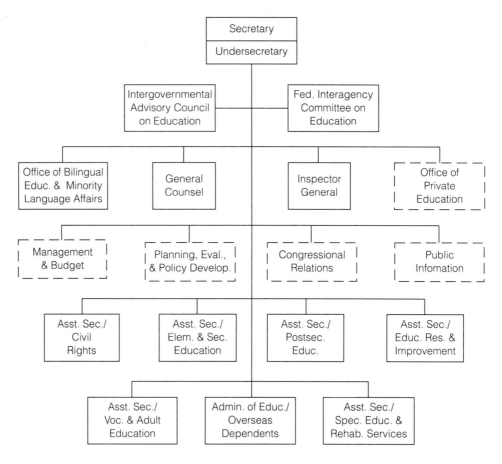

Department of Education

Key: Solid lines indicate offices stipulated in legislation.
Dotted lines indicated offices not stipulated in legislation.
Source: Office of Management and Budget.

FIGURE 4.2. Organization, United States Department of Education.
Reprinted with permission, G. Neill, 1979, Observers see danger, challenge in building Education Department. Phi Delta Kappan 61 (4), 236.

To accomplish such a broad range of purposes, the department is organized into several different units (see figure 4.2).

Following the opening of the Department of Education, many critics continued to challenge its purposes. Indeed, one of President Ronald Reagan's campaign goals was to dismantle the entire department and create an educational foundation. The new Foundation for Educational Assistance was to administer (1) block grants and consolidated aid, (2) student financial aid, (3) compensatory programs for the disadvantaged, handicapped, and others, (4) informational, statistical, and research services, and (5) investigations of complaints and compliance (Rosenau 1982). Contrary to President Reagan's wishes, Congress did not accept the removal of departmental status for education and the department is likely to continue this status well into the future.

NATIONAL ORGANIZATIONS

Teacher Unions

Teachers want some control over education, and they are as capable of developing sound education policy as are lay school boards (Retsinas 1982). As individuals, however, teachers have limited power. Therefore, they have banded together into teacher organizations to become a major force in controlling public education in the United States. Currently, the two major teacher organizations in this country are the National Education Association (NEA) and the American Federation of Teachers (AFT).

Teachers' organizations began in 1794 when the Society of Associated Teachers of New York City was founded. In the early 1800s several similar groups were developed, primarily in urban areas. With the growth of these urban organizations came the ability to organize on a state level. By 1860 approximately thirty such state organizations were in existence. In 1857 the National Teachers Association was formed in Philadelphia. This group combined with the National Association of School Superintendents and the American Normal School Association in the 1870s to become the National Educational Association. In 1906 the organization changed its name to the National Education Association (Armstrong, Henson, and Savage 1983; Pulliam 1987).

The American Federation of Teachers (AFT) was formed in 1916 when teachers' organizations in Chicago and the upper Midwest joined together. Unlike NEA, which was originally dominated by administrators and university professors, the AFT has always been primarily for teachers. While the NEA focused mainly on a broad array of educational issues, the AFT has always aimed its activities at teachers' benefits. Although never as large as the NEA, the AFT has had a major impact on education (Armstrong, Henson, and Savage 1983).

Both the NEA and AFT have grown dramatically since 1960. In 1957 the NEA had only seven hundred thousand members (Elam 1981); in 1978 the membership had grown to more than 1.6 million (Lieberman 1981). The NEA set as a goal to have a membership of 2 million by 1990 (NEA Handbook 1987–1988). AFT membership increased from forty thousand in 1940 (Armstrong, Henson, and Savage 1983) to five hundred thousand by 1978 (Lieberman 1981). The number of members in these organizations has enabled the groups to influence legislation at the state and national levels and to influence policy at local levels. With an average of six thousand members per congressional district, the NEA spent nearly $350,000 on the 1980 national elections (Elam 1981). At the 1983 NEA convention alone, a record $125,000 was raised for political contributions (Ficklen and McCormick 1983). Although their influence has been less than expected in some situations, both teachers' groups will continue to influence educational policies and legislation at the local and national levels.

NEA-PAC: HOW MUCH DO YOUR DOLLARS MATTER?

For a member of Congress, the nation's capital can be a very hectic place. Congress is bombarded by a never-ending stream of issues and ideas, pressures and demands.

In such an atmosphere, getting senators and representatives to pay close attention to any one issue—even an issue as important as education—isn't easy. That's where NEA-PAC, NEA's political action arm, comes in.

The dollars that NEA members contribute to NEA-PAC go to support candidates for Congress who support education. Those dollars help focus congressional attention on issues that would otherwise be lost in a sea of good ideas.

"Making an issue stand out in a crowd of important issues is what success in Washington is all about," notes independent Washington Lobbyist Les Francis. "That's why everyone involved in public education needs to understand the importance of the role NEA-PAC plays. In this town, the political pundits measure organizational clout by the volume of an organization's voluntary contributions. Without NEA-PAC, it's hard to imagine where education would be today."

But the best evidence of the difference NEA-PAC makes comes from members of Congress themselves.

Representative Charles Hayes (D-Ill.): "One of the reasons that first led me to decide to run for Congress was my desire to do something to improve young people's opportunities through education. Starting with my first campaign, teachers and school employees have been dependable volunteers. My NEA endorsement, the early contributions from NEA-PAC, and the resulting volunteers got my campaign off and running. I'll never forget what the NEA members did for me."

Representative Nancy Johnson (R-Conn.): "Receiving a NEA-PAC contribution from the NEA members in my district tells me a lot about them and their understanding of how government works. I know they've looked hard at my record and reassured themselves that I am truly committed to improving education. And I know they understand that it would be much harder for me, as a member of Congress, to continue that work without their support. Taking that extra step of voluntarily signing up to contribute to NEA-PAC is a very tangible way of saying, 'I know what it takes to make a difference for education.'"

Representative Dale E. Kildee (D-Mich.): "There is nothing more American, more in keeping with the ideals of our democracy, than getting politically involved. And nobody gets involved more actively than the NEA members in my district. They know my education record—which is 100 percent—thanks to NEA's Congressional Report Card. They interview the candidates on current education issues, and they prove they understand modern-day financial realities through their contributions to NEA-PAC."

Representative Bob Wise (D-W.Va.): "I still remember the early days before my first campaign. A lot of people, including many friends, said I couldn't win. I didn't have enough name recognition, and my opponent had too much money. But I entered the race despite the odds. Looking back, it was the trust our local NEA members had in me that led to my NEA endorsement. The incredible volunteer effort by teachers and that first NEA-PAC contribution, which let us do our first mailing, got our campaign off to a winning start."

NEA created NEA-PAC because federal law requires that direct financial assistance to federal candidates be raised voluntarily. Over the years since 1972, when NEA-PAC gave its first contribution to a candidate for Congress, NEA-PAC has grown substantially. Today NEA-PAC collects close to $2

continued

million per year in contributions from NEA members.

But the potential of 2 million NEA members to make an impact on Congress has only begun to be tapped. Currently, about 20 percent of members are contributing to NEA-PAC.

In this era of federal budget squeezes and underfunded education programs, NEA-

PAC needs to be as potent as it can possibly be. Interested in finding out how you can contribute to NEA-PAC's success? Just ask your local Association officers or UniServ staff.

National Education Association, April 1989.

Other National Organizations

Besides teachers' organizations, several other groups at the national level exert some control over public education. These include testing agencies, accreditation agencies, curriculum reform groups, textbook authors and publishers, foundations, citizens' advisory groups, and professional organizations.

Testing Agencies. As a result of the development of national, standardized tests, various testing agencies influence education. School boards, administrators, and teachers want students in their districts to perform well on such tests as the Scholastic Achievement Test (SAT), American College Test (ACT), and other group achievement measures. The emphasis for students to perform well on these tests leads some schools to modify curricula and teaching objectives to better prepare students to perform well.

Many countries use a national testing program that requires students to pass certain exams before completion of formalized schooling. These tests greatly affect the content of courses. While such a national testing program does not exist in the United States, the fact that only a few companies market most of the college entrance tests has a similar controlling effect on curricula. The ramifications are such that high schools have no choice but to offer their best students the majority of courses related to the subjects on college board exams (Koerner 1968).

The organization that is most important in college entrance testing is the Educational Testing Service (ETS) of Princeton (Koerner 1968). Most universities require that students complete the SAT, which is designed by ETS. Schools not requiring the SAT normally require the ACT, which is developed by the American College Testing Program (Jencks and Crouse 1982).

In 1900 several colleges attempted to relieve the burden of screening applicants for their schools by establishing the College Entrance Examination Board to administer one standardized test. As a result, the first SAT was administered in 1926. Since this beginning, colleges and universities have looked to ETS and others to a lesser degree to help determine which students to admit (Jencks and Crouse 1982). Indeed, the SAT "is being presented to the public—and apparently is increasingly accepted—as both the gatekeeper of college admissions and the single most important indicator of academic health at the college entry level" (Bracey 1980, p. 197).

Although recent studies have raised important issues about the ability of the SAT to predict college success, many high schools still attempt to formulate their curricula to prepare students for these entrance tests. If students do not do well on college entrance tests, students and their parents may be outraged. Schools, therefore, feel as though they have little to do other than try to prepare students to score well on the SAT and other admissions tests. Therefore, in effect, ETS and other test developers are controlling education to some degree.

Accreditation Agencies. Like testing agencies, accreditation agencies exert influence over public education in an unofficial manner. Accreditation of public schools has been done by universities, voluntary regional associations, and state education agencies. Universities began accrediting high schools in 1871 when the University of Michigan issued a notice to high schools that, after a visit to the school by university faculty, the school could be designated as meeting the quality standards that would allow its graduates to be admitted to the University of Michigan without further examination (Saylor 1982).

The accreditation of high schools by universities continued until after World War II. The University of Nebraska maintained the only authority to accredit high schools in that state until 1950 when the state legislature passed legislation granting the State Department of Education this responsibility (Saylor 1982).

With the discontinuation of accreditation of high schools by universities came the requirement of standardized tests for university admission and the growth of voluntary regional accreditation agencies. Accreditation by regional agencies serves to

- provide standards for the public to compare its schools;
- assure that schools will undergo periodic self-study;
- assure that faculty and teaching conditions meet certain minimum standards;
- indicate a commitment to quality education by schools. (Partners in Quality Education 1982)

The first voluntary regional accreditation agency was the New England Association of Secondary Schools, which started in 1885. As with later voluntary agencies, the New England Association was "extra-legal and not under public control" (Saylor 1982, p. 48). Following the establishment of the New England Association, several other regional agencies were developed (see table 4.2). Of the regional associations,

TABLE 4.2
Regional Accreditation Agencies

AGENCY	YEAR ESTABLISHED
New England Association of Colleges and Secondary Schools	1885
Association of Colleges and Preparatory Schools in the Middle States and Maryland	1888
Association of Colleges and Preparatory Schools of the Southern States	1895
North Central Association of Colleges and Secondary Schools	1895
Northwest Association of Secondary and Higher Schools	1918
Western College Association	1948

Source: Saylor, 1982.

the North Central and Southern Associations have become dominant (Saylor 1982).

The accreditation of teacher training programs by voluntary agencies also influences public education. The National Council for Accreditation of Teacher Education (NCATE) is the primary accreditation agency that accredits teaching training institutions. Founded in 1954, "NCATE was created in an attempt to establish a national, voluntary accreditation process for teacher education" (Watts 1983, p. 646).

Although voluntary, NCATE accreditation is sought by many institutions for reasons such as (1) prestige, (2) reciprocal transfer of credit among member institutions, (3) student recruitment, (4) job placement of graduates, and (5) certification (Watts 1983). Accreditation of teacher training programs supposedly adds credibility to the assumption that its graduates are competent (Huffman 1982). Some consider NCATE accreditation as essential in maintaining quality teacher education programs, while others consider it unnecessary, expensive, and contributing little to quality teacher education.

Curriculum and Reform Groups. Other groups that affect public education in this country also do not have official sanctions, but provide information and impetus for change. Among these are curriculum reform groups, often assembled by professional organizations, and other actions by professional organizations.

Curriculum reform groups have been impacting education in this country for only a brief time. The beginning of involvement by scholars in public education started in 1952 when a group of university professors and public school teachers founded a group to reorganize the teaching of math in public schools. While this action was small, it led to larger groups, such as the Physical Science Study Committee (PSSC), which was formed at the Massachusetts Institute of Technology to reform the high school physics curriculum. PSSC was the major curriculum reform group of the time and was the inspiration for many others that followed. As a result, high-school physics classes changed dramatically and up to twenty-five percent of students studying physics in high schools used the PSSC program (Koerner 1968).

Individuals involved in PSSC created Educational Services Incorporated (ESI), which was the umbrella organization for PSSC and other reform efforts. In 1962 the focus of ESI was expanded from the sciences to include social sciences. ESI is the largest group in the country focusing on curriculum reform and research (Koerner 1968).

In addition to private groups such as PSSC and ESI, various professional groups also have made efforts to influence the curriculum (see table 4.3).

Textbook Authors and Publishers. Another national force in education comes from the private sector relating to textbooks. Textbooks contain the majority of the content presented to students and often include suggestions for teaching style and methods. Although numerous text-

■ *Publishers of educational materials exert a great deal of influence over our educational system.*

INTRODUCTION TO EDUCATION

TABLE 4.3
Professional Groups Influencing Curriculum

GROUP	ACTIONS
Modern Language Association	■ Established a Committee of Twelve in 1896 that submitted a report in 1898 that continues to influence curriculum in secondary schools and colleges. ■ Established the Modern Foreign Language Study in 1924 that published seventeen volumes related to teaching foreign language.
American Historical Association	■ Established the Commission on the Social Studies in 1929 that prepared and published twelve volumes over a five-year period. Volumes on *The Social Studies as School Subjects and Methods of Instruction in the Sciences* provided guidelines for planning at the local and state levels.
National Council of Teachers of English	■ In 1935, published a broad, flexible plan for teaching English. The book, *An Experience Curriculum in English,* was one of the best guides ever prepared by a national committee for curriculum planning in a subject field.
Progressive Education Association (PEA)	■ Carried out curriculum experimentation with about thirty selected high schools in which schools chose their activities and received consultative services from PEA. This was called the Eight-Year Study. ■ The PEA Commission on Secondary School Curriculum established five committees to develop curricula for art, language and literature, science, math, and social studies. The reports from these committees did not have a great impact.

Source: Saylor, 1982.

book publishers prepare books for educational purposes, a few companies appear to control the market. The influence of these publishers and authors should not be discounted.

The influence of textbooks varies depending on the subject matter taught and the age groups of students. Limited influence results from textbooks at the kindergarten level while at the secondary level the content contained in books can be very influential. Subjects such as music, physical education, and vocational education are less influenced by textbooks than are biology, economics, history, and other more content-oriented subjects where the textbook may provide the only external curriculum plan available (Saylor 1982).

An example of the influence of textbooks would be in the teaching of economics. Some books might overemphasize capitalism as the only moral, appropriate economic system while others would fairly present other economic systems, including those that deviate greatly from capitalism. As another example, in the teaching of reading, textbooks that emphasize the phonics approach would influence the reading program in an elementary school. Textbook publishers and authors, therefore, have a great influence on education. While this influence may be hidden, it definitely pervades the educational system (Koerner 1968).

STATE LEVEL INFLUENCE

States derive most of their power over education by default. The Tenth Amendment to the United States Constitution states that "powers not delegated to the United States by the Constitution, nor prohibited by it to the states, are reserved to the states respectively, or to the people." As a result, states have assumed the major responsibility in education. Many different groups at the state level exert a great deal of influence over education, including state legislatures, teacher associations, administrator associations, and groups representing specific populations of students (Rosenthal and Fuhrman 1982). The power of these groups varies from state to state. The 1987 Gallup Poll of attitudes toward public schools revealed that a majority of respondents, fifty-five percent, felt that more influence over public schools should come from the state. Only twenty-one percent wanted less state influence (Gallup and Clark 1987).

State Government

State government influences education in the following ways:

1. Provisions in state constitutions
2. Enactment of statutory law
3. Court decisions
4. Powers granted state department/state boards of education
   a. Legal and regulatory powers
   b. Accreditation/standardization of schools
   c. Selection of textbooks and instructional materials
   d. Issuance of curriculum syllabi and guides
   e. Competency examinations (Saylor 1982, p. 78)

State Constitutions

All state constitutions include some provisions related to public education. Early constitutions contained limited details concerning education, with the primary focus being on the establishment of a public school system. However, many states are rewriting their original constitutions to contain more detailed guidelines on education. Even the rewritten constitutions most often give vast authority over education to state legislatures and do not include many specifics about educational systems. The granting of this power to legislatures together with the provisions made for taxes, enable state constitutions to influence education (Saylor 1982). The courts consistently have upheld the rights of states over local governments to control education (Strahan and Turner 1987).

Very Hostile Takeovers

Connie Leslie

More students drop out of the four neighborhood high schools in Jersey City than graduate. And last year 64 percent of the district's ninth graders flunked the state's basic high-school proficiency test. But if Jersey City is representative of the nationwide crisis in public education, it is only one of a thousand dim bulbs across the country. Last May the state Education Department declared the Jersey City schools to be "academically bankrupt," and New Jersey became the first state in the nation to try to take over operations of a local school district. Since then Kentucky has decided to seize control of one academically deficient school system, while West Virginia became the seventh state to authorize such drastic intervention. And last month the New York state regents threatened to eject the Board of Education in New York City's gigantic and very troubled school system. "It's very effective to say to people, 'If you're not going to do it right, someone else will'," says Bill Honig, state superintendent of schools in California, where legislators are considering an academic-bankruptcy law. "That gets people's attention."

State takeovers are reforms born of desperation. "When enough is enough," says New Jersey Education Commissioner Saul Cooperman, "*somebody* has to do *something*." But what? There is no evidence that administrators parachuting in from the state capital can do a better job than local officials. And a takeover is the antithesis of other reforms that preach greater local control of curriculum and finances. Nevertheless, these very hostile takeovers may be an idea whose time has come. According to a recent report by the Council of Chief State School Officers, 18 states have programs under which low performance triggers some kind of intervention, most well short of a complete takeover.

Nearly every state now attempts to apply some pressure on local districts, most often by using the functional equivalent of a warning note to parents. At least 48 states now require that students be tested regularly; many release the school-by-school results to the public. California, Illinois, West Virginia and New Jersey go even further. All issue annual report cards for each school in the state. Typically, the report cards give such measures of school success as scores on achievement tests, numbers of students held back, and rates of attendance, dropouts and graduation.

Public exposure, says Honig, "is a powerful way to turn a school around. Some people complain that teachers will then teach to the test. But if that means teachers will review mathematics or work with students on their reading and interpretation skills, that's what we want." Other states are putting more pressure directly on administrators and principals by requiring regular evaluations, toughening up licensing or certification requirements or increasing the minimum standards of education and experience that new applicants must have.

Money Trouble

Some states are not content to stop with mandating bureaucratic reforms. In New Jersey, for instance, the takeover law is the final step of a monitoring process that consists of three levels. If the state Education Department determines that a local school system cannot improve—and can document its case to the state Board of Education—the state can take over the district and operate it for five years or until it decides that local control should be re-established. Under a takeover, the school board is abolished; the job of superintendent and the central office positions responsible for curriculum, per-

continued

sonnel and business are abolished, and a state district superintendent is appointed to manage the district. Only 16 of New Jersey's 583 school systems are in some level of the review process. Jersey City superintendent Franklin Williams says his district is improving. He is fighting the state intervention in an administrative hearing. In the interim, Williams is operating the schools under a court order that says he must get permission from the state before making any purchase over $5,000 or taking any personnel action. "Jersey City's problem is not incompetence," says Williams. "It's money and a poor population."

All of those problems can be found across the river in New York City. Last month Martin Barell, the chancellor of the state Board of Regents, declared that "the time for accountability has arrived;" if city officials couldn't manage their schools, he threatened to have them removed. That is probably an empty threat because state Education Commissioner Thomas Sobol wants no part of running the 940,000-student district, but it may help focus even more attention on a faltering system. The regents ordered a series of remedial measures, including a pilot program for reading improvement, bilingual studies and drug education. But those are hardly large-scale solutions. In Sobol's view, the state is now home to "two unequal systems." In the largely black and Hispanic city schools, funding is lower, classes are bigger, and performance, on the average, poorer.

Local Control

Critics of the takeover concept charge that many states have fallen down on their job of providing adequate funding and instead are now blaming the school districts for their own neglect. "The state is expecting us to run the 100-yard dash, but they're tying our legs. Then when we don't run well, they want to kick us out," says Thomas A. Shannon, executive director of the National School Boards Association. "They should give us more tools and less rules." Indeed, several districts in Kentucky and West Virginia's economically depressed Appalachian Mountains region are being targeted by their states for takeover. Ron Hager, superintendent of Kentucky's Floyd County school system, says that inadequate state funding and the poverty in his district have prevented him from meeting state standards for dropout prevention, attendance and test scores. Tom Stevens, a U.S. Department of Education official who oversees the region, agrees with Hager and says that's why he backs the state intervention plans. "That's not a blanket indictment against local control, says Stevens. "It's just that people in areas like Floyd County, Ky., are more concerned about economics and jobs than education." That may be so. But it remains to be seen whether the proposed solution will solve the problems or merely be another example of good intentions gone wrong.

State Legislatures

Although many state-level groups affect education, in many states the legislatures have emerged as the powerful force. In some states they are even referred to as "the big school board" (Rosenthal and Fuhrman 1982, p. 4). For the most part, legislators who have been in office for the past ten to fifteen years and have been supportive of education are being replaced by new representatives and senators. While most legislators in the past were stable in their offices, today's legislators are likely to stay in office only four to eight years. As a result, they do not develop an advocacy role for many areas, education being one of them (Rosenthal and Fuhrman 1982).

In several states, recent actions by legislatures have usurped powers previously held by local school boards. For example, legislation passed in New Jersey allows the state to take over "educationally bankrupt" school districts from locally elected school boards. In Minnesota and Iowa, laws have been passed that provide some financial incentives for parents to take their children out of the public school system (Shanker 1989). These kinds of actions are giving states more power over local schools.

Legislators influence education via two legislative functions: budget and oversight. As state funds have diminished during the past decade, the budget appropriation role has become extremely critical. All state programs want more money. Prisons, social programs, higher education, transportation, and law enforcement have developed strong lobbies and demanded their fair share of state revenues. This leaves less for education, an area that often has had a fragmented lobbying effort (Rosenthal and Fuhrman 1982).

The oversight function of state legislatures enables legislators to evaluate previously approved programs to determine if they are effective and if schools are implementing them as intended. Such oversight functions now occur in thirty-five states. Because of the recent uproar over the quality of public education, legislators are more likely to get involved in oversight functions than in the past, making their impact on public education greater than ever.

> The professional dominance of education policy ended some years ago, and it is unlikely to recur. No longer will legislatures rubber-stamp policy decisions made by educators, by their associations, or by state departments of education. Currently, legislatures shape education policy—for better or for worse—and educators must reconcile themselves to that fact. (Rosenthal and Fuhrman 1982, p. 49)

State legislatures are heavily involved in the educational reform movements that began in the early 1980s. Several states have passed legislation implementing educational reforms ranging from teacher testing to school-year extensions. Legislatures probably will not give up their role in education; since they come from and represent a concerned constituency, they could not even if they so desired.

State Education Agencies (SEAs)

State departments of education are found in all fifty states. They are composed of specialists who provide assistance to the state board of education, to the state director of education, and to the local school districts. Personnel in the state departments collect information to ensure that directives and policies of the state boards of education are carried out (McCarthy and Cambron-McCabe 1987). Examples of activities with which state departments are involved include licensing teachers, ensuring that schools meet various state curricular standards, and providing technical assistance in special education and other specialized educational areas.

SEAs vary greatly from state to state. Some are extremely large with massive budgets, while others are relatively small with minimal funding. SEAs also may vary over the following:

- SEAs organize themselves to become more or less actively involved in the policies and practices of all local education agencies (LEAs) within their boundaries.

- SEAs organize themselves to provide something between a very high and a very low amount, as well as quality of, technical assistance to LEAs.

- SEAs vary greatly in the emphasis they give to the determination and the attempt to regulate LEA policies and standards of practice.

- SEAs vary widely along a continuum from low to high organizational efficacy. (Dentler 1984, p. 151–52)

Although SEAs vary greatly, most lack the necessary resources to be effective. They are hampered by limited budgets and rigid civil service requirements for employees. While many SEAs continue to maintain tight control over such areas as teacher and administrator certification, they are limited in their ability to perform more important roles such as inspecting schools, gathering research and data, making long-range plans, and providing educational leadership (Koerner 1968). A recent study by Dentler (1984) confirms these facts. After visiting the SEAs, the conclusion was that only fifteen to twenty of the fifty SEAs are capable of influencing positive changes in the quality of schools.

Even though many SEAs appear to lack the necessary components to effect major changes, they have the necessary power to do so in most states. Primary methods of influencing local education programs are in the areas of (1) accreditation/standardization schemes, (2) textbook selection, (3) issuance of curriculum syllabi and guides, and (4) competency exams (Saylor 1982). The effectiveness with which SEAs influence education through these avenues varies from state to state.

SEAs, therefore, have the power if not the means to greatly influence education. The educational reform movements begun in the early 1980s likely will provide more means to SEAs to accomplish reforms. "A great deal of effort in curriculum formulation will be mandated and directed by the state departments of education as they seek to dictate the educational outcomes to be attained by students in at least a portion of the instructional program of the school" (Saylor 1982, p. 115).

Voluntary Statewide Agencies and Groups

Several agencies and groups at the state level wield influence over public education. In most states one group that influences educational practices is the state organization of teachers, usually the state chapters of the National Education Association or the American Federation of Teachers. The state affiliates of the NEA are the most powerful of these state groups; in most states, state affiliates of the AFT have not as yet developed into a powerful group. The state NEA groups exert tremendous power with the legislatures in many states. Often their executive offices are in the capitol cities, and the groups are heavily involved in legislation affecting education (Koerner 1968).

One reason state affiliates are so powerful is that membership is greater at the state level than it is at the national level. Many states, including Kansas, Iowa, and Illinois, have a tradition of large, active state NEA associations. In these states, legislatures often have a great deal of difficulty getting legislation passed without the approval of the state NEA affiliate (Koerner 1968).

Other state groups that affect education include state professional associations such as the state federation of the Council for Exceptional Children, which focuses on special education. Professional associations attempt to influence legislation and educational practices that are related to their own specific concerns. The effectiveness of the groups varies from state to state depending on the particular power of each organization in each state.

LOCAL INFLUENCE

Many local groups influence education in this country. Indeed, many people believe that local groups control public education. Among these local groups are school boards, local teachers' organizations, local advisory boards, and the general public.

School Boards

American public schools are organized nationwide into approximately 1600 school districts. School districts can be defined as "local agents for the state, carrying out the state function of public education; they have an identity separate from cities or counties, even when boundaries and names may be similar or the same" (O'Reilly and Green 1983, p. 17). Each school district is under the control of a local school board. Although many forces exert control over public education, local boards still have some powers in setting policies and priorities and in providing the necessary incentives to ensure the quality of local educational programs (Nelson and Crum 1983). The three primary functions of local school boards are (1) long-range planning, (2) setting priorities, and (3) evaluating the superintendent (Moberly and Stiles 1978).

Many school boards control districts with fewer than five hundred students while a few govern districts with several thousand students. While individual board members have no power or authority, as a col-

■ *Local school boards have traditionally been thought of as the major controlling agency of schools.*

lective group, boards exert significant influence over local educational practices. Although school boards vary significantly, some generalizations can be made:

■ Rights and responsibilities of boards are rarely clearly defined.

■ Five to seven members serve on boards.

■ Board members are elected on a nonpartisan basis.

■ The majority of members are men.

■ Professional and business groups are generally represented.

■ Many board members have three to four years of experience.

■ Board members are solid citizens.

■ Boards meet regularly, weekly, biweekly, or monthly (depending on state laws and regulations) and in special meetings as needed.

(Koerner 1968; O'Reilly and Green 1983; and Hartrick, Underwood, Fortune, and Keough 1989)

School boards set policies that affect the local district. In a study of 130 school districts representing nearly six thousand schools and 3.5 million students, it was determined that school boards often set policies that are more stringent than state requirements in such areas as graduation requirements and teacher qualifications (Nelson and Crum 1983). Boards do have power, therefore, to set their own more rigorous standards even though state departments of education and legislatures also set standards. A great deal of ambiguity exists concerning the relationships between SEAs and LEAs (Dentler 1984). As a result, some local boards exercise a great deal of power and control while others tend to relinquish these powers to the SEA. As a result of the actions taken by many states during the most recent reform movement, local boards of education are losing some of their control over local education issues (Reecer 1989; Shanker 1989).

Local Advisory Groups

In addition to exerting influence over local educational practices through local boards of education, community members also exert power with advisory groups. These groups often are developed with the leadership of the school administration. Establishing advisory groups (1) creates strong ties between the community and the school, (2) helps disseminate information, (3) promotes public confidence, and (4) encourages evaluations by community members (Else 1983).

School districts can benefit directly from advisory groups. A vocational education advisory council in the Petersburg, Virginia, school district helped to determine the vocational needs of the community, identify goals and objectives, and, more important, assisted in developing and maintaining appropriate vocational programs (Murphy 1983). Therefore, although not legally formulated groups with actual powers, local advisory groups can exert influence over educational practices.

Local Associations

The Parent Teacher Association (PTA) has been a major force in local educational policy from time to time and from community to community. In some communities, PTAs are very active and involved while in others the organization is barely visible. In districts where the PTA is active, administrators and school boards must pay attention to the group's wishes because the group can exert a great deal of influence over local educational practices and policies.

Teachers

Certainly, at least in many districts, teachers influence local educational practices. This can be accomplished on an individual basis in the classroom or collectively when teachers are organized and express their views to the administration and school board. As they become more sophisticated, local teacher organizations—often the local chapter of the NEA or AFT—have begun to wield more power over local educational practices.

In many states, teachers have earned the legal right to collective bargaining. Even in states where this right has not been legally guaranteed, teachers often exercise the right through "sick outs" and other collective bargaining methods (Koerner 1968). As a result of teachers' bargaining powers, their ability to influence education at the local level has increased dramatically. Not only are teachers bargaining for salaries and fringe benefits, but they also are negotiating issues such as class size, extracurricular duties, and their rights to participate in local policy development.

Individually, teachers exert a great deal of control over what occurs in their classrooms. In this respect teachers are the ultimate curriculum planners. Teachers are in an excellent position to implement only the parts of the curriculum they desire. As a result, teachers are very influential in specific classroom actions (Good 1986).

School Administrators

School administrators, namely superintendents, assistant superintendents, and building principals, are obviously key individuals in local educational practices. Indeed, administrators ultimately are responsible for all that occurs in the schools. Therefore, the success of local schools depends a great deal on the quality of administration.

The role of administrators has changed in American education. Whereas these individuals initially were considered primarily as expert teachers and curriculum experts, their roles now include a vast array of functions, including fiscal planning and management, business management, personnel management, and school law (Podemski, Price, Smith, and Marsh 1984). This change of roles now mandates that school administrators assume a major leadership role in all aspects of education.

Although administrators work for school boards, they still are in a unique position to influence educational practices and policies in the local district. Most school board members are not educational specialists; rather they are professional members of the community. As a result, they often will weigh very heavily the recommendations made by administrators when discussing school policies and practices. This, in effect, makes administrators the primary force in educational policy and implementation (Koerner 1968).

FINANCING PUBLIC SCHOOLS

One important aspect of control over public schools is school finance. Like any other organization, schools require money with which to operate. Funds must be available to establish and maintain up-to-date educational programs, to pay salaries, to purchase supplies and equipment, to provide transportation, to maintain buildings and grounds, to construct new buildings, to contract for some services, and to provide staff development. Without funding for these activities, schools would not be able to provide appropriate educational programs for students, the basic purpose of public schools. The financing of public schools, therefore, is a controlling element in our educational system. As for any other public enterprise, the chief source of these funds is taxes. Schools receive tax dollars from local, state, and federal government levels.

The relative amounts contributed from these three sources have changed significantly during the past twenty-five years. In 1960, public schools received fifty-six percent of their funding from local governments, thirty-nine percent from the state, and only 4 percent from federal sources. In 1987, the local contribution had dropped to 44 percent, while the state contribution had increased to fifty percent. Federal contributions in 1987 amounted to only six percent of the school's total funds. This was a drop from the record ten percent provided by the federal government in 1980 (National Center for Education Statistics 1988).

Taxes

A tax is a payment to a government to pay for various services. The definition of taxes has not changed over the years and still can be considered "a compulsory contribution from the person to the government to defray the expenses incurred in the common interest of all with reference to special benefits conferred" (Seligman 1925, p. 432).

Schools receive tax money because public education is a matter of common interest. However, no relationship exists between the payment of a tax for education and the receipt of any direct benefit. The recipients of a public education are children, who pay no taxes; the taxpayer is an adult with or without children to be educated. No special benefits are received from the tax by the taxpayer. However, taxpayers benefit indirectly from publicly supported education programs by

- increasing the level of education in the community;
- attracting industry and additional tax base to the community as a result of having a sound educational program;
- increasing the earning power of local students, thereby increasing the tax base.

Classification of Taxes. Taxes can be classified in a number of ways. One important method is in terms of the effect of the tax upon the taxpayers. When related to the taxpayer's income, a given tax may be termed progressive, proportional, or regressive. A progressive tax is one where a person with a higher income pays a greater proportion of that income than an individual with a lower income. The federal and state income taxes are the closest approximation of progressive taxation, because individuals with different incomes pay different percentages of their taxable income (see table 4.4).

A proportional tax requires the same percentage of each person's income to be paid in taxes. A sales tax is an example, assuming that all income is spent in a manner subject to taxation. A regressive tax is one where a person with a lower income pays proportionally more in taxes than someone with a higher income. The property tax, which is based on the assessed value of a house, may be an example of a regressive tax. Two families occupying houses of the same value may have different incomes, yet may pay the same amount in property tax. Since the property tax bears no necessary relationship to income, it often is termed a regressive tax (Johns, Morphet, and Alexander 1983).

Tax Sources. Each level of government—local, state, and federal—theoretically may be able to tax the same things; however, this is generally

TABLE 4.4
Federal Tax Rates

■

SCHEDULE X SINGLE TAXPAYERS

Use this Schedule if you Checked Filing Status Box 1 on Form 1040-

| If the amount on Form 1040, line 37 is: | | Enter on Form 1040, line 38 | |
Over-	But not over-		Of the amount over-
$ 0	$ 2,300	-0-	$ 2,300
2,300	3,400	11%	3,400
3,400	4,400	$121 + 12%	4,400
4,400	6,500	241 + 14%	6,500
6,500	8,500	535 + 15%	8,500
8,500	10,800	835 + 16%	10,800
10,800	12,900	1,203 + 18%	12,900
12,900	15,000	1,581 + 20%	15,000
15,000	18,200	2,001 + 23%	18,200
18,200	23,500	2,737 + 26%	23,500
23,500	28,800	4,115 + 30%	28,800
28,800	34,100	5,705 + 34%	34,100
34,100	41,500	7,507 + 38%	41,500
41,500	55,300	10,319 + 42%	55,300
55,300	81,800	16,115 + 48%	81,800
81,800	—	28,835 + 50%	

■

not the case. The levels of government usually rely on different taxes as their primary sources of revenue. For the federal government, these sources are primarily individual and corporate income taxes. Many states also tax income, but, for the most part, states depend upon sales taxes, severance taxes, exise taxes on alcohol and tobacco, and, where legal, pari-mutuel betting and lotteries for their revenues. Local governments often have sales taxes, but their basic revenue source is from property taxes.

Local governments are prohibited from taxing states or the federal government on federal and state land and property within city limits. To compensate local governments for this loss of revenue, the federal government and many states make payments in lieu of taxation to local governmental units. Property such as military bases, parks, forest and grazing lands, wildlife areas, wilderness areas, and governmental buildings are examples of these kinds of properties.

Development of School Finance

Prior to the settlement of North America, the support of schools with tax funds was unknown in western Europe. Not until Prussia began the practice in the early eighteenth century did any European nation have public tax supported schools (Butts 1955). On this side of the Atlantic, the Massachusetts Bay Colony enacted the "olde deluder Satan" law of 1647. This act not only created tax supported schools, but it set an unfortunate pattern of permitting communities to evade their responsibilities by paying a fine rather than operating a school. Some towns found it cheaper to pay the penalty rather than operate a school (Pulliam 1987).

Therefore, the idea of spending tax funds to support public education—but only as little as possible—took root and still exists today. Only recently has the public's attitude toward raising taxes to support improvement in public education been favorable. In the most recent Gallup poll (Gallup and Elam 1988), sixty-four percent of the respondents indicated a willingness to pay more taxes to improve the schools. This is a significant change from the 1985 Gallup poll which indicated that only thirty-eight percent of the individuals were in favor of increasing taxes for schools (Gallup 1985).

School Finance during Colonial America. With the exception of Rhode Island, all of the New England colonies enacted versions of the "olde deluder" law in the seventeenth century (Pulliam 1987). In the Middle and Southern colonies, private- and church-supported schools were the rule. These, like the private schools in New England, depended upon charity and tuition payments. Public tax support of schools in the Middle and Southern colonies was not present in colonial America.

School Finance after the Colonial Period. Shortly after the end of the revolutionary war, the Continental Congress passed the Northwest Ordinances of 1785 and 1787. These laws granted section sixteen of every township in the Northwest Territory (later extended to all new territory added to the Union) for the use of education. This meant that the land could be used for a school location, it could be rented and the payment used to support a school, or it could be sold and the proceeds invested with the interest earned used for operating a school. The "Permanent School Fund" created by the latter option became the basis for school funding in the early days of the Republic. Aided by lotteries, gifts, and donations, schools were started in the new states, as well as in the older states where public education had fallen on bad times due to the waning influence of the Puritan church. In some communities, tax funds were spent on education; however, the communities were not legally required to do so and the practice was very limited.

The leadership of Thomas Jefferson and Horace Mann in the early nineteenth century made tax-supported schools more acceptable and accessible. However, "despite the advocacy of Jefferson and many others, tax-supported public education did not generally become available in the Middle Atlantic and Midwestern states until after 1830 and in the Southern states until the last quarter of the nineteenth century" (Johns, Morphet, and Alexander 1983, p. 235).

Battles over statewide referendums to use tax funds to support public schools were fought in New York and Pennsylvania. Finally, the United States Supreme Court in 1874 approved that taxes could be spent on high schools (Pulliam 1987).

By 1900 the principle of tax-supported schools was firmly established and the stigma associated with attending "charity schools" supported by tax money had been removed. Had this change of attitude not occurred, publicly supported education would not have become the foundation of the American educational system.

The turn of the century also marked the final chapter in the passage of compulsory school attendance legislation. Prior to 1900 thirty-two states had such laws; by 1920 all states had adopted them (Pulliam 1987). In 1900 only eight percent of the fourteen- to seventeen-year-old group was enrolled in public high schools (Johns, Morphet, and Alexander 1983). Following the passage of compulsory schools laws, this number expanded dramatically, largely at the secondary school level. Since secondary education programs are more costly than elementary programs, added pressure was placed on local, state, and even national authorities for additional funding for schools. Although federal aid to higher education existed as early as 1862, the beginning of the twentieth century marks the start of federal aid for public elementary and secondary schools, in the form of the Smith-Hughes Act and expanded state programs of aid to local districts. Current methods of financing schools are rooted in the developments of this era.

Local Support for Schools

Historically, the primary source of funding for public schools has been local taxation. Recently, however, this has been changing. States currently provide a larger share of support largely due to initiatives that have placed limits on property taxes, such as Proposition 13 in California and Proposition 2½ in Massachusetts. The property tax is still the backbone of local taxation and, therefore, a major source of funds for public education.

Property Tax. Each county within a state normally administers the property tax. Several officials are involved. The county assessor determines the value of the property to be taxed. This can be done on several different bases such as actual cash value, fair market value, or use value. Two different assessors can determine two different values even using the same method. As a result, most counties have Equalization Boards which review assessments when those assessments are challenged by the property owner. The board has the final decision as to the assessment.

Another factor adds confusion to property assessment. Many states use what are termed assessment ratios where the taxable assessment is a legally set percentage of the real value. Thus, a $100,000 home would be assessed at only $40,000 if the assessment ratio is set at forty percent.

Tax Rate. In most states, the tax rate on property is expressed as millage. A *mill* is a tenth of a cent or a thousandth of a dollar. Hence, millage rates can be expressed as either twenty mills or twenty dollars per thousand. Millage rates are at least partly set by elections. The voters determine the level of millage that they want to pay; this can be a problem with property tax income since this is the only form of taxation that requires a popular vote. An antitax mood cannot be taken out on federal or state taxes directly, but it can have an impact on local millage elections. Quite often local millage increases fail, which can be very harmful to school building programs and other activities in the district. School officials cannot easily convince taxpayers that they should vote to increase their taxes, especially when many of those taxpayers do not even have school-age children.

School Buildings. Although the idea of statewide authorities issuing school construction bonds to fund new school buildings is growing, construction of most new school buildings is the responsibility of local boards of education. If the district cannot build a new school from existing local funds, it must borrow the money by selling bonds. To sell the bonds, a millage amount sufficient to pay interest and retire the bonds within a set time frame, normally a twenty-year period, must be passed. School administrators are responsible for selling the need for this tax increase to fund new construction.

State Assessments. In most states, a state agency assesses railroad and utility properties, along with carriers such as aircraft and large trucks. This provides a standard method of assessment of these kinds of property within a state. Each county, school district, or other taxing authority is credited with the amount of the assessment that lies within its borders. Therefore, school districts receive a fair share of taxes paid by utilities and carriers.

Differences in Wealth. Differences obviously exist in the wealth of local school districts. Some will have more taxable property than others. In some districts the value of the property may be much higher than in other districts. For example, some suburbs, primarily populated by young professionals likely will have houses with a much higher average value than houses found in older, established cities with mostly older dwellings. An example of wide disparity was found in Texas, where at one time the poorest district had a taxable value per student of $25,000 compared to $6 million per student in a wealthy district (Wright and Inman 1988). Districts with more money may or may not have more children to educate. When one district has far more taxable wealth per pupil than another, it can afford to provide a superior education at the same level of tax effort than another district with less valued taxable property. A district may even be able to do this at a lower tax rate.

The child in the poorer district may not have the same educational opportunity as the child in the wealthier district. Wealthier districts can pay higher teacher salaries and, therefore, possibly attract better-qualified staff. They also can purchase state-of-the-art equipment, such as computer equipment, which can only enhance educational opportunities. This situation raises the issue of equity, which has been the concern of state aid programs for several decades; recently the courts have become involved with this issue.

Equity in Financing. Equity refers to many things in school finance. One example is equity for taxpayers. Should taxpayers in one school district be required to pay a much higher rate of taxation than taxpayers in another district to maintain the same level of public education? More important, should children receive a less-adequate education in one district than children in another district merely because one district has lower assessments per child and, therefore, fewer dollars to spend on school programs?

This issue has been debated for years. State aid programs have tried unsuccessfully to provide adequate solutions to the equity problem. The issue finally found its way to court in California in the case of *Serrano v. Priest.* In this case, the California Supreme Court declared that the state's school finance plan violated the California Constitution because it denied equal treatment to some children by allowing some districts to underfinance their educational programs. In its ruling, the court stated that the California financing plan "as presently constituted is not necessary to the attainment of any compelling state interest. Since it does not withstand the requisite 'strict scrutiny,' it denies to the plaintiffs and others similarly situated the equal protection of the laws" (Benson 1975, p. 85). A similar case, *Robinson v. Cahill* arose in New Jersey. The New Jersey Supreme Court stated that equal educational opportunity must exist throughout the state.

HIGHLIGHT

■

LEGISLATORS ATTACK PHANTOM STUDENTS, PROPERTY TAXES

Jonathan Roos

Summoning their legislative powers, the House and Senate have begun the task of exorcising phantom students from the budget ledgers of Iowa's school districts.

They've also taken after an even bigger bogeyman—the tax collector.

The fight over the nearly $2 billion in state aid and local property taxes that are spent on 433 school districts each year began Friday and continues Monday with vows to improve the formula by which all that money is distributed.

But even with computer projections to help legislators see into the future, no one knows for sure how much of an improvement the new finance plan will be over the old formula, which has been around for nearly 20 years.

"When we finish this, there are going to be some winners and losers. There's no way to avoid that," said Representative C. Arthur Ollie, a Clinton Democrat who is guiding an 88-page school spending bill through the House.

Going into Friday's lelgislative debate, the winners appeared to be the majority of Iowa's school districts, which have been able to use the non-existent students in the school aid formula to cushion themselves from the financial effects of declining enrollment.

Despite the eventual elimination of those phantom students under the new school-aid formula proposals, districts that in the past

continued

have been able to count a large number of those fictional pupils for budget purposes won't be penalized financially—at least not right away.

Other winners are the children who would benefit from a proposed $3 million increase in spending on programs for gifted and talented students and a $10 million appropriation for programs to help students at risk of dropping out of school. Then there's $6.9 million to help schools meet new accreditation standards.

The debate Friday focused on helping two other groups that, in the minds of some legislators, had been left out:

■ School districts with stable or growing enrollments that haven't been allowed to spend as much per actual pupil as districts able to count a large number of phantom students.

Although politicians promised to "put the money where the students are" in banishing phantom students from the school finance formula, proposals offered by Gov. Terry Branstad and legislators fall short of that goal. Under the House bill debated Friday, the gap in per-pupil spending among Iowa's school districts (about $1,700 currently) wouldn't close until the year 2035, said House Minority Leader Delwyn Stromer.

The House bill does contain a "catch-up" feature for low-spending districts; and attempts are expected to be made this week to strengthen it. The bill "moves in the right direction, but it doesn't move very quickly," said Representative Dorothy Carpenter, a West Des Moines Republican.

■ Property-tax payers. Since the biggest share of property taxes is spent in support of public schools, tax reform groups and their legislative allies have been waiting for revision of the school finance formula. Even though the existing formula has provided a large measure of property-tax relief, those who would revise taxes have wanted to shift even more of the tax burden from farmers and other property owners to income- or sales-tax sources.

Property-Tax Relief

Their argument is that property wealth, especially in rural areas where incomes tend to be lower, isn't necessarily related to one's ability to pay taxes.

As events in the Legislature showed Friday, property-tax foes are not satisfied with the property-tax relief provided through the new school-formula proposals. The Senate tentatively approved a $150 million state income-tax increase, earmarking the money to replace some of the property taxes raised through the school formula.

The personal income taxes would be raised by limiting to 50 percent the amount of federal income tax that could be deducted for state purposes.

The Senate-approved tax shift is only tentative. But it sends a message that the Senate is serious about property-tax relief, said Senate Majority Leader Bill Hutchins, an Audubon Democrat.

Although not unexpected, the injection of a property-tax fight into a debate about education issues threatens to disrupt what had been a surprisingly smooth and speedy effort to revise the school finance formula, which has been in effect since 1971.

Other Relief Proposals

Other property-tax relief proposals are in the works. Representative David Osterberg, a Mount Vernon Democrat, said he likes the Senate idea of limiting the amount of federal taxes Iowans can deduct on their state income-tax returns. But he believes it's unfair to give all property owners a big tax break.

He is preparing a plan to broaden a property-tax credit for the low-income elderly to include other Iowans with small incomes. Under current law, Iowans older than 65 or disabled and whose total incomes are $12,000 or less can subtract from their income-tax bill some or all of what they pay in property taxes. Those who make less than $5,000 receive a 100 percent credit, Osterberg said.

The property-tax issue also flared in both chambers over a proposal to allow school districts to exceed their budget limits by up to 10 percent annually over five years. Voter approval would be needed to exceed the limits for more than five years.

continued

Finally, a case involving equitable school financing reached the United States Supreme Court. In this case, *San Antonio Independent School District v. Rodriquez*, the Court declared that, since education was not a right guaranteed by the United States Constitution, relief would have to be sought at the state level. In making its decision, the Court indicated that "its decision should not be interpreted as placing a 'judicial imprimatur' upon the status quo. But the ultimate solution, said the Court, should come from the lawmakers in each of the states" (Campbell, Cunningham, Nystrand, and Usdan 1980, p. 41). As a result, more cases have been brought in state courts seeking equity. The supreme courts of Connecticut, Washington, West Virginia, and Arkansas have declared that equity was not being achieved under their state aid formulas. On the other hand, the courts in Arizona, Michigan, Ohio, Maryland, and Georgia have held that the inequities found in their states were acceptable. Equal access to an education is still an unsettled issue.

State Aid for Education

During the latter nineteenth century, states recognized the need for funding local schools at a higher level than many local districts could afford. State aid began as an equal amount per pupil whenever the pupil lived within the state's boundaries. This system was termed a flat grant, because it did not consider differences in local wealth.

By the 1920s state laws began to recognize the need to equalize educational opportunity through the equalization of funding. The New York legislature, in attempting to equalize school financing in that state, exacted the Strayer-Haig formula. The concept behind this approach was for the state to rank all of its school districts from top to bottom in terms of their expenditures. Then a district would be selected, and districts spending less than the amount expended by the selected district would receive state aid sufficient to bring it up to the level of the selected district.

This approach, although sound, led to several abuses. It did not consider the cost of educating children in different districts, and it did not look at the matter of local district effort. A district could be spending fewer dollars than the optimal district, because it had improperly lowered property assessments or tax rates. Although corrective actions were taken to alleviate some of these abuses, states continued to seek other solutions.

Minimum Foundation Programs. The concept of the Minimum Foundation Program was developed in the 1940s as a solution to equalizing school finance. This idea was based on the state's guarantee that every child should receive an educational program funded at an average minimal level. Wealthier, or higher taxing districts, could go beyond this minimum amount with local effort. Districts funding programs above the minimal level were termed "lighthouse" districts, because they set a pattern that other districts could model. This idea, adopted in several states, required the state to calculate the district's wealth. In the states where local assessment practices were questionable, an index of taxpaying ability was used. This index, using alternative measures of wealth rather than property assessments, was translated into a calculated tax base for the district, which then had to raise an appropriate amount of local tax revenues to receive state aid. Alternative measures included personal income, sales tax receipts, auto license fees, the value of farm products, and the preparation of nonfarm equipment.

How Minimum Foundation Aid Works. Minimum foundation aid works as follows: Each district's wealth is determined either by the use of actual assessment data or by a calculated tax base. Each district must levy a statewide millage on that base. Then the cost of educating children in the district is determined. The funds raised, or supposedly raised, by the local district are subtracted from the cost of education, and the difference is made up by state aid. Individual states have developed numerous variations to this concept. However, most are based on the same concept.

Only one state has solved the problem of equity in funding. This is Hawaii, which has only one school district and where all funding is on a statewide basis. Of the states with multiple school districts, Utah has come closest to solving the funding problem. In Utah, if a school district charges the required statewide millage and produces more revenue than it costs to run its schools, the excess funds are returned to the state, which then can distribute the funds to schools in other districts.

Costs of Educational Programs. The calculation of the cost of education for minimum foundation requires the recognition that the education of some children costs more than others. Some states have class size limits on primary grades. Vocational education, special education, science and computer literacy programs, and education for gifted children will require added funding. The method generally used to calculate these cost differences is called *weighting*.

Weighting. Weights are cost factors assigned to represent the average added cost of education for certain groups of students. They are expressed as percentages of costs for regular students. Weights can be calculated in two general ways: as teacher units and as weighted pupils.

Teacher Units. Teacher-unit weighting is expressed as a proportion of regular units. Assuming that a state has defined a teaching unit as twenty-five children, then a primary unit could be twenty students, a vocational class fifteen, and some special education classes ten or fewer students. The student population is totalled by category, regular students are divided by twenty-five, and the other categories are divided by the assigned numbers. The total number of units are then multiplied by whatever number of dollars the state has determined will be spent per teacher unit.

Weighted Pupils. The weighted-pupil approach works in a parallel fashion to teacher units. A regular child is weighted as 1.00. Assigning weights of 1.25 to a primary child, 1.65 to a child in vocational education, and 2.50 to a child in special education generates approximately the same amount of cost as using the teacher-unit method. The total number of weighted children is then multiplied by the dollar amount that the state has determined should be expended for each child.

Drawbacks to Minimum Foundation Plans. Although they are the most commonly used state funding method, minimum foundation programs are not without drawbacks. One, which became evident soon after the programs were started, is that although minimum foundation programs were enacted to ensure funding at a minimum level, the "minimum" became the standard in most districts. Rather than becoming the true minimum to be exceeded, the minimum became the standard to be attained. The result is that minimum foundation programs have not led to equity, because the expenditures of wealthy districts cannot be restricted. They can and do vastly exceed the minimum or guaranteed amount. This creates a highly inequitable situation, because children in one of the select districts will have a higher quality program available than the average child in the state due purely to the accident of residence. Therefore, efforts should continue to enact equitable opportunities for all children in a state.

Federal Support for Education

Federal aid to public education did not begin until the twentieth century. Prior to that time, federal interests were directed almost totally toward higher education, with the exception of the Northwest Ordinances. During the nineteenth century, Congress created the military and naval academies and passed the Morrill Acts, which gave land grants and operating funds to states for the operation of colleges and universities. As a result, each state has at least one land-grant university.

Federal involvement in precollegiate education began with the Smith-Hughes Act of 1917. This law provided for vocational education in secondary schools for agriculture, home economics, trade, and industrial education. Boards were created at both state and federal levels to oversee the distribution of these funds, which had to be matched by the states (Butts 1955).

Federal involvement in public education increased through programs such as school lunches, the Civilian Conservation Corps (CCC), and the National Youth Administration (NYA), which were developed during the depression of the 1930s. While these programs did not provide direct aid to the instructional process, they did have a positive effect on the public schools.

The late 1950s and early 1960s saw the establishment of large-scale federal aid to public education through the National Science Foundation (NSF), the National Defense Education Act of 1958 (NDEA), and the Elementary and Secondary Education Act of 1965 (ESEA). These actions, which were taken primarily in response to advances in science by the Soviet Union, set the trend for direct federal aid to public education. Other legislation passed by Congress during this period provided for Teacher Corps, Education Professions Development, Bilingual Education, Education for the Handicapped, and a flurry of other programs. Many of these programs were combined in 1981 by the Educational Consolidation and Improvement Act. By 1980 the annual total dollar figure of these programs for elementary and secondary schools exceeded seven billion dollars (Johns, Morphet, and Alexander 1983).

Unlike state aid to education, federal aid is not concerned with equity. Rather, it is concerned with special problems. Federal aid is categorical; it can only be spent for those purposes specified in the authorizing legislation, regardless of the school district's needs. It is distributed in two ways, by formula and by discretion. Formulas determine the division of most federal money, yet, in general, more programs have been funded by discretionary means.

The Future of Federal Aid. With school enrollments beginning to increase as a result of children of the baby-boom generation, aid to education will become a major political issue. In addition, as the education of the handicapped and other special groups continues to be recognized as a responsibility of schools, costs will continue to escalate. These facts, combined with the mood to improve public education in the United States, make it likely that federal aid to education will continue and may possibly increase. The nature of the aid, however, may change. The Reagan administration pushed hard for block grants rather than the categorical aid that has been the rule. Whether more aid is moved to the block category remains to be seen; however, substantial reduction in federal aid to education is unlikely.

CONCLUSIONS: WHO DOES CONTROL?

The control over education in the United States is obviously a complex question. Although the belief has long been held that local boards of education exert ultimate control, investigating the influences at the state and national levels shows that local boards of education are very limited in their control. The control of our schools is shared by many different groups, both formal and informal. Certainly the federal government's influence has grown dramatically during the twentieth century. Although the early 1980s saw an effort to shift the trend away from federal influence and back to states and local units, federal involvement in public education is so broad that any such efforts undoubtedly will result in only minor changes.

No one group controls American education. All three levels of government—local, state, and federal—are heavily involved; publishing companies, teachers' organizations, and testing companies exert indirect influence; the judiciary has set precedence of ruling on education issues; and local teacher and parent groups are gaining influence. The only conclusions that can be drawn are that (1) control of education in the United States is and will continue to be shared by a multitude of individuals and groups, and, (2) although the levels of influence may shift among groups, most of the variables influencing education currently will continue to have some impact in the future.

SUMMARY

This chapter has focused on the issue of control over American education. Many different forces exert influence. At the federal level, the executive branch, legislative branch, and judiciary branch are all involved. State legislatures have been gaining in involvement during the past two decades. At the local level, school boards still influence specific practices in local schools. In addition to government, many informal groups exert influence. These include testing agencies, accreditation agencies, and book publishers. Groups such as the right-wing coalition have become powerful influences. Teachers' organizations, through collective bargaining and strike actions, have added to their influence over what occurs in classrooms.

Control over education was shown to be a complex issue. No one group or level of government dominates public education in the United States. Rather, schools are influenced and controlled by a combination of government, lay, professional, and corporate groups.

IN THE FIELD

1. Do teachers feel they have a major role in decision making in the district? If so, how do they access the decision-making process?
2. Should teachers have a role in decision making? Why?
3. Do teachers primarily follow a teacher's guide or curriculum guide in their instructional activities? If not, what do they follow?
4. Do teachers use any state or district document relating to classroom objectives?
5. Does the district have a citizens' advisory group that is active? If so, what is its role?
6. Are school board policies available for review by teachers and students?
7. Is there a local teachers' organization? If so, does it have a role in district decision making?
8. Are the school and district accredited by a regional accreditation agency? If so, what agency, and when was the last accreditation visit?
9. How does the school district ensure compliance with state and federal regulations in areas such as special education?

REFERENCES

Armstrong, D. G., K. T. Henson, and T. V. Savage. 1983. *Education: An Introduction.* New York: Macmillan.

Benson, C. S. 1975. *Education Finance in the Coming Decade.* Bloomington, IN: Phi Delta Kappa Foundation.

Bracey, G. W. 1980. The SAT, college admissions, and the concept of talent: Unexamined myths, unexplained perceptions, needed explorations. *Phi Delta Kappan* 62(3), 197–99.

Butts, R. F. 1955. *A Cultural History of Western Education.* New York: McGraw-Hill.

Campbell, R. F., L. L. Cunningham, R. O. Nystrand, and M. D. Usdan. 1980. *The Organization and Control of American Schools* (4th ed.). Columbus, OH: Merrill.

Dentler, R. A. 1984. Ambiguities in state-local relations. *Education and Urban Society* 16(2), 145–64.

Elam, S. M. 1981. The national education association: Political powerhouse or paper tiger? *Phi Delta Kappan* 63(3), 169–74.

Else, D. 1983. Productive advisory committees keep parents happy and curriculums current. *The American School Board Journal* 170(6), 34+.

Ficklen, E. and K. McCormick. 1983. Repeated attacks on education put unions on the defensive. *The American School Board Journal* 170(10), 31–34.

Fischer, L. 1979. Law and educational policy. *Educational Forum* 44(1), 109–14.

Gallup, 1985. The 17th annual Gallup poll of the public's attitudes toward the public schools. *Phi Delta Kappan* 67(1), 35–47.

Gallup, A. M. 1986. The 18th annual Gallup poll of the public's attitudes toward the public schools. *Phi Delta Kappan* 68(1), 43–57.

Gallup, A. M. and S. M. Elam 1988. The 20th annual Gallup poll of the public's attitudes toward the public schools. *Phi Delta Kappan* 70(1), 33–46.

Gallup, A. M. and D. L. Clark 1987. The 19th annual Gallup poll of the public's attitudes toward the public schools. *Phi Delta Kappan* 69(1), 17–30.

Ginsburg, A. L., J. Noell, and A. S. Rosenthal. 1985. Is the federal "chapter I" education formula equitable? *Journal of Education Finance* 10(3), 360–74.

Good, H. G. 1956. *A History of American Education.* New York: Macmillan.

Good, T. L. 1986. What is learned in elementary schools. In T. M. Tomlinson and H. J. Walberg (Eds.), *Academic Work and Educational Excellence.* Berkeley, CA: McCutchan.

Good, H. G., and J. D. Teller. 1973. *A History of American Education.* 3d ed. New York: Macmillan.

Harder, J. C. 1983. The federal-state relationship: A traditionalist's view. *Education and Urban Society* 16(1), 81–93.

Hartrick, E. B., K. E. Underwood, J. C. Fortune, and K. E. Keough. 1989. Our 11th annual survey of school board members. *The American School Board Journal* 176, 19–24.

Huffman, J. 1982. The role of accreditation in preserving educational integrity. *Educational Record* 63(2), 41–44.

Jencks, C., and J. Crouse, 1982. Should we relabel the SAT . . . or replace it? *Phi Delta Kappan* 63(10), 659–63.

Johns, R. L., E. L. Morphet, and K. Alexander. 1983. *The economics and financing of education.* 4th ed. Englewood Cliffs, NJ: Prentice-Hall.

Kaestle, C. F., and M. S. Smith. 1982. The federal role in elementary and secondary education, 1940–1980. *Harvard Educational Review* 52(4).

Killian, M. G. 1983. Community poll defines key skills and assesses schools' performance. *Phi Delta Kappan* 65(3), 218–19.

Kirp, D. L., and D. N. Jensen. 1983. The new federalism goes to court. *Phi Delta Kappan* 65(3), 206–10.

Koerner, J. D. 1968. *Who Controls American Education? A Guide for Laymen.* Boston: Beacon Press.

Lieberman, M. 1981. Teacher bargaining: An autopsy. *Phi Delta Kappan* 63(4), 231–34.

McCarthy, M. M., and N. H. Cambron. 1981. *Public School Law: Teachers' and Students' Rights.* Boston: Allyn and Bacon.

McCarthy, M. M., and N. H. Cambron-McCabe 1987. *Public School Law: Teachers' and Students' Rights,* 2nd Ed. Boston: Allyn and Bacon.

Marvell, T., A. Galfo, and J. Rockwell (n.d.) *Student Litigation: A Compilation and Analysis of Civil Cases Involving Students 1977–1981.* Williamsburg, VA: National Center for State Courts.

Moberly, D. L., and L. J. Stiles. 1978. Getting a school board to address its primary tasks. *Phi Delta Kappan* 60(3), 236–37.

Murphy, M. C. 1983. How advisory councils can help. *Vocational Education* 58(4), 34–35.

National Center for Education Statistics. *The Condition of Education 1988.* Washington, D. C.: U.S. Department of Education.

NEA Handbook 1987–1988. Washington, D. C.: National Education Association.

Neill, G. 1979a. Department of education nears showdown in house. *Phi Delta Kappan* 60(10), 701–702.

Neill, G. 1979b. Observers see danger, challenge in building education department. *Phi Delta Kappan* 61(4), 236–37.

Neill, G. 1980. Education department explains its structure and purposes. *Phi Delta Kappan* 61(10), 670.

Nelson, J. L., and L. R. Crum. 1983. The power and challenges of local school boards. *American Education* 19(10), 10–16.

Pulliam, J. D. 1987. *History of Education in America.* Columbus, OH: Merrill.

Partners in quality education. 1982. The community, its schools, and the north central association. *The North Central Association Quarterly,* 57(2), 27–29.

Podemski, R. S., B. J. Price, T. E. C. Smith, and G. E. Marsh. 1984. *Comprehensive Administration of Special Education.* Rockville, MD: Aspen Systems.

Reecer, M. 1989. Yes, boards are under fire, but reports of your death are greatly exaggerated. *American School Board Journal* 176, 31–34.

Shanker, A. 1989. Al Shanker (of all people) wants a hard look at what's befallen school boards. *American School Board Journal* 176, 29–30.

Retsinas, J. 1982. Teachers: Bargaining for control. *American Educational Research Journal* 19(3), 353–72.

Robinson v. Cahill (62 NJ 473, 303 A.2nd 273).

Rosenau, F. S. 1982. Administrative proposal for dismantling ED awaits congressional action. *Phi Delta Kappan* 63(8), 509.

Rosenthal, A., and S. Fuhrman. 1982. State legislatures and education policy: An overview. *Educational Horizons* 61(1), 4–9+.

San Antonio Independent School District v. Rodriquez (411 US 1, 93 S. Ct. 1278, 36 L. Ed. 2d 16).

Saylor, J. G. 1982. *Who Planned the Curriculum? A Curriculum Plans Reservoir Model with Historical Examples.* West Lafayette, IN: Kappa Delta Pi.

Seligman, E. R. A. 1925. *Essays in Taxation.* 10th ed. New York: Macmillan.

Serrano v. Priest (487 P.2nd 1241).

Strahan, R. D., and L. C. Turner 1987. *The Courts and the Schools.* New York: Longman.

Silberman, H. F. 1980. Working in Washington, *Phi Delta Kappan* 61(7), 449–51.

Valente, W. D. 1987. *Law in the Schools*, 2nd Ed. Columbus, OH: Merrill.

Watts, D. 1983. Four views of NCATEs role and function. *Phi Delta Kappan* 64(9), 646–49.

Wright, L., and D. Inman. 1988. The impact of education reform on local school districts. *Journal of Education Finance* 14, 7–17.

Zirkel, P. A. 1978. *A Digest of Supreme Court Decisions Affecting Education.* Bloomington, IN: Phi Delta Kappa.

5

LEGAL ISSUES

ADVANCE ORGANIZERS

1. What is the constitutional basis for public education?
2. What is the role of state government in public education?
3. What are school boards, and how are they involved in public education?
4. What is the basis for separation of church and state?
5. What has been the general trend in the courts' rulings on issues such as prayer in public schools, released time for religious activities, and religious influences on school curriculum?
6. How did the *Tinker* case affect freedom of expression for students?
7. What do the courts say about dress and grooming codes for students?
8. What were the important court cases dealing with desegregation of public schools?
9. How do teachers' rights differ from the rights of other citizens?
10. What facts are necessary to show age or racial discrimination in hiring practices?
11. For what reasons can tenured teachers be dismissed?

INTRODUCTION

Our entire system of public education is based on a legal foundation. The United States Constitution, which provides the framework for our legal and social systems, is also the basis of our educational system. State constitutions, local governmental ordinances, and practices and policies of local education agencies overlap the Constitution to influence public schools. As previously discussed in chapter four, the control of American public education is shared among many different forces. This chapter will provide a framework for understanding the legal issues surrounding public education; information on numerous court cases will be discussed.

THE U.S. CONSTITUTION AND PUBLIC EDUCATION

The Constitution of the United States is the foundation for our entire legal and governmental system. It is a simple document that has withstood the test of time, having been an effective governing tool for more than two hundred years. The Constitution cannot deal with all of the issues found in our society, and education is one of those issues not specifically addressed. The Tenth Amendment of the Constitution states that "The powers not delegated to the United States by the Constitution, nor prohibited by it to the States, are reserved to the States respectively, or to the people." Since the Constitution does not delegate powers over education to the U.S. government, nor prohibit such powers to states, public education in this country has become a state responsibility. This is reflected in the fact that every state constitution includes public education as a responsibility of the state (O'Reilly and Green 1983). Therefore public education is primarily the responsibility of state governments by default, or by a failure of the U.S. Constitution to address public education issues.

During the past twenty-five years the role of the federal government in education has been increasing. Beginning in the mid-1950s with litigation dealing with civil rights issues, the federal government has taken on an increasingly important role in public education. Influence has come through legislation, litigation, and the financing of specific educational programs. As the federal role in education has increased, the debate has grown relative to the appropriate role of the federal government in public education.

STATE GOVERNMENTS AND PUBLIC EDUCATION

States have readily accepted the primary responsibility for providing public education to its citizens and have responded by including provisions in their state constitutions for public school programs. Examples include Georgia's constitution, which makes the state responsible for public education and in turn gives the responsibility to local school boards; the New York State constitution which requires the state to provide for free, common schools for all of its children; and Michigan's constitution which calls for the state to provide an education to all its children, regardless of "religion, creed, race, color or national origin," because religion, morality, and knowledge are prerequisites for good government (O'Reilly and Green 1983).

In attempting to provide educational services to children, states occasionally have become embroiled in conflict with parents. Often parents have viewed states' actions as efforts to circumvent their rights as parents concerning the education of their children (Strahan and Turner 1987). One area where this has been common, and still occasionally occurs, is in compulsory school attendance laws. Based on the premise that an educated citizenry is the best way to maintain a democratic society, states enacted compulsory attendance laws requiring children between certain ages to attend public schools. The legal basis for mandatory school attendance is the common-law doctrine of *parens patriae*, which suggests that the state is ultimately responsible to ensure the well-being of its citizens. Although widely accepted as within the power of the state, mandatory school attendance laws do have limitations. For example, the state cannot mandate attendance at public schools (parents may opt to send their children to private schools), and many states have now accepted the rights of parents to educate their children at home (Alexander and Alexander 1984).

State legislatures have utilized state agencies to ensure the implementation of state laws and provisions for public education. The names of these agencies vary from state to state, but are generally referred to as state boards of education. These boards provide for a state department of education, or state education agency (SEA), to carry out the legislative provisions of the state relative to public education (O'Reilly and Green 1983). Most state education agencies are organized into various divisions, such as elementary education, secondary education, and teacher certification, which specialize in oversight activities of the schools.

LOCAL BOARDS OF EDUCATION

Local boards of education, commonly called school boards, are a unique form of government; their counterpart is rarely found in other countries. Boards are created by state statutes for the purpose of administering local school districts. The boards derive their powers from the state constitution, state statutes, and court decisions. The expressed powers of the school board are specified in legislation or other guidelines; implied powers are those that the board assumes. If implied powers are challenged and sustained in the courts, those powers are considered to be based on statute (O''Reilly and Green 1983).

Although on the surface most citizens believe that local school boards are in control of the district's schools, the courts consistently have held that maintaining public schools is a state, not a local, responsibility (Strahan and Turner 1987). School boards are dependent on the existence of local school districts, which are created by and can be dissolved by state legislatures. In a sense, members of local boards of education are not local officials but state officials because their purpose is to carry out the functions of the state relative to public education (O'Reilly and Green 1983).

Regardless of the restrictions on local school boards, they do exert a great deal of influence over public education in this country. The following statements characterize local boards of education (O'Reilly and Green 1983):

- Legally, the local board of education is the governing body for the school district.
- State legislatures determine how school board members are elected or appointed, their terms of offices, duties and responsibilities, the procedures for removal from office, reimbursements for expenditures, and qualifications required for board members.

- Boards can act only as a body; individually, board members have no power.
- Primary responsibilities of local boards of education are goal setting and policy-making.
- A board of education's power to make and enforce policy and rules cannot conflict with state and/or federal provisions.
- Due process must be provided by the board regarding rules and regulations adopted by the board.

Boards of education are unique governing units which often appear to be more than they are, and at times are more than they appear. Although they are severely restricted in their powers, they wield a great deal of influence over local educational practices. This can be substantiated by the hotly contested local school board elections that now and then occur in every community. Membership on school boards is highly sought, even though memberships are unpaid and often unrewarded positions of government.

LEGAL BASIS FOR EDUCATION: CONCLUSIONS

The legal basis for public education in this country is complex. Because the U.S. Constitution did not directly mention education nor prohibit states from becoming involved in education, the Constitution created a situation where states have assumed the major role in providing public education. States, in turn, created school districts and local boards of education to ensure that state policies and statutes regarding education are implemented. Thus local school boards have been granted what many consider the major power over public schools.

In reality, the federal government is heavily involved in public education. The courts have taken a leading role in this involvement through protection of civil and individual rights guaranteed by the U.S. Constitution. The courts have interpreted and the legislative branch has enacted laws affecting schools. For instance, the legislature has created a cabinet-level office, the U.S. Department of Education, to carry out various functions related to public education. Federal agencies and departments have used different legal sources to justify their increased involvement in the schools. These include the *General Welfare Clause* of the Constitution, the *Commerce Clause* of the Constitution, and the First, Fourth, Fifth, Ninth, and Fourteenth Amendments to the U.S. Constitution (McCarthy and Cambron-McCabe 1987). Table 5.1 describes these sources.

The involvement of the federal courts with education issues has increased substantially over the past three decades. During 1957–1966, only 729 total cases in federal courts dealt with education compared to more than 8,500 during 1977–1986. The number of cases heard by the Supreme Court related to public schools increased from an average of 2.5 per decade from 1900 to 1949, to 9 in the 1950s, 22 in the 1960s, and

TABLE 5.1
Legal Sources for School Law

SOURCE	DESCRIPTION
General Welfare Clause	Part of Article I, Section 8, of the U.S. Constitution. Allows Congress to collect taxes to provide for the general welfare of citizens. Congress has used this as a rationale for getting involved in public education.
Commerce Clause	Part of Article I, Section 8, of the U.S. Constitution. Empowers Congress with power to regulate commerce. Congress has used this clause to justify involvement in labor/union activities.
First Amendment	Provides freedom of religion principle. Basis for separation of church and state.
Fourth Amendment	Protects citizens from unwarranted search and seizure. Basis for decisions regarding search and seizure of students.
Fifth Amendment	Protects citizens from being deprived of life, liberty, or property, and prohibits requiring an individual to testify against himself/herself. Used to support desegregation and rights of disabled children in District of Columbia. Provides protection for teachers related to outside work activities.
Ninth Amendment	States that the enumeration of certain rights in the Constitution does not deny other rights. Teachers and students have based their rights related to physical appearance and privacy on this amendment.
Fourteenth Amendment	Mandates that states may not deny equal protection to citizens. Most widely used basis for school litigation.

Source: McCarthy and Cambron-McCabe, 1987.

53 in the 1970s (Zirkel 1989). One of the reasons for the widespread growth in litigation during the 60s and 70s was the activism of proponents of the civil rights and special education movements. Since statutes regarding these areas have now existed for several years, the number of cases has begun to level off.

Recently, state legislatures have become more involved in local educational issues (Shanker 1989; Reecer 1989). Additionally, local boards of education have begun to express themselves as the "legitimate" leaders of public schools by making decisions regarding the educational reform movement of the 1980s.

The basis for our entire educational system is legal and occurs at all levels of government—federal, state, and local. The remaining parts of this chapter describe the relationships between certain practices in our schools and the law.

RELIGION AND PUBLIC EDUCATION

Originally, religion and education were closely linked in this country. The first attempt to secure tax money for this effort was to keep men knowledgeable about the Scriptures. *The New England Primer*, the textbook used to teach reading in much of New England during the late 1600s, used letters and pictures related to Bible stories. When Horace Mann led the common-school movement in the early 1800s, he advocated the separation of education and religion. Much of the opposition to the common-school movement actually came from clergy who wanted to maintain the schools as religious teaching vehicles. In the early twentieth century, most schools had morning religious activities, including prayer and Bible reading. It was not until the mid to late twentieth century that persons began questioning the role of religion in public education (Alexander and Alexander 1984).

Constitutional Basis

Religious activities were prevalent in our public schools during the first half of this century without much debate. Since the 1950s, however, there has been a great deal of legal dispute regarding the place of religion in public education. The basis for most of the legal controversy centers specifically on the First and Fourteenth Amendments to the U.S. Constitution. The First Amendment states that "Congress shall make no law respecting an establishment of religion, or prohibiting the free exercise thereof." The Fourteenth Amendment provides that no state shall "deny to any person within its jurisdiction the equal protection of the laws;" the Fourteenth has been used to apply the First Amendment provisions to education (Kemerer 1987).

The First Amendment contains two phrases dealing with education. The first part of the Amendment, known as the Establishment Clause, "requires that the government neither advance nor inhibit religion . . ." in effect erecting "a wall between church and state" (Kemerer 1987, p. 81). The second part of the amendment, the Free Exercise Clause, prevents interfering with anyone's practice of religion.

The United States Supreme Court issued its first major Establishment Clause decision in the *Everson v. Board of Education* case. In its ruling, the Court reviewed the First Amendment and concluded that the amendment was indeed intended to erect a wall between church and state. "Since 1970 the Supreme Court has applied a tripartite test in assessing most establishment clause claims. To withstand scrutiny under this test, governmental action must: (1) have a secular purpose; (2) have a primary effect that neither advances nor impedes religion; and (3) avoid excessive governmental entanglement with religion" (McCarthy and Cambron-McCabe 1987, p. 26). These three criteria were used by the Supreme Court in 1971 when it struck down salary increases for teachers in parochial schools and the purchase of educational services from parochial schools in *Lemon v. Kurtzman* (1971) (Alexander and Alexander 1984). Since this case, the three-criteria test has been called the Lemon Test (McCarthy and Cambron-McCabe 1987).

Religious Influences

From Colonial America into the mid-twentieth century, public schools in this country were involved in a variety of religious activities. Many schools sanctioned school prayer, school activities related to religious weeks and events, and assemblies with a religious focus. In the early 1960s, the Supreme Court issued two precedent-setting decisions stating that schools that sponsored daily Bible reading and daily prayer violated the Establishment Clause of the Constitution. Unfortunately, these decisions left many unanswered questions:

1. Can students, rather than school personnel, initiate devotional activities?
2. Can students participate in religious activities as long as such activities do not occur daily?
3. Can student religious groups hold meetings in school buildings if other student groups are allowed to meet in the school?
4. Can religious speech be differentiated from other types of free speech?

Many of these issues have not been resolved (McCarthy and Cambron-McCabe 1987). The question of religion in the schools is much more complex than it appears.

HIGHLIGHT
•
SECULAR HUMANISM IN THE DOCK

Kenneth L. Woodward

To Christian fundamentalists, secular humanism is as deadly and difficult to unmask as the Devil himself. Like Satan, the secular humanist assumes many disguises: he controls the government, the media and worst of all, public education. But in a federal district courtroom in Mobile, Ala., Judge W. Brevard Hand has at last trapped this protean evil spirit. Before him is a case, arranged by the judge himself, in which 600 parents and teachers are challenging four dozen textbooks used in Alabama public schools on the ground that they promote secular humanism at the expense of traditional religious faiths. Both sides have summoned an impressive array of religious and educational experts to debate the basic

issues: Is secular humanism itself a religion? And is it being taught in Alabama's public schools?

Now in its third week, the case has attracted national attention as a kind of courtroom exorcism. If secular humanism is indeed a religion, as the plaintiffs contend, then it has no more constitutional right to be taught in public schools than the Protestant, Roman Catholic or Jewish faiths. A victory for the parents would allow an apparently eager Judge Hand—or any other judge—to purge public classrooms of offending humanist texts. The defendants, state and local school boards, argue that the

continued

fundamentalists are using the issue of secular humanism as a cover to force their own sectarian values on the public schools.

Ignoring God

In the first two weeks of the nonjury trial, witnesses for the plaintiffs offered various definitions of secular humanism and testified to its pervasiveness as a functional equivalent of religion. Essentially, they argued that secular humanism is a philosophy of life that ignores or repudiates God and makes human reason the source of all values. Historically, European humanism included a belief in Biblical revelation. But as conservative Catholic scholar James Hitchcock of St. Louis University testified, secular humanism—as an "ism"—evolved out of 18th century rejection of revealed religion and the Enlightenment's faith in reason alone. "Often," Hitchcock said, "in academic and intellectual circles, humanism is indeed a religion."

Witnesses for the plaintiffs seemed unable to demonstrate that secular humanism has the coherence that is characteristic of a religion. Under cross-examination, University of Virginia sociologist James Hunter conceded that almost any secular enthusiasm—including feminism, vegetarianism and socialism—could be defined as the equivalent of a religion. To defense witness Paul Kurtz, a professor of philosophy at the State University of New York at Buffalo and the only acknowledged secular humanist to take the stand, the term "refers to humanistic development and is nonreligious. . . . It uses science, reason and evidence to test theory." In short, secular humanism seems to be the faith some people get when they don't get religion.

Far more telling was the testimony on how public-school textbooks studiously avoid religion. Prof. Timothy L. Smith, a distinguished historian of American religion at Johns Hopkins, said he was "profoundly shocked" by the almost total lack of religious references in the state's 11th-grade history texts. There was little mention, he said, of religion's role in the development of American pluralism or of the "absolutely central role" of Christians in the abolition of slavery. Psychologist Paul Vitz of New York University reported a "total absence of any references to American religious life of any kind, Protestant, Catholic or Jewish" in a series of primary-school books he studied for the National Institute of Education. He found no mention of God in any of the materials for five out of the eight grade levels. In one book, the Pilgrims' first Thanksgiving was mentioned, but not the God to whom they prayed. And even a story by Isaac Bashevis Singer for sixth graders was amended so that "Thank God" was converted into "Thank goodness."

Similarly, public schools were criticized for substituting psychology for hard moral reasoning. Among other examples, Dr. William Coulson, a professor of psychology at the United States International University in San Diego, cited a course on decision making in family life in which, he testified, never once "is it suggested that [what is morally] right can be known."

This week witnesses for the defense will include Harvard psychiatrist Robert Coles, whose testimony is likely to surprise both sides. Coles thinks that the parents are confusing culture with religion in their attack on secular humanism. In his view, secular humanism is a kind of odorless gas that permeates the entire society. Nonetheless, Coles believes, the parents have good reason to complain about what their children are being taught in school. "What you find in these texts is the exaltation of looking at the world through psychological theories, especially of the self and its needs," he observes. "There's no reference to the self as subject to something else."

Distorting History

Although the plaintiffs are Alabama fundamentalists, the issues they have raised transcend the Bible belt. At the very least, evidence introduced in this and earlier schoolbook cases indicates that American teachers and textbook publishers are so wary of discussing religion in the classroom that they are willing to distort history—and literature—in order to avoid the subject. Moreover, it appears that when questions of morality arise in public-school classes, they

continued

are routinely processed like cheese into the individualistic jargon of humanistic psychology. Thus, pupils are encouraged to discover their own "identities," to learn how to express their true "selves" and to "clarify" their values.

"Are students really better off with the theories of psychologists," asks Harvard's Coles, "than with the hard thoughts of Jeremiah and Jesus?" Indeed, the U.S. Supreme Court has allowed educators to find ways to teach about religion, so long as they do not proselytize. One way would be to include key books from the Bible along with the fables and fairy tales that now clog the curricula. That approach may not satisfy fundamentalists, who want it taught only as sacred Scripture. But it would introduce pupils to what, by any standard, are essential documents in the tradition of Western culture, which is built on religious humanism. Secular humanism may not be a religion, but Judaism and Christianity are most certainly humanistic.

From *Newsweek*, October 22, © 1986, Newsweek, Inc. All rights reserved. Reprinted with permission.

School Prayer and Bible Reading. Many cases dealing with religion and the schools have focused on school prayer and Bible reading. While not an issue until the mid-twentieth century, it is currently a topic that will not go away. In nearly every political contest—local, state, or national—the issue of school prayer is discussed. The first Supreme Court case dealing with school prayer was *Engel v. Vitale* (1962). In this case, the Supreme Court ruled that a prayer advocated by the New York State Board of Regents violated the Establishment Clause of the First Amendment. The Court stated that "the constitutional prohibition against laws respecting an establishment of religion must at least mean that in this country, it is no part of the business of government to compose official prayers for any group of the American people to recite as a part of a religious program carried on by government" (*Engel v. Vitale* 1962; Alexander and Alexander 1984).

In a companion case, the Supreme Court ruled in 1963 that laws in Pennsylvania and Maryland requiring daily school prayer and Bible reading were unconstitutional, even though students had the right to leave the classroom if they did not want to participate. The ruling in this case suggested that the use of the Bible in objective, secular teaching of history would not be considered unconstitutional (Alexander and Alexander 1984).

Other cases have dealt with variations of school-sanctioned prayers and religious readings. In 1985, the U.S. Supreme Court issued its first ruling on a period of silent prayer or meditation. The case, *Wallace v. Jaffree* (1985) dealt with an Alabama law that called for a daily period of silent prayer or meditation. The Supreme Court upheld the ruling of the Eleventh Circuit Court of Appeals in that the law violated the Establishment Clause of the First Amendment (McCarthy and Cambron-McCabe 1987).

In other cases, courts have ruled similarly on issues related to school-led prayer and voluntary prayer or meditation. The U.S. Circuit Court of Appeals, 5th Circuit, ruled that a Louisiana law requiring students to observe a period of silent meditation or classroom prayer (or leave the room) violated the First Amendment. The U.S. Court of Appeals, 11th Circuit, issued a similar ruling in a case dealing with two Alabama statutes allowing for voluntary prayer (Deskbook Encyclopedia of American Law School 1985).

A recent case focused on prayers before a high-school football game. In this case, *Jager and Jager v. Douglas County School District and Douglas County Board of Education,* (1987), a high-school band member filed suit requesting that the pregame invocations be disallowed. On February 27, 1987, the federal court issued an ambiguous opinion that found in favor of the plaintiffs regarding clergy giving the pregame invocation. The court, however, left the door open for someone rather than clergy to give a pregame motivational, inspirational speech. Other cases dealing with invocations before school activities have resulted in diverse opinions. Currently, there is no uniformly accepted decision regarding this issue (Walden 1987).

Exclusions/Exemptions for Religious Reasons. Several issues regarding students being excluded or exempted from various activities for religious reasons have found their way to the courts. These include released time for religious instruction, participation in patriotic observances, and full participation in the secular curriculum.

Released Time. A practice routinely found in schools until the 1960s was released time for religious activities. Students were allowed to voluntarily attend various religious activities during the school day. The first court case that dealt a blow to this practice was *McCollum v. Board of Education* in 1948. In this case, the court ruled that the practice of allowing students released time to attend religious instruction by Protestant, Catholic, or Jewish instructors violated the First Amendment establishment of separation of church and state (Alexander and Alexander 1984).

Other courts have ruled that schools can release students during the school day to receive instruction away from the school grounds. However, in one case, *Lanner v. Wimmer,* the 10th Circuit Court of Appeals ruled that such instruction in off-campus courses could not result in earning school credits for graduation (Alexander and Alexander 1984). Releasing students during the school day for religious activities, as long as these activities occur off school grounds, has therefore been ruled constitutional as long as the attendance at such activities is voluntary and students do not receive official school credits.

Exemption for Patriotic Activities. The courts have had to deal with several instances when parents contended that participation in various patriotic activities was against their religion. In the landmark 1943 case,

■ *Course content and teaching materials have received a great deal of attention in the courts.*

West Virginia State Board of Education v. Barnette, the U.S. Supreme Court ruled that children could not be required to salute the American flag if it violated their religious beliefs. In its opinion, the Court noted that refusal to salute the flag does not preclude other children from performing the action, nor is it disruptive. Other courts have applied the *Barnette* decision and allowed students to silently protest by remaining in their seats during the flag-saluting ceremony (McCarthy and Cambron-McCabe 1987).

Secular Curriculum and Religion. Some parents have contested various courses and course materials for their children on religious grounds. In a 1974 U.S. district court case in New Hampshire (*Davis v. Paige*) parents requested the exclusion of their children from a health course and music course for religious reasons. The court ruled that the parents did not show how participation in the two courses violated their religious freedoms; the court also ruled that the school had a vested interest to provide what it considered to be an appropriate educational curriculum (Deskbook Encyclopedia of American Law School 1985).

Parents often have been successful in getting their children exempted from certain courses, such as sex education and ROTC, and from specific class assignments in certain courses when alternative activities can meet the course requirements. In these situations where the courts found in favor of parents, the secular activities have not been altered, nor have schools been required to implement activities or procedures to prevent embarrassment of students who do not participate (McCarthy and Cambron-McCabe 1987).

Course content and teaching materials have received a great deal of attention in the courts. Probably the one topic that has attracted the most interest is creation-science. With the era of school reform and with an increase in the conservative influence on schools came demands from certain religious groups that the biblical description of creation be taught in schools. These groups wanted equal instructional time for creation-science and evolution. In 1982, the Louisiana legislature passed the Balanced Treatment for Creation-Science and Evolution-Science Act. In addition to requiring schools to teach creation-science when evolution was taught, the law "required the development of curriculum guides and the provision of research services for teaching creationism, limited the membership on a panel providing research services for science teachers to 'creation scientists,' and prohibited school boards from discriminating against anyone who 'chooses to be a creation scientist' or chooses to teach creation science" (Flygare 1987, p. 77–78). A group of teachers, parents, religious leaders, and school officials filed suit stating that the law violated the First Amendment to the Constitution. The federal district court and Fifth Circuit Court of Appeals ruled in favor of the plaintiffs. On June 19, 1987, the Supreme Court upheld the lower courts' decisions by a 7–2 vote (*Edwards v. Aguillard*, 1987).

HIGHLIGHT

·

SCIENTISTS, CREATIONISTS EACH CLAIM VICTORY IN TEXAS EVOLUTION VOTE

Robert Rothman

The Texas Board of Education last week adopted a controversial rule that would, for the first time, require publishers to include discussions of evolution in biology textbooks.

But in a move that pleased supporters of creationism, the board also amended the guidelines to mandate instruction in other "reliable" theories as well.

"We're very happy with what the board did," said Mel Gabler, a long-time anti-evolution textbook critic and activist.

"If it is observed," he said of the rule, "we'll see an entirely different type of teaching of evolution. For every argument for it, there will be an argument counter to

continued

the theory. That has been censored from students for a long time."

Eugenie C. Scott, executive director of the National Center for Science Education Inc., a California-based group that defends the teaching of evolution, said the board's action sends a "confused" signal to publishers, particularly in light of a recent policy on the subject adopted in California.

In January, the California Board of Education issued a policy statement urging teachers to reject "dogma" and restrict their teaching to "observable facts and testable hypotheses."

"Publishers are going to be confused," Ms. Scott said. "Here are the two biggest markets in the country. California is standing up strongly for scientific integrity. Texas takes one and a half steps forward and one step back."

The new guidelines are part of a proclamation the Texas Education Agency will send to publishers to solicit bids for textbooks for the 1991–92 school year.

The proclamation lists numerous topics, instuctional strategies, and materials that must be included if the books are to be adopted.

Publishers are expected to pay close attention to the guidelines, because Texas is the largest bulk purchaser of biology textbooks in the country. Although California buys more books, that state does not adopt high-school texts statewide.

As submitted to the board last month by the state's commissioner of education, William N. Kirby, the proclamation listed evolution as one of the topics that must be included in texts.

At the time, Texas Education Agency officials said the guidelines were aimed at bringing textbooks in line with classroom instruction, which has for years called for the teaching of evolution.

Science and civil-liberties groups hailed the move, saying it would send a stronger signal to publishers than the previous proclamation, which has resulted, critics say, in a watered-down treatment of the subject.

'Beyond Neutral'

But the proposal also provoked an outcry among some fundamentalist Christian groups, who contend that evolution is an unproven theory that conflicts with the biblical account of the creation of the earth. Those groups vowed to appeal to the board to either strike the evolution requirement or mandate "equal treatment" for creationism.

The groups launched a letter-writing campaign to urge board members to modify the guidelines.

"We asked our friends to contact board members and let them know how the public felt," Mr. Gabler said. "We were amazed by the volume of mail" the appeal generated.

At a meeting on March 10, a board committee charged with overseeing the regulations amended the guidelines. In addition to requiring instruction in evolution, the revised rules stated that textbooks should also include "reliable scientific theories to the contrary."

"Obviously, that caused us tremendous discomfort," said Michael Hudson, director of the Texas chapter of People for the American Way, a civil-liberties organization. "That goes beyond neutral."

The committee also agreed to require books to include content to develop skills in "examining alternative scientific evidence to test, modify, or refute" the thoey of evolution.

Both Sides Claim Victory

The following day, however, after lobbying by scientists and civil libertarians, the full board agreed to modify the revisions.

By a vote of 12 to 3, the board rejected the requirement to include content on evidence contrary to evolution, and instead specified that texts could include such information if there is any.

In addition, the board agreed to require materials to develop skills in examining evidence to "verify or refute" all theories, including the theory of evolution.

Mr. Hudson said the board's actions were a victory for science.

"We got 99 percent of the way back to a totally strong statement that evolution has to be included in textbooks," he argued.

continued

"The message to publishers is to stick to science and science only."

But Mr. Gabler, the evolution critic, also claimed victory. He conceded, however, that the board did not mandate the teaching of creationism.

"Teachers don't have to bring creationism into science class," he pointed out. "This is not a matter of teaching science or religion."

"The new proclamation," he predicted, "Will result in more honest and accurate science. Many scientific ideas have been kept away from students. We want students to have a well-rounded education."

Mr. Gabler added that he would continue to monitor the textbooks submitted for adoption to make sure they adhere to the guidelines.

"If publishers are willing to do so, they can give a fair presentation of evolution," he said.

Mr. Hudson predicted that the adoption process would reignite the "political battle" fought at the board meeting last week. "That will be a battle in which vigilance is going to be necessary," he said.

Reprinted with permission from *Education Week*, vol. VIII, no. 26, p. 1.

Sex education has been another curricular area frequently attacked on religious grounds. In most instances, the courts have ruled in favor of schools providing sex education, citing the fact that schools are promoting the health and welfare of the students and society through the course content (McCarthy and Cambron-McCabe 1987).

Religion and Public Education: Conclusions

During the past two decades the courts have been extensively involved in cases dealing with religion and public education. In most instances, state and federal courts at all levels have upheld the separation of church and state requirement and have extensively utilized the Establishment Clause of the First Amendment as reason to keep religion out of the public schools. Citing both the Supreme Court's decision in the Louisiana Balanced Treatment Law in 1987, and a previous Supreme Court ruling in 1985 declaring as unconstitutional an Alabama law requiring a minute of silence for meditation or prayer, Morris (1987) stated that "states will have a most difficult task winning Supreme Court approval for putting religion into public school classrooms" (p. 1). Although the attitudes of the courts do change over time, the trend continues toward strict interpretation of the First and Fourteenth Amendments as they relate to religion and public education.

STUDENTS' RIGHTS

An area that has been litigated extensively is students' rights, especially students' rights related to noninstructional activities. Areas such as freedom of expression, physical appearance, extracurricular activities, right to education, and issues related to disciplinary actions have all been dealt with through the legal system.

Freedom of Expression

Freedom of expression is a basic right guaranteed by the First Amendment of the U.S. Constitution. Prior to the antiwar movement in the 1960s and 1970s, it was generally accepted that schools could restrict the freedom of expression of students (Sorenson 1989). Students were required to adhere to strict dress codes, participate in group activities, and, in general, keep their opinions private. However, since the middle of this century, the Supreme Court has taken the position that students do not give up their First Amendment rights just because of their student status. The result has been an abundance of cases that upheld the freedom of expression rights of students.

Freedom of Speech. The landmark case dealing with freedom of expression was *Tinker v. Des Moines Independent School District*. In this 1969 case, the Supreme Court ruled that students in schools and out of schools are citizens who have the protection of the U.S. Constitution. The case involved three students who were suspended for wearing black arm bands to symbolize protesting the Vietnam War. In its decision, the Court included the same statements previously included in an appellate court's decision, "that a student may express opinions on controversial issues in the classroom, cafeteria, playing field, or any other place, as long as the exercise of such rights does not materially and substantially interfere with the requirements of appropriate discipline in the operation of the school or collide with the rights of others" (McCarthy and Cambron-McCabe 1987, p. 113; *Burnside v. Byars, 1966*).

The *Tinker* case did not grant students the right to say or do anything. Indeed, when schools can show that various student activities are disruptive, they can prohibit such actions. Insignias, buttons, or other methods of expression that express inflammatory messages can be prohibited by school authorities. Likewise, student sit-ins and walkouts can be disruptive and are therefore considered grounds for student disciplinary actions (*Tate v. Board of Education*, 1972; Alexander and Alexander 1984). In one Indiana case, a federal district court upheld the suspensions of several high-school students who were handing out leaflets that encouraged a student walkout (*Dodd v. Rambis*, 1981; McCarthy and Cambron-McCabe 1987).

Freedom of expression does not apply to defamatory, inflammatory, or obscene and vulgar expression (McCarthy and Cambron-McCabe 1987). In *Bethel School District No. 403 v. Fraser*, the U.S. Supreme Court overturned the lower court's decision and upheld the disciplinary action of a local school district that was imposed on a student who used sexual innuendos during a nominating speech for a friend (Flygare 1986b).

In summary: (1) schools can make and enforce reasonable rules even if these could encroach on freedom of expression; (2) armbands, buttons, and other symbolic expressions are protected by the Constitution as long as they are not inflammatory; (3) a reduction of students' rights must be reasonable and focus on the accomplishment of an educational objective; and (4) denying rights must be based on an objective prediction of disruptions.

Physical Appearance

The right of students to dress and groom themselves as they wish also has been frequently litigated. This is considered freedom of expression by some and simply a personal preference issue by others. Miniskirts, long hair, and clothing with obscene expressions have been involved in some of these cases. In trying to implement the general principle of controlling student conduct with reasonable policies, many schools have attempted to regulate students' physical appearance. "It has been said that it is in the interest of the school to divert the student's attention from the hemline to the blackboard, or from beards to books" (Alexander and Alexander 1984, p. 82).

Students' Clothing. There have been many attempts to regulate the clothing worn by students. Dress codes in some schools have included:

- girls cannot wear slacks;
- boys must wear socks;
- the hemlines of girls' dresses must fall below the knee;
- tie-dyed clothing is prohibited;
- clothing with various slogans or pictures cannot be worn.

For the most part, the courts have upheld the rights of students to wear whatever clothing they want as long as the clothing did not create a distraction. These rulings have been based on the Fourteenth Amendment. Schools wishing to implement dress codes must ensure that the purpose of restricting various clothing is to prevent disruptions of or distractions from the educational program.

Hairstyles. The Fourteenth Amendment as well as the First and Fourth Amendments have been used to uphold students' rights to wear their hair in various fashions. To this point, the U.S. Supreme Court has refused to hear appeals of cases dealing with hairstyles; decisions rendered by the appellate courts have been inconsistent. Courts in the first, fourth, seventh, and eighth circuits have ruled in favor of students, while courts in the third, fifth, sixth, ninth, and tenth circuits have favored the rights of schools to implement hairstyle policies. Although cases focusing on hairstyles have declined significantly during the past several years, there is still potential for such cases because there is no Supreme Court precedent with nationwide jurisdiction (Bartlett 1986).

Extracurricular Activities

Participation in extracurricular activities frequently has been dealt with in the courts. While the courts consistently have ruled that students cannot be denied access to schools without due process, students' rights to access extracurricular activities have been less clear. In general, the courts have upheld the criteria designated by schools as prerequisites for initial participation in extracurricular activities, as long as these requirements can be applied fairly and are related to the activity. For example, skill requirements for athletic teams and musical proficiency for bands and choruses have been upheld unless those requirements have been unfairly applied. The courts have been less consistent in dealing with suspensions from extracurricular activities (McCarthy and Cambron-McCabe 1987).

Tied to the recent educational reform movement has been the implementation in several states of academic prerequisites for participation in extracurricular activities. The so-called no pass, no play rule in Texas is an example. The Texas legislature passed a law stating that students must maintain a 70 percent average in all classes in order to retain eligibility for participation in extracurricular activities. This rule was challenged in *Spring Branch Independent School Dist., v. Stamos* in 1985. The Texas Supreme Court upheld the law, stating that it was related to the state's objective to provide a quality educational program to all students. A similar law in West Virginia also was upheld in a West Virginia Supreme Court decision in 1985 (McCarthy and Cambron-McCabe 1987).

In other factors related to extracurricular activities, the courts generally have upheld the schools' rights to require prerequisites for participation in extracurricular activities, such as: attendance at practice, participation in training, residency parameters, and age restrictions. The right of schools to charge fees to students who wish to participate in extracurricular activities has not been uniformly upheld by the courts; future challenges to this practice probably will be decided on a case-by-case basis, dependent on state law (McCarthy and Cambron-McCabe 1987).

Right to Education

The right for students to participate in the American educational system has been unquestioned for most children. Indeed, mandatory attendance laws require children of certain ages to attend schools; there is no choice. However, for children with disabilities and other health-related problems, as well as for those from minority populations, equal access to public education has not always been the case. Prior to the passage of Public Law 94–142 in 1975, schools frequently discriminated against students with disabilities and disallowed their admission into public schools. Public Law 94–142, however, along with landmark court decisions, gave disabled students the right to public education (Smith, Price, and Marsh 1986).

Students with Disabilities. The first landmark court case focusing on the right to education for students with disabilities was *PARC v. Pennsylvania* in 1971. This case, brought by the parents of children with mental retardation, resulted in a consent decree that made public educational services available to children in Pennsylvania with mental retardation. The *Mills v. Board of Education, Washington, D.C.* (1973) case expanded the *PARC* decision to all school-age children with disabilities (Smith et al. 1986).

Students with AIDS. The right to education for children with disabilities has been established for several years. A new group of children who are now fighting for their rights to public school programs are children with Acquired Immune Deficiency Syndrome (AIDS). Since AIDS is a relatively new medical problem, case law on children with AIDS and their access to school is very limited. A recent case dealing with an AIDS-afflicted child in a school setting was *District 27 Community School Board v. The Board of Education of the City of New York*, 130 Misc. 2d 398, 502 N.Y.S. 2d 325 (Sup. 1986). In this case, the judge ruled that a child could not be considered handicapped and therefore eligible for services under Public Law 94–142 simply because of a diagnosis of AIDS. The court, however, ruled that the child could be considered handicapped and therefore protected under Section 504 of the Rehabilitation Act of 1973. Since Section 504 provides many of the same protections and required services that are included in P.L. 94–142, specialized services in public schools are required (Whitley 1987).

The entire issue of the educational rights of children with AIDS is unresolved. A recent Supreme Court decision dealing with the rights of persons with contagious diseases apparently will have a major impact on children with AIDS. In the case, *Arline v. School Bd. of Nassau County*, a teacher was dismissed because she had tuberculosis. Although the federal district court upheld the termination, the U.S. Court of Appeals, 11th Circuit, upheld Arline's appeal and stated that her condition entitled her to the equal employment provisions guaranteed by Section 504. The school board's appeal to the U.S. Supreme Court resulted in a 7–2 decision on March 3, 1987, that upheld the appellate court's decision. Although it did not specifically deal with the AIDS issue, the *Arline* case has set a precedent that contagious diseases can result in a person's protection under Section 504 (Flygare 1987b).

With the expected rapid expansion in the number of AIDS patients, the number of court cases dealing with AIDS victims will dramatically increase. In the future, the courts will have to deal with several legal considerations. These include the Education of the Handicapped Children Act, Public Law 94–142, Section 504 of the Rehabilitation Act of

■ Brown v. Board of Education *set the stage for the desegregation of public schools.*

1973, the Fourteenth Amendment to the Constitution, and the issue of confidentiality (Whitley 1987).

Civil Rights Issues. Another area of case law that has been developed relating to the right of education includes discrimination on the basis of race and the resulting desegregation/integration litigation. The landmark court decision related to the desegregation of public schools was *Brown v. Board of Education, Topeka* in 1954. This case resulted in the tearing down of the dual system of public education based on race in this country. Prior to the *Brown* case, school districts provided educational opportunities to children of different races based on the principle of *separate but equal.* The most important case that formed the basis of the separate-but-equal public education system was *Plessy v. Ferguson,* in 1896. In this case, the Supreme Court ruled that separate facilties and services, as long as they were equal in nature, were constitutional. Although *Plessy* dealt with transportation, not public education, the principle of separate but equal was applied to public schools until the *Brown* decision.

The *Brown* case was first heard on December 9, 1952. It was reargued a year later on December 9, 1953, and a final decision was rendered in 1954 which nullified the separate-but-equal doctrine. In its decision, the Court said that, in regard to public schools, separate is "inherently inequal" and that the lower courts should act "with all deliberate speed" to desegregate public schools.

"Deliberate speed" turned out to encompass many years. Several legal efforts were made to circumvent the *Brown* decision, including closing public schools and providing vouchers for parents of white children. This practice was found to be unconstitutional in *Griffin v. County School Board of Prince Edward County* (1964). Another legal maneuver to avoid desegregation was implementing a so-called freedom-of-choice plan whereby students could choose which school they wanted to attend. The Supreme Court ruled on freedom-of-choice plans in the *Green v. County School Board of New Kent County* (1968) case. The ruling was that if freedom-of-choice plans actually led to desegregated schools, then they were constitutional; if they maintained segregation, then they were unconstitutional (Alexander and Alexander 1984).

One of the most important court cases after the *Brown* case that dealt with school desegregation was the *Swann v. Charlotte–Mecklenburg Board of Education* case in 1971. In this case, the Supreme Court ruled on four important points:

1. Using a strict mathematical ratio system to determine the number of white and black students in an entire district was not the intent of the court;
2. One-race schools can exist as long as the district can prove that the assignment of pupils is nondiscriminatory;
3. Neighborhood schools should be abolished in order to reverse *de jure* segregation.
4. Bussing should be considered as a major tool with which to desegregate schools.

Probably the most remembered aspect of the *Swann* case is the acknowledgement by the Court that bussing is a legitimate method to effect desegregation. This particular ruling has been challenged ever since its publication; even today proponents of neighborhood schools argue against bussing. Many other court cases have dealt with *de jure* (legitimate, or by law) and *de facto* (in deed, or by simple existence) segregation. Table 5.2 summarizes some of these cases.

TABLE 5.2
Cases Dealing with *De Jure* and *De Facto* Segregation

CASE	DESCRIPTION
Bell v. School City of Gary	▪ U.S. Seventh Circuit of Appeals ▪ Ruled that there is no constitutional requirement to alter legitimate *de facto* segregation caused by population shifts.
Milliken v. Bradley	▪ Supreme Court reversed lower court's decision. ▪ Stated that Detroit had not explicitly or implicitly done anything that resulted in *de facto* segregation. ▪ No action to desegregate required.
Columbus Board of Education v. Pencik and *Dayton Board of Ed. v. Brinkman*	▪ Supreme Court held that discriminatory acts by the school districts in Columbus and Dayton had resulted in *de jure* segregation. ▪ Required a dismantling of the segregated systems.
Crawford v. Board of Education	▪ California Supreme Court ruled that state school boards had an obligation to take steps to alleviate segregated schools, regardless of *de jure* or *de facto*.
Hoots v. Commonwealth of Pennsylvania	▪ Federal district court ruled that plans to create school districts would result in *de jure* segregation.

Source: Alexander and Alexander, 1984.

Disciplinary Issues

Many disciplinary issues have found their way to the court system. These include search and seizure, corporal punishment, and expulsions and suspension.

Search and Seizure. Search and seizure in public schools has long been a problem for school officials and law enforcement officers. The major reason is the interpretation of the Fourth Amendment in school settings. Rulings on search and seizure from lower courts have added to the confusion. What might be proper in one district might be considered unconstitutional in a nearby district. What is considered legally proper at one time might be considered a violation of student rights at a later period. The Supreme Court decision in *New Jersey v. T.L.O.* added some clarity (Rossow 1989).

New Jersey v. T.L.O. (1985). In this case, a fourteen-year-old girl, T.L.O., was caught smoking in the bathroom. She denied that she smoked, and the principal required her to empty the contents of her purse. During this search, a package of cigarettes and some rolling papers were found. Suspecting the papers were for marijuana, the principal carried out a more extensive search of the purse, and found evidence that indicated T.L.O was possibly selling marijuana (van Geel 1986). T.L.O moved to suppress the evidence found in her purse on the grounds that school officials violated her Fourth Amendment rights by conducting an illegal search. New Jersey argued that the Fourth Amendment did not apply because school officials were standing *in loco parentis* (Rossow 1989).

The U.S. Supreme Court ruled that the Fourth Amendment protections do apply to students in schools. While requiring schools to abide by the Fourteenth Amendment, the Court did say that school officials should not have to meet the probable-cause requirement of the Fourteenth Amendment, but should be able to conduct searches if reasonable suspicion is present (Zirkel and MacMurrie 1988).

In determining if the reasonableness standard is met, schools should be able to (1) justify the search at its beginning and (2) justify the scope of the search based on the student's age, sex, and the nature of the infraction. If schools could meet this two-part standard for reasonableness, then Fourteenth Amendment protections are considered to have been afforded.

Although the T.L.O. case gave schools some flexibility in conducting searches, the ruling did not set the precedent for unwarranted actions. In a related case, students filed suit asking the court to block the testing of urine samples by the Carlstadt-East Rutherford, New Jersey Regional Board of Education. The board had adopted a policy requiring all students to undergo physical exams, with the expressed intent of detecting any physical defects, illnesses, or communicable diseases. Part of the physical required a urine sample which was to be tested for the presence of various substances. The plaintiffs contended that the drug testing was an unreasonable search of their bodies and that school statistics revealed only a small number of students with drug problems. The court ruled in favor of the students, saying that the drug testing was a search that was not supported by reasonable suspicion (Flygare 1986).

Lockers and Other Property. Although the Supreme Court has ruled that school officials must provide protections afforded in the Fourth Amendment during school searches, most decisions regarding locker searches conclude that lockers are school property. While not allowed carte blanche, school officials can conduct locker searches as long as there is reasonable suspicion that the contents would reveal violations of law or school regulations (McCarthy and Cambron-McCabe 1987).

Several examples support the notion that lockers are school property. In a case heard by the Kansas Supreme Court (*State v. Stein* 1969), it was held that schools have the inherent authority to manage schools, which includes determining if lockers are being used for illegal purposes. In another case, the Tenth Circuit Court of Appeals ruled that schools have the duty to ensure that school property is not being used unlawfully (*Zamora v. Pomeroy*, 1981). The rulings in these cases agree that school personnel have both a responsibility and a legal right to inspect school property to ensure that unlawful or illicit activities are not being carried out by students (McCarthy and Cambron-McCabe 1987).

Personal Searches. Personal searches differ in several ways from searching lockers and other personal property. The Fifth Circuit Court of Appeals stated that "the fourth amendment applies with its fullest vigor against any intrusion on the human body" (*Horton v. Goose Creek Independent School Dist.* 1982; McCarthy and Cambron-McCabe 1987). Therefore, school personnel must be very cautious in personal searches. To ensure the legality of personal searches, school officials should go beyond the required reasonable-suspicion requirement for personal property searches and should make sure that probable cause exists. Common sense is a good rule for school personnel to follow. If a student is suspected of having a weapon that could in turn be used to harm someone, a personal search would be warranted. On the other hand, if a teacher thinks a student possesses marijuana simply because the student "looks like he has been smoking," a personal search is probably not a good idea.

Corporal Punishment. For many years, corporal punishment has been an accepted method of disciplining students in schools. Although corporal punishment still is being used in some schools, its use has declined steadily during the past several decades. The author of this textbook does not advocate corporal punishment as a disciplinary method. If teachers and administrators use corporal punishment, they must ensure that it is moderately administered with a proper instrument, and that the child's age, sex, size, and overall physical strength are taken into consideration. Excessive physical punishment will not be tolerated by the courts or by most parents (Alexander and Alexander 1984).

Corporal punishment in the schools is extremely controversial and has been extensively litigated. In most cases, the courts have assumed that corporal punishment has been administered reasonably by teachers and administrators; the burden to show malice and excessiveness generally has been on the parents (McCarthy and Cambron-McCabe 1987).

The U.S. Supreme Court has been involved in a limited number of cases on corporal punishment. In 1975 the Court let stand a lower court's decision that corporal punishment did not constitute "cruel and unusual punishment" from which citizens are protected under the Eighth Amendment and that schools did not have to obtain parental permission before administering corporal punishment (*Baker v. Owen* 1975). In a 1977 case, *Ingraham v. Wright*, the court majority ruled that corporal punishment in schools does not violate the Eighth Amendment nor the Fourteenth Amendment's guarantee of procedural due process. The

Court stated that litigation dealing with corporal punishment should be handled at the state level (McCarthy and Cambron-McCabe 1987).

Although federal courts have ruled that corporal punishment is not unconstitutional, several states have laws and policies regarding the use of corporal punishment. Additionally, most local school districts have written policies regarding the use of corporal punishment. Frequently this includes the mandatory presence of a witness and the completion of written reports following the administration of corporal punishment.

Expulsions and Suspensions. Another area frequently litigated and related to disciplinary actions is that of expulsions and suspensions. One disciplinary method schools and school districts have is the power to suspend and/or expel students from school. In using this power, schools must ensure that the due-process rights of students are not violated. "Failure to follow due process requirements can lead to reversals of the suspensions or expulsions, expunction of records or proceedings from student files, lawsuits seeking damages against the school and its board, and lawsuits against the board members individually" (Deskbook Encyclopedia of American Law School 1985, p. 342).

Expulsion. Expulsion occurs when students are barred from attending school for an extended period of time. Although the amount of time for which a student is expelled will vary from case to case and district to district, a frequent minimal expulsion is ten days. Most states and local districts have established policies for expulsion. It should be noted that infractions resulting in expulsion need not occur during school hours in the school building. They can occur before or after school on school grounds, during any school activity, or while students are involved in a school-sponsored extracurricular activity (McCarthy and Cambron-McCabe 1987). Students can be expelled for a variety of reasons. Table 5.3 includes a list of some typical behaviors that often result in expulsion.

Several cases have upheld the rights of schools to expel students as long as due process has been afforded. Due process means that individuals are treated fairly and have a right to contest various actions by governmental units. Due process is afforded an individual when the governmental unit taking actions against that person

- gives the person time to prepare a defense,
- gives the person the opportunity to confront individuals making accusations,
- gives the person the opportunity to challenge testimony or evidence that has been presented against him/her, and
- enables the person to present a defense.

TABLE 5.3
Behaviors Frequently Resulting in Expulsion

- Using—or encouraging others to use—violence, force, noise, coercion, or any other comparable conduct that interferes with school purposes
- Stealing or vandalizing valuable school or private property or repeatedly damaging or stealing school or private property of small value
- Causing or attempting to cause physical injury to a school employee or student
- Possessing a weapon
- Knowingly possessing, using, or transmitting intoxicants of any kind (with the exception of prescriptions from authorized physicians)
- Repeatedly failing to comply with reasonable directives of school personnel
- Engaging in criminal activity or other behavior forbidden by the law or state

Source: McCarthy and Cambron-McCabe, 1987.

Recently, questions have been raised concerning the rights of schools to expel students with disabilities. Although Public Law 94–142, Education for Handicapped Children Act of 1975, does not address expulsions, it does require schools to provide appropriate educational programs for students with disabilities. In an important case dealing with this issue (*S–l v. Turlington*, 1981), a group of parents of mentally retarded students who had been expelled from school for a variety of reasons filed suit stating that the school had to provide educational services to the students as a result of P.L. 94–142. The Fifth Circuit Court of Appeals upheld the lower court's ruling that the students' expulsions constituted a change of placement. In order to change the placement of a student in special education, a committee must convene and make the determination that a change of placement is required in order to provide appropriate educational services (Podemski, Price, Smith, and Marsh 1984).

Suspension. Suspensions include removing students from school activities for a short period of time and usually are imposed when the student's infraction does not merit expulsion. Prior to a 1975 ruling by the Supreme Court in a case that dealt with suspensions, there was little consistency in the courts on this matter. In the 1975 case, *Goss v. Lopez*, the court ruled that, even for short-term suspension, certain due-process rights had to be afforded students. While not specifically addressing short-term, one-period suspension, the court's decision implied that, even for suspension for this brief time period, due process must be afforded students. Specific protections that must be afforded students prior to suspensions include (McCarthy and Cambron-McCabe 1987, p. 209).

- oral or written notification of the nature of the violation and the intended punishment;

- an opportunity to refute the charges before an objective decision maker (such a discussion may immediately follow the alleged rule infraction); and
- an explanation of the evidence upon which the disciplinarian is relying.

Students' Rights: Conclusions

Students in public schools have the same protections as other citizens related to freedom of expression, including freedom of speech and freedoms associated with dress and grooming standards. The only time these guarantees are restricted is when they interfere with the ability of the school to carry out its mission of educating children. Therefore, when the exercise of these freedoms proves disruptive or inflammatory, schools have the legal authority to restrict certain behaviors.

Students also have a right to an education. Although the courts have ruled that the right to an education is not guaranteed by the U.S. Constitution, students are protected under the Equal Protection Clause of the Fourteenth Amendment. Therefore, if public education is made available for some students, it must be made available for all students, regardless of race or disability. Additionally, students have the right to be treated fairly regarding participation in extracurricular activities and disciplinary procedures used by the schools. The courts have ruled, however, that schools have the right to restrict participation in some extracurricular activities and they have the right to implement certain types of disciplinary actions as long as due process is afforded.

TEACHERS' LEGAL RIGHTS

Teachers, just as students, have a variety of legal rights they can rely on to ensure their fair treatment. Specific areas where legal precedents have been established regarding teachers include substantive constitutional rights, employment considerations, and collective bargaining.

Substantive Constitutional Rights

Teachers, like all citizens in this country, are entitled to certain rights and freedoms under the U.S. Constitution. These include the right to freedom of expression (including personal appearance), and academic freedom.

Freedom of Expression. Just as students have a right to freedom of expression, so do teachers. An important case affirming this right was *Pickering v. Board of Education* (1968). In this case, a teacher sent to a local newspaper a letter which criticized the school board and superintendent. As a result, the teacher was dismissed. The U.S. Supreme Court ruled in the case that teachers have constitutional rights that must be protected. In its ruling, the Court concluded that a balance of interests must be established between the right of the state to provide an orderly educational system and the right of free expression by teachers. The Court ruled in favor of the teacher's reinstatement (Alexander and Alexander 1984).

The ruling of a later Supreme Court case, *Connick v. Myers* (1983), reaffirmed the *Pickering* decision, but said that the public employee's speech was protected by the First Amendment only as long as it was a "matter of public concern." Therefore, while *Connick* did not specifically deal with teachers, the ruling affects teachers and all other public employees. Just a few years after the *Connick* decision, the Supreme Court ruled in the *Bethel School District No. 403 v. Fraser* (1986) case. In this case (previously discussed relative to freedom of speech for students), the Court ruled that schools could restrict speech which was vulgar or lewd. Although it has been suggested that this decision should be interpreted very narrowly, the ruling could give schools significant latitude in determining what free speech is appropriate and what is inappropriate (Sorenson 1989).

A recent Texas case appears to suggest the continued erosion of teachers' First Amendment rights. In this case, *Day v. South Park Independent School District* (1985), a teacher filed suit after she was terminated for challenging the content of her teaching evaluation. Although the teacher followed the grievance procedures established by the local board of education, the federal district court and the Fifth Court of Appeals ruled that her First Amendment rights had not been violated because her concerns dealt with a private matter—the contents of her evaluation—not a matter of public interest. The district court's decision even stated that the teacher's contract "would have been renewed had she not initiated the grievance procedure." (Flygare 1986c, p. 397) This case will likely "disturb many educators because it suggests that the federal courts will provide no remedy to a teacher who is fired because he or she followed a grievance procedure established by the school district" (Flygare 1986c, p. 397).

Teachers, like all citizens, enjoy the protection of the First Amendment for freedom of speech. However, as depicted in the cases cited, the freedom of speech enjoyed by teachers is somewhat restricted when compared to other citizens' First Amendment rights. With the Supreme Court and other courts seemingly limiting the freedoms of speech of teachers during the past few years, it will be interesting to see if the trend continues or if a reversal in court attitudes occurs (Flygare 1987c).

Personal Appearance. School boards and administrators have established dress codes for teachers as well as for students. These codes frequently have been challenged as an infringement on freedom of expression. In a few cases, the courts have ruled school dress codes for

■ *School boards and administrators have established dress codes for teachers as well as students.*

teachers unconstitutional. In a ruling issued by a Mississippi federal district court in *Conard v. Goolsby* (1972), the court stated that rules and regulations dictating the personal appearance of adults must be closely monitored. In this case, "the court found no legitimate state interest to justify applying a school board's student grooming policy to teachers in the absence of evidence that a certain manner of grooming would disrupt the educational process." (McCarthy and Cambron-McCabe 1987, p. 295–296).

Although *Conard* is an example where the courts have considered personal appearance as an individual prerogative, the majority of rulings on this issue have supported the school districts. The one Supreme Court ruling having a major impact on teachers' personal appearance rights was in *Kelley v. Johnson* (1976). In this case, the Court ruled that a hair-grooming policy for policemen was constitutional. The decision differentiated between the rights of government employees and other citizens regarding personal freedoms. Other cases where the courts have upheld physical-appearance codes for teachers include *Domico v. Rapides Parish School Board* (1982), where the Fifth Circuit Court of Appeals supported the policy barring employees from wearing beards, and *East Hartford Educational Association v. Board of Education* (1977) where the Second Circuit Court of Appeals supported the school board's right to implement policies regulating the appearance of teachers (Alexander and Alexander 1984). In rulings supporting dress codes for teachers, the courts have acknowledged the importance of individual liberties, but consider these less important than the rights of schools and school boards to govern the appearance of their employees.

Academic Freedom. Most people think of academic freedom being related to higher education, not to public education in general. Some litigation has dealt with academic freedom and the teachers of public-school grades K–12. In general, the courts have not upheld for K–12 teachers the academic freedom principles commonly accepted in higher education. Since there is no uniform precedent on this issue, rulings vary considerably from case to case, and jurisdiction to jurisdiction. Most of the issues dealing with academic freedom and K–12 teachers focus on teachers' rights in their classrooms. Table 5.4 summarizes some of these cases.

TABLE 5.4
Litigation and Academic Freedom

AREA OF LITIGATION	RULINGS
Course Content	▪ Tenth Circuit Court of Appeals ruled that teachers do not have the unlimited rights to structure content of their courses and that the school board has the authority to define curriculum (*Adams v. Campbell County School District*)
	▪ Seventh Circuit Court of Appeals ruled that teachers do not have right to omit prescribed course content (*Palmer v. Board of Education of the City of Chicago*)
	▪ Eighth Circuit Court of Appeals ruled that teachers do not have right to disregard a superior's instructional directives relative to course content (*Ahern v. Board of Educ. of School Dist. of Grand Island*)
Teaching Strategies	▪ Teachers can use materials that they have not been instructed otherwise not to use (*Keefe v. Geanakos* and *Mailloux v. Kiley*)
	▪ Even if certain instructional strategies are relative to course content, if they lack general support of the profession they may be barred (*Mailloux v. Kiley*)
	▪ Fifth Circuit Court of Appeals ruled that a teacher could use simulation methods to teach about the civil war because they were related to the class objectives. Parents had complained that the methods incited racial problems (*Kingsville Independent School Dist. v. Cooper*)

Source: McCarthy and Cambron-McCabe, 1987.

Employment Considerations

Of major interest to teachers are issues surrounding their employment. These include discriminatory employment practices and termination policies. A great deal of litigation has focused on both of these areas.

Discriminatory Employment Practices. Prior to the 1960s, protections from discriminatory employment practices were limited. However, as a result of the civil rights movement, of the advocacy for persons with disabilities, and of efforts to ensure equal opportunities for women, many legal protections now exist relative to employment practices.

Most litigation dealing with discriminatory employment practices is based on the Fourteenth Amendment to the U.S. Constitution, which requires states to provide equal protection under the laws for all persons. Discrimination based on race, sex, age, or other personal characteristics cannot be justified because of the Equal Protection Clause. Although the laws are unambiguous regarding equal protection, there have been and still are countless numbers of cases filed based on discriminatory employment practices.

Racial Discrimination. Members of racial minorities have filed many cases claiming discriminatory employment practices. One common basis for these suits has been that test requirements for conditions of employment are discriminatory. In most of these cases, the rulings of the courts have been based on whether or not the test is related to the job and whether the test has been validated for the purpose for which it is being used.

Examples of cases dealing with the testing issue include a U.S. Supreme Court case in 1976, *Washington v. Davis,* in which the Court ruled that a written-skills test used as an entrance test for admission into a police training course was not discriminatory. The rationale for the decision was based on several considerations, including data that supported a positive relationship between test scores and training course performance. In a 1986 decision by the Fifth Circuit Court of Appeals (*United States v. Lulac*), the court upheld the use of a basic skills competency test as a prerequisite for admission into teacher education programs. The court ruled that the state presented substantial data supporting the validity of the test, and concluded that educating and certifying people who could not pass a basic skills test was not required of the state.

The courts have ruled that test requirements for employment are not legal in cases where employers could not show a relationship between the test and job requirements. In *Griggs v. Duke Power Co.* (1971), the Supreme Court ruled that a preemployment test required for employees was not related to job requirements and was therefore a violation of personal rights. In *Albemarle Paper Co. v. Moody* (1975), the

Supreme Court ruled that testing requirements used by a company for seniority purposes again failed to be related to the job and was therefore a violation of the Civil Rights Act (Alexander and Alexander 1984).

Testing employees for job screening purposes has been ruled in favor of both plaintiffs and defendants. The key in rulings appears to be whether the test is related to the job. The courts have referred to this as test validation. A recent case dealing with the employment of teachers using the National Teachers Exam (NTE) reinforces this rationale. In this case, *United States v. State of South Carolina*, the court ruled that the NTE could be used as part of teacher employment practices because the test reflected knowledge about teaching; it was therefore considered a valid test for determining teaching knowledge (Alexander and Alexander 1984).

Racial discrimination also has been claimed by individuals from minority racial groups who were qualified for a position but were not employed, and the position remained unfilled. Cases of this nature are called *prima facie* cases. If plaintiffs can show that they were not employed for any reason other than for their minority racial status, there is a strong likelihood that the courts will rule in their favor. In these situations, however, it is difficult for the courts to determine discrimination if the employer provides some legitimate reason the person was not employed.

Sex Discrimination. Although discrimination on the basis of sex has not been as extensively litigated as on the basis of race, the number of court cases dealing with this issue has increased dramatically during the past ten years. Prior to the 1970s, discrimination based on sex was actually an accepted aspect of our society. It is very difficult to prove discrimination based on sex using the Fourteenth Amendment as a basis. As a result, most cases dealing with sex discrimination rely on the Equal Pay Act of 1963, on Title VII of the Civil Rights Act of 1964, and on Title IX of the Education Amendments of 1972 (McCarthy and Cambron-McCabe 1987).

Just as in cases dealing with racial discrimination, sex discrimination cases are frequently ruled in favor of the plaintiffs if the employer cannot provide legitimate reasons for not hiring female applicants for "male" positions or male applicants for "female" positions. As long as an applicant is the most qualified, various reasons for rejecting her or his employment, including the requirement of physical skills, have not been supported by the courts.

Age Discrimination. One of the last groups in this country to turn to litigation to ensure their equal protection under the Constitution are older individuals. The "graying" of America has created a group of older individuals who have begun to exploit their political clout through such lobbying organizations as the American Association of Retired Persons (AARP), which allows membership at age fifty-five.

Passed in 1967, the Age Discrimination in Employment Act prohibits discrimination against individuals between the ages of forty and seventy years old on the basis of age. The act was intended to provide protections for older individuals still in the employment market who might be discriminated against by employers simply because of their age. Protections provided by the act focus on areas of hiring, compensation, terms and conditions of employment, privileges, retirement benefits, and demotions (Alexander and Alexander 1984).

Just as sexual discrimination is difficult to prove, it also is difficult to convince the courts that age is the reason for not being employed. In order to determine discrimination based on age, the plaintiff must meet the same criteria as must members of minority racial groups, that:

- the person belongs to a special minority group;
- the person applied for and was qualified for the position;
- the person was rejected in spite of his or her qualifications;
- the position remained open and the employer sought other applicants.

Once these criteria have been established by the plaintiff, the employer must then show legitimate reasons why the individual was not employed (Alexander and Alexander 1984).

Termination. When school districts make the decision to terminate the employment of teachers and other school personnel, they must take into consideration the protections provided individuals under the Fourteenth Amendment of the Constitution and they must afford due process to the employees. The landmark Supreme Court case in 1972, *Board of Regents v. Roth,* provided a basis for due-process claims by stating that a "legitimate claim of entitlement must exist before due process protections apply" (Hooker 1986, p. 1). In this case, a professor hired by the University of Wisconsin for a fixed one-year academic term was not rehired for a second year. The professor filed suit stating that his due-process rights had been violated. The court's ruling noted that due-process procedures were not required when terminating probationary teachers unless those teachers can demonstrate that the school deprived them of their liberty or property rights (Alexander and Alexander 1984).

The courts have held that, in cases where untenured teachers are terminated, the burden of proof rests with the teachers to show how their termination was unconstitutional, not on the school to show just cause for termination. If the plaintiff can show that the termination may have been due to an impermissible reason, then the school board must show permissible reason for the termination. This has been held in *Steward v. Bailey* (1975) and *Mount Healthy City Board of Education v. Doyle* (1977).

Dismissal of teachers who hold tenure presents very different legal issues. However, despite some opinions to the contrary, tenured teachers can be dismissed by school boards for a variety of reasons, and the dismissals likely will be sustained by the courts as long as procedural due process has been accorded the teacher. Minimum due-process procedures that should be followed when teachers are dismissed include (McCarthy and Cambron-McCabe 1987, p. 388)

- notification of charges,
- opportunity for a hearing,
- adequate time to prepare a rebuttal to the charges,
- access to evidence and names of witnesses,
- hearing before an impartial tribunal,
- representation by legal counsel,
- opportunity to present evidence and witnesses,
- opportunity to cross-examine adverse witnesses,
- decision based on evidence and findings of the hearing,
- transcript or record of the hearing, and
- opportunity to appeal an adverse decision.

These are minimal due-process procedures. If they wish, schools can add additional rights for teachers and other employees.

Tenured teachers can be dismissed when schools show just cause in the dismissal. Tenure laws originally were created to provide job security to good teachers who continue to perform satisfactorily. While tenure does not guarantee employment for teachers, it does require that schools use due-process procedures in terminating tenured teachers. A variety of reasons can support a termination for cause. These include incompetence, immorality, insubordination, unprofessional conduct, neglect of duty, unfitness to teach, and the need to reduce professional staff (McCarthy and Cambron-McCabe 1987). Table 5.5 summarizes these reasons for termination and provides examples of litigation related to the issue.

Collective Bargaining

Collective bargaining can be defined as "a provision for negotiating with a school board by which teachers are represented not as individuals but as a group. A union or a professional organization may be the bargaining agency" (Pulliam 1987, p. 287). Collective bargaining for teachers usually is accomplished through the two major, national teacher organizations—National Education Association (NEA) and

TABLE 5.5
Reasons for Terminating Teachers with Tenure and Supporting Litigation

REASON FOR TERMINATION	SUPPORTING LITIGATION
▪ Incompetence	▪ *Blunt v. Marion County School Board* (1975) ▪ *Frank v. St. Landry Parish School Board* (1969)
▪ Discipline Problems	▪ *Board of Directors of Sioux City v. Mroz* 1980) ▪ *Gwathmey v. Atkinson* (1976)
▪ Insubordination	▪ *Fernald v. City of Ellsworth* (1975) ▪ *Christopherson v. Spring Valley Elementary School* (1980)
▪ Immorality	▪ *Bethel Park School Dist. v. Krall* (1982)
▪ Heterosexual Conduct with Students	▪ *Weissman v. Board of Education of Jefferson City School District* (1976)
▪ Public Homosexual Acts	▪ *Sarac v. State Board of Education* (1967)
▪ Public Lewdness	▪ *Wishart v. McDonald* (1974)
▪ Criminal Conviction	▪ *Board of Education v. Calderon* (1973)
▪ Drug Abuse	▪ *Dominy v. Mays* (1979)

Source: Alexander and Alexander, 1984.

American Federation of Teachers (AFT). As previously stated, these two organizations currently have approximately two million members and therefore represent one of the largest labor groups in the United States. Compensation is the major area considered in collective bargaining agreements between teachers and school districts. However, teachers' organizations also negotiate a host of other areas, including grievance procedures, length of contracts, involvement in curricular decisions, student placement, teacher assignments, teacher retention, and staff development (Goldschmidt and Painter 1987–1988). Considered a very unprofessional activity just a few years ago, contract negotiation between teachers and school districts is now accepted as a legal right and personal prerogative of teachers.

The legal right of teachers and other public employees to organize and bargain collectively has not always been clearly established. In 1935, Congress passed the National Labor Relations Act, known as the Wagner Act, which gave employees the right to bargain collectively with employers. The Act also created the National Labor Relations Board to guarantee these rights for workers. The legal right for public employees to join and participate in unions did not exist until the Supreme Court ruled in 1967 that employees of public agencies could not be required to give up their right to join unions or to engage in other forms of free association (McCarthy and Cambron-McCabe 1987). This case, *Keyishian v. Board of Regents* (1967) paved the way for NEA and AFT to legally engage in collective bargaining on behalf of teachers.

Teachers' Rights: Conclusions

Teachers, just as students and other citizens, are guaranteed certain rights by the United States Constitution. Although the courts have always taken the personal liberties of teachers into consideration when determining freedom of speech and other individual rights issues, they frequently have cited the interest of the public as having priority over these individual liberties.

Teachers do have a host of legally protected rights, including the right to equal employment practices, the right to gain tenure, the right to fair and reasonable termination, the right to join and participate in teacher unions, and the right to various personal freedoms as long as the exercise of these freedoms does not infringe on the best interests of schools.

SUMMARY

This chapter has presented information regarding legal issues in education. The first part of the chapter focused on the legal basis for education, with a discussion of the U.S. Constitution and of the different ways states and local boards of education have legal authority over public education. The next section dealt with the complex issue of religion and public education. Areas addressed in the discussion included the constitutional basis for separation of church and state and various religious influences found in public schools. Influences discussed included prayer and schools, religion and the curriculum, and released time for students to participate in religious activities. In most instances the courts have strictly upheld the separation of church and state principle and have not allowed religious activities to occur in conjunction with public education.

The next section of the chapter focused on students' rights. Freedom of expression, physical appearance, extracurricular activities, and the right to educational services were discussed. In each of these areas, the U.S. Constitution provides personal guarantees to students, as long as those rights, when exercised, do not disrupt the educational setting. The broad area of discipline and students was also included in this section. When and how schools may search students and seize information and evidence were discussed, as well as corporal punishment, suspensions, and expulsion. In most instances, schools have the authority to exercise their control over students and the school environment as long as personal, constitutionally guaranteed freedoms are not infringed upon.

The final section of this chapter dealt with the rights of teachers in public schools. Conditions of employment were discussed, with an emphasis on equal employment practices and various discriminatory practices used by some school districts in employing teachers. Teachers' constitutional rights, such as freedom of expression and personal appearance, were also discussed. It was pointed out that teachers have these rights, but only to the extent to which they do not interfere with the overall needs and goals of the schools. During the past several years, the trend in the courts has been to erode some personal freedoms of teachers in favor of the public organization. The final section of the chapter focused on termination issues. The conclusion in this section was that due-process procedures do not necessarily apply to nontenured teachers. For teachers with tenure, schools must show just cause in termination procedures, and due process must be followed.

IN THE FIELD

1. Does the school or the school district have a written policy on corporal punishment? If so, describe the policy.

2. Does the school or the school district have a written policy on suspensions and expulsions? If so, what is the policy?

3. Has the school district experienced litigation dealing with students' or teachers' rights? If so, what was the outcome?

4. What is the school's policy on school prayer and Bible reading?

5. Does the local teachers' organization collectively bargain for salaries, curricular input, and/or noninstructional duties for teachers?

6. Does the school district have an attorney on its staff?

7. Does the district have any written guidelines on student conduct during off-campus extracurricular activities?

8. Are students required to meet certain criteria prior to participating in extracurricular activities? If so, describe the criteria.

REFERENCES

Adams v. Campbell County School Dist., 511 F.2d 1242, 1247 (10th Cir. 1975).
Ahern v. Board of Educ. of School Dist. of Grand Island, 456 F.2d 399 (8th Cir. 1972).
Albemarle Paper Co. v. Moody, 422 U.S. 405, 95 S.Ct. 2362, 45 L.Ed.2d 280 (1975).

Alexander, K., and M. D. Alexander. 1984. *The Law of Schools, Students, and Teachers*. St. Paul, MN: West.

Arline v. School Bd. of Nassau County, 772 F.2d 759 (11th Cir. 1985).

Bartlett, L. D. Hair and dress codes revisited. *West's Education Law Reporter*, September 4, 1986, 7–18.

Baker v. Owen, 395 F. Supp 294 (M.D.N.C. 1975).

Bell v. School City of Gary, 324 F.2d 209 (7th Cir. 1963).

Bethel Park School District v. Krall, 67 Pa.Cmwlth. 143, 445 A.2d 1377 (1982).

Bethel School District No. 403 v. Fraser, 478 U.S. 675, 106 S.Ct. 3159, 92 L.Ed.2d 549 (1986).

Blunt v. Marion County School Board, 515 F.2d 951 (5th Cir. 1975).

Board of Directors of Sioux City v. Mroz, 295 N.W.2d 447 (Iowa 1980).

Board of Education v. Calderon, 35 Cal.App.3d 490, 110 Cal.Rptr 916 (1973).

Board of Regents v. Roth, 408 U.S. 564, 92 S.Ct. 2701, 33 L.Ed.2d 548 (1972).

Brown v. Board of Education, Topeka, 349 U.S. 294, 75 S.Ct. 753, 99 L.Ed.1083 (1955).

Burnside v. Byars, 363 F.2d 744, 749 (5th Cir. 1966).

Christopherson v. Spring Valley Elementary School, 90 Ill.App.3d 460, 45 Ill. Sec. 866, 413 N.E.2d 199 (1980).

Columbus Board of Education v. Penick, 443 U.S. 449, 99 S.Ct. 2941, 61 L.Ed.2d 666 (1979).

Connick v. Myers, 461 U.S. 138, 103 S.Ct. 1684, 75 L.Ed.2d 708 (1983).

Conard v. Goolsby, 350 F. Supp 713 (N.D. Miss. 1972).

Crawford v. Board of Education, 17 Cal.3d 280, 290, 130 Cal.Rptr. 724, 551 P.2d 28, 34 (1976).

Davis v. Paige, 385 F. Supp. 395 (D.N.H. 1974).

Day v. South Park Independent School District, 768 F.2d 696 (5th Cir. 1985).

Deskbook Encyclopedia of American School Law. 1985. Rosemount, MN: Data Research, Inc.

District 27 Community School Board v. Board of Education of the City of New York. 130 Misc. 2d 398, 502 N.Y.S 2d 325 (Sup. 1986).

Dodd v. Rambis, 535 F. Supp 23 (S.D. Inc. 1981).

Domico v. Rapides Parish School Board, 675 F.2d 100, 102 (5th Cir. 1982).

Dominy v. Mays, 150 Ga.App. 187, 257 S.E.2d 317 (1979).

East Hartford Educational Association v. Board of Education, 562 F.2d 838 (2d Cir. 1977).

Engel v. Vitale, 370 U.S. 421, 82 S.Ct. 1261, 8 L.Ed.2d 601 (1962).

Everson v. Board of Education, 330 U.S. 1, 15–16, 67 S.Ct. 504, 511–12, 91 L.Ed. 711 (1947).

Fernald v. City of Ellsworth Superintending School Committee, 342 A.2d 704 (Me. 1975).

Edwards v. Aguillard, 482 U.S. 578, 107 S.Ct. 2573, 96 L.Ed.2d 510 (1987).

Flygare, T. J. 1986. Court foils schools' efforts to detect drugs. *Phi Delta Kappan* 68(4), 329–330.

Flygare, T. J. 1986b. Is *Tinker* dead? *Phi Delta Kappan* 68(2), 165–166.

Flygare, T. J. 1986c. Teachers' first amendment rights eroding. *Phi Delta Kappan* 67(5), 396–397.

Flygare, T. J. 1987e. Supreme court strikes down Louisiana creationism act. *Phi Delta Kappan* 69(1), 77–79.

Flygare, T. J. 1987b. Supreme court holds that contagious diseases are handicaps. *Phi Delta Kappan* 68(9), 705–706.

Flygare, T. J. 1987c. Kentucky teacher hits the wall with Pink Floyd. *Phi Delta Kappan* 69(3), 237–238.

Frank v. St. Landry Parish School Board, 225 So.2d 62 (La.App.1969).

Goldschmidt, S. M., and S. R. Painter. 1987–1988. Collective bargaining: A review of the literature. *Educational Research Quarterly* 12(1), 10–24.

Goss v. Lopez, 419 U.S. 565, 95 S.Ct 729, 42 L.Ed.2d 725 (1975).

Green v. County School Board of New Kent County, 391 U.S. 430, 88 S.Ct. 1689, 20 L.Ed.2d 716 (1968).

Griffin v. County School Board of Prince Edward County, 377 U.S. 218, 84 S.Ct. 1226, 12 L.Ed.2d 256 (1964).

Griggs v. Duke Power Co., 401 U.S. 424, 91 S.Ct. 849, 28 L.Ed.2d 150 (1971).

Gwathmey v. Atkinson, 447 F.Supp. 1113 (E.D. Va. 1976).

Hooker, C. P. 1986. Due process of law: *Loudermill v. Cleveland Board of Education.* In T. N. Jones and D. P. Semler (eds.). *School Law Update 1986.* Topeka, KS: National Organization on Legal Problems in Education.

Hoots v. Commonwealth of Pennsylvania, 672 F.2d 1107 (3d Cir. 1982).

Horton v. Goose Creek Independent School Dist., 690 F.2d 470, 478 (5th Cir. 1982).

Ingraham v. Wright, 525 F.2d 909 (5th Cir. 1976), affirmed, 430 U.S. 651, 97 S.Ct. 1401, 5 L.Ed.2d 711 (1977).

Jager and Jager v. Douglas County School District and Douglas County Board of Education, 86–2037A (D.Ga. 1987).

Keefe v. Geanakos, 418 F.2d 359 (1st Cir. 1969).

Kelley v. Johnson, 425 U.S. 238, 96 S.Ct. 1440, 47 L.Ed.2d 708 (1976).

Kemerer, F. 1987. Court battles over religion in the school. *Kappa Delta Pi Record* 23(3), 81–85.

Keyishian v. Board of Educ., 385 U.S. 589, 87 S.Ct. 675, 17 L.Ed.2d 629 (1967).

Kingsville Independent School District v. Cooper, 611 F.2d 1109 (5th Cir. 1980).

Lanner v. Wimmer, 662 F.2d 1349 (10th Cir. 1981).

Lemon v. Kurtzman, 403 U.S. 602, 91 S.Ct. 2105, 29 L.Ed.2d 745 (1971).

McCarthy, M. M., and N. H. Cambron-McCabe. 1987. *Public school law: Teachers' and students' rights,* 2d ed. Boston: Allyn and Bacon.

McCollum v. Board of Education, 333 U.S. 203, 68 S.Ct. 461, 92 L.Ed. 649 (1948).

Mailloux v. Kiley, 323 F. Supp. 1387 (D.Mass. 1971).

Milliken v. Bradley, 418 U.S. 717, 94 S.Ct. 3112, 41 L.Ed.2d 1069 (1974).

Mills v. Board of Education of District of Columbia, 348 F. Supp. 866 (D.D.C. 1972).

Morris, A. A. 1987. Fundamentalism, creationism, and the first amendment. *West's Education Law Reporter,* October 15, 1987, 1–20.

Mount Healthy City Board of Education v. Doyle, 429 U.S. 274, 97 S.Ct. 568, 50 L.Ed.2d 471 (1977).

New Jersey v. T.L.O., 469 U.S. 325, 105 S.Ct. 733, 83 L.Ed.2d 720 (1985).

O'Reilly, R. C., and E. T. Green. 1983. *School Law for the Practitioner.* Westport, CT: Greenwood Press.

PARC v. Pennsylvania 334 F. Supp. 1257 E.D. Pa. (1971).

Palmer v. Board of Educ. of the City of Chicago, 603 F.2d 1271, 1274 (7th Cir. 1979).

Pickering v. Board of Education, 391 U.S. 563, 88 S.Ct. 1731, 20 L.Ed.2d 811 (1968).

Plessy v. Ferguson, 163 U.S. 537, 16 S.Ct. 1138, 41 L.Ed. 256 (1896).

Podemski, R. S., B. J. Price, T. E. C. Smith, and G. E. Marsh. 1984. *Comprehensive Administration of Special Education.* Rockville, MD: Aspen Systems.

Pulliam, J. D. 1987. *History of Education in America.* Columbus, OH: Merrill.

Reecer, M. 1989. Yes, boards are under fire, but reports of your death are greatly exaggerated. *The American School Board Journal* 176(3), 31–34.

Rossow, L. F. 1989. Search and seizure in the public schools. In G. P. Sorenson (ed.). *Critical Issues in Education Law: The Role of the Federal Judiciary in Shaping Public Education.* Topeka, KS: The National Organization on Legal Problems of Education.

Sarac v. State Board of Education, 249 Cal.App.2d 58, 57 Cal.Rptr. 69 (1967).

S–1 v. Turlington, 635 F.2d 342 (5th Cir. 1981).

Shanker, A. 1989. Al Shanker (of all people) wants a hard look at what's befallen school boards. *The American School Board Journal* 176(3), 29–30.

Smith, T. E. C., B. J. Price, and G. E. Marsh. 1986. *Mildly Handicapped Children and Adults.* St. Paul, MN: West.

Sorenson, G. P. 1989. Freedom of speech for students and teachers. In G. P. Sorenson (ed.). *Critical Issues in Education Law: The Role of the Federal Judiciary in Shaping Public Education.* Topeka, KS: National Organization on Legal Problems of Education.

Spring Branch Independent School Dist. v. Stamos, 695 S.W.2d 556 (Tex. 1985)

State v. Stein, 203 Kan. 638, 456 P.2d 1, 2 (1969).

Steward v. Bailey, 396 F.Supp. 1381 (N.D.Ala. 1975).

Strahan, R. D., and L. C. Turner. 1987. *The courts and the schools.* New York: Longman.

Swann v. Charlotte–Mecklenburg Board of Education, 402 U.S. 1, 91 S.Ct. 1267, 28 L.Ed.2d 554 (1971).

Tate v. Board of Educ., 453 F. 2d 975 (8th Cir. 1972).

Tinker v. Des Moines Independent School District, 393 U.S. 503, 511, 89 S.Ct. 733, 739, 21 L.Ed.2d 731 (1969).

United States v. LULAC, 793 F.2d 636 (5th Cir. 1986).

United States v. State of South Carolina, 445 F.Supp. 1094 (D.S.C. 1977).

van Geel, T. 1986. Search of students after *New Jersey v. T.L.O.* In T. N. Jones and D. P. Semler (eds.). *School Law Update 1986.* Topeka, KS: National Organization on Legal Problems of Education.

Walden, J. C. 1987. Are prayers at high school football games unconstitutional? *West's Education Law Reporter,* August 6, 1987, 493–501.

Wallace v. Jaffree, 472 U.S. 38, 105 S.Ct. 2479, 86 L.Ed.2d 29 (1985).

Washington v. Davis, 426 U.S. 229, 96 S.Ct. 2040, 48 L.Ed.2d 597 (1976).

Weissman v. Board of Education of Jefferson City School District, 190 Colo. 414, 547 P.2d 1267 (1976).

West Virginia State Board of Education v. Barnette, 319 U.S. at 642, 63 S.Ct. at 1187.

Whitley, T. 1987. A.I.D.S. in the classroom. *Kappa Delta Pi Record* 23(2), 40–44.

Wishart v. McDonald, 500 F.2d 1110 (1st Cir. 1974).

Zamora v. Pomeroy, 639 F.2d 662, 670 (10th Cir. 1981).

Zirkel, P. A. 1989. Federal courts and public schools: An overview. In G. P. Sorenson (ed.). *Critical Issues in Education Law: The Role of the Federal Judiciary in Shaping Public Education.* Topeka, KS: The National Organization on Legal Problems of Education.

Zirkel, P. A. and F. MacMurtrie. 1988. A quick quiz on supreme court decisions affecting public schools. *Kappa Delta Pi Record* 24(3), 92–96.

6

EARLY CHILDHOOD EDUCATION

Dr. Stephen B. Graves of the University of Alabama at Birmingham
is the author of this chapter.

OBJECTIVES

After reading this chapter you will be able to

- describe the ideas of the leading thinkers and early philosophers in early childhood education;

- discuss how the field of early childhood education emerged;

- discuss the role of federal involvement in programs for young children;

- describe the types of current programs in early childhood education;

- discuss major issues in early childhood education programs;

- describe current trends in kindergarten and prekindergarten programs.

OUTLINE

ADVANCE ORGANIZERS

1. What are the purposes of early childhood education programs?
2. How did the field of early childhood education emerge?
3. What leading thinkers influenced programs for young children?
4. What influenced federal involvement in early childhood education programs?
5. What were the goals of compensatory early childhood education programs?
6. What types of current programs are available for young children?
7. What are the current issues in early childhood education programs?
8. What are the trends in public school kindergarten and prekindergarten programs?
9. What is the most accepted practice concerning parent involvement in programs for young children?

INTRODUCTION

Early childhood education is a relatively new field, although the history of its development is rich. Its importance and status has increased during the past thirty years due to the research about children's learning, growth, and development. Many parenting and teaching techniques have been influenced by the research on children's early experiences. Studies on children's early years have shown that preschool experiences influence all areas of a child's development and later learning. Many more parents now recognize this fact, which has caused the general public to place attention on programs and schools for young children.

Early childhood education is generally defined as the education of children from birth to age eight. As a field, it has grown out of a distinguished historical tradition. It is important for the student and beginning teacher to examine the historical roots of early childhood education, because knowledge of the past helps us understand our recent direction and shapes our future course.

HISTORY OF EARLY CHILDHOOD EDUCATION

A clear historical perspective provides the source of many current philosophies and practices in programs for young children. The beginning teacher will recognize that many educational innovations already have been tried and written about.

As a specialization, early childhood education dates back to the nineteenth century. However, many of the practices and philosophies seen in today's programs were created by teachers, writers, religious leaders, and philosophers well before the nineteenth century. Many of the early leading thinkers were concerned with issues that concern educators today. Some of these issues are: the education of the whole child; the role of play in learning; the belief in universal education; and individual freedom in learning.

Of course, early childhood education as a field could not emerge until the concept of childhood as a developmental period was accepted. Prior to the sixteenth and seventeenth centuries, children were regarded as little adults and were given no special consideration or treatment.

Several teachers, writers, religious leaders, and philosophers have significantly shaped the thinking and practices in today's programs for young children.

Early Beginnings. Two of the earliest influences on current practice were Plato (428–348 B.C.) and Aristotle (384–322 B.C.). Plato was primarily concerned with developing a ruling class of people with strong values. Aristotle believed that a person's merits should determine his status. Both believed in the importance of beginning education with young children. They also viewed human beings as being essentially good and they worked to create a society of good people.

Martin Luther. Remembered as a religious reformer of the Renaissance, Martin Luther (1483–1546) was an advocate of universal education. He believed that a reformed church also needed a reformed educational system (Morrison 1988). During the sixteenth century, the emphasis was placed on formal education to teach people to read the Bible. This marked the beginning of teaching and learning in the people's native language as opposed to Latin, the official language of the Catholic church.

Luther believed that the purpose of schools was to develop the intellectual, religious, physical, emotional, and social aspects of children. Throughout his life, he wrote letters and preached sermons on the subject of education. Luther often argued for public support of education as he did in his 1524 *Letter to the Mayors and Alderman of All the Cities of Germany in Behalf of Christian Schools:*

> Therefore it will be the duty of mayors and council to exercise the greatest care over the young. For since the happiness, honor, and life of the city are committed to their hands, they would be held recreant before God and the world, if they did not, day and night, with all their power, seek its welfare and improvement. Now the welfare of the city does not consist alone in great treasures, firm walls, beautiful houses, and munitions of war; indeed, where all these are found, and reckless fools come into power, the city sustains the greatest injury. But the

highest welfare, safety, and power of a city consists in able, learned, wise, upright, cultivated citizens, who can secure, preserve, and utilize every treasure and advantage. (Painter 1928)

Luther advocated a compulsory school system which would be supported by the public. He believed that music and physical education should be added to the curriculum and that young women should be encouraged to teach. Other religious denominations emerged during the Reformation. Each of the denominations was interested in preserving the faith and keeping their followers, so most of the larger denominations established schools to provide knowledge about the faith. As a result of Luther's beliefs and efforts, then, the adult population began to consider educational practices for young children.

John Amos Comenius. A Czechoslovakian bishop, teacher, and writer of textbooks, John Amos Comenius (1592–1670) believed that all people were equal before God and were entitled to the same education. His commitment to starting education in the early years was made clear in *The Great Didactic:*

> It is the nature of everything that comes into being, that while tender it is easily bent and formed, but that when it has grown hard, it is not easy to alter. Wax, when soft, can be easily fashioned and shaped; when hard it cracks readily. A young plant can be planted, transplanted, pruned, and bent this way or that. When it has become a tree these processes are impossible. (Keatinge 1896, 1910)

Comenius saw education as beginning at birth in the "school of the mother's knee" and extending throughout the learner's lifetime. He also believed that education should follow the order of nature. This belief implies a time for different types of growth and learning: One must observe the natural sequence of events to avoid forcing learning before the time is right or before the proper foundation for future learning is built.

Comenius's teaching emphasized concrete experiences and sensory learning. In his *Orbis Pictus* (1658), the first picture book written for children, he helped children learn names of things and names of concepts through pictures and words. He recommended that teachers make learning easy and pleasant.

Jean-Jacques Rousseau. Writer, philosopher, and social theorist Jean-Jacques Rousseau (1712–1778) was born in Geneva, Switzerland, but spent most of his life in France. His book *Emile*, published in 1762, charted the life of a hypothetical child from birth to adolescence. In it, he presents the view that innate goodness will flower when people are brought out of the corrupt society and are free to learn from direct contact with nature. Some of Rousseau's ideas, which were considered radical, were reactions to what he viewed as a corrupt government and society. He rejected the notion of original sin and believed that a person's inherent goodness was spoiled by society.

Some historians of education point to Rousseau's work as the dividing line between the historical and the modern periods of education. His thoughts on young children are reflected in other innovators of educational practice such as Pestalozzi and Froebel. The view that children are essentially good and capable of achievements represents a common element in the work of Rousseau and other early thinkers. The belief that a child can become autonomous and self-directed is based on his philosophy.

The Field of Early Childhood Education Emerges

The next group of reformers and educational theorists were directly involved in the education of young children. Their work continues to have an impact on many modern educational practices.

Johann Heinrich Pestalozzi. Swiss educator Johann Heinrich Pestalozzi (1746–1827) was greatly influenced by the romantic philosophers, especially Rousseau. He was so impressed by Rousseau's back-to-nature ideas that he purchased a farm where he started a school called Neuhof. At Neuhof, he advocated sensory exploration, observation, self-discovery, and self-paced learning. Pestalozzi felt that the best way to learn many concepts was through manipulative experiences.

Johann Friedrich Oberlin. In about 1767, protestant minister Jean Friedrich Oberlin (1740–1826), developed the earliest reported school especially for young children. Although he is credited with founding the school in Alsace, an eastern province of France, he never taught in it. The school enrolled children as young as two or three years old, taught handicrafts, and included play and exercise. Oberlin's wife Madame Madeleine Oberlin, as well as Sarah Banzet and Louise Scheppler, who managed the Oberlin household, taught in the school. The children often gathered in a circle around Louise Scheppler, who talked to them as she knitted. She showed the children pictures from nature and history and helped them learn to speak in proper French as well as in their regional dialect.

The "knitting school" was quite popular, although some French citizens were suspicious that the teaching would be religious and anti-revolutionary. The school expanded to five neighboring village centers, but never grew further after the French Revolution.

Robert Owen. English industrialist, social philosopher, and reformer Robert Owen (1771–1858), established the Infant School in 1816. A disciple of Pestalozzi, Owen was deeply concerned with the poor conditions of the cotton mill workers and their families during the Industrial

Revolution. He worked for reform in those communities where children as young as six years of age worked in the mills. He raised the minimum working age in his mill from six to ten years and started schools for adults and children.

Owen called his school the Institute for the Formation of Character. The part of the school that was set aside for the youngest children was called the Infant School. The children were taught reading, writing, arithmetic, sewing, geography, natural history, modern and ancient history, music, and dance. Children often were taken on field trips to observe things as they were in the real world. Owen did not believe in punishing or pressuring children to learn.

The infant schools represented an important movement to provide a humane form of education for young children. Although the schools did not have lasting success, some of the practices originating in Owen's schools still can be found in today's programs for young children. These include child-chosen activities, learning through play, and a nurturing atmosphere guided by a nonpunitive teacher.

Friedrich Wilhelm August Froebel. Friedrich Wilhelm August Froebel (1782–1852) was born in Germany and was greatly influenced by the ideas of Comenius, Rousseau, and Pestalozzi. He not only advocated a system for teaching young children, but also developed a curriculum and methodology. Through this work, he earned the appellation of "father of the kindergarten."

His concept of how children learn was based on the idea of natural unfolding held by Comenius and Pestalozzi. The educator's role was to observe this unfolding process and provide activities that helped the child learn what he was ready to learn. Froebel believed that activity was the basis for knowing and that play was an essential component of learning.

The curriculum of Froebel's kindergarten included a set of "gifts and occupations." The gifts were objects like yarn balls, blocks, wooden tablets, and geometric shapes. The occupations included activities such as molding, cutting, folding, and bead stringing. These gifts and occupations were designed to enhance the development of the senses and to symbolize unity with God.

Froebel's practices reflected his belief that knowledge is transmitted through symbols and that education must begin with the concrete and move to the abstract. These views are still accepted today and the concepts have been documented through research. According to Froebel, the teacher was responsible for guiding and directing the child toward the end of being a contributing member of society. Besides establishing the first kindergarten, Froebel also established an institute to train young women to teach kindergarten.

Froebel's kindergarten program became popular throughout Germany. With a large migration from Germany to the United States in the mid-nineteenth century, the kindergarten idea came to America.

TABLE 6.1
Abstract From: Syllabus of Froebel's *Education of Man*

Education defined by the law of divine unity.

Free self-activity the essential method in education.

Unity, individuality, and diversity the phases of human development.

The several stages of childhood, boyhood, and manhood to be duly respected in their order.

The various powers of the human being to be developed by means of suitable external work.

Nature and value of the child's play.

The family is the type of true life and the source of active interest in all surroundings.

The games of boyhood educate for life by awakening and cultivating many civic and moral virtues.

The true remedy for any evil is to find the original good quality that has been repressed or misled, and then to foster and guide it aright.

The purpose of the school and its work is to give to the child the inner relations and meanings of what was before merely external and unrelated.

The essential work of the school is to associate facts into principles, not to teach isolated facts.

Mathematics should be treated physically, and mathematical forms and figures should be considered as the necessary outcome of an inner force acting from a center.

Writing and reading grow out of the self-active desire for expression and should be taught with special reference to this fact.

In the study of plants, animals, etc., then work proceeds from particulars to generals, and again from generals to particulars in varied succession.

From natural objects and the products of man's effort, the study should proceed to include the relations of mankind.

The prime purpose throughout is not to impart knowledge to the child, but to lead the child to observe and to think.

The general purpose of family and school instruction is to advance the all-sided development of the child and the complete unfolding of his nature.

Source: Froebel. *The Education of Man*, 1887.

The first American kindergarten was established by Margarethe Schurz in Watertown, Wisconsin, in 1856. She started the kindergarten in her home for her own children and the children of her relatives. Other German-speaking kindergartens were established in cities throughout America during this period.

The first English-speaking kindergarten was established in Boston by Elizabeth Peabody in 1860. Peabody traveled all over the country for many years speaking about the purpose and benefits of kindergarten. She helped establish kindergartens wherever she went. The first public-school kindergarten was started in 1873 by Susan Blow in St. Louis.

During the remainder of the nineteenth century, kindergartens were sponsored by churches, settlement houses, factories, and trade unions. These programs were developed independently from elementary education and the nursery school and were seen as critically important programs for the children of the poor.

Reform in the Kindergarten

At the end of the 1800s and the beginning of the 1900s, conflicting philosophies arose among leaders in the kindergarten movement. The conservative group generally held to Froebelian principles and prac-

TABLE 6.2
From Luther to Piaget: Basic Concepts Essential to Good Educational Practices

AS THEY RELATE TO CHILDREN

Everyone needs to learn how to read and write.

Children learn best through using all their senses.

All children are capable of being educated.

All children should be educated to the fullest extent of their abilities.

Education should begin early in life.

Children should not be forced to learn, but should be taught what they are ready to learn and should be prepared for the next stage of learning.

Learning activities should be meaningful to children.

Children learn through guided and directed play.

Children can learn through activities based on their interests.

AS THEY RELATE TO TEACHERS

One must show love and respect for all children.

Teachers should be dedicated to the profession.

Good teaching is based on a theory, a philosophy, and goals and objectives.

Children's learning is enhanced through the use of concrete materials.

Teaching should move from the concrete to the abstract.

Observation is a key to determining children's needs.

Teaching should be a planned, systematic process.

Teaching should be child-centered rather than adult-centered.

Teaching should be based on children's interests.

AS THEY RELATE TO PARENTS

The family is an important institution in education.

Parents are their children's primary educators.

Parents must provide guidance and direct young children's learning.

Parents should be involved in any educational program designed for their children.

Everyone should have some training for child rearing.

Source: Morrison. *Early Childhood Education Today,* 1988.

tices. A group known as the progressives placed a stronger emphasis on the child and the child's interests rather than on subject matter.

John Dewey. John Dewey (1859–1952) is credited with the theory of schooling called progressivism. Dewey was from Burlington, Vermont, and taught philosophy at the University of Chicago and at Columbia University. It is from his emphasis on the child and the child's interests that the terms "child-centered curriculum" and "child-centered schools" were coined. The progressive movement maintained that the schools should be concerned with helping children deal with the realities of the present, not just preparing children for the future. In his famous *My Pedagogical Creed,* Dewey described education as a process for living, not simply a preparation for future living.

Progressivism was a reaction to the traditional view that children should learn predetermined skills by rote memorization. In Dewey's classroom, the child was involved with social interaction, physical activities, discovering how objects work, and other intellectual pursuits. Dewey stressed daily living activities such as cooking and carpentry. He also believed that children should be given many opportunities for inquiry and discovery.

Although Dewey believed in responding to the interests of the child, he also valued using traditional subject matter that was appropriate for youngsters. Rather than impose knowledge on children, he felt that teachers should use the interests of children as a source for subject matter and as a catalyst for learning skills.

The progressive movement was criticized by those who believed that children were not learning the basic subjects well enough. Many educational historians now feel that Dewey was misinterpreted by some of his followers. Some became overly permissive and did not adequately encourage children to become responsible and self-directed.

Dewey's beliefs have made an impact on all areas of education in the United States. Although the influence of progressive education as a guiding philosophy has disappeared from most schools, it continues to remain a strong influence in programs for young children.

Maria Montessori. Maria Montessori (1870–1952) was the first woman in Italy to earn a medical degree. Working in the psychiatric clinic of the University of Rome, she discovered successful approaches for helping children learn who were thought to be incapable of learning. She founded the *Casa Dei Bambini* (Children's House) to test her methods on normal children. Through her work with handicapped and normal children and as a result of her being influenced by the work of Pestalozzi, Froebel, and Freud, Montessori concluded that intelligence was not fixed and could be shaped by the child's experiences. She believed very strongly that children learn through their direct sensory exploration. She also believed that children have a natural desire to explore and understand their world. The dignity of each child and the development of independence and responsibility were important components of the Montessori method.

Montessori's schools were very successful throughout Italy and eventually spread to many other countries. Montessori's ideas of creating a child-sized environment and her focus on using sensory materials were adopted in early childhood education programs throughout the world. Montessori education grew rapidly in the United States until the stock market crash and depression that followed in the 1930s. The Montessori method rebounded in the 1950s and remains popular in America today.

The Nursery School

Margaret McMillan. Margaret McMillan (1860–1931) and her sister Rachel established the first nursery school in London in 1911. Born in the United States, the McMillan sisters moved to England with their mother when she returned to her family home after the death of their father. Margaret, who studied music and acting in her early years, became very politically active and fought for social causes as a young adult. In 1894 she was elected to the school board of Bradford, England, and became an advocate for the needs of poor children in school. She was convinced that the children's medical and physical needs must be met before they entered school. She fought for medical examinations, school lunches, and school baths for the children.

The McMillans' nursery school stressed health and nutrition, perceptual-motor skills, the development of the imagination, and outdoor play and work. The role of the teacher in the nursery school was to nurture the natural development of the children and to enhance opportunities for creativity and play. The work of the McMillans in the nursery school movement contributed to the passage of the Fisher Act of 1918, which allowed the establishment of nursery schools in the public schools of England (Spodek, Saracho, and Davis 1987). Funds were not available to make the schools universal, but many British nursery school educators came to the United States to demonstrate their program. This movement prompted the establishment of many nursery schools in colleges and universities throughout the states.

Jean Piaget

Jean Piaget (1896–1980) is probably mentioned more often in the education and psychology literature than any other person. He devoted many years to studying the way children think. One of his contributions is the theory of cognitive development. According to this theory, children are active agents who interact with the social and physical world. Piaget found that children construct knowledge about their world through real experiences and through manipulating, changing,

■ *Jean Piaget identified the processes of cognitive development.*

and adapting information. He believed that knowledge is discovered and constructed through activity.

Through his observations of children, Piaget identified processes of cognitive development. Through the child's interaction process with the environment, the child develops organizing structures Piaget called "schemes." These schemes become the foundation upon which later mental structures are built. Piaget found that children use three processes to organize their experience into a framework for thinking: assimilation, accommodation, and equilibration.

Assimilation is the process by which learners integrate new information or experience into existing structures or schemes. Through this process, the child fits new information into her own structural framework for understanding. For example, a young child who sees a goat for the first time and calls it a dog is attempting to assimilate the new information into existing structures. The second process—accommodation—involves changing or modifying the schemes or structures to reflect the child's understanding of the world. If the child, through experience, is able to see the different traits, characteristics, uses, etc. of the goat, then she acquires the new scheme: goat. The third process involves reaching the state of equilibrium through the successful balancing of assimilation and accommodation. Imbalance between these two creates a state of disequilibrium. Through these three processes, intellectual growth occurs.

Using these three processes, the child progresses through very distinct developmental stages that are built upon the interaction of experience, existing mental structures, and maturation. These stages occur in a predictable sequence for children, but the exact age when a child enters each stage varies greatly among children. The four stages of cognitive development are discussed in Table 6.3 below.

FEDERAL INVOLVEMENT IN EARLY CHILDHOOD EDUCATION

The creation of the Children's Bureau in 1912 marked the first federal involvement in promoting the health, education, and welfare of young children. The primary responsibility of the Bureau was to investigate child health and labor conditions and to report the findings. There was little federal involvement in programs between the 1920s and the 1940s except for a few work-relief programs under President Franklin D.

TABLE 6.3
Piaget's Stages of Cognitive Development

STAGE	CHARACTERISTICS
Sensorimotor (Birth–18 mos.) (or 2 yrs.)	Uses sensorimotor systems of sucking, grasping, and gross body activities to build schemes. Begins to develop object permanency. Dependent on concrete representations. Frame of reference is the world of here and now.
Preoperational (2–7 yrs.)	Language development accelerates. Internalizes events. Egocentric in thought and action. Thinks everything has a reason or purpose. Is perceptually bound. Makes judgments primarily on basis of how things look.
Concrete operations (7–12 yrs.)	Capable of reversal of thought processes. Ability to conserve. Still dependent on how things look for decision making. Less egocentric. Structures time and space. Understanding of number. Beginning of logical thinking.
Formal operations (12–15 yrs.)	Capable of dealing with verbal and hypothetical problems. Ability to reason scientifically and logically. No longer bound to the concrete. Can think with symbols.

Source: Morrison. *Early Childhood Education Today*, 1988.

Roosevelt. Some nursery schools were also established to provide work for unemployed teachers.

During World War II, the Lanhan Act was passed to establish child care centers in war industry areas. Children in these centers were provided education and care, sometimes on a 24-hour basis, while their mothers worked. When the war ended, the federal government withdrew its involvement in early childhood education programs.

In 1959 the federal government established a Department of Health, Education and Welfare. This office was called the Office of Child Development in 1969 and was later called the Administration for Children, Youth, and Families. These agencies have focused on providing assistance to families unable to adequately care for their children. Programs have addressed such needs as health and nutrition, education, child care, and child abuse prevention.

During the 1960s and the early 1970s, a resurgence of interest in child care programs occurred. Research in child development and a national concern for social reform contributed to the renewed interest. Under President Lyndon Johnson's "Great Society" initiative, early childhood programs began to be viewed as relevant to our economic and social needs. In 1972, both the United States House of Representatives and the U.S. Senate passed a comprehensive child care services bill. The bill, which would have provided child care services for all who desired it, was vetoed by President Richard Nixon. Nixon justified the veto by stating that the bill threatened the stability of the institution of the American family. Child care legislation introduced in the 1980s has taken a more passive form than that of a comprehensive bill.

COMPENSATORY EARLY CHILDHOOD EDUCATION PROGRAMS

Programs have been sponsored by institutions, agencies, government, and other groups. Federal, state, and local governments, parent groups, churches, private entrepreneurs, businesses, and industries have provided programs for young children. The purpose and focus of these programs has varied greatly among sponsors.

The launch of Sputnik in 1957 contributed to a national fear that American children were not being adequately educated to compete in the world. This concern caused many educators to carefully examine their programs in elementary and secondary schools, especially in science and math. It was about this time when researchers and educators were suggesting that planned intervention in the early years could have very positive benefits in later life. Research by Jean Piaget, Benjamin Bloom, J. McVicker Hunt, and others rejected the notion that intelligence is static. Because of this new knowledge, many people believed early childhood education should claim a more significant role in the total educational process of children (Morrison 1988).

The focus on our educational systems, the new ideas about children's growth, development, and learning, and the political climate of the 1960s set the stage for a new era in early childhood education. During the John F. Kennedy administration, the Office of Economic Opportunity was created to aid in the so-called War Against Poverty. The whole nation became sensitized to the conditions and needs of the poor.

With this renewed interest and concern for the poor and their children, an interdisciplinary panel was formed and directed by the Office of Economic Opportunity to develop a program which would combat the effects of poverty on children. The panel was composed of professionals representing the fields of child development, education, pediatrics, and social services. It was hoped that the program would provide these poor children with opportunities for learning and a head start in their achievement.

Project Head Start

Project Head Start focused on the total development of the child and had seven objectives:

1. improving the child's physical health and abilities;
2. helping the social and emotional development of the child;
3. improving the child's mental processes and skills;
4. establishing patterns and expectations of success;
5. increasing the child's capacity to relate positively to family members while at the same time strengthening the family's stability and capacity to relate positively to the child;
6. developing a positive attitude toward society in the child and his or her family and fostering constructive opportunities for society to work together with the poor in solving their problems; and
7. increasing the sense of dignity and self-worth within the child and his or her family. (Hodges and Cooper 1981)

Head start began in 1965 as an eight-week summer program but soon grew into a full-year program. During the first summer, 500,000 children were enrolled in 11,000 centers. From 1965 through 1984, more than 8 million children were served in Head Start centers (Decker and Decker 1988). Through this program, early childhood education was viewed as a vehicle for school improvement and social change.

In an effort to continue serving low socio-economic level children and expand the services, other programs were developed. Home Start and Follow Through were two such programs. Home Start was designed to strengthen parents' abilities to enhance their child's development in the home. It utilized home visitors as parent trainers (Almy 1975). Follow Through was established in 1967 and administered by the United States Office of Education. One of its main purposes was to

EVERYBODY LIKES HEAD START

Connie Leslie

As a part of the day's arithmetic lesson, Richard Bettis sat at a table with two other 4-year-olds last week, cutting comic strips from a newspaper and placing them in a neat stack. For Richard, it was just another day at the Head Start program in Tate, Ga., a rural town 45 miles north of Atlanta. But for his mother, Saundra, the day was further proof of a remarkable transformation. "Before Richard enrolled in the Head Start program last August, he was angry, mad at the world," she says. Richard was suffering from the aftershocks of her recent divorce. So was she. Volunteering in the classrooms forced Saundra to get out of the house and leave her anomie behind. Eventually she became a member of the program's advisory council and, recently, she found a part-time job. "After the divorce, I didn't have a positive or negative attitude about anything," she says. "Now I'm involved. Head Start has made a difference in my life."

Project Head Start began in the summer of 1965 as part of Lyndon B. Johnson's War on Poverty. The federally sponsored preschool program was designed to give disadvantaged children the preparation they'd need to cope with traditional schooling and to help them and their families earn a living. "Head Start was always the model of what early childhood intervention should be about," says Edward F. Zigler, a psychology professor at Yale University, and one of the founders of Head Start. It's also the one poverty program no one hates. Even in his early cut-and-slash budgets, Ronald Reagan didn't try to eviscerate it. During the fall campaign, George Bush pledged his fealty to the program: "Give any American kid an equal place at the starting line and just watch what that kid can do. Head Start helps kids get that equal place." Last week Bush made Head Start one of the centerpieces of his "kinder, gentler" budget by proposing to spend $400 million more a year than the program's current $1.23 billion funding—a

40 percent boost by 1993. Since Head Start's inception, its most important components have been an emphasis on parental involvement and a broad approach to child development. Nationally, four out of five parents with kids in Head Start provide some volunteer service. At the Fort George Center in New York City, the staff offers free medical and dental checkups regularly and explains proper nutrition to each parent. If there is a family problem with alcohol or child abuse, the mental-health staff will work with parents individually, refer them to city social services and, if necessary, even accompany them to family court. "I see the nutrition, health and parental involvement as being more important than the education component," says diretor Lenore Peay.

The first assessments of Head Start graduates were disappointing because researchers strictly focused on increases in IQ levels. After initial increases, those gains invariably disappeared in the early grades of elementary school. Then, in the mid-'80s, new research that took a longer and broader view of the effects of early intervention programs began to paint a brighter picture. Researchers found that those who had gone through the program were more likely to graduate from high school (65 percent) than those who hadn't (52 percent). Other studies found that graduates were less likely to repeat a grade, be assigned to a special-education class, have trouble with the law or become teenage mothers. Those who became pregnant were more likely to return to high school for their degrees. Still other data revealed that as young adults, those who attended these preschools had significantly higher rates of employment and were more likely to attend college.

Despite its popularity and effectiveness, Head Start has never been funded at a level that would serve all impoverished pre-

continued

schoolers. The need is great: according to the Children's Defense Fund, 13 million children—1 in 5—live in poverty. In 1987 only 18.5 percent of all eligible children found places in Head Start (at a cost of $2,445 per child), down from 25 percent in 1978. "It was stupid not to make an investment that we knew would pay for itself five to 10 years down the road, and we're paying the price for it now," says Bill Honig, state superintendent of schools in California.

Salary Hikes

Now that Head Start is about to receive a windfall from the Bush budget, the question is, how should the money be spent? Instead of opening more Head Start outlets to accommodate more children, some proponents would prefer to raise the quality of existing programs. One way might be to increase staff wages. Salaries for teachers at the State Center near Atlanta average about $4.25 per hour; few centers offer pensions. Or, the new funds could be used to hire more teachers. Parents and others who volunteer as teachers' aides frequently graduate from Head Start's highly regarded

training program and move on to paying jobs in private child-care programs. The national teacher-student ratio for Head Start has gone from 1 in 5 in 1965 to 1 in 10 today. "There's nothing more important than staff ratios," says Zigler.

The new budget will also allow the programs to reconsider its structure. "I think it's time to modernize Head Start," says Douglas Besharov of the American Enterprise Institute. "The model is 25 years old." The big question is how many hours the programs should run. Head Start began as a half-day program, and 82 percent of the children still go for only four hours each session. Working parents, or parents who want jobs, need full-day care. Should Head Start offer more half-day classes and thus serve more kids, or sharply increase its daycare component and help their parents? People of good faith can differ on these questions. But there's a consensus on an important first principle: it's wiser—and in the long run cheaper—to spend money on children before their problems multiply.

---

observe the success of the Head Start children as they progressed through the third grade.

Although there has been some controversy about the lasting effects of Head Start, most early childhood educators agree that the gains have been significant. Researchers found that Head Start

1. produces substantial gains in children's cognitive and language development;

2. provides the greatest amount of benefits to the most needy children;

3. allows participants to perform equal to or superior to their peers when regular school begins;

4. provides positive contributions to the development of socially mature behavior;

5. supports generally better health and nutritional practices in children; and

6. lessens the likelihood of children being retained in grade or assigned to special education classes. (Spodek et al. 1987)

The Head Start research also found improvement in parenting abilities and more positive reactions between mothers and children (Cal-

INTRODUCTION TO EDUCATION

houn and Collins 1981). Zigler and Lang (1983) found that over 95 percent of Head Start parents favorably endorsed the program. Some offshoot programs of Head Start have survived and still can be observed, while others like Home Start have come and gone (Nurss and Hodges 1981).

Part of the Follow Through study involved tracking children who had experienced a wide variety of educational models in their preschool experience. These models were taken from different theories and represented very different philosophies and approaches in early childhood education. Each of the models was developed by a program sponsor which usually resided at a university or an educational research center.

The Preacademic Program was developed by Siegfried Englemann and Wesley Becker at the University of Oregon and Don Bushell at the University of Kansas. This model advocated a strong emphasis on teacher direction and behavior modification. The Discovery Model describes the models used at Bank Street College in New York and at the Educational Center in Massachusetts. These programs focused on setting up a stimulating classroom environment which offered a variety of learning opportunities for the children. The teacher's role in these programs was viewed as a facilitator. Several similar models, such as the Tucson Early Education Model in Arizona, the Cognitively-Oriented Curriculum model developed by David Weikart in Michigan, and the Responsive Environment model from the Far West Laboratory in California, were all considered "Cognitive Discovery" models.

CURRENT PROGRAMS

Child Care Centers

Child care centers are programs which provide care for young children. Many programs care for children as young as six weeks of age while others begin serving children at age two or three. Some programs also serve school-aged children after school hours. Most programs are open from early morning until late afternoon or early evening.

Centers are sponsored by a variety of groups including churches, schools, government agencies, businesses, and industries. The purpose of the centers may vary just as sponsorship does. Most programs have identified as their goals one or more of the following: (1) to provide for the education and care of young children, (2) to provide child care for working parents, (3) to enhance the intellectual, social, physical, and emotional development of the children, and (4) to provide education and support services for parents (Feeney, Christensen, and Moravcik 1987).

There is also great variety in the funding of centers. Most programs are privately funded, while some receive federal funds through a Social Services Block Grant. The children who are served in these federally funded centers typically have parents who are below current poverty guidelines. Federal funds which support these programs have decreased dramatically during the past decade (Edelman 1985). Licensing among programs also varies from state to state, but usually provides minimum guidelines regarding safety and health features.

Family Day Care Homes

Family Day Care Homes serve a small number of young children in group care. This alternative to center care is very prevalent in the United States and is a desired choice by many parents who prefer the home setting with fewer children. Family day care homes provide more toddler care than care for any other age groups. Many homes serve infants and some serve preschoolers as well as school-age children (Stevens 1982).

Preschools

Sometimes called nursery schools, preschools historically have been half-day programs. Preschools traditionally have focused on the social and emotional needs of the children. In programs today, preschools also focus on the intellectual development of the children. Sponsorship of preschools often is assumed by colleges, universities, and other educational institutions that provide a laboratory setting in which to train students.

Employer-Sponsored Programs

According to some researchers, employer-sponsored child care is the fastest growing type of child care (Burud, Collins, and Devine-Hawkins 1983). Interest in employer-sponsored child care has grown tremendously because of the changing work force. The reasons employers consider providing child care include to reduce employee turnover, reduce absenteeism, increase worker productivity and concentration on the job, improve employee recruitment, enhance worker morale, and enhance company image (Burud et al. 1983; Hicks and Powell 1983).

Public School Kindergartens

With Mississippi starting kindergarten programs in 1986, all fifty states now serve five year olds in public schools. There is, however, much diversity in how programs are carried out. Robinson's (1982) survey of early childhood education consultants in state departments of education revealed many differences among states in funding, availability of programs, and admission policies.

INTRODUCTION TO EDUCATION

■ *Preschools focus on social, emotional, and intellectual development.*

As in elementary and secondary schools throughout the states, the amount of funding allocated for each kindergarten child varies greatly. Some states rely heavily on local funds, while others rely more on state or federal monies (Morrison 1988). Some states have moved to a compulsory kindergarten program while others offer programs to the parents of five year olds on a voluntary basis. In a few states, children are selected on a lottery basis for admission.

The length of the kindergarten day also varies. There are full-day and half-day programs throughout the country and, in some states, both programs are present. Those who support half-day programs state that a half-day program is more appropriate to the child's readiness level and makes a good transition to the all-day first grade experience. Those who support a full-day program believe children can learn more during a whole day and already are ready for that type of comprehensive program.

The issues which traditionally have caused the most disagreement are what and how to teach kindergartners. Opinions generally can be

MAKING THE (FIRST) GRADE

Jean Seligmann

Playing Show and Tell, emptying the gerbils' cage and making cookies from Rice Krispies and peanut butter—kindergartners have a pretty easy life, right? Not in Georgia. As part of a broader effort to improve its public schools, the state has become the first in the Union to require five-year-olds to take a standardized achievement test before they can be promoted to the first grade. The 90-minute multiple-choice exam, mandated by the state legislature, was given during the past two weeks. It has stirred up a flurry of concern among teachers and child-development experts, who believe Georgia's 93,000 kindergartners are just the latest victims of a national testing mania.

How do you test children who, for the most part, don't know how to read yet? The teacher reads each question aloud. And the students, using a workbook, fill in the bubble that's under the picture they've selected as the right answer. Why bother? One rationale is that children of the same age aren't automatically at the same stage of development. "Readiness for first grade matters," says U.S. Secretary of Education William Bennett. "To enter when you're not ready can cause a lot of problems." Using the California Achievement Test, Georgia is measuring recognition of letters and language sounds (such as rhymes) and basic numerical concepts. At best, critics charge, testing won't reliably assess a five-year-old's skills; a bright child may be bored or another's performance might be affected by a minor trauma on the way to school. "Their bodies and minds just aren't ready for [testing] in kindergarten," declares Marilyn Gootman, assistant professor at the University of Georgia and a specialist in early learning. But she and other critics are even more concerned that teachers will now have to take class time away from helping kids grow developmentally in order to prepare them for the test.

When the test results are disclosed next month, officials expect a failure rate of about 10 percent. If a child flunks but his teacher thinks he's ready for first grade, he will be given the opportunity to take a different standardized test. While the grown-ups are aflutter, many of the test takers appear unruffled. Keith Bailey-Kopp, five, summed up the majority view of his classmates at Flat Shoals Elementary School in Rockdale County; "it was easy."

put into two very opposing views. One group believes that kindergarten should be structured more like first grade with many teacher-directed activities and formal learning experiences. The opposing group believes that young children learn through active, participatory, hands-on experiences, with the teacher serving as a facilitator.

In 1984 the Southern Association on Children Under Six (SACUS) published a position statement about the kindergarten experience. In the introduction, the authors stated ". . . recent trends to incorporate developmentally inappropriate teaching strategies such as workbooks, ditto sheets, and formal reading groups as well as academic skill-oriented curriculum content in kindergarten, raise serious concerns" (Swick, Brown, and Graves 1984).

This paper included a discussion of the importance of play and the importance of matching learning experiences to the children's developmental stages and needs. It also contained guidelines for designing appropriate learning environments for five year olds. The SACUS statement speaks strongly on young children's learning and development:

1. Kindergarten children constantly strive to understand and make sense of their experiences.

2. Kindergarten children develop understandings through play and other natural learning strategies.

3. The social, emotional, intellectual, and physical needs of kindergarten children are interrelated.

4. While kindergarten children follow similar developmental sequences, they do so in unique ways and at different rates.

5. Kindergarten children need adults to help them make sense of their experiences.

6. The best learning environment for kindergarten children is one in which they can actively participate by manipulating objects and by expressing their ideas through many curricular areas.

7. Kindergarten children learn best when all of their development/ learning needs and interests are nurtured through a broad and understandable curriculum.

8. The different learning styles, interests, and developmental needs of kindergarten children can best be facilitated through informal, flexible classroom arrangements which utilize interest centers and individualized activities and games.

9. Kindergarten children learn best when the curriculum is based on concrete experiences to which they can relate in meaningful ways. (Swick et al. 1984)

The National Association for the Education of Young Children (NAEYC) has also published a statement describing appropriate classroom practice for young children. This statement, by the country's largest early childhood education professional organization, is very much in agreement with the ideals addressed in the SACUS statement. The NAEYC statement recognizes that "a growing body of research has emerged recently affirming that children learn most effectively through a concrete, play-oriented approach to early childhood education" (Bredekamp 1987).

Other educational groups like the National Association of State Boards of Education and the Early Childhood Education Consultants in State Departments of Education have published papers supporting similar appropriate experiences for young children. A feature article in *Newsweek* (April 17, 1989), affirmed the major points of all these papers

TABLE 6.4
Full-Day Kindergarten Survey, April 1, 1988

STATE	ORGANIZATION			FINANCE FOR FULL-DAY EVERY-DAY KINDERGARTEN				KINDERGARTEN ATTENDANCE		STARTING AGE	
	Number Children Full Day, Every Day	Number Children Half Day	Number Children Full Day, Alternate Day	Number Children Other	State Finance	State Does not Finance	Other	Manda-tory	Not Manda-tory	State Uniform Starting Age	No Uniform Starting Age
ALABAMA	54,070				x				x	October 1	
ALASKA	2,284	7,469			x				x	November 2	
ARIZONA	State does not have this information					x			x	September 1	
ARKANSAS	31,025	3,935			x				x	October 1	
(1) CALIFORNIA	1,000	380,608			x				x	September 1	
(2) COLORADO	2,634	44,431				x			x		x
(3) CONNECTICUT	State does not have this information				x				x	January 1	
(4) DELAWARE	44	7,772				x		x		December 31	
FLORIDA	116,192	6,115			x			x		September 1	
GEORGIA	93,000				x				x	September 1	
HAWAII	14,252				x				x	December 31	
(5) IDAHO		17,310	799			x			x	October 16	
ILLINOIS	24,133	103,260	3,607		x				x	September 1	
(6) INDIANA	4,150	67,990				x			x	October 1	
IOWA	7,786	21,925	7,176	3,308	x					September 15	
KANSAS		27,305	9,053			x			x	September 1	
KENTUCKY	800	29,800	18,900			x		x		October 1	
LOUISIANA	67,752	1,574			x			x			x
MAINE	1,901	14,884			x				x	October 15	
MARYLAND	5,234	53,146				x			x	December 31	
MASSACHUSETTS	6,300	52,000	150		x			x			x
MICHIGAN	2,295	134,949	2,401		x				x	December 1	
MINNESOTA	State does not have this information.					x			x	September 1	
MISSISSIPPI	37,602	164			x				x	September 1	
MISSOURI	18,358	44,060				x			x	July 1	
MONTANA	State does not have this information.					x			x	September 10	
NEBRASKA	State does not have this information.				x				x	October 15	
NEVADA		13,202				x			x	September 30	
NEW HAMPSHIRE	28	6,200				x			x		x
(7) NEW JERSEY	13,019	65,233			x			x			x
NEW MEXICO	State does not have this information.					x			x	September 1	
(8) NEW YORK	109,000	73,000			x				x	December 1	
NORTH CAROLINA	83,833			3,751	x				x	October 16	

STATE	ORGANIZATION				FINANCE FOR FULL-DAY EVERY-DAY KINDERGARTEN			KINDERGARTEN ATTENDANCE		STARTING AGE	
	Number Children Full Day, Every Day	Number Children Half Day	Number Children Full Day, Alternate Day	Number Children Other	State Finance	State Does not Finance	Other	Mandatory	Not Mandatory	State Uniform Starting Age	No Uniform Starting Age
(9) NORTH DAKOTA		9,489		704		x			x	August 31	
OHIO	4,499	106,832	20,552	10,439		x			x	September 30	
(10) OKLAHOMA		45,009					x		x	September 1	
OREGON	1,061	27,000	260	12,000		x			x	September 1	
PENNSYLVANIA	18,500	99,950	2,583		x				x	January 31	
RHODE ISLAND		9,636				x			x	December 31	
SOUTH CAROLINA	5,040	40,992				x		x		November 1	
SOUTH DAKOTA	483	6,085	3,464	1,092			x		x	September 1	
TENNESSEE	State does not have this information.				x				x	September 30	
(11) TEXAS	See notes.				x			x		September 1	
UTAH		37,235							x	September 30	
(12) VERMONT	State does not have this information.						x	x		August 31–January 1	
VIRGINIA	46,310	32,562			x			x		September 30	
WASHINGTON	8,800	56,058			x				x	August 31	
WEST VIRGINIA	4,212	5,405	4,233		x			x		September 1	
WISCONSIN	5,040	57,860		540	x				x	September 1	
WYOMING	8,516					x			x	September 15	
	790,637	1,718,961	73,178	31,834	26	21	3	11	39		5

(1) State law prohibits holding kindergarten for more than four hours per day in a few districts. Therefore, full-day kindergarten is rare in California. A child must be at least four years and nine months of age on or before September 1 to enroll in]kindergarten.

(2) State provides full-day kindergarten funding for only 2,313 students based on a 1975 law which provided funding for full-day kindergarten. Districts cannot claim full-day funding for more students than they had in 1975.

(3) Approximately 35 of 166 school districts offer extended-day or full-day kindergarten.

(4) Full day is classified as extended day.

(5) Upon annual application and approval by the State Superintendent of Public Instruction, school districts are authorized to have kindergarten students in two sessions daily.

(6) Starting age will be moved back one month each year until uniform starting age is June 1.

(7) Kindergarten children attending a minimum day of 150 minutes are factored into the state equalization computations in exactly the same way as other elementary school children.

(8) Local schools may decide to admit younger children, but they may not deny entrance to those who comply with the December 1 rule.

(9) State finances 30 to 90 full days. The number in the "half-day" column includes those who attend 180 half days or 90 full days. The number in the "other" column includes those attending from 30 through 89 full days or equivalent in half days.

(10) State mandates schools to offer half-day kindergarten with funding at a full-day rate.

(11) There are 262,485 children who attend kindergarten in Texas. It is the local option of each school district to offer either half- or full-day kindergarten. State figures reflect only the total enrollment.

(12) The total kindergarten is 5,728 children. The state does not collect information by kindergarten organization. State aid monies are provided for total budgets, not just kindergartens.

Source: Evansville–Vanderburgh School Corporation. *A Longitundinal Study of the Consequences of Full-day Kindergarten: Kindergarten through Grade Eight*, 1988.

and discussed the growing agreement about developmentally appropriate practice. Through a "Primer for Parents," the article's authors list things to look for in a quality program for young children:

> (1) Teachers should talk to small groups of children or individual youngsters; they shouldn't just lecture.
> (2) Children should be working on projects, active experiments, and play; they shouldn't be at their desks all day filling in workbooks.
> (3) Children should be dictating or writing their own stories or reading real books.
> (4) The classroom layout should have reading and art areas and space for children to work in groups.
> (5) Children should create freehand artwork, not just color or paste together adult drawings.
> (6) Most importantly, watch the children' faces. Are they intellectually engaged, eager and happy? Do they look bored, or scared? (Kantrowitz and Wingert 1989)

Discussions about classroom practice for young children date back to the first public school kindergarten in St. Louis in 1873. There is growing agreement today among educators, school administrators, and professionals organizations. Developmentally appropriate practices, such as those outlined by SACUS, are solidly based on research in children's learning that has taken place over the past thirty years. These ideas have been emerging for some time and reflect ideas from progressivism, open education, and constructivism.

Prekindergarten Programs

By 1979 seven states had appropriated funds for public school prekindergarten programs. During the last decade, funds for early childhood programs have decreased even as a greater awareness of the benefits of good quality programs for young children has occurred. While the federal government has generally reduced its support for young children's programs, the states have recognized the need to fund programs for prekindergartners.

Along with states' efforts to increase funding and support for child care programs, the number of states that have funded public school prekindergarten programs has increased dramatically. By 1989, thirty-one states had appropriated funds for such programs and/or direct contributions to Head Start programs. Many of these programs are part-day and target at-risk four year olds. They generally are administered by the state departments of education and provided by the local school district. About half of these states, however, permit other state agencies to administer the programs. Among the newer state program sponsors are New Jersey, Florida, Vermont, Massachusetts, and Washington (Mitchell 1989).

Research in programs for young children has clearly revealed seven critical components in high quality programs:

1. A developmentally appropriate curriculum;
2. Supervisory support and inservice training for program staff;
3. Low enrollment limits and an adequate number of adults, with teaching/caregiving teams assigned to small groups of children;
4. Staff trained in early childhood development;
5. Parents involved as partners with program staff;
6. Sensitivity to the noneducational circumstances of the child and family; and
7. Developmentally appropriate evaluation procedures. (Schweinhart 1987)

PARENT INVOLVEMENT

The necessity of parent involvement in early childhood education programs has been well documented (Lazar 1981; Gordon 1976; Swick 1987; Schweinhart 1987). Some programs provide opportunities for parents to become directly involved in working with children in the classrooms. Many programs provide parent education classes which deal with parenting skills, child development, and child management techniques.

Parental status has changed. Parents no longer are mere recipients of services, but now have an opportunity to become active participants in the education of their child. Some programs, especially those serving handicapped children, require parents to become involved.

Traditionally, parental involvement in the educational process was somewhat vague and restricted. Teachers were reluctant to allow parents to assume a participatory role. In some cases, parents were perceived as problems or as the cause of problems in the child (Seligman and Seligman 1980). Parental attitudes toward professionals also were part of the historical problem. Some parents have blamed professionals for not recognizing the child's problem, disability, or handicap. As a result of these types of interactions, positive and effective relationships between the two groups were inhibited (Graves and Gargiulo 1989).

Fortunately, a new way of approaching parent-teacher partnerships is being exhibited. Professionals are now viewing parents as an untapped resource in working with young children. Both parties recognize that the process of building and maintaining effective partnerships must be created, nurtured, and cultivated (Berger 1987). Trust, respect, and cooperation are essential ingredients in the collaborative effort (Graves and Swick 1986). Strategies for programs serving young children must be supportive of parents (Swick 1987).

SERVING CHILDREN WITH SPECIAL NEEDS

The enactment of Public Law 99–457, the Education of the Handi-capped Act Amendments of 1986, demonstrated a new era of commit-ment to the nation's special-needs youngsters. It is the first major legislation affecting the special-needs child since Public Law 94–142 was passed in 1975. One of the unique features of this legislation is the recognition of the importance of family services in meeting the needs of the preschool child. Rather than using an Individualized Education Program (IEP) to guide the services for the child, this act requires that an Individualized Family Services Plan (IFSP) be written and used to best meet the needs of the child and family. This approach offers the professional and the parent an opportunity to become part of an in-terdisciplinary team which will work for the child and family.

Public Law 99–457 establishes a new federal initiative to assist states in developing and implementing comprehensive programs for hand-icapped young children. The program must be coordinated, interdis-ciplinary, and serve children and their families. It extends discretionary programs under parts of P.L. 94–142 including research, demonstration and outreach programs, and personal preparation. Under the Act, pre-

■ *Public Law 99-457 requires schools to serve preschool children with disabilities.*

INTRODUCTION TO EDUCATION

schoolers will be served and children two years old and younger may be served. These children must be at risk or show a developmental delay. Many types of services may be provided including family counseling, speech pathology and instruction, occupational therapy, physical therapy, psychological services, and early identification, screening, and assessment (Liaison Bulletin 1986). Because of this new law, many more handicapped young children will be served in comprehensive programs. Under this new Act, parent participation is no longer a privilege, but a right. P.L. 99–457 provides an open door for direct involvement as parents become participating members in a multidisciplinary team to provide appropriate services for children.

ADVOCACY AND PUBLIC POLICY

Professionals in early childhood education are becoming more politically active in efforts to change public policy which affects young children and their families. Groups like the Children's Defense Fund and the National Association for the Education of Young Children have taken the lead in lobbying efforts for children. Since the United States is the only major industrialized nation without a specific federal child care policy, advocates are making clear suggestions about the kinds of relationships they believe should exist for families. Four assumptions underlie the beliefs of children's advocates:

(1) Families have the ultimate responsibility for caring for and rearing their children, but society is responsible for supporting families and enabling them to better meet their child-rearing responsibilities.
(2) The self-sufficient family is a myth. Parents are executive coordinators of services for their children, selecting schools, doctors, and special programs. Families are not self-sufficient; they do not independently fulfill their own needs; many of the problems families face are beyond individual control.
(3) A wide variety of childrearing practices and family forms are equally successful in rearing competent children, although family policies in the past have not adequately recognized or supported this diversity.
(4) Interested adults have learned that children's needs must be promoted, and often can be met only through the political process (Goffin 1988).

During the past few years, early childhood education advocates have spoken out on two very important issues: developmentally appropriate educational experiences and the need for a national child care bill. Publications from the Children's Defense Fund and the National Association for the Education of Young Children are very important resources for advocates. One such book is *Speaking Out: Early Childhood Advocacy* (Goffin and Lombardi 1988).

Teachers in early childhood education have been slow to become child advocates for several reasons:

1. They feel advocacy is beneath their dignity.
2. They feel they are powerless to change anything.
3. They are unsophisticated about how the political process actually works (Lombardi 1986).

Some leaders in higher education are now recommending advocacy training in teacher education programs. It is hoped that, by including advocacy, teachers will feel better equipped to become a child advocate. According to Caldwell (1987), educators should be commited to three types of advocacy: personal advocacy, professional advocacy, and informational advocacy. Professional organizations are helping educators in the professional advocacy and informational advocacy areas. In each issue of journals such as *Young Children* and *Dimensions*, public policy reports inform the professional of current bills and of what types of action can be taken.

SUMMARY

This chapter has focused on early childhood education. Although the field of early childhood education is relatively young, its history is influenced by thinkers such as Plato and Aristotle, who date back to 384 B.C. Some historians point to the work of Rousseau as the dividing line between the historical and modern periods of education. His view that children were essentially good and were capable of achievements became common elements in works of other leading thinkers who were discussed in the chapter.

Froebel, the "father of kindergarten," believed that activity is the basis for knowing and that play is an essential component of learning. Many of his ideas were held by Comenius and Pestalozzi. John Dewey's beliefs have made an impact on all areas of education in the United States. It is from his emphasis on the child and the child's interests that the terms child-centered curriculum and child-centered schools were coined. Although the influence of Dewey's progressivism as a guiding philosophy may have disappeared from many schools, it continues to remain a strong influence in early childhood education programs.

Reform in the kindergarten, which was led by John Dewey's progressive movement, is discussed in the chapter. This movement placed a stronger emphasis on the child and the child's interests rather than subject matter. The Nursery School movement, beginning with Margaret McMillan's first nursery school in 1911, is discussed. Federal involvement and compensatory programs like Head Start and Follow Through are examined, as well as other program models. The influence of Maria Montessori and Jean Piaget on current programs is also explained.

The next section of the chapter discusses the different types of programs for young children including child care centers, family day care homes, preschools, and employer-sponsored programs. Programs are funded in a variety of ways and are sponsored by a variety of groups. Issues and trends in public-school kindergartens and prekindergartens are discussed. This discussion includes developmentally appropriate educational experiences and the critical components of quality programs.

Sections on parent involvement, on serving children with special needs, and on advocacy and public policy are contained in the last portion of the chapter. A recognition of the partnership potential in working with parents is discussed, and the necessity for parent involvement in programs for young children is well documented. Information about a new federal initiative to assist states in developing and implementing comprehensive programs for handicapped children is also discussed in the last section.

IN THE FIELD

1. What key issues of concern influenced the beginning of early childhood education programs?
2. How did Martin Luther's beliefs influence early efforts in education for young children?
3. Why did the federal government become involved in programs for young children?
4. Describe the reasons compensatory programs for young children were developed?
5. Are public-school kindergarten programs available for five-year-old children in every state? Are they mandatory?
6. Are prekindergarten programs available in public schools?
7. What are the benefits for employers who provide programs for young children? What are the benefits for the employees?
8. What are the current key issues in programs for young children?
9. Are parents generally involved in programs for young children? Has the research shown parent involvement to be beneficial to the overall program?
10. Are special-needs children served in public school programs? What is the public law which relates to programs for the handicapped?
11. Should teachers become involved in advocacy activities? Why?

REFERENCES

Almy, M. 1975. *The Early Childhood Educator at Work*. New York: McGraw-Hill.

Berger, E. 1987. *Parents as Partners in Education*. Columbus: Merrill.

Bredekamp, S., ed. 1987. *Developmentally Appropriate Practice in Early Childhood Programs Serving Children from Birth through Age 8*. Washington: National Association for the Education of Young Children.

Burud, S., R. Collins, and P. Devine-Hawkins. 1983. Employer supported child care: everybody benefits. *Children Today* 12(3) 2–7.

Caldwell, B. 1987. Advocacy is everybody's business. *Child Care Information Exchange* 54, 29–32.

Calhoun, J., and R. Collins, 1981. A positive view of programs for early childhood intervention. *Theory into Practice* 20, 135–140.

Decker, C., and J. Decker, 1988. *Planning and Administering Early Childhood Programs*. Columbus: Merrill.

Edelman, M. 1985. *A Children's Defense Fund Budget*. Washington: Children's Defense Fund.

Evansville-Vanderburgh School Corporation. 1988. *A Longitudinal Study of the Consequences of Full-day Kindergarten: Kindergarten through Grade Eight*. Evansville, IN: Evansville-Vanderburgh School Corporation.

Feeney, S., D. Christensen, and E. Moravcik. 1987. *Who am I in the Lives of Children?* Columbus: Merrill.

Froebel, F. 1887. *The Education of Man*. Trans. New York: D. Appleton.

Goffin, S. G. 1988. Putting our advocacy efforts into a new context. *Young Children* 43(3), 52–56.

Goffin, S. G., and J. Lombardi. 1988. *Speaking Out: Early Childhood Advocacy*. Washington: National Association for the Education of Young Children.

Gordon, I. 1976. *Building Effective Home-school Relationships*. Boston: Allyn and Bacon.

Graves, S. B., and R. Gargiulo. 1989. Parents and early childhood professionals as programs partners: Meeting the needs of the preschool exceptional child. *Dimensions* 17(2), 23–24.

Graves, S. B., and K. Swick. 1986. The relationship of parental locus of control, interpersonal support, and the young child's level of developmental functioning in a preschool setting. *Instructional Psychology* 13(3), 153–159.

Hicks, M., and J. Powell. 1983. Corporate day care, 1980's: A responsible choice. *Dimensions* 11(4), 4–10.

Hodges, W., and M. Cooper. 1981. Head start and follow through: Influences of intellectual development. *Journal of Special Education* 15(2), 221–237.

Kantrowitz, B., and P. Wingert. 1989. How Kids Learn. *Newsweek*, April 17, 1989, 50–56.

Keatinge, M., ed. 1896, 1910. *The Great Didactic of John Amos Comenius*. New York: Russell and Russell, trans. and ed., 1967.

Lazar, I. 1981. Early intervention is effective. *Educational Leadership* 38, 303–305.

Liaison Bulletin 12(12), 1986. National Association of State Directors of Special Education, Washington, DC.

Lombardi, J. 1986. Training for public policy and advocacy. *Young Children* 42, 65–69.

Mitchell, A. 1989. Old baggage, new visions: Shaping policy for early childhood programs. *Phi Delta Kappan* 70(1), 665–672.

Morrison, G. S. 1988. *Early Childhood Education Today*. Columbus: Merrill.

Nurss, J., and W. Hodges. 1981. *Encyclopedia of Educational Research*, 5th ed. Atlanta: Georgia State University.

Painter, F. 1928. *Luther on Education*. St. Louis: Concordia.

Robinson, S. L. 1982. Educational oportunities for young children in America. *Childhood Education* 59 (1).

Schweinhart, L. J. 1987. When the buck stops here: What it takes to run good early childhood programs. *The High/Scope Resource*. Ypsilanti: High/Scope Foundation.

Seligman, M. and P. Seligman. 1980. The professional's dilemma: Learning to work with parents. *Exceptional Parent* 10, 11–13.

Spodek, B., O. Saracho, and M. Davis. 1987. *Foundations of Early Childhood Education: Teaching Three-, Four-, and Five-year-old Children*. Englewood Cliffs, NJ: Prentice-Hall.

Stevens, J. 1982. The national day care home study: Family day care in the United States. *Young Children* 37(4), 59–66.

Swick, K. 1987. *Perspectives on Understanding and Working with Families*. Champaign, IL: Stipes.

Swick, K., M. Brown, and S. B. Graves, 1984. Developmentally appropriate educational experiences for kindergarten. *Dimensions* 12(4), 25.

Zigler, E., and M. Lang. 1983. Head start: Looking toward the future. *Young Children* 38(6), 3–5.

7

ELEMENTARY EDUCATION

ADVANCE ORGANIZERS

1. What are the purposes of elementary schools?
2. How do principals provide instructional leadership?
3. What are the advantages and disadvantages of graded and nongraded schools?
4. What are the roles of philosophy and policy in elementary education?
5. What influences elementary school curricula?
6. What do elementary teachers do?
7. How can teachers utilize classroom space?
8. What are the primary modes of instruction in elementary classrooms?
9. What special services are available in elementary schools?

INTRODUCTION

Elementary schools in the United States are the mandatory beginning point for public education (Good 1986). The elementary school was the basis for the common-school movement of Horace Mann in the mid-1800s (Binder 1974) and has become the foundation of free, public education. While many children do not attend vocational schools, do not graduate from high school, and may attend junior high school only with a well-documented record of failure, the majority of American children attend elementary schools, and without experiencing academic failure. It has been shown that the two major influences on children's academic performances in later school years are parents and the children's teachers in grades 1–3 (Entwisle and Hayduk 1988).

ELEMENTARY SCHOOLS

Elementary schools are the first and most important educational opportunity for many children. Although many children of middle- and upper-middle-class families attend day-care programs before reaching school age, for many others the public elementary school is their first organized educational experience. Even for the many children who attend several day-care programs, public elementary schools provide the first academic training they receive. Several factors help shape elementary schools in the United States. Among them are the administration, organizational arrangements, philosophy and school policies, curriculum, and teaching styles and methodologies.

Purpose of Elementary Schools

Elementary schools in the United States have many different purposes. Those most frequently stressed include

1. literacy,
2. citizenship education, and
3. personal development (Jarolimek and Foster 1985)

Literacy. Public schools in the United States have always had the responsibility to develop literacy in children. This initially began as reading instruction but expanded to include writing and arithmetic. Currently schools focus not only on instruction in the three basic academic areas but on knowledge of the world, science, and cultural awareness. "There is no way that an elementary school can receive a high rating without doing a respectable job of teaching children the fundamental skills of literacy" (Jarolimek and Foster 1981, p. 4).

Citizenship Education. The second goal of elementary schools is to provide citizenship education. Like literacy training, this goal has been present in elementary schools since the development of publicly supported educational programs. Citizenship education is provided through formal classes such as history and civics; children also experience citizenship training through informal activities with children from a cross section of society (Jarolimek and Foster 1985).

Personal Development. The final goal of the elementary school is personal development. Although not a primary focus of elementary education until this century, personal development is now thought of as a major responsibility of schools. Emotional, social, and physical growth are aspects of personal development that elementary schools attempt to facilitate (Jarolimek and Foster 1985). Another area of personal development includes multicultural education. Elementary-aged children need an awareness of the various cultures and ethnic groups that are represented in this country. Children from these racial and cultural minority groups need to be able to identify with their groups; multicultural education can greatly facilitate this process.

Administration of Elementary Schools

As in all educational programs, the administration of elementary schools is vital to all elements of the school. Superintendents, building principals, and educational supervisors all participate to some degree in the administration of elementary schools. While the board of education and school superintendent are major administrative forces in el-

■ *Citizenship education is a major purpose of elementary schools.*

ementary schools, principals have the most direct administrative and supervisory role in the total school program.

Principals perform many different roles and functions in elementary schools, including instructional leadership and management, personnel management, financial management, plant management, community relations, and student management. These roles are becoming increasingly complex (Duke 1987). They vary from school to school, district to district, and state to state. With so many different things to do, principals frequently find themselves going from one thing to the other, constantly having to shift gears (Morris, Crowson, Hurwitz, and Porter-Gehrie 1982). Even so, the public generally views elementary principals as doing an effective job. In the 1987 Gallup Poll on the Public's Attitudes Toward Schools, forty-seven percent of the respondents felt that elementary principals should receive an *A* or *B* for their efforts; another twenty-three percent gave the principals a *C* (Gallup and Clark 1987). Today's K–8 principals regard three types of experiences as critical to being a good administrator—on-the-job experience as a principal, classroom teaching experience, and experience as an assistant principal (Doud 1989).

Assistant principals are more prevalent in elementary schools today than in the past. During a ten-year period between 1978 and 1988, the number of assistant principals increased thirteen percent. Seventy-five percent of all elementary schools with more than 600 students employ assistant principals (Doud 1989). It follows that, if principals have assistant principals to assist in carrying out routine daily tasks, then they have more time to spend on other, more important issues.

Principals are bound by the administrative hierarchy of the school, by the chain of command. In school districts, principals usually report to the superintendent, unless the district is large enough to employ assistant superintendents. The larger the school bureaucracy, the more principals must concern themselves with groups of individuals in the chain of command rather than single individuals (Brieschke 1985). Regardless of the size of the administrative structure, principals still are directly in control of the actions that occur in their schools. As a result, the many functions performed by principals in elementary schools are critical to the functioning of the school.

Principals as Instructional Leaders. One of the most important functions of the principal is in the area of instructional leadership. Broadly defined, instructional leadership includes all actions taken by principals, or delegated to others, that promote learning in students. Principals view themselves as instructional leaders and even attend workshops and other staff development activities to improve their skills in this area (Cooper 1989). The fact that elementary principals indicated classroom teaching was the second most important kind of experience needed for being a good principal reveals the importance principals place on this role.

In today's era of educational reform, the role of instructional leader is more important than ever. Principals must be able to recognize poor teaching and be able to implement ways to make teaching better. At the same time, principals should recognize exemplary teaching skills and should develop incentives and rewards to encourage these teaching styles.

Hierarchy of Administration. The state's right and responsibility for providing public education are inferred from the United States Constitution, which did not reserve either for the federal government. States, in turn, have granted the power to operate local schools to local boards of education. Boards of education hire superintendents to carry out board policy, and superintendents employ other administrative personnel, such as assistant superintendents and principals, to assist in carrying out board policy.

At the top of the administrative hierarchy of public schools is the district superintendent. From this point, school districts vary considerably in their organizational structure. For example, in large districts, several administrative levels may exist between the superintendent and the principal. In small districts, on the other hand, principals report directly to the superintendent because the district does not employ assistant superintendents or curriculum coordinators.

In addition to the formal power structure, or the administrative hierarchy, there is an informal power structure. The formal power structure can be described as the traditional hierarchical design where power flows from top to bottom, whereas the informal power structure comprises interpersonal relationships among school staff and community members (Wood, Nicholson, and Findley 1979). The two structures also differ in that the formal structure describes the responsibilities for decision making, and the informal structure does not; communication channels in the formal structure are well-defined, but the informal structure depends on communication methods such as the infamous "grapevine" (Lipham and Hoeh 1974). Individuals in the formal power structure, such as superintendents and principals, must pay attention to the informal structure and consider its influence in decision making.

Organizational Arrangements of Elementary Schools

The movement of students in elementary schools is both vertical and horizontal, which requires that schools be organized both vertically and horizontally.

Vertical Organization. "Vertical organization is the plan of the school for identifying when and who is ready to enter, as well as the procedures for regulating pupil progress through the elementary school to a completion point" (Ragan and Shepherd 1977, p. 109). Without vertical organization, there would be no set beginning time for students, no plan as to when to move students to higher curricular areas, and no set time for the completion of the program.

Most organizational strategies can be dichotomized into *graded* and *nongraded.*

The general concept of the graded elementary school is to move students through the school in groups in a series of steps called grades. Each step, or grade, is usually one academic year in duration, with the number of grades varying among schools. During colonial America, graded schools did not exist; students with wide age ranges were simply assigned to a teacher, usually in a one-room schoolhouse with only one teacher. The notion of grouping students into grades based on chronological age was developed in Germany. American educators liked the idea, and, after the Civil War, there was a rapid growth of graded schools. The general concept was to assign students to groups based on chronological age and keep these students together from year to year (Jarolimek and Foster 1985). Characteristics of the graded school are the following:

1. The graded school recognizes chronological age as the primary, if not the only, determiner of entry. Chronological age and years in school are the major ingredients of the decisions that locate the child within the vertical sequence.

2. The graded school has identified a body of skills, knowledge, and appreciations and has placed them in a sequence of six or seven positions called "grades." Each position equals one school term, or approximately nine months.

3. As a result of these positions and their sequence, graded textbooks were developed. Textbooks are typically assigned to a position within the sequence, and pupils at that position study the assigned text.

4. The decisions governing the vertical movement of pupils through the sequence are made at the end of the school term. Some variations have been introduced to provide for quarterly or semester promotions.

5. Promotion from one position to the next higher position within the sequence is dependent upon the pupil's having completed, with average or above success, all the work of the preceding position.

6. Graded schools may utilize the horizontal organizations of the self-contained classroom, departmentalization, platoon, or team.

7. The symbols expressing a graded organization are 1–6, or K–3 and 4–6, as applied to a building. For a school district the symbols, elementary through secondary, might be: K–5, 6–8, 9–10, and 11–12, or K–8 and 9–12. These symbols represent the vertical organization and the commitments of the district to kindergarten, middle school, mid-high, and high school.

8. At its lowest level, gradedness is essentially a lockstep system. (Ragan and Shepherd 1977, p. 111–12)

The graded organization has some definite strong points: (1) it reduces some variability among students; (2) it exposes all children to the same curriculum; (3) educational materials can be developed for chronological age interests; (4) similar chronological age among students facilitates social interactions; (5) it is efficient; (6) teachers are able to specialize their teaching by focusing on a particular age group; and (7) minimum standards can be established for each grade level. Limitations of the graded approach include locking students into certain groups, regardless of ability levels, and encouraging teachers to teach to the group with a rigid curriculum (Jarolimek and Foster 1985).

The aim of the nongraded school is continuous progress. Rather than locking students into a step system, nongraded schools allow students to progress through a curriculum at their own pace. The advantages of a nongraded approach are obvious, the greatest advantage being that students are not locked into a level irrespective of their skills and abilities. Capable students are able to progress in one year through two or more traditional grade levels. Likewise, students whose progress is slower than average avoid the stigma of having to repeat a grade or of being passed onto the next grade without having mastered the competencies required for that level. While nongraded programs vary in name and type, the following features are common to most:

1. Students progress at their own rates throughout the school year.
2. Identification of skills, knowledges, and appreciations in content areas, not length of time, are the key to moving on to higher curricular levels.
3. Competencies, not the number of years in school, are used to determine pupils' locations along the curricular sequence.
4. Extensive reporting and record keeping are required to chart student progress.
5. Students are provided with successful experiences regardless of their location in the curriculum. (Ragan and Shepherd 1977)

At first glance, the nongraded approach would appear to have many advantages over the graded system. Although as many as twenty-five percent of elementary schools have tried the nongraded organization, fewer than ten percent maintained the system (Ragan and Shepherd 1977). Probable causes for the lack of popularity of the nongraded system include (1) too much record keeping, (2) great deviation from the traditional graded approach, (3) the likelihood that teachers were trained for the graded system, and (4) the likelihood that many parents do not understand the nongraded format.

Horizontal Organization. Besides organizing the way students move through elementary schools, students and teachers need to be organized into instructional groups. This is called horizontal organization. The two basic approaches to horizontal organization are self-contained classrooms and departmentalization.

Students placed in self-contained classrooms receive the majority of their instruction in the same classroom from one teacher. This is the traditional approach and the most popular. A 1968 survey of more than two thousand elementary principals determined that more than ninety-five percent of the schools used self-contained classrooms in primary grades, eighty-eight percent in the fourth grade, eighty percent in the fifth grade, and seventy-one percent in the sixth grade (National Education Association 1968).

Many arguments support the self-contained classroom. First, by having the same group of students all day for all subjects, teachers have a great deal of time to learn about, observe, and evaluate their students. Self-contained classrooms also facilitate an interrelated curriculum. Teachers are better able to tie material together across subject areas. In self-contained classrooms, students also have a better opportunity to participate in group activities, and there is a great deal more flexibility with time than in departmentalized schemes where students must go to another classroom at a certain time (Ragan and Shepherd 1977). The most viable argument for maintaining self-contained classrooms is tradition. Just as tradition makes nongraded vertical organization difficult to implement, it also helps to maintain the self-contained classroom that was used in the one-room schoolhouse.

The self-contained approach does have limitations:

- Pupils and teachers are isolated from other students and teachers.
- Students are primarily forced to interact with students in the same classroom.
- Cliques are easily established.
- Many teachers are not capable of teaching all subject areas.
- Leaders remain leaders and followers remain followers.

In departmentalized elementary schools, teachers specialize in a particular curricular area or areas. In contrast to the teacher in a self-contained classroom who must be somewhat of a generalist, teachers in a departmentalized scheme have time to concentrate on one or two teaching areas. Rather than teaching all subjects to twenty to thirty children daily, they may teach one or two subjects to one hundred children daily. The advantage of the departmentalized approach is that teachers have the opportunity to become experts in a limited number of subject areas.

Most of the disadvantages of the departmentalized approach relate the advantages of the self-contained approach. Namely, teachers in a departmentalized school have less time to get to know students well, subject matter may not be coordinated among the different teachers, and teachers and students are locked into specific time restraints.

In today's schools, specialized "pull-out" programs for students create scheduling problems even in schools using a self-contained organizational model. Students frequently are pulled out of classes for special education, enrichment, speech therapy, and chapter programs. "This reality results in repeated interruptions, loss of instructional time, fragmented programs, and frustration. . . . (Canady 1988, p. 65). Parallel block scheduling which parallels pull-out programs with regular classes, enables teachers to spend more instructional time with students who remain in class and at the same time accommodate those students involved in pull-out programs (Canady 1988).

Philosophy and School Policies

The philosophy and policies of schools give each school a unique personality. What occurs in schools and classrooms has a direct relationship to the underlying philosophy of the school and classroom. "Decision about goals and curriculum rest solidly upon the school's ideas and beliefs about the nature of the child and how the child learns; about ethics, economics, and other great issues" (King-Stoops 1977, p. 5). For example, some schools may have the reputation of being tough on discipline and academic requirements, while others may be more lax and include some extracurricular opportunities in the curriculum. While the philosophy and policies of individual schools reflect the philosophy and policies of the local school board and superintendent, principals and teachers can influence these two elements to some degree, thereby giving the school a different personality than other schools.

The philosophy and policies of schools affect disciplinary methods, academic expectations and requirements, dress codes, curriculum, and school climate. Persons who influence the philosophy and policies of schools include administrators, teachers, school staff, parents and other community members, and students.

Although many would say that school boards and superintendents dictate school philosophy and policies, many variations exist among schools in the same district. Administrative leadership style is a key factor in how individuals are brought into decision making and how school district philosophies and policies are implemented. Administrators can affect district philosophy and policies by choosing to implement directives, at the expense of the school, or by refusing to implement directives for the sake of the school (Brieschke 1985).

Refusing to implement district directives or policy is called creative insubordination. It can be accomplished either by attempting to directly go against policies or by two or more principals agreeing to not implement certain directives. A third method is to openly refuse to meet deadlines. Regardless of the modes of insubordination chosen, administrators must believe that their actions are better for the school than the results of following district guidelines (Brieschke 1985).

In addition to building administrators influencing district philosophy and policies, the actions of many groups have an impact (see table 7.1).

Curriculum in Elementary Schools

The curriculum adopted and implemented by a school is more than a listing of subjects to be taught. The curriculum includes not only the

TABLE 7.1
Groups Influencing District Philosophy and Policies

GROUP	INFLUENCE
Parents	Actions by parent groups Actions by individual parents
Teachers	Actions by teacher organizations Actions by individual teachers Actions by teacher committees
State Department of Education	Development of curriculum guides Development of policies
Professional Groups	Curriculum suggestions in publications Development of standards
Accreditation Groups	Development and monitoring standards

intellectual content of subjects but the methods used to teach, the interactions that occur between teachers and students, and school-sponsored activities. A curriculum includes all student experiences for which the school accepts responsibility: formal courses, school-sponsored clubs, athletics, and band.

The school's curriculum is derived from several different sources. Tyler (1949) suggested that a curriculum results from society, subject-matter specialists, and students (see figure 7.1). The role of society in curricular development is essential; what a particular society values must be incorporated into public school programs. After all, members of society are the taxpayers who support public education. Subject-matter specialists are needed in curricular development to help determine how much of a particular subject should be included in each grade level. Students participate, not by deciding what they should and should not learn, but by others determining the needs of students as viewed by society and subject-matter specialists (Fain, Shostak, and Dean 1979).

The elementary school curriculum is in a constant state of change; it never remains static but changes relative to the outside world. Throughout history, various influences have had an impact on school curricula (see table 7.2). A school's curriculum reflects the attitudes, values, and concerns of society. As a result of this relationship between curriculum and external forces, the current curriculum used in schools can be expected to undergo changes during the coming decades. For instance, in looking at what the future holds for school curricula, Wassermann (1984) indicates a preference for including areas that cannot be taught using computers and technology: (1) nurturing of children's feelings, (2) promotion of interpersonal skills, (3) promotion of higher-order cognitive skills, (4) nurturing of creativity and imagination, and (5) development of moral integrity.

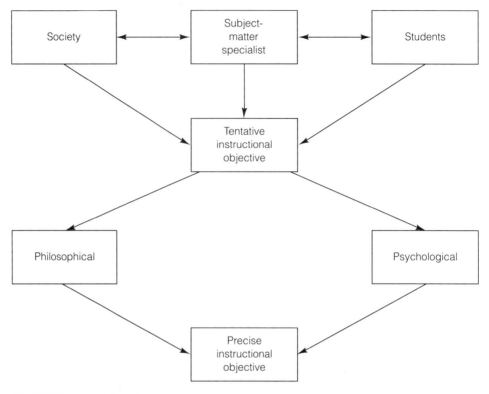

FIGURE 7.1. *Tyler's Rationale.*
Source: Tyler. Basic Principles of Curriculum and Instruction, 1949.

TABLE 7.2
Major Influences on Curriculum

TIME	INFLUENCE
1635–1770	Religion; schools expected to promulgate the religious beliefs in the country.
1770–1860	Political; schools should educate the public to ensure the preservation of democracy.
1860–1920	Economic; schools should educate people to fill new jobs in a rapidly expanding economy.
1920–present	Mass Education; schools should provide equal educational opportunity to all citizens.
1957–present	Excellence in Education; schools should do a better job in educating American youth. This movement resulted from the discovery in World War II that many graduates were very weak in mathematics and science. Sputnik also was a major influence.

Although every school district may have a slightly different curriculum, most elementary schools provide basic academic instruction in similar areas. These include reading, mathematics, and writing, commonly referred to as the three Rs. A former secretary for the U.S. Department of Education expressed the importance of the basic academic curriculum in elementary schools when he said, "It is imperative that elementary educators focus on the acquisition of basic skills and good habits through which children will be able to extend the reach of their learning in later years" (Bennett 1986, p. 11).

In addition to these basic academic areas, several other areas normally are found in the curriculum of elementary schools. Areas such as science (Besvinick 1988); social studies (Maxim 1987); language arts, including written and verbal expression (Monson, Taylor, and Dykstra 198); drug education (Sylwester and Hasegawa 1989); and even listening skills (Winn 1988) have received emphasis during the past several years. The curriculum in elementary schools must be in a constant state of change in order to meet the ever-changing needs of its students (Bennett 1986).

Elementary school curricula in the future must take into consideration the needs of society; it must be responsive to the rapidly changing world. In view of the rapid growth of knowledge and increased specialization, a task force studying future trends in curriculum planning recommended that common themes be treated in an interdisciplinary fashion, that facts as well as processes be stressed, and that materials in addition to textbooks be used in education (Troutman and Palombo 1983). Another important component of the curriculum of the future should be an emphasis on teaching students to relate language to culture. This need will become more pronounced as daily interactions among culturally diverse individuals increase (Miel 1984). The curriculum should reflect multicultural education components to enable children to understand, accept, and identify with cultural and ethnic groups other than their own.

Variables that affect what a district includes in its elementary curriculum include the size and location of the district, socioeconomic factors in the community, priorities of the district, pupil-teacher ratios, and desired student outcomes. For example, small districts located in rural, agricultural communities likely stress different subjects than large, urban, industrialized districts. The teacher also has a major role in determining what part of the school's curriculum is taught (Good 1986).

Although elementary students may not have a great deal of impact on the school's curriculum, they do have a preference for various subjects. A recent study compared the subjects preferred by elementary students in 1988 to preferences in a 1977 survey. The results showed that art was the most preferred and English the least preferred in both

HELPING KIDS LIKE THE LAB

Sharon Begley

One day last week the fourth graders at Piney Branch Elementary School in Maryland eagerly filed into Craig Logue's class for a lesson on chemical reactions. They were smiling because they knew they didn't face a lecture on electron exchange, catalysts and other sleep inducers. Rather, Logue, 37, was making alchemists of them. Working in pairs, the students added 20 drops of vinegar from a squeeze bottle to each of five little cups of "mystery powders." They stirred the sludge with a Popsicle stick and recorded the look and texture of the mixtures that fizzed, got hot, developed lumps and otherwise put on a good show. The bell rang but no one wanted to leave. "When you get plain old lectures, you don't learn anything," said Alex Patchen, nine. His friend Scott Collins agreed. "We learn more because we get to see it for ourselves. And it's funner."

"It" is hands-on science, and it's part of the biggest push to improve science education in the United States since the Soviets orbited Sputnik 1 in 1957. Then the goal was to groom elementary and high schoolers for college science and swell the nation's ranks of researchers and engineers. No one would mind if that happened this time around. But today the emphasis is more on reaching the ordinary student, not the one who will cure AIDS but the one who will vote on whether AIDS carriers should be quarantined. The rationale is simple. Crucial political decisions increasingly depend on science and technology—everything from deploying the Strategic Defense Initiative to releasing genetically engineered bacteria. The scientifically illiterate "are foreigners in their own culture," says Paul DeHart Hurd, professor emeritus of science education at Stanford University. Ignorant of science, they can't understand the debate, much less shape it.

The symptoms of the ills in science education are legion. One-third of Americans don't know what a molecule is, reports Jon Miller of Northern Illinois University, who surveyed adults in 1985. Five out of six don't understand the basics of genetic engineering; more than two-thirds have no clear understanding of radiation. The causes of this ignorance are clear, too. Science tends not to be taught, or to be taught poorly, in most public schools. The average third grader spends 18 minutes a day on science; the average sixth grader, 29 minutes. About one-third of science and mathematics courses are staffed by teachers who are not qualified to teach the subject. High schools have only minimal science requirements for graduation, particularly compared with schools in the Soviet Union. Science education is, in part, an unintended victim of the back-to-basics movement. Educators, pressured to teach Johnny to read and add, neglected to teach him biology, chemistry or physics. And since schools are often rated on reading and math scores, many don't seem to care as much as they might whether their pupils know what DNA is.

Gradually, however, science education is changing. Tedious lectures on batteries or magnetism or photosynthesis are disappearing. In their place is the kind of hands-on science offered at the East Los Angeles Science Center, one of eight in the school district where teachers take their charges for mesmerizing demonstrations that go beyond show and tell. Last week fifth and sixth graders watched in awe as light beams bounced off mirrors, bent through prisms and burst into rainbows. It was a painless way to get acquainted with optics and the discoveries of Isaac Newton.

continued

Perhaps the biggest hit among students lately are lessons based on cutting-edge research. The science story of 1987, for example, was superconductivity, in which special materials conduct electricity with no loss of power. Already, thousands of high schools are using a $25 superconductivity kit developed by chemist Arthur Ellis of the University of Wisconsin. For many students at Madison West High School in Wisconsin, David Braunschweig's senior seminar was one of the few times science wasn't drudgery. During one recent experiment, 17-year-old Deborah Chagnon watched with delight as she levitated a magnet above a superconducting pellet amid wisps of liquid nitrogen. It looked like magic, but the students were demonstrating a key property of superconductors: their ability to repel magnetic fields. "I had to go through three years of science classes before I had fun," Chagnon says.

Flying Trains

The levitation experiment sent the students' imaginations soaring, too. They envisioned a world of uses for superconductors, forseeing a tomorrow in which hockey players float above superconducting ice rinks and trains fly along superconducting rails. "I like the idea of taking ideas that are usually science fiction and making them practical," says Chagnon.

The need to hook students before they get turned off by science has made elementary schools the focus of many of the reforms. Traditional lessons "do a good job of killing our kids' natural curiosity," says Bassam Shakhashiri of the National Science Foundation. To keep it alive, classes are getting away from rote learning, especially of vocabulary. As part of its drive to replace the tedious, old ways, the NSF gave $2.2 million to the Technical Education Research Centers in Cambridge, Mass., to develop curricula for grades four through six. Next week 200 schools will begin testing the program. It shouldn't bore anyone. In the unit on acid rain, for instance, the students collect pond, tap and rainwater, measure its acidity, enter the results into a computer and compare them with what kids across the

country have found. The idea is not only to teach students about acidity but to expose them to the collaboration and conflicting results of real science. "This is a far more appropriate educational strategy than the usual fact-and-formula approach," says TERC's Robert Tinker.

The trend of linking science to contemporary issues such as acid rain addresses one of the most serious failings of education: that it teaches the facts of science, not its process. Educators may endlessly debate whether physics or biology is more important, but most everyone agrees that the real need is to produce citizens who can think critically and reason logically. "We want students to know why the results of experiments are sometimes different, how conclusions are reached," says Anthony Galitsis, science director of the New York City schools. "We don't want them to take everything they hear and read as gospel." The curriculum at Nathan Bishop Middle School in Providence, R.I., has brought such lofty sentiments to life. Last year students learned about garbage incinerators, an emerging environmental issue. They visted a landfill, made up a questionnaire on the pros and cons of incineration, heard from experts and built a model incinerator. Finally, they staged a mock talk show, debating the policy implications of incineration. They saw how scientists working with the same facts can honestly reach different conclusions, a process that baffles most laymen.

New Recruits

Despite the advances, science education still faces consideration hurdles. The most innovative curriculum won't do any good if the teacher is too science-phobic to tackle it, for instance. Some states are addressing the problem by hiring scientists and engineers to teach now and pick up education credits later. Beginning next August, Mills College in California will be training midcareer scientists and mathematicians to be teachers. And for researchers who want to lend a hand in the classroom but not abandon the lab entirely, there are programs such as a

continued

surveys (Eicher, Wood, Webster, and Gullickson 1988). Table 7.3 summarizes the results of the study.

ELEMENTARY CLASSROOMS

Individual classrooms comprise the structure of the schools. If the vertical organization of the school is graded, these classroom units will represent various grades. In schools that use a nongraded organization, classroom units represent a level of subject matter. Regardless of the organizational structure, the elementary classroom unit is a crucial element in elementary education.

The Elementary Teacher

The elementary teacher is the professionally trained individual who is in charge of the education of students. Although aides may be present in the classroom, individual teachers still are responsible for the educational accomplishments of students.

TABLE 7.3
School Subjects Preferred by Elementary School Children

SCHOOL SUBJECT	1987 RANK ORDER	1988 RANK ORDER
Art	1	1
Science	2	3
Music	3	6
Arithmetic	4	4
Health	5.5	7
Spelling	5.5	5
Reading	7	2
Handwriting	8	8
Social Studies	9	9
English	10	10

Source: Eicher, Wood, Webster, and Gullickson. School subjects preferred by elementary school children in South Dakota: Ten years later, *Education* 109(2), 1988.

INTRODUCTION TO EDUCATION

Roles of Elementary Teachers. Elementary teachers perform many roles in facilitating the education of their students: social model, evaluator, walking encyclopedia, moderator, investigator, ombudsman, morale builder, leader of the group, substitute parent, target for frustrations, and friend (Jarolimek and Foster 1985) (see table 7.4). Wassermann (1984) described the roles of the elementary teacher as diagnosing learning problems, facilitating independent learning, and developing curricula. While these lists differ somewhat, they illustrate the numerous roles that elementary teachers play in the education of children. Being an elementary teacher is no easy task; elementary teachers are busy people.

While teachers must perform many varied roles, their primary role is that of instructor. As an instructor, the elementary teacher imparts knowledge, guides students' learning experiences, and determines students' progress. Many of the other roles of elementary teachers are required to facilitate the overall role of instructor.

TABLE 7.4
Roles of Elementary Teachers

ROLE	DESCRIPTION
Social Model	Models appropriate moral values and social values, lifestyles and career goals expected by the community
Evaluator	Includes formal and informal evaluation of all aspects of students' performance, including academic, behavior, and social
Walking Encyclopedia	Has a vast amount of knowledge to impart to children, but more importantly provides a model for children to find information on their own
Moderator	Includes moderating personal differences among children; teacher actions must be viewed as fair
Investigator	Determining who is at fault, if thefts occur, etc.; should be performed in a very constructive manner
Ombudsman	Enables students to confide in the teacher concerning various anxieties and problems
Morale Builder	Provide successful learning experiences for children; helps build self-confidence in students
Group Leader	Includes classroom management and instructional planning for a group of children as opposed to one-on-one activities
Substitute Parent	Especially important with young children; teacher becomes the child's daily "parent" during school hours
Target for Frustrations	Attempt to understand children's frustrations and adverse behavior directed at teacher
Friend	Serve as the child's friend without becoming so friendly that the teacher-student role cannot be maintained

Source: Jarolimek and Foster. *Teaching and Learning in the Elementary School*, 3d ed., 1985.

Elementary teachers are required to fill a variety of roles and job assignments. A recent study (McDaniel-Hine and Willower 1988) investigated how elementary teachers spend their days. Data gathered through observing five elementary teachers revealed that teachers average 37.5 hours in school each week and spend an additional 6.6 hours on after-school work. Instructional time accounted for 45.1 percent of the teacher's time, with the remainder of the day spent on recess, playground, and other support activities. Table 7.5 summarizes the findings of this study.

Characteristics of Good Teachers. Being an effective elementary teacher requires various professional competencies and personal characteristics, such as

1. able to organize
2. likes children
3. understands teaching modes and strategies
4. able to adjust teaching strategies to specific children
5. maintains a healthy self-concept (Jarolimek and Foster 1985)

TABLE 7.5
Elementary School Teachers' Work Behavior

ACTIVITY	PERCENTAGE OF TOTAL TIME
Instructional Activities	
Group Instruction	3.8
Question-Answer	14.0
Individual Help	16.8
Giving Directions	2.7
Giving Tests	1.4
Reading to Class	0.9
Organizing	5.5
Subtotal	45.1
Non-Instructional Activities	
Transition-Supervision	6.8
Recess-Supervision	7.6
Clerical-Mechanical	1.4
Desk Work	12.3
Travel	3.1
General Conversations (Staff)	8.1
Planning with Staff	4.0
Conversations (Students)	6.0
Planning with Students	0.7
Private	1.9
Miscellaneous	2.9
Subtotal	54.7

Source: McDaniel-Hine, and Willower. *Journal of Educational Research* 81(5) 1988.

INTRODUCTION TO EDUCATION

HIGHLIGHT
■

TEACHER PREPARATION TIME GAINS APPROVAL

Bruce Orwall

The state would have to give elementary school teachers class preparation time for the first time under a bill approved Monday by the House Education Committee.

State law has given Minnesota high school and junior high teachers an hour a day for planning for more than 30 years. But elementary teachers often have had to squeeze in preparation time on an informal basis—something that has angered them increasingly, especially at contract time.

The bill, sponsored by Rep. Alice Johnson, DFL [Democrat]–Spring Lake Park, would require the state Board of Education to adopt a rule on preparation time for elementary teachers by May 1990. The board then would ask the Legislature for the funds to pay for the extra preparation time—probably up to $15 million.

Rose Hermodson, lobbyist for the Minnesota Federation of Teachers, said elementary teachers currently get the preparation time on a district-by-district basis, with some getting 10 minutes a day and some getting an hour. More and more, she added, elementary school teachers are refusing to ratify contracts that don't include provisions for adequate planning time.

"We never have time to prepare for the basic program, which is kids," said Hermodson, an elementary school teacher.

Secondary teachers have had mandatory preparation time since 1957.

The Minnesota School Boards Association is opposed to the bill because it doesn't identify exactly what the costs will be. Lobbyist Carl Johnson said the board is afraid the districts will get stuck paying for the extra planning time without additional compensation from the state.

"We wouldn't have much trouble with any kinds of mandates you would pass if they are funded," Johnson said.

The legislation next will be considered on the House floor.

Source: *St. Paul Pioneer Press Dispatch*, March 14, 1989.

Instructional behaviors that enhance achievement include the ability to present information clearly, the use of variety in planning learning experiences, enthusiasm, task orientation, and the presentation of repeated opportunities for learning (Jarolimek and Foster 1985).

Teacher Education. Being able to perform the many varied tasks of an elementary teacher requires considerable training. Most states require that a qualified elementary teacher complete a program of study at a college or university with an approved teacher education program. Upon successful completion of the college or university training program, individuals are eligible for certification as an elementary teacher. Teacher training programs vary somewhat, as do state certification requirements for elementary certification.

While there are variations, teacher training programs and certification programs have much in common. Most states require that students complete coursework in the following general areas before being eligible for certification as an elementary teacher: language arts, methods courses for various subject areas, measurement, learning theory, and curriculum. Some training programs have individual courses for these topics, while others combine several areas into one course. For example, a training program may have only one methods course for elementary teachers rather than specific methods courses for each subject.

Curricular Variations Within Classrooms

Although school boards, superintendents, and building administrators adopt the curricula they want implemented in individual classrooms, elementary teachers can have a dramatic impact on the ways the curriculum is carried out (Good 1986). Methods of modifying the curriculum include use of textbooks, use of materials, use of space, teaching strategies or methods, and grouping for instruction. The teacher also is largely responsible for the classroom milieu.

Use of Textbooks. Textbooks for elementary schools usually are selected by a textbook committee appointed to act for the local school

■ *Classroom curriculum is partially determined by individual teachers.*

district. In many states, schools must select books that are on a state approved list of acceptable textbooks. Although teachers may be asked to provide input into the selection process, and many elementary teachers may actually serve on the local district selection committee, some elementary teachers have limited impact on the books adopted by the district. Even in these situations, teachers can modify the curriculum to some degree.

Teachers may use a great deal of supportive materials to reinforce the content of textbooks, to supply additional information, or to present information in a different manner than is found in the adopted text. Teachers do not have to follow the content of the state and district adopted text without using supplemental materials. As long as students are achieving at appropriate levels, teachers probably will not be asked to explain why they are teaching material differently than is prescribed by an adopted textbook.

Use of Classroom Materials. Unlike textbooks, which may have been selected with limited teacher input, other teaching materials are largely left up to the teacher. School budgets usually are very limited for teaching materials, and teachers often make their own materials or modify materials given to them by local businesses and other groups to fit the needs of children in classrooms. By making or modifying materials, teachers control the kinds of materials available for student use. However, some states have developed guidelines to assist teachers in determining which materials have appropriate multicultural and non-sexist content.

Use of Space. As with materials, teachers have a great deal of flexibility in their use of classroom space. The way space is used may be directly related to the success of students. Modifications in space may be required to take advantage of various activities and to meet the particular needs of individual students. Many elementary classroom teachers organize their classrooms in the traditional row-by-row design. While this organization may facilitate structure, a more flexible approach may better suit various types of children found in the classroom. Berkowitz and Sheridan (1979) suggest that the utilization of space in a classroom be determined using a trial-and-error method. By becoming sensitive to the relationships between children's stimulation levels and the physical environment, teachers found that (1) rugs could be added or taken away to adjust noise levels, (2) furniture could be moved to create open or closed spaces for various type of activities, (3) certain toys should be removed if they are too distracting, and (4) some activities could best be conducted outside the classroom.

Another method of adjusting classroom space is through the use of learning centers, spaces for individuals or small groups that include materials about specific topics. A learning center "enlarges the learning

■ *Elementary teachers perform many different roles.*

environment, contributes to the development of self-actualizing learning, and provides for a greater range of learning rates, styles, and developmental levels" (Ragan and Shepherd 1977, p. 210). Learning centers permit teachers to occupy children with various learning activities while the teachers work more intensely with other children.

Individual learning should be encouraged with learning centers. Students are able to go to a learning center, perform the required activities, evaluate the work, and move on to another center or back to the base desk. Teachers can develop learning centers by pushing extra desks together in a corner of the room, acquiring small tables, or even using the teacher's desk (King-Stoops 1977). Materials at learning centers can be commercial, teacher-made, or student-made. Typical learning centers include science, math, language arts, and sensory training. Learning centers need not be elaborate, expensive, or difficult to make. Used properly, learning centers can take advantage of limited space in classrooms and create opportunities for individual initiative.

Methods of Instruction. A variety of teaching methods are available for elementary teachers (Reisman and Payne 1987). One method is not necessarily superior to others in all circumstances. The most commonly used method in secondary schools—lecturing—rarely is used in elementary classrooms. Elementary teachers most often use question-and-answer activities and provide individual help. Occasionally they use worksheets and other individual desk activities or read to students (McDaniel-Hine and Willower 1988).

The way teachers teach is a very critical element in students' learning. Delisle stated that "it's how we teach, not what we teach that makes a lasting impact on our students" (1988, p. 24). The teaching style used by teachers includes such components as classroom rules, classroom climate, methods of reinforcement, attitude toward students, and interactions with students.

HIGHLIGHT

•

CHANGE FROM THE BOTTOM UP

Connie Leslie

The people who run the West Haven, Conn., schools recognized last year that they had a problem. Too many kids were dropping out; too many classes were boring. What were they to do? Instead of focusing their efforts on junior high and high school, they tried a different approach: change from the bottom up. By shifting to a new "developmentally appropriate" curriculum, West Haven aims to turn them on to school.

Teacher Linda Mathews, 39, is one of West Haven's new childsavers. On this day she's sitting on the floor with a hand puppet, teaching math. "Little bear is telling me a story about the time he went to meet a friend but was late and his friend started to cry," she says. "He doesn't have a watch, so how can he measure time without a clock?" She wants her first graders at the Alma E. Pagels Elementary School to grasp the concept of time and learn how to estimate it by counting seconds. The kids pair off with their "math buddies" to play the pendulum game. One student stands, swinging a ball of clay attached to a long string, and counts the number of seconds it takes the other student to snap 20 plastic links together to make two sets of 10. Mathews walks around listening and correcting the students as they count. Seven-year-old Stephanie Piscitelli says she counted to "a killion" but isn't sure how to write that number down. Mathews smiles and shrugs: sometimes the right answer isn't everything.

A Collaboration

To help teachers enter this brave new world, West Haven officials have brought in consultants from the Greenfield Center School, a private school in Greenfield, Mass. Run by

continued

refugees from public education, Greenfield specializes in methods that gear lessons to a child's stage of development. "What you teach is a decision that the teacher has to make based on what she knows the children know," says Marlynn Clayton, a Greenfield teacher and consultant. "We see everything as a collaboration between child and teachers."

That union begins as soon as the kids come to class. At 8:25 A.M., Mathews's first graders arrive and immediately start to devise their own schedules by filling out a daily plan sheet. The classroom is carefully organized into learning activity areas for art, group work, math and independent projects, among others. The plan sheet has a space for the child's name, the date and a list of about 15 choices of activities in words and drawings. Each morning, Mathews writes every student's name on the blackboard along with one assigned activity. She helps each student write down the assignment or color in the illustration on a plan sheet along with the child's choice of one additional activity.

By 9:20, work has begun. The teacher rings a bell when it's time for the children to "freeze" and then "melt" to attend mandatory classwide discussions or switch to one of their two activities. The first work of the day is one of their favorites, a daily journal which everyone, even the preliterate, must keep. Using a developmental technique called "process writing," the children start the year by drawing a picture each day. At first, Mathews writes down what the child says about the picture as a caption. Later in the year, the children begin to scribble and write words the way they sound using "invented spelling." (Apple, for instance, is rendered as apel or apl.) Throughout the year, Mathews meets with each child to help translate the invented spellings into correct English. Then she types the child's captions onto the drawing page and eventually binds each student's work together to make a book, which children love because they get to think of themselves as authors.

After daily journal comes the morning meeting. Everyone sits on the rug either to do a math problem or to read the newspaper aloud to each other. Sometimes students read together from oversized books that everyone can see or sing songs or chants. As she engages each child in the activity, Mathews discusses concepts such as nouns, vowels, contractions and new vocabulary words. Next, the children complete their daily assignments.

After lunch is checking time, when Mathews reviews mistakes with each student. (Any child who misbehaves while Mathews is working is asked to sit in the "time-out chair.") The final lesson involves social studies, science or art. By then the children are tired. Mathews talks with each child and evaluates his or her day. She helps each one draw a happy or sad face on the plan sheet. They leave and Mathews remains behind to prepare for the next day. She doesn't evaluate herself, but after an exhausting day in class, she can't stop smiling.

Grouping for Instruction. Teachers sometimes group students for instructional purposes (Polloway, Patton, Payne, and Payne 1989). Students can be taught in large groups, small groups, or individually. If grouped together, the issue is whether to group homogeneously or heterogeneously. Although several studies have investigated homogeneous/heterogeneous grouping, the results are inconclusive (Good 1986). In determining which grouping is best suited for a particular group of children, teachers should consider the effectiveness, efficiency, and social benefits of the various options (Polloway et al. 1989).

Heterogeneous grouping does not attempt to categorize students on any specific criteria such as ability or interest. Students are randomly placed in instructional groups (although grouping by age is characteristic of a graded system) without any preselection for other characteristics. The advantages of heterogeneous grouping include: (1) students can interact with a broad range of students; (2) students have a wider variety of peer role models; and (3) a heterogeneous classroom closely resembles the characteristics of society. The disadvantages of heterogeneous grouping include: (1) teachers may teach to the middle, leaving brighter students and students who require extra help to make it on their own; (2) the same students are in leadership roles; and (3) teachers have many different academic levels to teach.

Homogeneous grouping places children with similar characteristics together. The one characteristic normally considered when grouping is academic ability. However other characteristics that could be used include cultural background, psychomotor development, age, personal and social adjustment, and interest (Jarolimek and Foster 1985). Using age as the criterion for grouping is most common in school districts where entry into the first grade is mandatory for children in certain age groups and where admission before the target age is reached is prohibited.

The major advantage of homogeneous grouping is that teachers have similar students to teach. When grouping is based on academic abilities, teachers can gear instruction to the students' level of intellectual development without needing to consider students at extreme ends of the continuum. The disadvantages are that students in homogeneous classes do not get a chance to interact with a variety of children and, often, teachers of low academic students expect less from those students than they should, which often leads to less teacher output and less student achievement than are possible.

Classroom Milieu. The milieu, or environment, in elementary classrooms is largely determined by the teacher. Does the teacher have an open, trusting environment, or is the teacher continuously suspicious of all students, thinking that they are ever plotting to circumvent class rules? Does the teacher lavishly give out praise and "warm fuzzies," or does the teacher expect students to work on-task and recognize students only when their behavior is inappropriate? These variables, along with many other subtle and overt influences by the teacher, compose the classroom milieu.

The most critical environmental factors include the definition of a good student, classroom rules, student-teacher interactions, and student-student interactions. The following statements briefly describe each component:

1. Definition of a good student. Teachers like some students better than others. This probably is determined by values held by the teacher related to what constitutes a "good" student.

■ *Homogeneous grouping allows teachers to work with students with similar characteristics.*

2. Classroom rules. Classroom rules and teacher behaviors definitely affect student behavior. Students need to be aware of the classroom rules and the probable consequences of breaking the rules. Classroom rules must be applied equally to all children.

3. Student-teacher interactions. Teachers vary a great deal in their interactions with students. Some are very warm and interactive; others are more formal, rarely hugging, touching, or smiling. This aspect of milieu can affect feelings of stress and anxiety by students.

4. Student-student interactions. Peer interaction is a basic part of milieu. Some students are ostracized by peers and others are very popular. Teachers should recognize these relationships and encourage positive interactions among all students.

SPECIAL SERVICES

Elementary schools serve some children who require services beyond those provided for the majority of children. These include special education services, services for gifted and talented children, and counseling services. Without the provision of these services, equal educational opportunities would not be possible.

Special Education Services

Approximately ten percent of the school population is handicapped to such a degree that special services are warranted. As a result of federal and state legislation and litigation, schools are now required to provide appropriate educational services to all school-age children, regardless of the children's disabilities. The major federal legislation that mandated these services was Public Law 94–142, passed in 1975. This legislation required that schools

- locate handicapped children;
- individually assess handicapped children;
- develop individual educational programs for handicapped children;
- provide appropriate services to handicapped children in the least restrictive setting (with nonhandicapped children); and
- annually review the progress of handicapped children to determine the effectivenes of the services provided. (Patton, Payne, and Beirne-Smith 1986)

Elementary schools serve many handicapped children, mostly those with mild disabilities such as educable mental retardation and learning disabilities. The resource-room model, where students attend regular classrooms part of each school day and receive extra help in the resource part of the day, is the primary model used to serve handicapped children (Smith, Price, and Marsh 1986). Regular elementary teachers and school administrators must share in the responsibility of educating handicapped children. Chapter nine focuses entirely on special education and provides a great deal of information concerning services to handicapped children in public schools.

Gifted Education Services

Gifted children have been in and out of favor more than any other group of children. In the late 1950s gifted education received much emphasis and money following the launch of Sputnik by the Soviet Union. This was short-lived, however, because the federal emphasis shifted to disadvantaged and handicapped children. Recently, programs for gifted and talented children have been revived.

Whereas gifted children previously were defined only in terms of academic abilities, current definitions include high performance in creativity, leadership, and visual and performing arts (Gallagher 1985). As a result of this broader concept, elementary school programs must be expanded to provide meaningful experiences in a variety of areas.

The following program adaptations for gifted students can be made in elementary schools:

1. Enrichment in regular classes—Special materials and lessons are provided to enhance learning.
2. Consultant teacher—Specially trained teachers act as consultants to regular classroom teachers to suggest activities for gifted children.
3. Resource room—Gifted children go to a resource room for a portion of the school day to work with a gifted-education specialist.
4. Mentor—Community members with specialized skills work with gifted students either individually or in small groups.
5. Independent study—Gifted students are allowed to carry out independent studies under the supervision of a teacher.
6. Special-interest class—Classes in specialized content fields are offered to gifted students.
7. Special class—Gifted students are homogeneously grouped in self-contained classes or subject areas.
8. Special schools—Gifted children attend schools specifically designed for gifted students. (Gallagher 1985)

Although gifted education in elementary schools grew substantially during the early 1980s, the gains made in providing appropriate educational programs for these children may not be permanent. If history repeats itself, an emphasis on programming for gifted children may diminish as other, more pressing needs of the schools surface.

Counseling Services

Although counseling programs originally were developed for secondary schools, they recently have become common in elementary schools. Professionals realized that young children also have counseling needs. Children with emotional problems, and those with characteristics that suggest the eventual development of problems, have been targeted for intervention. Although many schools still do not have elementary counseling programs, the trend is that such programs will be available in most schools within the next few years. Elementary school counselors may be assigned to a single school or they may serve several schools in a shared relationship. Regardless of the physical assignment, elementary school principals are beginning to use counselors to meet immediate needs of young children; today there are more counseling personnel in elementary schools than ever before (Hume and Hohenshil 1987).

Unfortunately the need and benefits of elementary counseling programs have not been greatly documented. Gerler (1985) reviewed studies published in *Elementary School Guidance and Counseling* from 1974 to 1984. Conclusions from this review revealed that elementary counseling programs can have positive effects on the affective, behavioral, and interpersonal skills of children, and therefore impact positively on academic performance. Elementary school counselors need to use these data to increase support for their programs.

SUMMARY

This chapter has focused on the elementary school. Elementary schools were the first to develop in this country, and they remain as the beginning point of education for most children. Although training in the basic academic skills was the original purpose of elementary schools, other purposes have been added, including citizenship education and personal development. Currently elementary schools are asked to accomplish much more than academic instruction.

As in all school organizations, the administration of elementary schools is a critical element. Without administrative support for programs, the likelihood that elementary-aged children will receive appropriate educational experiences is significantly reduced. Elementary school principals do not function in a vacuum but must administer schools within the administrative hierarchy of the district. Still, the success of schools greatly depends on the skills and attitudes of building principals.

Elementary schools are organized both vertically and horizontally. Vertical organizational arrangements include graded and nongraded schools, and horizontal organizations are either self-contained or departmentalized; each organizational structure has several advantages and disadvantages. Elementary school curriculum focuses on academic training, as well as other experiences directed at child growth and development. Although every school district may have a different curriculum, most include academic instruction in the basic subject areas of reading, writing, and arithmetic. The curriculum of a given elementary school is affected by many different variables, including the community, financial resources, and philosophy.

The second section of the chapter focused on the elementary classroom. Within the classroom, the teacher is the key professional, being responsible for implementing school policies and philosophies. Although instruction is a primary role for elementary teachers, they must also address the personal growth of students, evaluate students' progress, and perform a host of other duties. Teachers have a great deal of flexibility in their classrooms concerning how they implement the curriculum and how they teach children.

The final section of the chapter discussed some special services available to students in elementary schools. These included special education, gifted education, and counseling services. Students enrolled in elementary schools in the United States make up a very diverse group. They come from all kinds of backgrounds and require different services to enable them to benefit from school programs. Special services provided in elementary schools attempt to provide for the unique needs of many children.

IN THE FIELD

1. Are there stated purposes for the elementary school and district elementary education program? Discuss.

2. Describe activities performed by the principal related to the role of instructional leadership.

3. What is the practice in the school related to the principal visiting classrooms?

4. Is the school graded or nongraded? How long has the organization been in place?

5. Describe one instructional behavior by the teacher you observed that seemed to be particularly effective.

6. Does the school have a school counselor? If so, what activities are performed by this individual?

7. Are there any administrators other than the principal at the school? If so, what are their job responsibilities?

8. Does the school use the self-contained or departmentalized model? How long has the model been in place?

9. Does the school's curriculum primarily result from state guidelines?

10. What kinds of educational materials are available in classrooms?

11. What kinds of materials are available in the school library?

12. Does the school have audio-visual materials? If so, what kinds of equipment and materials?

13. Are students grouped for instructional purposes? If so, what criteria are used for grouping?

14. Does the school have a program for gifted and talented students? If so, what is the nature of the program?

REFERENCES

Bennett, W. J. 1986. A critical look at curriculum goals. *Principal* 66(2), 11–15.

Berkowitz, J., and M. Sheridan. 1979. Group composition and use of space in a preschool setting. *Teaching Exceptional Children* 11, 154–57.

Besvinick, S. L. 1988. Twenty years later: Reviving the reforms of the '60s. *Educational Leadership* 46(1), 52.

Binder, F. M. 1974. *The Age of the Common School, 1830–1865*. New York: John Wiley & Sons.

Brieschke, P. A. 1985. Principals in schools: Insubordination in discrectionary decision making. *The Educational Forum* 49(2), 157–69.

Canady, R. L. 1988. A cure for fragmented schedules in elementary schools. *Educational Leadership* 46(2), 65–67.

Cooper, L. A. 1989. The principal as instructional leader. *Principal* 68(3), 13–16.

Delisle, J. R. 1988. Test your teaching style. *Learning* 16, 24–25.

Doud, J. L. 1989. The K–8 principal in 1988. *Principal* 68(3), 6–12.

Duke, D. L. 1987. *School Leadership and Instructional Improvement*. New York: Random House.

Eicher, C., R. W. Wood, L. Webster, and A. Gullickson. 1988. School subjects preferred by elementary school children in South Dakota: Ten years later. *Education* 109(2), 191–195.

Entwisle, D. R., and L. A. Hayduk. 1988. Lasting effects of elementary school. *Sociology of Education* 61, 147–159.

Fain, S. M., R. Shostak, and J. F. Dean. 1979. *Teaching in America*. Glenview, IL: Scott, Foresman.

Gallagher, J. J. 1985. *Teaching the Gifted Child*. 3d ed. Boston: Allyn and Bacon.

Gallup, A. M., and D. L. Clark. 1987. The 19th annual Gallup poll of the public's attitudes toward the public schools. *Phi Delta Kappan* 69(1), 17–30.

Gerler, E. R. 1985. Elementary school counseling research and the classroom learning environment. *Elementary School Guidance and Counseling* 21(1), 39–48.

Good, T. L. 1986. What is learned in elementary schools. In *Academic Work and Educational Excellence*, edited by T. M. Tomlinson and H. J. Walberg. Berkeley, CA: McCutchan.

Hume, C. W., and T. H. Hohenshil. 1987. Elementary counselors, school psychologists, school social workers: Who does what? *Elementary School Guidance and Counseling* 22(1), 37–45.

Jarolimek, J., and C. D. Foster. 1985. *Teaching and Learning in the Elementary School*, 3d ed. New York: Macmillan.

Jarolimek, J., and C. D. Foster. 1981. *Teaching and Learning in the Elementary School*. 2d ed. New York: Macmillan.

King-Stoops, J. 1977. *The Child Wants to Learn: Elementary Teaching Methods*. Boston: Little, Brown.

Lipham, J. M., and J. A. Hoeh, Jr. 1974. *The Principalship: Foundations and Functions*. New York: Harper & Row.

Maxim, G. W. 1987. *Social Studies and the Elementary School Child*. 3d ed. Columbus, OH: Merrill.

McDaniel-Hine, L. C., and D. J. Willower. 1988. Elementary school teachers' work behavior. *Journal of Educational Research* 81(5), 274–280.

Miel, A. 1984. Making room for the future in the curriculum. *Kappa Delta Pi Record* 21(1), 14–16.

Monson, D. L., B. M. Taylor, and R. Dykstra. 1988. *Language Arts: Teaching and Learning Effective Use of Language*. Glenview, IL: Scott, Foresman.

Morris, V. C., R. L. Crowson, E. Hurwitz, Jr., and C. Porter-Gehrie. 1982. The urban principal: Middle manager in the educational bureaucracy. *Phi Delta Kappan* 63(10), 689–92.

National Education Association, 1968. *The Elementary School Principalship in 1968: A Research Study.* Washington, DC: Department of Elementary School Principals.

Patton, G. J., J. S. Payne, and M. Beirne-Smith. 1986. *Mental Retardation,* 2d ed. Columbus, OH: Merrill.

Polloway, E. A., J. R. Patton, J. S. Payne, and R. A. Payne. 1989. *Strategies for Teaching Learners with Special Needs,* 4th ed. Columbus, OH: Merrill.

Ragan, W. B., and G. D. Shepherd. 1977. *Modern Elementary Curriculum.* New York: Holt, Rinehart & Winston.

Reisman, F., and B. Payne. 1987. *Elementary Education.* Columbus, OH: Merrill.

Smith, T. E. C., B. J. Price, and G. E. Marsh. 1986. *Mildly Handicapped Children and Adults.* St. Paul, MN: West.

Sylwester, R., and C. Hasegawa. 1989. How to explain drugs to your students. *Middle School Journal* 20, 8–11.

Troutman, B. I., and R. D. Palombo. 1983. Identifying future trends in curriculum planning. *Educational Leadership* 41(1), 49.

Tyler, R. W. 1949. *Basic Principles of Curriculum and Instruction.* Chicago: The University of Chicago Press.

Wassermann, S. 1984. What can schools become? *Phi Delta Kappan* 65(10), 690–93.

Winn, D. D. 1988. Develop listening skills as a part of the curriculum. *The Reading Teacher* 42(2), 144–146.

Wood, C. L., E. W. Nicholson, and D. G. Findley. 1979. *The Secondary School Principal: Manager and Supervisor.* Boston: Allyn and Bacon.

8

SECONDARY EDUCATION

ADVANCE ORGANIZERS

1. What is the structure of secondary education in the United States?
2. What are the purposes of middle schools compared with junior high schools?
3. What three curricular tracks are found in most secondary schools?
4. How are secondary schools organized vertically?
5. What subjects are generally included in the common curriculum?
6. What is the current status of science and math education?
7. What are the purposes of vocational education?
8. What is the current status of vocational education?
9. What problems exist in secondary schools?

INTRODUCTION

Public secondary education in the United States is a relatively recent occurrence. The early education provided in colonial times through the common-school movement of the nineteenth century focused on young children in elementary schools. Although high schools date from Boston in 1821 and the Massachusetts Law of 1827, large numbers of secondary schools became operational much later. In 1860 there still were only 300 high schools in the entire country, with 100 of them being in Massachusetts (Binder 1974). At the turn of the century, only 6.4 percent of the 17-year-old population graduated from high schools. The number of graduates did not reach 50 percent until the 1939–1940 school year (Digest of Education Statistics 1988).

While public secondary education in this country is relatively recent, it still set the trend internationally. Great Britain's secondary schools had an enrollment of only 109,000 in 1900 and did not provide secondary education for children who could not afford fees until 1907. After World War II Great Britain began public educational programs for fourteen- to eighteen-year-olds. Other European countries, with the possible exceptions of Holland, Switzerland, and the Scandanavian countries, followed similar patterns of development (Commager 1983).

Secondary education in the United States today is big business. Since the beginning of the twentieth century, growth has been phenomenal. The number of students graduating from high schools increased from 95,000 in 1890 to 311,000 in 1920, 1.2 million in 1940, and 1.8 million in 1960. The number of high school graduates peaked at 3.15 million in 1977. Since then the numbers have declined due to a general school-age population decrease. The number of seventeen-year-olds who graduate now stands at approximately seventy-five percent (Digest of Education Statistics 1988). (See table 8.1)

TABLE 8.1
Number of High School Graduates

1900	95,000
1910	156,000
1920	311,000
1930	667,000
1940	1,221,000
1950	1,200,000
1960	1,858,000
1970	2,889,000
1980	3,043,000
1987	2,693,000

Source: *Digest of Education Statistics*, 1988.

STRUCTURE OF SECONDARY SCHOOLS

Secondary education in the United States comprises two levels: intermediate schools and high schools. The high school was the first to develop, starting in the late nineteenth century. This was followed by the development of intermediate schools in the early twentieth century.

Intermediate Schools

Intermediate schools initially were designed to bridge the gap between the relatively easy curriculum of elementary schools and the demanding academic curriculum of high schools. Many psychologists also began to recognize the need to provide students in their preadolescent and early adolescent years with experiences that were more appropriate for their maturational levels. Charles Elliott, the president of Harvard University, was instrumental in the development of intermediate schools as a result of his serving as chairperson of the Committee on Secondary School Studies. Under his leadership, the committee recommended that students be allowed to take subjects such as algebra, geometry, and foreign languages toward the end of their elementary years. At this time [1893], elementary schools were usually eight years in duration. The recommendation, therefore, suggested that elementary schools be reduced to six years and that secondary schools be expanded to six years (Tomlinson and Walberg 1986).

Junior High Schools. The first form of intermediate school to be developed was the junior high school. Junior high schools became a part of the public educational system around 1910 (Tomlinson and Walberg 1986). In the beginning the appropriate name for these schools was an issue. Names such as "subhigh school," "upper grammar school," "higher primary school," "departmental school," and "intermediate school" were used. Junior high school, however, became the predominant label for these early intermediate schools (Armstrong and Savage 1983).

By the early 1920s junior high schools were clearly established as an intermediate step between elementary schools and high schools. Although some emphasis was still placed on the special needs of young adolescent children, junior high schools soon came to focus almost entirely on academic preparation for high schools. This shift of purpose created a situation where unique psychological and social needs of these children were not being met. Critics began to question the overemphasis on academics and the limited focus on personal development (Tomlinson and Walberg 1986). Armed with research from developmental psychologists and physiologists, these critics proposed a reorganization of the intermediate school to enhance the focus of child growth and development during the pre- and early adolescent years. The name chosen for the reorganized school was borrowed from European education—middle schools (Armstrong and Savage 1983).

Middle Schools. Middle schools have always attracted a great deal of attention (Laven and McKeever 1989). However, unlike many educational innovations, the middle school has endured for many years. George (1988) even said that "The middle school movement is American education's longest-lived innovation" (p. 14). Middle schools are now the most popular school organization between elementary and high schools (Lounsbury 1987). Although most middle schools include grades 6–8, some begin with the fifth grade (Tomlinson and Walberg 1986). For the most part, middle schools attempt to serve students based on their needs, not on their chronological age grouping. This results in a curriculum that includes academic, physical, social, and emotional components (Lounsbury 1987).

Basic characteristics of middle schools include (Lounsbury 1987)

- a block of time (rather than separate periods) scheduled for academic subjects, under the direction of an interdisciplinary team of teachers,
- an extensive program of enrichment, exploratory, and special-interest classes and activities;
- a developmental skills program that emphasizes reading and other communication and learning skills;
- a teacher-based guidance program that helps students develop positive attitudes, values, and self-esteem;
- a program that recognizes and accommodates the social needs of early adolescents;
- a positive school climate and a schoolwide atmosphere of cooperation and caring (Lounsbury 1987, p. 45).

Middle schools likely will continue as the option used by most school districts to provide a transitional program from elementary to high schools.

High Schools

Secondary education actually started with public high schools. These schools, which evolved from private academies, were developed to provide educational opportunities for children beyond the elementary school years. High schools have developed into a stable educational institution to prepare adolescents for higher education or the world of work.

American high schools today no longer solely focus on academic preparation but include activities that deal with socialization, vocational preparation, homemaker preparation, and a host of extracurricular activities such as clubs and athletics. They follow a comprehensive model by providing a variety of programs to a very diverse student population. Comprehensive high schools provide educational opportunities to prepare students for postsecondary academic education, vocational training opportunities, and jobs. Although they differ significantly from each other, comprehensive high schools share many common factors. In general, "[S]econdary schools pursue the egalitarian ideal: They hold out the promise of social, political, and economic equality for all. Because they are open to all, secondary schools are generally large, diverse, and comprehensive; they are publicly funded from state taxes and local property taxes; and since state taxes are allocated on a per-pupil basis, the schools are accountable to the voting and taxpaying public" (Tomlinson and Walberg 1986, p. 138).

In general, high schools group students horizontally by age and vertically by program track; programs comprise various subjects taught by teachers certified in those areas; students are exposed to subjects in various classes each day; and the social activities of students are many and varied (Sizer 1983).

OBJECTIVES OF SECONDARY EDUCATION

A constant problem in secondary education has been to define its goals and objectives. In the 1800s it was assumed that elementary schools should focus on teaching basic skills, such as reading, writing, and arithmetic, while the limited number of secondary schools should prepare students for higher education or entry into vocations. In 1918 the Commission for Reorganization of Secondary Education issued its report, The Cardinal Principles of Secondary Education, which indicated that secondary schools should prepare students for (1) health, (2) command of the fundamental processes, (3) worthy home membership, (4) vocational efficiency, (5) civic competence, (6) worthy use of leisure time, and (7) ethical character (Clark and Starr 1981).

■ *Secondary schools provide comprehensive education for students with a wide variety of needs.*

These objectives laid the foundation for the comprehensive high school focusing on much more than academic training. Gross (1978) modified these seven principles into what he called "Seven New Cardinal Principles." These included personal competence and development, family cohesiveness, skilled decision making, moral responsibility and ethical action, civic interest and participation, respect for the environment, and global human concern.

The debate continues: should public secondary schools attempt to educate all children in all aspects of life, or should they restrict their efforts to more academic tasks? Boyer (1984) studied state legislation in all fifty states to determine the legal mandates of secondary schools. The results indicated a variety of mandated missions (see table 8.2).

Secondary schools must have a well-defined mission and set of purposes to be effective. These should include

1. training students in thinking and writing skills;
2. educating students using a core curriculum that should include literature, the arts, foreign language, history, civics, science, mathematics, technology, and health;
3. preparing students for work; and
4. preparing students for community service. (Boyer 1984)

TABLE 8.2
State Mandated Mission of High Schools

STATE	MANDATE
Idaho	The school program shall be organized to meet the needs of all pupils, the community, and to fulfill the state objectives of the school.
Mississippi	The purpose of education is to provide appropriate learning experiences to promote the optimum growth and development of youth and adults throughout life.
Oregon	Each individual will have the opportunity to develop to the best of his or her ability the knowledge, skills, and attitudes necessary to function as an individual . . . a learner . . . a producer . . . and a family member.
Maine	The public school must teach virtue and morality for not less than one-half hour per week. This includes principles of morality and justice and a sacred regard for truth, love of country, humanity, a universal benevolence, sobriety, industry and frugality, chastity, moderation and temperance, and other virtues that ornament human society.
California	Each teacher shall endeavor to impress upon the minds of the public the principles of morality, truth, justice, patriotism, and a true comprehension of the rights, duties, and dignity of American citizenship, including kindness toward domestic pets and the humane treatment of living creatures, to teach them to avoid idleness, profanity, and falsehood, and to instruct them in manners and morals and the principles of a free government.

Source: Boyer. Clarifying the mission of the American high school. *Educational Leadership* 41(6) 1984.

Secondary schools attempt to meet the needs of a variety of students: academically talented, academically deficient, college-bound, vocationally oriented, disadvantaged, and the majority of students who fit in the middle group of intellectual abilities and career aspirations. Some schools attempt to meet the needs of these students through a multifaceted program; others offer specialty areas such as the arts and vocational training. Many people have been critical of the comprehensive high school, including Admiral Hyman G. Rickover and Werner von Braun, who believed that academically talented students were being neglected as a result of comprehensive programs attempting to be all things to all students. Because of these kinds of criticisms, many people have advocated splitting the comprehensive high school into specialized programs, such as vocational schools, alternative schools, and even private schools supported by tax dollars (Tanner 1979). The future of comprehensive high schools is in question. However, the success of this secondary model has been such that any significant changes will likely come slowly, if at all.

There is no consensus concerning the goals and objectives of secondary schools in the United States. While the debate will continue, secondary education in this country will probably remain comprehen-

TODAY, CLASS, WE'LL LEARN ABOUT SOAP

Mark Starr and Lynda Wright

High schools are no longer refuges from reality—if ever they were. With handguns in lockers, pregnant girls in gym class and AIDS lectures part of the biology curriculum, America's schools offer an abundance of lessons in real life. Last week two more were added, albeit comparatively benign ones. Six schools began showing a daily TV news program called "Channel One" that included paid commercials. And in the San Francisco Bay Area, the first 7-Eleven outlet opened in a high school. Two NEWSWEEK correspondents visited the campuses. Here are their reports:

"Channel One" has been on the air only a week now and critics have already decried it as the worst thing to happen to American youth since . . . well, since television itself. The 12-minute news and information show ("like a 'Today' show for teenagers," say its producers) is being broadcast daily to classrooms in six public schools for a seven-week trial. The debate centers on just two of those minutes—the four 30-second spots that are being sold to commercial sponsors. "When television first started, there was a huge debate about whether you should advertise to children at all," says Peggy Charren, president of Action for Children's Television. "Now it's stuck right in the middle of the curriculum."

Christopher Whittle, whose eponymous company is producing the program, says "Channel One" addresses two serious problems: the ignorance of the kids and the poverty of the schools. "The notion of using TV as a teaching resource has been around for decades," says Whittle's editor in chief, William Rukeyser. "But it has moved at a glacial pace because of the expense. The commercials are what's finally making it feasible." As part of the arrangement, the schools have received $50,000 worth of equipment for free, including a satellite dish, a VCR and color-TV monitors. "If I had an option I'd go strictly for the instruction without the commercials," says Lionel Brown, the principal of Cincinnati's Withrow High School. "But this is America, and somebody's got to pay."

First Run

During the first weeks, the six advertisers are paying an undisclosed "test market" fee. By the fall of 1990 Whittle hopes to place "Channel One" in 8,000 schools, creating an audience of 6 million to 7 million teenagers—twice that of any prime-time show. Then, Whittle says he expects to raise his prices to $120,000 per 30-second ad, or about half the rates for a first run of "The Cosby Show."

Schools will be able to use the equipment as they see fit. The new technology could bring innovative programming into the schools from groups such as the Children's Television Workshop, creator of "Sesame Street." "It's time to use television to deal with . . . the failure of millions of American children to acquire the . . . skills they need to make their way in a technological society," CTW chairwoman Joan Ganz Cooney wrote recently in The Washington Post. Cooney has declined to comment directly on "Channel One."

Whittle will have to overcome the opposition of the education establishment. "Channel One" has been denounced by national associations of school boards, principals and teachers. Children should not be made a captive audience to corporate America, argues Patricia Graham, dean of Harvard's Graduate School of Education. For his part, Whittle points out that no one complains when corporations sponsor "trivial" things like school uniforms.

For all the hand-wringing, the first shows went off uneventfully. They featured timely

continued

news reports on Eastern Air Lines, John Tower and Salman Rushdie as well as a five-part segment on teenagers in the Soviet Union. The audiences were not much different from those found at home: some kids watched, some talked, and a few nodded off. Anyway, they'd all seen the commercials before: Levi's jeans, Head & Shoulders and Snickers are staples of their viewing habits. "They're worried we're going to be corrupted," says Kerri Little, a senior at Billerica (Mass.) Memorial High, another pilot school. "I think people underestimate students."

. . .

It's not your ordinary school store. The staff works to the exacting standards of a corporate giant, where every situation has a rule-book solution. The product line runs to 500 different items. And the sign in the window isn't the modest work of the wood-shop boys but the bold and familiar red, white and green 7-Eleven logo. In a converted classroom at James Logan High School in Union City, Calif., 75 business students have opened a mini-version of a mini-mart. "It's kind of a win-win situation," says Margaret Chabris of 7-Eleven's parent, Southland Corp. "It provides the business class with good hands-on experience, and we hope to recruit some of these kids for our stores."

The students use equipment donated by a local franchise and 7-Eleven's procedures—but it is up to them to do all the purchasing, inventory control, sales work and accounting. The student body is financially responsible for the store, and reaps all of its profit. Already, the young managers have learned an important lesson in starting a small business: the initial costs can be ter-

rifying. The student government, which is underwriting the project, has already incurred $3,700 in debt. "I'm leery of the whole thing," says Bill Honig, state superintendent of schools. "I understand it is not a commercial venture, but it could be, and that's what I'm worried about. Where will it all end?"

Pretty Neat

Logan's store is part of its academic program. To qualify for a job, students must first complete a year of business classes. Their work is unpaid and accounts for up to 20 percent of an advanced business-course grade. They are supervised by business teacher Maile Seney and Marlene Borlaug, a 7-Eleven franchisee who came up with the idea. The students like it. "It keeps kids from going off campus," says Traci Wise, 16. "I think it's pretty neat." So does Henrietta Schwartz, dean of San Francisco State University's School of Education. "This idea brings a reality dimension to the classroom," she says. "As long as the commercial aspect doesn't become a 13-foot neon sign on the building, I'm delighted."

According to students, adults worrying about crass commercialization invading campuses shouldn't waste their time. Many of the students who have after-school jobs say this experience is more valuable. "In this class I'm responsible for the merchandise that I'm manager over. I think that's a lot different from just being a salesperson," says Manicea Gober, 17, who orders and stocks the store's magazines. Alex Keaton, your time has come.

sive, either through comprehensive schools or separate, specialized schools. The needs of most American youth will be addressed.

ORGANIZATION OF SECONDARY SCHOOLS

Secondary schools are organized using several patterns. One major organizational pattern has been the division of secondary education into junior high schools or middle schools and high schools. This particular format has been implemented in most school districts except those with very low enrollments that dictate combining students into one organization.

Secondary schools also are organized by the type of curricular program. Most secondary schools offer three basic types of curricular options: general, academic, and vocational. The general curriculum is designed for students who do not anticipate attending colleges or universities and who plan on entering the job market or technical training after high-school graduation. The academic program focuses on preparing students for higher education programs. Students who choose the academic curriculum most often have definite plans for attending colleges or universities. The third curricular option, vocational education, provides training in vocational areas designed to prepare students to enter the job market following high-school graduation. Vocational education programs can be general in nature or job specific.

Of the three tracks, students most often select the academic track, with the general track a close second choice. In the spring of 1980, 38 percent of the high-school seniors were in an academic program, 37.2 percent were enrolled in a general program, and the remaining 24.8 percent were taking part in a vocational education program (National Center for Education Statistics 1983).

Another method of organizing secondary schools is through graded or nongraded programs. Nongraded secondary programs provide students with the opportunity to progress at their own rates rather than being tied to grade levels. The concept is based on continuous progress education. Pupils complete courses at their own rate and then progress to other course options (Wood, Nicholson, and Findley 1985).

The more common organizational arrangement for instruction is the graded system. This approach organizes courses around grade levels; students enroll in various courses that are tied to grade levels and continue in the course for a semester or academic year. This is by far the more traditional approach and is found in the majority of secondary schools. While students may be allowed to enroll in courses designed for other grade levels, usually they take courses for their grade. For example, most freshmen enroll in freshman English, general math or algebra, a particular history course such as World History, and general science or biology. Likewise, some courses are primarily geared for upper-level secondary students. Trigonometry, for example, is considered a junior- or senior-level course in most high schools; civics or American government is also geared for upper-level students in most schools.

Secondary schools, therefore, may be organized by several criteria. Although differences do exist among most secondary schools, the majority follow a traditional model. Most are graded, most districts have junior high schools or middle schools and high schools, and most provide general, academic, and vocational curriculum tracks.

CURRICULUM OF SECONDARY SCHOOLS

Like elementary schools, secondary schools revolve around the curriculum, the sum total of all secondary-school experiences designed for students. The curriculum of secondary schools has been debated a great deal. Questions such as the following are continually discussed:

1. Is there a core curriculum that all secondary students should complete?
2. What subjects should be included in a core curriculum at the secondary level?
3. How many units of various subjects should be required of students for graduation?
4. Should curricular requirements be different for students seeking different post-school objectives?
5. Should schools include in their curriculum subjects such as death education, sex education, creation-science, and peace education?
6. What is the role of multicultural education in the secondary curriculum?

State departments of education to some degree control the curriculum of secondary schools by imposing minimum graduation requirements. However, many of these issues are resolved locally by the administration and the school board with considerable input from the constituents of the school district.

Common Curriculum

Most secondary schools require a common curriculum for all students. A common curriculum can be defined as "a study of those consequential ideas, experiences, and traditions common to all of us by virtue of our membership in the human family at a particular moment in history" (Boyer 1984, p. 21). Courses in the common curriculum should include literature, the arts, foreign language, history, civics, science, mathematics, technology, and health (Boyer 1984). Secondary schools require that students complete a certain number of units in many of these subject areas before graduation requirements can be considered met.

One result of the reforms initiated during the early 1980s was the strengthening of high school graduation requirements. The *A Nation at Risk* report (National Commission on Excellence in Education 1983) found that high school students enrolled in as few math and science courses as allowed, more often selecting elective coursework. To correct this, many states revised minimum graduation requirements. At the end of the 1986 school year, the average number of years of coursework required for graduation included math, 2.7; science, 2.3; English,

4.0; foreign language, 1.4; and social studies, 3.0 (National Center for Education Statistics 1988).

Science. Science education has received a great deal of interest at various times, while at other times it falls out of public and professional attention. Following the launching of the satellite Sputnik by the Soviet Union in the late 1950s, the federal government made a strong effort to improve science education in this country (Besvinick 1988). While the motivation was political, the results were positive for public schools. Curriculum reform, inservice training for teachers, and funds for materials and equipment were made available. Unfortunately, this push in science education did not last. With the Kennedy and Johnson administrations emphasing educational opportunities for disadvantaged and handicapped students, fewer federal dollars were available for science education. During the same period the United States apparently had regained the scientific advantage over the Soviet Union, thereby reducing the political need to expand science education (Glatthorn 1987).

In the late 1970s and early 1980s, interest shifted back to science education. Critics of public education clamored for more instruction in science for American children and youth. In the post-Sputnik years, back-to-the-basics became a strong movement but did not include science. Instead, it focused on the basic academic skills of reading, writing, and math. By 1984 it was very clear that there was a serious crisis in science education (McNeil 1985). Some of the problems included

- too much emphasis on textbooks;
- most teaching materials developed by non-scientists (Besvinick 1988);
- most students considering the content in their science classes useless (Yager 1988); and
- teachers primarily using the lecture approach, thereby limiting students' opportunities for hands-on learning (Glatthorn 1987).

Several suggestions were made to alter the negative trend in science education. Sigda (1983) recommended that students take science courses each year and that teachers combine content-oriented and process-oriented instructional methods. McNeil (1985) recommended that new materials be developed that were related to students' everyday problems. Finally, a content-oriented instruction method was recommended to focus on learner involvement. Yager (1988) recommended an approach called science/technology/society (S/T/S). In this method, students use local resources to investigate real problems found in their community. In science education, then, the thrust appears to be toward making science more functional and process oriented.

Math. Most high schools require students to complete some coursework in math. Too often this is a minimal requirement. Math education, like science education, is in a crisis: students often choose to take only the minimal math requirements in secondary schools; they often elect to take general math rather than algebra or more difficult math subjects when they have the option; math electives are rarely taken by many students; many math teachers meet only minimal teaching qualifications (Stefanich and Dedrick 1985).

Except for a brief period following Sputnik, the math curriculum in our schools has changed little since the beginnings of public education. One exception to this was in the mid-1960s when "new math" emerged. Prior to this effort, math education primarily had been based on learning computation skills. As a result of criticism, a new approach to math was developed (Glatthorn 1987). The new-math approach focused more on conceptual theories and less on computation. Unfortunately, the developers of this approach failed to consider the practical applications of the new curricula. Consequently, many educational reformers returned to a more traditional math curriculum focusing on practical computational skills (McNeil 1985).

Today both traditional and new math can be found in schools. Several trends have been suggested to improve math education: (1) integration of math with other subject areas; (2) increased use of technology in teaching math; and (3) community involvement in planning and implementing math curricula (McNeil 1985).

Many of the recommendations for improving science education also would improve math programs. Just as science teachers can rely on creativity to make science classes appealing, math teachers can do similar activities to encourage students to enroll in math classes or to motivate students already enrolled in required math classes. Schall (1984) described how teachers could make math classes more fun and more practical. For example, students can learn a variety of math facts and how to apply them simply by using the outdoors as the classroom and natural objects as materials.

Social Studies. Social studies could conceivably include the study of everything about human beings and their environments. In practice, however, more traditional definitions are used which emphasize subjects such as history, civics, geography, psychology, and sociology (Nelson and Michaelis 1980). Social studies is an important area in the secondary school curriculum. It can and should include components related to social justice, equity, and social problems.

The social studies curriculum in the 1950s focused on social literacy or the development of socially desirable behavior. During the 1960s more than 40 social studies curriculum projects were funded nationally to develop new social studies programs. Many professionals involved in these projects could not agree on what should be included in the curriculum. For the most part, though, these programs focused on inductive reasoning by students, or the ability to make generalizations from data (McNeil 1985).

The 1970s back-to-the-basics movement was highly critical of the new social studies curriculum (Glatthorn 1987). Programs were criticized for overemphasizing values and social awareness issues and for not teaching enough traditional social studies content. As a result, many schools returned to a more basic social studies curriculum. McNeil (1985) concluded that "the social studies curriculum is in disarray" (p. 314). Some of the current trends in the area include 1) increasing the social studies requirement for graduation, 2) becoming more flexible in organizing the sequence of social studies coursework; 3) increasing concerns about global issues; and 4) refocusing on moral educational issues (Glatthorn 1987). Many changes will likely occur in the next five years in this curricular area.

Specialized Curricular Areas

Beyond the basic, common curriculum, schools frequently offer specialized programs for students dependent on the students' postschool goals. For example, students who plan to attend college usually will complete extra units in English, mathematics, and science, while students enrolled in a vocational program may only complete the minimum units in the basic curriculum and then complete courses designed for their vocational interest.

Several subjects that are not related to common academic pursuits or vocational education are available to some secondary schools. These include sexuality education, drug education, multicultural education, and others.

Sexuality Education. One curricular area that has received a great deal of attention in American schools is sexuality education. Should schools provide sexuality education, or is this an area that belongs to parents? Over the past decade, there have been major increases for adolescents in sexual activity, pregnancy, abortions, and out-of-wedlock births (Kennedy and Orr 1984).

Public awareness of increased teenage sexual activity and pregnancy provides support for sexuality education. Research indicates that (1) there is broad support for sexuality education in the schools and (2) parents support sexuality education in the schools. The advantages of sexuality education provided through public schools are that it can reach all children before they become sexually active and it is relatively inexpensive. The latest report by the Sex Information and Education Council of the U.S. (1988) indicated that thirteen states currently require sexuality education in schools and another twenty-two states have recommendations or guidelines for sexuality education in health classes (State Update on Sexuality Education and AIDS Education 1988). These figures have increased significantly during the past three years.

The task, however, is great. Sexuality education programs must "modify, in a few hours of classroom instruction, the messages that young people receive every day from their friends, the mass media, and other sources" (Kenney and Orr 1984, p. 494). Although sexuality education is popular with parents, many schools still face major challenges from some groups when they initiate sexuality education programs. Some groups object on religious and other grounds. Others object on the grounds that the courses are ineffective. For instance, the majority of the public believes that schools are not capable of dealing effectively with teenage pregnancy (Gallup and Elam 1988). As a result, these programs will likely continue to be an optional component of most secondary schools.

For several decades, sexuality education focused on helping young adolescents understand the physical changes of puberty, the reproduction system, and family responsibilities. This rather simplistic approach to sexuality education has given way to diverse programs. Today's programs range from short units on menstruation to long, comprehensive courses on family life. Some of the programs begin in kindergarten; others are offered at the secondary level.

A major component in sexuality education courses today is AIDS education. Gallup and Elam (1988) reported that ninety percent of the respondents in the most recent Gallup Poll on Attitudes Toward the Public Schools favored AIDS education in public schools. Of this total, forty percent felt that the programs should begin with children ages 5–9, while another forty percent favored beginning the programs with children ages 10–12.

Drug Education. Drug education is an extremely important component of the secondary education curriculum. Even if teachers are not designated as drug-education teachers, they still will be expected to know the answers to questions related to drug use. Since many students begin experimenting with drugs during their middle-school years, that is an optimal time to emphasize drug education. Although the majority of the public has little or no confidence in the school's ability to deal with drug problems (Gallup and Elam 1988), it is still imperative for schools to provide information on this very important topic. Sylvester and Hasegawa (1989) suggest that drug education programs include information on (1) why people use drugs, (2) what are drug molecules and (3) the effects of drugs on the brain. Current knowledge about drugs makes it possible to present this information in very understandable terminology.

Multicultural Education. While not a specific subject to be included in secondary curricular options, multicultural education should be a part of every course taught in secondary schools. Berry (1979) indicated the importance of multicultural education in the secondary curriculum by stating that it was a principle that should not have been excluded from the seven Cardinal Principles of 1918 and 1978. "The secondary school pupil has a moral responsibility to learn, understand, and respect the values inherent in other races and religions, and to practice behaviors that will insure human dignity and civil rights to males and females of cultural groups different from their own" (Berry 1979, p. 745).

Multicultural education goes far beyond teaching courses labeled ethnic studies or social assimilation. While it does include teaching such courses, it also includes changing schools to provide equal educational opportunities for all children, regardless of ethnic background. Educators interested in making their schools multicultural must evaluate their school environments and curricula to determine to what extent it is monoethnic and Anglo–Centric. Once this determination is made, systematic efforts can be made to implement necessary changes to bring about multicultural education (Banks 1981).

Other Curriculum Areas. Occasionally various groups will express their support for increased emphasis in certain existing curricular areas.

These include foreign language, death education, education about the nuclear threat, creation-science, and economics education. Often these topics create controversy in schools. For example, the area of creation-science has been the focus of several court cases. The diversity of our population will always mean that some topics considered important for the curriculum by some will be considered inappropriate by others. The constant fluidity of our curriculum is one of the novel characteristics of our public educational system.

Vocational Education

In addition to the academic curriculum available to students enrolled in public schools in the United States, many schools offer students training referred to as vocational education. All secondary students are not interested in pursuing extensive education or training beyond the twelfth grade. For some students, high-school graduation signals an end to formal, academic education and training. At the approximate age of eighteen years, these students attempt to enter the job market. Unfortunately, without preparation for employment, many of these students will have significant adjustment difficulties.

Many school districts use the vocational education model to facilitate the success of students who terminate their educational experiences upon high-school graduation.

Vocational education has been a component in many public schools for several years. Since around World War I, various aspects of vocational education have been in some schools (D'Alonzo 1983). During the past two decades, vocational education has grown significantly (Bottoms and Copa 1983). Marsh and Price (1980) suggest that two of the major reasons for the recent growth in vocational education programs have been the shifting of the economy from an agrarian to an industrialized base and the corresponding population shift from rural to urban. Not only are schools expected to train students in specific skill areas, they also may be severely criticized when students graduate from high school without specific, salable skills.

What Is Vocational Education? Unfortunately, vocational education is a misunderstood program. Some of the misconceptions concerning vocational education include

- vocational education is only on the periphery of the high-school curriculum (Lotto 1985).
- vocational education only focuses on the needs of low-achieving students, (Silberman 1986)
- vocational education only attracts students from low socioeconomic classes,

■ *The aim of vocational education is to prepare students for employment.*

■ vocational education primarily serves the needs of boys, and
■ secondary vocational education programs have low status in secondary schools (Lotto 1985).

Vocational education has been defined by many different groups and individuals in many different ways. The definition used by the federal government states that vocational education

> means organized education programs which are directly related to the preparation of individuals for paid or unpaid employment, or for additional preparation for a career requiring other than a baccalaureate or advanced degree; and, for purposes of this paragraph, the term "organized education program" means only (a) instruction related to the occupation or occupations for which the students are in training, or instruction necessary for students to benefit from such training, and (b) the acquisition, maintenance, and repair of instructional supplies, teaching aids, and equipment, and the term "vocational education" does not mean the construction, acquisition, or initial equipment of buildings, or the acquisition or rental of land. (Title 45, U.S. Code of Federal Regulations 1979, p. 166)

Basically, the definition means training directly related to the preparation of students for employment or other training related to employment. The distinction is made between preparation for occupations that do not require a university degree and those that do.

Purposes of Vocational Education. Vocational education programs have many purposes, including:

1. providing skills and experiences considered valuable by students;
2. facilitating the mastery of avocational and vocational skills by students;
3. providing hands–on learning opportunities;
4. providing a curriculum that is closely related to everyday life needs; and
5. possibly providing an alternative for potential school dropouts. (Lotto 1985)

In addition to these, Weisberg (1983) indicates that supporters of vocational education programs believe that vocational education (1) can help integrate children from the lower economic sector, (2) can help with national economic problems, (3) can provide an appropriate curriculum for the approximately half of the student body not suited for a more academic program, and (4) can help with the broader problems posed by youth, such as crime, gangs, and teenage pregnancy.

Vocational education should incorporate multicultural components. Students in vocational education programs need to be aware that race, cultural background, sex, handicapping conditions, and socioeconomic status should have no bearing on vocational opportunities. The idea should be stressed that all students, within their physical and intellectual limitations, can enter any vocational area.

Current Status of Vocational Education. Vocational education is an option available to students in many American secondary schools. The number of students enrolled in vocational education programs has increased slightly over the past five years. Currently, 7.3 million high-school students are enrolled in secondary vocational education programs, compared with 7.1 million five years ago (Frantz, Strickland, and Elson 1988). Approximately twenty-five percent of high-school students are enrolled in vocational education programs, and more than ninety percent of today's graduates have completed at least one vocational course. Some schools require all students to complete exploratory courses such as home economics and industrial arts (Campbell 1986). Of the 20 million students enrolled in vocational education programs, sixty-three percent are in programs at public secondary schools, with the remainder being in private schools and other settings (National Center for Education Statistics 1983). (See table 8.3)

TABLE 8.3
Number of Students Enrolled in Vocational Education

PROGRAM	NUMBER OF STUDENTS	PERCENT-AGE
Public Secondary Schools	12,513,000	65%
Private Secondary Schools	22,000	1%
Public Noncollegiate Postsecondary	741,000	4%
Private Noncollegiate Postsecondary	989,000	5%
2–Year Institution of Higher Ed.	4,423,000	23%
4–Year Institution of Higher Ed.	309,000	2%
Totals	19,339,000	100%

Source: National Center for Educational Statistics. *The Condition of Education*, 1983.

Vocational Education Programs. There are seven areas of concentration for high school vocational education. These include

- agriculture
- business education
- distributive education (marketing)
- health occupations
- home economics
- technical education
- trade and industrial education (Campbell 1986, p. 10)

The types of students who enroll in these programs vary considerably. Some are full-time vocational-education students, while others are only taking minimal vocational-education coursework (Campbell 1986).

Future of Vocational Education. Vocational education is a popular program option for many students. It goes well beyond its original purposes, especially beyond the focus of simply preparing students for a particular vocation. Although some educators question the role of vocational education in American secondary education, it likely will remain a strong aspect of secondary schools. The reform reports issued in the late 1970s and early 1980s could negatively affect vocational education programs. However, once education and government leaders see the probable negative effects of some of the reforms, vocational education likely will regain its status in secondary education.

For vocational education to remain a strong component of public secondary education in the future, some changes need to be made. These include

- offering more field-based training options;
- responding more to the needs of industry and business;

- ensuring continued and increased support from local, state, and federal sources; and

- providing more realistic job training to students.

Extracurricular Activities

In addition to the academic curriculum, most secondary schools provide many extracurricular activities for students. The purpose of extracurricular activities is to enable students to participate in events not a part of the regular academic curriculum but viewed as important for overall growth (Weber and McBee 1988). Examples include athletics, subject-matter clubs, debating, drama, band, student government, honorary clubs, and cheerleading. A large percentage of secondary students participate in these kinds of activities. In 1982, fifty-one percent of the high-school seniors were involved in some form of athletics (National Center for Education Statistics 1988). Table 8.4 summarizes the participation in various extracurricular activities.

Public support for extracurricular activities has been consistently shown (Gallup 1984). However, in the wake of the reform movements, many states have initiated policies to prohibit participation in extracurricular activities by students who violate rules, fail to pass courses, are insubordinate, or abuse drugs (Weber and McBee 1988). The state of Texas was a leader in this movement. In 1984 the Texas Legislature passed a law, commonly referred to as the No-pass-no-play law. This law prohibited participation in extracurricular activities by students who did not maintain a passing grade in all subjects. In 1985 the Texas Supreme Court upheld the rule allowing the state to regulate extracurricular activities in public schools (Flygare 1985). In 1986 the U.S. Supreme Court refused to hear a case involving the Texas law, thus upholding a lower court's decision to allow the law to stand (Chase and Jacobs 1987).

The one extracurricular area that has generated the most controversy is competitive athletics. Commager (1983) states that high school competitive athletics have, in too many communities, become the focus of the community. Even with this sort of criticism and with the movement to restrict participation, there remains strong support for high school competitive athletics. Skinner (1988) states that the virtues of athletics, such as building character, self-esteem, and teaching teamwork, far outweigh the negatives.

METHODS OF INSTRUCTION

Often students lose interest in their classes because teachers use the same methods over and over. Montague (1987) states that "nothing is deadlier to student interest than a teacher who follows the same passive methodology every day" (p. 65). Today, teachers can use a variety

TABLE 8.4
Participation of High School Seniors in Extracurricular Activities, by Selected Student Characteristics: 1972 and 1982

STUDENT CHARACTERISTICS	ATHLETICS[1]	DEBATING, DRAMA, BAND, CHORUS[2]	SUBJECT-MATTER CLUBS	VOCATIONAL EDUCATION CLUBS	NEWSPAPER, MAGAZINE, OR YEARBOOK CLUBS	STUDENT COUNCIL, GOVERNMENT, POLITICAL CLUBS	HOBBY CLUBS	CHEERLEADERS, PEP CLUB, MAJORETTES	HONORARY CLUBS
1	2	3	4	5	6	7	8	9	10
All 1972 seniors	**44.5**	**32.9**	**25.8**	**23.0**	**20.4**	**19.6**	**18.7**	**17.3**	**14.8**
Sex									
Male	58.2	26.9	20.4	16.0	14.7	18.6	23.7	5.3	11.1
Female	32.1	39.8	31.2	29.8	26.7	21.0	13.3	29.6	19.4
Race									
White	44.5	32.6	25.0	21.9	20.7	19.2	18.3	17.3	15.7
Black	49.7	40.6	33.1	33.1	21.2	25.5	19.7	20.5	11.6
Father's highest level of education									
Less than high school	39.3	31.1	24.1	30.0	19.4	15.4	16.9	15.6	12.5
High school graduate[3]	46.7	32.9	25.7	21.9	21.4	20.2	18.0	19.6	16.1
College graduate[4]	51.4	40.2	28.6	12.4	24.2	27.6	20.8	17.5	23.1
High school curriculum									
General	43.3	33.0	22.3	24.3	17.5	15.5	19.4	15.5	7.0
Academic	53.4	39.7	29.6	14.8	25.7	26.7	17.7	20.2	25.2
Vocational	31.3	21.9	22.9	37.2	15.4	12.1	18.7	15.2	6.6

PERCENT OF SENIORS PARTICIPATING IN ACTIVITIES

TABLE 8.4 — Continued

Participation of High School Seniors in Extracurricular Activities, by Selected Student Characteristics: 1972 and 1982

STUDENT CHARACTERISTICS	PERCENT OF SENIORS PARTICIPATING IN ACTIVITIES								
	ATHLETICS[1]	DEBATING, DRAMA, BAND, CHORUS[2]	SUBJECT-MATTER CLUBS	VOCATIONAL EDUCATION CLUBS	NEWSPAPER, MAGAZINE, OR YEARBOOK CLUBS	STUDENT COUNCIL, GOVERNMENT, POLITICAL CLUBS	HOBBY CLUBS	CHEERLEADERS, PEP CLUB, MAJORETTES	HONORARY CLUBS
1	2	3	4	5	6	7	8	9	10
All 1982 seniors	**51.5**	**34.6**	**20.6**	**23.6**	**18.3**	**16.3**	**20.0**	**13.7**	**15.6**
Sex									
Male	61.7	25.8	16.4	20.2	13.3	13.1	23.5	4.1	12.1
Female	41.8	42.9	24.6	26.7	23.1	19.3	16.7	22.8	18.8
Race									
White	51.1	34.0	19.7	22.2	19.1	15.6	19.1	13.5	16.8
Black	54.5	43.1	23.9	30.0	16.0	19.7	19.5	16.8	12.5
Father's highest level of education									
Less than high school	43.4	29.4	21.2	31.0	14.6	12.2	18.4	11.8	10.6
High school graduate[3]	52.4	33.8	19.8	24.1	17.9	15.9	19.9	14.6	14.9
College graduate[4]	62.6	42.4	23.1	13.4	25.9	24.1	21.0	14.4	26.8
High school curriculum									
General	49.5	33.1	16.7	22.9	15.0	11.6	20.8	12.6	7.7
Academic	61.1	41.9	25.4	12.7	25.5	24.7	19.6	15.7	28.4
Vocational	40.7	26.0	18.7	40.2	12.4	10.5	19.5	12.4	7.7

[1]In 1972, includes participation in team athletics, intramurals, letterman's clubs, and sports clubs. In 1982, includes varsity athletic teams and other athletic teams—in or out of school.

[2]In 1972, includes debating, drama, band, and chorus. In 1982, includes debating, drama, band, orchestra, chorus, and dance.

[3]Includes attendance at a vocational, trade or business school, or 2-year college, or attendance at a 4-year college resulting in less than a bachelor's degree.

[4]Includes those with a bachelor's or higher level degree.

Source: National Center for Education Statistics. *Condition of Education,* 1988.

■ *Individualized instruction is one technique for educating at the secondary level.*

of teaching methods. These most often include lecture, classroom discussion, independent study, and individual instruction.

Lectures

Lecturing is the most frequently used method of instruction in secondary schools. In a study of high-school seniors, Wagenaar (1981) found that over eighty percent of the students reported that they were in classes which emphasized lectures. The lecture method has received a great deal of criticism; during the late 1960s and early 1970s, the lecture method was nearly doomed because of new teaching techniques and criticisms. However, the lecture method has been retained and still is the major method used in secondary school (Michel and Weaver 1984).

Some past criticisms of the lecture method are still a concern. Namely, many teachers who use this method lack sensitivity toward students, are not effective presenters, and are not sufficiently prepared (Michel and Weaver 1984). Several actions can be taken by teachers to meet these concerns and be better lecturers (see table 8.5). What should be

TABLE 8.5
Actions to Improve Lectures

Improve sensitivity to students

Use humor

Be organized

Capture students' attention

Take time for adequate preparation

Use examples frequently

Source: Michel, Weaver. Lecturing: Means for improvement. *The Clearing House* 57(9) 1984.

remembered is that the lecture method is not necessarily bad. When used properly, it is an effective method of instruction. It does, however, place the responsibility for selecting, organizing, and sequencing information on the teacher, not the student (Gold 1984). Teachers who rely on this instructional method must realize this and be prepared to take appropriate preparatory actions.

Classroom Discussion

The discussion method of instruction is also used extensively in secondary schools. Nearly sixty percent of the seniors studied by Wagenaar (1981) reported that they were in classes that used the discussion method of instruction. However, beginning teachers often have difficulty with classroom discussions. They need to learn to ask leading and appropriate questions at the proper time to stimulate the discussion, to be good listeners, and to know how to respond to students' questions to keep the discussion going (Armstrong and Savage 1983).

One effective method of promoting discussion is to require students to read textbook assignments and base the discussion on the reading selection. Alvermann (1984) studied the use of discussion in middle-school social studies classes and determined that very little actual discussion took place. More time was spent on listening and reciting information than on discussions. Also, almost as much time was spent on social, off-task talking as on classroom discussion. Alvermann pointed out that this did not have to be the case. Used properly, discussions can be effective in following textbook reading assignments.

Independent Study

The independent-study technique can be effective with some children; the key is in determining which children can benefit from this form of instruction. Children who are self-motivated and who work well without close supervision are likely candidates for independent studies.

■ *Extracurricular activities provide students with many enjoyable activities.*

On the other hand, children who require a great deal of structure would not do well with an independent-study assignment. After determining which students could benefit from an independent study assignment, teachers must decide (1) what students are to do, (2) what materials are necessary, (3) how grades will be assigned, and (4) activities for students not involved in independent study (Armstrong and Savage 1983).

Independent studies allow some students to venture into activities that would not be possible to address in large groups. This method of instruction is excellent for gifted students but also can be effective with students of average academic abilities and students who have learning difficulties. Teachers should be cautious in using the independent-study model; it takes a great deal of planning. Teachers cannot assume that this particular model makes teaching easy. Quite the contrary. If students are to benefit from an independent study assignment, it must be well planned, monitored, and evaluated.

Individual Instruction

Similar to the independent-study method is individual instruction. Individual instruction differs in that students in a class are all studying the same thing, whereas in independent study, individual students study different topics. Individual instruction is important in secondary schools because teachers must teach students with varying abilities. For example, a high-school history teacher not only has a majority of students who are functioning at a similar level, but also has students who are academically superior and those who have learning difficulties. Regardless of the abilities of the high achievers or the type of problem experienced by students with difficulties, individual instruction allows teachers to teach to the student's appropriate level, using the appropriate methods.

Several steps must be followed when individualizing instruction. These include determining the functioning level of students, establishing objectives, choosing appropriate materials, presenting information, and evaluating students' progress (Post 1984).

SCHOOL PHILOSOPHY AND POLICIES

The philosophy and policies of secondary schools greatly affect students, teachers, and parents. Often these are determined by the school board and state department of education. Individual school administrators and teachers, however, must implement the philosophy and policies of the school district. Areas affected by school philosophy and policies include discipline, appearance codes, and student rights.

Discipline

Probably one of the most talked-about topics in secondary schools is discipline. How are students to be disciplined? Whose responsibility is discipline? What disciplinary methods are effective? School discipline is consistently noted as a major concern of parents and school personnel (Barth 1980; Polakowski 1984, Gallup and Elam 1988). Respondents in the latest annual Gallup poll on attitudes toward public schools listed discipline as the second major problem of public schools (Gallup and Elam 1988). The National Center for Education Statistics (1988) reports that 40 percent of public school teachers believe that behavior problems interfere with their teaching either to a great or moderate extent.

Discipline in schools is essential if learning is to take place. Critics often say that discipline is too lax, while others may say that discipline is too harsh (Barth 1980). Professional educators are often caught in the middle. Knowing how to maintain discipline is a difficult task, but it can be made easier if certain principles are followed.

First, school policies must be made clear to students. The policies must be written down and clearly explained (Thomas 1988).

Second, disciplinary standards must be consistent. "Inconsistency in policies and approaches to dealing with discipline problems, in expectations by teachers from one room to another, in interpretation of rules and policies, and in types of punishment used is the most serious detriment to a good school discipline system" (Lordon 1983, p. 59).

Third, teachers who attempt to enforce school rules must have administrative support. Nothing defeats teachers' attitudes as much as the belief that they will not be backed up by administrators in disciplinary matters. Likewise, teachers must be supportive of each other and the administrator. If administrators try to enforce school rules and teachers circumvent them, the climate is ripe for disciplinary problems. Rules are a primary component of discipline programs (Curwin and Mendler 1988); however, they are only as good as the support they have (Polakowski 1984).

Probably the best and most effective disciplinary program is preventive in nature: keep problems from occurring in the first place (Maynard 1983). If the school climate is positive and not overly restrictive, students are less likely to create disciplinary problems. Establishing a positive school climate requires the collaborative efforts of teachers, administrators, and students (Helm 1984).

Once school or classroom rules have been broken, teachers and administrators must be prepared to deal with the situation. When punishing students for breaking rules, teachers and administrators must consider several things. First, they must ask if the disciplinary action is fair. If students were aware of the rules and the consequences for breaking them and if the punishment fits the infraction, then the action probably is fair. Second, school personnel should not make an example of rule breakers. Finally, adequate records should be maintained. With the public's bent on accountability for educators, and with the courts getting involved in disciplinary cases, teachers and administrators must protect themselves with documentation (Nolte 1985).

Teachers and administrators in secondary schools can take myriad disciplinary actions with students. Consequences to misbehavior should be considered on an individual basis. What is effective punishment for one child might not be effective for another; a critical element in disciplining students is that the adversive treatment given to the child indeed be considered adversive by that child (Heitzman 1983). Disciplinary options include those typically thought of, such as detention hall, extra work, reduced privileges, and suspensions, as well as some less popular but effective measures, such as in-school suspension (Diem 1988), time out (Engelhardt 1983), individual behavior management plans (Thomason and Pedersen 1984) and mediation (Graham and Cline 1989). Whatever disciplinary approach is used, school personnel should make sure that policies are explicit, that students understand policies, and that consequences are made clear before the rule violation occurs.

Appearance Codes

Appearance codes, especially dealing with dress and hair length, have been challenged in schools during the past several years. During the 1970s, students began challenging school policies in these areas as being repressive and denying them their right to free expression. The courts have been inconsistent in their rulings on these issues. Some courts have upheld school policies related to dress and appearance of students; other courts have rejected them as being unnecessary. The one principle that has emerged is that schools apparently have the right to impose various dress and appearance standards when they can be shown to be related to the preservation of safety and to the orderly functioning of the school program (Armstrong and Savage 1983).

Expulsion and Suspension

Expulsion and suspension have been used as disciplinary measures against students for many years. Students who violate certain rules have been automatically expelled for long periods of time or suspended for a few days. During past years these disciplinary actions have been challenged as excessive. As with dress codes, the courts have at times upheld expulsion and suspension policies and at times have rejected them. Suspending and expelling students are now used most often when schools can show that the continued presence of a particular student is dangerous or severly disruptive to the school program. Even under these circumstances, schools must follow due process procedures and allow students to present their side of the issue. Schools that use expulsion and suspension should ensure that students' rights have not been infringed upon (Armstrong and Savage 1983).

Search and Seizure

The right of school officials to search students' lockers and personal areas has been an issue during the past several years. For example, do school personnel have the right to search a student's locker for suspected drugs without the student's permission? Many court cases have dealt with this subject. Although some of the rulings have denied schools the right to search students' property without their permission, other rulings have given schools this authority. The key to these rulings is that the Fourth Amendment to the United States Constitution prohibits unreasonable searches, not all searches. Courts have upheld cases where there was probable cause—in other words, in cases where school officials have demonstrated evidence to support a belief that a student is guilty of a particular offense (Armstrong and Savage 1983).

After reviewing several search and seizure litigation cases, Sendor (1984) recommended that school officials consider two things. First, evidence should be searched for only if it is related to a student's alleged offense; and second, a school policy for regular, unannounced locker searches should be developed and publicized. While the courts have upheld students' right to privacy, school officials do have the right to search private areas under appropriate circumstances. Teachers must be familiar with school policies and procedures related to search and seizure.

Other School Policies

In addition to policies on discipline, appearance codes, suspension and expulsion, and search and seizure, schools frequently have policies on topics such as

- use of school facilities during after-school hours
- field trips/excursions away from school
- grading
- graduation
- school-sponsored social activities

Without policies on these and other topics, school personnel may be at a loss as to what to do in certain circumstances. Policies, developed by the local board of education in compliance with state and federal regulations, enable school personnel to establish and implement guidelines that are necessary for the day-to-day functioning of the school.

PROBLEMS FACING SECONDARY SCHOOLS

Many problems currently face secondary schools in the United States. Examples include school dropouts, discipline, declining academic performance, and general problems facing adolescents, including alcohol and drug abuse, teenage pregnancy, and suicide. Although many of these reflect general problems of society, schools are expected to deal with these problems as they relate to school-age children.

School Dropouts

Schools can use social, psychological, behavioral, physical, and academic characteristics to identify potential dropouts and intervene to reduce the numbers of dropouts (Soderberg 1988). One program that attempts to do this was initiated in Gateway High School, Aurora, Colorado. Called the Experimental Program for Orientation (EXPO), this program identified sixty students who were considered potential dropouts. Of these sixty, thirty were enrolled in the program (on a volunteer basis) and thirty were considered a control group. The program assigned mentors to students to help them with any problems and provided workshops on study skills, assertiveness, time management, team building, self-image, and decision making. After one year, the thirty students enrolled in the EXPO program exhibited several characteristics superior to those in the control group: (1) less truancy, (2) higher grade-point average, and (3) fewer dropouts (only one student in the EXPO program dropped out, while seven in the control group dropped out). This program, therefore, was considered a huge success. (See table 8.6).

Many programs have been developed to help prevent students from dropping out of school. Some ideas that can help include (1) providing support programs, (2) providing alternative classes, (3) encouraging cocurricular activities, (4) encouraging positive group interactions, and (5) working with families (Mahan and Johnson 1983). Preventing students from dropping out of school before they complete the regular school program requires a great deal of time and effort from all school personnel and family members.

Declining Academic Performance

One of the major reasons for the reform reports of the late 1970s and early 1980s was the declining academic performance of students as measured by norm-referenced, standardized tests. Scores on the Scholastic Achievement Test (SAT) are quickly pointed to by critics of education as evidence of declining academic performance. The National Commission on Excellence in Education report, A Nation at Risk, issued

TABLE 8.6
Characteristics of Potential Dropouts

- More Mobile Than Other Students
- Behavior Problems
- Absenteeism or Truancy
- Lower Income Home
- Low/Under Achievers
- Feelings of Rejection
- Limited Participation in Extracurricular Activities
- Frequent Health Problems
- Personal Problems
- Loners
- Poor Communication Between School and Home
- Poorly Educated Parents
- Sibling is Dropout
- Friends are Outside the School
- Fail Grades Frequently

Source: Neill. *Keeping Students in School: Problems and Solutions.* 1979.

in 1983, pointed out that SAT scores have declined steadily from 1963 to 1980 and that science achievement test scores of seventeen-year-olds have declined in testings in 1969, 1973, and 1977. The report further indicated that remedial math courses offered by colleges and universities increased seventy-two percent between 1975 and 1980 (National Commission on Excellence in Education 1983).

Although some reports indicate that test scores for top students have remained relatively constant, the concern is for the majority of students whose scores have declined. Secondary educators must be concerned about declining test scores. Following the Nation at Risk report and other reform reports of the late 1970s and early 1980s, many state departments of education and state legislatures adopted policies to help reduce this academic decline. Whether some of the measures have a positive, long-term effect remains to be seen. At least for now, college entrance examination scores have begun to increase. Scores on the American College Testing (ACT) Program and SAT have risen in the past few years. This, associated with recent increases in Stanford Achievement Test scores, may signify a reversal of the declining academic performance trend that started in the 1960s (Stedman and Kaestle 1985). Educators, however, must still be aware of the past trends and maintain efforts to improve students' score.

Problems of Adolescence

For many, the adolescent years are marked by turbulence. During this period, generally thought of as the teenage years, individuals must deal with physical, physiological, and emotional changes. These are the years when children mature into young adults. This period "seems to hold the sweetest and most painful experiences" (Stevens-Long and Cobb 1983, p. 12). Educators who teach adolescents must be aware of adolescent needs and problems. Although most individuals pass through adolescence without major problems, some experience traumatic events that significantly affect their lives.

Alcohol and Drug Abuse. Alcohol and drug abuse were once considered problems for a small, select segment of the adolescent population. Currently, however, abuses of these substances among American youth is an acknowledged fact.

Alcohol abuse is considered by some as America's number one mental health problem (Stevens-Long and Cobb 1983). That adolescents in the United States are drinking too much is becoming an accepted fact. Although alcohol use by adolescents has declined since 1979, the rate of use remains very high. In 1987, approximately sixty-six percent of the high-school seniors had used alcohol during the past thirty days; ninety-two percent had used alcohol at one time in their life (National Center for Education Statistics 1988).

286

■

SCHOOL-NIGHT WORK LIMIT ADVANCES

Bill Salisbury

Students ages 16 and 17 would be barred from working past 11 P.M. on school nights under a bill given preliminary approval by the Minnesota House on Monday.

"This is a strong measure to help protect our children," the bill's sponsor, Rep. Len Price, DFL [Democrat]-Woodbury, told his colleagues before the vote.

The House approved the measure 95–35. Seventy-five DFLers and 20 Independent-Republicans voted in favor, while 32 IRs and three DFLers voted "no."

Price said the legislation is needed because some employers intimidate high school students into working late, and those students often perform poorly in school.

A companion bill, sponsored by Sen. A. W. Diessner, DFL-Afton, is pending in a Senate committee.

"Working late into the night does affect school performance," Price said. "Testimony from parents, teachers and students indicates that students are so tired that they often do not do the homework assignments, they fall asleep in class, and as a result have poor grades."

Price, a teacher, said he has often seen such cases firsthand.

But critics said the bill won't get teenagers off the streets or stop them from watching television after 11 P.M.

"What you need is a statewide curfew," said Rep. Terry Dempsey, IR [Republican]-New Ulm.

Sixteen- and 17-year-olds who don't attend school won't be affected by the bill, so they will take late-night jobs to make money, Dempsey said. "You've created an incentive to drop out of school," he asserted.

Rep. Steve Sviggum, IR-Kenyon, argued that parents and children should have the right to choose whether to work late.

"The issue before us is whether government knows best. I don't think it does," Sviggum said.

Price responded that many parents requested the work curfew so they don't have to argue with their children over working late.

Late-night work hours are common for teen-agers, he said. A recent survey of Anoka and Blaine high school students showed 60 percent to 70 percent of them work, and about one-fourth of those with jobs work past 11 P.M. at least one night a week.

Other proponents of the legislation said students work whatever hours employers assign them because they fear being fired.

"There is exploitation of our most fragile people, our young people," said Rep. James Rice, DFL-Minneapolis.

Under the bill, an employer who violated the curfew would be fined $50 for each underage employee. A repeat violator could be charged with a gross misdemeanor.

The measure would strengthen existing child labor laws, which ban employing minors under age 14 and those under 16 during school hours and after 9 P.M. on school nights. There are no similar restrictions on 16- and 17-year-olds under the law now.

Source: *St. Paul Pioneer Press Dispatch*, March 14, 1989.

Drug abuse is defined as the use of drugs contrary to medical and legal regulations and/or norms. Professional and popular literature present data supporting the contention that drug abuse exists in all segments of our society, crossing barriers of race, socioeconomic status, age, and geographic location. The National Center for Education Statistics (1988) reported that nearly twenty-five percent of the high-school seniors in 1987 had used illegal drugs during the past thirty days and forty-one percent had used illegal drugs during the previous twelve months.

Teenage Pregnancy. Approximately 1.2 million adolescents get pregnant each year; nearly half of these pregnancies result in live births, with the remaining pregnancies ending in either spontaneous or induced abortions or maternal death (Anastasiow 1983). Teenage pregnancy, therefore, is a large problem in the United States.

In increasing numbers, pregnant adolescents are opting to give birth and keep their children. This often results in young families with low incomes, low socioeconomic status, and low educational attainment (Stevens-Long and Cobb 1983). The future outlook for these families is bleak.

Children born to teenage mothers have been found to be more susceptible to problems than children born from older mothers. For example, in women under age fifteen, the risk for low birth-weight and premature births increases. These factors have been associated with various disabilities later in life. There also is an increased likelihood for "failure-to-thrive infants, emotional disturbance among pre-schoolers, and lower academic and more frequent grade retention, particularly among males" (Anastasiow 1983, p. 398).

Teenage pregnancy occurs more than one million times each year and can result in difficulties for young families and learning and behavior problems for children later in life. Educators need to be cognizant of the problems resulting from teenage pregnancies and must understand the needs of students who must deal with an unwanted pregnancy.

Suicide. Adolescent suicide in the United States has increased 300 percent during the past two decades (Hunter 1988); it is the leading cause of death among fifteen- to twenty-four-year olds. The number is far too high "because promising young lives are destroyed" (Konopka 1983, p. 391).

Although long-term solutions for teenage suicides must come from the community and society (Hunt 1987), schools have a major responsibility in helping to prevent suicides (Guetzloe 1988). Research has accumulated a large set of data concerning teenage suicides. Some of the signs that could indicate suicidal behavior include:

- fatigue;
- excessive concern for physical health or body image;
- growing inability to absorb or retain information regardless of the effort made;
- sudden decline in scholastic achievement;

SOUTH TAKES AIM AT HIGH TEEN PREGNANCY RATE

LaBarbara Bowman

Giving youngsters hope, jobs and sex education can reduce the South's teenage pregnancy rates—the highest in the USA—Southern governors say.

Their report out Wednesday says teen-age girls with bad grades, no fathers living at home and low self-esteem are most vulnerable to pregnancy.

"People that think they have hope for their future, that think they have good skills, that are going places, they tend not to have these problems," said Mississippi Gov. Ray Mabus, releasing the report supported by the 17-member Southern Governors Association.

In 1985, the South had 47 percent of the nation's births to girls 17 and under while only 37 percent of girls that age lived in the South.

The group proposed sex education, teaching boys pregnancy prevention and expanding programs to make sure poor children—most at risk of becoming dropouts and teen-age parents—to learn to like school and read and write.

Males need to learn pregnancy prevention because focusing solely on females "ignores half the problem," the report said.

Says Mabus: "When our children have children, everybody loses. We pay for it in so many ways. It's cheaper to prevent it than to pay for it."

Price tag: The 17 Southern states spent $3.5 billion in 1986–87 on welfare, food stamps and medical insurance for teen-age mothers and their children.

Copyright May 25, 1989, *USA Today*. Reprinted with permission.

Births to Teen-age Mothers

Percentage of 1986 births that were to teen-age mothers (Southern states—as defined in the study—are listed in **bold**):

Ala.	**17.4%**	**Ky.**	**17.4%**	Ohio	13.3%
Alaska	8.7%	**La.**	**16.8%**	**Okla.**	**15.6%**
Ariz.	13.8%	Maine	11.6%	Ore.	10.9%
Ark.	**19.0%**	**Md.**	**11.7%**	Penn.	11.3%
Calif.	10.9%	Mass.	8.3%	R.I.	10.3%
Colo.	10.2%	Mich	12.3%	**S.C.**	**16.6%**
Conn.	8.8%	Minn.	7.3%	S.D.	9.7%
Del.	**13.2%**	**Miss.**	**20.5%**	**Tenn.**	**17.0%**
D.C.	17.0%	**Mo.**	**13.4%**	**Texas**	**15.2%**
Fla.	**13.8%**	Mont.	10.1%	Utah	9.3%
Ga.	**17.0%**	Neb.	8.9%	Vt.	9.2%
Hawaii	9.6%	Nev.	11.9%	**Va.**	**12.0%**
Idaho	10.8%	N.H.	7.7%	Wash.	10.4%
Ill.	12.5%	N.J.	9.4%	**W. Va.**	**17.1%**
Ind.	14.0%	N.M.	15.3%	Wis.	9.9%
Iowa	9.2%	N.Y.	9.7%	Wyo.	10.7%
Kan	11.5%	**N.C.**	**15.9%**	USA	12.6%
		N.D.	8.0%		

Source: Children's Defense Fund

- restlessness and an exaggerated effort to keep busy;
- constant need for new and different kinds of risk or thrill-seeking stimulation to avoid thinking;
- crying;
- sleeplessness and loss of appetite;
- sudden changes in personality;
- withdrawal from friends;
- giving away treasured personal belongings;
- preoccupation with talking or writing about death. (Hunter 1988, p. 93–94)

Schools should have a plan to be alert for these kinds of signals and should have an intervention program to help prevent suicides.

SUMMARY

This chapter focused on secondary education in the United States. Although secondary education was a rather late occurrence, it has grown dramatically during the twentieth century. Secondary education in the United States is organized into high schools and either junior high schools or middle schools. Middle schools are a more modern development than junior high schools and are intended to allow educators to consider the unique needs of early adolescence.

The objectives of secondary education have been and will continue to be debated. Should secondary schools attempt to be all things to all children, or should they focus their efforts only on academic tasks? Secondary schools are organized along several different criteria, including curriculum tracks and vertical organization, or graded versus nongraded.

One major section of the chapter dealt with the curriculum found in secondary schools. Most schools have a common curriculum consisting of English, math, science, and social studies. In addition, specialized courses are available, such as sex education, drug education, and multicultural education. Extracurricular activities are also offered at most secondary schools. With vocational education programs also being available to most students, American secondary schools can easily be classified as "comprehensive."

The methods used to instruct secondary students were also discussed. These include lecture, discussion, independent study, and individual instruction. Another section of the chapter focused on the school philosophy and policies, especially as they relate to such issues as discipline, appearance codes, expulsion and suspension, and search and seizure.

The final section of the chapter dealt with problems facing secondary schools in the United States, including (1) school dropouts,

(2) declining academic performance, and (3) problems experienced by adolescents, such as drug and alcohol abuse.

Secondary education in the United States is widespread. Although it developed later than elementary education, it has become a world standard as a model for educating the masses. Although problems in secondary education in the United States exist today, educators have to assume that solutions will be found. The resolution of such difficulties will call upon the collective wisdom and skill of the professional and the public.

IN THE FIELD

1. Does the district have middle schools or junior high schools, or a combination of both? How long has the current organizational structure been used?

2. Are there stated objectives for the secondary school and secondary education in the district? If so, are these objectives available to students and teachers?

3. What suggests that the high school is a comprehensive high school?

4. What types of curricula are offered at the high school?

5. What are the required courses for graduation? Have these changed recently? If so, why?

6. Do requirements differ for college-prep students and other students? If so, what is the rationale for the difference?

7. Are special topics, such as sex education, drug education, and multicultural education, included in any courses?

8. What are the school's policies on discipline, dress codes, and suspension and expulsion?

9. Are there any programs to address adolescent problems such as pregnancy and drug abuse? If so, what is their nature?

10. Are there prerequisites for participation in extracurricular activities? If so, what are they, and are they considered effective?

11. Does the school have a vocational education program? If not, is there a special vocational school or program available to the school's students?

12. What vocational education options are available to students?

REFERENCES

Alvermann, D. E. 1984. Using textbook reading assignments to promote classroom discussion. *The Clearing House* 58(2), 70–72.

Anastasiow, N. J. 1983. Adolescent pregnancy and special education. *Exceptional Children* 49(5), 396–401.

Armstrong, D. G., and T. V. Savage. 1983. *Secondary Education: An Introduction.* New York: Macmillan.

Banks, J. A. 1981. *Multiethnic Education: Theory and Practice.* Boston: Allyn and Bacon.

Barth, R. S. 1980. Discipline: If you do that again. *Phi Delta Kappan* 61(6), 398–400.

Berry, G. L. 1979. The multicultural principle: Missing from the seven cardinal principles of 1918 and 1978. *Phi Delta Kappan* 60(10), 745.

Besvinick, S. L. 1988. Twenty years later: Reviving the reforms of the '60s. *Educational Leadership* 46(1), 52.

Binder, F. M. 1974. *The Age of the Common School, 1830–1865.* New York: John Wiley & Sons.

Bottoms, G., and P. Copa. 1983. A perspective on vocational education today. *Phi Delta Kappan* 64(5), 348–54.

Boyer, E. L. 1984. Clarifying the mission of the American high school. *Educational Leadership* 41(6), 20–22.

Campbell, P. B. 1986. Vocational education: Access, equity, and consequence. *Educational Horizons* 65 (1), 10–13.

Chase, C. I., and L. C. Jacobs. 1987. The impact of grade point average requirements for participation in school activities. *The High School Journal* 71(2), 69–73.

Clark, L. H., and I. S. Starr. 1981. *Secondary and Middle School Teaching Methods.* New York: Macmillan.

Commager, H. S. 1983. A historian looks at the American high school. *American Journal of Education* 91(4), 531–48.

Curwin, R. L., and A. N. Mendler. 1988. Packaged discipline programs: Let the buyer beware. *Educational Leadership* 46(2), 68–71.

D'Alonzo, B. J. 1983. *Educating Adolescents with Learning and Behavior Problems.* Rockville, MD: Aspen Systems.

Diem, R. A. 1988. On campus suspensions: A case study. *The High School Journal* 72(1), 36–39.

Digest of Education Statistics, 1988. Washington, D.C.: U.S. Department of Education.

Engelhardt, L. 1983. This system called for time out on student discipline problems. *The American School Board Journal,* June 21–24.

Flygare, T. J. 1985. Texas Supreme Court upholds 'no pass/no play' rule. *Phi Delta Kappan* 67(1), 71.

Frantz, N. R., D. C. Strickland, and D. E. Elson. 1988. Is secondary vocational education at risk? *Vocational Education Journal* 63(7), 34–37.

Gallup, G. H. 1984. The 16th annual Gallup poll of the public's attitudes toward the public school. *Phi Delta Kappan* 66(1), 23–36.

Gallup, A. M., and S. M. Elam. 1988. The 20th annual Gallup poll of the public's attitudes toward the public schools. *Phi Delta Kappan* 70(1), 33–46.

George, P. 1988. Education 2000: Which way the middle school? *Clearing House* 62(1), 14–16.

Glatthorn, A. A. 1987. *Curriculum Leadership.* Glenview, IL: Scott, Foresman.

Gold, S. 1984. What's wrong with telling? A veteran teacher re-examines her classroom style. *The Clearing House* 57(7), 331–32.

Graham, T., and P. C. Cline. 1989. Mediation: An alternative approach to school discipline. *The High School Journal* 72(2), 73–76.

Gross, R. E. 1978. Seven new cardinal principles. *Phi Delta Kappan* 80, 291–93.

Guetzloe, E. 1988. School prevention of suicide, violence, and abuse. *The Pointer* 32, 4–6.

Heitzman, A. J. 1983. Discipline and the use of punishment. *Education* 104(1), 17–22.

Helm, D. J. 1984. To discipline or not to discipline. *The Clearing House* 57(7), 333.

Hunt, C. 1987. Step by step: How your schools can live through the tragedy of teen suicides. *The American School Board Journal* 174(2), 34–35.

Hunter, B. E. 1988. Adolescent suicide: Cries for help. *NASSP Bulletin* 72(510), 92–94.

Kenney, A. M., and M. T. Orr. 1984. Sex education: An overview of current programs, policies, and research. *Phi Delta Kappan* 65(7), 491–96.

Konopka, G. 1983. Adolescent suicide. *Exceptional Children* 49(5), 390–94.

Laven, D., and W. McKeever. 1989. Program quality review in California middle schools. *Thrust* 18(5), 45–46.

Lordon, J. F. 1983. Establishing a climate for school discipline: The total perspective. *NASSP Bulletin* 67(62), 58–60.

Lotto, L. S. 1985. The unfinished agenda: Report from the national commission on secondary vocational education. *Phi Delta Kappan* 66(8), 568–73.

Lounsbury, J. H. 1987. Why I believe middle school is better than junior high school. *American School Board Journal* 174(9), 45+.

Mahan, G., and C. Johnson. 1983. Portrait of a dropout: Dealing with academic, social, and emotional problems. *NASSP Bulletin*, April, 80–83.

Marsh, G. E., and B. J. Price. 1980. *Methods for Teaching the Mildly Handicapped Adolescent.* St. Louis: C. V. Mosby.

Maynard, B. 1983. Is your discipline policy part of your discipline problem? *The Executive Educator*, 26–27.

McNeil, J. D. 1985. *Curriculum: A Comprehensive Introduction.* Boston: Little, Brown.

Michel, T. A., and R. L. Weaver. 1984. Lecturing: Means for improvement. *The Clearing House* 57(9), 389–91.

Montague, E. J. 1987. *Fundamentals of Secondary Classroom Instruction.* Columbus, OH: Merrill.

National Center for Education Statistics, 1988. *The Condition of Education.* U.S. Department of Education.

National Center for Education Statistics. 1983. *The Condition of Education.* Washington, DC: U.S. Government Printing Office.

Neill, S. B. 1979. *Keeping Students in School: Problems and Solutions.* Sacramento, CA: American Association of School Administrators.

Nelson, J. L., and J. U. Michaelis. 1980. *Secondary social studies: Instruction, curriculum, evaluation.* Englewood Cliffs, NJ: Prentice-Hall.

Nolte, M. C. 1985. Use caution in punishing kids who break the rules. *The American School Board Journal* 172(5), 42.

Polakowski, K. 1984. Some ideas on discipline. *The Clearing House* 58(2), 83–84.

Post, L. M. 1984. Individualizing instruction in the middle school: Modifications and adaptions in curriculum for the mainstreamed student. *The Clearing House* 58(2), 73–76.

Schall, W. E. 1984. Take math outdoors. *Instructor* XCIII(8), 46–49+.

Sendor, B. 1984. Student drug searches: Can you risk the frisk? *The American School Board Journal*, 171(3), 27+.

Sigda, R. B. 1983. The crisis in science education and the realities of science teaching in the classroom, *Phi Delta Kappan* 64(9), 624–27.

Silberman, H. F. 1986. Improving the status of high school vocational education. *Educational Horizons* 65(1), 5–9.

Sizer, T. R. 1983. High school reform: The need for engineering. *Phi Delta Kappan* 64(10), 679–83.

Skinner, A. 1988. Time out: Criticism notwithstanding, school sports still are the best game in town. *The American School Board Journal* 175(7), 22–23.

Soderberg, L. J. 1988. Educators knowledge of the characteristics of high school dropouts. *The High School Journal* 71(3), 108–114.

State update on sexuality education and AIDS education. 1988. *SIECUS Report*, November/December 1988.

Stedman, L. C. and C. F. Kaestle. 1985. The test score decline is over. Now what? *Phi Delta Kappan* 67(3), 204–10.

Stefanich, G., and C. Dedrick. 1985. Addressing concerns in science and mathematics education: An alternative view. *The Clearing House* 58(6), 274–77.

Stevens-Long, J., and N. J. Cobb. 1983. *Adolescence and Early Adulthood.* Palo Alto, CA: Mayfield.

Sylwester, R., and C. Hasegawa. 1989. How to explain drugs to your students. *Middle School Journal* 20, 8–11.

Tanner, D. 1979. Splitting up the school system: Are comprehensive high schools doomed? *Phi Delta Kappan* 61(2), 92–97.

Thomas, W. 1988. To solve 'the discipline problem,' mix clear rules with consistent consequences. *The American School Board Journal* 175(6), 30–31.

Thomason, J. and J. Pedersen. 1984. Perfect 10: A discipline alternative. *The Clearing House* 57(8), 353–55.

Tomlinson, T. M., and H. J. Walberg 1986. *Academic Work and Educational Excellence.* Berkeley, CA: McCutchan.

Vocational Education Regulations. Title 45, *U.S. Code of Federal Regulations*, 1979.

Wagenaar, T. C. 1981. High school seniors' views of Themselves and their schools: A trend analysis. *Phi Delta Kappan* 63(1), 29–32.

Weber, L. J., and J. McBee. 1988. Excluding students from participating in athletic and other extracurricular activities. *The High School Journal* 71(4), 155–160.

Weisberg, A. 1983. What research has to say about vocational education and the high schools. *Phi Delta Kappan* 64(5), 355–59.

Wood, C. L., E. W. Nicholson, and D. G. Findley. 1985. *The Secondary School Principal: Manager and Supervisor.* Boston: Allyn and Bacon.

Yager, R. E. 1988. Achieving useful science: Reforming the reforms of the '60s. *Educational Leadership* 46(1), 53–54.

9

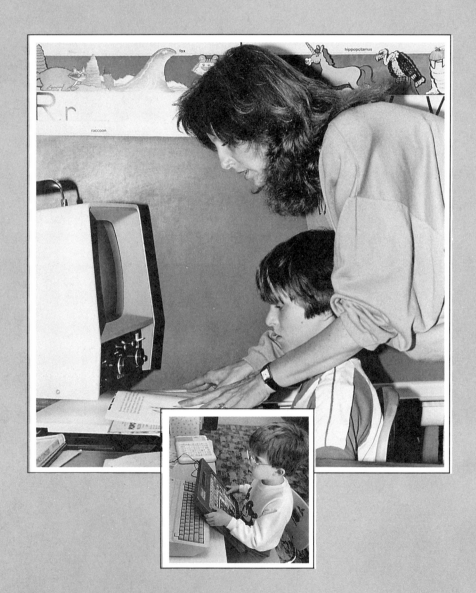

SPECIAL EDUCATION

OBJECTIVES

After reading this chapter, you will be able to

- trace the history of treatment and education of handicapped persons to the present;
- outline the major legislative acts that preceded Public Law 94–142;
- describe Public Law 94–142;
- describe the key parts of Public Law 99–457;
- discuss the major litigation cases dealing with special education;
- describe the categorical classification model;
- discuss the benefits of generic classification;
- list the major services in a traditional service delivery system; and
- describe the cascade of service model.

OUTLINE

ADVANCE ORGANIZERS

1. How were disabled individuals treated prior to 1750?
2. What is the magnitude of special education today?
3. What legislation led to the passage of Public Law 94–142?
4. What are the key components of Public Law 94–142?
5. What court cases are considered landmarks in special education?
6. How did the civil rights movement affect special education?
7. What are the categories used to classify handicapped children using the traditional classification system?
8. What is the definition of "mildly handicapped"?
9. What service options were available using the traditional service delivery system?
10. What options should be available along a continuum of services model?

INTRODUCTION

Special education has been provided for students with disabilities for most of the twentieth century; however, the magnitude of special education has grown dramatically since the 1950s. As a result of legislation and litigation, special education is available to students with disabilities in all public schools in the United States. Disabled children currently receive special education and related services at an unprecedented level. While special education was a small program just a few years ago, it now serves approximately 10.6 percent of the school population, or approximately 4.4 million students (United States Department of Education 1988) and touches all teachers and adminstrators in a school district. Madeleine Will, former assistant secretary for the Office of Special Education and Rehabilitative Services, U.S. Department of Education, noted the recent growth in special education: "The past decade has produced results for students with disabilities that were considered unobtainable and unthinkable only a few years earlier. Little more than a decade ago, many children were left completely out of the nation's school systems" (Will 1984, p. 11).

The impetus for expanded services is the federal government. Federal legislation, funding, and court decisions have brought about increased services for the handicapped. Special education in the 1980s has been shaped a great deal by federal involvement during the 1970s.

Special education once was limited to educational services provided for handicapped students, primarily mentally retarded students, in a self-contained classroom by a special education teacher. Regular classroom teachers rarely saw these students or their teachers. At present the focus is to provide educational and therapeutic services to all handicapped children in an integrated setting. Children with disabilities are educated with nondisabled children as much of the time as is appropriate. The education of disabled children, therefore, has become a shared responsibility among special education personnel, regular classroom teachers, and school support personnel.

HISTORY OF TREATMENT OF THE HANDICAPPED

Handicapped people have not always been afforded special education and other necessary services. Hundreds of years ago, individuals with disabilities were actually put to death. The treatment and education of disabled individuals has evolved during the past two thousand years to what currently is considered special education, with the most rapid advances in services occurring since the mid-1900s.

Education and Treatment Prior to 1750

Prior to the middle 1700s, the plight of handicapped people was dismal. The first written reference to the handicapped appeared in the therapeutic Papyrus of Thebes, an Egyptian papyrus dated 1552 B.C. Other ancient works, including the Bible, Talmud and Koran, also contained references to the handicapped; however, during this era many handicapped people were forced to beg for survival (Blackhurst and Berdine 1985). In the Greek city states of Sparta and Athens, handicapped individuals frequently were left to die or actually put to death. The philosophy of the time was that individuals unable to take care of themselves should be done away with.

The life for handicapped people improved little during the next several hundred years. A few would be chosen for duty as court "fools," with the responsibility of making people laugh, but the majority, if allowed to live, were destined to a meager life of begging. During the Middle Ages, the church began to provide some of the basic necessities for handicapped people. Although no formal training or education was provided, at least food, water, and shelter were provided.

During the Renaissance and Reformation periods, individuals were caught up in witchcraft, demonology, exorcism, and the persecution of the handicapped. Such persecution was even practiced by religious leaders of the time. "Martin Luther and John Calvin, for example, accused the mentally retarded of being 'filled with Satan', and many were put in chains and thrown into dungeons" (Blackhurst and Berdine 1985, p. 14).

Changes began to occur by the 1600s. A hospital in Paris began treating emotionally disturbed people, a manual alphabet for the deaf was developed, and John Locke differentiated between the mentally retarded and mentally ill (Blackhurst and Berdine 1985). From the beginning of recorded history, individuals have attempted to change the view of the populace toward people with disabilities. These individuals, however, were always frustrated in their attempts at improving the lives of disabled people (Gearheart 1980).

Education and Treatment Since 1750

Itard and the Educational Movement (1750-1900). The educational era for disabled people started with the work of a French physician named Jean Itard. Itard became personally involved in trying to educate and socialize a boy who had been found in the Aveyron forest in southern France in 1799. The boy, given the name of Victor, had been abandoned for several years and had somehow managed to survive in the wilderness. Itard obtained custody of Victor and attempted to educate him, even though many thought Victor was incurable. The program for Victor was not successful, but it was an attempt to provide educational training to an individual with functional mental retardation, something that had not been attempted before.

Education and Treatment in the United States. People with disabilities in colonial America were no better off than their peers in Europe. Mentally retarded people were kept at home, placed in poorhouses, or auctioned off to bidders who took care of them and received work in return (Blackhurst and Berdine 1985).

As a result of Itard's work, things began to change in the United States in the 1800s. The first residential school for the deaf was established by Thomas Hopkins Gallaudet in 1817 in Connecticut, and Samuel Howe established the first residential school for the blind, the Perkins School for the Blind, in Massachusettes in 1829 (Kirk and Gallagher, 1989). Many other individuals also pushed for increasing services to the disabled. These included Sequin, a colleague of Itard, who immigrated to the United States and did a great deal of work with the mentally retarded (Gearheart 1980), as well as Dorothea Dix, a retired school teacher who campaigned tirelessly for the rights of mentally ill people (Cartwright, Cartwright, and Ward 1981).

Education and Training since 1900. Services for disabled children and adults have grown tremendously since the turn of the century. One major action that facilitated improved services was the testing movement. Prior to the development of an individual intelligence test by Binet in 1905, there were no good measures of intelligence or aptitude. As a result of Binet's efforts, the testing movement was launched in which many assessment instruments were developed that aided in the provision of appropriate services to disabled individuals.

■ *Public Law 94-142 required schools to provide appropriate services for students with disabilities.*

Several other trends occurred during the first part of the twentieth century. These included

1. an increase in the number of public school classes for the educable mentally retarded;
2. an increase in the number of residential schools for lower-functioning mentally retarded, visually impaired, and hearing impaired children;
3. the beginning of classes for the physically handicapped;
4. establishment of speech therapy services in the public schools; and
5. the beginning of classes for the emotionally disturbed (beginning around 1950). (Gearheart 1980)

These trends greatly enhanced the educational and training opportunities for disabled children, but they were only a sign of things to come. During the 1960s and 1970s, legislation and litigation provided disabled children and adults with the right to appropriate educational programs and other services. Public schools and other government agencies began providing services that previously had been denied. The era of full opportunities had arrived.

SPECIAL EDUCATION TODAY

Educational and support services provided for disabled children in public schools are more extensive than ever before. The growth of special education has been largely the result of two factors: legislation and litigation.

Students Served

The growth of special education programs has enabled schools to serve many more students. The Office of Special Education, U.S. Department of Education, annually reports to Congress on the status of services to children with disabilities. The following information from two of these reports indicates the rapid growth in special education programs:

- The number of handicapped children who receive special education and related services continues to grow.
- In the 1982–1983 school year, 4.2 million children with disabilities received special education and related services. In the 1986–1987 school year, this number was 4.4 million.
- The number of children served in the 1982–1983 school year reflected a 16 percent increase since the 1976–1977 school year. The 1986–1987 school year showed an additional 3 percent increase.
- The percentage of the school population receiving special education and related services in the 1981–1982 school year was 10.47; the percentage receiving services in the 1986–1987 school year was 10.64.
- The number of preschool children served increased 23 percent from 1976–1977 to 1982–1983. (U.S. Department of Education 1984; U.S. Department of Education 1988)

A wide variety of disabled children are currently being provided with special education and related services. During the 1986–1987 school year, children classified as learning disabled were the largest special education group served. Table 9.1 lists each category of disability, the number of children served, and the percent of the total disabled population. The learning disabilities category, which has grown so rapidly during the past decade, grew by 53,000 students between the 1985–86 and 1986–87 school years (National Center for Education Statistics 1988).

The 1988 annual report to Congress (U.S. Department of Education 1988) reflected an increase in the number of students served, but the number of children identified and served through special education is expected to level off soon. With approximately 10 percent of the school population identified as disabled, all teachers and administrators must understand the special needs of disabled students and the legal responsibility of educators to provide these students with appropriate educational services.

TABLE 9.1
Students Served Under Federal Programs by Handicapping Condition

HANDICAPPING CONDITION	NUMBER	PERCENT[a]
Learning Disabled	1,926,097	43.6
Speech or Language Impaired	1,140,422	25.8
Mentally Retarded	664,424	15.0
Emotionally Disturbed	384,680	8.7
Multihandicapped	99,416	2.2
Hard of Hearing and Deaf	66,761	1.5
Orthopedically Impaired	58,328	1.3
Other Health Impaired	52,658	1.2
Visually Handicapped	27,049	.61
Deaf-Blind	1,766	.04
All Conditions	4,421,601	100

[a]Percent of total children served in special education.

Source: U.S. Department of Education. 1988. Tenth annual report to Congress on the implementation of Public Law 94–142.

HIGHLIGHT

EXTRA $3,555 SPENT PER HANDICAPPED CHILD

Christopher Connell

WASHINGTON—Schools spent an extra $3,555 for each of the 4.4 million handicapped children receiving some form of special education in the 1985–86 academic years, according to a study prepared for the government.

The total cost for special education students was $6,335 on average, or 2.3 times the $2,780 cost for regular classwork, the report said. About 11 percent of the nation's school children receive special education in some way.

The new $1.8 million study, done by a private research and analysis firm, Decision Resources Corp., breaks down the special education costs by the different approaches used to teach children with handicaps, ranging from physical disabilities to mental disorders.

It examined both "resource programs," or those serving pupils for less than half of the regular 30-hour school week, and "self-contained programs"—defined as those which occupied more than 15 hours per week.

Looking only at what was spent on special education, the resource programs spent $2,463 per pupil versus $5,566 per pupil in the self-contained programs.

But the schools also incurred regular education costs for these pupils—the full regular cost of $2,780 for those in resource programs, and about half as much, $1,347, for those in self-contained programs.

That boosted the total per pupil costs to $5,243 for those in resource programs and to $6,913 for those in self-contained programs, the study said.

"It's an erroneous comparison to say, 'If I had all the kids in resource programs, I could save a lot of money,'" said Mary

continued

Moore, vice president of Decision Resources Corp. and project director for the study. "The difference is only about $1,700, not $3,000."

The study, based on visits to 60 school districts in 18 states, also found average per pupil costs of:

■ $4,750 for preschool special education programs, plus $973 in regular education costs for a total of $5,723.

■ $29,108 for residential programs, plus $389 in regular education costs for a total of $29,497.

Most special education pupils were enrolled in resource programs, and they spent 80 percent of their time in regular education.

Fifteen percent of those in self-contained programs spent no time in regular education. The rest spent an average of 28 percent of their time in regular classes.

The study said special education costs rose 10 percent after inflation between 1977–78 and 1985–86, versus a 4 percent increase for regular education.

Instruction accounted for 63 percent of the special education costs, assessment 13 percent, support services 11 percent, related services 10 percent and transportation 5 percent. Moore said the percentages added to more than 100 percent because of rounding up.

The average caseload for teachers in resource programs was 26 students.

In self-contained programs, there was one teacher for every four hard-of-hearing students; one per five autistic or multihandicapped students; one per seven deaf or visually handicapped students, one per eight mentally retarded or orthopedically impaired students; one per nine speech impaired or seriously emotionally disturbed students, and one per 13 learning disabled students.

Transportation was the most expensive related service provided handicapped students. Thirty percent needed special transportation services, at an average cost of $1,583. Assessment cost an average of $1,206, physical therapy $993, occupational therapy $918, psychological services $867, speech language pathology $648 and guidance and counseling $553.

Federal dollars provided 5 percent of the local district's instructional budget for the handicapped, but 17 percent of their budget for support services.

Moore discussed the report in an interview and provided a set of tables prepared for a recent briefing for special education groups. The full report, "Patterns in Special Education—Service, Delivery and Cost," will be available early next year.

Source: *The Birmingham News*, December 25, 1988.

Legislation

Federal legislation affecting handicapped children in public schools dates back to 1823 when Public Law 19–8 was passed. This legislation provided a federal land grant to establish an asylum for the deaf in Kentucky (Boston 1977). Other early federal legislation that affected disabled children included:

■ P.L. 45–186. In 1879 this legislation was passed to provide $10,000 to the American Printing House for the Blind to produce Braille materials.

■ P.L. 66–236. This act, passed in 1920, made civilians eligible for vocational rehabilitation benefits that were provided for World War I veterans.

■ P.L. 80–617. In 1948 this bill was passed to eliminate discrimination in hiring physically handicapped persons.

- P.L. 83–531. Passed in 1954, this legislation provided funds for educational research in the area of mental retardation. (Boston 1977)

Since the mid-1950s, more federal legislation has had a significant impact on special education (see table 9.2). These legislative actions culminated with the passage of P.L. 94–142, the Education for All Handicapped Children Act of 1975.

P.L. 94-142. Passed in 1975, Public Law 94–142 has had a profound impact on the education of handicapped children. Support for such a law came from a variety of sources.

Forces Leading to the Passage of P.L. 94–142. The 1950s and 1960s were the decades for civil rights activities. In 1954, the landmark United States Supreme Court's decision in *Brown v. Board of Education, Topeka, Kansas,* legally eliminated racial discrimination in public education. P.L. 94–142 is an extension of civil rights legislation for racial minorities. "Basically, this Act is Civil Rights as well as educational legislation, and can be fully understood only from that perspective" (Corrigan 1978, p. 10). Following litigated victories by minorities, parents of handicapped children decided to pursue equity through the courts and legislative lobbying.

TABLE 9.2
Early Legislation Dealing with Special Education

LEGISLATION	DATE	DESCRIPTION
PL 85–926	1958	Provided funds for universities to prepare teachers for mentally retarded children
PL 88–164	1963	Provided funds to prepare special education teachers for all types of handicapped students
PL 89–10	1965	Known as the Elementary and Secondary Act, provided funds to schools to assist the disadvantaged and handicapped
PL 89–36	1965	Created the National Institute for the Deaf
PL 89–750	1966	Created the Bureau of Education for the Handicapped and a National Committee on the Handicapped
PL 91–61	1969	Etablished National Center on Educational Media and Materials for the Handicapped
PL 91–205	1970	Required buildings constructed with federal funds be accessible to the physically handicapped
PL 93–112	1973	Assured rights of the handicapped in employment and educational institutions; also known as Section 504
PL 93–380	1975	Forerunner to P.L. 94–142; assured due process, nondiscriminatory assessment, and protection of school records

The actions of parent advocacy groups was another force that led to the passage of P.L. 94–142. Parents of handicapped children, who began to lobby state and national legislators and file suit in the courts, began to realize that together they could be a much stronger force than as individuals. Parent groups expanded rapidly and became an important factor in the passage of P.L. 94–142.

The group of parents that has taken a leadership role in the struggle for the rights of the disabled is the National Association for Retarded Citizens (NARC). Beginning in 1950, NARC has worked hard to generate support for appropriate legislation for disabled people. Following the lead of NARC, other parent groups were formed, such as the Association for Children with Learning Disabilities (ACLD), which also has been extremely influential in gaining the passage of federal and state legislation.

Professional associations, like parent groups, also lobbied for strong state and federal legislation to support educational opportunities for disabled children. Probably the one organization that had the greatest impact was the Council for Exceptional Children (CEC), which expanded from 141 chapters in 1950 to 967 in 1980 (Lord 1981). This advocacy group, made up primarily of professionals serving handicapped children in public school programs, played a key role in the development and ultimate passage of P.L. 94–142.

The passage of P.L. 94–142 also was helped along by litigation. Parents of handicapped children began filing suit in the early 1970s to force public schools to provide their children with appropriate educational programs. Courts often ruled in favor of the parents. Litigation victories made legislators aware that the courts likely would mandate certain services unless they were required by legislation.

Purposes of P.L. 94–142. The basic purpose of P.L. 94–142 is to ensure that every handicapped child receives a *free appropriate public education in the least restrictive environment.* The act contains provisions to

1. assure that all handicapped children have available to them a free appropriate public education;
2. assure that the rights of handicapped children and their parents are protected;
3. assist states and localities to provide for the education of handicapped children;
4. address and assure the effectiveness of efforts to educate such children. (A Free/Appropriate Public Education 1977, p. 20)

P.L. 94–142 was no doubt the most comprehensive legislation ever passed by Congress related to special education. It is very broad and complex, and it addresses many different areas.

Key Component of P.L. 94–142. The component of P.L. 94–142 that has most affected the way handicapped children are educated is the requirement that handicapped children be educated in the least restrictive environment. This mandates that handicapped children be educated with their nonhandicapped peers as much of the time as is possible. Although P.L. 94–142 did not include the term *mainstreaming*, most people have interpreted the least-restrictive-environment concept to mean mainstreaming (Biklen 1985).

The writers of P.L. 94–142 envisioned that schools would match children's placements with their individual needs. A continuum of services should be made available, and children should be placed in the appropriate setting along the continuum that corresponds with their needs. The goal always is to move the child toward the least restrictive setting, toward full-time regular classroom placement.

To determine the least restrictive setting for a child, an individual evaluation must be conducted by a trained, qualified individual. Following the evaluation, a committee of professionals, along with the parents of the child, analyze the evaluation results and determine programming needs and the placement that will best meet the child's unique educational needs.

Another component of P.L. 94–142 that has had a significant impact on schools and teachers is the requirement that every handicapped child have an *individual educational program (IEP)*. The legislation makes Individualized Educational Programs a reality for handicapped children by requiring that a written IEP be developed and implemented for every handicapped child served. The phrase Individual Educational Program should and does convey some important concepts: (1) the IEP is designed for a single child, not similar children in a group; (2) the IEP should only include elements related to the child's educational program; (3) the IEP is not a plan, but a specific program (Weintraub 1977). Educators should integrate the IEP into actual instruction (Sugai 1985).

At a minimum, IEPs must include a statement concerning the current functioning level of the child, annual goals and short-range objectives, services that will be provided, dates for the services, and an evaluation plan. Although the act makes these specific requirements for IEPs, the implementation of the IEP requirement has been somewhat less than intended by Congress. Scanlon, Arick, and Phelps (1981) conducted a study to determine who participates in the development of IEPs. Results revealed that, except for parents and special education teachers, attendance by administrators and other support staff was very low. P.L. 94–142 calls for involvement from all individuals who are involved in the child's program and, when appropriate, even the child (Gearheart, Weishahn and Gearheart, 1988).

By law, parents should be extensively involved in developing the IEP. Unfortunately, many parents feel intimidated by professionals and are rarely full participants in the IEP development. To rectify this situation, several strategies should be implemented by the school, such as the appointment of a school employee to act as the advocate for the parent at the IEP meeting. This method of parental support has been found to be very effective (Goldstein and Turnbull 1982). Parental input is so important that teachers should make every effort to ensure that the collaboration with parents is mutually beneficial (Price and Marsh 1985; Elksnin and Elksnin, 1989).

P.L. 94–142 also defined the handicapped population. Regulations implementing the act state that handicapped children are those evaluated as being "mentally retarded, hard of hearing, deaf, speech impaired, visually handicapped, seriously emotionally disturbed, orthopedically impaired, other health impaired, deaf-blind, multihandicapped, or as having specific learning disabilities, who because of these impairments need special education and related services" (Federal Register, Vol. 42, No. 163, August 23, 1977, Sec. 121a5). The definition excludes gifted and talented children and, therefore, does not extend the rights granted by P.L. 94–142 to this group of children.

Still another component of P.L. 94–142 is its requirement for *nondiscriminatory assessment*. Individuals who test children using normreferenced, standardized test instruments are aware that these tests often may be discriminatory toward some cultural and/or socioeconomic groups. For example, non-Anglo children and children from poor families cannot be expected to do as well on some tests as children who belong to the majority culture, or middle- or upper-class children. In an effort to avoid misclassification and labeling, P.L. 94–142 requires that children be assessed nondiscriminatorily. The act provides guidelines to prevent discriminatory assessment (see table 9.3).

TABLE 9.3
Nondiscriminatory Assessment Procedures

- Tests and other evaluation materials must be administered in the child's native language or other mode of communication, be administered by trained personnel, and be validated for the purpose for which they are used.

- Tests and evaluation materials should include areas of academic need, not solely provide a single intelligence quotient (IQ).

- Tests administered to children with various sensory, manual, or speaking skills reflect the child's aptitude, not the child's deficits in sensory, motor, or speaking skills.

- No single procedure is to be used as the sole criterion for determining an appropriate program.

- A multidisciplinary team should be involved in the assessment.

- The child should be assessed in all areas of suspected disability.

Source: Federal Register, Vol. 42, No. 163, Tuesday, August 23, 1977.

INTRODUCTION TO EDUCATION

Assuring *due process* rights for parents and children is another major feature of P.L. 94–142. The right to due process, a procedure meant to ensure fair treatment, is a requirement of the Fifth and Fourteenth Amendments to the United States Constitution. "Without a means of challenging the multitude of discriminatory practices that the schools had habitually followed, the children would have found that their right to be included in an educational program and to be treated nondiscriminatorily (to receive a free appropriate education) would have a hollow ring" (Turnbull and Turnbull 1978, p. 1).

Due-process requirements guaranteed by P.L. 94–142 include the right to examine school records, the right to obtain an independent evaluation, the right to receive prior notice before a change of program, and the right to disagree with and appeal a decision made by the school concerning special education services. This right to appeal provides parents an option to request a due-process hearing, conducted by an impartial hearing officer, in which both parties to the disagreement present their side of the conflict (see table 9.4).

TABLE 9.4
Due-Process Requirements of Public Law 94–142

REQUIREMENT	EXPLANATION	REFERENCE
Opportunity to examine records	Parents have a right to inspect and review all educational records.	Sec. 121a.502
Independent evaluation	Parents have a right to obtain an independent evaluation of their child at their expense or the school's expense. The school pays only if it agrees to the evaluation or is required by a hearing officer.	Sec. 121a503
Prior notice; parental consent	Schools must provide written notice to parents before the school initiates or changes the identification, evaluation, or placement of a child. Consent must be obtained before conducting the evaluation and before initial placement.	Sec. 121a.504
Contents of notice	Parental notice must provide a description of the proposed actions in the written native language of the home. If the communication is not written, oral notification must be given. The notice must be understandable to the parents.	Sec. 121a.505
Impartial due process hearing	A parent or school may initiate a due-process hearing if there is a dispute over the identification, evaluation, or placement of the child.	Sec. 121a.506

Source: Final regulations, P.L. 94–142. Federal Register. Washington D.C.: U.S. Government Printing Office. 42(163).

Parents and schools have used the due-process hearing extensively since P.L. 94–142 was implemented. Smith (1981) conducted a national survey to determine the status of due-process hearings. Findings included:

- Thirty-eight states reported that more than 3,500 hearings had been held.
- Placement was the issue most often represented in hearings.
- Parents requested the majority of hearings.
- Rulings were in favor of the school the majority of the time.

P.L. 94–142 also requires that handicapped students receive *related services* when these services are required to enable a child to benefit from special education. Services include:

> transportation and such developmental, corrective, and other supportive services as are required to assist a handicapped child to benefit from special education, and includes speech pathology and audiology, psychological services, physical and occupational therapy, recreation, early identification and assessment of disabilities in children, counseling services, and medical services for diagnostic or evaluation purposes. The term also includes school health services, social work services in schools, and parent counseling and training. (Sec. 121a.13)

The bottom line in determining if a child is eligible to receive a related service is whether the service required is necessary in order for the child to benefit from special education. Unfortunately, this is not always clear. For example, when is a medical service diagnostic, and when is it treatment? As physicians become more involved with disabled children (Levine 1982), these questions are likely to surface regularly.

P.L. 98-199. Funds for planning statewide comprehensive services for children ages 0–5 were provided through this legislation passed in 1985.

P.L. 99-457. This law, which was the 1986 amendments to P.L. 94–142, will likely have as big an influence on services to children with disabilities as did P.L. 94–142. It mandates that schools serve all children with handicaps, ages 3–5 years, by the 1990–1991 school year. In effect, it lowers the age requirement for P.L. 94–142 and provides incentives for states to serve children in the birth through two-year range. Key components of the legislation include:

- lowers the age of mandatory services to include children ages 3–5 who have disabilities defined in P.L. 94–142;
- provides financial incentives for schools to provide services to infants and toddlers (ages 0–2) who are disabled or who are at risk for developing disabilities;

- requires service providers of infants and toddlers to develop and implement an Individualized Family Service Plan (IFSP);
- requires the IFSP to include goals and objectives for the child and the family; and
- provides the same due-process protections for children and their families as required by P.L. 94–142.

The law is viewed as landmark legislation because it requires schools to provide appropriate intervention services to children heretofore considered too young to be served by public schools.

Litigation

A force equal to legislation in shaping special education services has been litigation (Prasse 1988). Parents of handicapped children realized in the early 1970s that one method to obtain services for their children was through the courts. Certainly, racial minority groups had established the precedent in the 1950s and 1960s for access to equal opportunities through litigation.

Litigation in Education. Prior to the 1950s, the courts did not play a major role in education. This changed, however, with the landmark decision by the United States Supreme Court in the *Brown v. Board of Education, Topeka, Kansas,* decision in 1954. During the past ten years, court cases involving most aspects of education have been heard at all levels of the court structure. "Topics of litigation have included students' rights to free expression, compulsory attendance and mandatory curriculum offerings, school finance reform, employment practices, student discipline, educational malpractice, sex discrimination, collective bargaining, employees' rights to privacy, desegregation, and the rights of handicapped and non-English-speaking students" (McCarthy and Cambron 1981, p. 13).

Litigation in Special Education. Since the mid-1970s, litigation in special education has been extensive. In a study of civil rights cases involving students, Marvel, Galfo, and Rockwell (1981) found that approximately 46 percent of the cases involved special education issues. As early as 1974, Laski (1974) noted that "Handicapped persons are in court. They are in courtrooms throughout the land asserting their rights under the U.S. Constitution, federal and state statutes, including their right to services from the public sector. In increasing numbers, they are finding the judicial branch of government an effective forum to secure rights long denied" (p. 15). It is highly likely that the trend of courts being more involved with special education issues will continue into the 1990s.

Literally hundreds of court cases have dealt with special education. A few are recognized as landmark decisions that have had a significant impact on schools and handicapped students.

Pennsylvania Association for Retarded Citizens (PARC) v. Pennsylvania. Known as the PARC case, this suit is considered the landmark right-to-education case in special education. The suit was filed in 1971 by the Pennsylvania Association for Retarded Citizens (PARC) and thirteen mentally retarded children on behalf of all mentally retarded children being denied an education in public schools. The action challenged Pennsylvania laws that denied educational programs to mentally retarded children because they were considered "uneducable." Expert testimony presented was so convincing that both parties entered into a consent decree, with the state of Pennsylvania acknowledging its responsibility to provide appropriate public education to all children (Laski 1974).

Mills v. Board of Education of the District of Columbia. As in the PARC case, this case was brought by parents who were attempting to gain educational services from public schools for their handicapped children. The court's ruling extended the rights to education beyond the mentally retarded category to all handicapped children and specifically indicated that the poor could not be subject to discrimination.

Diana v. State Board of Education. This case dealt with the right to fair classification and placement. Parents of Spanish-speaking children filed suit to challenge the classification of their children as mentally retarded. This court's ruling was that minority children, specifically Mexican-American and Chinese, were to be tested in their native languages and that all children in California should be reassessed to determine if appropriate placements had been made due to discriminatory assessment practices.

Armstrong v. Kline. A landmark decision related to extended-year programming resulted from this case. The parents of three severely handicapped students filed suit in 1978 challenging Pennsylvania's law prohibiting funds for educational programs for handicapped children beyond 180 days per year. The parents claimed that this law was contradictory to P.L. 94–142, which indicated that a handicapped child's IEP should determine the program, not a state law refusing certain services (Stotland and Mancuso 1981). In June 1979 the court ruled in favor of the parents, stating that some handicapped children may legitimately require extended-year programming. The court was quick to point out that this in no way mandated summer programming for all handicapped children, but only for those who truly needed continuous services during the summer months.

Board of Education of the Hendrick Hudson Central School District Board of Education v. Rowley. This case, known simply as the Rowley case, was the first case that dealt with P.L. 94–142 that was ruled on by the United States Supreme Court. In this case, the parents of a deaf child wanted the local school district to provide the services of a sign-language interpreter in all of the child's academic classes. The school refused, and its decision was upheld by the New York State Commissioner of Education. At this point the Rowleys filed suit in federal court. The federal district court, and the appeals court, ruled in favor of the Rowleys, stating that the denial of a sign-language interpreter in effect denied the child the right to a free, appropriate education.

The United States Supreme Court, to the surprise of many special education advocates, reversed the lower courts' decisions. In doing so, the Court ruled that the intent of Congress in P.L. 94–142 was to guarantee access to public education, not equality of educational opportunity (Heaney 1984).

Department of Education v. Katherine D. This case from the state of Hawaii focused on the issue of least restrictive environment and homebound placement. The court ruled that services being provided in a homebound setting for a child with multiple health impairments did not meet the least restrictive setting requirement of Public Law 94–142. The school was ordered to move the child into an integrated school setting with medical support services.

Irving Independent School District v. Tatro. This was the second case heard by the U.S. Supreme Court that dealt with Public Law 94–142. The court ruled in 1984 that catheterization was a legitimate related service for a child with physical disabilities.

Cleburne v. Cleburne Independent Living Center. In this Texas case, the U.S. Supreme Court ruled in 1985 that cities cannot use various zoning laws to prevent the establishment of a group home for persons with mental retardation. The case is considered landmark in establishing rights for group homes in residential areas.

MULTICULTURAL SPECIAL EDUCATION

Multicultural considerations must be made in special education. Many children identified as disabled and referred for special education are from minority cultural groups. Black children and Mexican-American children form the majority of this group. In addition, many children served in special education programs are from poor homes, which also causes multicultural considerations. Migrant children are another group that represent a high risk in developing problems and therefore require multicultural considerations (Baca and Harris 1988).

Multicultural Concerns

Several concerns related to racial and cultural minority children in special education have been noted, including

1. overrepresentation of minority children in special classes, especially classes for children with mental retardation (Reschly 1988);
2. discriminatory assessment procedures (Clark-Johnson 1988);
3. stigmatizing labels (Smith, Price, and Marsh 1986);
4. negative teacher attitudes toward the potential of minority children (Jones and Wilderson 1976).

Studies have substantiated that more children from racial and cultural minorities are in special education classrooms than would be expected based on prevalence estimates. This is particularly true in classes for the mentally retarded (Reschly 1988). The primary reason for the overrepresentation probably is discriminatory assessment procedures.

Professionals recognize that many of the norm-referenced tests used to determine eligibility for special education are biased against certain minority groups. Test designers are working to develop tests that are culturally fair. Unfair testing may bring out overidentification of minority children for special education, placement of children in slow tracks, and may impede minority children from entering postsecondary educational programs (Clark-Johnson 1988).

Responding to the Multicultural Problem

Public Law 94–142 attempted to address some of the problems and concerns of multicultural special education. One of its strong requirements is that schools must use nondiscriminatory assessment practices in determining eligibility for special education. One method of eliminating some of the bias found in assessment instruments is to test the child in the native language of the home. This at least gives the child the opportunity to listen to questions and provide responses in his or her primary language. As long as some tests are used that are inherently discriminatory, totally nondiscriminatory assessment will not be possible. That attention has been focused on discriminatory assessment procedures has greatly facilitated the efforts to correct the situation.

Total parental involvement in the decision process, parental permissions, notifications, and the right to due-process hearings should help in limiting problems associated with multicultural special education. Requiring that all handicapped children served in special education have an Individualized Education Program (IEP) also should reduce some of the concerns related to multicultural special education. No longer should students be placed in particular classes or tracks because of minority status. Every child should be evaluated, and, based on an individual's strengths and weaknesses, programs should be developed to provide appropriate educational programming (Baca and Harris 1988).

HANDICAPPED CHILDREN

Special education is for handicapped children, or children with disabilities. To determine if a child is eligible for special education services, the child must exhibit one of several different handicapping conditions. The final regulations implementing P.L. 94–142 list eight handicapping categories, including mental retardation, learning disabilities, serious emotional disturbance, orthopedic handicaps, visual impairment, hearing impairment, speech impairment, and other health impairment (Federal Register, Vol. 42, No. 163, August 23, 1977). Each category is designed to group children with similar disabilities and needs.

Traditional Classification System

Classifying children into specific disabling categories, such as those noted in P.L. 94–142, has been the traditional method of classifying

■ *The noncategorical classification system focuses on learning needs, not clinical labels of children.*

handicapped children. The major reason for this tradition has been that various groups of disabled children have come to the attention of educators at different times. For example, learning disabilities is a relatively new category, having only been recognized during the past ten to fifteen years. Since many state statutes, as well as P.L. 94–142, recognize special education eligibility by children fitting into one of several categories of disabilities, all educators should be aware of the different categorical groups.

Mental Retardation. Children classified as mentally retarded have been served in special education classes in some public schools for many years. The generally accepted definition of mental retardation was published by the American Association on Mental Retardation (AAMR).

> Mental retardation refers to significantly subaverage general intellectual functioning existing concurrently with deficits in adaptive behavior, and manifested during the developmental period. (Grossman 1983, p. 1)

The definition is not very understandable unless various conditions are explained. In general terms the AAMR says that individuals can be classified as mentally retarded if they have an intelligence test score of seventy or below, have deficits in the ability to adapt, and have had the condition since before the age of eighteen (Grossman 1983).

Within the category of mental retardation there have been numerous subcategories; the model that is used most often was published by the AAMR. It contains four different groups: mild, moderate, severe, and profound (see table 9.5). More than 650,000 students with mental retardation received special education services in 1986–1987 (U.S. Dept. of Education 1988)

Learning Disabilities. The newest category used to classify handicapped children is learning disabilities. Until 1960 there were no classes for children with learning disabilities in public schools; however, since the 1970s this category has grown into one of the largest being served (Kirk and Gallagher, 1989). The report to Congress submitted by the Department of Education in 1988 indicated that learning disabilities is the largest single category of handicapped children currently served in public school programs. In the 1986–1987 school year, 1.9 million students were served in this category (U.S. Department of Education 1988).

One of the problems of the learning disabilities category is a lack of agreement on a definition. The definition issued by the federal government in 1977 has been adopted by most states for use in determining eligibilty for speical education.

> Specific learning disability means a disorder in one or more of the basic psychological processes involved in understanding or in using language, spoken or written, which may manifest itself in an imperfect

TABLE 9.5
Characteristics of Categories of Mental Retardation

CATEGORY	CHARACTERISTICS
Mild	▪ IQ 55–70 ▪ Possible academic achievement to third-grade level ▪ Capable of living independently as adults ▪ Potential for employment good
Moderate	▪ IQ 35–55 ▪ Possible academic achievement to first-grade level ▪ Capable of employment in sheltered workshop ▪ Capable of sheltered living
Severe	▪ IQ 20–35 ▪ Communication difficulties ▪ Possible physical disabilities ▪ Need supervised living ▪ Possible ability to work in sheltered environment
Profound	▪ IQ 0–20 ▪ Communication difficulties ▪ Possible physical disabilities ▪ Need supervised living

ability to listen, think, speak, read, write, spell, or to do mathematical calculations. The term includes such conditions as perceptual handicaps, brain injury, minimal brain dysfunction, dyslexia, and developmental aphasia. The term does not include children who have learning problems which are primarily the result of visual, hearing, or motor handicaps, or mental retardation, or of environmental, cultural, or economic disadvantage. (Federal Register 1977, p. 42478)

Basically, a learning disabled person is one who has average or above-average intelligence, but who has trouble in academic areas that cannot be explained. With such a nebulous definition, the category has been abused, with many more children being classified as learning disabled than should be.

Characteristics associated with learning disabilities include

▪ average or above average intelligence

▪ academic deficit area(s)

▪ hyperactivity

▪ perceptual-motor problems

▪ impulsivity

▪ emotional swings

▪ attention disorders

▪ disorders of speech and hearing

Learning disabilities is a little understood category (Coplin and Morgan 1988). School districts vary considerably in their interpretation of eligibility requirements for the learning disability category. Children classified as learning disabled in one school district might be deemed nonhandicapped in a neighboring district. Suffice it to say that the learning disability category is one that creates a great deal of disagreement among professionals and parents (Rivers and Smith 1988).

Emotional Disturbance/Behavior Disorders. This category is plagued, as are several others, by problems with definitions and characteristics. The term *emotional disturbance* had many forerunners, including lunacy, psychosis, neurosis, and schizophrenia, to name a few. The social stigma associated with a condition of mental aberration is "craziness," and historically "crazy" people have had a difficult time receiving appropriate services. P.L. 94–142 uses the term *Seriously Emotionally Disturbed* (SED) to describe these children and defines the category as follows:

> The term means a condition exhibiting one or more of the following characteristics over a long period of time and to a marked degree, which adversely affects educational performance:
>
> (A) An inability to learn which cannot be explained by intellectual, sensory, or health factors;
> (B) An inability to build or maintain satisfactory interpersonal relationships with peers and teachers;
> (C) Inappropriate types of behavior or feelings under normal circumstances;
> (D) A general pervasive mood of unhappiness or depression; or
> (E) A tendency to develop physical symptoms or fears associated with personal or school problems.
>
> The term includes children who are medically diagnosed as schizophrenic or autistic. The term does not include children who are socially maladjusted, unless it is determined that they are seriously emotionally disturbed. (Federal Register, Vol. 42, No. 163, August 23, 1977, p. 42478)

Slightly different from emotional disturbance is the category of *behavior disorders.* P.L. 94–142 does not include such a handicapping category, but some states use this nomenclature rather than SED, or in addition to SED. Succinctly defined, a behavior disorder is a deviation from age-appropriate behavior which significantly interferes with the child's growth and development and/or the lives of others (Kirk 1972). The behavior disorder category, therefore, is less severe than the emotionaly disturbed or SED category called for in P.L. 94–142.

As with other disabilities, there are many different methods of subclassifying emotionally disturbed children. Quay (1975) divided emotional disturbance into conduct, personality, and immaturity problems. Conduct disorders included striking other children and being disobedient, personality problems included withdrawing and being shy, and immaturity problems included passivity, short attention spans, and clumsiness.

Hearing Impairment. Hearing impairment is a familiar disability to most people. Most individuals know of someone, perhaps an older person, who has difficulty hearing. It is a disability that is common in older individuals, but also occurs in school-age children. Individuals are classified as hearing impaired if they have a decibel (dB) loss as measured by an audiometer. There are two categories of hearing impairment: hard of hearing and deaf. Persons with dB losses of twenty-five to ninety are considered hard of hearing, while individuals with a loss of ninety or greater are classified as deaf.

Educators have adopted more functional definitions that allow them to discern certain hearing abilities from the label. Most schools have accepted the definition of hearing impairment for educational purposes reported by Moores (1978) that was adopted by the Conference of Executives of American Schools for the Deaf. According to the definition a deaf person is one whose hearing is disabled to an extent that precludes the understanding of speech through the ear alone, with or without assistance of an amplification device. A hard-of-hearing person is one whose hearing is disabled to such an extent that speech is difficult to understand through the ear alone, with or without a hearing aid. Most children classified as hearing impaired do have some residual hearing (Heward and Orlansky 1988).

Visual Impairment. Like hearing impairment, visual impairment is a disability that is frequently found in the population. Many persons wear glasses; without them they might have a severe visual problem. Older individuals frequently find themselves losing their vision. However, the category of visual impairment used in special education is for school-age children whose disability cannot be corrected with glasses.

There are two major groups of visually impaired individuals: blind and partially sighted. Individuals are classified as legally blind if they have a visual acuity of 20/200 or less in the better eye with best correction, or if they have a field restriction of 20 degrees or less. Partially sighted persons are those with a visual acuity of 20/70 to 20/200 in the better eye with best correction. These definitions, considered legal or medical definitions, may be useless to educators.

School personnel have adopted more functional definitions for use with children who experience visual problems. Children are classified as educationally blind when they cannot read print and are classified as partially sighted, or low vision, if they have visual problems but are able to read print. These more functional definitions alert educators to the functional ability of students regarding their abilities to see letters.

Physically Handicapped. This group of children is extremely heterogeneous. Because of the wide variety of disabilities included in the category it is virtually impossible to define. For example, children who would be labeled physically handicapped could include those with spina bifida, cerebral palsy, amputations, muscular dystrophy, or general paralysis. P.L. 94–142 uses the category *orthopedically impaired* and defines it as a severe orthopedic impairment which adversely affects a child's educational performance. The term includes impairments caused by congenital anomaly (e.g., clubfoot, absence of some member, etc), impairments caused by disease (e.g., poliomyelitis, bone tuberculosis, etc.), and impairments from other causes (e.g., cerebral palsy, amputations, and fractures or burns which cause contractures). (Federal Register, Vol. 42, No. 163, August 23, 1977, p. 42478)

Other Health Impaired. Another category that consists of many different disabilities is *other health impaired*. The federal definition states that children are placed in this category if they have limited attention, vitality, or stamina that results from one of several conditions, including diabetes, asthma, epilepsy, lead poisoning, or a heart condition (Federal Register, Vol. 42, No. 163, August 23, 1977).

Speech and Language Disorders. A succinct definition of all communication disorders that has been widely accepted is that a person has a communication disorder if his or her speech differs from the speech of others to the extent that it calls attention to itself, interferes with the message that is intended, or causes distress to the speaker or listener (Van Riper 1978). There are three general categories of communication disorders: nonverbal, language disordered, and speech impaired. Nonverbal children are those who, for a variety of reasons, do not have speech and language ability. This may be due to brain damage, emotional problems, or as a result of severe mental retardation. Many children are erroneously regarded as nonverbal who have receptive and inner language ability but who are unable to use expressive language. They are certainly not nonverbal. Another relatively small group of children has problems of dysfluency, usually characterized as stuttering, or voice disorders. The majority of children with speech disorders have articulation problems such as omissions, substitutions, or distortions of sounds. Most such conditions occur during the elementary school years and yield rapidly to remediation. Ordinarily the regular classroom teacher will have little difficulty managing and supporting such children.

Generic/Noncategorical Model

Although the different disability categories are still used in many states and school districts, there is a trend to implement a new classification model. Some professionals in special education believe that categorical labels have little practical usefulness (Smith and Neisworth 1975; Lilly 1979; Hallahann and Kauffman 1978; Marsh, Price, and Smith 1983; Smith, Price, and Marsh 1986). Specific criticisms of the categorical model include:

1. The categories are educationally irrelevant.
2. Categorical groupings overlap.

3. Categories label children as "defective," implying that the cause of the educational or developmental deficiency lies only within the child.

4. Special educational instructional materials and strategies are not category-specific.

5. Preparation of teachers along traditional categorical lines results in redundancy of coursework and barriers within the profession.

6. Patterns of funding for special education have perpetuated the categorical approach. (Smith and Neisworth 1975, pp. 8–9)

One primary reason to move toward the noncategorical or generic model to serve handicapped children is that categorical descriptions of mildly handicapped children are meaningless in a system that is gravitating rapidly toward the inclusion of additional groups of handicapped persons and the inclusion of new services for handicapped persons. The "mild" conditions that emerged in the field during the past several years—namely the mildly or educable mentally retarded, the learning disabled, and the mildly emotionally disturbed/behaviorally disordered—compose the largest number of children who are regarded as handicapped (Smith, Price, and Marsh 1986). These categories overlap in all dimensions—psychologically, educationally, and behaviorally (Katims 1988). Lilly (1979) totally abandons the categories and refers simply to exceptional children as those who require special services of a substantive nature and degree to assume optimum learning and educational development.

This rationale is opposed by traditional special educators who prefer the strict categorical approach to special education. However valid some of the arguments presented by this group, the trend clearly is toward the noncategorical approach. One major reason for this trend is the current emphasis on delivering services to handicapped children in public schools using the resource room model. Handicapped children are less likely to be segregated into separate classrooms and are more likely to be mainstreamed into regular classrooms at least a portion of each school day.

Mildly handicapped is therefore a new category for handicapped children. Children no longer will be considered seriously handicapped simply because of a categorical label. As a result of the noncategorical model, labels will be more functional and less stigmatizing. Only a relative minority of handicapped children will be considered severely handicapped: those mentally retarded at the low end of the intellectual continuum and those severely emotionally disturbed children who may be dangerous to themselves or others. Others, including the physically handicapped, health impaired, and vision and hearing impaired, will be considered mildly handicapped and will attend regular classrooms in increasing numbers.

The following summary points stress the important issues related to the mildly handicapped category:

1. The similarities among handicapped students of various categories are greater than their differences. Characteristics associated with one condition or another overlap significantly, and materials useful for one diagnostic category are also appropriate for another. In the same vein the differences among children labeled within one category are greater than their similarities. Characteristics are significant only as they are applied to a particular student.

2. Teaching should be based on what the student can and cannot do, on what the curricular sequence should be in response to specific, individual objectives, and on what the teacher should or should not do to improve change and learning in the student.

3. Instructional methods and materials should be selected to meet the needs and characteristics of an individual learner rather than chosen from those that seem to be appropriate for a label or certain type of group assignment deemed appropriate for children who share certain theoretical characteristics. (Marsh, Price, and Smith 1983, p. 9)

The trend is away from categorical labels to noncategorical/generic classification. The following definition of the mildly handicapped was developed by Smith, Price, and Marsh (1986):

> The term mildly handicapped refers to the large group of students who differ from nonhandicapped students in cognitive-academic, sensori-physical, and socioemotional characteristics to such an extent that special education and related services are required, but not to the degree that segregated special class placement is essential. These are children who violate the norms of the school in some way: deviation from norms of behavior, academic expectations, acquisition of standard English in spoken and written forms, motivation and aspirations for achievement, or exceeding the school's traditional resources to provide instruction.

SPECIAL EDUCATION SERVICES

The philosophical underpinnings of serving handicapped children is *normalization*. "Normalization is the creation of as normal as possible a learning and social environment for the exceptional child and adult" (Kirk and Gallagher 1989, p. 41). As a result of litigation, legislation, and advocacy, handicapped children are being provided free, appropriate education in the mainstream. While the normalization movement started in the Scandinavian countries (Nirje 1969), the changes that have occurred most specifically in America and Canada are unique within the cultural contexts of each country.

One result of normalization has been mainstreaming. P.L. 94–142 requires that handicapped children be educated in the least restrictive setting. This requires that each handicapped child be evaluated and a decision made concerning the child's least restrictive setting. Some mildly handicapped children may be able to benefit from regular classroom placement several hours daily, while others may not be able to benefit from any regular classroom placement. The mainstreaming movement differs significantly from the more traditional service delivery system that was used extensively in special education prior to the passage of P.L. 94–142.

Traditional Service Delivery Model

Following the pressure exerted by parents in the early 1950s, some schools began providing educational services to some handicapped children. The services were provided using categorical groupings and physical segregation.

Categorical Grouping. The delivery of special education services has been, until the late 1970s, exclusively along categorical lines—that is, by category of handicapping condition. Mentally retarded children, learning disabled children, emotionally disturbed/behaviorally disordered children, and physically handicapped children were grouped by label for special education. The training of teachers, certification standards for teachers, and funding patterns to support special education were all based on categories. Professionals have been concerned that categorical labels applied to children are damaging in many ways, including self-esteem and expectations of teachers and peers.

Self-contained Classes. For most of the history of special education, children were classified by category and segregated from their nonhandicapped peers in self-contained special education classrooms. Students remained in the same classroom with the same teacher for the entire school day. This model has become a major point of contention in special education. Johnson (1983) noted that self-contained services were attacked as a result of the civil rights movement and high national productivity and affluence. The efficacy of such placement has been seriously questioned as well as the discriminatory nature of such programming for any class of student, no matter how defined (Algozzine, Morsink, and Algozzine, 1988).

Special Schools. Another model used extensively in the past was to use public funds to operate a segregated facility for all handicapped children in a school district. In essence, this is not different from the self-contained classroom except that it is a much more blatant form of segregation. While special schools for handicapped children still exist, the number of children served in such settings has been greatly reduced.

Institutional Settings. Still another service option using the categorical approach is institutional, which was an early method of intervention for all handicapped individuals. The current trend is toward *deinstitutionalization*, moving individuals from institutions into community programs. This is a major component of the normalization philosophy and has greatly reduced the institutional population in the United States (Scheerenberger 1976).

Current Service Delivery Model

The traditional model of providing educational services to handicapped children has changed during the past several years. Now, rather than providing most special education in self-contained programs, the majority of schools educate handicapped children using the resource room model (Friend and McNutt 1984). Several factors led to the adoption of the resource room model.

■

SHORTAGE OF QUALIFIED SPECIAL EDUCATION PERSONNEL DECLARED NATIONAL EMERGENCY

The shortage of qualified professionals in special education and related services has reached a crisis of such proportions that it has been declared a national emergency by six organizations. They warn that future personnel shortages, will seriously jeopardize the provision of special education and related services guaranteed by federal law.

The warning was delivered in a joint statement entitled "A Free Appropriate Education: But Who Will Provide It?" by the American Speech-Language-Hearing Association, the Council of Administrators of Special Education, the Council for Exceptional Children, the Council of Graduate Programs in Communication Sciences and Disorders, the Higher Education Consortium for Special Education, the National Association of State Directors of Special Education, and the Teacher Education Division.

Testifying on behalf of the organizations before the Senate Subcommittee on the Handicapped, and the House Subcommittee on Select Education, Dr. William

Carriker, Professor of Special Education at the University of Virginia, noted, "According to figures released by the U.S. Department of Education, the number of special education teachers that are needed has been steadily increasing over the last decade with the shortage growing by more than 10,000 between 1984 and 1986."

Highlights of the report include:

■ As serious as the shortfall identified by the U.S. Department of Education is, it may underrepresent the magnitude of the problem. For example, several states failed to report any personnel needs and reports for several others represent figures substantially inconsistent with other states. Furthermore, it may inadequately represent the number of persons practicing in special education who do not meet state standards, a figure reported to be 30 percent nationally.

■ Projected increases in the school age population suggest that there will be an increase in the number of students requiring

continued

the assistance of special education professionals, while at the same time a significant cohort of the special education professionals will be retiring. A major aging out of persons in leadership positions, including university faculty, administrators, and supervisors, will take place within 10 years to be followed by a similar exodus of direct service personnel over the next 20 years. The problem is further exacerbated by the large numbers of special education professionals who, annually, leave the profession for reasons other than retirement.

■ There has been a continuing decline over the past decade in special educators graduating from personnel preparation programs. The National Center for Education Statistics reports a 35% decline of such graduates within the decade. Data indicate that while there are serious problems in the number of persons being prepared for careers in education overall, the shortfall in special education is of substantially greater magnitude than in any other area other than bilingual education.

■ If the shortage of qualified personnel is not reversed, the county could experience a major deterioration of the availability and quality of special education which will result in increases in the number of persons with handicaps lacking the knowledge and skills necessary to function independently, escalating costs to society for services to care for individuals with disabilities, and growing legal problems as school districts try to meet mandated requirements for special education.

The statement calls for a collabortive effort on the part of professional associations, state and local educational agencies, colleges and universities, the federal government, and the private sector to solve the problem.

The following are some of the recommendations proposed:

■ There needs to be both an increase and improvement in the financial support available to students pursuing careers in special education both at the entry and leadership levels.

■ A major coordinated campaign needs to be initiated to recruit persons for careers in special education, with particular attention given to ethnic populations and persons with disabilities.

■ Better data needs to be collected, analyzed, and disseminated regarding the special education and related services work force.

■ All levels of government must exert greater responsibility to assure that persons employed to provide special education are qualified by virtue of their preparation.

■ Attention must be given to assure that institutions of higher education have the capacity to prepare the qualified personnel needed.

■ There is a need for an expanded effort to prepare special education leadership personnel, including persons from ethnic populations and with disabilities.

■ Greater attention needs to be given to examining the reasons for the high attrition rate of special education personnel and strategies developed and implemented to increase the retention rate.

Source: *News and Notes*, May 1989. American Association on Mental Retardation.

Efficacy Studies. Probably the single, most important development that encouraged the adoption of the resource room model was a group of studies published that questioned the efficacy of self-contained special education programs. In the professional literature, the research became known as *efficacy studies*, or a comparison of the performance of educable mentally retarded children in self-contained and regular classrooms (Yoshida 1984).

The most famous and perhaps influential attack on traditional, segregated special education services came from Dunn (1968), who criticized the practice of special education for mentally retarded children and called for a reexamination of the procedures employed in schools to educate handicapped children. His article, "Special Education for the Mildly Retarded—Is Much of it Justifiable?" created the atmosphere for change. Later, Dunn (1973) outlined a series of negative conclusions about the effectiveness of traditional special education classes:

1. As a group, mildly retarded pupils make as much or more progress in regular classes as their counterparts in special classes.
2. Mentally retarded children do not work up to their mental age capacity whether they are in regular classrooms or special classes.
3. Special class children do not achieve academically above randomly selected regular-class-placed mentally retarded children.
4. Mentally retarded students with higher IQs develop a dislike for special class placement and an increase in their feelings of self-derogation about such placement.
5. Low IQ children who make the best progress in the regular grades are those who come from ethnic minorities and who are adjusted and accepted in their communities.

On the whole, Dunn was of the opinion that the effectiveness of special, segregated or self-contained classes could not be demonstrated. He recommended that such classes be eliminated. Other voices that joined Dunn included Blatt (1960), Johnson (1962), Fisher (1967), Johnson (1969), Christopolos and Renz (1969), Jansen, Ahm, Jensen, and Leerskov (1970). Still other professionals stood firm and defended special class placement for many mentally retarded children. Kolstoe (1976), one of the leading defenders of self-contained placement, has continued to argue in support of special classes.

Johnson (1983) suggested that all programs that segregate handicapped children are now considered bad, regardless of their true quality. Regardless of the concern about the dismantling of a large portion of self-contained classrooms, the tide turned. Normalization and mainstreaming have spread effectively throughout the school systems and are undeniably civil rights trends. Whether the efficacy studies were good research is of little consequence now, because they played an important part in the professional deliberations that helped to usher in the mainstreaming movement and to alter conceptualizations of handicapping conditions that are now referred to as mild conditions. P.L. 94–142 mandated that handicapped children be served in the least restrictive setting. For many children now considered mildly handicapped, this means regular classroom placement for a large portion of the school day.

Continuum of Services Model. P.L. 94–142 calls for a continuum of educational services because it requires schools to provide appropriate educational services on an individual basis. As a result, schools must be prepared to provide educational services in a variety of settings, with the placement decision of each child depending on unique characteristics, strengths, and weaknesses.

The model that closely parallels the requirements of P.L. 94–142 is Deno's (1970) Cascade of Services. This model has been incorporated into federal and state guidelines and laws, and forms the basis for implementing the least restrictive environment requirement (Peterson, Zabel, Smith, and White 1983). The Cascade of Services model

- aids conceptualization of a continuum of services (Podemski, Price, Smith, and Marsh 1984);
- presents a base of service options for exceptional students (Merulla and McKinnon 1982);
- focuses on aspects of placement other than physical and mechanical (Reid and Hresko 1981);
- emphasizes appropriate assignment of special education students in order that they advance toward eventual regular class placement (Cegelka and Prehm 1982).

The model consists of seven levels, ranging from full-time placement in a regular classroom to full-time placement in an institution (see table 9.7). Table 9.6 provides the most recent enrollment figures of students with disabilities in each placement option.

Level I, Full-time Regular Classroom. Level I represents the least restrictive setting possible. For some mildly handicapped children, accommodations made by regular classroom teachers are sufficient to circumvent manifested disabilities. These accommodations could consist of changing seating arrangements, reading tests orally, and giving extra time for assignments to name a few.

Level II, Full-time Regular Classroom with Assistance. Level II enables children to be placed full-time in regular classrooms, and at the same time receive special, supportive services. One of the strategies subsumed under this arrangement is the itinerant teacher model similar to the model that schools have used for several years to provide speech therapy services to students. Another type of special service using this model includes mobility training for visually impaired students. The itinerant teacher, who would go into regular classrooms to provide support for disabled students, is the primary support person when using this model.

Gearheart, Weishahn, and Gearheart (1988) state that the itinerant model is not as practical as the resource room model for some types of disabled children, because it does not provide daily services. For other children who do not require daily intervention, however, the itinerant model works well.

TABLE 9.6
Number and Percent of all Handicapped Children and Youth Served in Nine Educational Environments by Age Group During School Year 1985-86

ENVIRONMENT	3-5 YEARS		6-11 YEARS		12-17 YEARS		18-21 YEARS	
	Number	Percent	Number	Percent	Number	Percent	Number	Percent
Regular Class	109,431	36.89	726,586	35.88	277,424	15.60	21,908	9.66
Resource Room	58,718	19.79	807,144	39.86	849,989	47.81	75,429	33.25
Separate Class	78,487	26.46	408,345	20.16	500,315	28.14	72,601	32.01
Public Separate School Facility	22,797	7.68	40,955	2.02	71,870	4.04	28,451	12.54
Private Separate School Facility	18,577	6.26	22,199	1.10	23,784	1.34	6,507	2.87
Public Residential Facility	3,659	1.23	9,532	0.47	18,018	1.01	10,673	4.71
Private Residential Facility	330	0.11	3,420	0.17	9,567	0.54	2,487	1.10
Correction Facility	38	0.01	197	0.01	7,948	0.45	5,073	2.24
Homebound/ Hospital	4,614	1.56	6,813	0.34	18,952	1.07	3,709	1.64

Data as of October 1, 1987.

Source: U.S. Department of Education. 1988. *Tenth Annual Report to Congress on the Implementation of Public Law 94-142.*

TABLE 9.7
Cascade of Services

Level I	Regular classroom with or without supportive services
Level II	Regular classroom plus supportive services
Level III	Part-time special class (Resource room)
Level IV	Full-time special class (Self-contained room)
Level V	Special stations (Segregated schools)
Level VI	Homebound
Level VII	Hospital or residential setting

Source: Adapted from E. Deno, Special education is developmental capital, *Exceptional Children* 37, 1970.

Level III, Part-time Special Class. Level III is the most popular service model used today (Smith, Price, and Marsh 1986). During the 1985–1986 school year, nearly 40 percent of children with disabilities, ages 6–11, were served in resource rooms. For children ages 12–17, 47.8 percent received services in a resource room (U.S. Department of Education 1988). The resource room is the special education setting where level III is implemented. Students are placed in regular classrooms and attend the resource room part of the day to receive intensive assistance in problem areas from special education teachers. The resource room model is a bridge between total special education placement and total regular classroom placement. Two needs led to the development of the resource room model: (1) provide more direct services to more handicapped children, and (2) provide regular classroom teachers with support services (Mandell and Gold 1984).

Resource rooms can be of several types, as indicated by Wiederholt, Hammill, and Brown (1978) (see table 9.8). Although there are differences, there are also many commonalities among resource rooms:

1. The student divides the day between the resource room and the regular classroom.

2. Resource room scheduling is usually done, so that only small groups of students are in the resource room at any one time.

3. Instruction is almost totally individualized and centers around the goals and objectives of the IEP for each student.

4. The focus of instruction may include remediation of the student's basic skills or assistance in passing regular class subjects, an approach termed *accommodation.*

5. The teacher should be a certified special educator with experience and training in management of a resource room.

6. Successful resource room programs require extensive interaction and cooperation between the special education program and the regular classes in the building. (Marsh and Price 1980)

TABLE 9.8
Types of Resource Rooms

TYPE	DESCRIPTION
Categorical	The children who attend are from one area of exceptionality.
Cross-Categorical	Children are assigned according to instructional level not label.
Noncategorical	Children in this model may or may not be labeled handicapped, but they do have mild or moderate learning and/or behavior problems.
Specific Skill Program	Teachers usually work on a specific skill area, typically with nonlabeled children who need assistance.
Itinerant Resource Teacher	Services are provided to more than one district, with the teacher serving part-time in each district.

Adapted from Wiederholt, Hammill, and Brown. 1978. *The Resource Teacher: A Guide to Effective Practices.*

Level IV, Full-time Special Class. Full-time placement in special classes was the most popular service model for special education before P.L. 94–142 emphasized serving handicapped children in regular classrooms as much as possible. In the self-contained model, one special education teacher has the primary responsibility for the entire educational program of students placed in the classroom. Students remain in the self-contained room all day every day, with the possible exception of attending music or other nonacademic classes, having lunch with nonhandicapped students and attending assemblies. Although not as popular as before the mainstreaming movement, approximately 25 percent of all children with disabilities still receive services in separate classes (U.S. Department of Education 1988).

From 1950 to 1970, the self-contained special classroom became the preferred organizational strategy for educating special education students served in public school programs (Reynolds 1973). Although displaced in popularity by the resource room model, the self-contained approach has some advantages (see table 9.9).

Levels V through VII. These lower levels of the Cascade of Services model are inappropriate for most mildly handicapped children. They are primarily reserved for more severely handicapped children, such as severely and profoundly mentally retarded, seriously emotionally disturbed, autistic, and medically fragile students. However, when determining appropriate placements for these more severely handicapped children, schools are still required by P.L. 94–142 to determine the least restrictive placement. In fact, there has been movement during the past few years to place more severely disabled students in regular school programs (Stainback, Stainback, and Stainback, 1988).

TABLE 9.9
Summary of Possible Advantages and Disadvantages of the Self-Contained Classroom Model

■

ADVANTAGES

1. Full-time interaction with the teacher may allow more scheduling flexibility.
2. Students are able to spend more time in small groups with peers, which may foster friendships.
3. Parents may form closer relationships with one teacher than when dealing with several teachers.
4. Grouping for instruction may be easier to accomplish.
5. It may be easier for one teacher to assume complete responsibility for the student's performance.

DISADVANTAGES

1. The student's opportunities to interact with peers and other adults are restricted.
2. Teachers may be isolated from other staff members.
3. There is limited opportunity for special education students to have experiences with students of other ability levels.

Source: Adapted from Cegelka and Prehm. 1982. *Mental Retardation: From Categories to People.*

■

TRENDS IN SPECIAL EDUCATION

Several trends appear to be gaining momentum in the area of special education. Two of these include the Regular Education Initiative (REI) and Transition and Supported Employment.

The Regular Education Initiative movement has had great impetus from several different factions including the Office of Special Education, U.S. Department of Education, and various professional and advocacy groups, such as The Association for the Severely Handicapped (TASH). Succinctly stated, REI focuses on the integration of regular education and special education into one system (Braaten, Kauffman, Braaten, Polsgrove, and Nelson 1988).

One of the early leaders of the REI was Madeline Will, then assistant secretary for special education and rehabilitation in the U.S. Department of Education. Will (1986) argued that many children with mild disabilities should be able to be served with minimal accommodations in regular classrooms. The call for such an overhaul of the special education model currently in place has resulted in an emotional debate (Davis 1989). On the one hand are those professionals questioning the efficacy of our current special education delivery system, and on the other are those professionals who are inclined to support the current system until research proves that REI is a better method of serving children with disabilities (Kirk and Gallagher 1989).

■ *The regular education initiative supports serving children with disabilities in regular classes the majority of the time.*

One other area that has received a great deal of attention during the past few years and which appears to be gaining widespread acceptance is transition programming and supported employment. Transition can be viewed as the "process of movement through life phases or the methodology associated with the life development process of persons as they move from the structure of one social institution or service delivery system to that of another" (Ianacone and Stodden 1987 p. 3). In essence, this means the movement from one service delivery setting, such as the high school, to the world of work. The successful transition of young adults with disabilities from high school to the adult world requires close collaboration between educators and vocational rehabilitation staff.

One method of assisting young adults with disabilities in their movement from school to the postschool environment is supported employment. Supported employment can be described as permanent, ongoing work for pay in an integrated setting. To this point, the focus of supported employment programs has been on persons with severe disabilities (Wehman, Moon, Everson, Wood, and Barcus 1988).

Research using the supported employment model, where job coaches work with persons with disabilities at the job site, has consistently found that the model is very effective. Frequently the end result is a person with a disability who is trained and successful on a competitive job (Bellamy, Rhodes, Mank, and Albin 1988).

SUMMARY

This chapter focused on special education. The beginning section discussed the history of treatment of disabled persons. Handicapped people were treated badly for much of history, even being persecuted and killed during various historical periods. Benevolent treatment for the disabled began around 1600; however, services were not truly expanded until the twentieth century.

Currently in the United States more than four million students are served in special education programs in public schools. The number has grown tremendously during the past decade. Federal legislation and litigation primarily have been responsible for the growth. Since the mid-1950s a great deal of federal legislation has been passed that has had an impact on special education. The one piece of legislation that had the most impact was Public Law 94–142, the Education for All Handicapped Children Act. The key components of this act were discussed, as well as actions that led up to its passage.

Another section of the chapter was a discussion on traditional and current categorizing of disabled people and services provided. The traditional classification system used with disabled individuals placed individuals into categories such as mental retardation, learning disabilities, and visual impairment. The discussion then moved to focus on the current classification model, generic or noncategorical classification.

Finally, services provided to disabled students in special education were discussed. The traditional method of delivering services to this population—segregating students into self-contained classrooms—has given way to mainstreaming students into regular classrooms. Using this model, known as the resource room model, students leave the regular classrooms and go to the resource room for specialized instruction. The pros and cons of this current model of service delivery were discussed, as well as other recent trends.

IN THE FIELD

1. Does the school have a special education program?
2. Is the special education categorical or noncategorical?
3. How many resource rooms are in the school? How many self-contained rooms?
4. What did you observe to indicate the relationship between regular classroom teachers and special education teachers?

5. What administrative actions indicate support for the special education program?

6. Approximately what percentage of the school's students receive special education?

7. Are there any variations for special education students relative to pass/fail and graduation requirements?

8. Can special education students participate in extracurricular activities? If so, which activities?

REFERENCES

Algozzine, B., C. V. Morsink, and K. M. Algozzine. 1988. What's happening in self-contained special education classrooms? *Exceptional Children* 55(3), 259–265.

Baca, L. and K. C. Harris, 1988. Teaching migrant exceptional children. *Teaching Exceptional Children* 20(5), 32–35.

A free appropriate public education. 1977. *AMICUS* 2(3), 20.

Bellamy, G. T., L. E. Rhodes, D. M. Mank, and J. M. Albin, 1988. *Supported Employment: A Community Implementation Guide*. Baltimore: Brookes.

Biklen, D. P. 1985. Mainstreaming: From compliance to quality. *Journal of Learning Disabilities* 18 (1), 58–61.

Blackhurst, A. E., and W. H. Berdine, 1985. Basic concepts of special education. In A. E. Blackhurst, and W. H. Berdine, eds., *An Introduction to Special Education*. Boston: Little, Brown.

Blackhurst, A. E., and W. H. Berdine, 1981. Basic concepts of special education. In A. E. Blackhurst, and W. H. Berdine, eds., *An Introduction to Special Education*. Boston: Little, Brown.

Blatt, B. 1960. Some persistently recurring assumptions concerning the mentally subnormal. *Training School Bulletin* 57, 48–59.

Board of Education of the Hendrick Hudson Central School District Westchester County v. Rowley ex rel. Rowley, 458 U.S. 176 (1982).

Boston, B. O. 1977. *Education Policy and the Education for All Handicapped Children Act (P.L. 94–142)*. Washington, DC: Institute for Educational Leadership, The George Washington University.

Braaten, S., J. M. Kauffman, B. Braaten, L. Polsgrove, and C. M. Nelson. 1988. The regular education initiative: Patent medicine for behavior disorders. *Exceptional Children* 55(1), 21–28.

Cartwright, G. P., C. A. Cartwright, and M. E. Ward. 1981. *Educating Special Learners*. Belmont, CA: Wadsworth.

Cegelka, P. T., and H. J. Prehm. 1982. *Mental Retardation: From Categories to People*. Columbus, OH: Merrill.

Christoplos, F. and P. Renz, 1969. A critical examination of special education programs. *Journal of Special Education* 3, 371–79.

Clark-Johnson, G. 1988. Black children. *Teaching Exceptional Children* 20 (4), 46–47.

Coplin, J. W., and S. B. Morgan. 1988. Learning disabilities: A multidimensional perspective. *Journal of Learning Disabilities* 21 (10), 616–622.

Corrigan, D. 1978. Political and moral contexts that produced P.L. 94–142. *Journal of Teacher Education* 29, 10–14.

Davis, W. E. 1989. The regular education initiative debate: Its promises and problems. *Exceptional Children* 55(5), 440–447.

Deno, E. 1970. Special education as developmental capital. *Exceptional Children* 37, 229–37.

Dunn, L. M. 1968. Special education for the mildly retarded: Is much of it justified? *Exceptional Children* 35, 5–22.

Dunn, L. 1973. *Exceptional Children in the Schools: Special Education in Transition.* New York: Holt, Rinehart, and Winston.

Elksnin, L. K., and N. Elksnin. 1989. Collaborative consultation: Improving parent-teacher communication. *Academic Therapy* 24(3), 261–270.

Fisher, H. K. 1967. What is special education? *Special Education in Canada* 41, 9–16.

Federal Register 1977. Washington D.C.: U.S. Government Printing Office 42 (163).

Friend, M. and G. McNutt. 1984. Resource room programs: Where are we now? *Exceptional Children* 51 (2), 150–55.

Gearheart, B. R. 1980. *Special Education for the 80s.* St. Louis: C. V. Mosby.

Gearheart, B. R., M. W. Weishahn, and C. J. Gearheart. 1988. *The Exceptional Student in the Regular Classroom.* 4th ed. Columbus, OH: Merrill.

Goldstein, S., and A. P. Turnbull. 1982. Strategies to increase parent participation in IEP conferences. *Exceptional Children* 48 (4) 360–61.

Grossman, H. J. 1983. *Manual on Terminology and Classification in Mental Retardation, 1983 Revision.* Washington, D.C.: American Association on Mental Retardation.

Hallahan, D. B. and J. W. Kauffman. 1978. *Exceptional Children.* Englewood Cliffs, NJ: Prentice-Hall.

Heaney, J. P. 1984. A free appropriate public education: Has the Supreme Court misinterpreted Congressional intent? *Exceptional Children* 50 (5), 456–62.

Heward, W. L., and M. D. Orlansky. 1988. *Exceptional Children,* 3d ed. Columbus, OH: Merrill.

Ianacone, R. N., and R. A. Stodden Transition issues and direction for individuals who are mentally retarded. In R. N. Ianacone and R. A. Stodden (Eds.), *Transition Issues and Direction.* Reston, VA: Council for Exceptional Children.

Jansen, M. J., P. E. Ahm, D. L. Jensen, and A. Leerskov. 1970. Is special education necessary? Can this program possibly be reduced? *Journal of Learning Disabilities* 3 (9), 11–16.

Johnson, G. O. 1962. Special education for the mentally retarded—A paradox. *Exceptional Children* 29, 62–69.

Johnson, G. O. 1983. Inconsistencies in programming. *Education and Training of the Mentally Retarded* 18 (2), 101–102.

Johnson, J. L. 1969. Special education in the inner city: A challenge for the future or another means of cooling the markout? *Journal of Special Education* 3, 241–51.

Jones, R. L., and F. B. Wilderson. 1976. Mainstreaming and the minority child: An overview of issues and a perspective. In R. L. Jones, ed., *Mainstreaming and the Minority Child.* Minneapolis: Leadership Training Institute.

Katims, D. S. 1988. Effective teaching and learning in the noncategorical classroom. *Academic Therapy* 24 (2), 199–206.

Kirk, S. A. 1972. *Educating Exceptional Children.* Boston: Houghton-Mifflin.

Kirk, S. A., and J. J. Gallagher. 1989. *Educating Exceptional Children*, 6th ed. Boston: Houghton Mifflin.

Kolstoe, O. P. 1976. *Teaching Educable Mentally Retarded Children.* New York: Holt, Rinehart, and Winston.

Laski, F. 1974. Civil rights victories for the handicapped—I. *The Record* 1 (15), 15–20.

Levine, M. D. 1982. The child with school problems: An analysis of physician participation. *Exceptional Children* 48 (4), 296–304.

Lilly, S. 1979. *Children with Exceptional Needs: A Survey of Special Education.* New York: Holt, Rinehart, and Winston.

Lord, F. E. 1981. The attainment of professional stature, 1950–1980, part I. *Exceptional Children* 47 (6), 438–52.

McCarthy, M. M. and N. H. Cambron. 1981. *Public School Law: Teachers' and Students' Rights.* Boston: Allyn and Bacon.

Mandell, C. J. and V. Gold. 1984. *Teaching Handicapped Students.* St. Paul: West.

Marsh, G. E., and B. J. Price. 1980. *Methods for Teaching the Mildly Handicapped Adolescent.* St. Louis: C. V. Mosby.

Marsh, G. E., B. J. Price, and T. E. C. Smith. 1983. *Teaching Mildly Handicapped Children: Methods and Materials.* St. Louis: C. V. Mosby.

Marvell, T. A. Galfo, and J. Rockwell. 1981. *Student Litigation: A Compilation and Analysis of Civil Cases Involving Students 1977–1981.* Williamsburg, VA: National Center for State Courts.

Merulla, E., and A. McKinnon. 1982. "Stuck" on Deno's cascade: *Journal of Learning Disabilities* 15, 94–96.

Moores, D. F. 1978. *Educating the Deaf: Psychology, Principles, and Practices.* Boston: Houghton Mifflin.

National Center for Education Statistics. 1983. *The Condition of Education*, 1983 edition. Washington, D.C.: U.S. Government Printing Office.

National Center for Education Statistics. 1988. *The Condition of Education*, 1988 edition. Washington, D.C.: U.S. Government Printing Office.

Nirje, B. 1969. The normalization principle and its human management implications. In R. B. Kugel and W. Wolfensberger (eds.). *Changing Patterns in Residential Services for the Mentally Retarded.* Washington, D.C.: U.S. Government Printing Office.

Peterson, R. L., R. H. Zabel, C. R. Smith, and M. A. White. 1983. Cascade of services model and emotionally disabled students. *Exceptional Children* 49, 404–10.

Podemski, R. S., B. J. Price, T. E. C. Smith, and G. E. Marsh. 1984. *Comprehensive Special Education Administration.* Rockville, MD: Aspen Systems.

Prasse, D. P. 1988. Legal influence and educational policy in special education. *Exceptional Children* 54 (4), 302–308.

Price, B. J., and G. E. Marsh. 1985. Practical suggestions for planning and conducting parent conferences. *Teaching Exceptional Children* 17 (4), 274–78.

Quay, H. C. 1975. Classification in the treatment of delinquency and antisocial behavior. In H. Hobbs, ed., *Issues in the Classification of Children. Vol. I.* San Francisco: Jossey-Bass.

Reid, D. K., and W. P. Hresko. 1981. *A Cognitive Approach to Learning Disabilities*. New York: McGraw-Hill.

Reschly, D. J. 1988. Minority MMR overrepresentation and special education reform. *Exceptional Children* 54 (4), 316–323.

Reynolds, M. C. 1973. Changing roles of special education personnel. Paper presented to University Council on Education Administration, 1973.

Rivers, D., and T. E. C. Smith. 1988. Traditional eligibility criteria for identifying students as specific learning disabled. *Journal of Learning Disabilities* 21 (10), 642–644.

Scanlon, C. A. J. Arick, and N. Phelps. 1981. Participation in the development of the IEP: Parents' perspective. *Exceptional Children* 47 (5), 373–74.

Scheerenberger, R. C. 1976. *Deinstitutionalization and Institutional Reform*. Springfield, IL.: Charles C. Thomas.

Smith, R. M. and J. T. Neisworth. 1975. *The Exceptional Child: A Functional Approach*. New York: McGraw-Hill.

Smith, T. E. C. 1981. Status of due process hearings. *Exceptional Children* 48 (3), 232–36.

Smith, T. E. C., B. J. Price and G. E. Marsh. 1986. *Mildly Handicapped Children and Adults*. St. Paul: West.

Stainback, G. H., W. C. Stainback, and S. B. Stainback. Superintendents' attitudes toward integration. *Education and Training in Mental Retardation* 23 (2), 92–96.

Stotland, J. F. and E. Mancuso. 1981. U.S. Court of Appeals decision regarding *Armstrong v. Kline:* The 180 day rule. *Exceptional Children* 47 (4), 266–70.

Sugai, G. 1985. Case study: Designing instruction from IEPs. *Teaching Exceptional Children* 17 (3), 233–39.

Turnbull, R. H., and A. P. Turnbull. 1978. Precedural due process and the education of handicapped children. *Focus on Exceptional Children* 9 (9), 1–12.

United States Department of Education. 1984. Sixth annual report to Congress on the implementation of public law 94–142: The education for all handicapped children act. *Exceptional Children* 51 (3), 199–202.

United States Department of Education. 1988. *Tenth Annual Report to Congress on the Implementation of Public Law 94–142*. Washington, D.C.: Author.

Van Riper, C. 1978. *Speech Correction: Principles and Methods*. 6th ed. Englewood Cliffs, NJ: Prentice-Hall.

Wehman, P., M. S. Moon, J. M. Everson, W. Wood, and J. M. Barcus. 1988. *Transition from School to Work*. Baltimore: Paul H. Brookes.

Wiederholt, J. L., D. D. Hammill, and V. Brown. 1978. *The Resource Room Teacher: A Guide to Effective Practices*. Boston: Allyn and Bacon.

Weintraub, F. J. 1977. Understanding the individualized education program (IEP). *Amicus* 2 (3), 26–31.

Will, M. C. 1984. Let us pause and reflect—but not too long. *Exceptional Children* 51 (1), 11–16.

Yoshida, R. K. 1987. Perspectives on research. In E. L. Meyen (ed.), *Mental Retardation: Topics of Today—Issues of Tomorrow*. Lancaster, Pa.: Lancaster.

10

EDUCATIONAL ADMINISTRATION

OBJECTIVES
■

After reading this chapter you will be able to

- describe a typical administrative hierarchy in a public school district;

- list the responsibilities of the local school board;

- discuss the history of local boards of education;

- describe the roles of the district superintendent;

- list various assistants found at the district level;

- discuss the roles of the principal;

- describe the role of disciplinarian;

- discuss the ways principals evaluate personnel and programs;

- list groups that hold expectations for the principal;

- describe the various career options for school administrators; and

- discuss how to become a school administrator.

OUTLINE
■

ADVANCE ORGANIZERS

1. What is an administrative hierarchy?
2. How did local control of public schools evolve?
3. What are the specific responsibilities of local boards of education?
4. What is the relationship between the superintendent and the board of education?
5. In what roles do superintendents become involved?
6. What roles do assistant central office staff fill?
7. What are the primary roles of school principals?
8. What are the major management responsibilities of principals?
9. How do principals influence the school climate?
10. How does a typical principal spend a day?
11. What expectations do various groups have for principals?
12. What career opportunities are there for school administrators?
13. How can you become a school administrator?

INTRODUCTION

Like businesses, social organizations, and institutions, schools are complex organizations which must have leaders (Rallis 1989). In schools leaders are called school administrators. Without administrators schools would have no direction; they would be leaderless institutions functioning in a haphazard fashion without any common purpose or goals. School administrators definitely perform a vital role in public education. As more emphasis is placed on effective schools, the role of school administrators will become even more critical.

ADMINISTRATIVE HIERARCHY

Public schools are administered by an administrative hierarchy that, while differing from school to school, most often fits a similar pattern. At the top of the hierarchy is the local school board, a group of constituents. The local board hires the school superintendent, who is the chief local school officer. The superintendent, in turn, employs other central office administrative staff as well as building principals. Each level of the hierarchy serves a specific purpose involving the administration of the public schools (see figure 10.1). School administrators are for the most part bound by the chain of command that is established in the hierarchy (Brieschke 1985).

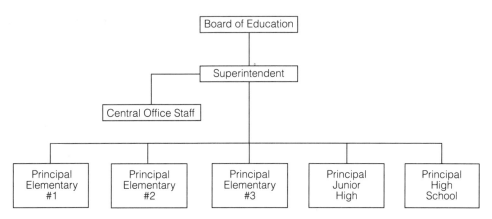

FIGURE 10.1. Typical Organizational Chart of a Middle-size School District.

LOCAL BOARD OF EDUCATION

In the 1986–1987 school year, there were 15,713 local school districts operating in the United States (National Center for Education Statistics 1988). Most of these districts are administered by a local school board that is either elected or appointed. In the majority of districts, school board members are elected.

Local control of education by lay persons began in the New England colonies. The Massachusetts School Ordinance of 1642 delegated the responsibility for education to the "townsmen." This trend was reinforced with the Massachusetts School Ordinance of 1647 and in subsequent amendments passed in 1671 and 1683. Even stronger than the Massachusetts laws were the Connecticut Laws of 1650. These laws were specific in the description of duties and responsibilities of individuals selected to oversee the schools (Pulliam 1987).

The laws enacted in the New England colonies directing the public to control the schools became the pattern throughout the rest of the country. Not until 1721 in Boston, however, were individuals responsible for overseeing the schools set apart from the local governmental structure of the community (Campbell, Cunningham, Nystrand, and Usdan 1980). Following this lead, other states and communities started separating the administration of schools from local governments.

Powers and Responsibilities of Boards

Today the powers and responsibilities of local school boards are established by state statutes. State laws dictate the size of boards, terms of office, methods to fill vacancies, meeting requirements, and the duties of board members.

Specific duties frequently cited include

- selecting the Chief Executive Officer (CEO) of the school district (superintendent)
- approving budgets
- determining school sites and attendance boundaries
- entering into contracts
- collective bargaining
- establishing criteria for employing school district personnel
- determining the curriculum (Guthrie and Reed 1986)

Local boards also have some discretionary powers. For example, they may exceed various state requirements for graduation, teacher qualifications, or course offerings; they may pay teachers more than the state-mandated minimum salary; they may set salaries in states without minimum teachers' salaries; or they may elect to offer a wide variety of extracurricular activities or none at all. Therefore, while local boards of education are obligated by state law to accomplish certain activities, they also can make many decisions at the local level that are not bound by state or federal statutes or litigation decisions.

Specific responsibilities of local boards of education include the following:

- To delegate to the superintendent responsibility for all administrative functions, except those specifically reserved through board policy for the board chairperson. Those reserved areas might include: conducting board meetings and public hearings, approving the agenda and minutes and other activities incidental to, and associated with, serving as presiding officer of the board.
- To support the superintendent fully in all decisions that conform to professional standards and board policy.
- To hold the superintendent responsible for the administration of the school through regular constructive written and oral evaluations of the superintendent's work. Effective evaluation is an ongoing effort and should be linked to goals established by the board with the assistance of the superintendent.
- To provide the superintendent with a comprehensive employment contract.
- To give the superintendent the benefit of the board's counsel in matters related to individual board members' expertise, familiarity with the local school system, and community interests.
- To hold all board meetings with the superintendent or a designee present.
- To consult with the superintendent on all matters, as they arise, that concern the school system and on which the board may take action.

- To develop a plan for board-superintendent communications.
- To channel communications with school employees that require action through the superintendent, and to refer all applications, complaints, and other communications, oral or written, first to the superintendent in order to assure that the district processes such communications in an effective, coordinated fashion and is responsive to students and patrons.
- To take action on matters only after hearing the recommendations of the superintendent.
- To establish a policy on the effective management of complaints.
- To provide the superintendent with sufficient administrative help, especially in the area of monitoring teaching and learning. (Roles and Relationships: School Boards and Superintendents 1981, pp. 3–4)

Local boards of education comprise community members who are either elected by the local citizenry or appointed by elected officials and who have the responsibilities of operating the local school district. Individuals who make up local school boards vary from wealthy to poor, educated to uneducated, and interested in the schools to interested in self-advancement. While school board members represent all segments of the community, they most often are from higher educated, upper-middle-class groups. The latest survey of school board members published in The American School Board Journal (Hatrick, Underwood, Fortune, and Keough 1989) describes the typical school board member as white, male, in his forties, and earning between $40,000 and $50,000 annually. Other characteristics include married with one or two children, home owner, college graduate working in a profession or managerial position, and served on the board from one to four years. Table 10.1 provides additional information about current school board members. The composition of school boards has not changed significantly from past years, when studies also found them to be primarily composed of white, educated, middle-aged males (Alvey, Underwood, and Fortune 1986).

PROFESSIONAL ADMINISTRATIVE STAFF

Before 1900 the number of individuals employed as "professional" educational administrators was extremely small. As cities and schools grew in the 1800s, the need became apparent for full-time professionals to manage the schools. In June, 1837, the Buffalo, New York City Council employed a superintendent of the city's common schools. Following this action, many other large cities employed professional managers for their schools. The profession of school administration had begun.

TABLE 10.1
Characteristics of School Board Members

CHARACTERISTIC	PERCENTAGE
Sex	
Male	68.1
Female	31.9
Ethnic Background	
White	93.7
Black	3.4
Hispanic	1.3
Other	1.3
Age	
25 or less	0.2
26–35	7.3
36–40	15.4
41–50	44.5
51–60	20.0
Over 60	12.6
Family Income	
Under $20,000	3.4
$20,000–$29,000	7.9
$30,000–$39,000	15.6
$40,000–$49,000	17.5
$50,000–$59,000	15.7
$60,000–$69,000	11.0
$70,000–$79,000	7.6
$80,000–$89,000	4.6
$90,000–$99,000	3.3
Over $100,000	10.0

Source: Hatrick, Underwood, Fortune, and Keough. *The American School Board Journal* 176(1), 1989.

By 1980 there were 160,000 school administrators in the United States (Guthrie and Reed 1986).

Today schools are administered by a host of professional staff, with the superintendent being the chief school officer hired by the local school board. Responsible to the superintendent are many other professionals involved in school administration, including central office staff, principals, and assistant principals.

Districtwide Administrative Staff

Administrative staff that oversee all activities within the district are housed in the central office. These include the superintendent and any assistant administrators who may be employed to assist the superintendent in carrying out districtwide activities.

Superintendents. Most school districts employ a superintendent as the chief executive officer of the school. This person, the resident expert on education, filters information between schools and the board of education (Reecer 1989). The superintendent generally is hired by the board of education and serves at the pleasure of the board. As a result, superintendents are responsible to their boards for all of the activities within the school district. In addition to serving as the school district's CEO, the superintendent also is the most visible member of the community on educational issues (Guthrie and Reed 1986).

The duties and responsibilities of superintendents vary among districts as a result of the size of the district, the financial condition of the district, and the expectations of the local school board and community members. However, most superintendents perform certain functions regardless of the district in which they serve. Examples of these duties include (1) maintaining relationships with the board, (2) organizing staff, (3) maintaining positive relationships among the community, and (4) ensuring that all legal requirements are met by the district (see table 10.2). In 1980 the American Association of School Administrators published *Roles and Relationships: School Boards and Superintendents*. Specific responsibilities of the superintendent included the following:

1. To serve as the board's chief executive officer and advisor.
2. To serve as the school system's educational leader.
3. To keep the board informed about school operations and programs.
4. To keep the community informed about board policies, programs, and district procedures.
5. To interpret the needs of the school system to the board.
6. To present and recommend policy options along with specific recommendations to the board when circumstances require the board to adopt new policies or revise existing policies.

TABLE 10.2
Roles of School Superintendents

ROLE	DESCRIPTION
Maintain relations with board	Keeps in contact with board Informs board of staffing decisions Advises board on policy decisions Informs board of school activities Informs board of the needs of the schools
Educational leader	Stays informed about educational practices Facilitates staff development Secures necessary teaching materials and equipment Encourages educational innovations
Maintain positive relations with the community	Disseminates information about school programs Forms community advisory groups Informs parents about school activities Facilitates contacts between school staff and community

7. To develop and inform the board of administrative procedures needed to implement board policy.
8. To provide leadership for the district's educational programs.
9. To develop an adequate program of school-community relations.
10. To manage the district's day-to-day operations.
11. To evaluate personnel and keep the board informed about evaluations. (Roles and Relationships: School Boards and Superintendents 1980, p. 5)

These roles have not changed dramatically during the 1980s. In order to perform these duties effectively, superintendents must possess skills in human relations, conceptual skills, and skills regarding technology (Hoyle 1989).

The district superintendent, therefore, is a key individual in the functioning of any local school district. The individual occupying this position "is obviously the most important member of the administrative team at the district level . . . " (Gorton 1983, p. 121). This person must give information and counsel to a host of groups, including other administrators, board members, teachers, parents, and students (Doremus 1985). There are approximately fourteen thousand superintendents in the United States. The majority of school superintendents are white males, between the ages of 48 and 55, and have held their current jobs for more than five years (Education Vital Signs 1988). (See table 10.3)

Central Office Staff. In large school districts, the superintendent is assisted by one or more assistant superintendents. In smaller districts, all central office functions are carried out by the superintendent. Large districts, however, require so many actions by the central office that assistant superintendents and other administrative staff are necessary. Approximately fifty thousand administrative staff in school districts assist superintendents in carrying out central office duties. These individuals, primarily assistant superintendents, directors, or supervisors, carry many different titles. These titles include assistant superintendent, assistant superintendent for areas such as personnel, director of elementary/secondary education, director of finance, elementary/secondary supervisor, art supervisor, and science consultant (Campbell et al. 1980).

Most school districts do not employ all of these administrative staff; on the other hand, in large school districts all of these positions, plus others, may be filled. The number and variety of administrative staff in the central office varies, primarily as a result of district size and financial condition.

The duties performed by central staff administrators are determined by their specific roles. For example, in a small district there may be only one assistant superintendent. This individual may be assigned the re-

TABLE 10.3
Characteristics of Superintendents

CHARACTERISTIC	PERCENTAGE
Sex	
Male	95
Female	5
Ethnic Background	
Black	1
White	91
Hispanic	1
Other	1
Age	
Under 30	0
30–35	4
36–41	17
42–47	20
48–55	40
56–65	18
Over 65	1
Years in Current Job	
1 or less	14
2–3	32
3–5	14
More than five	41
Percentage who consider compensation adequate	51

Source: *Education Vital Signs,* Vol IV, 1988/1989.

sponsibilities for transportation, food services, and the curriculum. In large districts, these duties may be divided among several central office staff members.

Building-Level Administrative Staff

At the building level, principals are the key administrators. Many schools also employ assistant principals, department heads, and supervisors to assist the principal in carrying out the administrative duties found at the building level.

Principals. Similar to superintendents, who oversee the operations of the entire district, principals are responsible for all activities that occur within their school buildings. "The principal is perhaps the only individual who can see the whole picture in his or her school (Rallis 1988 p. 644). During the past twenty-five years, the roles and responsibilities of principals have changed dramatically as a result of many different factors, including federal legislation, the economy, and the reform movement (see table 10.4). Certainly the role of school principals has changed from the days when the teacher in charge of older students

TABLE 10.4
Factors Affecting the Role of Principals

FACTOR	IMPACT
Demographic Changes	Decline in school enrollments Increase in school enrollments Difficulty in estimating future enrollments Changes in tax base
State of Economy	Unemployment and reduced tax base Tax-revolt movement Difficulty in passing millage increases
Collective Bargaining	Adversarial relationship between principals and teachers Collective decision-making Teacher assignment difficulties Forced reallocation of school budgets
Federal and State Government	Legislation mandating actions Funds for certain programs Regulations and paperwork Court-imposed activities
News Media	Negative publicity Positive publicity Generalizations resulting from media coverage

Source: Gorton. *School Leadership and Administration,* 1983.

in the Boston Primary School was called the principal teacher and was responsible for administrative duties (Pulliam 1987). No longer can schools simply promote male teachers or athletic coaches into the job of principal. The position currently is far too complex and requires many different skills (Duke 1987). The roles increasingly involve more than the infamous three Bs: buses, boilers, and budgets (Spillane 1989).

Roles of Principals. Principals are expected to perform many varied roles in today's schools, including manager, instructional leader, disciplinarian, human relations facilitator, evaluator, and conflict manager (Gorton 1983). In small, rural schools the roles of principals often go beyond expectation. Wilkens (1983), in detailing his activities as a principal in such a school, revealed that his roles included working on school buses, herding cows from the playground, looking for a child's first lost tooth on the playground, and "discussing" a child's discipline problems with an irate, aggressive father. Although the principal's role as instructional leader is considered by many to be the primary role, without expertise and leadership in the noninstructional activities, the school would have a difficult time functioning.

A major function of the principal is to manage all aspects of the school, including the instructional program, school plant, food services, transportation, pupil and personnel services, and budget. With all these different areas to manage, principals need to be well skilled in management.

The principal as instructional leader is the role that is frequently mentioned when discussing what principals do (Snyder and Anderson 1986). Instructional leadership can be defined as "leadership that informs and guides teachers' decision-making so that practice can mesh with policy . . . " (Rallis 1988, p. 643). Principals actually view themselves as primarily instructional leaders, too (Cooper 1989). The principal should be heavily involved in the curriculum of the school and the instructional process. As an instructional leader the principal should (Rallis 1988)

- speak for teachers;
- establish the direction of instruction;
- know and interpret research findings;
- explain "best practices";
- take risks in instruction;

- *The instructional leadership role includes being aware of what takes place in classrooms.*

- work well with and support teachers;
- encourage sharing;
- help teachers assess and evaluate their impact;
- know how to teach; and
- be accessible to teachers.

Many teachers actually look to the principal for guidance related to teaching. Too often principals get overly involved in activities such as management and discipline, and the instructional program may suffer as a result. Principals should, however, make a strong effort to get into classrooms and stay involved in the instructional program of the school.

Although many different activities occupy the principal's time each school day, principals must return to the instructional leadership role, the role that actually began the profession. Other responsibilities such as scheduling, record keeping, and staff development must be addressed by principals. However, realizing that these functions are secondary to instructional leadership in facilitating the school's instructional goals may help keep principals more involved in the instructional program (Pinero 1982).

School discipline has been the major concern expressed by many Americans during the past several years (Gallup and Elam 1988). In the opinion of many, especially parents and students, a primary role of the principal is that of disciplinarian. The role of disciplinarian is time consuming for many principals. Principals often reject this role because of its negative perception, because the disciplinarian is the one who punishes students (Gorton 1987). However, adequate discipline must be maintained in schools if the goals and objectives of the school are to be met. The instructional program, student and teacher morale, and community support can all be negatively affected by schools without adequate discipline. Since the principal is the chief administrative officer of the school, the ultimate responsibility for discipline belongs to that office.

Principals must establish a positive climate for good discipline. To do so, they must view discipline from the total school perspective, not merely isolated cases of inappropriate behavior. Lordon (1983) suggests that principals determine (1) the commitment of the school staff for out-of-class discipline, (2) the clarity of school policies, (3) the attitudes of teachers about discipline, (4) the consistency of disciplinary policies in the school, and (5) the clarity of supervision policies. By scrutinizing these areas, principals are in a better position to implement a consistent, well-founded school discipline policy.

Limited new theory related to discipline has surfaced. As a result, principals must take the initiative during this information lull to educate and/or reeducate their teachers concerning classroom management techniques. With no new ideas, school professionals must hold on to the theories of discipline that have proven effective (Tauber 1989).

Another primary role of principals is evaluation, including program evaluation and personnel evaluation. Program evaluation is a multi-faceted activity with many different evaluation models (Podemski, Price, Smith, and Marsh 1984). Regardless of the model used, the principal must do several things in order to carry out the evaluation function, including

- determine who should be involved in the evaluation;
- establish evaluation criteria;
- select methods of evaluation;
- collect data;
- analyze data;
- draw conclusions and develop recommendations;
- report findings; and
- implement recommendations (Gorton 1983, p. 74).

Personnel evaluation is a major responsibility of the principal. Since the reform movement began in the early 1980s, improving the performance of teachers has been in the headlines. As a result, principals must be able to determine who are the good teachers, which teachers need improvement, and how to make those improvements. Too often administrators are not trained in substantive personnel evaluation (Buser and Pace 1988). In Fairfax County, Virginia, principals evaluate teachers on their abilities to

1. demonstrate knowledge of content and curriculum;
2. provide appropriate learning experiences;
3. demonstrate appropriate planning;
4. manage instruction and student behavior;
5. demonstrate human relations and communication skills;
6. monitor and evaluate student outcomes;
7. use available resources; and
8. accept and fulfill professional responsibilities (Spillane 1989).

Clinical supervision is another method principals use to evaluate teachers. In this time-tested method, 1) principals and teachers agree on specific skills and practices of effective teaching; 2) teachers' behaviors are observed; 3) feedback is provided to the teacher by the principal; 4) areas for improvement are determined; and 5) plans for future instruction are agreed upon (Sullivan and Wircenski 1988).

Other personnel evaluation models include (Haefele 1980): (1) performance of students on standardized tests; (2) gains students make during the school year, as determined by standardized tests; (3) test scores of students compared among classes; (4) informal observations of the teacher; (5) systematic observation of the teacher by the principal or supervisor; (6) systematic observation of the teacher by peers; (7) students' ratings of the teacher; (8) scores earned on the National Teachers Examination (NTE); (9) students' performance on a predetermined set of teaching objectives; (10) scores on the Teacher Perceiver Interview (TPI); (11) teacher responses to written descriptions or films of classroom problems; and (12) attainment of goals predetermined by the teacher and principal or supervisor.

Through evaluation, principals can determine strengths and weaknesses in the instructional program and in personnel. If weaknesses exist, principals may need to intervene with program modifications or

■ *Personnel evaluation is a major role of principals.*

with personnel counseling in the case of inadequate performance by staff. Ongoing evaluation enables principals to be aware of the success of the school's programs and provide additional support to certain aspects of the program that may need improvement (Rice 1989).

Still another role of the principal is collective bargaining (Gorton 1987). As a result of the National Education Association (NEA) and the American Federation of Teachers (AFT) more than doubling their memberships between 1964 and 1975, their power in collective bargaining increased dramatically (Goldschmidt and Painter 1987–1988). A recent survey revealed that seventy percent of the principals are in schools where teachers have collectively negotiated their contracts (Doud 1989). The end results are that principals must negotiate and collaborate with teachers on a daily basis; that in most schools, the ultimate authority of the principal has been diminished. Barth (1988) concluded that principals must now share leadership with teachers.

A new role emerging for principals is that of adult developer. In this role, principals deal with teachers, staff members, and parents. Because of the increased demand by these adults to participate in school decision-making, principals must understand adult development and facilitate its process. No longer can principals simply focus their attention on children. Although activities with students will continue to occupy the largest part of the principal's time, involvement with adults will demand more and more attention. Therefore, understanding adults is critical in the success of principals (Levine 1989).

Other roles and responsibilities include acting as a change agent or innovator, and working with the community in community relations. The role of change agent is one that many principals relish. This role gives principals the opportunity to assume a leadership role in instigating changes in the school. The changes may be in the areas of instruction, curriculum, personnel policies, discipline, or any other area. Principals set the tone or atmosphere in their buildings. If principals are supportive and encouraging of change and innovation, changes and innovations are more likely to occur than if principals are nonsupportive (Sivage 1982; Mechling 1983).

Principals also must perform a major role related to community relations. Although the "neighborhood school" may not be as common as it once was in this country, the community that is located near a school is vital to the success of the school. Principals must help foster its support. Gaining and maintaining active community support is difficult. The first group that should be involved is parents. Parents who are involved in the school operations provide principals with much needed political support. More important, however, parents who are involved in decision-making in the school are more likely to support those decisions than if those decisions were simply imposed upon them (Jenkins 1981).

Expectations of Principals. Principals are expected to do many different things for different groups of people, such as teachers, students, central administration personnel, state departments of education, and the local community. (see figure 10.2).

Specifically, students expect principals to have a personal relationship with them. This is the most important, ardent expectation expressed by students in several studies (Gorton 1987). Students also want fewer and more reasonable rules. Different students expect different things from their principals. Academically inclined students may be in favor of principals supporting higher academic standards, providing higher level courses, and holding lower academic students responsible for their poor performance. Students whose primary interest is athletics likely will have different expectations of their principals. They will want the principal to be understanding of their travel and practice requirements, to encourage teachers to be flexible in homework assignments, and to generally support school athletics.

Because of the central role teachers play in the educational process, principals must attend to the expectations teachers have of them. Common expectations held by teachers include (Gorton 1987) (1) supporting teachers on discipline problems, (2) treating teachers as

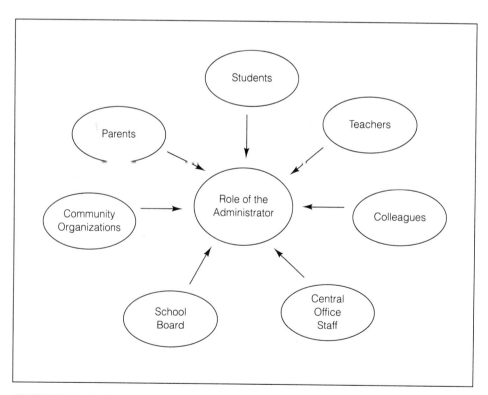

FIGURE 10.2. Groups Holding Expectations of Principal
Source: Gorton. School Leadership and Administration, 1987.

professional colleagues, and (3) enabling teachers to participate in decision-making.

Parents also have some specific expectations of principals. These may include providing instructional leadership, collaborating with parents, and keeping the interest of students foremost (Gorton 1987). These expectations are broad but cover most of the specific expectations that parents can voice. While not having to respond to all of the expectations held by parents, principals definitely need to be aware of these expectations and attempt to meet those that would have a positive effect on the school.

Principals also must adhere to the expectations of their superiors, namely the superintendent and school board. Although the principal in most districts is hired by the superintendent in conjunction with the board, principals must be aware of the expectations held by both groups. Some expectations held by the principals' superiors would include

- carrying out school policy;
- maintaining a positive relationship with community members;
- providing instructional leadership;
- maintaining student discipline;
- maintaining staff morale; and
- effectively managing the school.

Although principals cannot always meet the expectations of everyone, they must at least determine the feasibility of meeting the expectations, the impact on the school and on their personal life if the expectations are not met, and the importance of the expectations to the goals and objectives of the school. Principals cannot be all things to all people; they must make decisions related to which expectations are in the best interests of the school.

Typical Day of Principals. As has been described, principals have many different roles and functions and are expected to please many groups. Taken together, all of these tasks appear to be overwhelming. Howell (1981) studied the ways principals spend their days by having fourteen middle school and junior high principals record their activities every fifteen minutes on a particular day. The results indicated that paperwork was the major activity performed, taking up approximately 33 percent of the principals' time. Other activities included parent conferences (13.5 percent), personnel conferences (13.5 percent), discipline (9 percent), scheduling (9 percent), cafeteria duties (9 percent), supervision (7.5 percent), and instructional leadership (2.5 percent). Less time was spent on instructional leadership than any other major activity, a finding not inconsistent with other studies.

Principals, therefore, are burdened with many responsibilities that take away time that could be used in the instructional program. Although Howell's (1981) times are probably representative of many principals at all levels, principals in effective schools likely spend more time related to the curriculum and instruction.

Principals of Today. As you can see, principals are key individuals in schools. They must fill a host of roles and they are required to satisfy the expectations of many different individuals. In a recent survey, Doud (1989) profiles the K–8 principal. In general, today's elementary principal is a white male, age 47, who serves as a full-time administrator over a school with just fewer than 500 pupils. Table 10.5 provides additional characteristics of today's typical principal.

Assistant Principals. Some schools employ assistant principals to help principals carry out their many and varied responsibilities. Assistant principals perform many activities, depending on the wishes of the principal. Marsh (1981) described the many different roles he performed while serving as an assistant principal for several different principals. These included assisting the principal with duties associated with (1) the lunchroom, (2) transportation, (3) books and supplies,

TABLE 10.5
Characteristics of Principals

CHARACTERISTIC	PERCENTAGE	
	HIGH SCHOOL	ELEMENTARY
Sex		
Male	97	67
Ethnic Background		
Black	6	7
White	91	90
Hispanic	3	3
Other	1	1
Age		
Under 30	1	0
30–35	6	9
36–41	19	20
42–47	23	26
48–55	40	29
56–65	11	15
Over 65	0	1
Years in Current Job		
1 or less	6	8
2–3	28	24
3–5	14	13
More than five	53	55
Percentage who consider compensation adequate	37	43

Source: *Education Vital Signs*, Vol. IV, 1988/1989.

■ *Assistant principals perform many varied roles in the school, sometimes even cafeteria supervisor.*

(4) bicentennial program planning, (5) assemblies, fire drills, and special events, (6) policy-making decisions, and (7) curriculum. Marsh (1981) pointed out that his role as an assistant principal varied considerably from one principal to the next. Some principals had openly involved him in most school activities, while others had severely restricted his activities.

When used effectively, assistant principals can prove a valuable resource to the principal. If not properly used, assistant principals can be more of a burden than an asset. Principals need to learn how to best utilize assistant principals to relieve some of their work load while increasing the efficiency of the school.

CAREERS IN ADMINISTRATION

Educational administration is a career for many individuals. As previously indicated, approximately 64,000 superintendents and other central office staff serve in public school programs. Added to this number are principals and assistant principals. With approximately

85,000 elementary and secondary schools in this country, it could be estimated that there are 85,000 principals. Although not every school employs a principal, the majority do. Therefore, there may be approximately 150,000 positions in administration in American public schools.

How to Become an Administrator

Most school administrators start out as classroom teachers. This seems to be the best way to become a school administrator. Most states have specific certification requirements for administrators that go beyond the requirements for a teaching certificate. These certificates are usually job-specific; that is, there is a state-issued elementary principal certificate, secondary principal certificate, supervisor certificate, and superintendent certificate. The requirements for these certificates vary from state to state, but usually they include college coursework at the graduate level and years of experience as a teacher. Some states (e.g., Michigan) do not yet require a specific license for administrators.

Although school administrators have been trained using a traditional, graduate education model for many years, many of these programs have been "fragmented, unfocused, and lacking a carefully sequenced curriculum" (Hoyle 1989, p. 376). In order to correct this, Hoyle recommends that in the future school administrators be trained using a professional-studies model that is intellectually challenging and practically oriented. Some actions recommended include:

- strengthen admission criteria;
- integrate coursework with professional practice;
- reward professors of educational administration for clinical work; and
- encourage intuition and creativity.

Individuals interested in becoming a school administrator should write the state department of education in the state where the certificate is desired. The request generally should be addressed to the state certification office.

Benefits of School Administration

School administrators receive many benefits, including

- higher salaries than teachers;
- management responsibilities;
- opportunities for advancement in administration; and
- leadership opportunities.

School administrators receive better pay and benefits than teachers. In a recent survey of school administrators, Carter and Rosenbloom

(1989) reported that the median base salary for superintendents was $62,000 in districts with between 1,000 and 2,499 students. The median salary for teachers in the same size districts was $26,800. Table 10.6 presents salary data for superintendents and teachers in districts with differing enrollments. In 1987, the average salary of principals was $39,988, a $33,000 increase over the average principal's salary in 1958 (Doud 1989).

In addition to better salaries, administrators also receive benefits that are not available to teachers. These include housing, automobiles, extra health benefits, and college tuition for dependents (Carter and Rosenbloom 1989). Table 10.7 describes some of these benefits.

SUMMARY

This chapter focused on educational administration. The beginning section discussed the administrative hierarchy found in schools. Although differing to some degree among districts, the administration

TABLE 10.6
Salaries of Administrators and Teachers by Size of District

DISTRICT SIZE	MEDIAN SALARY SUPERINTENDENTS	MEDIAN SALARY TEACHERS
Under 1,000	$49,500	$25,000
1,000–2,499	$62,000	$26,800
2,500–4,999	$64,250	$27,500
5,000–9,999	$64,480	$24,055
10,000 +	$85,000	$28,960

Source: Carter and Rosenbloom. The Peat Marwick/AS&U compensation survey for school and university administrators. *American School and University* 61, 1989.

TABLE 10.7
Fringe Benefits for Administrators

DISTRICT SIZE	BENEFIT			
	CAR AV. $	PROF. DEV. AVG. $	PROF. ASSOC. AVG. $	RETIRE CONT. AVG. $
Under 1,000	0	344	225	2,246
1,000–2,499	3,290	970	313	3,874
2,500–4,999	2,425	612	243	2,934
5,000–9,999	3,171	806	200	3,955
10,000 +	3,117	825	150	5,364

Source: Carter and Rosenbloom. The Peat Marwick/AS&U compensation survey for school and university administrators. *American School and University* 61, 1989.

hierarchy of public schools is fairly similar. At the top is the local school board. The board has powers that have been established by state statutes. Superintendents are hired by the board to carry out board policy, and they, in turn, employ principals and other professional administrative staff to carry out the functions of the school.

The local board of education most often is an elected body of lay persons from the community. Boards have legislated, specific powers, such as building buildings, and discretionary powers, such as establishing policies that go beyond the state minimum requirements for graduation. Local boards must work closely with the superintendent, since that individual is the chief administrative school official.

Superintendents have many responsibilities, but the most important ones are to advise the board and to serve as the school district's educational leader. Superintendents are key individuals in the effectiveness of the school district and must respond to the wishes of many groups, including the board, staff, and parents. In some districts, superintendents have the assistance of other central office administrators. The number of these assistants usually is determined by the size and wealth of the school district.

At the building level, principals are the chief administrative officers. They oversee the entire operation of their particular school and are expected to perform a variety of jobs. These include instructional leader, manager, disciplinarian, facilitator of human relations, conflict manager, evaluator, and change agent. Each of these roles was discussed in the chapter.

In performing these many and varied roles, principals must consider the expectations of many groups. The superintendent and central office administrative staff, teachers, parents, students, and community members all have expectations of the principal. Principals spend their days doing a host of different jobs, and research has determined that principals too often are bogged down with paperwork and other administrative chores at the expense of the instructional leadership role. Still, there are many effective principals. For the most part, effective principals do get involved in the school's instructional program and juggle other duties in an appropriate priority.

The final section of the chapter focused on how to become a school administrator and the benefits of school administration. In most states, the prerequisite for becoming a school superintendent or principal is to be qualified or certified by the state department of education or state department of public instruction. This usually requires various degrees and a certain number of college credits in administration coursework. Salaries and fringe benefits for administrators usually surpass those for teachers. Therefore, for individuals so inclined, school administration is a rewarding vocation.

IN THE FIELD

1. Is the local board of education in the district elected or appointed? How many individuals make up the board and what are their terms?

2. Who makes up the local board of education?

3. Does the board have a set of board and district policies? If so, are they accessible to students and teachers?

4. What are included in local district policies?

5. Is there a list of duties and responsibilities for the local superintendent?

6 What other central administrative staff are there in addition to the superintendent? What are their duties?

7. Are there any assistant principals in your building? If so, what are their specific duties and responsibilities?

8. What activities of the principal suggest that he/she is an effective administrator?

9. What different roles does the principal fulfill?

10. What are some of the expectations of teachers and students of the principal?

11. How does the school principal spend a typical day?

REFERENCES

Administrative Information Report. 1984. Salary report #1: Principals and assistant principals. Reston, VA: National Association of Secondary School Principals.

Alvey, D. T., K. E. Underwood, and J. C. Fortune. 1986. Our annual look at who you are and what's got you worried. *American School Board Journal* 173(1), 23–27.

Barth, R. S. 1988. Principals, teachers, and school leadership. *Phi Delta Kappan* 69(9), 639–642.

Brieschke, P. A. 1985. Principals in schools: Insubordination in discretionary decision making. *The Educational Forum* 49(2), 157–69.

Buser, R., and V. D. Pace. 1988. Personnel evaluation: Premises, realities, and constraints. *NASSP Bulletin* 72(512), 84–87.

Campbell, R. F., L. L. Cunningham, R. O. Nystrand, and M. D. Usdan. 1980. *The Organization and Control of American Schools.* Columbus, OH: Merrill.

Carter, M., and C. Rosenbloom. 1989. Compensation survey for school and university administrators. *American School and University* 61(5), 21–25.

Cooper, L. S. 1989. The principal as instructional leader. *Principal* 68(3), 13–16.

Doremus, R. R. 1985. The superintendent as teacher. *Educational Leadership* 42(5), 82–84.

Doud, J. L. 1989. The K–8 principal in 1988. *Principal* 68(3), 6–12.

Duke, D. L. 1987. *School Leadership and Instructional Improvement.* New York: Random House.

Education vital signs, Vol. IV, 1988/1989. 1988. *American School Board Journal* 175(10), A1–A25.

Gallup, A. M., and S. M. Elam. 1988. The 20th annual Gallup poll of the public's attitudes toward the public schools. *Phi Delta Kappan* 70(1), 33–46.

Goldschmidt, S. M., and S. R. Painter. 1987–1988. Collective bargaining: A review of the literature. *Educational Research Quarterly* 12(1), 10–18.

Gorton, R. A. 1983. *School Administration and Supervision.* Dubuque, IA: William C. Brown.

Gorton, R. A. 1987. *School Leadership and Administration.* Dubuque, IA: William C. Brown.

Guthrie, J. W. and R. J. Reed. 1986. *Educational Administration and Policy.* Englewood Cliffs, NJ: Prentice-Hall.

Haefele, D. L. 1980. How to evaluate thee, teacher–Let me count the ways. *Phi Delta Kappan* 61(5), 349–52.

Hatrick, E. B., K. E. Underwood, J. C. Fortune, and K. E. Keough, 1989. Our 11th annual survey of school board members. *The American School Board Journal* 176(1), 19–24.

Howell, B. 1981. Profile of the principalship. *Educational Leadership* 38(4), 333–36.

Hoyle, J. R. 1989. Preparing the 21st century superintendents. *Phi Delta Kappan* 70(5), 376–379.

Jenkins, P. W. 1981. Building parent participation in urban schools. *Principal* 61(2), 21–23.

Levine, S. L. 1989. The principal as adult developer. *Principal* 68(3), 17–18.

Lordon, J. F. 1983. Establishing a climate for school discipline: The total perspective. *National Association of Secondary School Principals Bulletin* 67(462), 58–60.

Marsh, L. 1981. Nobody knows the principals I've seen. *Educational Leadership* 38(7), 542–43.

Mechling, K. R. 1983. Taking charge: How principals can improve school science programs. *Principal* 62(3), 16–21.

Pinero, U. C. 1982. Wanted: Strong instructional leaders. *Principal* 61(4), 16–19.

Podemski, R. S., B. J. Price, T. E. C. Smith, and G. E. Marsh, 1984. *Comprehensive Administration of Special Education.* Rockville, MD: Aspen Systems.

Pulliam J. D. 1987. *History of Education in America.* Columbus, Ohio: Merrill.

Rallis, S. 1988. Room at the top: Conditions for effective school leadership. *Phi Delta Kappan* 69(9), 643–647.

Reecer, M. 1989. If you want to lead the way, it's nice to know where you're going. *The American School Board Journal* 176(2), 19–21.

Rice, E. K. 1989. The changing principalship: A principal's perspective. *Principal* 68(3), 21–22.

Roles and Relationships: School Boards/Superintendents. 1981. Arlington, VA: American Association of School Administrators.

Sivage, C. R. 1982. Oiling the gears: How the principal helps, or hinders, change. *Principal* 61(4), 20–23.

Snyder, K. J., and R. H. Anderson. 1986. *Managing Productive Schools.* New York: Harcourt Brace Jovanovich.

Spillane, R. R. 1989. The changing principalship: A superintendent's perspective. *Principal* 68(3), 19–20.

Sullivan, R. L., and J. L. Wircenski, 1988. Clinical supervision: The role of the principal. *NASSP Bulletin* 72(510), 34–39.

Tauber, R. T. 1989 Discipline theory: Making the most of what works now. *NASSP Bulletin* 73(516), 1–4.

Wilkens, E. R. 1983. Lives of a rural principal. *Principal* 62(5), 27–29.

11

CAREERS IN EDUCATION

OBJECTIVES

After reading this chapter you will be able to

- describe the early role of teachers in American public education;
- discuss teaching as a profession;
- list characteristics of good teachers;
- discuss the status of teaching, including supply and demand, salaries, and other benefits;
- describe some of the shortcomings of teaching; and
- list educational occupations other than teaching.

OUTLINE

ADVANCE ORGANIZERS

1. What was the nature of teaching in colonial America?
2. How many teachers are currently employed in public schools?
3. What benefits do teacher organizations provide?
4. What are some characteristics of good teachers?
5. What is the supply and demand for teachers?
6. What are some potential shortcomings of teaching?
7. What other professional opportunities are there in public education?

INTRODUCTION

Many different professional opportunities exist in education, including classroom teaching, administration, and a host of support positions such as counselors, therapists, social workers, dietitians, and health personnel. Of these various positions, teaching is the one that is considered the cornerstone of education.

Teaching is a noble profession; it requires an ability to impart knowledge, provide leadership, instill values, and help prepare young individuals for the future. Teaching is definitely an awesome responsibility (Newbrough 1983). Teachers possess great power; they affect students not only during short periods of instruction in classrooms, but beyond. "The profession of the teacher is a high calling, for along with the parents, teachers more than any other group in society fashion the world they will not live to see" (Perkin 1979, p. 658).

Great teachers never die. Plato and Aristotle live because of their teaching. Teachers leave behind scores of former students who carry on with ideas, values, and abilities imparted to them (Robinson and Brower 1982).

Teachers, like education in general, have come under a great deal of criticism during the 1980s. They have been labeled lazy, incompetent, uncaring, unmotivated, and products of poor training. However, teachers do make a difference in their students (Ornstein 1984), and, if education is to continue to be the mainstay of our culture, really good, inspiring teachers must be applauded for their unselfish efforts in the face of the challenges confronting public education (Dedrick and Raschke 1984).

The jobs of teachers have been made difficult during the past thirty years by external forces. These include

1. racial desegregation, which started with the 1954 landmark court case, *Brown v. Board of Education;*

2. the panic to catch up with the Soviet Union after the launching of Sputnik in 1957;

3. criticisms in the 1960s by groups opposed to the overemphasis on traditional education;

4. new requirements imposed by the Elementary and Secondary Education Act of 1965;

5. the back-to-the-basics movement in the 1970s;

6. the role of social problem solver thrust upon the schools in the late 1970s; and

7. federal and state legislation mandating that schools provide appropriate educational programs for all children including those with disabilities, e.g., P.L. 94–142. (Dedrick and Raschke 1984)

These actions have made the teaching profession responsible for much more than merely instructing children in various subject areas. In light of these demands placed on teachers by society, the performances of teachers have been, for the most part, extremely good. However, where there is a public there are critics, and teachers have been on the receiving end of some criticism about education for the past several years. Despite the criticisms, people are still interested in becoming teachers, and veteran teachers are continuing in the profession.

People are attracted to teaching for many reasons. Some enter the teaching profession because of a great teacher they had who strongly influenced them (Kile 1987). Stated another way: "I am a teacher because of teachers" (Yerger 1983, p. 44). For another, "The major satisfaction of being a teacher lies, for me, in the knowledge that I have made a difference in the lives of children" (Freeman 1979, p. 255).

TEACHING AS A PROFESSION

Whether teaching is a profession has long been debated. Medicine, law, and other vocational areas have been considered professions since their beginning. Teaching, on the other hand, has only begun to emerge as a profession. Many people still argue that teaching is more of a craft than a true profession.

Early Status of Teaching as a Profession

Over time, the roles of teachers have changed dramatically. In colonial America, for example, the qualifications of individual teachers varied considerably. Some teachers, especially of lower schools for the masses, "were often poorly educated and possessed, at best, only a rudimentary knowledge of the basic skills of reading, writing and arithmetic. Some of them were bond-servants; others were students of the ministry or the law who kept school to support themselves until they were able to enter their preferred profession" (Gutek 1970, p. 131–32). In parochial schools, whichever church supported the school selected the teacher. The teacher's religion was considered more important than academic and teaching abilities (Gutek 1970).

The Latin grammar school had better qualified teachers. Since the role of these schools was to prepare students in the areas of Latin and Greek, teachers had to be better educated. Not until the common-school movement, however, was serious attention paid to teacher education (Gutek 1970), and, even as late as the 1860s, teachers in some locations were minimally prepared. Bullough (1982) described teachers who taught in Utah in the late 1860s. The typical teacher of the time was "female, poorly educated, religiously motivated, hard working, in need of extra income and committed to education as a vehicle for 'uplifting' young heathens" (Bullough 1982, p. 199).

Teaching during the early years of this country was not a profession at all. Rather it was a job held by individuals with various backgrounds and with various purposes. Some were individuals who taught while receiving training for more respected professions, while others were women who taught because they needed extra money. Most of the teachers in early America had no training in teaching and limited basic academic training and abilities.

Current Status of Teaching as a Profession

Today teachers make up an educated, diverse group of individuals. Approximately 2.2 million teachers are employed in public schools in the United States, and another 280,000 work in private schools (National Center for Education Statistics 1988). The number of teachers is overwhelming. Public education is the largest, single employer in the United States. The question of whether teaching is a profession still troubles individuals who choose to enter, and then remain, in the teaching vocation. Is education a profession, or is it simply a job viewed as being at the level of blue-collar labor?

Teaching, a Profession. Many education majors, and possibly beginning teachers, do not care whether teaching is classified as a profession or some other level of employment. Within the educational community, however, the issue is of vital importance. Reasons educators care about the perception of education include status, salary, and benefits. If teaching is considered a profession by the public, a certain amount of status will be associated with the position. Likewise, as a profession, teachers should be in a better position to demand higher salaries and better benefits than if teaching is simply viewed as a run-of-the-mill occupation. As a profession, educators are in better positions to seek gains for the overall quality of education.

Is teaching a profession, or should it be relegated to "semi-" professional status? While few would agree that teaching is currently accepted as a legitimate profession, its status has been changing in that direction (Ondovcsik 1988). Ornstein (1988) believes that eight different practices have facilitated this change:

1. professional practice boards;
2. teacher centers;
3. mediated entry, or inducting persons into the profession in stages;
4. staff development;
5. researcher-teacher collaboration;
6. merit pay;
7. master teachers; and
8. new alliances between education and business.

Levels of Jobs. There are basically three levels of jobs in the United States labor market: professions, semiprofessions, and nonprofessions (O'Neill 1988). Professions emerge from crafts, which use trial and error to learn knowledge. In their later stages of development, *professions* have a distinctive body of knowledge that was developed through research and analysis (Smith 1980).

One thing that must occur if teaching is to be advanced as a profession is to change the attitudes of teachers. Too often teachers consider their jobs as vocational insurance, a job they can always get if they cannot find a more suitable and financially rewarding position. This attitude does not convey professionalism. Teachers must convey to their students the professional aspects of teaching and the commitment required by teachers to improve the quality of education (O'Neill 1988). "Teaching cannot survive as a pseudo-profession . . ." (Marczely 1985, p. 703).

Another change that is necessary to promote teaching as a profession is increasing the sharing of leadership between administrators and teachers. Although an uncomfortable position for many administrators, empowering teachers to share leadership will only benefit our schools. Teachers have a great potential for leadership and are "a major untapped resource for improving U.S. schools" (Barth 1988, p. 639). Without an opportunity to share in leadership however, teachers often resort to boring, unimaginative teaching that negatively impacts the entire educational system (McNeil 1988). Empowering teachers to be involved in decision-making only increases their professionalism. "For a teacher, empowerment means—more than anything else—working in an environment in which the teacher acts and is treated as a professional" (Maeroff 1989, p. 6).

Teaching and the Labor Movement. One growing practice of teachers that has eroded the professionalism of teaching in the minds of some is the active involvement of educators in unions. The National Education Association (NEA) and American Federation of Teachers (AFT) are the largest teacher organizations and are increasingly acting similar to labor unions. Teacher unions are here for the foreseeable future (Finn 1985).

Membership in teacher organizations makes teaching one of the most unionized occupations in the United States, especially among so-called white-collar workers (Finn 1985). In 1964 the membership of the NEA and AFT combined totalled approximately 1 million. That number has more than doubled (Goldschmidt and Painter 1987–88); in 1987 the NEA had 1.8 million members and had a membership goal of 2 million by 1990 (NEA Handbook 1987).

There is nothing wrong with professional associations, one of which the NEA considers itself. Physicians and lawyers, for example, both have their associations in the American Medical Association and the American Bar Association. What primarily makes teacher organizations different from these two groups is that teacher organizations engage in collective bargaining and, at times, resort to strike actions (Goldschmidt and Painter 1987–88). Although physicians and other noted professionals have engaged in strikes, their status as professionals has not been questioned by society.

Teacher organizations do provide benefits to their members besides collective bargaining, such as

- a sense of belonging to a professional group;
- group insurance benefits;
- group liability insurance;
- cut-rate tours and excursions; and
- the enhancement of the profession.

This last benefit is one of the most beneficial for education. Through professional organizations such as the NEA and AFT, teachers and other members can exert their influence on state and federal policy as it relates to education. Unorganized teachers could not have such an impact. One way of promoting the profession is through the publication and dissemination of materials. At one time, the NEA was the largest producer of educational materials in the United States (Elam 1981).

Whether teacher organizations have promoted education as a profession or created a unionized atmosphere that makes it more difficult for the public to accept education as a profession in inconclusive. For those who believe that teachers should teach and not worry about their own personal gains, teacher organizations have obviously hurt professionalism. On the other hand, many people consider teachers well within their rights to form groups and lobby for both personal improvement and the improvement of education. For these people, militant teacher organizations have enhanced the image of education as a profession.

CHARACTERISTICS OF TEACHERS

What are teachers like? Are they mostly male or female? Do they stay in the profession long, or do they burn out and "retire" after only a brief fling at teaching? Do they have bachelor's or graduate degrees? These are only a few of the questions that could be asked about characteristics of teachers. Like most professions, individuals engaged in teaching represent a broad-based group; no one type of person enters the teaching profession.

General Characteristics

Teachers represent all types of Americans—male and female; majority and minority culture; all ages; new and experienced. A general composite of the teacher in today's public schools would be white, female,

▪ *Teaching is being more accepted as a true profession.*

35–39 years old, elementary teacher, with a bachelor's degree and 11–15 years of experience (National Center for Education Statistics 1988c). Table 11.1 summarizes characteristics of public school teachers.

Characteristics of Good Teachers

Ask various people what they feel a good teacher is and you will receive a wide range of responses. Some would likely include the following:

- Good teachers love children.
- Good teachers set proper examples for children.

TABLE 11.1
Characteristics of Public School Teachers

TEACHER CHARACTERISTIC	NUMBER	PERCENT
Sex		
Male	650,000	32.3
Female	1,362,000	67.7
Race/Ethnicity		
White, non-Hispanic	1,725,000	85.7
Minority	288,000	14.3
Age		
Under 30	329,000	16.4
30–34	287,000	14.2
35–39	460,000	22.9
40–44	321,000	15.9
45–49	232,000	11.5
50 and over	384,000	19.1
Level		
Elementary	1,326,000	65.9
Secondary	687,000	34.1
Highest Degree Earned		
Bachelor's	1,030,000	51.2
Master's/Ph.D.	963,000	47.0
Other	20,000	1.0
Years Full-Time Teaching		
Under 6	307,000	15.3
6–10	439,000	21.8
11–15	491,000	24.4
16–20	358,000	17.8
21–25	211,000	10.5
Over 25	206,000	10.2
Region		
West	387,000	19.2
North Central	488,000	24.2
Northeast	398,000	19.8
South	741,000	36.8

Source: National Center for Education Statistics. *Survey Report: Moonlighting among Public School Teachers 1988*, 1988.

- Good teachers provide knowledge to children.
- Good teachers have community-acceptable morals.
- Good teachers motivate children to learn.
- Good teachers know they are not in it for financial rewards.
- Good teachers work well with parents.
- Good teachers keep children under control.

Some people agree with some of these statements while disagreeing with others. The key is that there is no consensus about what is a good teacher; everyone has an opinion on the issue. Definitions of good teachers vary from district to district (Wise, Darling-Hammond, Berry, Berliner, Haller, Praskac, and Schlechty 1987).

In general most Americans think that good teachers are working in our public schools. Gallup and Clarke (1987) found that forty-nine percent of the sample surveyed said they would give teachers either an A or a B rating related to their performances. Another twenty-five percent graded teachers a C. Only three percent indicated that teachers would receive a failing grade. Although people disagree over what makes a good teacher, a majority of Americans surveyed by Gallup and Clarke (1987) would rate teachers either an A, B or C on their job performance.

Teachers themselves also think they are doing a good job. In the Gallup Poll of Teachers' Attitudes Toward the Public Schools, Gallup (1985) found that fifty-nine percent of the teachers surveyed felt that public school teachers made a more significant contribution to society than any other profession. Only twenty-nine percent of the general population agreed with this assessment.

A great deal of literature has been written to describe good effective teaching. Teaching has been described as an art form by several professionals (Pellicer 1984; Gage 1984). Good teaching, when viewed as an art, involves much more than providing information to students. "It requires improvisation, spontaneity, the handling of a vast array of considerations of form, style, pace, rhythm, and appropriateness in ways so complex that even computers must lose the way, just as they cannot achieve what a mother does with a 5-year-old" (Gage 1984, p. 88).

To be a good teacher, individuals must understand the many different ways students learn and that there is no single, best teaching method for all children (Wise et al. 1987). Unfortunately, some teachers feel that their primary role is information dissemination and that information can be disseminated in the same way to all students. These are not good teachers. They may provide valuable learning experiences for some students, but the learning experiences could be much more beneficial for all students if teachers simply realized that learning is different for most students. Taking this basic premise into consideration and altering styles for different students helps make good teachers.

■ *Good teachers display a number of characteristics, including the ability to provide knowledge to students.*

There are many different characteristics of good teachers. Kysilka (1988) includes

- establishing an environment conducive to learning;
- having respect for students;
- determining individual needs of students and implementing programs to meet those needs;
- encouraging questioning and thinking among students; and
- being enthusiastic about learning.

Examples of "good teachers" as perceived by students are described in some of their quotes (Delisle 1988):

- "The best teachers can be honest and can speak to the class, not at it" (a Virginia 6th grader).
- "A Good teacher can give you help when you need it and not say, 'Sit down and figure it out yourself' " (a Louisiana 5th grader).

- "I like teachers who can understand my feelings, ideas, and thoughts, and give us the right amount of help with them" (a Louisiana 5th grader).

These are not the only qualities of good teachers. Teachers also need to understand child and adolescent development and psychology, have a working knowledge of educational psychology, understand learning theory, and be able to organize classroom activities. They also need to be genuine, warm, empathetic, and caring. When teachers have a genuine affection for students, their instruction will reflect this relationship; teachers who want and expect their students to learn will be more successful than those who have lower expectations.

STATUS OF TEACHING

A great deal is happening in public education today. The entire public education structure is being attacked by critics; teacher education is being described as being inadequate and attracting inferior students to the profession, and dollars needed to support public education continue to shrink. Despite the problems found in public education, teaching is still considered an exciting and rewarding career. Hundreds of thousands of outstanding teachers provide appropriate learning experiences for children and youth; many top high-school students annually choose teaching as a career. Although under fire from many angles, teaching is still considered an excellent vocational choice.

Supply and Demand

All prospective teachers are concerned whether jobs will be available after graduation. The number of teaching jobs has declined over the past decade as public school enrollments have dropped. As the number of job opportunities have declined, fewer students have chosen to enter teacher training programs. This has resulted in a sharp reduction in the number of graduates with teaching credentials, which in turn has created teacher shortages in many different fields.

In 1971 an estimated 314,000 new teachers graduated from universities for which only 163,000 job openings existed. In 1973, undergraduate degrees in education were awarded to 194,229 students. This number declined annually to only 87,221 in 1986. Figure 11.1 summarizes this decline in undergraduate education degrees. The number of Master's degrees awarded in education also has declined, from forty percent of all Master's degrees granted in 1976 to fewer than thirty percent of the degrees granted in 1986 (National Center for Education Statistics 1988).

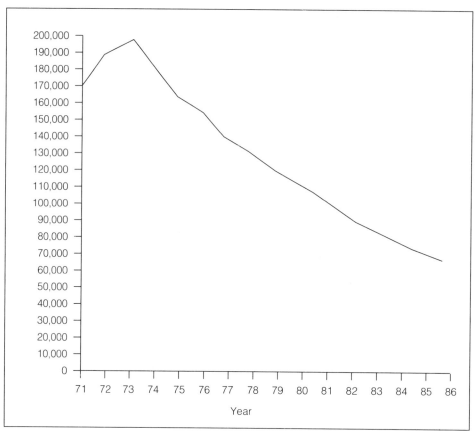

FIGURE 11.1 Bachelor's Degrees in Education, 1971–1986
Source: National center for education statistics. Survey report 1988: Moonlighting among public school teachers, *U.S. Department of Education. 1988.*

Now, some parents who live here—on the outer fringes of suburbia 45 miles up river from New Orleans—are trying to turn the image around.

A citizens' committee—led by Henrietta Millett, a caterer, and John Crose, a food inspector—is trying to find teachers for an anticipated 80 September vacancies.

In six months, the parents have persuaded local businesses and the parish (county) government to offer financial incentives to new teachers; the state ethics commission and local teachers' union to bless the idea; and the school board, usually bitterly divided, to adopt the program 11-0.

"I've lived in St. John for 48 years," Keller says. "This is the first time I've seen a mesh of community government and school system on a project."

Crose says he'd like to see about six applicants for every St. John vacancy and "then we could hire the best of the six."

Next step, Keller says: make St. John's pay scale competitive. Beginning teachers here earn $17,353; average for all teachers is $21,500. That's even lower than the Louisiana average, 45th in the USA at $22,470.

The St. John package is similar to incentive programs blossoming across the USA as school districts—even states—compete for a limited supply of good people.

"It's a seller's market. Good, qualified teachers can name the school they want to teach in," says Brian Porter of Prince George's County, Md., which pioneered a financial incentive package similar to St. John's four years ago. It includes free rent for a month, low-cost car loans, moving expenses, discounts on other services.

Government forecasters see about 50,000 teaching vacancies across the USA this fall, growing to 86,000 by 1995.

Adding to the problem: 20 percent of the 11,000 teachers responding to a recent Carnegie Foundation survey say they're unqualified to teach the classes to which they're assigned. Albert Shanker, president of the American Federation of Teachers, calls these widespread misassignments "education's dirty little secret."

In St. John Parish, Keller says 51 of 318 teachers aren't certified for their assignments.

Some solutions:

■ Alternate teacher certification, bypassing traditional teachers' colleges, exists in 38 states. It was pioneered in New Jersey five years ago.

In Georgia, anyone with a bachelor's degree in science, math or a foreign language can attend an eight-week summer institute to be certified to teach those subjects.

■ East Orange, N.J., sends recruiters to campuses like Harvard and Yale—not known for training teachers—to seek graduates for its alternate certification program.

■ Houston placed mid-winter ads in Chicago newspapers urging teachers to "leave the cold weather" for Texas. They lured 13 Chicagoans.

■ New York City schools are starting a Teacher Corps to recruit and train students at local colleges. It's similar to the way the city recruits and trains police officers.

At college job fairs, Prince George's County recruiters disdain the customary small table in a large room filled with dozens of other school districts. To promote their district, and its financial incentives for new teachers, they rent a hospitality suite with couches, soft chairs and a TV set that doubles as door prize.

"When we started all this," Porter says, "a lot of districts pooh-poohed it. Now we get reports that others are trying it, but maybe not with the audacity and pizazz we do. But you have to wave the flag if you want to be noticed."

The Prince George's plan and its imitations are similar to the effort in St. John with one big exception: The others were conceived by school officials.

In Louisiana, it was launched by Henrietta Millett on the day last fall when her daughter came home from school, read the latest newspaper story about the school board's attempts to fire the superintendent, and asked: "Mom, what's going on?"

Millett, until then not involved in local politics, replied: "I don't know, but I'm sure going to find out."

She found a long history of problems:

■ A 43-day teachers' strike in 1985, longest in Louisiana's history, produced a new,

continued

thriving teachers' union in a traditionally non-union state.

- The yearlong effort to fire the former superintendent, by a bitterly split school board, produced statewide headlines and TV coverage. The fired superintendent is suing to get his job back.

- An equally bitter dispute erupted over who should be the new superintendent. Keller, an assistant, was promoted.

- Voters recalled one board member and are attempting to oust a second.

"We're fortunate," says Alfred Donaldson, the schools' new personnel director, who's on the recruiting road with the bag full of incentives. "We're now at the bottom so we can't go anyplace but up."

Ford dealer Robert Passman moved here three years and says, "All I knew was I didn't want my kids to go to the public schools." They don't.

Passman's agency is offering the 15-percent discount on car repairs. He says he heard about the program on TV and volunteered to contribute.

"But I didn't want to limit it to just the new people coming in," he says. The offer is open to all school employees, from principals to janitors.

The citizens' committee also paused amid its recruitment campaign to let current teachers know they're appreciated. Businessmen paid $50 each for the privilege of cooking and serving a crawfish dinner for the teachers this month. They raised $1,200.

Linda Prudhomme, vice president of Landmark Land Co., offers 3 percent off its new homes and will pay closing costs and up to three points on a mortgage.

"When Louisiana upgrades education," she says, "we'll be able to make smarter decisions—including electing people who will keep this state moving forward. And we'll overcome the banana republic image."

Even as the supply of new teachers has declined, though, the number of new teaching jobs in public schools has begun to increase, as a result of increasing enrollments and of reforms which reduced student/teacher ratios. In 1988, an estimated 128,000 new teachers will be needed to fill vacancies. This number is expected to increase more than thirty-five percent, to 174,000 by 1996. The greatest demand will be in secondary education, where demand for new teachers will be eighty percent higher than in 1988. The need for elementary teachers will increase by eleven percent over the same period (National Center for Education Statistics 1988).

The ratio of new graduates and available jobs has changed dramatically in favor of graduates over the past years. In certain teaching fields, severe teacher shortages exist. For example, seventy-two percent of principals had difficulty hiring fully qualified physics teachers in the school year that ended in 1986. Other teaching fields where severe shortages exist include chemistry, computer science, mathematics, and foreign languages. Table 11.2 describes the subject areas where hiring difficulties exist, as well as the variables of school size and community type.

In addition to varying by teaching field, the need for teachers also varies by region of the country. Some areas of the country have a high teacher demand, while other areas continue to be saturated with more teachers than jobs (see table 11.3). Even in the regions with a high

TABLE 11.2
High School Principals Who Reported Having Difficulty Hiring Fully Qualified Teachers for Vacancies, by School Size, Type of Community, and Subject: School Year Ending 1986

	SIZE OF SCHOOL*			TYPE OF COMMUNITY		
Subject	Total	Small	Medium	Large	Rural	Urban	Suburban
	Percent of principals						
Physics	72	73	72	67	77	67	65
Chemistry	63	64	64	56	69	60	52
Computer science	62	65	62	47	70	59	48
Mathematics	57	61	52	47	67	52	40
Foreign language	52	55	60	31	57	46	49
Biology/life science	38	44	33	18	50	33	13
Physical science	38	43	30	28	48	26	24
Earth/space science	38	43	30	27	49	30	14
Special education	37	41	31	31	48	29	16
General science	27	35	11	15	38	16	10
Social studies	6	5	10	6	7	8	4

*Small = fewer than 800 students
Medium = 800–1,400 students
Large = more than 1,400 students

NOTE: Schools that indicated "No vacancies/does not apply" for a particular subject were not included in the analysis for that subject. High school is defined as any school containing at least one of grades 10 through 12.

SOURCE: Iris R. Weiss, *Report of the 1985–86 National Survey of Science and Mathematics Education*, Research Triangle Institute, 1987; and personal communication with the author. From National Center for Education Statistics. *Condition of Education.* 1988.

teacher demand, job availabilities fluctuate. For example, in a state with an overall teacher surplus, rural areas may still reflect a high demand for certain teaching areas.

Small schools have a particular problem securing teachers for some disciplines. In 1946 the United States had more than one hundred thousand districts; this number now stands at approximately sixteen thousand. Still, small districts make up the bulk of school units. Eighty percent of all students in the United States attend schools in districts with fewer than twenty-five hundred students while fifty-five percent are enrolled in districts with fewer than one thousand students (Digest of Education Statistics 1988).

These small districts have major problems with teacher shortages. Smaller districts have a higher turnover rate than larger districts, get fewer applicants for vacant jobs, get no fully qualified applicants for jobs such as science and math, and have a high percentage of teachers who were born and raised in the community (Dunathan 1980). The problem created by teacher shortages nationwide is thus compounded for small districts.

TABLE 11.3
Teacher Supply/Demand by Field and Region

REGION FIELD	ALASKA	HAWAII	1	2	3	4	5	6
Agriculture	3.00	3.00	3.50	2.50	2.67	3.33	3.67	3.00
Art	2.00	2.00	1.60	1.29	1.60	2.43	3.13	2.00
Bilingual Ed.	3.00	4.00	4.50	4.14	3.75	4.25	4.29	4.67
Business	3.00	3.00	2.80	3.50	3.33	3.29	3.00	3.25
Computer Programming	3.00	—	4.40	4.50	4.00	4.17	4.50	4.75
Counselor-Elem.	2.00	4.00	4.50	2.43	3.10	3.67	2.86	2.50
Counselor-Sec.	4.00	4.00	4.50	2.57	3.10	3.83	2.71	2.50
Data Processing	3.00	3.00	4.60	4.33	4.00	4.20	4.20	4.50
Driver Ed.	3.00	3.00	3.20	2.00	3.00	2.20	2.57	2.67
Elem.-Primary	3.00	2.00	2.40	3.29	2.67	2.00	3.25	3.00
Elem.-Intermediate	3.00	2.00	2.40	3.29	2.67	2.00	3.25	2.60
English	4.00	4.00	3.10	3.14	2.79	3.29	3.75	3.25
Health Education	2.00	2.00	1.40	1.50	2.80	2.67	2.13	1.33
Home Economics	4.00	3.00	3.33	4.00	3.13	2.60	2.50	2.50
Industrial Arts	3.00	4.00	3.67	3.80	2.88	3.00	4.00	4.00
Journalism	3.00	3.00	1.75	3.33	3.33	3.50	2.63	1.75
Language, Mod.-French	3.00	3.00	3.25	2.57	3.50	3.57	3.57	4.50
Language, Mod.-German	3.00	3.00	3.00	2.43	3.60	3.57	3.14	4.00
Language, Mod.-Spanish	3.00	3.00	3.60	2.71	3.40	3.43	3.75	5.00
Library Science	4.00	4.00	3.00	3.00	3.50	3.86	4.00	3.75
Math	3.00	4.00	4.80	4.86	4.29	4.43	5.00	4.60
Music-Instrumental	5.00	3.00	4.20	3.29	3.50	3.71	3.38	3.00
Music-Vocal	4.00	2.00	4.00	2.71	3.50	3.14	4.57	2.50
Physical Education	2.00	2.00	1.20	1.67	1.42	1.33	1.88	2.00
Psychologist (school)	4.00	—	4.00	3.50	3.38	4.20	3.60	3.75
Science-Biology	3.00	4.00	3.20	3.29	3.25	3.29	3.88	3.80
Science-Chemistry	4.00	4.00	4.20	4.43	4.08	4.14	4.63	4.60
Science-Earth	2.00	4.00	3.60	3.43	3.40	3.50	4.00	4.00
Science General	3.00	4.00	3.40	3.29	3.50	3.29	3.83	3.75
Science-Physics	4.00	4.00	4.40	4.43	4.42	4.71	4.43	4.50
Social Science	3.00	2.00	1.40	2.00	2.40	2.00	2.57	1.75
Social Worker (school)	—	—	2.67	2.67	3.50	3.00	2.40	1.00
Speech	2.00	2.00	2.20	2.80	3.13	2.86	2.75	2.33
Special-ED/PSA	4.00	3.00	4.40	4.20	4.60	4.00	4.14	4.20
Special-Gifted	5.00	3.00	3.25	3.67	4.13	4.50	4.00	4.33
Special-LD	4.00	4.00	3.60	4.00	4.60	4.14	3.63	4.40
Special-MR	4.00	3.00	3.80	4.00	4.60	3.43	3.57	4.00
Special-Multi. Hand.	4.00	4.00	4.00	4.00	4.60	4.17	4.00	4.00
Special-Reading	4.00	3.00	3.80	3.14	3.75	3.17	3.71	3.75
Speech Path./Audio.	3.00	—	3.38	3.67	4.67	4.00	4.20	4.50
COMPOSITE	3.20	3.17	3.34	3.24	3.42	3.40	3.50	3.49

Regions are coded as follows: Alaska, Hawaii, 1–Northwest, 2–West, 3–Rocky Mountain, 4–Great Plains/Midwest, 5–South Central, 6–Southeast, 7–Great Lakes, 8–Middle Atlantic, 9–Northeast. Alaska and Hawaii are not included in the Continental United States totals.

5 = Considerable Shortage, 4 = Some Shortage, 3 = Balanced, 2 = Some Surplus, 1 = Considerable Surplus
From October, 1984 survey of Teacher Placement Officers, James N. Akin, Kansas State University
Reprinted with permission. J. N. Atkin, 1986, 21–22.

TABLE 11.3— *Continued*
Teacher Supply/Demand by Field and Region

7	8	9	CONTINENTAL UNITED STATES							
			1985	1984	1983	1982	1981	1980	1976	
3.50	2.66	—	3.11	3.44	4.02	4.36	4.46	4.73	4.06	Ag.
1.83	2.00	2.00	2.04	1.89	1.92	1.84	2.00	2.45	2.14	Art
4.75	3.50	3.50	4.12	4.04	3.83	4.13	4.10	4.21	—	Bil. Ed.
3.50	4.00	3.00	3.32	3.11	3.24	3.47	3.50	3.80	3.10	Bus.
4.67	4.29	4.00	4.37	4.34	—	—	—	—	—	Comp. Prog.
3.67	2.50	2.83	3.05	2.80	3.03	2.72	3.05	3.38	3.15	Couns.-El.
4.00	2.50	2.67	3.08	2.67	2.83	2.79	3.13	3.76	2.69	Couns.-Sec.
4.33	4.25	4.00	4.30	4.18	4.36	3.86	4.35	—	—	Data Proc.
2.80	2.50	2.67	2.65	2.61	2.94	2.77	2.87	2.98	2.44	Dr. Ed.
1.83	2.50	2.00	2.57	2.13	2.11	2.02	2.24	2.77	2.78	El.-Prim.
2.33	2.50	1.50	2.53	2.20	2.11	2.26	2.56	2.84	1.90	El.-Inter.
3.33	2.88	2.60	3.14	3.13	2.90	3.21	3.37	3.51	2.05	English
2.00	2.25	2.00	2.08	1.90	1.76	1.90	2.24	2.17	2.27	Health Ed.
2.67	2.67	2.33	2.79	2.43	2.44	2.43	2.54	2.85	2.62	Home Ec.
3.00	4.33	4.25	3.65	3.50	3.96	4.36	4.72	4.77	4.22	Ind. Arts
3.33	2.80	2.00	2.74	2.60	2.63	2.61	2.77	2.98	2.86	Journ.
4.00	3.00	2.20	3.31	3.00	2.59	2.49	2.58	2.68	2.15	French
3.33	3.00	2.20	3.11	3.08	2.51	2.48	2.58	2.70	2.03	German
4.17	3.13	2.40	3.43	3.18	2.77	2.68	2.95	3.34	2.47	Spanish
3.50	3.00	3.00	3.49	3.30	3.09	3.12	3.31	3.58	—	Libr. Sci.
5.00	4.88	4.50	4.71	4.78	4.75	4.81	4.79	4.80	3.86	Math
3.50	2.17	2.83	3.29	3.25	2.97	3.28	3.33	3.65	3.03	Instr.
3.33	2.17	2.50	3.19	3.00	2.89	2.95	3.06	3.32	3.00	Vocal
2.00	2.38	1.60	1.75	1.61	1.54	1.72	1.80	1.82	1.74	P.E.
3.83	3.67	3.00	3.65	2.98	3.19	3.56	3.70	3.87	3.09	Psych.
3.67	3.75	4.20	3.58	3.40	4.10	3.66	3.89	3.50	2.97	Biol.
4.67	4.50	4.50	4.42	4.25	4.30	3.13	4.42	4.18	3.72	Chem.
3.50	4.13	4.60	3.79	3.70	3.80	3.89	4.08	3.64	3.44	Earth
3.83	3.88	4.20	3.65	3.65	—	—	4.31	4.10	—	General
4.83	4.63	4.80	4.57	4.45	4.46	4.41	4.56	4.28	4.04	Physics
2.17	2.14	2.60	2.17	1.91	1.75	2.11	2.05	1.98	1.51	Soc. Sci.
3.40	2.75	3.00	2.81	2.33	2.27	2.34	—	—	—	Soc. Wrk.
3.17	3.29	3.67	2.91	2.70	2.51	2.76	2.65	2.50	2.46	Speech
3.83	4.00	2.80	4.02	3.84	4.08	3.98	4.22	4.36	3.42	ED/PSA
4.25	3.50	3.00	3.85	3.74	3.80	3.81	4.10	4.33	3.85	Gifted
4.83	4.00	2.50	3.95	3.98	4.09	4.20	4.47	4.48	4.00	LD
3.33	4.33	3.00	3.76	3.55	3.71	3.84	4.14	4.23	2.87	MR
3.60	4.00	3.00	3.94	3.77	3.82	3.93	4.13	3.87	—	MH
3.50	3.50	2.50	3.39	3.48	3.39	3.73	4.21	2.23	3.96	Reading
4.33	3.83	3.75	4.01	3.83	3.62	3.95	4.27	4.17	3.68	Sp./Aud.
3.52	3.31	2.97	3.36	3.19	3.14	3.20	3.39	—	—	COMP.

Salaries

An obvious area of interest for future teachers is the salaries teachers earn. The 1986 Gallup Poll of the Public's Attitudes Toward the Public Schools revealed that forty-nine percent of the respondents thought that teachers' salaries were too low (Gallup 1986). The attitude poll of teachers indicated that ninety percent of all teachers surveyed felt that salaries were too low (Gallup 1985). While historically the pay for teachers has been low in comparison to other college-degree areas, the salaries paid to teachers have improved. One reason for this improvement was the reform reports of the late 1970s and early 1980s which said that better teachers need to be attracted to the classrooms and good teachers need to be convinced to stay in the classrooms.

HIGHLIGHT

MISSISSIPPI STUDENTS DO BETTER ON TESTS

JACKSON, Miss. (AP)—Mississippi teachers' salaries are off the bottom thanks to four years of big raises, and educators in the nation's poorest state are starting to see dividends: higher scores on national achievement tests.

But state education officials say the efforts that moved teacher pay from 50th to 45th in the United States must continue.

"We have to make a bold commitment to our children that we don't want them to be 50th," said Olon Ray, education assistant to Gov. Ray Mabus. "An important part of that is having a good teacher in every classroom."

The 1988–89 national average teacher salary was $29,567. The State Department of Education estimates the average in Mississippi at $22,677. The 1988–89 average in the Southeastern states was $24,863.

Education leaders hope the prospect of fatter paychecks will attract better teachers and help enhance student performance.

A U.S. Department of Education report released May 3 showed that Mississippi students scored worst among those in 28 states where the American College Testing Program, or ACT, is the predominant college entrance examination.

However, state officials noted that performance had improved with the average Mississippi ACT score up 0.7 point to 16.2 in 1988 over 1987. Nationwide, the average score was up 0.1 point to 18.8, and declines were shown in 11 states. The test is scored on a scale of 1 to 36.

Officials credit the 1982 Education Reform Act, which made sweeping changes in Mississippi's education system, for the improvements and Mabus has promised to propose an "Education Reform II" package this year.

Mabus made education improvements in general, and teacher salaries specifically, a cornerstone of his successful 1987 campaign.

He pushed through the legislature's 1988 session a teacher pay raise averaging $3,800 over two years. The second half takes effect in July.

That money, added to $3,000 in 1986 and $2,400 in 1987, helped move Mississippi teacher salaries from next to last place to 45th among the 50 states and the District of Columbia as of March 16, state education officials said. They said Monday that, based on

continued

INTRODUCTION TO EDUCATION

National Education Association figures, Mississippi now is followed by Louisiana, North Dakota, Oklahoma, West Virginia, Arkansas and South Dakota.

"Teacher pay is the key issue to being able to both recruit and retain good people into the classroom," Ray said.

Mabus wanted in 1988 to raise state teacher salaries to what was then the Southeastern average. But the Mississippi Association of Educators, the state's largest teacher organization, wants salaries to reach the national average by 1995.

Dr. Joe Ross of Vicksburg, chairman of the state Board of Education, said Mississippi has made progress but he believes the state should continue pressing toward the Southeastern average.

"There's no question but that we've made great strides in the past couple of years, but everybody else keeps going up, too," Ross said.

"I think the fact is that nobody who went into education ever went in with the idea that they could get rich," state Education Superintendent Richard Boyd said. "It was a field where people thought they could do some good for humanity. But it makes it more attractive if they know that they can make a decent living."

Ross said students entering college would look more favorably at teaching if they knew they could make a reasonable living.

"A lot of people like to talk about education being a calling," said Peggy Peterson, president of the 13,000-member MAE. "Yes, you have to be dedicated, but you can't live on dedication and you can't live on chalk dust."

Source: *The Birmingham News*, June 6, 1989.

Over the ten-year period from 1976–1977 to 1986–1987, salaries for teachers doubled from $13,354 to $26,704 (National Center for Education Statistics 1988). Table 11.4 reflects the growth of teachers' salaries over the past twenty-five years. The most current data on salaries (Carter and Rosenbloom 1989) indicate that the median base salary is $25,000 for teachers in districts with fewer than 10,000 students; the median is $28,960 for teachers in larger districts.

Teachers' salaries generally rise based on degree and number of years of experience. A teacher with a bachelor's degree and no experience would start at the bottom of the district's salary schedule. That teacher would move up the schedule with step increases each year, and would possibly move over on the schedule if additional hours and/or degrees are earned (see table 11.5).

Other Benefits

In addition to salaries, teachers normally receive a package of additional benefits provided by the school district. Normally these benefits include (Carter and Rosenbloom 1989):

- participation in a teacher retirement plan;
- health and dental insurance;
- disability insurance and sick leave;
- professional liability insurance and personal days;

TABLE 11.4
Estimated Average Annual Salary of Teachers in Public Elementary and Secondary Schools: Selected School Years Ending 1960-1987

YEAR	ALL TEACHERS	ELEMENTARY TEACHERS	SECONDARY TEACHERS
1960	$4,995	$4,815	$5,276
1962	5,515	5,340	5,775
1964	5,995	5,805	6,266
1966	6,485	6,279	6,761
1968	7,423	7,208	7,692
1970	8,635	8,412	8,891
1971	9,267	9,021	9,568
1972	9,705	9,424	10,031
1973	10,176	9,893	10,507
1974	10,778	10,507	11,077
1975	11,690	11,334	12,000
1976	12,600	12,280	12,937
1977	13,354	12,989	13,776
1978	14,298	13,845	14,603
1979	15,032	14,681	15,450
1980	15,970	15,569	16,459
1981	17,644	17,230	18,142
1982	19,274	18,853	19,805
1983	20,693	20,226	21,288
1984	21,917	21,456	22,554
1985	23,595	23,185	24,197
1986	25,206	24,667	25,842
1987	26,704	26,141	27,351

*Based on the Consumer Price Index, prepared by the Bureau of Labor Statistics, U.S. Department of Labor, and adjusted to a school-year basis.

NOTE: Data for some recent years have been revised from previously published figures.

SOURCE: National Education Association, *Estimates of School Statistics*, various years, copyrighted from National Center for Education Statistics. *The Condition of Education 1988*, 1988.

- professional development; and
- professional association membership.

The exact benefit package will differ among school districts. In some districts, teacher associations actually bargain for certain benefits. In other districts, teacher bargaining is limited, and the school administration and school board determine the benefits package.

SHORTCOMINGS IN TEACHING

Teaching is an excellent profession. It is hard to convince good teachers who enjoy their positions that they should be doing something different. Dedicated, *career* teachers are likely to stay in the profession for their entire working lifetime (Turner 1987). However, the teaching profession does have pitfalls. Some of these include burnout, low job status, low salaries, and some of the results from the current reform movement.

TABLE 11.5
Sample Salary Schedule

STEP	YEARS OF EXPERIENCE	SALARY
B/0	1	18,300
B/1	2	18,300
B/2	3	18,300
B/3	4	18,300
M/0	1	18,300
B/4	5	18,300
M/1	2	18,300
M/2	3	18,300
B/5	6	18,300
B/3	4	18,303
B/6	7	19,000
M/4	5	19,000
B/7	8	19,615
M/5	6	19,745
B/8	8	20,380
M/6	7	20,562
B/9	10	21,228
M/7	8	21,500
B/10	11	22,138
M/8	7	22,320
B/10+	12	23,083
M/9	10	23,251
B/11	13	23,551
B/11+	14	24,200
M/10	9	24,211
B/12	15–16–17	24,497
B/12+	18–19	25,039
M/10	12	25,181
B/13	20–21	25,493
M/11	13	25,715
B/13+	22–23	26,095
M/11+	14	26,195
B/14	24+	26,580
M/12	15–16–17	26,668
M/12+	18–19	27,124
M/13	20–21	27,740
M/13+	22–23	28,216
M/14	24+	28,785

B/ = Bachelor's Degree/Step
M/ = Master's Degree/Step

Burnout

Burnout can be defined as losing the edge, losing the desire to be the best, losing the ability to reap rewards. Teachers can and do burn out. Many excellent teachers enter the profession with enthusiasm only to retire to some other job in a few years. The number of teachers who experience job burnout is growing. In 1962 more than twenty-five percent of all teachers in the United States had twenty or more years of experience. In 1976 this number had been reduced by one-half (Walsh 1979).

The causes of teacher burnout include physical assaults, harassment by the administration, paperwork, and isolation. Pressures can result in high absenteeism, alcohol abuse, and ultimately leaving the profession (Walsh 1979). These factors occur even though teaching has many advantages. Salaries, although low, are improving; working days are short; job security is high in districts where tenure is awarded; vacations are long and frequent; and good fringe benefits are provided (Bardo 1979).

Teachers must be aware that they are vulnerable to burnout. They need to be aware of the characteristics that foreshadow the beginnings of burnout and be prepared to deal with them before getting too despaired. Although school administrators are not ultimately responsible, they should be cognizant of the burnout problem and initiate steps to keep good teachers from leaving the profession.

While more money may not be available to entice teachers to stay in teaching, administrators can do several things to reduce the chances of burnout among their teachers. These include:

- Provide rewards other than financial, such as travel money to professional conferences.
- Reduce class sizes. Although this may not be possible on a permanent basis, teachers could receive lower student/teacher ratios on a rotating basis.
- Rotate unpopular classes among all teachers.
- Reduce paperwork to a bare minimum.
- Reduce extra duties, such as lunchroom, hall monitors, and playground monitors. While administrators must staff these roles, they could use aids and other staff (depending on state law).
- Provide opportunities for good in-service training that is developed with teacher input.

Low Job Status

Teachers often are looked upon by the public as unprofessionals who are incapable of earning a living in any other vocation. In the Gallup Poll of Teachers' Attitudes Toward the Public Schools (Gallup 1985), only one percent of the teachers surveyed felt that teaching was regarded as the highest status profession in the community. Although nineteen percent of the general public rated the teaching profession as highest in the community, this figure still reflects a fairly low status. The majority of the general public still does not consider teaching a profession (Cain 1987).

■ *Teachers must be aware of burnout and its characteristics.*

One reason for the low status of teaching is that some still consider it a job for women. "The myth remains that teaching is almost always a second income and that the majority of teachers are female and are tied to their location by their husband's (better paying) job" (Ondovcsik 1988, p. 46). Until these kinds of misperceptions are corrected, teaching will be thought of as a low-status vocational endeavor, and the professionalization of the field will be limited.

Job status is an intangible; it is something that is difficult to improve. However, it is a real issue for teachers. Individuals in any profession like to feel that their jobs are viewed as important and with a certain amount of prestige. That teachers and the general public have low opinions of teaching can only add to teacher burnout.

Low Salaries

The problems of teachers' salaries already have been discussed. Male teachers, who are expected to be the major income earners in the majority of American families, have a difficult time justifying teaching when they could make more money in many other jobs. Likewise, women teachers, as a result of the equal-pay/equal-opportunity movement for women, could earn substantially more money in many other vocations.

The reform movements of the 1970s and 1980s provided some improvement in salaries for teachers. Still, a large gap exists between what teachers earn and what individuals in many other professions earn. While the gap may be shrinking, it will take many years to improve teachers' salaries to a level that can attract and hold many individuals who could make major contributions to education.

Actions from Reform Movements

The educational reforms that were initiated in the late 1970s and early 1980s were viewed by most teachers as very positive. Better pay for teachers, higher standards for students, and a stronger commitment from states for education were all needed. However, several suggested actions from these reform proposals were received negatively by teachers.

Merit Pay. Many of the reform reports suggested that teachers be paid using a merit-pay system, paying teachers not merely on years of experience and levels of training. This appears to be an excellent proposal. Certainly, good teachers who go the extra mile should be rewarded. The problem for many teachers is not the concept but how the concept will be implemented.

Many teachers view merit pay as a means for administrators to reward their pets while punishing other teachers. Some teachers are concerned that merit-pay increases will be given to teachers based on criteria that have little to do with effective teaching (Ornstein 1988). Since the products of effective teaching are difficult to identify and measure, basing teachers' pay raises on merit would be difficult.

Despite the many concerns about merit-pay plans, the movement appears to be gaining momentum. Illinois, New York, and Ohio are considering plans to implement state-funded merit programs. Other states, namely California, Tennessee, North Carolina, Kentucky, and Pennsylvania, have adopted the career ladder plan (Ornstein 1988). The career ladder concept provides incentives for teachers to improve themselves at their own pace (Engelking and Samuelson 1986).

Teacher Testing. Some of the reform reports indicated that teachers should be tested with incompetent teachers being weeded out. Again, the idea is sound. The problem arises when deciding how to measure competent teaching. Paper-and-pencil tests are unlikely to ascertain effective instruction. While some would agree that new teachers should be tested to confirm their cognitive abilities, the testing of veteran teachers has met with stiff opposition. Regardless of the controversy, many states have adopted plans to assess skill levels of teachers. Thirty-six states currently use certification tests and twenty-three states evaluate professional skills with tests (Eissenberg and Rudner 1988).

Despite the negatives in the teaching profession, prospective teachers should not change their goals to be teachers. Teaching is a profession that gives life not only to the students in classrooms, but also to the teachers who teach them and to society in the future. While not perfect, teaching enables individuals to make their mark and help prepare future leaders and citizens of the world. Teachers do make a difference.

OTHER EDUCATION PROFESSIONS

In addition to teaching, education offers many other professional opportunities, including administration, counseling, social work, school health, and support personnel. While these positions all require professional training in Colleges of Education, major differences exist in the training curricula, job expectations, and job benefits.

Educational Administration

All schools have status leaders called administrators. These include superintendents and assistant superintendents in the central administration, building principals and assistant principals, and supervisors. Chapter ten discussed administration as a career.

School Counseling

School counselors are employed and active in most secondary schools, and there are more counselors in elementary schools than ever before (Humes and Hohenshil 1987). Most states require specific certification to be a school counselor. Most often this encompasses graduate training beyond an undergraduate degree in education. Most states also require that school counselors have some classroom teaching experience.

The roles of school counselors vary from school to school. However, in general they are available to provide to students counseling, assessment of educational and psychological needs, scheduling, and career guidance (Humes and Hohenshil 1988).

Social Work

Although not as common as school counselors, school social workers are found in many districts, especially in larger schools. To become a school social worker, individuals must possess training in social work. Most states do not have separate social-work certification. Licensure by professional associations is usually the primary eligibility criterion.

School social workers act as a liaison between the school and the family. In situations where students have problems, such as having disabilities, being victims of child abuse, or being delinquent, school social workers attempt to alleviate these problems by working with the parents, child, and various social agencies. Currently a very important role for social workers is with special education students (Humes and Hohenshil 1988).

School Health

Most school districts employ certain health personnel. Primarily, these are school nurses. School nurses in most states require no additional certification, licensure, or training than for any regular nursing position. This means that school nurses must successfully complete approved nursing programs and receive professional licensure.

School nurses perform a multitude of duties, including vision and hearing screening, information dissemination, and, probably the most important, administering to the health needs of students (Collis and Dukes 1989). Although not regarded as the top of the career ladder for nurses, school nurses do have several advantages over nurses in other settings, including shorter hours, long vacations, and less stressful activities.

Other Professional Support Personnel

Schools often employ many individuals for support roles within the school environment. These include physical and occupational therapists for physically handicapped students, school psychologists for counseling and assessment activities, and speech therapists for speech-impaired children. All these individuals are vitally important for the day-to-day functioning of the school. Although often serving in less visible roles than teachers and administrators, these support staff are critical to the success of the school.

TEACHING: SUMMATION

Teaching is the critical profession in the American education system. Teachers are in daily contact with students and lead them into learning activities. They identify students with special needs, individualize instruction as much as possible for all students, act as counselors, and frequently fill the role of parent-on-the-scene.

Without teachers, public education in the United States would not have achieved its applauded status around the world. Although critics like to say that American public schools, their teachers, and their students are substandard compared with some other industrialized nations, the public education system in the United States is very sound. A major reason for this is the quality and dedication of its teachers.

Teachers have to be dedicated. They have to overlook the low status the profession has in some circles, the low pay, the stress, and the criticisms voiced daily by some parents and others. For the most part, schools are doing an excellent job, and teachers should get the credit. The dedication of teachers is exemplified by the Educator's Oath, which is taken by new graduates from the teacher education program at Michigan State University. The oath is as follows:

> I hereby affirm my dedication to the profession of education. With this affirmation I embrace the obligations of professional educators to improve the general welfare, to advance human understanding and competence, and to bring honor to the endeavors of teaching and learning. I accept these obligations for myself and will be vigilant and responsible in supporting their acceptance by my colleagues.
>
> I will always be mindful of my responsibility to increase the intelligence of students through the disciplined pursuit of knowledge. I will be steadfast in this commitment, even when weary and tempted to abdicate such responsibility or blame failure on obstacles that make the task difficult. I will be persistent in my commitment to foster respect for a life of learning and respect for all students.
>
> To perform faithfully these professional duties, I promise to work always to better understand my content, my instructional practice, and the students who come under my tutelage. I promise to seek and support policies that promote quality in teaching and learning and to provide all engaged in education the opportunity to achieve excellence. I promise to emulate personally the qualities I wish to foster, and to hold and forever honor a democratic way of life that cannot exist without disciplined, cultivated, and free minds.
>
> I recognize that at times my endeavors will offend privilege and status, that I will be opposed by bias and defenders of inequality, and that I will have to confront arguments that seek to discourage my efforts and diminish my hope. But I will remain faithful to the belief that these endeavors and the pursuit of these goals make me worthy of my profession, and my profession worthy of a free people.
>
> In the presence of this gathering, I bind myself to this oath (Lanier and Cusick 1985, p. 712).

SUMMARY

This chapter has dealt with careers in education. The primary focus was on teaching as a career. The teaching profession has come under a great deal of pressure and attack during recent years. Some of the reasons include desegregation, education for handicapped students, accountability, and the reform movements of the 1970s and 1980s.

Teaching—is it a profession or simply a vocation? This issue was discussed in detail, emphasizing the historical place of teaching and the current professional status of teaching. The role played by teacher organizations in the perception of teaching as a profession was also discussed.

Another topic included was the status of teaching. The demand for teachers dropped significantly during the 1970s and resulted in fewer college students majoring in education. This in turn created a situation of teacher shortages in many different fields and several regions of the country, particularly in rural areas.

The final section of the chapter dealt with shortcomings in the teaching profession. Specific items discussed were teacher burnout, low job status, low salaries, and suggested reforms from the reform movement. Also discussed were other career options in education, including administration, school health, counseling, and support activities. In conclusion, teachers are critical in the public education system in the United States, teaching is a rewarding profession, and many of the criticisms of the educational system are unfounded.

IN THE FIELD

1. What do teachers in your school think make their jobs the most difficult?

2. What intangible benefits do teachers in your school feel they receive?

3. Do teachers consider themselves professionals or simply workers? Why do they feel this way?

4. Are the teachers organized into a teachers' organization? If so, is the organization associated with either the NEA or AFT? If not, how is it organized?

5. What do teachers think make good teachers?

6. What actions did you observe that you consider good teaching practices?

7. Does the district have difficulty in hiring teachers who are fully certified in all areas? If so, what specialty areas?

8. What is the current salary schedule for the district? Has the schedule changed much during the past five years?

9. Is teacher testing required in your state? If so, what is the nature of the test that is required? What are the attitudes of teachers in the district concerning teacher testing?

10. What staff are employed in the district/school other than teachers and administrators?

REFERENCES

Bardo, P. 1979. The pain of teacher burnout: A case history. *Phi Delta Kappan* 61(4), 252–53.

Barth, R. S. 1988. Principals, teachers, and school leadership. *Phi Delta Kappan* 69(9), 639–642.

Bullough, R. V., Jr. 1982. Teachers and teaching in the nineteenth century: St. George, Utah. *Journal of Curriculum Theorizing* 4(2), 199–206.

Cain, J. 1987. I'm teaching as fast as I can. *Kappa Delta Pi Record* 23(3), 86–88.

Carter, M., and C. Rosenbloom, 1989. Compensation survey for school and university administrators. *American School and University* (5) 21–25.

Collis, J. L., and C. A. Dukes. 1989. Toward some principles of school nursing. *Journal of School Health* 59(3), 109–111.

Dedrick, C., and D. Raschke. 1984. Plaudits for educators. *Educational Forum* 48(4), 489–95.

Delisle, J. R. 1988. Test your teaching style. *Learning* 16(3), 14–16.

Digest of Education Statistics. 1988. Washington, DC: U.S. Department of Education.

Dunathan, A. T. 1980. Teacher shortage: Big problems for small schools. *Phi Delta Kappan* 62(3), 205–206.

Eissenberg, T. E., and L. M. Rudner. 1988. State testing of teachers: A summary. *Journal of Teacher Education* 39(4), 21–22.

Elam, S. M. 1981. The National Education Association: Political powerhouse or paper tiger? *Phi Delta Kappan* 63(3), 169–74.

Engelking, J. R., and E. V. Samuelson. 1986. Career ladders. *The Clearing House* 60(3), 137–140.

Finn, C. E., Jr. 1985. Teacher unions and school quality: Potential allies or inevitable foes? *Phi Delta Kappan* 66(5), 331–37.

Freeman, J. 1979. The joy of teaching: Another case history. *Phi Delta Kappan* 61(4), 254–56.

Gage, N. L. 1984. What do we know about teaching effectiveness? *Phi Delta Kappan* 66(2), 87–93.

Gallup, A. M. 1986. The 18th annual Gallup poll of the public's attitudes toward the public schools. *Phi Delta Kappan* 68(1), 43–57.

Gallup, A. 1985. The Gallup poll of teachers' attitudes toward public schools part 2. *Phi Delta Kappan* 66(5), 323–30.

Gallup, A. M., and D. L. Clark. 1987. The 19th annual Gallup poll of the public's attitudes toward the public schools. *Phi Delta Kappan* 69(1), 17–30.

Goldschmidt, S. M., and S. R. Painter. 1987–1988. Collective bargaining: A review of the literature. *Educational Research Quarterly* 12(1), 10–18.

Gutek, G. 1970. *An Historical Introduction to American Education*. New York: Thomas Y. Crowell.

Humes, C. W., and T. H. Hohenshil. 1987. Elementary counselors, school social workers, school psychologists: Who does what? *Elementary School Guidance and Counseling* 22(1), 37–45.

Kysilka, M. L. 1988. Partnerships in education: Pathways to excellence. *Kappa Delta Pi Record* 24(3), 67–71.

Lanier, J., and P. Cusick. 1985. An oath for professional educators. *Phi Delta Kappan* 66(10), 711–12.

McNeil, L. M. 1988. Contradictions of control, part 1: Administrators and teachers. *Phi Delta Kappan* 69(6), 333–339.

Maeroff, G. I. 1989. The principles of teacher enpowerment. *NASSP Bulletin* 169, 6–9.

Marczely, B. 1985. Teacher education: A view from the front lines. *Phi Delta Kappan* 66(10), 702–706.

National Center for Education Statistics. 1988. *Survey report: Moonlighting among public school teachers 1988*. Washington DC: U.S. Department of Education.

National Center for Education Statistics. 1988. *The Condition of Education 1988*. Washington, DC: U.S. Department of Education.

NEA Handbook 1988. Washington, DC: National Education Association.

Ondovcsik, M. 1988. Is the teaching profession growing? *Learning* 16(9), 46–50.

O'Neill, G. P. 1988. Teaching as a profession: Redefining our concepts. *Action in Teacher Education* 10(2), 5–10.

Ornstein, A. C. 1988. The changing status of the teaching profession. *Urban Education* 23(3), 261–279.

Ornstein, A. C. 1984. A difference teachers make: How much? *Educational Forum* 49(1), 109–17.

Pellicer, L. O. 1984. Effective teaching: Science or magic? *The Clearing House* 58(2), 53–56.

Perkin, J. R. C. 1979. The teacher as the key. *Phi Delta Kappan* 60(9), 655–58.

Robinson, T. E., and W. A. Brower. 1982. Teachers and their survivors. *Phi Delta Kappan* 63(10), 722+.

Smith, B. O. 1980. Research bases for teacher education. *Phi Delta Kappan* 66(10), 685–90.

Turner, R. R. 1987. To teach or not to teach. *Learning* 16(3), 57–60.

Yerger, C. W. 1983. Why I teach. *English Journal* 72(3), 43–44.

Walsh, D. 1979. Classroom stress and teacher burnout. *Phi Delta Kappan* 61(4), 252.

Wise, A. E., L. Darling-Hammond, B. Berry, D. Berliner, E. Haller, A. Praskac, and P. Schlechty. 1987. Effective teacher selection. *The Education Digest* 102(3), 14–18.

12

TEACHER PREPARATION

OBJECTIVES

After reading this chapter you will be able to

- provide factual data concerning the status of teacher education;

- discuss some of the current criticisms about teacher education;

- describe actions being recommended and taken to reform teacher education;

- describe how teachers are certified and recertified; and

- discuss alternative certification programs.

OUTLINE

1. What is the status of teacher education?
2. What are the major criticisms of teacher education?
3. How have universities responded to criticisms related to teacher training?
4. How are teachers certified in most states?
5. What is alternative certification and what is its status?

INTRODUCTION

To become a teacher or other professional in the educational vocation, certain training is required. This is similar to other professions, such as medicine, law, and business, which require that certain skills and competencies be acquired before entering into the profession. Educational professionals believe that certain prerequisites must be met before someone can be a teacher.

Teacher education is a major endeavor in this country. Never before has the process been under such scrutiny as during the past several years (Bush 1987). Although there has been a great deal written and discussed about how to prepare teachers, several general questions remain (Keith 1987, p. 20):

1. What is adequate qualification for a teacher?
2. What is the place of pedagogy in teacher preparation?
3. What specialized or general academic content constitutes "vastly more" knowledge than a teacher is required to teach?

TEACHER EDUCATION

Teacher preparation is a vital component of the public education system in the United States (Gage 1984). The quality of teachers became a concern as early as the mid 1880s. Steps taken to increase the knowledge and skills of teachers during this period included testing potential teachers for licensure, conducting one-day and five-day institutes for inservice training, and requiring teachers to participate in a reading circle (Graham 1974).

During the past fifty years, significant contributions have been made by teacher education institutions. In the 1930s the average teacher, especially in rural areas, had two or fewer years of college; many only had a high-school diploma. Currently, teachers must have a minimum of a bachelor's degree, and approximately one-third have a master's degree or higher. Today's teachers have a much broader academic background, a better understanding of child growth and development, and more knowledge about teaching methods than at any previous time in the history of American education (Smith 1980). Much of this improvement is the result of teacher education programs.

Status of Teacher Education

Approximately thirteen hundred institutions of higher education offer teacher education programs in the United States (Sirotnik 1988). This equates to nearly seventy percent of all four-year colleges and universities in the country (Clark 1984). Forty percent of the institutions are private colleges with enrollments of fewer than one thousand students, and the remaining sixty percent are state-operated universities (Smith 1980).

Despite the large number of teacher education programs, the enrollment in these programs has declined sharply since 1970. In 1969, twenty-four percent of all college-bound students in the United States planned to major in teacher education. This number had dropped to less than five percent in 1982 (Weaver 1984a). From 1970 to 1986 the number of students graduating from teacher education programs dropped from 314,000 to under 90,000 (National Center for Education Statistics 1988a). One reason for the drop in numbers has been the decline in the status of teaching. Gallup (1984a) reported that in 1969 seventy-five percent of parents indicated that they would like a son or daughter to enter the teaching profession. This number had declined to thirty percent in 1987 (Turner 1987).

HIGHLIGHT
■

EDUCATION SCHOOLS' ENROLLMENT RISES FOR THIRD STRAIGHT YEAR, STUDY SHOWS

Lynn Olson

ANAHEIM, CALIF.—Enrollment in undergraduate teacher-education programs has increased for the third year in a row, according to preliminary data released here during the annual meeting of the American Association of Colleges for Teacher Education.

But those gains may be leveling off after a year of striking growth, findings from the national survey of teacher-training programs indicate.

Enrollment in undergraduate teacher-education programs jumped by 20.2 percent between 1985 and 1986, according to the study. But researchers said they expected to find an increase of only about 10 percent between 1986 and 1987.

Gary R. Galluzzo, an associate professor of education at Western Kentucky University who helped analyze the enrollment data

continued

for the research team, said the apparent "slowdown" in enrollments could be temporary or a reflection of the institutions that were sampled.

"Nationally, when you talk to folks, everybody's enrollment seems to be up," Mr. Galluzzo said. "It's the rare institution whose enrollment is not up."

He attributed the surge of interest in teaching as a career, in part, to the availability of jobs and increases in teachers' salaries.

But the researchers also found that minority enrollment in undergraduate teacher-education programs has remained relatively stable over the past three years, never exceeding 5 percent of the total.

The enrollment data and other survey findings were made public here earlier this month as part of AACTE's "Research About Teacher Education" project.

The new survey is based on data gathered from 77 representative institutions over the past year by AACTE's committee on research and information. The enrollment data were drawn from a subset of 38 institutions that have participated in all three years of the survey. They reflect institutional enrollments for the fall semester of 1987.

In addition to enrollment data, the survey includes demographic and attitudinal information gathered from some 1,141 elementary-education students and 253 professors in that field.

The participating colleges and universities were randomly selected from three kinds of institutions: smaller colleges that grant only bachelor's degrees, medium-sized institutions that grant bachelor's and master's degrees, and larger universities that also offer doctorates.

Elementary-Education Majors

The survey this year focused on the preparation of elementary-school teachers.

Its results indicate that slightly more than three-fourths of the elementary-education students do not have an academic major other than education. And almost the same proportion—72.1 percent—reported that they did not have an academic minor.

The findings appear to corroborate a repeated criticism regarding the preparation of elementary-school teachers: that their training focuses too much on pedagogy and not enough on the academic subjects they will teach.

However, the survey does not provide details on the content of the elementary-education majors.

Antoine M. Garibaldi, chairman of the department of education at Xavier University of Louisiana, said that after several years of discussion on the need to redesign teacher-education programs, "there are still a number of institutions out there that have not changed their degree requirements for teacher education, especially in the elementary-education area."

But Nancy L. Zimpher, an associate professor of education at Ohio State University who analyzed the student data with Mr. Garibaldi, suggested that the findings may reflect "past practices" rather than current trends.

States are moving to ensure that students take more credit hours within academic subjects, she said, but those changes may not have been picked up by the survey. She added that prospective elementary teachers often take as many as 20 semester hours of coursework outside their major in subjects they are likely to teach.

Over three-quarters of the students surveyed said they believed that general studies in the arts, sciences, and humanities were very important for prospective elementary teachers, and 21.4 percent said they were somewhat important.

Those beliefs were particulary widespread among students in four-year colleges. There, 9 out of 10 students rated courses in general studies as very important for future elementary teachers.

The survey also asked faculty members how difficult it is to provide students with a well-rounded liberal education and the needed professional coursework within a four-year undergraduate program.

Approximately 41 percent said it was somewhat difficult; more than 26 percent said it was very difficult.

continued

'A Parochial' Group

As in previous years, the population preparing to teach was found to be overwhelmingly white and female.

"Both the faculty and the students stand in stark contrast to what the student population is in our schools," said Kenneth R. Howey, a professor of education at Ohio State University and chairman of the committee on research and information.

The preponderance of female students—92 percent—was particularly noticeable this year, researchers said, because of the survey's focus on prospective elementary teachers.

Students in this year's sample were also slightly older on average than those surveyed last year—25 years old versus 24.3 years old.

"The notion that students in higher education are all 18 to 21 years old is obviously passé," said Ms. Zimpher. She also noted that about one-third of the group was married this year, compared with one-fourth in 1987.

More students in this year's survey also reported that the largest share of their financial assistance for college came from family support—approximately 41.3 percent, up from 37 percent in 1987.

Mr. Garibaldi said the increase was interesting in light of the decline in federal financial-aid programs. "I think that's a very critical issue for minority students in particular," he said, especially as college costs continue to climb.

In general, the findings portray what Ms. Zimpher described as a relatively "parochial" student body, with little interest in teaching in urban areas.

Seventy-three percent of the students surveyed attended school less than 100 miles from their home, and said they would like to stay close to their hometown to teach.

Slightly more than half grew up in rural or small towns, compared with approximately one-fifth from urban areas.

More than half of the students said they would like to teach in suburbia, and about one-fourth said they would like to teach in rural areas. Only 19 percent expressed an interest in teaching in urban settings—a finding that has remained relatively constant over time.

Multicultural Settings

Both students and faculty members provided extremely positive ratings for the quality of their professional-preparation programs, with students giving even more positive ratings than faculty members.

Approximately 73.5 percent of faculty members and 80.9 percent of students rated their programs as above average or excellent.

But Mr. Howey, who analyzed the program data, cautioned against placing too much emphasis on these self-reports.

"Typically, what happens in studies of teacher-education students is that perceptions of the quality of their training programs diminish over time, as they get more of a reality base and assume full responsibility for teaching," he said.

In addition, a sizable minority of students expressed some apprehension about their ability to teach about computers, handle disciplinary problems, and work with exceptional and high-risk students in culturally diverse settings.

Only one-third of the students polled, and one-fourth of the faculty members, thought that students were more than adequately prepared to teach in culturally diverse settings or to work with "at risk" students.

Three-fifths of the students also reported that they spoke no language other than English, and only 14.4 percent of those who spoke another language considered themselves fluent in that language.

Positive View of the Future

Researchers said they were heartened, however, by the quality of the students and by their positive view of teaching as a career.

The combined scores of education students on the Scholastic Aptitude Test averaged 898, compared with an average of 906 for all entering freshmen in 1987. Prospective teachers also tended to be in the top third of their graduating high-school class.

"I'm convinced, from three years of data, that people who do train to teach look like

continued

the typical entering college freshman," said Mr. Galluzzo, alluding to reports that prospective teachers are not as academically able as their counterparts in other fields.

Education students also reported a very rosy view of their future as teachers:

- Almost 95 percent said they were "positive" or "very positive" about teaching as a career, up from 91 percent in 1987.
- Ninety-three percent said they planned to teach after graduation, up from 87 percent last year. The majority also planned to remain in teaching for at least 11 years.
- Nearly three-quarters of those surveyed felt that teachers' salaries were "adequate" or "more than adequate" to support a single person. But 89 percent felt that they were not adequate to support a family.

When students were asked if they were familiar with the concept of a "career ladder," almost three-fourths responded in the affirmative. And 91 percent said the availability of a career ladder would serve as an incentive to remain in teaching.

AACTE will publish final results from the survey later this year.

Reprinted with permission from *Education Week*, vol. VIII, no. 26, p. 7.

The reasons for declining enrollments in teacher education programs are complex and include more than lower teacher status. One obvious reason for the lower number of education majors is the lack of available jobs. In the 1960s teaching jobs were taken by approximately 25 percent of all college graduates. When the market became oversupplied with qualified teachers at the end of the 1960s, graduates from liberal arts programs who could become certified with minimal additional training found that no jobs were available. The result was that fewer undergraduates majored in education. Now the ratio of graduates to job openings has reversed. The number of public school teachers in schools is expected to increase from the present 2.2 million to more than 2.4 million in 1992 (Center for Education Statistics 1988b). This larger demand for teachers should lead to an increase in the number of undergraduate majors in teacher education.

Criticisms of Teacher Education

Another reason for the declining number of students majoring in education during the past decade is the criticism launched against teacher education programs. Teacher education in the 1980s came under attack from all sides (Ishler 1984; Clark 1984; Ohanian 1985; Pinar 1989; Tafel and Christensen 1988). Politicians, students, parents, and the general public have all accused teacher education programs of being the primary problem with American public education. Many problem areas have been enunciated. Those most commonly emphasized included:

1. Admission standards are so low that anyone can enroll in teacher education.

2. Education majors take too much coursework on "how to teach" and not enough coursework on "what to teach."

3. The general education program for prospective teachers is less rigorous than that required of other majors.

4. Anyone who gains admission to a teacher education program will undoubtedly graduate, because the academic standards are so low. (Ishler 1984, p. 121)

Other criticisms included the overall quality of education majors, poor abilities of teacher education faculty, and the lack of general education courses taken by education majors.

Quality of Education Majors. Teacher education programs traditionally have attracted students who are not as academically talented as those who choose to major in other areas. For example, high-school seniors who planned to major in education in 1982 averaged thirty-two points below the national average on the Scholastic Aptitude Test (SAT) verbal subtest and forty-eight points below the national average on the math subtest (Schoolteaching Profession in Crisis 1983). Clark (1984) stated that teacher education majors consistently have come from the bottom third of their high-school graduating classes. A study conducted by the New Jersey Department of Education determined that "In 1982 the Scholastic Aptitude Test (SAT) scores of New Jersey high school graduates who planned to major in education were lower than those of graduates who planned to major in 22 of 24 fields of study at the college level" (Cooperman and Klagholz 1985, p. 692). Other reports have indicated similar statistics regarding the quality of education majors (Haberman 1987).

More recent data indicate that the quality of education majors differs among regions and institutions. For example, Minnesota reported that fifty percent of their teacher education institutions who reviewed SAT scores found that their education majors had higher mean scores than state and national college-bound juniors (Haberman 1987). Nelli (1988) reviewed several studies focused on the academic skills of undergraduate teacher majors and concluded that the results "refute charges that teacher education graduates are academically inferior to non-education graduates, or that they have less of a grasp of the subject matter they studied in their majors" (p. 126). Other reports echo these conclusions (Tafel and Christensen 1988).

Inadequate Curriculum. Another criticism voiced by many critics of teacher education is that education majors take too many education courses, especially "methods" courses (Raimo 1983). The basic training program in most colleges of education has changed little during the past fifty years (Bush 1987). During these fifty years, a great deal of knowledge has been obtained related to teaching. Unfortunately, much of that knowledge has not been used to change the training program for teacher education majors. Changing teacher education is a very difficult and complex process (Keith 1987; Tafel and Christensen 1988).

Ishler (1984) found vast differences among colleges of education in the course requirements for graduation in education. The range of professional education courses required for elementary education majors ranged from twelve to seventy-eight credit hours, with a mean of thirty hours. Nineteen percent of the training programs required more than fifty semester hours of professional education courses. For secondary education majors, the range was from twelve to forty-seven hours, with a mean of twenty-eight hours; thirty-six percent required more than thirty semester hours for graduation.

The facts do support the criticism that education majors are required to take a large portion of their coursework in education. Still another criticism related to coursework is the nature of the education courses that are required. Some of the criticisms include:

- Efforts to develop a science of teaching have not been successful (Pinar 1989).

- Courses are irrelevant and too theoretical (Gage 1984).

- Courses contain too much information about learners and learning and not enough about teachers and teaching (Gage 1984).

- Courses are full of mechanical activities such as lesson planning and deplete in the areas of personal and developmental characteristics of students (Clabaugh, Feden, and Vogel 1984).

- Courses concentrate on developing too many materials and providing students with too many cookbook ideas and ignore showing future teachers how to find their own solutions to problems (Ohanian 1985).

- Courses focus too much on the subject matter to be taught when students may already know more than their education professors (Gage 1984).

Clark (1984) stated that secondary education majors miss out on a concentrated period of study in the teaching field, opportunities for socialization with peers, and chances for practice in a variety of settings. Elementary education majors suffer as a result of their not having a major in any subject area and limited practicum experiences (Clark 1984).

These criticisms were not all well-founded; however, many teacher education professors agreed, at least to some degree, with some of the points made. Consumers of teacher education programs tend to view their programs much more positively than the critics. In the Gallup Poll of Teachers' Attitudes Toward the Public Schools, eighty-two percent of the teachers surveyed gave their teacher training programs a C or better, with forty-nine percent rating their programs as either A or B (Gallup 1984b). The voices of critics, therefore, should not be accepted as reality. As a result of the national reform reports of the late 1970s and early 1980s, critics looked for reasons for the state of public education. Teacher education happened to be one of the targets for this blame. This is not to say that teacher education could not be significantly improved; it could.

Reforms in Teacher Education

Colleges of education around the country are currently engaged in major revisions of their training programs to better meet the needs of students. Some of these changes have been implemented as a result of local initiatives. However, the major impetus for change has come from a report from the Holmes Group and a report from the Carnegie Corporation (Keppel 1986; Lanier and Featherstone 1988). The Holmes Group, composed of approximately 100 research universities, represents an effort to change teacher education from within higher education (Wheeler and Giese 1988). The Carnegie Corporation financed a Task Force on Teaching as a Profession which resulted in a report calling for major revisions in teacher education programs (Bush 1987).

The Holmes Group recommended five different areas for change (Murray 1986):

1. Abandon undergraduate teacher education programs for a liberal arts undergraduate emphasis and a Master's level focus on pedagogy.
2. Create the position of career professional teacher who would be involved with teaching, administration, and teacher education.
3. Implement evaluation models for teachers and university training programs.
4. Create partnerships between schools of education and school districts.
5. Develop models for collaboration between teachers and administrators.

HIGHLIGHT
.

HOLMES GROUP FINDS MIXED RESULTS IN UNIVERSITIES' FIRST REFORM EFFORTS

Lynn Olson

ATLANTA—Initial attempts to improve how teachers are prepared at leading research universities have produced mixed results, according to a new study.

The forthcoming report by the Holmes Group, a consortium of 96 higher-education

continued

institutions, cites "unmistakable" signs of progress in some areas but says they coexist with minimal change and continued obstacles in others.

A draft of the unusually frank document, "Work in Progress: The Holmes Group One Year On," was obtained during the organization's third annual meeting here Jan. 27–29.

It provides the first indication of how seriously research universities have taken their pledge to reform teacher training since joining the Holmes Group in 1986.

The document summarzies the progress reports submitted by 71 institutions after their first year in the consortium.

Although 25 universities did not submit formal reports, some of them are also engaged in innovative work on their campuses, according to Holmes officials.

The Holmes Group's 1986 manifesto, *Tomorrow's Teachers*, sent shockwaves through the education community, particularly its recommendation that the undergraduate education major be replaced with a prolonged sequence of study—including a liberal-arts major and more extensive professional preparation for future teachers.

Many critics publicly doubted whether Holmes Group institutions would pursue the creation of longer and more costly programs for their students.

But according to the new report, nearly half of the Holmes universities that submitted progress reports have or are trying to create five-year programs that would provide more time for professional studies.

These programs typically combine an undergraduate major in the liberal arts with education coursework and a supervised internship. They lead either to a bachelor's degree or a master's degree plus certification.

Other campuses are focusing on the creation of "fifty year" programs that concentrate all education studies in a final year, usually after students have completed their baccalaureate. In addition, many of the larger Holmes institutions are pursuing the creation of multiple programs.

While some of these institutions may move toward the use of five-year programs exclusively, the report notes, others will continue to offer a combination of programs in the future, or will mount small-scale experiments that may or may not lead to larger efforts.

Fewer than a dozen institutions reported "no progress" in providing more time for the professional preparation of teachers, the study found.

Holmes officials questioned the commitment of such institutions to the organization's goals, but said they plan to work with them in the future.

"It's premature to crack the whip," said Gary Sykes, primary author of the report and assistant to the Holmes Group's president. "We're not drumming anyone out of the corps at this point."

Professional Studies

According to the report, the Holmes Group does not advocate any "particular" program structure. Rather, its goal is to make the education of teachers more intellectually rigorous.

Simply providing more liberal-arts courses, eliminating the undergraduate degree, or requiring students to take a fifth year of study will not necessarily satisfy this aim, the report cautions.

Instead, it argues, educators must rethink the content of what is taught and how it is taught within both schools of education and colleges of arts and sciences.

Rethinking the professional-education program, in particular, is the "central intellectual challenge facing Holmes Group institutions," the report states. "The credibility of the Holmes reforms rests here."

More 'Authentic' Studies

Acording to the progress reports, many institutions are struggling to redefine their professional curriculum. These attempts at change include assigning students to small groups that move through the curriculum together, creating new courses within a compressed program of "core studies" about teaching and learning, and using early, extended field experiences that provide students with an opportunity to reflect on what they have learned.

continued

The process of producing these new courses is "remarkable" on several counts, according to the report. First, they represent a "philosophical agreement" about the content of professional preparation that has often eluded education programs. Second, many institutions are trying to draw on the knowledge of expert, practicing teachers in more "authentic" ways by allowing them to help create and design courses.

The report predicts, however, that experimentation with the intellectual content of teacher education is likely to continue for the foreseeable future.

Although the notion of identifying a "knowledge base" for teaching and learning is "beguiling," the report notes, "the selection and organization of such knowledge into preparation programs is problematic."

Moreover, on the majority of campuses, teacher educators alone have participated in rethinking the professional-education program, with only limited participation by their liberal-arts colleagues.

'Most Difficult Goal'

The report cites this lack of collaboration between liberal-arts faculty members and their education-school peers as one of the major obstacles confronting Holmes institutions.

To improve the preparation of teachers, it notes, their liberal-arts training must emphasize broader, more interdisciplinary approaches, model good teaching, and promote a better understanding of how disciplines are structured and taught.

"[T]his has proven a most difficult goal at this stage of Holmes efforts," the document states. "Many reports are largely silent about any relations with the liberal arts. . . . And those universities which have tackled this issue report tensions and difficulties."

According to the report, education schools are having trouble influencing general education from their relatively weak vantage point within the university.

"Education faculty have little influence over the majority of their students' course-work," the report states, "while arts-and-sciences faculty on most campuses resist overtures to reform curriculum and teaching in the liberal arts."

In addition, the report notes, there are few existing incentives for either education or liberal-arts faculty members to pursue "genuinely liberal teaching and learning."

Some Progress Seen

Nonetheless, there has been progress on some campuses. Examples cited in the report include the formation of joint committees of liberal-arts and education faculty to plan new courses; the service of arts-and-sciences faculty members on admissions boards, mentor teams, and other committees within schools of education; and experiments in faculty "restructuring" to allow education professors to hold joint appointments in liberal-arts divisions.

The report cautions, however, that many of these initiatives are limited to small groups of individuals, while the promotion of "broader, more systematic collaboration is quite difficult."

Noted one institutional representative: "We do not and are never likely to have enthusiastic collaboration with the majority of faculty in the arts-and-sciences disciplines. Most simply do not value collaboration with school-of-education faculty and have no interest in the preparation of teachers."

On the positive side, the report found that most universities are working to strengthen the connection between clinical practice and students' professional studies.

Many of the extended programs, for example, either have or plan to offer a year-long or semester-long internship that would place students in one or more schools. They are also creating more formal positions on their campuses for teachers who serve as clinical faculty members, including the provision of salary, status, and perquisites.

Teaching-Hospital Model

But the report cautions that plans and projects to create "professional development schools," in particular, are still in their infancy. And some institutions, it says, may never undertake this challenge.

Creation of such schools, modeled after teaching hospitals for physicians, was a major recommendation of *Tomorrow's*

continued

Teachers. But according to the progress report, a number of obstacles are yet to be overcome.

Few Rewards for Teachers

Most universities, for instance, have few mechanisms for locating outstanding teachers within school districts and convincing them to participate in such programs. In addition, the creation of settings that require substantially different roles for both teachers and professors requires delicate and often prolonged negotiations between schools, universities, and teachers' unions.

"In a number of instances," the reports states, "promising starts have been slowed by turnover in key administrators, budget cutbacks, new state mandates, or the emergence of conflict around sensitive issues."

In part because of such problems, the report could cite few universities that have pursued the notion of differentiated staffing for teachers—another central proposal of the Holmes Group.

"Experiments are under way in many states and districts," the report notes, "but universities have played little role in these developments and can exert most influence in shaping school staffing patterns."

Minority and Part-time Students

The report also points to two demographic trends that universities will have to confront in efforts to improve teaching. One is the continued shortage of minorites in both the enrollments and faculties of schools of education.

"The problem is systemic," Mr. Sykes said. "There is a sense on many campuses that you can't find minority students to go into education because there are so few" on campus in general.

The report describes substantive efforts in this area that have been undertaken by some 15 or 20 Holmes institutions and go beyond scholarship and loan-forgiveness programs. They include making a commitment to hire several minority faculty per year; assigning full-time staff members to work on minority recruitment and retention; and developing collaborative projects with urban school districts to encourage young minority students to enter teaching.

In the future, Mr. Sykes said, ways will have to be found to build on and model such efforts.

The other demographic problem confronting many Holmes institutions is a growing number of part-time students, many from minority and working-class backgrounds. If such students cluster in certain programs, the report warns, it could lead to systematic differences in teacher preparation along race and class lines.

"Universities cannot afford to run elite and second-class professional programs side by side," the document states. "No report addressed this issue, but the creation of multiple programs on many campuses suggests that vigilance will be necessary to avoid inequities in program quality."

Reprinted with permission from *Education Week*, vol. VIII, no. 2, p. 1.

The Carnegie Report focused on similar areas and resulted in similar recommendations. One additional recommendation made by this report suggested the creation of a National Board of Professional Teaching Standards to determine the knowledge and skills teachers need to have and how to assess those skills (Keith 1987).

Probably the three most interesting and controversial recommendations coming out of these reports include (1) eliminating undergraduate teacher training, (2) reorganizing the teacher education curriculum, and (3) developing linkages between schools of education and local schools (Pinar 1989). Although these recommendations are supported by many different groups, their widespread, total adoption has not occurred. One reason for this, as concluded by Wheeler and Giese (1988), is the lack of involvement of many faculty members in the implementation process. Without involvement in the adoption process, some faculty members resent the changes. Other studies have indicated that some public school personnel are not in favor of the many changes recommended by the Holmes and Carnegie reports (Tracy, Sheehan, and McArdle 1988).

Colleges of education around the country are currently engaged in major revisions of their training programs to better meet the needs of students. Some of the changes include (1) improving the quality of teacher education majors, (2) revising the training curriculum, (3) increasing funding for teacher education, and (4) developing alternative certification requirements. Many of these recommendations are currently being implemented.

Improving the Quality of Teacher Education Majors. One of the easiest reforms to implement in teacher education focuses on improving the quality of students majoring in education (Clark 1984). Most profes-

■ *Teacher education programs are implementing reforms to counter recent criticism.*

sionals agree that more selection criteria and better screening procedures need to be developed concerning requirements for admission into teacher education. The issues are what criteria and what procedures should be adopted (Draba and Steinkellner 1977).

Methods used to increase admission requirements have varied considerably. In some states, legislatures or state departments of education have mandated changes; in other states, individual universities have taken their own steps to change admission requirements. Where states have mandated universal standards, test scores are most often used as the key entrance requirement. Most states now require minimum test scores to enter teacher education programs (Eissenberg and Rudner 1988). Universities most often use a student's grade point average (GPA) as the primary admission requirement. In these universities, the trend has been to raise the minimum GPAs required for admission into teacher education (Marker 1984). Ishler (1984) studied admission and graduation requirements in 103 institutions training teachers and found that the GPA required for admission into teacher education programs ranged from 2.0 to 3.0. Forty-six percent of the institutions in the study indicated that a GPA of 2.0 was required, twenty-three percent required a GPA of 2.1 to 2.25, twenty-seven percent required a GPA of 2.5, and three percent required a 3.0 or above GPA.

Improving the Training Curriculum. Most would agree that some improvement could be made in the teacher training curriculum. However, like admission requirements, there is no consensus as to what should be included in the curriculum. Suggestions range from making the curriculum more practical to increasing the length of teacher training programs from four to five years.

Teacher education professors cannot agree on a common curriculum for teacher education majors. A comprehensive list of "professional domains" students should be exposed to include

- different instructional approaches, including use of existing and emerging media;
- the relationship between diverse characteristics of learners and instructional strategies;
- curriculum models and theories, especially in subjects for which a given teacher will be responsible;
- small-group processes;
- professional responsibilities and obligations;
- consultation skills to work with other professionals, including knowledge of their roles and of the organization and administration of schools;
- parent/professional relations (including community relations);

- a capacity for inquiry and design to meet the specific needs of individual learners, including diagnosis, instructional and curricular design, and evaluation skills;
- classroom and behavior management; and
- self-awareness, or the ability to be in touch with oneself. (Gideonse 1982, p. 16)

Ohanian (1985) adds that the coursework in education should be geared toward helping prospective teachers develop their own ways of solving problems rather than providing them with long lists of how-to's. Marczely (1985) described this as putting "academic fiber" in college of education courses.

Another critical area in the teacher education curriculum is hands-on experience. Most often called student teaching, this course offers students opportunities to practice what they have learned in classes. Student teaching is the major linkage between teacher education programs and public schools. Students enrolled in student teaching spend from ten to thirty weeks in a classroom, either on a full- or half-day schedule. In most situations, the student is supervised by the cooperating teacher and a university faculty member (Griffin 1989). Two common concerns related to student teaching are that (1) students have to wait until the end of their coursework to student teach and (2) one

- *Most states now require testing for certification.*

semester of hands-on experience is not sufficient. Buchanan (1982) suggests that students get into classrooms after they have completed only twelve hours of education courses. By having this early experience, students would be able to relate their coursework to actual experiences and also find out early in their program if they really like teaching.

Some university training programs require more field experience than student teaching. For example, in a program developed at Oregon State University and Western Oregon State College, students enroll in three different field experiences. In addition to the normal student teaching, education majors enroll in an introductory field experience early in their programs and finally complete a senior-year practicum where they are involved in a school-improvement project with a cooperating local school district (Barr 1984).

Implementing Exit Criteria. In addition to implementing better screening of students at the beginning of teacher education programs, many colleges of education have begun to require teachers to pass exit examinations such as the National Teachers Examination (NTE). Even if the university does not require an exit test, thirty-six states currently require tests as a requirement for teacher certification. Three other states will implement the certification test requirement by 1991 (Eissenberg and Rudner 1988). Of the tests used, the NTE is required most often. Table 12.1 summarizes the testing requirements of states.

Testing new teachers is a controversial issue. The National Education Association, long opposed teacher testing, only recently reversed its opposition to teacher testing. The American Federation of Teachers has

TABLE 12.1
A Summary of State Testing of Teachers

STATE	DATA REVISED	TEST	PASS RATE	PASSING SCORES
Alabama	1987	Custom	80%	
Alaska	1987	—		173,172,174
Arizona	1987	PPST	79(1986)	
Arkansas	1987	—		
California	1987	CBEST	77(1986)	
Colorado	1988	CAT	58(1986)	75%ile
Connecticut	1987	Custom	55(1986)	
Delaware	1987			
Florida	1988	SAT, ACT		40%ile
Georgia	1987	—		
Hawaii	1987	—		
Idaho	1988	—		
Illinois	1987	—		
Indiana	1988	—		
Iowa	1987	—		

TABLE 12.1 – *Continued*
A Summary of State Testing of Teachers

STATE	DATA REVISED	TEST	PASS RATE	PASSING SCORES
Kansas	1988	—		
Kentucky	1987	CTBS	63(1985)	12.5 GES
Louisiana	1988	NTE		—,645,644
Maine	1987	—		
Maryland	1988	—		
Massachusetts	1988	—		
Michigan	1988	—		
Minnesota	1988	—		
Mississippi	1988	COMP		170
Missouri	1987	SAT, ACT		800,18
Montana	1988	—		
Nebraska	1988	PPST		170,171,172
Nevada	1987	PPST	95(1985)	169,169,170
New Hampshire	1988	—		
New Jersey	1988	—		
New Mexico	1987	Misc		
New York	1988	—		
North Carolina	1988	NTE		636,631,—
North Dakota	1988	Misc		
Ohio	1987	Misc (Planned for 1991)		
Oklahoma	1987	Misc		
Oregon	1987	CBEST	77(1986)	
Pennsylvania	1988	—		
Rhode Island	1988	—		
South Carolina	1988	Custom	81(1987)	
South Dakota	1988	—		
Tennessee	1988	PPST		169,169,172
Texas	1987	PPST	71(1987)	171,172,173
Utah	1987	Misc		
Vermont	1988	—		
Virginia	1988	—		
Washington	1987	Custom,SAT,ACT,		80,700,16
West Virginia	1988	PPST,COMP	81(1987)	172,172,171
		PPST (Planned for 1989)	95(1987)	17
Wisconsin	1987	CAT		
Wyoming	1988			70%ile
Totals		26	Mean = 76	

ACT = the American College Testing Program. CAT = the California Achievement Test. COMP = the College Outcomes Measure Project. CTBS = the California Test of Basic Skills. SAT = the Scholastic Aptitude Test. PPST = the Pre-Professional Skills Test. CBEST = the California Basic Education Skills Test.
Passing scores for the PPST are for the reading, mathematics, and writing portions. Passing scores for the NTE are for the general knowledge communication skills, and the professional knowledge portions Passing rates may be cumulative, per administration, or for the most difficult subtest. Because of the different definitions, the mean value is only approximate.

Source: Eissenberg and Rudner. State testing of teachers: A summary. *Journal of Teacher Education* 39(4), 1988. Printed with permission of The Journal of Teacher Education.

a long-term record of support for teacher testing. The AFT president Albert Shanker has even called for a national teacher's test (Williams and Howard 1984, p. 53). In addition to testing new teachers, some states have passed, or are considering passing, testing requirements for veteran teachers. In 1983, the Arkansas legislature passed legislation requiring all teachers to take a one-time teacher competency test. The test was administered for the first time during the spring of 1985. As could be expected, the test was challenged by the NEA and many Arkansas teachers.

Expanding Teacher Education Programs to Five Years. For many years, some critics of teacher education have encouraged colleges and universities to expand training programs to five years. The recent Holmes Group and Carnegie reports have both recommended graduate-level training for teachers, in effect converting current teacher education programs to five years. Programs at the University of Kansas (Scannel 1984) and the University of Florida (Smith, Carroll, and Fry 1984) both require a fifth year to earn a teaching certificate.

The Quality Assurance Program in North Carolina requires teachers with an undergraduate degree to teach two years in a probationary status. During this period teachers earn their master's degree and permanent certification through involvement with the university and the local school district (Schaffer and Wolfe 1988). The program at Pacific University in Forest Grove, Oregon, is a similar program. The Cooperative Fifth-Year program leads to a Master of Arts in Teaching (Nagel 1988).

TEACHER CERTIFICATION

Although some states are beginning to implement alternate certification programs, most states continue to certify teachers using a traditional model. Students who enroll in colleges of education wth state-approved teacher education programs and successfully complete the requirements for degrees in those training programs are eligible for state certification.

Traditional Certification Programs

Colleges of education vary considerably in their requirements for graduation. However, all closely follow the state department of education requirements for teacher certification. Although the certification requirements vary from state to state, there are many similarities. For example, most require that all individuals have a bachelor's degree before they can be certified. Most states also require that students earn a minimal number of credit hours in various courses, including general education courses, professional education courses, courses in the student's teaching field, and student teaching.

Ishler (1984) conducted a study to determine admission and graduation requirements for teacher education. The results from 103 teacher training programs that are members of the Association of Colleges and Schools of Education in State Universities and Land Grant Colleges and Affiliated Private Universities revealed major differences in degree requirements (see table 12.2).

Weible and Dumas (1982) studied the fifty states to determine the certification standards in secondary education (see tables 12.3 and 12.4).

TABLE 12.2
Graduation/Certification Requirements

| AREAS | NO. OF CREDIT HOURS REQUIRED | |
	ELEMENTARY	SECONDARY
Content Areas	12–38 X = 29	24–66 X = 35
Student Teaching	6–19 X = 12	5–15 X = 9
Professional Education	12–78 X = 30	12–47 X = 28
Cumulative GPA	2.0–3.0 X = 2.25	2.0–3.0 X = 2.25
GPA in Content Areas	2.0–3.0 X = 2.25	2.0–3.0 X = 2.25
GPA in Professional Education Courses	2.0–3.0 X = 2.25	2.0–3.0 X = 2.25

Source: Ishler. Requirements for admission to and graduation from teacher education. *Phi Delta Kappan* 66(2), 1984.

TABLE 12.3
Secondary Teacher Certification Standards in General Education

| DISCIPLINE | NUMBER OF SEMESTER HOURS | |
	RANGE	MEAN
History/Social Science	2–12	9
Natural Science	0–12	5
Mathematics	0–6	2
English Composition	0–12	6
Humanities	0–15	6
Oral Communication	0–3	1
Health/PE	0–6	2

Source: Weible and Dumas. Secondary teacher certification standards in fifty states. *Journal of Teacher Education*, 1982.

TABLE 12.4
Secondary Teacher Certification Standards in Professional Education

COURSE/COMPETENCY AREA	PERCENT REQUIRING
Reading in Content Area	54
Educational Psychology	97
Social Foundations	69
Org./Admin. of Schools	31
Early Field Experiences	38
Exceptional Child/Mainstreaming	36
Tests and Evaluation	38
Multi-Cultural Education	31
General Teaching Methods	74
Special Methods	59
Educational Media	23
Student Teaching	100

Source: Reprinted with permission. Weible and Dumas. Secondary teacher certification standards in fifty states. *Journal of Teacher Education* 32(4), 1982.

The range in requirements is great in many areas, meaning that students majoring in secondary education in one state may complete a significantly different program of study than those in another state.

In addition to state requirements for initial teacher certification, forty states have requirements for recertification. Recertification requirements typically have focused on teachers earning a certain number of graduate hours during a specified period of time. However, an emerging trend is to allow teachers to meet recertification requirements by participating in inservice activities planned and provided by the local school district. Twenty-nine states, fifty-eight percent, either have or plan to implement such options. The requirements for recertification vary considerably from state to state in such areas as (1) recertification period, (2) semester hours required, and (3) whether the recertification requirements can be met through district-planned activities (Hanes and Rowls 1984) (see table 12.5).

Alternative Certification Programs

Some states have responded to the call for educational reform through alternative certification for teachers. With teacher shortages being severe in some areas—for example, science and math—and emerging criticisms of traditional teacher education programs, states have opted to initiate alternative methods to certify teachers other than through traditional college of education degree programs. Twenty-one states have implemented alternative certification provisions since the mid-

TABLE 12.5
Recertification Requirements

	RECERTIFICATION REQUIRED?	RECERTIFICATION PERIOD (IN YEARS)	SEMESTER HOUR RECERTIFICATION REQUIREMENT	RECERTIFICATION VIA DISTRICT-PLANNED ACTIVITIES?	RECERTIFICATION SOLELY VIA DISTRICT-PLANNED ACTIVITIES?	% RECERTIFICATION CREDIT ALLOWED VIA DISTRICT ACTIVITIES
Alabama	yes	8–12*	6–9*	yes*	yes*	NA
Alaska	yes	5	6	yes	no	50%
Arizona	yes	6	5	no	NA	NA
Arkansas	yes	6–10*	6	no	NA	NA
California	yes	5(pending)	24(pending)	yes	no	pending
Colorado	yes	5	6	yes	no	66%
Connecticut	no	—	—	—	—	—
Delaware	no†	—	—	no†	—	—
Florida	yes	5	6	yes	yes	NA
Georgia	yes	5–10*	6	yes	yes	NA
Hawaii	no	—	—	—	—	—
Idaho	no	—	—	—	—	—
Illinois	no	—	—	—	—	—
Indiana	yes	5–10*	12–M.S.**	no	NA	NA
Iowa	yes	6–10*	6	yes	no	50%
Kansas	yes	3–5*	6–8*	yes	yes‡	50%
Kentucky	yes	10	3–M.S.*	yes	no	33%
Louisiana	no	—	—	—	—	—
Maine	yes	5	6	yes	yes	NA
Maryland	yes	5–10*	6	yes	yes §	50%
Massachusetts	nc	—	—	no	—	—
Michigan	yes	6	18**	no	—	—
Minnesota	yes	5	9	yes	yes	NA
Mississippi	yes	5–10*	6	yes	no	50%
Missouri	no	—	—	—	—	—
Montana	yes	5*	4*	yes	yes	NA
Nebraska	yes	3	6	no	NA	NA
Nevada	yes	5–6*	6	yes	yes	NA

TABLE 12.5 – *Continued*
Recertification Requirements

	RECERTIFICATION REQUIRED?	RECERTIFICATION PERIOD (IN YEARS)	SEMESTER HOUR RECERTIFICATION REQUIREMENT	RECERTIFICATION VIA DISTRICT-PLANNED ACTIVITIES?	RECERTIFICATION SOLELY VIA DISTRICT-PLANNED ACTIVITIES?	% RECERTIFICATION CREDIT ALLOWED VIA DISTRICT ACTIVITIES
New Hampshire	yes	3	3	yes	yes	NA
New Jersey	no	—	—	—	—	—
New Mexico	yes	4–10*	8	yes	no	50%
New York	no	—	—	—	—	—
North Carolina	yes	5	6	yes	yes	NA
North Dakota	yes	5	4	no	NA	NA
Ohio	yes	4–8*	6–18*	no	NA	NA
Oklahoma	yes	5	8	no	NA	NA
Oregon	yes	3–5*	9–24*	yes	yes	NA
Pennsylvania	yes	6*	24**	yes	yes	NA
Rhode Island	yes	3–5*	6–M.S.*/**	yes	no	33%–50%*
South Carolina	yes	5	6	yes	yes	NA
South Dakota	yes	5	6	yes	no	50%
Tennessee	yes	10	6	no	NA	NA
Texas	yes	3–5*	6*/**	yes	pending	pending
Utah	yes	5	6	yes	yes	NA
Vermont	yes	5	6	yes	yes	NA
Virginia	yes	5	6	yes	no	50%
Washington	yes	4**	10*	no	NA	NA
West Virginia	yes	3–5*	6	no	NA	NA
Wisconsin	pending	5	6	yes	yes	NA
Wyoming	yes	5–10*	5–10*	yes	yes	NA

NA = not applicable

* Contingent on candidate's years of successful teaching experience, certificate level, and/or highest degree attained.
** One to several renewals are allowed, leading toward permanent certificate.
† Recertification is required only after dormant period; district alternative to recertification is allowed.
‡ District alternative to recertification is sole option for recertification of teachers with master's degrees and beyond.
§ District alternative to recertification is sole option for first renewal only.

Source: Reprinted with permission. Hanes and Rowls. *Phi Delta Kappan 66*(2), 1984. Teacher certification: A survey of the states.

1980s. The entry requirements of most of these programs have at least equal requirements for admission into preservice teacher education programs (McKibbin 1988). Table 12.6 summarizes states' criteria for alternative certification.

The state of New Jersey responded to shortages in various teaching fields in 1982 with a long-term study related to alternative ways to certify teachers. The result was that in 1985 local school districts in New Jersey started to offer the first district-administered training programs leading to teacher certification in the United States (Cooperman and Klagholz 1985).

TEACHER EDUCATION: CONCLUSIONS

Teacher education in the United States is currently under a great deal of criticism. Among the charges are that students who enroll in colleges of education are of poor quality, the teacher education curriculum is irrelevant, and funds are insufficient to adequately prepare teachers.

Colleges of education have responded. New, tougher admission requirements have been implemented in many universities, training curricula are being scrutinized, and professors in teacher education are being encouraged to engage in relevant research to provide empirical bases for teacher education.

Some of the criticism is the result of critics looking for a scapegoat for the perceived poor status of public education in the United States. Some of the criticisms are valid and require immediate action on the part of teacher education professors. As a result, some needed changes will improve the quality of teacher education programs, with the end result of better teachers to staff public schools. Clark (1984) suggests that college of education faculty take four major actions to counteract much of the criticism and to improve teacher education training:

- Establish a better relationship between research on teaching and teaching effectiveness and teacher education.
- Recommit to research and scholarly activities.
- Expand research to include policy development.
- Develop new teacher training programs that are based on empirical data, not simply tradition.

SUMMARY

This chapter focused on teacher education. Teacher education has come under a great deal of criticism lately, with critics emphasizing the low quality of teacher education students and the teacher education curriculum. Current reforms in teacher education were presented, along

TABLE 12.6
Alternative Certification Requirements

STATE	DEGREE REQUIREMENTS	RESPONSIBLE PARTY(IES)	TEACHERS ELIGIBLE	TESTING REQUIREMENT	TRAINING PROGRAMS	PRACTICUM
Alabama	B.A.	College	Majors other than education	Yes	39 semester hours	300 hours student teaching
Arkansas	B.A.	College	All	State certification	College program	Internship
Arizona	B.A.	College	Majors other than education	Basic skills	College program	Internship
California	B.A.	District	Shortage areas	Basic skills/NTE	288 clock hours in largest district	Internship
Connecticut (planned)	•	•	•	•	•	•
Delaware	B.A.	•	Academic shortage areas	Preprofessional skills	Special institutes	Internship
Florida	B.A.	District	Secondary	Performance	90 hours + 6 semester units	Internship
Georgia	B.A.	District	Critical need	State certification and performance	250 clock hours	
Kentucky	B.A.	•	Shortage areas	State certification	Yes	Yes
Louisiana	B.A.	College/district	Secondary	State certification	Joint development	Internship
Maryland	B.A.	•	All	State certification	•	Internship
Massachusetts (planned)	•	•	•	•	•	•

TABLE 12.6 – *Continued*
Alternative Certification Requirements

STATE	DEGREE REQUIREMENTS	RESPONSIBLE PARTY(IES)	TEACHERS ELIGIBLE	TESTING REQUIREMENT	TRAINING PROGRAMS	PRACTICUM
Mississippi	B.A.	•	All	NTE	12 semester hours/3 years	•
New Jersey	B.A.	District	All	State certification	200 clock hours	Internship
New Mexico	B.A.	College business district	•	State certification	Summer program	•
North Carolina	B.A.	College/district	Shortage areas	State certification	Joint program	Internship
Oklahoma	B.A.	District/college	Shortage areas	State certification	Enrolled in professional education	
South Carolina	B.A.	District/college	Shortage areas	NTE	2-week program	•
Texas	B.A.	College	Shortage areas	Basic skills	1-year program	Internship
Virginia	B.A.	College/district	Secondary	State certification	Demonstration of competency or coursework	Yes
West Virginia	B.A.	College	Shortage mid-career, retired	State certification	University program and demonstration of competency	

Sources: Chronicle of Higher Education (1988) and Cornett (1988). Reprinted with permission. McKibbin. Alternative teacher certification programs. *Educational Leadership 46(3)*, 1988.
• Indicates data were not available to the author.

with the implications of these reforms. Reforms specified include improving the quality of teacher education students, revamping the teacher education curriculum, implementing exit criteria for certification, increasing funding for teacher education, and improving the quality of teacher education faculty.

Teacher certification was also discussed, focusing on traditional approaches and alternative programs.

IN THE FIELD

1. Have enrollment figures in the college of education where you attend bottomed out? What is the current trend in enrollment? What factors contribute to this trend?

2. Do you agree with some of the stated criticisms of teacher education? What factors in the teacher education program at your university do you consider good? What factors do you consider bad?

3. Has your college of education initiated any reforms in the teacher education program during the past five years? If so, what are they?

4. Does your college of education faculty feel as though the college receives its fair share of funding compared with other academic units on campus? If not, why?

5. What are the state certification requirements in your area of emphasis? Have these changed during the past five years, or are they expected to change in the near future?

6. Does your state have alternative certification programs? If so, what are they? Do college of education faculty members support such alternative programs?

REFERENCES

Barr, R. D. 1984. New ideas for teacher education. *Phi Delta Kappan* 66(2), 127–29.

Buchanan, R. 1982. Out in the field. *Phi Delta Kappan* 63(7), 458–59.

Bush, R. N. 1987. Teacher education reform: Lessons from the past half century. *Journal of Teacher Education* 38(3), 13–17.

Clabaugh, G. K., P. D. Feden, and R. Vogel. 1984. Revolutionizing teacher education: Training developmentally oriented teachers. *Phi Delta Kappan* 65(9), 615–16.

Clark, D. L. 1984. Better teachers for the year 2000: A proposal for the structural reform of teacher education. *Phi Delta Kappan* 66(2), 116–20.

Cooperman, S., and L. Klagholz. 1985. New Jersey's alternate route to certification. *Phi Delta Kappan* 66(10), 691–95.

Draba, R. E. and L. L. Steinkellner. 1977. Screening applicants for teacher training. *Educational Forum*, 42(1), 101–10.

Eiseenberg, T. E., and L. M. Rudner. 1988. State testing of teachers: A summary. *Journal of Teacher Education* 39(4), 21–22.

Gage, N. L. 1984. What do we know about teaching effectiveness? *Phi Delta Kappan* 66(2), 87–93.

Gallup, A. 1984a. The Gallup poll of teachers, attitudes toward the public schools. *Phi Delta Kappan* 66(2), 97–107.

Gallup, G. H. 1984b. The 16th annual Gallup poll of the public's attitudes toward the public schools. *Phi Delta Kappan* 66(1), 23–38.

Gideonse, H. D. 1982. The necessary revolution in teacher education. *Phi Delta Kappan* 64(1), 15–18.

Graham, P. A. 1974. *Community and Class in American Education, 1865–1918*. New York: John Wiley & Sons.

Griffin, G. A. 1989. A descriptive study of student teaching. *The Elementary School Journal* 89(3), 343–363.

Haberman, M. 1987. Lessons from the media: What the public is conditioned to believe about teacher education. *Action in Teacher Education* 9(4), 7–10.

Hanes, M. L., and M. D. Rowls. 1984. Teacher recertification: A survey of the states. *Phi Delta Kappan* 66(2), 123–26.

Ishler, R. E. 1984. Requirements for admission to and graduation from teacher education. *Phi Delta Kappan* 66(2), 121–22.

Keith, M. J. 1987. We've heard this song . . . or have we? *Journal of Teacher Education* 38(3), 20–25.

Keppel, F. 1986. A field guide to the land of teachers. *Phi Delta Kappan* 69(1), 18–22.

Lanier, J. E. and J. Featherstone. 1988. A new commitment to teacher education. *Educational Leadership* 46(3), 18–22.

Marczely, B. 1985. Teacher education: A view from the front lines. *Phi Delta Kappan* 66(10), 702–706.

Marker, G. W. 1984. The new crisis: Teacher education responds. *Educational Horizons* 62(6), 55–59.

McKibbin, M. D. 1988. Alternative teacher certification programs. *Educational Leadership* 46(3), 32–35.

Murray, F. B. 1986. Goals of the reform of teacher education: An executive summary of the Holmes Group report. *Phi Delta Kappan* 68(7), 28–32.

Nagel, N. 1988. One university's response to teacher education reform. *Educational Leadership* 46(3), 23–24.

National Center for Education Statistics. 1988a. *The Condition of Education*. Washington, DC: U.S. Department of Education.

National Center for Education Statistics. 1988b. *Targeted Forecast*. Washington DC: U.S. Department of Education.

Nilli, E. 1988. A research-based response to allegations that education students are academically inferior. *Action in Teacher Education* 9(2), 119–26.

Ohanian, S. 1985. On stir-and-serve recipes for teaching. *Phi Delta Kappan* 66(10), 696–701.

Pinar, W. F. 1989. A reconceptualization of teacher education. *Journal of Teacher Education* 40(1), 9–12.

Raimo, A. M. 1983. Methods courses are still a vital component in teacher education. *Kappa Delta Pi Record* 19(2), 42–44.

Scannell, D. P. 1984. The extended teacher education program at the University of Kansas. *Phi Delta Kappan* 66(2), 130–33.

Schaffer, E. C., and D. M. Wolfe. 1988. An innovative design for excellence in teacher education. *Action in Teacher Education* 10(1), 31–38.

School teaching profession in "crisis," new Carnegie analysis finds. 1983. *Chronicle of Higher Education*, August 31, 1983, 6.

Sirotnik, K. A. 1988. Studying the education of educators: Methodology. *Phi Delta Kappan* 70(3), 241–247.

Smith, B. O. 1980. Pedagogical education: How about reform? *Phi Delta Kappan* 62(2), 87–89.

Smith, D. C., R. G. Carroll, and B. Fry. 1984. PROTEACH: Professional teacher preparation at the University of Florida. *Phi Delta Kappan* 66(2), 134–35.

Tafel, L., and J. Christensen. 1988. Teacher education in the 1990s: Looking ahead while learning from the past. *Action in Teacher Education* 19(3), 1–6.

Tracy, S. J., R. Sheehan, and R. J. McArdle. 1988. Teacher education reform: The implementors' reactions. *Action in Teacher Education* 10(3), 14–21.

Turner, R. R. 1987. To teach or not to teach. *Learning* 16(3), 57–60.

Weaver, W. T. 1984. Solving the problem of teacher quality, part 1. *Phi Delta Kappan* 66(2), 108–15.

Weible, T., and W. Dumas. 1982. Secondary teacher certification standards in fifty states. *Journal of Teacher Education* 33(4), 22–23.

Wheeler, R., and R. Giese. 1988. Teacher education faculty perceptions of Holmes Group Membership. *Action in Teacher Education* 10(2), 22–27.

13

EDUCATIONAL TECHNOLOGY

OBJECTIVES
— ∎ —

After reading this chapter you will be able to

- describe instructional television;
- list advantages and disadvantages of instructional television;
- describe the use of closed-circuit television in schools;
- indicate the use of audiovisual kits;
- describe the uses of computers in education;
- discuss computer-assisted instruction;
- list barriers to implementing computer-assisted instruction;
- discuss other technologies of instruction; and
- describe some needed new directions in educational technology.

OUTLINE
— ∎ —

ADVANCE ORGANIZERS

1. What is instructional television?
2. How much is instructional television used today?
3. What are some advantages and disadvantages of instructional television?
4. How can closed-circuit television be used in instruction?
5. How are audiovisual kits used in schools?
6. What are some advantages and disadvantages of audiovisual kits?
7. What is the history of using computers in education?
8. What is computer-assisted instruction?
9. What are some advantages and disadvantages of computer-assisted instruction?
10. What barriers block the implementation of computer-assisted instruction?
11. How can software be evaluated?
12. What new directions does educational technology need?

INTRODUCTION

The world is in a technological revolution. New technologies are being developed every day. Beginning with radios in the early 1900s, moving to televisions in the 1950s, and finally microcomputers in the 1980s, technological advances have heavily affected the everyday life of most Americans. There is no sign that the technological revolution is slowing down. Indeed, with recent developments like FAX (facsimiles transferred via telecommunication) machines, the spread of new technologies appears to be increasing at a more rapid pace than ever.

Technology in education has long been an interest of professional educators. How can the latest technology be implemented to assist in the learning process? What is the most cost-efficient method of teaching children using technology? How can technological advances complement teachers in classrooms? These are but a few of the many questions asked by educators relative to technology and education.

Educational technology has long been associated with the audiovisual movement (Chan 1984). Today educational technology is primarily associated with computers, especially microcomputers. Educational technology, however, encompasses much more than either audiovisual materials or computers. It "embraces every possible means by which information can be presented. It is concerned with the 'gadgetry' of education and training, such as television, language laboratories and the various projected media, or, as someone once said, 'everything from computers to dinner ticket dispensers' " (Percival and Ellington 1988, p. 13). Technology of instruction can be defined "as the application of our scientific knowledge about human learning to the practical tasks of teaching and learning." (Heinich, Molenda, and Russell 1982, p. 19). Some of the components of educational technology include instructional television, audiovisual kits such as filmstrips, videocassette technology, closed-circuit television, and computers.

One problem with educational technology is that it is too closely associated with mechanization, machinery, and gadgetry. For educational technology to be better understood and accepted, a more humanistic and aesthetic approach must be taken. The following would enhance this perception of educational technology:

- Educational technology should address broader goals than simply instruction and training.
- Educational technology must be more oriented to humanistic compassion than simply mechanical activities.
- Educational technology must attempt to solve educational problems using a holistic approach.
- Educational technology must use scientific inquiry as a guide, not as a dictum.
- Educational technology should address concerns such as school organization and community involvement in addition to immediate learning by students. (Chan 1984)

Educational technology, therefore, includes many components. While it is often equated with machinery, mechanical responses, and restricted creativity, it can and should go beyond these perceived parameters. The most obvious technologies are in the area of machines and equipment (Hatch 1984); however, many other forms of educational technology can be effective in public schools for instructional purposes. The primary purpose of instructional technology is to facilitate instruction (Gagne' 1987).

INSTRUCTIONAL TELEVISION

Instructional television (ITV) began in the United States in the 1960s. It was presented as a way to solve many of the problems facing educators and the schools: providing high-quality teaching to students, increasing the productivity of students and teachers, and providing education in the home as well as the school. Because of the sudden adoption of ITV, the development of ITV materials grew dramatically. Schools of education began to include ITV as a part of the teacher training curriculum. Demonstration projects were funded, and some states initiated statewide distribution plans of ITV materials (Rockman

1985). However, much of this enthusiasm quickly faded as "teachers found ITV inconvenient to use off-air (from live shows) and intimidating to use on tape" (p. 27). Currently, ITV is experiencing a resurgence in popularity. As a result of the growing availability of VCRs and a general decline in teachers' fears of machinery, instructional television is again growing in use (Strohmer 1989).

Recent data collected by the Corporation for Public Broadcasting, the National Center for Education Statistics, and Quality Education Data, Inc. indicate that many schools use ITV. These findings included:

- seventy percent of the classrooms in the United States have televisions;
- fifty-five percent of the classrooms in the United States use televisions for instruction.
- 18.5 million students receive some of their instruction through television, and
- 14.5 million students use televisions as a regular part of their instructional day. (Rockman 1985)

These figures indicate that ITV is heavily used in public school programs for instructional purposes. Although not considered as glamorous as computers, ITV continues to be a form of educational technology that is often used in schools.

A recent development using ITV is the Star Schools Program. Enacted by Congress in 1987, the program authorized the federal government to fund four recipients for demonstration grants totalling $19 million. The 1988 awards will provide more than five hundred schools in thirty-nine states with equipment, personnel training, and technical assistance (Bruder 1988b).

The Star Schools Program will enable high-school students in rural communities to enroll in a variety of courses, ranging from anatomy to Japanese. Students enrolled in courses view a live lecture beamed from a training site. They can interact with the instructor by asking questions through a cordless telephone handset. Exams, handouts, and other course materials are provided through a low-cost dot-matrix printer. The cost for equipping each school is approximately $15,000. Schools only have to provide classroom space, telephone line, and a class facilitator to operate the equipment and provide supervision for the class (Cumuze 1989). The Stars School Project has added a new boost to ITV.

As with any educational technology, ITV has several benefits over regular instruction. These include (1) increased student motivation, (2) illustration of material that is difficult to teach, and (3) ability of teachers to use a common stimulus for teaching (Rockman 1985). Additional advantages include the facts that information is presented using color, moving pictures; programs can be transmitted over long distances; cost per student can be low; and learners can even be reached in their own homes (Heinich, Molenda, and Russell 1982).

Along with advantages of ITV come disadvantages, which include:

- The complexity of the technology creates opportunities for problems.
- Many programs are poorly developed and produced.
- Weather conditions may disrupt signals.
- Images received on television monitors may be too small for large classes.
- ITV is a one-way mode of communication. (Heinich, Molenda, and Russell 1982)

CLOSED-CIRCUIT TELEVISION

Another use of televisions for instructional purposes is through closed-circuitry. In closed-circuit television the sender and receiver are physically linked with wires. The most simple arrangement is a single camera hooked to a single television; more elaborate systems would connect several classrooms to a television studio (Heinich, Molenda, and Russell 1982). Closed-circuit television (CCTV) can provide many advantages in various teaching situations. Menis (1982) suggested the use of closed-circuit television as a substitute for the science laboratory. Instead of having all students do actual work in the lab, live demonstrations can be provided that enable students to see directly what is taking place in the lab. In days of high costs for lab equipment and materials, this method of presentation could greatly reduce costs and still allow students to see actual experiments conducted.

Other advantages are that closed-circuit televisions

1. enable teachers to focus the students' attention to a particular task while neutralizing the effects of the surrounding environment,
2. enable the enlargement or magnification of small items on the screen for easy viewing and detail recommendations,
3. introduce different effects by using different cameras with different lighting and angles,
4. insert enriching sections during the lecture and/or explanation of activities,
5. provide students with the opportunity to see successful experiments. Unsuccessful experiments are discarded or taped over so students only see what should occur. (Menis 1982)

Still another advantage, primarily administrative, is that since the signals used in CCTV do not travel over the airways, they are not regulated by government agencies; therefore, anyone with the equipment can use CCTV without a great deal of bureaucratic red tape.

Closed-circuit television as an educational technology has not been utilized as often as possible. Video cameras can be purchased relatively inexpensively (approximately $1,000), and videocassette recorders and tapes are readily accessible to most schools. Teachers should explore ways to use closed-circuit television instruction in their classes.

AUDIOVISUAL KITS

Audiovisual kits, usually in the form of filmstrips, tapes, or other audiovisual items and printed information, have been used in schools for instructional purposes for several decades. These kits enable teachers to focus on a particular topic and provide individual learning experiences to students (Smith and Ingersoll 1984). While computers are in the limelight as the possible "salvation" for American education, audiovisual kits continue to be used a great deal by teachers. They are effective, cost efficient, and available. Other advantages are that film-

■ *Closed circuit television (CCTV) can provide many advantages in various teaching situations.*

strips and filmstrip projectors are portable, easy to manipulate, present information in a sequential manner for learning purposes, enable the pace and level of instruction to be controlled by the teacher, and are especially useful in independent studies (Heinich, Molenda, and Russell 1982). Smith and Ingersoll (1984) conducted a study in 1982, with a followup study in 1983, to determine the use of audiovisual kits in public schools in the United States (see table 13.1). These studies showed a steady if not growing use of audiovisual kits. Most teachers felt that audiovisual kits were available for their use, and approximately one-third of the teachers used the kits at least weekly. The use of the kits was greater in elementary schools than high schools.

Even though audiovisual kits are not considered as important as some other forms of educational technology, future teachers should be aware of the availability of such materials and of their usefulness in the teaching process. These kinds of materials can still motivate students and enable teachers to focus on specific learning tasks.

VIDEOCASSETTE TECHNOLOGY

A relatively new entry in educational technology is videocassette recorders and recordings. The first videocassette recorders (VCRs) were marketed in the early 1970s. The growth of this industry has been phenomenal; sales of videocassette recorders in 1984 alone topped fifteen

TABLE 13.1
Use of Audiovisual Materials in Schools

	ELEM. SCHOOLS	MIDDLE SCHOOLS	HIGH SCHOOLS	ALL
% Teachers Reporting Availability of Audiovisual Kits in 1982	81.8	74.0	77.9	80.2
% Teachers Reporting Availability of Audiovisual Kits in 1983	72.8	70.3	71.3	71.0
% Teachers Reporting Weekly Use of Audiovisual Kits in 1982	41.2	23.2	17.9	32.9
% Teachers Reporting Weekly Use of Audiovisual Kits in 1983	29.4	19.5	20.8	26.0
% Teachers Reporting No Use of Audiovisual Kits in 1982	4.5	10.6	20.4	7.8
% Teachers Reporting No Use of Audiovisual Kits in 1983	7.7	14.5	14.0	11.0

Source: Smith and Ingersoll. Audiovisual materials in U.S. schools: A national survey on availability and use. *Educational Technology* 24(9), 1984.

■ *Teachers use a variety of audiovisual kits to focus on particular topics.*

hundred thousand units, which represented a 100 percent increase over the 1983 sales figures (Reider 1984).

Although expensive at first, videocassette recorders currently can be purchased for less than three hundred dollars, and blank videocassette tapes can cost as little as three dollars. The mass production of these devices, as well as their limited cost, makes the acquisition of VCRs easy for many individuals and most school districts. A recent report on technology in the schools reported that in the 1986–1987 school year, VCRs were available in ninety-six percent of the public schools and eighty percent of all private schools (Goodspeed 1988).

Professionals in education have begun to realize the value in VCR technology to instruction. Some of the advantages to using this technology in education include:

- the technology is a conventional type of media;
- the technology is very accessible (due to cost and production levels);
- VCRs can be used to tape all kinds of educationally relevant materials;
- the technology can easily be controlled by teachers;
- the technology offers many of the advantages of film while not including many of the disadvantages; and

- VCR technology has many advantages over filmstrips, primarily the utilization of a moving image. (Reider 1984)

VCR technology is available today, relatively inexpensive, can take advantage of materials presented on television at any time, and provides students with a highly motivating audiovisual mode of processing information. Again, even though this device is not the glamour item in educational technology today, teachers need to be aware of the potential for using VCRs.

VIDEODISC PLAYERS

The newest technology being adopted in some schools is the videodisc player. This audiovisual tool can present slides and play motion pictures at any time and in any sequence desired. The materials are durable, easy to use, and can provide high quality narration and natural backgrounds. The laser videodisc player is basically a record player that uses laser technology instead of direct contact with the disk (Phillipo 1988).

The videodisc playback features a combination of those options found in more traditional audiovisual equipment, such as a VCR, tape recorder, or record player. The difference is that the videodisc player provides all these options with one unit. As the price of this technology inevitably decreases, more schools will take advantage of the flexibility of the system (Phillipo 1988). Six percent of public and private schools currently own videodisc players (Goodspeed 1988).

HIGHLIGHT
▪
A NEW SPIN ON VIDEODISCS

Michael Rogers

The world of consumer electronics is cruelly competitive: gadgets that don't catch on rarely last more than a single Christmas season. But the laser videodisc, introduced a decade ago, is one technology that has refused to die. A single shiny silver platter, the size of a phonograph record, can hold a full two-hour movie, offering razor-sharp images and theater-quality sounds. Impressive credentials. Even so, videodiscs have been a flop, kept alive by industrial and educational users—and a fiercely loyal coterie of movie buffs.

Videodiscs are about to make a comeback. This summer several firms, including Philips, Pioneer and Sony, will introduce new videodisc players, some for less than $500. And many of the new machines will also be able to play compact discs. These machines promise a double payoff for manufacturers eager to maintain their rates of growth. Sales of videocassette recorders have slowed; almost 60 percent of American households already own one VCR. Also,

continued

---

while compact discs are dominating the recording industry, many consumers have been reluctant to spring for a new piece of hardware. Videodisc-CD combo players may be too tempting to resist.

The combination players work because both compact discs and videodiscs use a laser beam to read the grooves on the platter, just as a phonograph needle traces grooves in traditional records. The new players can read discs from 3 to 12 inches in diameter, carrying anything from a handful of songs to a full-length motion picture. Record companies are now experimenting with hybrid compact discs that deliver a short music video followed by 20 minutes of music without video.

Just five years ago videodiscs appeared to be dead when RCA killed its Selectavision disc system, which relied on a needle instead of a laser. Despite pouring more than $500 million into the project, RCA couldn't match the appeal of VCR's. That gigantic failure was widely misinterpreted as the end of all videodiscs. But video connoisseurs stuck with the more sophisticated laser technology. "It's always been the choice for people who want the closest reproduction of a theatrical experience in their homes," says Rockley Miller, publisher of the newsletter Videodisc Monitor.

Videodisc buffs shop mail-order outlets like Laser Island in Brooklyn, paying as much as $150 for the latest videodiscs from Japan, where titles are more plentiful. Laser Island's average customer owns more than 500 videodiscs; the store's current top seller is the Japanese copy of Disney's "20,000 Leagues Under the Sea." For $125 the viewer gets high-quality sound that gives the sensation of riding a diving submarine; on the screen, the picture is framed in a "letterbox format," which leaves black stripes at the top and bottom but shows the entire width of the movie.

In the United States, video buffs covet the wares of Los Angeles publishers Voyager, whose Criterion line presents movies ranging from "Bladerunner" to "The Wizard of Oz." Criterion videodiscs often feature bonus material: "Oz," for example, includes composer Harold Arlen's home movies of the production, excerpts from the 1925 silent version and material from the director's scrapbook. Criterion's "Black Narcissus" includes commentary by director Martin Scorsese.

Now movie studios are enthusiastically embracing the videodisc market, selling movies at prices far below the specialty and import discs. Three thousand titles are currently available, with another 90 or so appearing each month, and most prices range from $25 to $30. "If the volume increases, prices could drop to $15," says Douglas Pratt, editor of the Laser Disc Newsletter. Pratt also foresees a booming rental market for the discs. "A video cassette can look awful after too many rentals," he says. "But videodiscs never wear out."

Videodiscs may also become a schoolroom staple, for a single disc can hold more than 100,000 still images as well as moving video—essentially both slides and movies in the same package. "Potentially it could replace all other audiovisual methods," says Bev Hamilton, a south San Francisco elementary-school teacher. One science videodisc from Optical Data has an animated segment showing two dinosaurs battling; midway in the sequence, Hamilton freezes the action with the touch of a button, then leads her fifth graders in a discussion of which dinosaur is likely to win. "It's much more interactive than movies or videotapes," says Hamilton. The only shortcoming is a lack of hardware and school-oriented discs, but publishers are beginning to turn to that market now. Next month Encyclopaedia Brittannica will release more than 100 of its educational films and filmstrips on videodisc.

Cooks and Crooks

Videodiscs have already found a niche in business, since it's easy to repeat a given section as many times as necessary for training or sales. Sizzler Restaurants train their cooks with videodiscs; an IBM videodisc literacy program is used in prisons throughout the United States. And travel agencies can now lease a videodisc system from Los Angeles-based Laser Travel; if a client is interested in the Bahamas, the agent

continued

simply hands over a videodisc about the destination, complete with hotel and cruise information.

At home, the videodiscs will benefit from the increasing popularity of large-screen, high-resolution TV's. The larger the screen, the better videodiscs look compared with videotape. A television's sharpness is measured by the number of individual elements that can be seen in a horizontal line on screen. The best of the modern televisions can show 400 or more lines—far more than the 240 lines delivered by standard videocassette recorders. Videodiscs yield over 350 lines.

Newer videodiscs also offer surround sound, which provides theater-quality effects. "The sound of the best discs is truly awesome," says Harry Pearson, publisher of The Perfect Vision, a high-end video magazine. "Bullets fly around your head, ocean waves crash at your feet, planes fly overhead. In a horror movie, footsteps come up behind you." Several studios offer European opera and symphony performances on videodisc, as well as full-length pop-music concerts. After a decade of gestation, the theater-at-home quality of videodiscs may prove to be the answer to couch-potato prayers—with a bonus for those with younger spuds. "These discs are just about indestructible," says Pratt. "Even if your kid smears peanut butter on it, you just have to wipe it clean.

COMPUTERS

The newest, most talked about, and most highly sought after technology for education today is the computer. Computers are here to stay. Somewhat of a computer revolution has taken place in the United States since the beginning of the 1980s. Whereas computers were once thought of as big, expensive, and difficult-to-operate machines, today's computers are portable, relatively inexpensive, and easily operated. Many persons who are not in computer vocations have computers in their homes. Persons who just a few years ago would have said that computers are for intellectuals now have their own computers at home for home management, instruction, games, and a host of other activities.

Computers in Education

Computers are the most active form of educational technology in the schools today. The growth of the number of computers and the use of computers in schools is difficult to imagine. The number of schools with microcomputers increased from 13,986 in 1982 to 30,493 in 1983, an increase of 118 percent (National Center for Education Statistics 1984). During the 1986–1987 school year, more than 2 million microcomputers were in use in the public schools (Goodspeed 1988). Schools not only have computers available, but many are using computers in computer-assisted instruction (CAI). A survey of 202 schools indicated that the use of computers in CAI ranged from a low of 56.5 percent in kindergarten to a high of 81.5 percent in the third grade. At the secondary level, the greatest use of computers in CAI was in math (92.1

percent) and science (85.7 percent) (Nelson and Waack 1985) (see table 13.2).

History of Computer Use in Education. In the 1960s and 1970s the idea of using computers for educational purposes received a great deal of attention. Proponents of using this technology in public schools viewed computers as an unprecedented aid to teaching and learning. Still there were skeptics. Computers of this era were large monsters. They were designed for carrying out complicated mathematical calculations, for which they were very effective if the user understood the highly sophisticated language required to operate the hardware (Heinich, Molenda, and Russell 1982).

Then, about 1975, microcomputers were developed. The development of microcomputers was made possible by the invention of the silicon chip, a tiny microprocessor that could perform functions previously possible only on large mainframe computers. By 1980 approximately one million microcomputers were already in use (Heinich, Molenda, and Russell 1982). The development of microcomputers renewed the enthusiasm of some concerning the future role of computers in education. Microcomputers, the "Model T of the computer industry," have made computer technology readily accessible to most school districts (Holmes 1982).

The number of microcomputers on the market and their relatively low cost has enabled public education to implement computer tech-

TABLE 13.2
Uses of CAI

GRADE LEVEL	% USING CAI
K	56.5
1	73.2
2	76.9
3	81.5
4	80.6
5	75.5
6	66.6
7	21.4
8	28.7
Secondary/Math	92.1
Secondary/Science	85.7
Secondary/Business Education	82.2
Secondary/English, Language Arts	75.1

Source: Nelson and Waack. The status of computer literacy/computer-assisted instruction awareness as a factor in classroom instruction and teacher selection, *Educational Technology* 25(2), 1985.

nology into daily instructional activities. The movement to incorporate computer technology into education has basically been a grassroots phenomenon, led by classroom teachers who were interested in adding a new dimension into their classrooms (Donhardt 1984). The use of microcomputers in education is growing at a tremendous rate and should continue to increase in the future.

Close investigation of the use of computers in classrooms, however, indicates that their use has not been as successful as the numbers might indicate. Problems that continue to block the widespread use of microcomputers in education include (1) lack of availability of computers in schools; (2) lack of policy in schools relatd to computer use; (3) inadequate software; and (4) inadequate teacher training (Bonner 1984).

The use of computers, which potentially could revolutionize education, could fail, as have other technologies in the past where the purchases have come before the adequate planning and preparation of practitioners. To avoid this, Boyer (1984) suggests three priorities. First, students need to learn about technology. This includes teaching students about the social impact of technology and computers, not hands-on instruction. The second priority is to teach students how to learn with computers. Learning with computers includes using computers to gather information. Finally, students should learn from computers. This requires interactive learning between students and computers, or "conversing" between students and computers to improve thinking skills.

While computers are capable of becoming a major force in education, some concerns need to be mentioned. Some professionals argue that the overuse of computers and other technologies can have a negative effect on education. For example, the technology in education can "isolate us from the very processes by which we define our humanity" (Hatch 1984, p. 243). These human processes, defined as those things that differentiate humans from other living organisms—such as loving, knowing, and making decisions—can become devalued as a result of overdependency on technology.

Uses of Computers in Education

Computers, primarily microcomputers because of their low cost, high availability, and easy operation, can be used in education in several different ways. The three primary uses include computer-assisted instruction (CAI), computer science, and administration.

Computer-assisted Instruction. Computer-assisted instruction is a main use of computers in schools today. CAI can be defined as interaction between the learner and computer. The student is an active participant in the learning process; direct two-way communication

■ *Today schools use computers mainly for computer-assisted instruction (CAI).*

between the learner and computer take place in the form of questions, responses, and feedback. Passive learning is not possible with CAI (Lockard, Abrams, and Many 1987). When using CAI, learning is individualized and ranges from remediation for students having problems to enrichment activities for gifted students. The goal of CAI, simply stated, "is to use computers as a tool to increase student learning" (Long 1985, p. 27).

There are several common types of CAI: drill-and-practice, tutorial, and simulation. Drill-and-practice programs are the most common form of instructional programs. Programs are highly repetitious and primarily serve to reinforce previous learning (Lockard et al. 1987).

Tutorial applications of CAI focus on teaching new materials, as opposed to drilling on materials already taught (Willis 1987). The process includes (1) information presented by the computer; (2) student response to questions related to content; (3) computer evaluation of student responses; and (4) computer determination of next learning step (Merrill, Tolman, Christensen, Hammons, Vincent, and Reynolds, 1986).

In simulation applications, students interact with computer-generated models. For example, biology students can dissect a frog form on a computer rather than a real frog in the lab. "Simulations can also allow students to experience phenomena which would otherwise be too expensive or time consuming" (Merrill et al. 1986, p. 10).

Advantages and Disadvantages. As with any instructional methodology, CAI has both advantages and disadvantages. Specific advantages include

- individual pacing
- immediate feedback
- opportunities for drill
- overlearning (Smith, Price, and Marsh 1986)

Still other advantages include generating a high level of interest in students, enabling some students to learn materials that they would not be capable of learning in a normal classroom situation (Long 1985), and meeting individual learning needs (Lockard et al. 1987).

Although these advantages appear to support the implementation of CAI, certain disadvantages must be considered. First, CAI is directly related to the teacher's ability to structure the course and to impose order on the content. Because many teachers have not been trained in CAI, this may create significant problems. Second, CAI traditionally has been used as a supplement to traditional classroom instruction. Also, CAI programs usually present single-concept material, human interactions are missing, and the CAI program may have little relationship to the curriculum (Smith, Price, and Marsh 1986). Long (1985) adds that only a limited amount of software is available for CAI, and there is a dearth of materials appropriate for lower elementary students.

Barriers to Implementing CAI. Regardless of the advantages and disadvantages in CAI, schools that want to implement the use of such methodologies should be aware of some barriers that are likely to present problems. These include the costs of equipment and software, maintenance, the attitudes of personnel, attitudes of parents, and attitudes of students (Holmes 1982). Schools that want to implement CAI must consider these barriers, as well as the disadvantages of CAI, before attempting to develop a CAI component.

Roles of Personnel in CAI. Certain individuals both inside and outside the school play a vital role in the development of a CAI program. These include administrators, teachers, and students. Administrators have been characterized as key individuals in change and attitude development of school staff. They have been found to be vital in the success of almost every school activity. School administrators, basically because they control the budget, must be positive about CAI before it can be successfully implemented. Individuals in these roles usually proceed with change cautiously, because change itself can be extremely disruptive to the school. If CAI can be shown to be beneficial to administrators, their support is more likely than if they cannot see any positive result from implementing the new program. In the area of CAI, two possible benefits to which administrators might respond include peer approval and the possibility of receiving outside funding for the program (Holmes 1982).

Individuals interested in generating administrative support for CAI programs must work to garner this support. Examples of ways to get this support include

- inviting principals and other school administrators to visit schools that have implemented effective CAI programs;
- seeking outside funding from government or private sources to support the implementation of CAI programs;
- inviting school administrators to participate in a CAI planning session; and
- making administrators realize that a great deal of positive publicity could result for the school following the successful implementation of a CAI program.

- *Computers can be used in conjunction with videocassette recorders.*

While these actions may not win over administrators, they at least plant the idea that could result in administrative support over a period of time.

Teachers are also key individuals in the successful implementation of a CAI program. If teachers are supportive, CAI will more likely be successful than if teachers have negative attitudes about the program. After all, teachers are the ones who will have to implement the CAI program. Adminstrators can purchase computers and software and even mandate that CAI be used; however, without the willing cooperation of the teachers who are responsible for implementing CAI, the program will not likely be successful.

Often teachers are apprehensive about change because they do not understand their new role. As long as they are expected to teach five sections of history, or four sections of math, or all subjects to second graders, they understand where they fit in the system. CAI creates the possibility that their role in the educational process will be lessened. Although this is not the case, many teachers may fear that computers will replace them or undermine their status in the schools (Holmes 1982). To garner the support necessary from teachers for CAI, they must be made to understand their new role in a CAI program. Teachers must see the personal advantages inherent in CAI. Administrators could do this by encouraging teachers to attend workshops on computer use in instruction, providing funds for inservice programs, providing funds for college-credit courses, and simply indicating that administrative support would be available when CAI is implemented.

The third group of individuals who are critical to the successful implementation of CAI are the students (Holmes 1982). Students must want to use computers and software before they will be successful in using them. Although computers have been shown to be a motivating factor for many students, all students may not be receptive to their use. Computer anxiety is a real issue that must be overcome if students are to feel comfortable enough to try CAI, which is a major change from the traditional student-teacher learning process. One way to change students' attitudes about computers is to orient them to the technology. Administrators and teachers could sponsor a computer day for students, where local industries and computer dealers bring displays to the school and students get the opportunity to take a computer for a "test drive." Once students have the opportunity to see, touch, and operate a computer, many anxieties will be alleviated.

Parents of students also play a role in the successful implementation of CAI. If the community has a group of parents who want CAI in the schools, and this group is vocal in its support, the local school board probably will attempt to implement the program. Likewise, a group of vocal parents who oppose the introdution of computers could have a negative impact on the school's attempting to implement a CAI program. Parents, like students, could be invited to the school for the computer day so that they can gain a better understanding of the role computers would play in instruction were a CAI program initiated. One definite component for parents in the computer day should be a session pointing out the many personal and educational advantages students would have if the students were computer literate.

Other community members could also have an impact on CAI. For example, school districts in towns with certain industries are likely to get support, both political and financial, from private sources if students trained in CAI would be more likely candidates for jobs. Public schools often overlook the private sector in their attempts to implement new programs. School administrators need to court this group when attempting to implement new programs, especially those which have a high startup cost like CAI.

Software. CAI depends on programs commonly called *software.* The *hardware* is the machine, the computer, and peripherals (input-output devices); the software is the material that makes up the computer program (the step-by-step instructions that tell the computer what to do and how to do it). The majority of states are providing the same or more funding for software in 1988 compared to 1987 (Bruder 1988a). However, a lack of available, good software has been one of the criticisms often voiced about CAI. The software available for educators has increased dramatically in the 1980s, along with the use of computers in classrooms. Although much software is available, educators must know how to select software to get the best for the money. Just because numerous programs dealing with certain educational areas are available, they are not necessarily all good and worth the money.

Software in CAI is similar to textbooks in traditional instruction. To avoid selecting textbooks of poor quality, explicit procedures are followed by state departments of education and local school districts in textbook adoption. Unfortunately, similar procedures are not always followed in the selection of computer software. Too often teachers are asked to purchase materials without adequate information. They may be told one morning that they must spend five hundred dollars before the end of the day in order to keep from losing the money, and that they should buy computer programs. After looking at computer software catalogs, teachers might decide to purchsae certain programs because of many variables unrelated to the quality of the program, such as format of the advertisement, testimonials presented in advertisements by other supposed teachers, and cost. In the end, schools often purchase programs that are of little value to students.

Selecting good software for CAI presents many problems. First, many companies do not like to loan software to schools for review purposes for fear that the programs will be copied and returned without a sale. Also, most teachers are unaware of the different types of educational software (Wallace and Rose 1984). Further, since there is limited empirical data revealing the characteristics of good software, reviewers have a difficult time determining which software is appropriate (Jolicoeur and Bergen 1988).

Reviewing educational software should include a review of the content, the screen presentation, the interaction process, and the human values criteria. If this is done, then educators will more likely purchase software that (1) fits the curriculum, (2) is at the appropriate reading level for students, (3) reflects quality, (4) is compatible with the teacher's style, and (5) maintains sound educational practice (Wallace and Rose 1984). A systematic form could be used when reviewing educational software for CAI (see figure 13.1). Although this form can be modified to meet any school's particular needs, it does reflect the necessary components to ensure adequate software review.

Jolicoeur and Berger (1988) recommended evaluating software following its adoption by a school, too. They suggest the following eight steps to determine the effectiveness of the materials:

1. Specify the overall goals of the implementation procedures.
2. Select appropriate software.
3. Develop software support materials.
4. Randomly assign students to comparable groups.
5. Schedule and implement computer time for students.
6. Test student skills at regular intervals.
7. Evaluate the success of the software implementation procedures.
8. Evaluate the results of the issues examined. (p. 7)

Computer Science. Some schools actually offer computer science courses to their students. This application of computers in education is more likely to occur in the middle- and high-school level rather than in elementary schools. Computer science instruction basically teaches advanced computer literacy. Students learn about computing and some programming skills (Long 1985). The basic difference between computer science and CAI is that CAI is a means of instructing students in courses found in the regular curriculum. Computer science is not a method, but rather a course in itself. CAI is a means, computer science is a product.

Computer science courses in schools have some advantages and disadvantages. The chief advantage is that computer science will help students understand about computers. Since computers are here to stay and our society and world will become more and more computerized, students would be well-advised to learn about and understand computers. Some advocates of computer science courses also believe that learning how to program can actually lead to improved logical thinking skills in students. The major disadvantage of computer science is that too often schools do not have faculty with the expertise necessary to

---

Educational Software Review Form

PART I: SUMMARY

Identification

Program name: ....

.... Single program   .... Series

Program available for microcomputer brands: ....

Memory required: ....4K ....16K ....32K ....48K 64K
Format: .... Cassette Tape   ....5'' Diskette
         .... Cartridge   (Drives ....One ....Two)

Peripherals required:

        .... Printer
        .... Paddles/joystick   .... Voice/sound
        .... Color monitor   Other: ....;.

Description of Program: ....
....
....

Recommendation About Use:
    Appropriate for intended group: .... Yes   .... No
                               Group: ....
    Not appropriate
      for: ....

	Excellent	Acceptable	Poor
Appropriateness for student users	....		
Instructional Approach	....		
Content	....		
Presentation design of material	....		
Interaction process	....		
"Human values" criteria	....		

Other Comments: ....
....
....

(Continued)

FIGURE 13.1. Educational Software Review Form

teach such courses (Long 1985). Schools that implement computer sci‹ence courses simply because of popularity may end up with poor programs. Administrators would better serve students if the development of computer science courses resulted from long-range planning and if the capabilities of teachers were taken into consideration. If a school wanted to develop such a program, but had no qualified teachers to

Use:

Single user ....   Small team/group ....   Class ....
    .... Drill/practice   .... Simulation   .... Testing
    .... Instructional game   .... Problem solving   .... Management
    .... Tutorial   .... Data base
            Other ....
Target Audience: ....
Average Run Time: .... minutes

Management System:

Yes	No	
....	....	Keeps track of individual student performance.
....	....	Allows teacher to determine individual student levels within the program.

Directions for student user:

Yes	No	
....	....	Appropriate reading level.
....	....	Clear and understandable.
....	....	All contained and presented in the program.
....	....	Can be easily reviewed during use of the program.

PART II: EDUCATIONAL VALUE

Content:

Yes	No	None or NA	
....	....	....	Instructional objectives clearly stated.
....	....	....	The program has instructional significance.
....	....	....	Is compatible with other instructional materials.
			Levels of difficulty available:
			Determined by: program pretest ....,
			user selection ...., teacher selection ....
....	....	....	Material is free of content errors.
....	....	....	Language free of:
....	....	....	sex bias,
....	....	....	race bias,
....	....	....	cultural bias.
....	....	....	Women are proportionately represented in text.
....	....	....	Minority group members represented in text.
....	....	....	Contributions of all racial and ethnic groups and women and men presented in realistic and/or accurate ways.
....	....	....	A variety of ages are represented.
....	....	....	Disabled are represented in a variety of roles.

(Continued)

FIGURE 13.1. (Continued)

serve as the instructor, the school might want to send an interested teacher to school to become prepared to teach such a course and to share learning received with colleagues.

Adminstration. The third use of computers in schools is in the area of administration or management. Frequently schools do not restrict the

Instruction and Motivation:

Yes	No	None or NA	
....	....	....	User clearly knows when the computer is waiting for input.
....	....	....	User knows what kind of input the program expects.
....	....	....	The program runs without disruption.
....	....	....	The screen display is easy to read and understand.
....	....	....	The user can correct entries.
....	....	....	The software provides correct answer after the user responds incorrectly: Number of entries (errors/guesses) allowed ....
....	....	....	The input into the computer is appropriate for the objective of the program.
....	....	....	User can exit from the program without completion of the full program.
....	....	....	Motivators for the user are non-violent.
....	....	....	Motivational rewards are for correct rather than incorrect responses.
....	....	....	Motivators will be effective for racial and ethnic minority students.
....	....	....	Motivators will be effective for female students.
....	....	....	The program emphasizes cooperation.
....	....	....	The program emphasizes thinking and creativity.
....	....	....	Provides a summary of performance: .... during, ... at the end of program.

PART III: TECHNICAL VALUE

Check the appropriate boxes for use of different presentation styles.*

Presentation	ATTRACT ATTENTION	DIRECT INSTRUCTION	SUPPORT INSTRUCTION	MOTIVATION FOR USER
Highlighted Text	....	....	....	....
Color	....	....	....	....
Sound	....	....	....	....
Still Graphics	....	....	....	....
Animation	....	....	....	....

*If different segments of the program use different presentation styles, code the segments.

ADDITIONAL COMMENTS:

Note to Readers: This evaluation form may be reproduced for education and training activities, provided that credit is given to *Educational Technology* Magazine and stating that it is used with permission.

FIGURE 13.1. (Continued)
Source: EDUCATIONAL TECHNOLOGY, October 1984.

use of available computers to students. Two primary areas where computers are used in management activities are in the school office by school administrative staff and by teachers (Long 1985). In the school office, computers are often used for attendance records, student records, enrollment projections, or bus routing. Teachers most often use computers for management purposes, for word processing, grade keeping, test scoring, and grades calculation.

Teacher Training in Computers

Computer use in education is here to stay; the applications have been tested too often with favorable results. CAI, computer science, and management are three important uses of computers in the educational setting. Unfortunately, too few teachers take advantage of this technological revolution. Granted, many teachers have made a prompt and positive response to the use of computers in education (Sandoval 1984). Many have purchased their own computers, designed and/or purchased their own programs, and implemented the use of computers in their classrooms. This still is a minority of teachers. The majority do not have the skills or knowledge necessary to take advantage of the computer technology available.

The fact that many practicing teachers do not have computer literacy is understandable. However, new graduates from teacher education programs are also deficient (Glenn and Carrier 1989). There are several reasons for inadequate training in computer technology at the undergraduate level (Bruder 1989): (1) limited time in the undergraduate curriculum; (2) college faculty who are resistant to technology; and (3) diverse competency requirements.

Teachers need training in computer applications in education. The question is what kind of training and how much. At a minimum, computer users need to understand some basic terms frequently used related to computers (see table 13.3). Bitter (1989) suggests that all undergraduate education majors take a minimum of one course in computers in education. This course should include the following topics:

- the microcomputer in education
- the history of computer use
- the microcomputer system: hardware and software
- methods, curriculum and the microcomputer
- word processing
- spreadsheets
- data processing
- data bases
- graphics
- telecommunications and integrating software
- computer-assisted instruction
- choosing software for the classroom
- ethics and social concerns of computer use
- trends in teaching with computers (p. 34)

TABLE 13.3
A Brief Glossary of Computer Technology

BASIC—(Beginner's All-purpose Symbolic Instruction Code) a simple programming language based on the English language.

Bit—smallest unit of information (from BInary digiT).

Byte—generally, a single, alphanumeric character (e.g., one letter of the alphabet).

CRT—(Cathode Ray Tube) a computer display screen, same as television set.

Hardware—physical components of computer system.

Mainframe—a large, high speed business/scientific computer; often entails time sharing.

Microprocessor—a tiny chip incorporating an integrated circuit that is able to execute complex instructions electronically.

MODEM—(MOdulator/DEModulator) device that translates computer signals for transmission over telephone lines.

Peripherals—auxiliary devices that can be attached to a basic computer (e.g., a voice synthesizer, hard-copy printer, MODEM).

PLAN—(Program for Learning in Accordance with Needs) a computer-based instructional management system for diagnosis and record-keeping developed in 1967 by Westinghouse with American Institutes for Research and 13 school districts.

Plato—a powerful computer system designed especially for instructional use; begun in 1960 at University of Illinois, now marketed by Control Data Corp.

RAM—(Random Access Memory) the major memory mechanism of a computer, a "blank slate" to hold the program currently being used and then to be erased.

ROM—(Read Only Memory) contains program(s) permanently wired into the circuitry of the computer (e.g., the BASIC language).

Software—the programs that control the computer operation.

TICCIT—(Time-shared Interactive Computer-Controlled Information Television) like Plato, a computer system custom designed for instructional purposes; it was developed by Mitre Corp., and Victor Bunderson of Brigham Young University, and is now marketed by Hazeltine Corp.

Source: reprinted with permission. Heinich, Molenda, and Russell. *Educational Media and the New Technologies of Instruction,* 1982.

For teachers already in the field, inservice training is required. Janssen (1989) describes two different programs for practicing teachers: a summer institute and training tapes. The summer training institute was composed of twenty different three-hour sessions. Sessions address issues such as new software, applications in specific subject matter, and computer lab/class configurations. Video training tapes offer an alternative for teachers unable to attend the summer institute. Software preview and limited teacher preparation time are topics presented on the tapes.

OTHER EDUCATIONAL TECHNOLOGIES

In addition to ITV, CCTV, audiovisual kits, VCRs, videodisc players, and computers, there are many other components of educational technology. These include (1) programmed instruction, (2) programmed tutoring, (3) personalized system of instruction, (4) audio-tutorial systems, and (5) simulations and gaming. Although not often thought of as educational technology, these components are definitely a part of the overall area (see table 13.4).

EDUCATIONAL TECHNOLOGY: NEEDED DIRECTIONS

The computer revolution in the world affects everybody's daily lives. Bank machines, soft-drink machines with audio components, cash registers that talk are all possible because of computer technology. Without question, computers and other electronic technologies will have a major impact on education. If educators are to meet the challenges of these electronic technologies, several actions must be taken.

1. As the electronic technologies become the defining technologies, educators must gain an understanding of the history of technology, the role of technology in change, the social and psychological impacts of technology, and the implications of current changes for education.
2. Education must take a hard look at its traditional goals, particularly in the area of literacy.
3. Educators must devise new definitions of classroom learning consistent with the revolution in the cognitive sciences.
4. Educators must find a new metaphor for the learning environment. The school as factory is anathema.
5. Educators must abandon the lockstep, competency-based curriculum and devise new instructional strategies.
6. Educators must not only know about the electronic technologies, they must learn how to develop software for use with the visual media and the computer that facilitate learning.
7. Educators need to devise a curriculum whose content prepares students for thinking "by" computers, thinking "about" computers, and thinking "with" computers.
8. Education must emerge from its disciplinary narrowness. (Norton 1985, p. 18–20)

SUMMARY

This chapter focused on educational technology. The first section dealt with perceptions about educational technology. Too often educational technology is associated only with machinery and gadgetry, not learning. If educational technology is to be better understood, efforts must be made to humanize the ways educational technology is used in public schools.

TABLE 13.4
Characteristics of Technologies of Instruction

	PROGRAMMED INSTRUCTION	PROGRAMMED TUTORING	PERSONALIZED SYSTEM OF INSTRUCTION	AUDIO-TUTORIAL SYSTEMS	SIMULATION AND GAMING	COMPUTER-ASSISTED INSTRUCTION
A teaching/learning *pattern*	Small units of information requiring practice, followed by feedback	Small units of information requiring practice, followed by feedback	Large units of information in sequential order; passing a test is required before proceeding (mastery)	Core of instruction is on audio tape, used in lab setting independently; small group and large group sessions are added	Small group activity, may entail representation of reality and/or competition	Small units of information presented on display screen, frequent practice required, followed by immediate feedback
Designed to provide *reliable,*	Program recorded in printed form	Tutor follows directions; learner uses structured workbook	Course organization is clearly spelled out; based on print materials and standardized tests	Core material recorded on audio tape and other audiovisual materials	Procedures are enforced by means of game directions and play materials	Instructions are coded into a computer program and displayed on a screen
Effective instruction	Programs must be learner tested and revised during development process	Programs are learner tested and revised during development process	Materials themselves are not validated, but mastery is assured by testing/correction cycle	Materials themselves are not validated, but mastery is assured by test/review sessions	May be learner tested for effectiveness	Programs must be learner tested and revised during development process: computer capability facilitates data gathering

TABLE 13.4—Continued
Characteristics of Technologies of Instruction

	PROGRAMMED INSTRUCTION	PROGRAMMED TUTORING	PERSONALIZED SYSTEM OF INSTRUCTION	AUDIO-TUTORIAL SYSTEMS	SIMULATION AND GAMING	COMPUTER-ASSISTED INSTRUCTION
To *each* learner	Allows individual pacing	Allows individual pacing plus highly flexible, responsive branching via human tutor	Allows individual pacing plus one-to-one discussion of test errors and questions	Allows individul pacing in independent study portion of course	Usually group paced, with individuals assigned to compatible groups	Allows individual pacing and some branching
Through application of *scientific* principles of human learning	Reinforcement theory: verbal response followed by knowledge of results	Reinforcement theory: verbal or other overt response followed by knowledge of results plus social reinforcers Constant personalized human contact Variety	Rather frequent response to tests over content followed by immediate correction Occasional personalized human contact Mastery requirement ensures that learner is working at his level of comprehension	Conversational relationship with instructor via tape High use of audiovisual and other concrete media Occasional personalized human contact Active involvement in challenging tasks	Meaningful organization of content (in simulation) Frequent practice with immediate feedback Social interaction with small group Emotional involvement Repetition of drill-and-practice without tedium High motivation	Reinforcement theory: verbal response followed by knowledge of results plus branching May involve audiovisual display Appearance of personalized human contact May apply mastery concept Highly motivated for at least some learners

Source: Reprinted with permission. Heinich, Molenda, and Russell. *Educational Media and the New Technologies of Instruction*, 1982.

The next section presented the major educational technologies found in schools today. Included were instructional television, closed-circuit television, audiovisual kits such as filmstrips, videocassette technology, and finally computers. Each of these technologies was presented with information related to its use in schools, as well as its advantages and disadvantages in the learning process.

The final section of the chapter focused on computers in education. Computers are currently the major area of interest in educational technology. The three methods of using computers in schools were presented, including computer-assisted instruction, computer science, and management. Methods of application for each of these were presented, along with barriers to their use in the schools.

Finally, programs to better train teachers in the area of computer-assisted instruction were discussed. Too few teachers are adequately capable of using computers in instruction. Suggestions to alleviate this situation were presented. The major suggestion discussed, related to increased teachers' skills, was preservice training. Colleges and universities that train teachers must do a better job of preparing teachers to work with computers and CAI.

IN THE FIELD

1. Does the school use instructional television? Is so, how?
2. Does the school use closed-circuit television? If so, how?
3. Does the school use audiovisual kits? If so, how?
4. Does the school use videocassette machines? If so, how?
5. Are computers used in the school? If so, how?
6. How many microcomputers are available for instruction?
7. Has the number of microcomputers available for instruction increased during the past three years?
8. Does the administration use computers?
9. Does the school have a review process before purchasing computer software?
10. Have teachers in the district received any inservice training regarding computers in education? If so, what has been the nature of the training?

REFERENCES

Bitter, G. 1989. Preservice computer education: Introductory requirements. *Electronic Learning* 8(4), 34.

Bonner, P. 1984. Computers in education: Promise and reality. *Personal Computing* 8(9), 64–77.

Bork, A. 1984. Computers in education today—And some possible futures. *Phi Delta Kappan* 66(4), 239–43.

Boyer, E. L. 1984. Education's new challenge. *Personal Computing* 8(9), 81–85.

Bruder, I. 1989. Future teachers: Are they prepared? *Electronic Learning* 8 (4), 32–38.

Bruder, I. 1988a. Electronic Learning's 8th annual survey, *Electronic Learning* 8 (2), 38–45.

Bruder, I. 1988b. "Star Schools" awards $19.1 million to four distance learning projects. *Electronic Learning* 8(3), 22.

Chan, T. V. 1984. In search of the artistry in educational technology. *Educational Technology* 24(4), 7–12.

Cumuze, J. B. Education in the airwaves. *Alabama School Boards* 10(4), 2–4.

Donhardt, G. L. 1984. Microcomputers in education: Elements of a computer-based curriculum. *Educational Technology* 24(4), 30–32.

Gagné, R. M. 1987. *Instructional Technology: Foundations.* Hillsdale, NJ: Lawrence Erlbaum Associates.

Glenn, A. D. and C. A. Carrier. 1989. A perspective on teacher technology training. *Educational Technology* 29(3), 7–11.

Goodspeed, J. 1988. Two million microcomputers now used in U.S. schools. *Electronic Learning* 7(8), 16.

Hatch, J. A. 1984. Technology and devaluation of human processes. *Educational Forum* 48(2), 243–51.

Heinich, R., M. Molenda, and J. D. Russell. 1982. *Educational Media and the New Technologies of Instruction.* New York: John Wiley and Sons.

Holmes, G. 1982. Computer-assisted instruction: A discussion of some of the issues for would-be implementors. *Educational Technology* 22(9), 7–13.

Janssen, E. 1989. Two ways to reach teachers: A summer institute and training tapes. *Electronic Learning* 8(4), 29–30.

Jolicoeur, K. and D. E. Berger. 1988. Implementing educational software and evaluating its academic effectiveness: Part I. *Educational Technology* 28(9), 7–13.

Lockard, J., P. D. Abrams, and W. A. Many. 1987. *Microcomputers for Educators.* Boston: Little, Brown.

Long, C. 1985. How are today's elementary schools using computers? *Educational Technology* 25(5), 27–29.

Menis, Y. 1982. Educational technology research: Substituting closed-circuit television for the science laboratory. *Educational Technology* 22(4), 24–27.

Merrill, P. F., M. N. Tolman, L. Christensen, K. Hammons, B. R. Vincent, and P. L. Reynolds. 1986. *Computers in Education.* Englewood Cliffs, NJ: Prentice-Hall.

National Center for Education Statistics. 1984. *The Condition of Education, 1984 edition.* Washington, D.C.: U.S. Department of Education.

Nelson, P., and W. Waack, 1985. The status of computer literacy/computer-assisted instruction awareness as a factor in classroom instruction and teacher selection. *Educational Technology* 25(2), 23–26.

Norton, P. 1985. An agenda for technology and education: Eight imperatives. *Educational Technology* 25(1), 15–20.

Percival, F., and H. Ellington. 1988. *A Handbook of Educational Technology.* London: Kogan Page.

Phillipo, J. 1988. Videodisc players: A multi-purpose audiovisual tool. *Electronic Learning* 8(3), 50–51.

Reider, W. L. 1984. Videocassette technology in education: A quiet revolution in progress. *Educational Technology* 24(10), 12–15.

Rockman, S. 1985. Success or failure for computers in schools? Some lessons from instructional television. *Educational Technology* 25(1), 48–50.

Sandoval, H. R. 1984. Teacher training in computer skills: A call for a redefinition. *Educational Technology* 24(10), 29–31.

Smith, C. B., and G. M. Ingersoll. 1984. Audiovisual materials in U.S. schools: A national survey on availability and use. *Educational Technology* 24(9), 36–38.

Smith, T. E. C., B. J. Price, and G. M. Marsh. 1986. *Mildly Handicapped Children and Adults.* St. Paul: West.

Strohmer, J. C. 1989. ITV: From talking head to cognitive processing. *Educational Technology* 29(1), 27–28.

Wallace, J., and R. M. Rose. 1984. A hard look at software: What to examine and evaluate (with an evaluation form). *Educational Technology* 24(10), 35–39.

Willis, J. W. 1987. *Educational Computing: A Guide to Practical Applications.* Scottsdale, AZ: Gorsuch Scarisbrick Publishers.

THE FUTURE

OBJECTIVES

After reading this chapter you will be able to

- define futurism;

- describe the purposes of futurism;

- discuss the difficulties in predicting the future;

- describe worldwide population trends;

- discuss the impact of declining natural resources;

- list reasons for studying the future of education;

- describe population trends in the United States and their impact on public education;

- discuss the likelihood that school reform will continue;

- describe forces that will impact the curriculum in the future;

- discuss the future role of technology in education; and

- list predictions made concerning education.

OUTLINE

ADVANCE ORGANIZERS

1. What is futurism?
2. Why should futurism be studied?
3. What is the global population trend?
4. What are the projected dates for the depletion of some natural resources?
5. What role does geopolitics play in the future?
6. How can the educational system change to meet the needs of the future?
7. What is the population trend in the United States?
8. How does the U.S. population trend affect planning for public education?
9. How can educational reforms be evaluated?
10. What will the curriculum in the future include?
11. What role will technology play in the future?
12. What is the status of predictions made in 1974 concerning education?

INTRODUCTION

Predicting the future is difficult, if not impossible. However, the challenges that face the educational system in the United States today will basically be the same in the next century (Anthony 1984). The future of public education is a big question mark. Interest in public education in the United States has swung back and forth, as on a pendulum. At various periods of history, the public has been heavily involved and interested in public education. At other times, unfortunately, other issues have usurped education in the public focus. Most recently, beginning with the critical reports issued concerning public education in the late 1970s and early 1980s, the public interest skyrocketed. Politicians, parents, professionals, business leaders, and people from other sectors clamored for better educational programs and for more influence in public education. Since the mid-1980s, the fervor of the reform movement has subsided. Even though reforms to our public educational system are being devised, debated, and often implemented, the intensity of the movement has decreased. Whether the call for reforms will become stronger as we approach the twenty-first century remains to be seen. What can be said is that the future of education and the future of humanity are very complex issues. Studying the future and applying predictions to specific issues like education are not easy tasks.

Predicting the future of education is definitely linked, however, to the future of our society.

FUTURISM

The future is tomorrow and the day after. It is the entire period ahead of us. It "holds great promise for each of us if we think rather than daydream about it, if we plan rather than wait, if we accept rather than reject the inevitability of change" (Day and Speicher 1985, p. 7). The study of the future has been called futurism. Futurism is "a philosophical position and a movement in education designed to shift emphasis from the current era to the needs that will emerge in a period of rapid change" (Pulliam 1987, p. 289). By studying the future, policymakers and leaders are more capable of preparing for what will occur in the next twelve, twenty or even fifty years. Several different topics of study interest futurists, including world geopolitics, population, human resources, and natural resources. Education is another topic studied by futurists.

Studying and forecasting the future are important for several reasons. First, people cannot continue to let history repeat itself. The world has experienced many failures; if people can learn from these failures and prevent their recurring, then humanity will be better off. While people are capable of destroying the planet, they are also able to save it (Schreyer 1980).

The future, from the 1980s on, will change rapidly and dramatically. The year 2000 will undoubtedly be significantly more different from 1980 than the year 1800 was from 1780 (Platt 1980). And, "If the twenty-first century is as different from the twentieth as the twentieth was from the nineteenth, children entrusted to the care of educators may expect changes that stagger the imagination" (Pulliam 1987, p. 255). Indications suggest the future will change at an even faster pace.

Toffler (1980) stated that "we are the final generation of an old civilization and the first generation of a new one . . ." (p. 11). During the past two decades major changes have occurred. For example, we now live in the shadow of nuclear holocaust; television may be changing the family, school, commerce, politics, and our thinking; electronics has changed science and government and will affect every future society (Platt 1980). For the first time in history, we are able to

- manipulate, control, and change our own biological genetic substance;
- carry out collective self-destruction by interacting with the elementary building blocks of our world;
- create a worldwide communications and information network of an extent and effectiveness never before dreamed;

- throw off the shackles of our planet in the course of spreading out in the universe. (Puttkamer 1983, p. 4)

With changes occurring so rapidly, trying to study and predict the future becomes extremely difficult. However, without these efforts humanity may be faced with problems too overwhelming to conquer. It is only by getting a head start on tomorrow's problems that mankind can hope to find appropriate solutions.

GLOBAL CONCERNS AND THE FUTURE

Several concerns of the future are not unique to any one community, discipline, or country. These global concerns include changes in the population, geopolitics, and human and natural resources. Changes that occur in these areas and others across the planet can affect each of our lives in our local communities (Amara 1980). Without knowing what to expect in these global areas, predicting public education is perfunctory. Unfortunately, forecasting the future often has proved to lead to inaccurate predictions (Pulliam and Bowman 1975). Efforts in the area of futurism, however, are necessary to prepare for occurrences that, unanticipated, could lead to global catastrophies.

Population Trends

The world population is increasing extremely rapidly. In 1975 the world population was estimated to be just over 4 billion. This number is expected to increase to 6.3 billion by the year 2000, representing a fifty-five percent increase in only twenty-five years (Almanac and Yearbook 1986). The rate of population increase has climbed steadily through history.

Efforts to curb the spiraling increase in the population have met with religious, economic, and even governmental barriers. The Roman Catholic church, for example, while supporting population control, is officially opposed to birth control methods. The largest increases in the population are occurring in third world countries where poverty is frequently rampant and where the education level of individuals is low; this only hampers efforts at world population control. The largest projected population increases from 1975 to 2000 are in Africa (104 percent) and Latin America (96 percent) (Almanac and Yearbook 1986).

Natural Resources

The worldwide population explosion has had a severe effect on natural resources. Petroleum, once considered in sufficient supplies to be used uncontrollably by the large industrial countries, is now realized to be in dwindling quantities. Current rates of consumption would deplete

■ *Overpopulation threatens the availability of natural resources.*

petroleum reserves by the year 2021 (Almanac and Yearbook 1986). Although the oil shortage of the 1970s, which was primarily caused by world political forces, was reversed in the mid-1980s by an oil surplus, projections still indicate a real shortage of oil after thirty-five more years.

A world without oil could spell disaster for industrialized nations and have a devastating effect on developing countries. Researchers, therefore, are trying to develop alternative energy sources, such as nuclear power, solar power, and wind power, to take the place of many of the oil-dependent activities of the world. The efforts of this research will undoubtedly determine, to a great extent, many aspects of the future.

Many other natural resources are also being depleted rapidly. These include water, natural ores, and forests. For example, the U.S. Energy Department forecasts that natural gas reserves could be used up by the year 2047 and uranium reserves could be depleted by the year 2017 (Almanac and Yearbook 1986). Scientists are working diligently to guard against exploitation of these and other natural resources. Developing substitutes and determining ways to replenish natural supplies are among the many alternatives being investigated.

Food

The overpopulation of the world not only affects natural resources but also the ability of the world to feed itself. Third world, developing countries often are not able to produce enough food to feed their people. In the early 1980s droughts and natural disasters, political struggles, and poor planning resulted in hundreds of thousands of people starving to death. The mass starvation in the Sudan and Ethiopia in the early 1980s brought the plight of millions of individuals to the television screens of the United States and other countries. The world responded with aid; even rock singers banded together in an effort to provide relief to the hundreds of thousands of individuals starving to death. While the efforts were somewhat successful, the future will see many other crises related to a lack of food and the resultant starving masses.

Geopolitics

The world of the 1980s is not at peace and will probably never be. Although global conflicts have not occurred since the 1940s with World War II, hundreds of localized military conflicts have continued to plague many parts of the world. Civil wars in many African and South American countries, the Arab-Israeli conflict, and other smaller wars have continued unabated. Add to this the continuing political differences among the superpowers and the result is constant world tension. Developments in the Soviet Union in the late 1980s, namely *perestroika* and *glasnost* implemented by Mikhail Gorbachev, are signs for optimism. However, only time will tell how successful these overtures will prove.

Whether humanity survives these conflicts and possible future conflicts will depend on the common sense of the world's leaders. Living under the constant threat of nuclear holocaust definitely will affect the lives of all individuals living on earth. Many countries hold different political ideologies; this creates tension which will only make it more difficult to solve the problems that will face earth for the remainder of the twentieth century and into the twenty-first century.

THE FUTURE OF PUBLIC EDUCATION IN THE UNITED STATES

Like predicting the future of global issues, predicting the future of education is complex and difficult. Making predictions is easy; making accurate predictions, on the other hand, is extremely difficult (Broudy 1974). Even with these realities, forecasting educational trends is necessary to best prepare for the future. "The educational arena is filled with numerous examples of once-proud and effective school districts that failed to anticipate or accept purposeful change to enhance educational programs for students" (Day and Speicher 1985, p. 7).

■ *The general public agrees that the role of education to the future of the United States is critical.*

Many different elements in education will change throughout the twentieth-century. These include population trends, the fate of reforms that began during the early 1980s, curriculum, emerging technologies, and the support of citizens for public education. Specific developments that will impact education in the future include computers, materials, fiber optics, and science (Day and Speicher 1985).

Many individuals have tied the future of the world to the future of education. While the future cannot be forecasted totally accurately, the nature of changes that will occur can be determined (Lewis 1983). The many problems that citizens of earth will face during the next twenty to thirty years may be insurmountable unless educational systems adapt to better prepare the children of today for the world of tomorrow. To meet the challenges of the future, Allen (1974) believes that the educational system must make the following changes:

1. Education should move to the center of societal interaction by implementing cross-generational, nonformal, location-free social service programs.

2. Education should reorient itself to a new conception of information based on interdependence and cooperation, and on a new psychology of man based on Maslovian principles and diversity.

3. Our present values about educational change—sameness and objectivity—must be radically altered.

4. In the schools that remain after we have transposed to education for social service, flexible scheduling and differentiated staffing should be implemented. (Allen 1974, p. 18)

By the year 2000 the population will need education to a greater extent than today (Broudy 1974). "More and more careers will require backgrounds in science, mathematics, and computer science. Fewer careers will be open to the undereducated" (Lewis (1983, p. 10). Schools will have to adjust to meet the needs of the future population. The changes required of the public education system in the United States are significant. The question is whether the system can be altered to meet the challenges of the future.

The general public agrees that the role of education is critical to the future of the United States. In the 1984 Gallup Poll of the Public's Attitudes Toward the Public Schools, ninety-five percent of the respondents indicated that developing the best educational system in the world was very important or fairly important in determining America's strength over the next twenty-five years (Gallup 1984). In contrast, only eighty-one percent felt that building the strongest military force in the world was very important or fairly important. With the acknowledgement from the public that the role of education is critical to the future of the United States, implementing reforms that improve American public education should be easier.

Population Trends in the United States

Just as the population of the world affects the future, the population of the United States has a major impact on the future of public education. Unlike world population, which will have a significant impact due to massive expansion, the population trends in the United States resulted in fewer schoolchildren. While this trend may recently have been reversed at the lower elementary level, a changing school population will continue to impact the educational system for several more years.

Since the middle 1960s, the population growth in the United States has slowed markedly. Between 1955 and 1965 the average increase in the U.S. population was 2.8 million. Since 1965 the average has decreased to less than 1.9 million. During the 1980s the growth is estimated to be approximately 2.2 million per year, with only 1.5 to 2.0 million projected for the 1990s (Morrison 1979).

■

SENIOR BOOM: THE FUTURE'S NEW WRINKLE

Anita Manning and David Proctor

We're hip. We've always been hip. And, let's face it, we'll always *be* hip.

We're the baby boomers. By virtue of our numbers—76 million—we've always called the shots. How we look, what we do, think, say, care about and listen to sets the pace.

Moving through the stages of life, the biggest segment of society has been likened to a pig in a python—a giant bulge that can't be ignored.

And now, as we begin to push—and pass—age 40, the implications of an impending tidal wave of old folks are of growing interest. "There have been baby booms before, but there has never been a senior boom," says psychologist Ken Dychtwald, author of *Age Wave* (Jeremy P. Tarcher Inc.), . . . "The era of the U.S. as a youth-focused culture is coming to an end and will never be seen again."

The first of us, those born in 1946, will turn 65 in 2011. Those born in 1964, the last year of the boom, will reach that magic age in 2029. In our wake, the physical world, society and its institutions will change drastically.

Dychtwald's book, written with Joe Flower, provides a glimpse into a future like nothing we've ever seen.

■ Stoplights will be timed to accommodate slower-moving people.

■ Newspapers and magazines will have larger print.

■ Music and loudspeaker announcements will be re-pitched so older people can hear them better.

■ Medicine bottles and food containers will be easier to open; clothes will fasten with Velcro.

■ Chairs will have higher seats and arms long enough to provide support for getting in and out.

But it won't be a world outfitted only for the aged frail. Dychtwald says. Most of us won't be frail.

Because of medical advances and our interest in healthful eating and fitness, we'll tackle old age in new ways, experts say. We're more likely to follow the lead of the Ronald Reagans and George Burnses of today—remaining active and vigorous well into our 70s, 80s and 90s. This means:

■ We'll have several careers, punctuated by stints back at school for retraining.

■ Marriage-for-life will be less common; serial monogamy normal.

■ Plastic surgery and gerontology will be the busiest medical specialties of the 21st century.

■ Every major industry will develop new products and marketing strategies to meet our needs.

"Most of us are not aware that the man-made physical environment has been perfectly sculpted to match the form of youth," Dychtwald says. Bucket seats in cars and buses with high steps are fine for lithe young bodies, not so great for aging limbs and eyesight. "In the future, you'll see huge industries fall and others rise to meet the needs of people in the second half of life."

Already, forward-thinking segments of USA society are gearing up to cater to the needs and desires of older baby boomers. Dychtwald's company, Age Wave Inc., an Emeryville, Calif., marketing and communications firm, counts among its clients such giants as AT&T, McDonald's, Bank of America and Time Inc., all looking to the not-too-distant future.

And this week at Walt Disney World Village in Florida, experts in health care, social service and gerontology are attending a conference on technology for an aging population. The focus: new communications devices, environmental designs and medical innovations.

continued

Beyond thinking of our physical needs during our second 50 years, futurists also are imagining our social needs. And they predict that, as with all generations, the passions of our youth will carry into our older years.

"There will definitely be 70-year-old rock 'n' rollers," says Tim Willard of the World Future Society, who, at 38, is a self-described "archetypal baby boomer."

"There will be more people changing careers and coming into music in their 60s," he says. "Late bloomers in all fields of the arts will be much hailed. This self-congratulatory generation will be very pleased to see people in their 70s or 80s having their first art exhibition or recording their first record."

Ours is a generation that questions authority. Always has, always will.

"*Reader's Digest* reported that 22 percent of people now question, challenge or contradict their doctors," says Joseph Coates, president of J. F. Coates Inc., a Washington, D.C., think tank that does futures research. "Twenty years ago, no one questioned the doctor. He was a god.

"What's reflected in that is the rise of the individual as his or her own authority. Baby boomers believe there's nothing you can't learn."

That translates into a lifelong quest for experience and education, something already hinted at in the current boom in both adventure travel and adult education, he says.

It will also mean the anti-war activities of the '60s will rise again, Willard says.

"The people who were attracted to anti-war activism now are engaged in environmental activism, Mothers Against Drunk Driving, many groups for peace efforts. As that group keeps moving up the python, we can expect to see elders' rights groups."

Not surprisingly, he says, we'll see elders doing a lot we haven't seen in the past, including "ripping off the system." "If, say, you're not going to get your Social Security check or pension as promised, you'll see people thinking, 'Well, I'll just patch into the computer system and divert that money.'"

Living arrangements will be different, too, Willard predicts. Instead of retiring to a community full of strangers, people will remain active, perhaps working into their 80s, and live in groups according to similar interests. There will be "old jocks homes," he says, or a fraternity or professional group. Others will cluster with friends and relatives of several generations.

"We'll be seeing the rest home of the future as the commune of the future," he says. "One person practicing tai chi, a group of people getting ready to protest at the bank because of service charges, people heading off to a specially designed acoustic concert of the Grateful Dead, now in their 70s. They'll be wheeling Jerry Garcia onto the stage."

The concept of "acting your age" will change, Dychtwald says. "You'll see 60- and 70- and 80-year-olds who look and act like 30- and 40- and 50-year-olds. People will be going on adventures, falling in love, training for marathons."

Our image of beauty, always focused on the stage of life at which we happened to be, will expand. Youth will not be the only standard.

"We're seeing a redefinition of our sense of beauty now," Willard says. "On *thirtysomething* we see people with gray hairs and, hey, they look pretty good. We'll come to believe young people are beautiful, middle-aged people are beautiful and old people are pretty darn sexy, too."

"What may emerge is an aspirational image of aging," Dychtwald says. "The idea that growing old may be something we aspire to experience. Instead of looking at aging as extended youth, we'll look at it as an experience itself."

By the year 2000 the entire population will need education to a greater extent than today (Broudy 1974). Recently, the U.S. Department of Labor issued a report regarding the future trend in the work force. The report suggests that most of the new jobs that will be developed for the twenty-first century will require better academic skills in reading, following directions, and mathematical calculations. Even new jobs created during the next ten years will require some sort of postsecondary education or training (Hudson Institute 1987). The public education system will have to make significant changes to meet the needs of the future population. The question is whether the system can make those changes in order to meet the challenges of the future.

Although the overall population growth in the United States has declined, the number of school-age students is on the increase and will likely increase until the end of the century (Snyder 1988). Public school enrollment in grades K–12 reached a low in 1984 with 39.2 million students. Since then there has been a steady increase. In 1987 there were 40.2 million students in grades K–12, and this number is expected to increase to 43.9 million in 1997 (National Center for Education Statistics 1988). (See table 14.1)

Concomitant with the increased enrollment in public schools is an increase in the number of teachers needed. Unfortunately the supply of teachers is usually behind the demand. As a result of declining public school enrollments in the 1970s, and a general decline in the perception of the teaching profession, fewer college students enrolled as education majors. The result is beginning to show up as a teacher shortage. Although enrollment figures for education majors is increasing, "the supply of newly graduated teaching candidates is expected to satisfy only about 60 percent of the demand over the next five years" (Darling-Hammond 1988, p. 3). Figure 14.1 shows the projected demand for new teachers in the 1990s.

Maintaining the School Reforms

Many extensive educational reforms were initiated in the early 1980s as a result of the critical reports published concerning public education. The content of these reports and the resulting reforms have been substantially documented in previous chapters. The question now is whether the reform movement can be maintained. Will the general public continue to support educational changes, at a financial cost, or will the public interest in improving education wane and be replaced by other issues, such as the economy or geopolitics?

The prediction of Kirst (1986) that the pace of educational reforms would slow significantly during the latter 1980s has been proven. States are passing fewer and fewer major reform acts and local districts are implementing fewer and fewer sweeping changes at the district level. What could result is the same thing that has happened to other major

TABLE 14.1
Enrollments for Public Schools, K-12

FALL OF YEAR	GRADES K-12*
1969	45,619
1970	45,909
1971	46,081
1972	45,744
1973	45,429
1974	45,053
1975	44,791
1976	44,317
1977	43,577
1978	42,550
1979	41,645
1980	40,987
1981	40,099
1982	39,652
1983	39,352
1984	39,295
1985	39,509
1986	39,837
1987	40,200
1988 (projected)	40,200
1989	40,337
1990	40,752
1991	41,306
1992	41,879
1993	42,444
1994	43,014
1995	43,442
1996	43,775
1997	43,960

*In millions.

Source: National Center for Education Statistics. 1988.

reform movements in this country, such as cleaning up the environment and revitalizing inner cities. In each of these cases, the reform movements started out strong but fizzled after the initial discovery and crisis phases to mere policy phases.

To prevent the same negative results from happening to the educational reform movement, policymakers and the public must be kept apprised of the results of the reforms and the need for additional

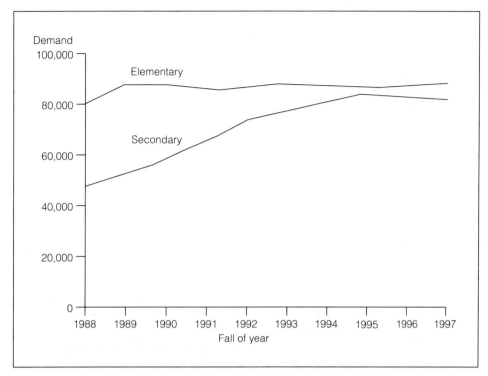

FIGURE 14.1. Projections for Teachers.
Source: National Center for Education Statistics. 1988. From National Center for Education Statistics, Projections of Education Statistics to 1997–98, forthcoming.

changes. This leads to the need for comprehensive evaluation of the reforms that have been implemented. Several different kinds and levels of evaluation should occur, including

1. performance indicators;
2. overall studies of the financial impact of reforms;
3. analysis of cost-effectiveness of various state interventions with the same specific objectives;
4. program evaluation;
5. impact of evaluation of several state interventions with the same general goal;
6. studies of the cumulative effects of all state reforms in omnibus bills; and
7. research that isolates cause-and-effect relationships. (Kirst 1986, p. 343–45)

Curriculum for the Future

Predicting the curriculum of future public schools is difficult. Various factions will contend for control of the curriculum in the future, reflecting the "splintering of common interests and the polarization of the larger society" (Apple 1983, p. 321).

Two of the political issues that will affect the curriculum will be (1) determining the "basics" and (2) determining the relationship among schools, business, and labor. The movement to return schools to teaching basic subjects has been present for several years. The issue is who will determine what should be included in the basic curriculum. Conservative groups have begun to exert influence on the curriculum and seem to focus on basic academic subjects at the exclusion of other topics. Other groups, however, want to include courses beyond the basic academic subjects. For example, what role should be reserved for bilingual education? Should creation-science be taught along with or to the exclusion of evolution? These types of conflicts will continue in determining what exactly should be included in the basic curriculum (Apple 1983).

Along with the controversy over what should be included in the basic curriculum will come increased pressures from business and labor to influence the curriculum content of the schools. In times of declining tax bases and, therefore, limited school budgets, schools have to rely on a closer relationship with the private sector for support. Too often coupled with this support comes efforts to control (Apple 1983).

Some conclusions concerning the future curriculum for schools can be drawn from the literature. First, the basic academic curriculum will continue to be stressed. The nature of this "basic curriculum" will be determined at state and local levels. There will, however, be an increased emphasis on math and science (Apple 1983) along with technology.

A general conclusion concerning the curriculum of the future is that many groups previously not involved in curricular planning will want to participate. These groups include conservatives, liberals, business, labor, professional groups, and even state legislatures. While the outcome of such heterogeneous input is difficult to predict, it at least should lead to a curriculum well planned and debated, which has not always been the case in the history of American education.

Technology in the Future

The role of technology in education has been increasing dramatically. With the advent of the microcomputer age, schools have joined the technological revolution. The question is not whether technology, particularly computers, will be a major part of education in the future, but exactly what role it will play.

Just within the current decade, advances made in technology will have the potential to

1. improve instruction in conventional subjects;
2. allow the efficient teaching of types of knowledge and skills previously too expensive to include in the curriculum (such as sophisticated laboratory procedures and advanced music);
3. improve research into the teaching/learning process; and
4. expand the number of students per teacher without increasing costs or decreasing quality. (Dede 1983, p. 22)

Certain obvious facts are predictable regarding technology and computers in the future of education, including:

- the number of computers in schools will increase;
- commercial companies will increase efforts to sell computers to schools and to develop more educational software;
- computers will continue to become more sophisticated at even lower prices;
- computers will become more and more user-friendly;
- new computer systems will be outdated almost as soon as they go into production; and
- more vocational, educational, and personal computing will occur in the home.

What is yet to be determined is the exact role computers and other technology will play in instruction. On the one hand, schools and teachers could continue to operate as today, using computers and technology as mere supplements to teacher-oriented instruction. On the other hand, schools and teachers could revolutionize education with the use of technology. Computers could become the impetus for new curricula, new instructional techniques, and a different organization of the school and the role of the teacher (Bork 1984). Only time will tell which direction the role of computers and technology takes. Many other educational innovations, such as educational television, never lived up to their expectations. Although computers should, the verdict is still out.

PAST PREDICTIONS OF THE FUTURE OF EDUCATION

The preceding pages have outlined some predictions about the future of public education in the United States. Whether these predictions will be proved accurate remains to be seen. Throughout history, professionals have attempted to predict the future of education, noting that such predictions are difficult. In a 1974 publication, *The Future of Education: 1975–2000*, several authors made predictions about the future of education. The predictions of two of the authors are summarized below to be evaluated by today's realities. While reading these predictions, determine which ones have proved accurate to this point, which ones are still under consideration, and which ones are obviously going to be proved wrong.

Predictions by Theodore Hipple (1974)

1. Financing of public education will be enlarged and its base broadened.
2. Concomitant with increased funding for education will be an increase in teacher's salaries.
3. Alternative forms of education will continue to flourish, especially beyond elementary school.
4. The school will be a community center as well as a user of community facilities to enhance its educational program.
5. To permit students to use the community facilities constructed near the schools, it seems probable that the time students spend in actual classrooms will be shortened.
6. Some of the "teachers" at the nearby playgrounds and youth centers will be high-school youth who are using their free time to work, on a paid basis, at the centers.
7. The curricula of the schools—that which is taught in them and which students are presumed to learn—will change in the last quarter of the twentieth century, but perhaps not as radically as some educational seers have suggested.
8. Curricula that focus on problem solving and on values clarification activities will call for new instructional strategies.
9. Education for young children will expand; colleges and universities will become more specialized; private colleges will continue to have a difficult time; and junior and community colleges will expand.
10. Many problems will continue to plague education.
11. Educators should make schooling enjoyable.

Predictions by Max Rafferty (1974)

1. The oversupply of teachers will get worse and will have perfectly splendid spinoffs.
2. There will be better education in the big cities without forced busing.
3. The frequency of teacher strikes will decline to zero.
4. Mandated statewide use of standardized tests will be universal.

SCHOOLS THAT NEVER CLOSE

Connie Leslie

Why do our schools sit empty most of the time? Inside are gyms, libraries and cafeterias. The buildings are childproof and they're paid for, but unless there's basketball practice or a Friday-night dance, the doors are shut at 3 P.M. "We've got well over a trillion dollars invested in these schools," says Yale University professor Edward F. Zigler. "Why don't we use them more fully?"

In Zigler's view, the public schools should be home to the nation's child-care programs—all of them. And he's not alone. "The school of the year 2010 will be different from today," says Thomas A. Shannon, executive director of the National School Boards Association. "There will be a substantial child-care and early-childhood-education component. The schools will be like more of a community center." In many local districts across the country, the future is now. Already 31 states offer prekindergarten classes for 4-year-olds, a fourfold increase over the last decade. And according to a new report by Wellesley College's School-Age Child Care Project, about 15 percent of the nation's local districts now offer some form of child care, or allow community groups to use their buildings. Many programs continue during vacations, and a few run even in the summer; some extend into junior high school.

Zigler who is often referred to as the godfather of Head Start, is closely watching a new child-care project in two school districts in Missouri. The schools in Independence and neighboring Platte County have become the hub for child care in their communities. Starting as early as 6 A.M. at some schools, the programs provide full-day and before- and after-school care for kids 3 to 12 years old. The schools also offer parenting classes and can refer families to local adults who take in children of working parents. State education officials in Connecticut plan to launch similar programs in three school districts next fall. And U.S. Sen. Christopher J. Dodd is sponsoring legislation that would give $500,000 to every state to set up demonstration projects in at least one school district.

Overhead Costs

The Missouri services depend on private funds and fees from parents. Independence is a sprawling suburban district with 13 elementary schools, while Platte County is a small bedroom community near Kansas City. Together, the two raised $175,000 in private donations to remodel classrooms, buy equipment and train workers for their programs. Parents pay $45 to $55 per week for full-day care and $18 to $24 for the before- and after-school service. Both districts provide privately funded scholarships for needy families. The program in Independence is already paying for itself. Robert Henley, superintendent of the Independence schools, says he already has to pay the overhead costs of keeping the buildings clean and heated. "Basically the parent is paying for the staff."

Like all states, Missouri exempts school systems from state licensing requirements for child-care operations. But to keep quality high, the two districts keep their day-care staff/student ratio at 10 to 1; the before- and after-school service uses a ratio of 16 to 1. The programs include physical activities, computer classes, arts and crafts and music practice. Safety, and a convenient location (the existing school-bus system is used when necessary) are other benefits. "For a parent, it makes life tremendously easier if you know your child is in a safe environment," says Sharon Williams, school-board president in Independence.

Not all child advocates favor the conversion of schools into child-care centers.

continued

"Schools are a partner that should be woven into the nation's existing structure of child-care services," says Amy Wilkins, a program associate at the Children's Defense Fund. "We worry that schools will become the only sources, and I don't think that schools are prepared to be sole providers." Early-childhood educators charge that the prekindergarten programs would inevitably adopt a rigid and formal structure, which they think is harmful to a young child's development. But given the proper supervision, Zigler believes that schools can do the job. "I'm not ready to hand this over to school administrators or sixth-grade teachers who've never seen a 3-year-old child," says Zigler. "The programs must have early-childhood educators trained to do this kind of work—and many are."

Lack of Space

Anne Mitchell, an associate dean at the Bank Street College of Education, recently completed a national study of prekindergarten programs in public schools and found "an incredible range" in quality. "In most urban districts with the kids who most need better child-care services, the public schools are already overcrowded," she says. "The places where Zigler's proposal works best are in middle-class and upper-middle-class communities where there is a declining school enrollment and where parents have enough money to pay for services."

By the turn of the century, schools may start taking on even more responsibilities in their communities, acting as a kind of community center. "As we have more and more senior citizens, they're going to be attracted to the schools, too; we may be feeding them," says Shannon. "And one wonders about the economy of having a library in the school strictly for schoolchildren, and then building another library down the street for everybody else in the community." California, Arizona and Utah have had community-center acts on the books for more than a decade. Shannon, for one, predicts that other states will soon adopt similar laws and put the statutes to work. That would put the neighborhood back in the schools.

5. More and better vocational education is in the cards, and for a lot more children than are getting it now.

6. Ethnic studies will be as important in the curriculum as Etruscan tomb-carving, and no more so.

7. Merit pay for teachers and modifications of tenure laws are coming up around the bend of the time stream.

8. Better textbooks are already on the way.

9. Both a longer school year and school day seem in the cards.

10. More student participation in school administration will be occurring.

11. More part-time students and off-campus courses.

12. School and teacher accountability will be demanded.

13. There will be a change in the selection and training of school administrators.

Conclusions on Predictions of 1974

Obviously some of these predictions made more than two decades ago are on their way to coming to fruition; others will never occur. Still others, while not achieved at this point, still have a chance to occur. Predicting the future of education is difficult; however, without futurists attempting to predict what will occur in the schools of tomorrow, there would be no time to prepare for needed changes. Futurism in schools is vital; without it the educational system would attempt and accept changes much less easily than is necessary. Everything needed to solve the problems of the future cannot be taught to children. However, by studying the future, educators will be in a better position to prepare today's students for tomorrow's world. Disregarding the future can only lead to a major breakdown in the survival chances of our species.

HIGHLIGHT
.

IN MINNESOTA, CHOOSE YOUR OWN SCHOOL

Pat Ordovensky

Kathy Kuipers and Phyllis Van Buren, who are sending their kids to schools outside their own districts, are part of this year's hottest trend in public school reform.

It's called the free market. In school jargon, it's "choice."

The idea is to let parents choose a school as they would a new car or loaf of bread, says Ruth Randall, state superintendent in Minnesota, where the USA's first statewide choice program is in its second year.

Kuipers, of Chanhassen, Minn., lets her third-grade daughter walk a block to the Minnetonka School District, where she rides a bus to a school that's closer than the one she was assigned. It also has "less of a rural orientation."

Van Buren drives her two children 10 miles from their home in Clearwater, Minn., to school in St. Cloud. After school, the kids walk to their grandparents' home where their mother, a language professor at St. Cloud State University, later picks them up.

They're among 435 Minnesota children crossing district lines this year in the program conceived by Gov. Rudy Perpich, praised by Presidents Bush and Reagan and looked at by a dozen other states.

It allows, with some restrictions, parents to choose for their children any public

school in Minnesota. For next school year, more than 3,000 have requested transfers.

Bush calls it "the single most promising" idea to improve schools. Reagan, before he left office, called it "that wonderful program in Minnesota that is fostering unprecedented competition among public schools."

Key to the free-market concept: $2,700 to $3,000 in state aid moves as each student moves. Public schools, say proponents must offer a better product or go out of business.

"We can choose our spouses, our significant others, our places of worship, our grocery stores," says state superintendent Randall. "We can choose our preschool experience and our (college) experience, but we have that little chunk in there between kindergarten and 12th grade where we haven't been able to make those choices."

But local school administrators say most of the choices are being made not for better schools but for convenience.

"From what I've seen, choices are not being made on quality, they're being made on geography," says superintendent Richard Berge in Faribault, 50 miles south of Minneapolis. "It's being marketed and sold for something that simply isn't there."

continued

In suburban St. Louis Park, where 70 parents have asked to leave next year and 80 have asked to transfer in, superintendent Carl Holmstrom says "95 percent (of the decisions) are for convenience—the baby sitter lives over there."

Says Randall: "If the decision's made because of child care, of proximity to the Y, because they don't like the school board, because they'd rather have a different principal—that's fine."

The national attention, fanned by a recent White House conference on school choice and by Perpich preaching its gospel across the USA, has spread the trend:

■ California State Superintendent Bill Honig backs legislation, introduced last month, authorizing statewide public school choice. Californians now are allowed to attend school where a parent works.

"Allowing parents to choose their children's schools," says Honig, "is an excellent way to cement the parents' commitment to those schools."

■ In Arizona, a bill allowing choice passed the House last year, but died in the Senate.

■ Iowa high school students, starting in 1990, can move to get courses that aren't available where they live. State tax dollars will move with them.

■ North Carolina Gov. James Martin is expected to offer a statewide choice plan, similar to Minnesota's, to his legislature this spring.

■ Gov. Michael Dukakis last year vetoed a Massachusetts bill allowing free movement between cities and suburbs. The state Education Department is working on a new plan.

School choice has been around under many names—magnet schools is one—for many years. It usually is confined to one school district or one metropolitan area.

Magnet schools—specializing in certain curricula and drawing students from throughout an area—grew in the 1970s as a voluntary alternative to court-ordered busing for desegregation.

In Hillsborough County (Tampa), Fla., as large as Rhode Island, choice has been allowed for the 22 years Ray Shelton has been superintendent. Students can move to any school in the county, says Shelton, for "a good reason."

This year, about 6,000 of Hillsborough's 120,000 students changed schools. Shelton, like his Minnesota colleagues, finds most are moving for parents' convenience.

"It's not a very big deal," he says. "We don't think it provides any competition to improve schools at all."

In Minnesota, the folks who produced choice think it's a very big deal.

"It's a major power shift from the education establishment to the customer," says Connie Levi, ex-state House majority leader who authored the open enrollment law.

"I like to take on big systems," says Levi, now executive director of the Minneapolis Chamber of Commerce. "I looked at the education system and the comfort level was too great. The rigidity within the system was not too healthy."

Critics say choice can be—and has been— used by coaches to lure better athletes.

So what?, says Randall, "Athletics is a legitimate reason for choosing a school. If we don't believe that children learn from athletics, then we shouldn't be spending all these dollars on them in the educational program."

Minnesota's teachers and school boards fought the proprosal as it moved through the legislature. Now the largest teachers' union, the Minnesota Education Association, thinks it might produce good results.

MEA president Robert Astrup—like other Minnesotans—says consolidation of small districts is the ultimate goal.

Of Minnesota's 435 school districts, 187 have fewer than 500 students. If they lose students to schools with more courses, their funds could dwindle toward insolvency.

Mergers "may well happen," says Robert Wedl, deputy state superintendent. "But that's not the primary motivation."

Just in case, the legislature is offering a $60-per-pupil bonus to small districts that work together to offer cooperative programs. More than half the rural districts, says Wedl, are taking it.

"There may be some consolidations," says Levi, the program's legislative mother. "That's not so terrible. If they come, they will be generated by the people affected most—the schools' customers."

PREDICTIONS BY JOHN PULLIAM (1987)

More recently, educational futurist John Pulliam made the following predictions concerning education.

1. Education will become lifelong and will be year-round. Computers and other technological devices will assist young learners, and adults will not finish school but will be involved throughout their adult life.

2. Traditional credit/semester courses will be replaced by methods of determining competency; industry and businesses will become more involved in educational endeavors.

3. The curriculum will be significantly expanded to include new discoveries, leisure, travel, human values, and a host of topics making the curriculum as broad as life.

4. Fewer teachers will be needed in the classroom, but an increase in the number of teachers will be required to facilitate lifelong education. Teachers will become more learning facilitators than "directive" teachers.

5. The future will be characterized by less standardization, less grouping, and less pressure on students.

6. Schools will be replaced by a variety of alternative learning centers where children will begin school earlier than present.

7. Technology will revolutionize the educational process.

8. Education will be more closely linked with the environment.

AUTHOR'S PREDICTIONS

With knowledge of past predictions made concerning the future of education, and with more insight into the future than was available in 1974 and even 1987, the author makes the following predictions.

1. Education will continue to become lifelong education. The education of young children, birth through age six, will expand. With more and more mothers joining the work force, the need for day care will continue to escalate. Traditional daycare centers will become more formalized educational centers. Likewise, education for older Americans will expand. With the American population becoming older, the need for formalized, publicly supported educational programs for adults will increase.

2. Financing of public education will broaden to include a major involvement with the private sector. Business and industries will expand their role of financial support to education. Along with this support will come an increased demand for influence in the curriculum.

■ *The curriculum of the future will be determined by a variety of factors.*

3. Teachers will be better trained. The reform movement of the 1980s related to teacher education will result in better-trained teachers. More emphasis will be placed on field experiences and psychology, with less emphasis on traditional methods courses. Along with better training for teachers will come better salaries and merit-pay plans.

4. Accountability will increase both for teachers and students. Standardized testing will begin to decline as the primary method of ensuring accountability; alternative quality-assurance methods will be developed.

5. Schools will become year-round centers for learning. This will include longer school years for all students, but also flexible scheduling so that school plants are open and activities occur all year.

6. Opportunities for minorities will continue to be a priority. This includes improved educational opportunities for students with disabilities as well as minority racial and cultural groups.

7. School curricula will expand to include required subjects such as peace education, ecology, and geopolitics. Increased emphases on math, science, and computer technology will continue.

8. Computers will become a major part of each school. The role of the teacher, while changing, will remain primary instructional leader in each classroom.

9. The role of the federal government will continue strong in public education. Federal funding, as well as federal regulation, will increase to ensure quality of educational opportunity for all segments of the society. The federal government will realize that a sound educational system is the best guarantee of a strong country.

10. The influence of various public groups, such as conservatives and liberals, will become less noticeable due to the increased involvement of more citizens, the private sector, and government.

11. Teaching will become an accepted profession with teachers sharing more leadership responsibilities with administrators.

SUMMARY

This chapter focused on the future of education in the United States. The beginning section dealt with futurism and the broader implications of the future of the world. Several variables will have a significant impact on the world and consequently the United States. These include the population explosion, depletion of natural resources, food shortages, and geopolitics. All of these variables are interrelated. For example, the population explosion directly affects the depletion of natural resources and the world hunger situation. World geopolitics can create an environment that is conducive for solving these problems or one that presents a barrier for common actions that could reduce the impact of these negative forces.

The focus of the chapter then moved to the future of education. Although predicting the future of education in the United States is a difficult process, a lack of predictions could lead to an inadequate educational system, one not capable of dealing with the problems of the next generation. Several different aspects of the future of education were discussed, including population trends in the United States, the future of school reforms, curriculum of the schools, and technology. Each of these factors was discussed, with implications presented for future planning.

The final section presented predictions of education provided by two authors in 1974 one in 1987, and the predictions of the author. Some of the earlier predictions were viewed as having been accomplished, while others were still considered in progress or were determined to be unattainable. The future of education in the United States definitely is tied to the future of the world. While predicting the future is extremely difficult, it is an exercise that must be constantly undertaken and updated. The problems faced by humanity in the twenty-first century will be substantial; without adequate predicting and planning, these problems could be overwhelming. Planning for the future increases the likelihood that humanity will endure.

IN THE FIELD

1. Does the school have a long-term plan (five years or more)?
2. What enrollment changes are predicted for the district?
3. Are educational reforms that have been implemented being evaluated? If so, how?
4. Does the district have a plan to deal with teacher shortage or too many teachers? If so, what is it?
5. How are computers currently being used and how will they be used in the future?
6. What are some predictions concerning education in your district made by teachers and administrators? Is there consistency in these predictions?

REFERENCES

Allen, D. 1974. What the future of education might be. In T. W. Hipple, ed. *The Future of Education: 1975–2000.* Pacific Palisades, CA: Goodyear.

Almanac and Yearbook. 1986. Pleasantville, NY: Reader's Digest.

Amara, R. 1980. Thinking globally, acting locally. In F. Feather, ed. *Through the 80s: Thinking Globally, Acting Locally.* Washington, DC: World Future Society.

Anthony, R. B. 1984. Education in the year 2000. *The Clearing House* 58(3), 104.

Apple, M. W. 1983. Curriculum in the year 2000: Tensions and possibilties. *Phi Delta Kappan* 64(5), 321–26.

Bork, A. 1984. Computers in education today—And some possible futures. *Phi Delta Kappan* 66(4), 239–43.

Broudy, H. S. 1974. Education: 1975–2000. In T. W. Hipple, ed. *The Future of Education: 1975–2000.* Pacific Palisades, CA: Goodyear.

Darling-Hammond, L. 1988. The futures of teaching. *Educational Leadership* 46(3), 4–10.

Day, C. W., and A. D. Speicher. 1985. Planning for the 21st century. *American School & University* 58(3), 7–8.

Dede, C. 1983. The likely evolution of computer use in schools. *Educational Leadership* 41(1), 22–24.

Gallup, G. H. 1984. The 16th annual Gallup poll of the public's attitudes toward the public schools. *Phi Delta Kappan* 66(1), 23–36.

Hipple, T. W. 1974. Some (specific and not-so-specific) notions about the (distant and not-so-distant) future of education. In T. W. Hipple, ed. *The Future of Education: 1975–2000.* Pacific Palisades, CA: Goodyear.

Hudson Institute. 1987. *Workforce 2000, Work and Workers for the 21st Century.* Indianapolis: Author.

Kirst, M. W. 1986. Sustaining the momentum of state education reform: The link between assessment and financial support. *Phi Delta Kappan* 67(5), 341–45.

Lewis, A. J. 1983. Education in the 21st century. *Educational Leadership* 41(1), 9–10.

Morrison, P. 1979. Beyond the baby boom: The depopulation of America. *The Futurist* 13(2), 131–38.

National Center for Education Statistics. 1988. *The Condition of Education, 1988 Edition* Washington, DC: U.S. Department of Education.

Platt, J. 1980. The greatest evolutionary jump in history. In F. Feather, ed. *Through the 80s.* Washington, DC: World Future Society.

Pulliam, J. D. 1987. *History of Education in America,* 4th ed. Columbus OH: Merrill.

Puttkamer, J. V. 1983. The future: Do we have a choice? *Educational Leadership* 41(1), 4–8.

Rafferty, M. 1974. American education: 1975–2000. In T. W. Hipple, ed. *The Future of Education: 1975–2000.* Pacific Palisades, CA: Goodyear.

Schreyer, E. R. 1980. The mystery of the future. In F. Feather, ed. *Through the 80s: Thinking Globally, Acting Locally.* Washington, DC: World Future Society.

Snyder, T. D. 1988. Trends in education. *Principal* 68(1), 26–30.

Toffler, A. 1980. The third wave. In F. Feather, ed. *Through the 80s: Thinking Globally, Acting Locally.* Washington, DC: World Future Society.

EPILOGUE

Education in the United States continues to be at a crossroads. Never in the history of public education in this country has so much attention been focused for such a long time on public schools, teachers, administrators, students, and teacher education institutions. The reform movements that began with critical reports of education issued in the late 1970s and early 1980s continue to have an impact on our public schools. Although the fervor of reform has declined, evidence of positive changes in public schools are still very apparent. The end result—what schools will be like if and when the current reform period ends—remains to be seen. Previous reform periods in public education often resulted in little or no positive change. However, since the public and the profession of teaching have been so engrossed by the changes, it is anticipated that sound, positive, longlasting changes will take place. To summarize the text, the following few pages will present some of the major themes previously discussed and possible future directions of these areas.

CONTROL OF AMERICAN EDUCATION

The control of American education is a complex issue. Long thought of as being controlled by local boards of education, public schools are actually controlled by a complex group of forces. These include local, state, and federal governments; teacher unions; parent groups; textbook publishers; accreditation agencies; and administrators. All these groups have some influence over public education.

No one group has more control than the others. While local boards of education establish policies, these policies must conform to certain state standards. Federal legislation and litigation must also be considered when developing policies for the public schools. Although boards may develop policies, the actual implementation of those policies rests with teachers and administrators, two groups which have a great deal of freedom within individual schools and classrooms.

Still other groups which exert influence are textbook publishers, who control the curricula used in schools to a great extent, and accreditation agencies, private groups which decide that schools must offer certain courses and/or experiences to students and that teachers and administrators must meet certain standards for schools to receive and keep creditation.

In the future, state governments and the federal government are likely to continue to have a great impact on schools, especially in this era of reform when legislation and court decisions are mandating certain educational practices. Even in the current era of reform, other forces exert great influence over education. Publishing companies and authors will continue to have a great impact on the curriculum; accreditation agencies will continue to set standards; teacher unions will continue to have an impact on what occurs in classrooms; administrators will still implement policies in their schools; and parents will have some control through direct contact and school board elections. Control will continue to be determined by a complex, interrelated set of variables.

REFORM MOVEMENTS OF THE 1980s

Educational reform reached a fever pitch in the United States in the early 1980s. Resulting from several stinging critical reports on the status of American public education, the reform movements included

- improved teacher education;
- increased standards for teachers, including teacher testing;
- longer school days and more days in the school year;
- more emphasis on basic academic subjects, including math and science;
- more required courses for graduation;
- less emphasis on athletics and other extracurricular activities;
- better pay for teachers;
- merit pay for teachers;
- requirements for students to do homework;
- more funding for educational programs; and
- applied research to investigate learning and teacher training.

While some of these changes undoubtedly will have positive effects on the quality of education offered in American public schools, the effects of others are questionable. For example, more of the same, if the same is inferior, is not necessarily a solution to quality educational programs. Therefore, simply extending the school day and the school year will not automatically lead to better educational programs. Still, the reform movements of the 1980s have had a positive effect by focusing the nation's attention on education. A not particularly popular subject, education has become publicized in newspapers, magazines, television, and even election campaigns. The pace of reform has slowed, but changes in our public system of education continue. Many of the initially discussed reforms that had limited support have been pushed aside for more substantive modifications of the system. The end result should be a better public education system in this country.

The increased awareness of the need to improve the educational system in the United States can only benefit the public school system and American schoolchildren. The key is not to let the attention focused on education in the early 1980s disintegrate when other issues become more popular. Education must stay in the limelight.

ELEMENTARY AND SECONDARY EDUCATION

The basic elements of the American public educational system are the elementary and secondary schools. Elementary schools were the beginning level of public education in the United States. They developed out of private schools and the common-school movement of the mid-1800s. Secondary schools, on the other hand, were not established on a large scale in the United States until the twentieth century. Still, they were the model for secondary education for the world. Few countries had publicly supported educational programs for adolescents until well into the twentieth century.

The future of elementary and secondary public schools depends on many issues. The organizational structure of the elementary school will undergo few changes. At the secondary level, however, changes are possible. Some critics believe that the comprehensive high school, the one that tries to be all things to all different types of children, is obsolete. These critics would argue for differentiated education at the secondary level, where brighter students are afforded opportunities in academic areas and other students have options that would focus more on vocational areas. The comprehensive high school, however, has been the basic element of public education at the secondary level for many years and will probably remain so in the near future.

SPECIAL EDUCATION

A subject not requiring much attention ten years ago, special education today is a relevant issue for all educators. As a result of federal and state legislation, and a multitude of litigation, providing appropriate educational programs for handicapped children is now a shared responsibility among all educators, both regular teachers and special education teachers. Administrators, who previously had little to do with special education programs, were also affected by the changing service model.

The major legislation mandating services for handicapped children was Public Law 94–142. Passed in 1975, and effective in 1978, this legislation mandated that every handicapped school-age child be afforded a free, appropriate education, regardless of the severity of the handicapping condition. A major requirement of the legislation was that the education provided had to be in the least-restrictive environment; that is, these children have to be educated in regular classrooms with non-handicapped children, by regular classroom teachers, as much as is feasible. This requirement has had a tremendous impact on regular classroom teachers. Before the legislation went into effect, regular teachers rarely saw handicapped children; after the requirement was passed, handicapped children were mainstreamed into regular classes a large portion of each school day.

Even though some attempts have been made to alter the requirements of P.L. 94–142, especially by the Reagan administration in the early 1980s, the requirements have not been changed. The lobby for the handicapped population is so strong that a major retrenchment from the requirements of P.L. 94–142 is highly unlikely. In fact, the most recent federal initiative in special education was the passage of Public Law 99–457 in 1986. This law mandates that schools provide services to children with disabilities, ages 3–5, beginning in 1990. The impact of this law on the schools will be significant. This means that all educators must continue to share in the responsibility of educating this group of children. Closer collaboration as well as better training will greatly facilitate this shared responsibility and enable handicapped children and nonhandicapped children to receive a better, higher quality education.

EDUCATION AS A PROFESSION

While many would agree that there can be no more noble a profession than teaching, many negative aspects are associated with teaching as a career. These include low pay, low status, high stress, burnout, and being a scapegoat for education ills. However, teaching does have its rewards, many of which cannot be related to material benefits. Some have said that teachers are the ones who help shape the future more than any other group, including parents. Often teachers spend more time, especially one-to-one, with children than the children's parents. As role models and imparters of knowledge, teachers play a critical role in the lives of children.

Teachers provide knowledge and information to students; facilitate students' learning; act as a role model for social skills, values, and attitudes; and act as a friend and stand-in parent. Teachers are definitely involved in more than instruction. If teachers only lectured, and made assignments from textbooks, computers could more easily and efficiently do the job. Teachers do a tremendous job in American schools. Even though they are frequently accused of being uncaring members of labor unions, most teachers are dedicated to the job of educating children and youth. The future should continue to find excellent individuals serving as teachers in public schools.

Thus, teachers are key individuals in the instructional process. How they become teachers has been an issue during the early 1980s. Along with criticisms of the educational programs offered in public schools have been criticisms of teacher education programs. Some of the common criticisms have included (1) low quality of students, (2) too much emphasis on how to teach, rather than child growth and development and educational psychology, (3) easy curriculum, (4) easy entrance and exit requirements for teacher education majors, and (5) poor quality of instruction from professors in teacher education.

Not all of these issues are valid. Although all colleges of education could improve in some areas, most are already doing an excellent job of preparing teachers.

The reports issued by the Holmes Group and the Carnegie foundation focused attention on needed reforms in teacher education. While some of these reforms have been adopted, others are controversial and are still being debated. Many colleges of education have initiated their own reforms. Some of these include:

- higher admission standards to teacher education;
- modified curriculum that focuses less on methods courses;
- increased emphasis on applied research by faculty in colleges of education;
- higher exit standards for teacher education graduates.

These are but a few of the reforms initiated by many teacher education institutions. The future should reveal that more colleges of education have taken a hard look at their programs and instituted many valuable reforms. The end result will definitely be better-trained teachers for American schools.

TECHNOLOGY IN THE SCHOOLS

The uses of technology in education include videotape, filmstrips, films, educational television, and microcomputers. Since the late 1970s, microcomputer technology has exploded. Millions of machines are currently on the market, and educational software has become a major business.

As more schools purchase, or are given, computers for their students, the selection and use of software becomes more important. Schools should use precise, careful methods in the selection of software, similar to those for the selection of textbooks. Once purchased, school officials must ensure that teachers know how to use both the machinery and software for maximum educational purposes. Computer technology in education is too valuable to wind up on a shelf collecting dust.

During the past decade, great strides have been made in the uses of computers in education. Initially they were primarily machines for drill. However, recent uses have included activities that actually facilitate learning in ways other than rote memory or drill. The appropriate uses of computers in instruction can greatly enhance the educational program of any school.

In addition, school personnel are just beginning to learn how to best utilize computer technology in areas other than instruction. The future should see increased uses of computers in schools, both in instructional and administrative areas.

ORGANIZATION AND FUNDING OF SCHOOLS

Schools are similar to businesses in that they must have leaders. In schools these individuals are called administrators. School administrators serve many varied functions, depending to a large degree on their actual administrative role. For example, superintendents are the chief school officers of the district. They are employed by a lay board of directors, usually elected by the community. In turn, superintendents recommend that the school board employ a principal to act as the chief administrative officer of a particular school. Administrators have roles that range from communicating with the school board to establishing and implementing a discipline policy for a particular school.

Administrators must be managers, disciplinarians, evaluators, facilitators, communicators, change agents, and fiscal managers. School administration is no longer a job that should go to retired athletic coaches simply because they contributed to the district. The roles of school administrators are so complex that the job requires a highly skilled, highly trained individual. In the future more school administrators will be career administrators, individuals who move up to administration through the teaching ranks. These individuals will have an inside view of the classroom and other aspects of public education and should lead the way to more effective administration in public schools.

A major requirement of schools is to educate students. To do this, they must have money. Public schools are supported by taxes at all levels of government: local, state, and federal. Types of taxes generally used to support schools include income taxes, primarily at the federal level, sales taxes at the state level, and property taxes at the local level.

One problem that has plagued educational finance since public support was first started has been the issue of equitable educational programs. Some schools, because of their local tax base, are able to offer higher cost, probably more effective, programs than other districts that have limited funds. States have made serious efforts to equalize the finances available to local districts. Unfortunately, most of these efforts have not been totally successful. Still, efforts must be made to develop methods of equity in school finance. Children in all districts should have access to equal educational opportunities. The future should see improved efforts in equitable school financing, as well as increased efforts at all levels of government in financing quality public education programs.

CONCLUSIONS

Public education in the United States is big business. The public schools employ more people and serve more individuals than any other industry or agency in the country. While many problems do exist in American public schools, for the most part the educational system is sound. Compared with other educational systems in the world, the American system is excellent. The reform movements of the 1970s and 1980s have resulted in public attention being focused on quality education. The outcome from this refocusing of attention will be more quality educational programs.

Public schools are sound. The ideas on which public education is based are sound. Teacher training is sound. Governmental and public support for public education are sound. Although there are problems, the most critical of these are being addressed, and the result will be a major improvement in an already excellent national program. Individuals wanting to become teachers will have an exciting career in public education. The future is ours; if mediocrity is our goal, it can easily be achieved. If excellence is our goal, it can also be achieved through extraordinary investment and effort. The final determination rests with the attitudes and willingness of the American public to fund, support, and rally for quality educational programs for children.

APPENDIX 1

AGENCIES AND PROFESSIONAL ASSOCIATIONS

American Association of Colleges for
  Teacher Education
One Dupont Circle
Washington, D.C. 20036

American Association for Counseling and
  Development
5999 Stevenson Avenue
Alexandria, Virginia 22304

American Society of Educators
1511 Walnut Street
Philadelphia, Pennsylvania 19102

American Vocational Association
1410 King Street
Alexandria, Virginia 22314

American Federation of Teachers
555 New Jersey Avenue, N.W.
Washington, D.C. 20001

Association for Childhood Education
  International
11141 Georgia Avenue, Suite 200
Wheaton, Maryland 20902

Association for Supervision and
  Curriculum Development
125 North West Street
Alexandria, Virginia 22314

Association of Teacher Edcators
1900 Association Drive
Reston, Virginia 22091

Council for Exceptional Children
1920 Association Drive
Reston, Virginia 22090

Home Economics Education Association
1201 Sixteenth Street, N.W.
Washington, D.C. 20036

International Reading Association
800 Barksdale Road
P.O. Box 8139
Newark, Delaware 19714–8139

Kappa Delta Pi
P.O. Box A
West Lafayette, Indiana 47906

National Association of Biology Teachers
11250 Roger Beacon Drive, #19
Reston, Virginia 22090

National Association of Elementary School
  Principals
1801 North Moore Street
Arlington, Virginia 22209

National Association of Secondary School
  Principals
1904 Association Drive
Reston, Virginia 22091

National Council for the Social Studies
3501 Neward Street, N.W.
Washington, D.C. 20016

National Council of Teachers of English
1111 Kenyon Road
Urbana, Illinois 61801

National Council of Teachers of
  Mathematics
1906 Association Drive
Reston, Virginia 22901

National Education Association
1201 16th Street, N.W.
Washington, D.C. 20016

National School Boards Association
1680 Duke Street
Alexandria, Virginia 22314

Parent Teachers Association
700 North Rush
Chicago, Illinois 60611–2571

Phi Delta Kappa
Eighth and Union
P.O. Box 789
Bloomington, Indiana 47402

Society for Research in Child
  Development
5801 Ellis Avenue
Chicago, Illinois 60637

United States Department of Education
Washington, D.C. 20202

APPENDIX 2

IN-THE-FIELD ACTIVITIES REPORT FORM

NAME: _____ DATE: _____

CHAPTER NUMBER AND TOPIC: _____

CLASSROOM SETTING WHERE OBSERVATIONS TOOK PLACE: _____
_____

QUESTION/ACTIVITY: _____

FINDINGS: _____
_____

QUESTION/ACTIVITY: _____

FINDINGS: _____
_____

QUESTION/ACTIVITY: _____

FINDINGS: _____
_____

QUESTION/ACTIVITY: _____

FINDINGS: _____
_____

QUESTION/ACTIVITY: _____

FINDINGS: _____
_____

GENERAL COMMENTS:

APPENDIX 3

FEDERAL LEGISLATION AFFECTING EDUCATION

LAND ORDINANCE OF 1785

- First legislation passed at the national level that had an impact on education.
- Required one section of each township established in the Northwest Territory be reserved for the establishment of public schools.

NORTHWEST ORDINANCE OF 1787

- Expressed general commitment for education by the federal government.
- Stated that "Religion, morality, and knowledge being necessary to good government and the happiness of mankind, schools and the means of education shall forever be encouraged."
- Considered by many as the foundation for public education.

MORRILL LAND GRANT ACT OF 1862

- Gave thirty thousand acres of federal land to each state for each elected representative to Congress.
- Purpose of the land was to establish a college for agriculture and mechanical arts.
- Eventual donation of seventeen million acres of land.

THE SMITH-HUGHES ACT OF 1917

- Provided funds to states to train teachers in the area of vocational education.
- Primarily assisted high schools; however, some funds used in junior colleges.
- Helped establish an extensive network of vocational education in the country.

NATIONAL DEFENSE EDUCATION ACT OF 1958 (Public Law 85–865)

- Passed after the launching of Sputnik.
- Primarily enacted as a defense action.
- Provided unprecedented amounts of federal money for public education.
- Emphasized educational improvement in the areas of science and foreign languages.

VOCATIONAL EDUCATION ACT OF 1963 (Public Law 88–210)

- Expanded federal support for vocational education.
- Main purpose was to assist states in maintaining, extending, and improving existing vocational education programs and to provide part-time empolyment for youths.
- Provided for $60 million during fiscal year 1964 and $225 million per year thereafter.

BILINGUAL EDUCATION ACT OF 1964

- Provided funds for school districts to develop and operate special programs for students with limited English speaking skills.
- 1974 amendment removed requirements that students in the program be from low income homes.

ELEMENTARY AND SECONDARY EDUCATION ACT OF 1965 (Public Law 89–10)

- Most extensive federal legislation passed dealing with public education.

- Focused public education efforts on children from poverty homes.
- Provided funds for library support.
- Established services for academic support and remedial instruction.
- Provided funding for research activities by universities.
- Funded programs at state education agencies to support personnel training and planning.

ECONOMIC OPPORTUNITY ACT OF 1965

- Continued efforts at providing services to poor children.
- Funded Head Start programs.

REHABILITATION ACT OF 1973 (Public Law 93–102)

- Basically civil rights legislation for the handicapped.
- Prevented discrimination against children and adults due to disabilities.
- Applied safeguards for school-age disabled children.

EDUCATION FOR ALL HANDICAPPED CHILDREN ACT OF 1975 (Public Law 94–142)

- Required the provision of a free, appropriate public education for all handicapped children.
- Mandated that all handicapped children have an Individualized Educational Program (IEP).
- Required that handicapped children be educated with nonhandicapped children as much as possible.
- Provided parents, students, and schools with due process safeguards.
- Required that parents be involved in the education of their handicapped children.
- Mandated that nondiscriminatory assessment practices be used with children.

DEPARTMENT OF EDUCATION ORGANIZATION ACT OF 1979 (Public Law 96–88)

- Established the Department of Education.
- Functions came from the Department of Health, Education, and Welfare.

EDUCATION CONSOLIDATION AND IMPROVEMENT ACT OF 1981 (Public Law 97–35)

- Consolidated forty-two programs into seven programs.
- Funding came from elementary and secondary block grant authority.

REHABILITATION AMENDMENTS OF 1984 (Public Law 98–221)

- Revised and expanded Rehabilitation Act of 1973 (Section 504).
- Provided for the Helen Keller National Center for Deaf/Blind.

REAUTHORIZATION OF THE EDUCATION OF THE HANDICAPPED ACT AMENDMENTS (Public Law 99–457)

- Reauthorized three-year programs under Public Law 94–142.
- Mandated services for children with disabilities, ages 3–5, by 1990–1991.
- Provided financial incentives to serve children 0–2 years with disabilities.

THE DRUG-FREE SCHOOLS AND COMMUNITIES ACT OF 1986 (Public Law 99–570)

- Authorized funding for FY 87–89.
- Part of Anti-Drug Abuse Act of 1986.
- Established programs for drug abuse education and prevention.

APPENDIX 4

IMPORTANT COURT CASES AFFECTING EDUCATION

COMMONWEALTH v. HARTMAN (1851)

The Pennsylvania Supreme Court ruled that the state constitution and school laws only establish minimum requirements and that schools could establish more stringent requirements, in this case, mandatory education.

SPRINGFIELD, v. QUICK (1859)

The United States Supreme Court ruled that states could collect taxes and tax funds for public educational programs.

KALAMAZOO CASE (1874)

The Michigan Supreme Court ruled that the Kalamazoo school district could levy taxes to support high schools.

PLESSY v. FERGUSON (1896)

The United States Supreme Court upheld a Louisiana law that required railways to provide separate-but-equal facilities for white and black individuals.

ATTORNEY GENERAL OF MICHIGAN v. LOWREY (1905)

The United States Supreme Court upheld the right of state legislatures to make and change boundaries of school districts.

PIERCE v. SOCIETY OF SISTERS (1925)

The United States Supreme Court ruled that state laws may require the attendance of children in school, but could not regulate whether the school is private or public.

COCHRAN v. LOUISIANA STATE BOARD OF EDUCATION (1930)

The United States Supreme Court ruled that state funds could be used to purchase textbooks for all school-age children, including those attending private, sectarian schools.

ILLINOIS ex. rel. v. BOARD OF EDUCATION (1948)

The United States Supreme Court ruled as unconstitutional a school program that permitted students to attend religious instruction in school during school hours.

ILLINOIS ex. rel. McCOLLUM v. BOARD OF EDUCATION (1948)

The United States Supreme Court ruled that school programs permitting religious instruction during school hours, and allowing students to leave their regular classes for the religious classes, was unconstitutional.

SWEATT v. PAINTER (1950)

The United States Supreme Court ruled that a black student could not be denied admission to the University of Texas Law School for the sole reason of race.

BROWN v. BOARD OF EDUCATION, TOPEKA KANSAS (1954)

The United States Supreme Court ruled that children could not be denied admission to public schools on the basis of race; ruling declared segregated public schools to be unconstitutional based on the Fourteenth Amendment to the Constitution.

ENGEL v. VITALE (1962)

The United States Supreme Court ruled that a New York State law that required the reading of a twenty-two-word, nondenominational prayer unconstitutional.

ABINGTON SCHOOL DISTRICT v. SCHEMPP, MURRAY v. CURLETT (1963)

The United States Supreme Court ruled as unconstitutional a law that required the reading of ten Bible verses and recitation of the Lord's Prayer during school hours, on school grounds, conducted by school personnel.

EPPERSON v. ARKANSAS (1968)

A law forbidding the teaching of evolution was ruled unconstitutional by the United States Supreme Court.

GREEN v. COUNTY SCHOOL BOARD (1968)

The United States Supreme Court declared that a "freedom of choice" plan in a previously segregated school district offers little likelihood for desegregation. The ruling required that an effective plan for desegregation be implemented.

TINKER v. DES MOINES INDEPENDENT COMMUNITY SCHOOL DISTRICT (1969)

The United States Supreme Court ruled as unconstitutional the suspension of students wearing armbands or other symbolic expressions unless the wearing of such interferes with school.

SWANN v. CHARLOTTE-MECKLEN-BURG BOARD OF EDUCATION (1971)

Federal court ruling upheld busing as a legitimate means for desegregating schools. It gave district courts wide discretion in remedying longstanding segregated school systems.

PENNSYLVANIA ASSOCIATION FOR RE-TARDED CITIZENS (PARC) v. PENNSYL-VANIA (1971)

Federal court required local schools to provide a free, appropriate public education for all school-aged mentally retarded children.

SAN ANTONIO INDEPENDENT SCHOOL DISTRICT v. RODRIQUEZ (1973)

Federal court upheld a state funding model where local property taxes are used to provide a minimum educational program for all students.

SLOAN v. LEMON (1973)

The United States Supreme Court ruled as unconstitutional a law allowing for partial reimbursement by the state for tuition paid by parents sending their children to private schools.

MILLIKEN v. BRADLEY (1974)

The United States Supreme Court, in a five to four decision, overturned lower court rulings that required the bussing of children between Detroit and suburban school districts to desegregate the Detroit system.

BAKER v. OWEN (1975)

The United States Supreme Court ruled that a statute allowing for reasonable corporal punishment was constitutional as long as certain procedural rights were afforded.

WOLMAN v. WALTER (1977)

The United States Supreme Court ruled that states may supply secular texts, standardized tests, diagnostic speech, hearing, and psychological services, and guidance and remedial services provided on religiously neutral territory to religious, private schools.

BATTLE v. COMMONWEALTH (1980)

Third Circuit Court of Appeals ruled that some handicapped children should be afforded extended school year services in cases where significant regression would occur during the summer.

BOARD OF EDUCATION v. ROWLEY (1982)

The United States Supreme Court ruled that Public Law 94–142 guaranteed the right of disabled children to a minimally appropriate educational program, not a program designed to maximize the educational performance of students.

NEW JERSEY v. T.L.O. (1985)

The United States Supreme Court ruled that while students had Fourth Amendment Rights relative to search and seizure, schools could use "reasonable suspicion" as a reason for searches rather than "probable cause."

SPRING BRANCH INDEPENDENT SCHOOL DIST. v. STAMOS (1985)

The Texas Supreme Court upheld the "no-pass no-play" rule in Texas requiring students to meet certain academic standards before being eligible for extracurricular activities.

DAY v. SOUTH PARK INDEPENDENT SCHOOL DISTRICT (1985)

This case, which will likely disturb educators, upheld the right of a school district to terminate an employee simply because the employee had used the employee grievance procedure.

DISTRICT 27 COMMUNITY SCHOOL BOARD v. THE BOARD OF EDUCATION OF THE CITY OF NEW YORK (1986)

The court ruled that a child with Acquired Immune Deficiency Syndrome (AIDS) could be considered handicapped under Section 504 of the Rehabilitation Act of 1973, and therefore eligible for certain protections under the law.

JAGER AND JAGER v. DOUGLAS COUNTY SCHOOL DISTRICT AND DOUGLAS COUNTY BOARD OF EDUCATION (1987)

This case resulted in an ambiguous opinion that made it unconstitutional for clergy to give a pregame invocation at a high school athletic event. The decision left the door open for other than clergy to give the invocation.

EDWARDS v. AGUILLARD (1987)

The U.S. Supreme Court upheld a lower court's decision that the Louisiana law, the Balanced Treatment for Creation-Science and Evolution-Science Act, was unconstitutional.

HOENIG v. DOE (1988)

In this case, the U.S. Supreme Court ruled that schools had to keep a child with emotional problems in the placement pursuant to the individualized educational program (IEP) unless the parents and school agreed to a change, or until the due process procedures for changing placement were carried out.

APPENDIX 5

IMPORTANT DATES IN AMERICAN EDUCATION

1636   Harvard University chartered.

1642   Law of 1642 enacted in Massachusetts.

1647   Old Deluder Satan Act passed in Massachusetts.

1690   First appearance of the *New England Primer.*

1693   William and Mary College chartered.

1701   Yale University chartered.

1746   Princeton University chartered.

1749   Benjamin Franklin introduced his Proposal Relating to the Education of Youth in Pennsylvania.

1751   First academy established in United States.

1754   Columbia University chartered.

1785   Land Ordinance of 1785 passed by national government.

1787   Northwest Ordinance of 1787 enacted by national government.

1788   United States Constitution ratified.

1802   Pauper School Act in Pennsylvania.

1806   First Lancastrian School established in New York.

1812   New York State has first state school officer.

1818   First Infant School begun in Boston.

1821   English Classical School of Boston established, first American high school.

1825   University of Virginia opens.

1827   Massachusetts law compelling high schools passed.

1837   Massachusetts first state school board established.
Horace Mann becomes first secretary.

1839   First public normal school established.

1840   Rhode Island compulsory education law becomes effective.

1849–50   General tax support for education in New York.

1852	Massachusetts compulsory education law.
1855	First American kindergarten established.
1857	National Education Association (NEA) established.
1859	Darwin's *On the Origin of Species* published.
1861	Massachusetts Institute of Technology founded; first engineering school.
1862	Morrill Act passed.
1866	Federal Department of Education established; became the Office of Education after one year.
1872	Kalamazoo law case establishes legal right of city to establish high school.
1881	Tuskegee Institute, first black normal school, founded.
1890	Second Morrill Act passed.
1892	Committee of Ten established by NEA to standardize high schools.
1896	*Plessy v. Ferguson* law case.
1899	Dewey's *The School and Society* published.
1909	First junior high school established at Berkeley, California.
1910	First junior college established at Fresno, California.
1916	American Federation of Teachers (AFT) established.
1917	Smith-Hughes Act passed.
1918	NEA establishes Commission on the Reorganization of Secondary Education.
1919	Progressive Education Association organized.
1924	Scopes "monkey" trial.
1926	Establishment of the Commission on the Social Studies in the Schools.
1944	First G.I. Bill passed.
1950	Establishment of the National Science Foundation.
1950	National Commission on Accrediting established.
1954	*Brown v. Board of Education* law case.
1957	Societ Union launches Sputnik.
1957	Federal troops ordered to Little Rock to ensure school desegregation.
1958	National Defense Education Act passed.
1964	Civil Rights Act passed.
1965	Elementary and Secondary Education Act passed.
1968	Bilingual Education Act passed.
1971	*Swann v. Charlotte-Mecklenburg* court case.
1975	Education for All Handicapped Children Act (P.L. 94–142) passed.

1979   Department of Education created.

1983   *Nation at Risk Report* issued.

1986   Congress passes Public Law 99–457.

1986   *A National Prepared: Teachers for the 21st Century,* released by the Task Force on Teaching as a Profession of the Carnegie Forum on Education and the Economy.

1986   *Tomorrow's Teachers: A Report of the Holmes Group* issued.

1989   First set of standards for national certification of teachers issued.

APPENDIX 6

IMPORTANT PARTS OF THE UNITED STATES CONSTITUTION

Amendment I

Congress shall make no law respecting an establishment of religion, or prohibiting the free exercise thereof; or abridging the freedom of speech, or of the press; or the right of the people peaceably to assemble, and to petition the Government for a redress of grievances.

Amendment IV

The right of the people to be secure in their persons, houses, papers, and effects, against unreasonable searches and seizures, shall not be violated, and no Warrants shall issue, but upon probable cause, supported by Oath or affirmation, and particularly describing the place to be searched, and the persons or things to be seized.

Amendment V

No person shall be held to answer for a capital or otherwise infamous crime, unless on a presentment of indictment of a Grand Jury, except in cases arising in the land or naval forces, or in the Militia, when in time of War or public danger; nor shall any person be subject to the same offense to be twice put in jeopardy of life or limb; nor shall be compelled in any criminal case to be a witness against himself, nor be deprived of life, liberty or property, without due process of law; nor shall private property be taken for public use, without just compensation.

Amendment X

The powers not delegated to the United States by the Constitution, nor prohibited by it to the States, are reserved to the States respectively, or to the people.

Amendment XIV

Section 1. All persons born or naturalized in the United States, and subject to the jurisdiction thereof, are citizens of the United States and of the State wherein they reside. No state shall make or enforce any law which shall abridge the privileges or immunities of citizens of the United States; nor shall any State deprive any person of life, liberty, or property, without due process of law; nor deny to any person within its jurisdiction the equal protection of the laws.

Section 2. Representatives shall be apportioned among the several States according to their respective number, counting the whole number of persons in each state, excluding Indians not taxed. But when the right to vote at any election for the choice of electors for President and Vice President of the United States, Representatives in Congress, the Executive and Judicial officers of a State, or the members of the Legislature thereof, is denied any of the male inhabitants of such State, being twenty-one years of age, and citizens of the United States, or in any way abridged, except for participation in rebellion, or ther crime, the basis of representation therein shall be reduced in the proportion which the number of such male citizens shall bear to the number of male citizens twenty-one years of age in such State.

GLOSSARY

Academy American secondary school during colonial times; stressed practical subjects.

Accountability Responsibility related to quality of educational programs.

Accreditation Acknowledgment by an outside group that an educational institution or program meets certain standards.

Administrative Hierarchy Administrative organization of a local school district.

Aesthetics Philosophy related to beauty.

Alternative Certification Teacher licensure obtained through other than traditional coursework in education courses.

American College Testing Program (ACT) College entrance exam used by many universities.

American Federation of Teachers (AFT) A national teachers' organization second only to the National Education Association in membership.

Assistant Principal Administrative position in an individual school that primarily assists the principal in administrative duties.

Assistant Superintendent Administrative position in a school district that primarily assists the superintendent in administrative duties.

Attitude Preconceived notions or ideas that affect behavior toward certain groups of people or programs.

Audiovisual Kit Instructional materials, usually in the form of filmstrips, tapes, and other audiovisual items and printed information.

Axiology Area of philosophy that focuses on values.

Back-to-the-basics Movement to return schools to emphasizing basic academic subjects in the curriculum.

Behaviorism Educational philosophy and practice that emphasizes reinforcing appropriate behavior or learning. Includes the concepts of stimulus and response.

Bilingual Education Educational programs aimed at providing equal opportunities to limited-English-speaking students.

Bill for the More General Diffusion of Knowledge Bill presented by Thomas Jefferson in Virginia that would have made three years of elementary education available for all children. Although defeated, this bill laid the foundation for public education.

Board of Education A group of citizens at the local and state levels, usually elected but occasionally appointed, that set policies for schools.

Building Level Administration Administration of individual schools.

Burnout The process of losing interest and motivation in teaching or other fields.

Cardinal Principles Seven goals for secondary education developed by the NEA in the early twentieth century.

Career Education A concept that aims at preparing students for adulthood, with emphasis on careers and vocations; can be infused into existing curricula K–12.

Carnegie Report A report issued by a task force organized by the Carnegie Foundation with suggestions for revising teacher education.

Career Ladder A system of incentives developed for teachers to improve and reward their professional skills.

Categorical Aid Financial assistance provided to local schools for specific programs or purposes.

Censorship The act of censoring materials such as library books and textbooks.

Central Office Refers to the district administration level of local school districts.

Certification Teacher licensure.

Change Agent A role of school administrators related to making and influencing innovations in schools.

Closed-Circuit Television A form of educational technology using a television and video camera.

Colonial Period Period in American education from 1607 to 1788.

Committee of Fifteen A committee appointed in 1895 by the National Education Association that reversed the findings of the Committee of Ten.

Committee of Ten NEA committee established in 1893 to standardize high schools.

Common School Free, publicly supported schools for all children; movement began in the mid-1800s.

Competency Ability to perform certain skills at appropriate levels.

Comprehensive High School Secondary schools that provide a variety of curricular options for students.

Compulsory Education Legal mandated education for all students within certain age groups.

Computer-Assisted Instruction (CAI) Programmed instruction using a computer.

Computer Science The study of computers and computer programming.

Conservative Movement Movement to influence educational programs by conservative groups.

Consolidation Combining smaller school districts into larger districts.

Core Curriculum Required curriculum for all students.

Creation-Science The study of the development of humanity based on the Bible.

Cultural Pluralism A society composed of many varied cultures forming a unified cultural group.

Curriculum All experiences provided students in schools.

Curriculum Reform Movements to change basic curricular options for students.

Declining Enrollments Trend in schools during the past decade.

Department of Education Cabinet-level office within the federal government responsible for education.

Discipline Actions in response to inappropriate behavior or actions that prevent inappropriate behaviors.

Discretionary Funds Federal funding for specific programs granted after specific needs are identified and documented.

Due Process Procedural safeguards afforded students, parents, and teachers that protects individual rights.

Education Philosophy Application of formal philosophy to the field of education.

Educational Technology Technology applied to educational practices, primarily instruction.

Educational Television Educational programs broadcast by either commercial stations or specialized educational networks that emphasize educational subjects.

Education Trends Forecasted patterns in education.

Elementary Schools Grades 1-6 or K-6.

English Grammar School Model of elementary education in colonial America.

Enlightenment Period Period in Europe during eighteenth century.

Epistemology Branch of philosophy that focuses on the nature of knowledge.

Essentialism Area of philosophy that believes a common core of knowledge and ideals should be the focus of the curriculum.

Ethics Philosophy that studies values.

Evaluation Assessing the quality and effectiveness of programs for individuals and groups.

Evolution The study of the development of humanity based on scientific data that proposes human beings developed from lower life forms.

Exceptional Children Students with disabilities or talents that require specialized programs.

Existentialism Philosophy that emphasizes individuals and individual decision-making.

Federal Government Governmental actions that occur within the national government of the United States.

Federal Role Role of the federal government in education.

Formula Grants Educational funding based on the number of children eligible for various programs.

Fringe Benefits Any number of benefits provided employees in addition to salary. Examples include insurance programs, retirement programs, and liability insurance.

Full-Time Equivalency (FTE) Funding model used at many universities where programs are funded based on the number of full-time students enrolled.

Futurism The study of the future, including global concerns and more regional or local matters.

General Curriculum Basic curriculum required of all students.

Geopolitics Political status of all countries in the world.

Gifted and Talented A group of students whose abilities are above those of most students; these students require specialized programs.

Global Trends Forecasted developments that have an impact on the entire world, such as geopolitics, hunger, population.

Graded Schools Schools organized using a step system whereby students are usually grouped related to chronological age rather than abilities.

Graduation Requirements Courses required of all students for graduation.

Handicapped Children Students who deviate from the norm due to physical, emotional, or mental disabilities.

History of Education Historical study of education.

Holmes Group A group of about one hundred research universities that issued a report calling for major reforms in teacher education.

Hornbook A single page, usually attached to a wooden paddle, containing the alphabet, syllables, a prayer, and other simple words; this "book" was used extensively in colonial schools.

Idealism A philosophy that emphasizes global ideas related to moral teachings.

Individualized Educational Program (IEP) Individual program of study mandated by federal and state laws for all handicapped students in special education programs.

Individualized Instruction Instruction designed to meet the needs of an individual student. Every student's individualized program is different.

Instructional Television Televised lessons broadcast for schools usually on educational television.

Intermediate Unit A level of educational organization between local school districts and the state department of education.

Kindergarten School programs for preschool age children; term coined by Froebel.

Latin Grammar School Secondary school whose curriculum emphasized Latin and Greek and focused on preparing students for college.

Learning Disability A handicapping condition where students of average or above-average intelligence have difficulty with academic subjects.

Least-Restrictive Environment Educational setting that is closest to a normal classroom for handicapped learners.

Legislation Acts passed by state legislatures and Congress that become laws.

Litigation Court actions, suits.

Local Education Agency (LEA) Local school districts. This is the basic educational unit in all states.

Mainstreaming The practice of integrating handicapped students into regular classrooms and programs as much as possible; implementation of the least-restrictive environment.

Measurement Another term used interchangeably with evaluation.

Medieval Period Period in Europe from 476 to 1300.

Melting Pot Theory Theory that people from all cultures form a common culture.

Mental Retardation A handicapping condition related to intellectual deficits; usually defined in terms of limited IQ scores and adaptive behavior.

Merit Pay Salary paid to an employee based on the employee's abilities or competencies, regardless of number of years of service.

Metaphysics Philosophy that studies the nature of reality.

Microcomputer Personalized computer the approximate size of a television set or smaller.

Middle School An organized educational unit between elementary school and high school; usually includes grades 5–8.

Mill A tenth of a cent or a thousandth of a dollar. Used to assess the rate of property taxes.

Minimum Competency Testing Evaluations to determine if students have minimum skills necessary for progressing to the next grade or graduation.

Minimum Foundation Program Funding model found in most states that attempts to guarantee a basic educational program for children funded at an average minimal level.

Monitorial Schools School model where brightest students were instructed and in turn they taught other students.

Motivation Willingness or drive to accomplish something.

Nation at Risk Report National report developed by the National Commission that indicated public education in the United States has serious problems.

National Commission on Education A study group formed in the early 1980s to investigate the status of public education in the United States.

National Council for the Accreditation of Teacher Education (NCATE) Accreditation agency that certifies the quality of teacher education programs nationwide.

National Education Association (NEA) Largest teachers' organization in the United States.

National Period Period in American education from 1788 to the present.

Negative Reinforcement Removal of an adversive stimulus when appropriate behavior is exhibited.

New England Primer Early textbook used in colonial schools.

New Right Term used to refer to extremely conservative groups that attempt to influence educational programs.

Nongraded School An organizational pattern for schools that use students' abilities for grouping rather than assigning students to certain grades based on chronological age.

Normal School First college training programs that trained teachers.

Northwest Ordinance Early legislation passed by the national government prior to the ratification of the United States Constitution.

Open Classroom Physical organization of schools where room dividers are deleted; students are educated in groups in large, open areas.

Overpopulation A condition when there are more people than a particular landmass can accommodate.

Paraprofessional Teachers' aides and others who assist teachers in educational programs.

Parent Teachers Association (PTA) National organization composed of parents and teachers that advocates for public education.

Pedagogy Science and art of teaching.

Perennialism Educational philosophy that believes in the existence of unchanging universal truths.

Personnel Evaluation Evaluation of individual teachers and administrators.

Philosophy of Education Application of philosophy to educational programs and practices.

Piagetian Theory Theory of child development based on the writing of Jean Piaget.

Population Trends Forecasted patterns of population growth and decline.

Pragmatism Philosophy that focuses on practical application of knowledge; John Dewey was a leading proponent.

Principal Administrator in charge of individual schools.

Program Evaluation Evaluation of specific programs regarding their effectiveness.

Progressive Tax A tax where individuals with higher incomes pay more taxes than individuals with lower incomes.

Progressivism Educational philosophy emphasizing experiences.

Property Assessment Determination of property values to assign taxes to individuals.

Property Tax Taxes assessed on local properties to use to finance public education.

Proportional Tax Taxes that require individuals to pay the same percentage of their incomes regardless of income level.

Public Law 94-142 Education for All Handicapped Children Act. Passed in 1975, this act mandates a free, appropriate public education for all handicapped children.

Public Law 99-457 A federal law passed in 1986 that mandates schools to serve children with disabilities, ages 3–5, by 1990–1991.

Punishment Application of something unpleasant to a child following inappropriate behavior.

Puritan Influence Influence over education by Puritans in the New England colonies during colonial America.

Realism Philosophy that emphasizes natural sciences and gaining knowledge through experiences.

Reform Movements of the 1980s Educational reforms initiated in the early 1980s in response to several national reports concerning the quality of public education.

Reinforcement Stimulus provided following a behavior; may be positive or negative.

Reinforcement Schedule Schedule used to determine when reinforcers are given to a person.

Regressive Tax Taxes where persons with lower incomes pay proportionally more taxes than individuals with higher incomes.

Reliability The technical aspect of a test that indicates that students' scores will be stable over time.

Renaissance and Reformation Period in Europe between 1300 and 1700.

School Counselor Professionals in schools who provide counseling for students who need affective intervention.

School Social Worker Social worker who works in schools to provide social work services to students and their families.

School Superintendent Chief school administrator at the local district level; usually appointed by the local board of education.

Secondary Reinforcer A reinforcer paired with a primary reinforcer designed to influence behavior after the primary reinforcer is no longer provided.

Secondary Schools Schools that provide educational programs for older students; usually includes grades 9–12 or 10–12.

Secretary of Education Cabinet-level official in charge of the United States Department of Education.

Self-Contained Classroom Classroom organization where students remain in the same room with the same teacher all day.

Sexism Practice of discrimination based on gender.

Shaping The process of providing reinforcers to alter a child's behavior into appropriate forms.

Software Computer programs.

Special Education Specialized programs developed for the education of children with disabilities.

Standardized Test A test that is norm-referenced and has specific administration standards so scores can be compared.

State Department of Education State unit responsible for public and private educational programs in states.

Symbolic Representation Most abstract of representation commonly referred to as verbal learning or problem solving.

Superintendent Chief school administrative officer in local school districts.

Supervisor Administrator responsible for specific programs in public schools, e.g., supervisor of special education, vocational education supervisor, supervisor of elementary education.

Supply and Demand Comparison between the number of teachers trained and the number needed for open positions.

Taxes Payments to a government to pay for various services.

Tax Revolt Movement to decrease taxes during the 1970s.

Tax Shifting The process of having someone else or some other group pay taxes for you.

Tax Sources Sources of tax revenue.

Teacher Education Programs designed to train prospective teachers in pedagogy.

Teacher Testing A movement begun in Arkansas in the early 1980s to test teachers in basic skills.

Teacher Unions Teachers' organizations that lobby for educational programs and teachers' rights and benefits. The NEA and AFT are the two largest national teacher unions in the United States.

Teacher Unit A method of funding public education programs based on the number of teachers needed for a particular district or program.

Technology Use of technical materials and equipment in schools.

Tenth Amendment United States Constitution Amendment that reserves to states areas not specifically mentioned in the Constitution.

Tenure An employee benefit that makes it difficult to terminate someone; usually provided to teachers after several years of successful teaching experience.

Textbook Censorship The process of groups determining which textbooks meet their standards.

Tracking Practice of channeling students into certain courses based on ability levels.

Ungraded Schools School organization where students progress based on their ability level rather than chronological age.

Validity Technical aspect of tests indicating that they measure what they purport to measure.

Values Clarification A teaching program that focuses on students understanding and expressing their own values.

Videocassette Technology Equipment consisting of a television and videocassette camera for use in educational settings.

Vocational Education Educational programs that emphasize career preparation. Training of students for particular jobs or skills.

Weighted Pupil Method A method of state funding for public education based on the needs of types of students.

INDEX